FEAR ITSELF

Fear Itself

*Enemies Real & Imagined
in American Culture*

Edited by
Nancy Lusignan Schultz

PURDUE UNIVERSITY PRESS

West Lafayette, Indiana

03 02 01 00 99   5 4 3 2 1

⊗ The paper used in this book meets the minimum
requirements of American National Standard for Information Sciences—
Permanence of Paper for Printed Library Materials, ANSI Z39.48-1992.

Printed in the United States of America

Library of Congress Cataloging-in-Publication Data

Fear itself : enemies real and imagined in American culture / edited by Nancy
Lusignan Schultz.
p. cm.
Includes bibliographical references (p.) and index.
ISBN 1-55753-114-5 (cloth : alk. paper). —ISBN 1-55753-115-3 (pbk. : alk.
paper)
1. United States—Civilization. 2. Fear—Social aspects—United States. I.
Schultz, Nancy Lusignan, 1956–
E169.1.F287   1998
972—dc21   98-13790
                                                                   CIP

"America . . . is attacked by unnatural enemies without and still more wicked wretches within who are aiming to destroy her. . . . [M]ay they fall into those very pits they themselves have digged for her and . . . be hanged on the very gallows they have erected for others."
—*Amicus Reipublica* (1776)

"Those who direct the Illuminati are against Christ and for Satan. They always remain in the dark, unidentified, and generally unsuspected. They use all peoples to serve their diabolical purposes. . . . Their primary goal is to form a one world government to have complete control over the entire world, destroying all religions and governments in the process."
—*<http://www.prolognet.qc.ca/ clyde/illumin.html>* (1997)

Contents

Contents

viii

Contents

ix

Preface

Publishing has done lust, gluttony, greed. It's had flings
with anger, envy, jealousy. Happiness and joy have been
steady sellers over the years. Now it's fear. Fear is hot.
Fear is the emotion du jour, if the books that have been
piling up on my desk lately are anything to go by.
—Diane White

Boston Globe columnist Diane White refers above to a spate of new popular books about fear, including Gavin de Becker's *The Gift of Fear,* Doreen Orion's *I Know You Really Love Me,* and *The Paranoid's Pocket Guide* by Cameron Tuttle.[1] In recent trade and academic publishing, Barbara Ehrenreich's *Blood Rites* theorizes that fear is a primal instinct that forged the psychic template for war and Elaine Showalter's *Hystories* examines the *paranoid style* that typifies so much of American culture, past and present.[2]

The French essayist Michel Montaigne once remarked, "The thing I fear most is fear," perhaps giving rise to Franklin D. Roosevelt's famous utterance, "the only thing we have to fear is fear itself."[3] As the title of this collection suggests, American culture has been particularly susceptible to imagining and persecuting enemies in every dark corner of its history, with some devastating results. Indeed, Kristina Bross's contribution on the Colonists' fear of the "Praying," or Christianized, Indians illustrates that even before the founding of the United States, Europeans mixed their penchant for demonizing the Other into the Nation's cultural foundations. We are familiar with the way Native Americans as savages—either primitive or noble—constituted an Other for the Colonists. But Bross's essay suggests that even as the American notion of the melting pot was forming with the first assimilating group, the Praying Indians, this boiling away of difference would become one of our most enduring myths.

The two quotations at the front of this anthology span better than two hundred years of our history:

America . . . is attacked by unnatural enemies without and still
more wicked wretches within who are aiming to destroy her. . . .
[M]ay they fall into those very pits they themselves have digged
for her and . . . be hanged on the very gallows they have erected for
others.—Amicus Reipublica (1776)

Those who direct the Illuminati are against Christ and for Satan.
They always remain in the dark, unidentified, and generally
unsuspected. They use all peoples to serve their diabolical purposes. . . . Their primary goal is to form a one world government to have complete control over the entire world, destroying all
religions and governments in the process.
—<http://www.prolognet.qc.ca/clyde/illumin.html> (1997)

"Amicus Reipublica" is quoted in James L. Walsh's essay on the demonization of the Loyalist supporters in the New Hampshire press at
the dawn of the American Revolution. It includes a reference to earlier
times in which witches were hanged from the gallows, including those
in Salem, Massachusetts. The second, with its distinctly *fin de siècle*
source (the Internet, in the sunset of the twentieth), is from Brian Marcus's essay on Freemasons and the Illuminati; this quotation warns of a
plot by the Illuminati to join with Satan to take over the world. The
centuries and media have shifted, but the sentiments remain strikingly
similar: American culture has feared the new, the different, the marginal, and has historically cast outsiders as being in league with Satan.
Fear Itself explores the historical continuum of fear that has centered on
enemies real and imagined in American culture.

The New England American Studies
Association Conference at Salem

On the weekend of 3–4 May 1997, the New England American Studies
Association held its annual conference on the campus of Salem State
College, in Salem, Massachusetts. As noted earlier, the site was appropriately chosen for its historical connection to the Salem witch hysteria. Twelve different panels featuring thirty-two presentations on the
subject of fear were presented over the two-day period, as well as a ple-
nary session entitled "Homophobia in American Culture" and a sneak-
preview screening of Arthur Dong's award-winning film, *Licensed to
Kill*. Winner of the 1997 award for the best documentary director and
the Filmmakers Trophy Award at the Sundance Film Festival, *Licensed
to Kill* offers what *Variety* has called "a harrowing look at homophobia

and gay bashing." The film uses interviews, videotaped confessions of perpetrators, news reports, and evidence from police files to examine the environments of men whose contempt for gays led them to murder. The appearance by Arthur Dong and the excellent panel of respondents, organized by Thomas Doherty of Brandeis University, was considered to be one of the highlights of the conference.

The NEASA Conference offered an opportunity for scholars from around the United States, Canada and Great Britain to examine many aspects of fear, represented by essays in this book. For example, John Regan, Jackson Schultz, an associate professor at Berklee College of Music, and I gave presentations on the fear that the Ursuline Convent in Charlestown, Massachusetts, generated before its destruction by mob in 1834. Jackson Schultz and I put together a slide presentation on a history and contemporary art exhibition, *Lifting the Veil*, which visual artist Nancy Natale and I had organized in 1997 at the Somerville (Massachusetts) Museum.

The idea for this meeting was developed by several of the NEASA officers (including last year's president, Stephen Nissenbaum) and coordinated by the current NEASA vice president, Dane Morrison. Cynthia Larsen designed the striking logo that helped attract so much interest. The contributions of Vice President Albert Hamilton and Dean Anita Shea of Salem State College, several members of the Salem State History Department, including the chairperson, Joan Maloney; faculty members Tad Baker, Larry Davis, Paul Marsella, Chris Mauriello, and Donna Vinson; and graduate students Kevin Goddu, Kara Markey, and Peter Williams, enabled the Salem campus to act as host to over a hundred conference participants. The idea for this book developed because of the outstanding efforts of the organizers and the high quality of papers presented at the NEASA conference. As one of the presenters, I was excited to have the opportunity to make these papers more widely available in this book.

Fear Itself

This volume contains twenty-seven essays that explore various manifestations of fear throughout American history. The seven sections are arranged by topic and proceed largely in chronological order. "Grand United Fear Theory" has two theoretical pieces that establish a context for many of the essays to follow. These two essays, by Corey Robin and Peter Knight, examine theoretical constructions of fear from Classical times to the present. Robin suggests that fear is so interwoven into the concept of freedom that since the nineteenth century emancipatory politics have employed it as a motivating factor. Knight's essay traces the increasing acceptance—indeed, "normalization"—of paranoid thinking in American culture since the 1960s. Together, they provide a theoretical context that prepares for the essays to follow.

"Rooted Fears in American Culture" contains five essays that explore the historical roots of intolerance in the United States. This section, which includes the essays by Bross and Walsh, offers a chronological examination of various groups targeted from our nation's beginnings through the end of the nineteenth century. The section continues with Jeffrey W. Taylor's study of the way nineteenth-century anti-mission Baptists feared the blurring of the boundaries between church and state. John Regan's article on the convent burning contributes a new understanding of antebellum culture's uneasiness about girls' boarding schools, which helped spark the violence against the Ursuline convent in Charlestown, Massachusetts. In the closing essay of this section, Elizabeth DeWolfe's study of the perceived threat of the Shakers throughout the antebellum period takes us chronologically to the Civil War. The debate and battle over slavery then overshadowed most of the earlier anxieties surveyed in this section.

With the start of the Civil War, the attention of the nation turned to the subject of race. "Fear of the Dark," the next section, contains four essays examining anxiety about racial Others. While "Rooted Fears" largely centers on the connection between religion and intolerance, the essays in "Fear of the Dark" examine race as a fear-inducing element. Eve Allegra Raimon and Amanda Frisken explore the "race card" as it factored into the 1864 and 1872 presidential elections. Both Raimon and Frisken revisit the myth of the melting pot as a political factor, but this time with the melting away of racial difference through miscegenation, a practice that provoked deep anxiety. Matthew Guterl next explores the way fears of mixing races dominated the eugenics movement of the 1920s and 1930s, led by Madison Grant. Mari Yoshihara's essay concludes "Fear of the Dark" and spotlights the period in American culture when the Oriental became an abiding racial and cultural fear. Specifically, Yoshihara critiques the Japanese character studies done by anthropologist Ruth Benedict in *The Sword and the Chrysanthemum* (1946), especially the ways in which Benedict served American political purposes by melding stereotypical cultural characteristics with gender stereotypes to emasculate and feminize the enemy Japan. (The essay by Jason Loviglio, included in a later section, touches on this fear of the Oriental during the late 1930s, leading up to the period just before the Second World War.) Building on the earlier explorations in the book about the relationship between faith and fear, this section identifies race as a provocation to anxiety with potential for eruption at any time.

Expressions of fear in literature are the subject of the four essays that make up "Literary Fears." This section explores the expression of cultural anxieties in selected literary works. Two of the essays examine nineteenth-century texts, both classic and popular. Anne Baker looks at the peculiar manifestation of American agoraphobia in *Moby-Dick*, a big book about a big whale, significantly appearing during a period of phenomenal territorial expansion. Elaine Frantz Parsons examines popular temperance novels for their paradoxical fascination with alcohol, which, Parsons demonstrates, undergirds so much of this late-nineteenth-century genre. Returning to the classic writers of the turn of the century—including Henry James, William Dean Howells, and Edith Wharton—Adam Sweeting traces a new anxiety expressed in American literature that develops out of growing class consciousness, reflected in the architectural design of the characters' residences. Finally, María DeGuzmán explores fear of fascism as an overriding theme in the work of contemporary Hispanic writer Floyd Salas. These expressions of fear in literary texts from the nineteenth century to the contemporary period suggest a fertile area for further research.

Throughout the nation, interest in the 1950s continues to grow, and the section entitled "Cold War Anxieties" contains three essays exploring manifestations of fear during this era. Lee Bernstein's essay on Lucky Luciano picks up on many of the themes touched upon earlier in "Fear of the Dark." The swarthy Luciano, both an insider and outsider, was an important cultural icon in America during the Cold War, when fears of crime within American borders matched fear of enemies conspiring without. James Young also explores paranoia about enemies within who are controlled by outsiders in his examination of the anti-union activity in Erie, Pennsylvania, which branded many members as communists. Finally, Anna Creadick's essay looks at science-fiction films from the 1950s to examine new anxieties about the effect of the atomic age on the virility of the American male. The Cold War period, commonly associated with McCarthyism and other paranoias, is a classically fearful era meriting its own section.

The last two sections of the book, "Anxieties of the Modern Age" and "Futurephobia," further explore the twentieth century. "Anxieties of the Modern Age, the longest section in this book, contains six essays about a variety of fears expressed in modern culture. The modern age ushered in a host of new anxieties in addition to those flourishing during the Cold War. The contributors in this section have flagged many fears that have manifested themselves during this century. Mark C.

Smith studies the incubation of the war on drugs and the use of fear tactics, which began with Richard Pearson Hobson and continues to this day with the strategies of William Bennett, Joseph Califano, and CASA. Jason Loviglio's piece, mentioned earlier in connection with Orientalism, examines the rise of radio drama and the corresponding notion of the intimate public. Michael Smith's essay takes us to a more recent decade for a look at the population bomb crisis that seemingly threatened to explode during the period of civil turbulence of the late 1960s and early 1970s. The diaphragm, which is the subject of the contribution by Rosanne L. Welker, might well have helped to offer a practical solution to this crisis, but as Welker points out, beginning at the turn of the century, access to it was restricted and controlled by the courts and the largely male medical profession. The final essays in the section, by Jacqueline Ellis and Richard Horwitz, explore two other contemporary anxieties: fear of working-class women, personified in the larger-than-life Roseanne of TV fame, and fear of corporate take-overs—specifically, of the family pig farm. Taken together, "Anxieties of the Modern Age" highlights some currents of paranoia that flow through twentieth-century America.

The essays in this volume, from a range of disciplines in American studies, cover topics from nearly every era in American history. The book concludes with a seventh section, "Futurephobia." First comes the essay by Brian Marcus on the sweeping history of fear of the Freemasons and Illuminati, which I alluded to earlier. The essay by Philip Lamy and Devon Kinne on "ufology" (the study of UFOs) and James Hewitson's essay on postmillenialism in American popular film conclude the book. The essays by Marcus and by Lamy and Kinne rely on Internet sources to read paranoid trends in contemporary culture, while Hewitson examines the portrait of the postmillenial period in several recent films. These three essays paint the future as a frightful place— but as we look back through this collection, it is probably no more frightful than where we've already been.

Notes

1. Diane White, "Cashing in on the Fear Frenzy," *Boston Globe*, July 17, 1997, E1.
2. Barbara Ehrenreich, *Blood Rites* (New York: Metropolitan, 1997); Elaine Showalter, *Hystories: Hysterical Epidemics and Modern Culture* (New York: Columbia University Press, 1997). The *paranoid style* refers to the classic

text by Richard Hofstadter, *The Paranoid Style in American in American Politics and Other Essays* (New York: Alfred A. Knopf, 1965).

3. The full quotation, from Roosevelt's inaugural address in 1933, is "Let me assert my firm belief that the only thing we have to fear is fear itself—nameless, unreasoning, unjustified terror which paralyzes needed efforts to convert retreat into advance."

Acknowledgments

Thanks to John Steele, English Department chairperson; Dean Anita Shea of the School of Arts and Sciences; Dr. Albert Hamilton, vice president for Academic Affairs; and President Nancy Harrington at Salem State College for their support of this project. Christine Geiger and Gail Rankin of the Salem State College Information Technology Department kindly provided technical support under a tight deadline. Leo Cotter, Robert Davies, Elyse Cotreau Ferris, Peter Forrester, Bob Kelley, Guadalupe Pierce, and Nahila Sabri were careful readers who contributed to the development of this book.

I especially wish to acknowledge the capable assistance of Kimberly Underhill, who worked marvels with the technical aspects of the project, fearlessly and in a timely manner. Thanks also to Bill Coyle, Frank Devlin, Eileen Margerum, and Patricia Johnston of Salem State College and to Thomas Doherty of the American Studies Department at Brandeis University. I am deeply indebted to Dane Morrison of the Salem State College History Department for his generous help with all phases of this project. In addition to his outstanding work coordinating the NEASA conference at Salem State College, he is a most valued colleague and friend. Thanks to Thomas Bacher and Margaret Hunt at Purdue University Press for their confidence in me.

My parents, Carolyn and Henry Lusignan, always offer their help generously. Finally, to Jackson Schultz Jr. and Jackson Schultz III, my loving appreciation for the uncountable ways they enrich my life.

PART I

GRAND UNITED FEAR THEORY

Why Do Opposites Attract?

Fear and Freedom in the Modern Political Imagination

Corey Robin

Fear is an ancient topic in the history of politics and political thought. According to Thucydides, the Athenians claimed that fear was one of the three "strongest motives" for human action, the other two being honor and interest.[1] Aristotle devoted part of the *Ethics* to a searching discussion of courage and cowardice, which he saw as the boundaries of virtue and vice.[2] Machiavelli made the notorious assertion that given the choice between being feared or loved, a prince ought to cultivate fear among his subjects because "it is much safer to be feared than to be loved when one of the two must be lacking."[3] Formulating what was to become one of the most paraphrased statements of moral philosophy, Montaigne commented, "The thing I fear most is fear."[4] And finally Hobbes, the master theorist of fear and its role in political matters, wrote that fear lay at the foundation of all political life. "The original of all great and lasting societies consisted not in the mutual good will men had toward each other, but in the mutual fear they had of each other."[5]

In the modern era, fear came to assume a particularly important role among political theorists. As the ideal of freedom inspired wave after wave of thought and political practice, political theorists turned their sights against fear as the great enemy of civilization. They argued that under no circumstances could fear and freedom be reconciled. The free individual was not to be found among the intimidated. Kant believed that fear was one of the main impediments that intellectually self-reliant men and women faced in attempting to develop their capacity for freedom. Enlightenment became the equivalent of liberating

3

humanity from fear and enabling individuals to exercise their independent rational faculties. "The motto of enlightenment is therefore: *Sapere aude!* Have courage to use your own understanding!"[6] A century after Kant, Henry Sidgwick stated the opposition between fear and freedom as if it were an utter truism: "But in another part of its meaning—which from our present point of view is more important—'freedom' is opposed not to physical constraint, but to the moral restraint placed on inclination by the fear of painful consequences resulting from the action of other human beings."[7]

Even though most modern theorists and many liberal political elites have agreed that fear is the *"summum malum"*[8] of political life and that it should be reduced significantly—if not eliminated outright—in order to develop a free society, I argue here that this commitment has been undermined in two ways. First, despite the belief that fear and freedom occupy two distinct poles of the human experience, modern theorists persistently have expressed an apprehension that some kind of fear may lie at the very heart of human selfhood. Fear, according to these theorists, stimulates human action and awakens the self to a more robust form of individual identity. Without fear, they have implied, there might be no self left to be free. Second, several theorists and intellectuals have argued that modern life makes for psychologically weak individuals who are all too happy to betray their own freedom. They have further argued that by developing a fear of that inner tendency—by developing a fear of ourselves—we will secure our freedom. In the concluding section, I argue that the mobilization of fear on behalf of freedom has been a basic animating feature of counterrevolutionary and antidemocratic politics since the nineteenth century. I conclude that freedom, particularly as it is equated with the ideal of autonomy, is crucial to the cultivation of fear. Although the idea of freedom has inspired centuries of emancipatory politics, it has also been used to create fear.

Fear, Freedom, and the Self

At the same time that modern political theorists have taken their stand against fear in the name of individual freedom, a few thinkers have argued that fear might very well be a necessary condition of human selfhood. Even more interesting is that this proposition has not been found among the more agitated currents of modern thought. The proponents of this view do not belong to the familiar cast of dark characters from the counter-Enlightenment, that is, de Sade, Nietzsche, and Foucault. Instead, the champions of this view include the patron saints of both modern liberalism and modern conservatism, John Locke and Edmund

Burke. In Locke's case the will to act is premised on the experience of anxiety; and in Burke's case selfhood itself depends upon the apprehension of a subdued kind of terror.

Locke claims that human freedom contains two attributes: first, the exercise of the will, that is, the capacity to make a decision or formulate a preference; and, second, the ability to act upon that decision.[9] In order to be free, we must be able to will. As he writes, "liberty cannot be where there is no thought, no volition, no will" (chap. 21, sec. 8, p. 316). Regarding the formation of the will, Locke is particularly concerned about what motivates the individual to will a new course of action. Why does an individual decide to act in a new way? He answers, "The motive for continuing in the same state or action, is only the present satisfaction in it; the motive to change is always some uneasiness: nothing setting us upon the change of state, or upon any new action, but some uneasiness" (chap. 21, sec. 29, p. 331). Individuals seldom choose to make decisions that break with established patterns of conduct unless they experience "uneasiness." This uneasiness might be occasioned by the recognition that one either does not possess some desired object or does not enjoy some desired benefit or experience. Uneasiness might also be the product of actual pain or displeasure. No matter what the cause, individuals will only change their actions in order to eliminate uneasiness. Individuals do not act in new ways out of a positive desire for some good. They do not pursue their own happiness. One might contemplate how pleasant life could be if one attained a certain good, but if the absence of that good does not generate anxiety or discomfort, one will not make a decision to pursue it. In other words, some experience of pain is necessary in order for people to act. "*Good*, the *greater good,* though apprehended and acknowledged to be so, does not determine the will, until our desire, raised proportionably to it, makes us uneasy in the want of it" (chap. 21, sec. 35, p. 335). Locke concludes that "a little burning felt pushes us more powerfully than greater pleasures in prospect draw or allure" (chap. 21, sec. 34, p. 334).

The human experience of uneasiness and anxiety is central to Locke's moral psychology. At times, he even indicates that without uneasiness, the individual might cease to act altogether. "The chief, if not only spur to human industry and action is *uneasiness*" (chap. 20, sec. 6, p. 304). Without uneasiness, there would be no need to make difficult decisions at all—for no one would or could choose to depart from a state devoid of uneasiness. There would be no circumstance or situation for the exercise of a robust will. Therefore, there would be no occasion for wondering whether the individual was free in any sense that mattered. Without uneasiness, individuals would merely continue doing the same thing over and over again, and that would require very little from the will. "When a man is perfectly content with the state he is in—which is when he is perfectly without any uneasiness—what industry, what action, what will is there left, but to continue in it?" (chap. 21, sec. 34, p. 334). In other words, without uneasiness and anxiety, the will to act vigorously would disappear.

Uneasiness upon the absence of a potential good or upon the experience of oppressive pain is more than merely a motivating source of the will. In fact, uneasiness proves to be a kind of universal solvent for Locke. It is constitutive of many human passions, including fear. He defines uneasiness as "all pain of the body, of what sort soever, and disquiet of the mind" (chap. 21, sec. 31, p. 333). Fear, in turn, is a particular form of uneasiness, "an uneasiness of the mind, upon the thought of future evil likely to befal us," whereas uneasiness is the actual experience of pain and discomfort—either physical or psychological—by the individual (chap. 20, sec. 10, p. 305). Fear, however, belongs strictly to those agitations of the mind involving thoughts of a potential (even probable) experience of evil, "which is apt to produce or increase any pain, or diminish any pleasure in us: or else to procure us any evil, or deprive us of any good" (chap. 20, sec. 2, p. 303). In other words, fear is the expectation or suspicion that one probably will experience a form of pain or a loss of pleasure in the future. Fear is the experience of uneasiness about the probability of experiencing future uneasiness. It shares with uneasiness the anxious sense that some pleasure will be absent or some pain will be present. Both sensations—uneasiness and fear—involve feelings of discomfort and the absence of any feeling of calm repose.

I do not wish to exaggerate the connections between fear and uneasiness. Locke is a careful chooser of words, and the fact that fear appears so seldom in his account of the will suggests that fear and uneasiness are proximate—not identical—experiences. What I do want to stress is that the apprehension of pain, the experience of anxiety upon expecting some potential danger, and the dissatisfaction occasioned by the absence of some potential good are all central to Locke's account of the will and, by extension, of freedom. Behind his idea of the willful self lurks a version of the self wallowing in habitual action, never able to break with patterns or custom. Hence without the pricks of anxiety and nervousness, the self would not be active. While these sensations of uneasiness and anxiety are not necessarily the same as fear, they bear a family resemblance. Their repeated appearances throughout the *Essay* reveal a suspicion on Locke's part that the self is in need of the disquieting, jarring sensation of anxiety in order to generate the impetus to change.

Burke takes Locke one step further by showing, with disarming honesty, how fear is crucial to all forms of human agency. While Locke believed that without anxiety the self would decide not to change course, Burke held that without anxiety the will would disappear entirely and the self would gradually erode. Burke begins *A Philosophical Enquiry into the Origins of Our Ideas of the Sublime and the Beautiful* with the proposition that left to their own devices, individuals are neither tempted by the possibility of pleasure nor tormented by the prospect of pain. Instead, "the human mind is often, and I think it is for the most part, in . . . a state of indifference."[10] In this state, individuals cannot undertake any kind of strenuous activity or decisive action. The temptations of pleasure only exacerbate that indifference. After either experiencing or contemplating some form of pleasure, the individual lapses into a "soft tranquility, which is tinged with the agreeable colour of the former sensation" (32). Pleasure induces passivity and dulls the individual's capacity to exert his or her will. The possibility of attaining pleasure does not generate a more willful self; pleasure does not tempt the individual to act in order to achieve it. Instead, pleasure induces a gentle implosion of the self:

> The head reclines something on one side; the eyelids are more closed than usual, and the eyes roll gently with an inclination to the object, the mouth is a little opened, and the breath drawn slowly, with now and then a low sigh; the whole body is composed, and the hands fall idly to the sides. All this is accompanied with an inward sense of melting and languor . . . relaxing the solids of the whole system. (135–36)

The experience of danger, however, can awaken a certain "delight" in the individual. "If the pain and terror are so modified as not to be actually noxious; if the pain is not carried to violence, and the terror is not conversant about the present destruction of the person," then the mind experiences a "delightful horror," which is the "strongest of all the passions" (123). The reason for this odd response to pain and danger, according to Burke, can be explained by comparing the individual when contemplating danger to the individual when faced with nothing threatening at all. In the absence of imagined terror, the individual wallows in "a state of rest and inaction." Far from providing an opportunity to pursue one's aims, the absence of fear causes "all the parts of our bodies" to "fall into a relaxation, that not only disables the members from performing their functions, but takes away the vigorous tone of fibre which is requisite for carrying on the natural and necessary secretions"

(122). Repose and ease are physically debilitating; the lack of exertion only makes the body physically incapable of carrying out its basic biological functions.

Even more frightening, however, is the emotional harm that inactivity threatens. "Melancholy, dejection, despair, and often self-murder," writes Burke, "is the consequence of the gloomy view we take of things in this relaxed state of body" (122). The only prophylactic against the possibility of bodily dissolution is physical labor. For the mind, however, labor is insufficient. If the mind is on the verge of losing its capacity to make decisions and exercise its sway over the body, then only "a mode of terror" can restore it to its rightful efficacy. Strength of mind is the crucial quality that the contemplation of terror awakens in the self, for it restores to the individual the capacity for willful action. Danger stimulates the self to a more agitated, alert state of mind, and that state induces the self to think clearly and act decisively. In certain respects, we might say that pain and danger are crucial to Burke's idea of selfhood, if by selfhood we mean individuals' experience of themselves as agents, as active beings capable of exerting their wills and activating the world around them with their imagination. Pleasure and ease, while pleasant experiences, merely promote a more relaxed, more passive sense of self.

In asserting that individuals are always on the verge of lapsing into a state of inaction, which threatens the body and mind with decomposition, Burke is not making the rather commonplace assertion that the individual must face adversity and difficulty in order to grow into a mature, powerful adult. His is the more radical claim that the self's contemplation of terror provokes the most strenuous exercise of the mind and body, and that this apprehension of terror is fundamentally connected to the experience of the sublime, which he claims is "the strongest emotion which the mind is capable of feeling" (36). He is not saying that the direct experience of danger or pain is necessary for awakening the self; in fact, the immediate experience of pain has the capacity to freeze the self. But the idea of danger and threat—a sustained engagement with fantasized danger—can stimulate the self to come to life. It can force the individual to act in and upon the world.

As theories of individual development, both Locke's and Burke's accounts seem relatively innocuous. After all, if the kind of terror that Burke recommends as necessary for developing the self is imaginary and aesthetic, why should we worry about it? As a mode of fantasy, fear is probably unproblematic. For example, many of us delight in scary movies or in screaming our way through a terrifying roller-coaster ride. This hardly means that we seek or would enjoy a life of real intimidation and terror. We are a long way away from the idea that this positing of anxiety as necessary for selfhood challenges the antipathy of modern political theorists toward regimes that systematically promote fear.

What the discussions of both Locke and Burke do reveal, however, is a concern among political and moral theorists that selfhood is not threatened solely by external constraints, physical coercion, or tyrannical governments. Locke and Burke suggest that the self is also threatened by contentment, pleasure, beauty, ease, and the absence of anxiety or fear. These experiences induce inactivity. Those who worry about the freedom of the will should attend to these dangers, recognizing that fear is necessary in order to ward off a more alarming loss of self.

Fear and Freedom in Politics

In the wake of the French Revolution, political theorists and intellectuals hostile to democracy have analyzed the relationship of fear to the self through the lens of politics. In their hands, the self who dissolves in the absence of fear becomes the symbol of democracy, a symptom of the breakdown of feudalism and the rise of egalitarianism. These antirevolutionary writers have equated the weak self with the democratic self. Because the greatest danger to freedom lurks within the democratic psyche, it makes perfect sense that we should cultivate a fear of our own capacity for internal collapse. That fear of ourselves goes hand in hand with a fear of certain aspects of democracy. This fear of ourselves is championed precisely because it will lead to freedom—both of the self and of society. If we are afraid of our tendency to inner collapse, we will take the necessary actions to ward off this collapse. Our fear will help make us free.

I take my examples of this political mobilization of fear on behalf of freedom from the arguments of Alexis de Tocqueville and Arthur Schlesinger—representative intellectuals of the democratic age who in their writings sought to strengthen the fragile self by having it march under the banner of antirevolutionary politics. They demonstrate how politically potent the image of the dissolving self becomes during the Age of Revolution. In *Democracy in America* and *The Vital Center,* Tocqueville and Schlesinger respectively claim that the democratic individual is threatened not by external danger but by internal anxiety. As I will show, this model of the anxious democratic individual who loses all will is quite similar to Burke's dissolving self and Locke's indolent individual. Against this crippling anxiety, which leads to internal collapse, both Tocqueville and Schlesinger recommend that we develop a revivifying fear. That fear of ourselves will push us to overcome our own desire to forsake our freedom. We will develop a stronger will, finding our freedom precisely in a fear of ourselves. The means to bringing about that fear is, for both Tocqueville and Schlesinger, political activity that defends certain portions of the democratic inheritance and does battle against its revolutionary implications.

Tocqueville claims that with the breakdown of feudalism, modern democratic societies occasion social dislocation and uncertainty. Either through political revolutions or because of the gradual evolution of equality, men and women are liberated from the figures of authority that formerly held society together. Aristocrats no longer preside over their servants; nor do they provide the guidance and firm hand of discipline that was so evident in feudal societies.[11] Religion also loses its sway. Although religion as a popular institution survives, religious authority and a belief in the providential will no longer command assent. In the past, religion and the aristocracy organized individual belief and conduct. Without them, individuals lack the markers that once gave them direction (444).

As this form of traditional authority in the social and religious spheres disappears, modern individuals are, according to Tocqueville, released from their bonds, only to find themselves entirely alone. Without authority, individuals are thrown back on themselves as the source of all understanding and knowledge. The feudal individual's fear of his or her master had brought the individual a certain measure of protection from others. Without that enabling fear, individuals face more extreme forms of anxiety. Far from liberating the self to go out and conquer new worlds, the alleged emancipation of democratic egalitarianism only breeds anxiety, despair, and loneliness. The ironic result of the revolution in politics and culture—where traditional authority is delegitimized in favor of modern notions of consent and individual rights— is that individuals are more afraid, more uncertain, and therefore more desperate for the comforting voice of authority and tradition. As Tocqueville writes:

> Such a state inevitably enervates the soul, and relaxing the springs of the will, prepares a people for bondage. Then not only will they let their freedom be taken from them, but often they actually hand it over themselves. When there is no authority in religion or in politics, men are soon frightened by the limitless independence with which they are faced. They are worried and worn out by the constant restlessness of everything. With everything on the move in the realm of the mind, they want the material order at least to be firm and stable, and as they cannot accept their ancient beliefs again, they hand themselves over to a master. (444)

In other words, individuals experience a kind of vertigo when faced with the loss of authority and the resulting loneliness of egalitarian society. All decisions become a source of even more anxiety because there is no foundational ground for choosing. Freedom becomes an unbearable burden, a permanent reminder of their lost state. Thus these individuals would prefer nothing more than to hand their freedom over to another.

Under Tocqueville's system, anxious individuals seek the restoration of a firm and decisive authority in order to relieve themselves permanently of the anxieties of freedom. This authority can come in a number of forms. The individual may conform to the anonymous power of the crowd, adjusting his or her beliefs and tastes to suit the demands of popular opinion.[12] Or this individual may make accommodations to the power of the centralized state, happily handing over basic rights and powers to a bureaucratic institution which takes over the management of the individual's daily affairs.[13] Finally, the individual may submit to a dictator, whose all-encompassing presence eclipses the individual, enabling this person to hide.[14] In each of these scenarios, the individual resolves the anxieties of living an independent, free existence by handing over his or her freedom to an alien structure of authority. The central motif of these modern tyrannies is the dissolution of the individual into a larger structure of power—public opinion, the bureaucratic state, the dictator. It is not that these tyrannies terrorize individuals or repress instincts; it is that they *absorb* the individual into their structures of operation. Modern men and women discard their personal identities and become part of a larger collective power. Only that kind of process of absorption relieves them of the anxieties that attend the exercise of freedom.

Modern tyrannies can operate in this fashion only because of the particularly weak character of democratic individuals, who long to belong to a uniting structure of authority. Tocqueville has transposed Locke's insight about the nature of the self into a sociological critique of democracy. For Tocqueville, the inner weakness of the self is not a function of human nature, as it was for Locke, but a condition endemic to the democratic mass. Aristocratic individuals "have something of greatness and strength which is all their own." Their sense of honor gives "extraordinary strength to individual resistance." Because they hold "a high idea of their individual worth," they are not frightened by their isolation. They feel confident enough in themselves that they do not need the approval of others. Thus, they dare "in isolation to resist the pressure of public authority." Democratic individuals lack that sense of inner confidence and strength. They are especially dependent on maintaining the esteem of their peers. Of the democratic individual Tocqueville notes,

"Finding nothing that raises him above their level and distinguishes him, he loses his self-confidence when he comes into collision with them."[15] Because of the overthrow of paternalistic authority, democratic individuals lose the structures that formerly shaped their will. Their desire to accept external authority is merely symptomatic of the absence of traditional structures of authority. In the absence of those structures, they lose the contours of a sharply defined self with its own interests and purposes; they become, in effect, living embodiments of the kind of self Burke had in mind when discussing the individual who has not witnessed a certain kind of terror.

The psychological character of the democratic individual provides the point of entry for threatening tyrannical power. In certain respects, the most powerful weapons of the despot are democratic individuals for they bring about their own oppression. "As equality spreads and men individually become less strong, they ever increasingly *let themselves* glide with the stream of the crowd and find it hard to maintain an opinion abandoned by the rest" (520; emphasis added). Because the inner character of the democratic individual is the despot's most powerful weapon, it becomes the greatest object of fear; it is the chief danger of which democratic men and women should be afraid, if not the chief danger against which democratic individuals should take precaution. Tocqueville's analysis of the dangers of modernity is not merely the neutral account of a spectator; it is also a warning which he expects his readers to heed. Tocqueville very much believes we *should* fear this alleged tendency toward inner collapse. His text is as much about creating fear in his readers as it is about describing fear. For it is only in fearing ourselves that we will overcome our inner desire to collapse. Fear will restore us to a sense of willful purpose and enable us to protect our freedom. As he writes near the end of *Democracy in America*, "Let us, then, look forward to the future with that salutary fear which makes men keep watch and ward for freedom, and not with that flabby, idle terror which makes men's hearts sink and enervates them" (702). It is only by mobilizing individual fear, which transforms the permeable democratic self into a solid integer, that Tocqueville believes modern individuals will be free.

Tocqueville is not making the rather commonplace argument that we must fear a society of fear and then fight against it in order to establish a society based on freedom. He is arguing that a healthy fear of ourselves will lead us to guard against external influence and thereby enable us to exercise our freedom. Tocqueville's conception of freedom involves an active will, which imposes itself on the world, usually in the context of battle. He contrasts this self with weak, flabby individuals who allow themselves to be influenced and ruled by others. He imagines a society of strong spirits, individuals capable of rising above drabness and who can add color to democratic life. These are individuals who will make the desert of modernity bloom. These are individuals who find their true home in conflict, in some kind of warfare where passions are elevated and heroic spirits are summoned. But in what kind of war, and against what kind of enemy, should the individual do battle?

First, Tocqueville seems to entertain the possibility that military engagement—particularly that involving colonial adventures—might produce an impermeable self. Perhaps it is no coincidence that, throughout his life, Tocqueville expressed a romantic infatuation with warfare.[16] In 1840, during a temporary crisis involving Egypt and Turkey that threatened to draw France into war, he wrote to his friend Gustave Beaumont that while he thought entering the war was probably a bad idea, "these wise reflections do not prevent me, at the bottom of my heart, from seeing all this crisis with a certain satisfaction. You know what a taste I have for great events and how tired I am of our little democratic and bourgeois pot of soup."[17] Not long after, he confessed to John Stuart Mill that the threat of war "has caused me a great deal of confusion and difficulty." While he remained ambivalent about whether France should enter the war, he wrote that peace might be just as dangerous. After all, "the greatest malady that threatens a people organized as we are is the gradual softening of mores, the abasement of the mind, the mediocrity of tastes; that is where the great dangers of the future lie" (*Letters*, 151).

A second, more enticing, option for political battle was the struggle of counterrevolution. Tocqueville could not conceal his own delight at the prospect of civil war and conflict in 1848. That year promised to liberate him from "the incessant uncertainty in which I had to live" during the peaceful July Monarchy. The eighteen years of parliamentary peace that preceded the Revolution were marked by "mediocrity and monotony," during which Tocqueville was forced to endure "the triviality of the passions." What he found so exhilarating about the Revolution was that he could finally set out boldly on a course without misgiving or ambivalence, without the flabbiness of will that he believed had consumed him during the preceding years.[18] Democratic revolutions were the perfect enemies because they not only provided opportunities for willful action but also reminded people of the consequences of inner weakness and loss of self. Revolutions led to a desire for material comforts, they dulled aristocratic sensibilities, they softened the passions, and they produced individuals who acted out roles from the past.[19] In each of these respects, revolutions produced or reflected weakness. As the clearest manifestations of the inner demons of the democratic self, revolutions provided an object lesson about the nature of internal weakness and the loss of will. They were the perfect enemy against which to do battle. In 1848, Tocqueville campaigned for political office on two planks—the healthy fear of revolution and the love of freedom. In his eyes, these twin commitments were inextricably linked as political brothers under the skin. "This bold profession of anti-revolutionary had been preceded by one of republican faith; the sincerity of the one seemed to bear witness to that of the other."[20] This was a political posture that would find its ultimate home in the twentieth-century struggle against communism.

In the hands of Arthur Schlesinger, the avatar of postwar American liberalism, Tocqueville's argument for freedom and against revolution is marshalled on behalf of liberalism's war against both international and domestic communism. Schlesinger begins *The Vital Center* precisely where Tocqueville leaves off *Democracy in America*. He writes, "Western man in the middle of the twentieth century is tense, uncertain, adrift. We look upon our epoch as a time of troubles, an age of anxiety. The grounds of our civilization, of our certitude, are breaking up under our feet, and familiar ideas and institutions vanish as we reach for them, like shadows in the falling dusk." As did Tocqueville, Schlesinger argues that the overthrow of traditional structures only liberates individuals to face the terrifying emptiness of the universe. Without "the protective tissues of medievalism," modern individuals experience freedom as "a release from external restraints rather than a deep and abiding sense of self-control." In the absence of the guiding lights of religion or traditional authority, individuals must confront an array of decisions but lack any ground from which to choose. Rather than exercise their free will, modern individuals "prefer to flee choice, to flee anxiety, to flee freedom." The best, most reliable means of escaping freedom is "to surrender that individuality to some massive, external authority."[21]

For Schlesinger, totalitarianism preys upon this individual weakness and the desire to be subsumed into some all-embracing structure. Totalitarian movements—whether of the left or of the right—promise to deliver men and women from "the loneliness and rootlessness of . . . free society." The authoritarian politics, the firm discipline, the absolute submission of the individual to the collective "promises the security and comradeship of a crusading unity, propelled by a deep and driving faith." As Schlesinger writes, "members of a totalitarian party *enjoy* the discipline, they revel in the release from individual responsibility, in the affirmation of comradeship in organized mass solidarity." In the context of Cold War America, there is only one institution that can offer the individual such an escape from freedom. That is the Communist Party. "Communism fills empty lives," writes Schlesinger, diagnosing the appeal of the party to the mass individual in American society. These individuals, however, are not an isolated minority. After all, "America has its quota of lonely and frustrated people, craving social, intellectual and even sexual fulfillment they cannot obtain in existing society. For these people, party discipline is no obstacle; it is an attraction. The great majority of members in America, as in Europe, *want* to be disciplined." The party insinuates itself into many aspects of American life, including the powerful labor movement and an increasingly active African-American community.[22] Within the larger circles of the party's orbit, totalitarianism is able to make its appeal to the considerable number of anxious men and women of American society.

Even though he writes in 1949, on the verge of the Soviet Union's explosion of the atomic bomb and just as the United States is about to enter the Korean War, Schlesinger is emphatic that the greatest threat to freedom comes from within American society. "The crisis of free society has assumed the form of international collision between democracies and the totalitarian powers; but this fact should not blind us to the fact that in its essence this crisis is internal." The reason the greatest threats spring from within American society is that there is a "Stalin in every breast." In other words, the Soviet Union need not invade the United States; it does not need to infiltrate with spies or other traditional means of subterfuge. Instead, at the heart of the American soul, there is a deep passion for submission to some kind of tyranny. The longing for total authority, the desire to lose oneself in a tight structure of discipline and unity, is so overpowering that it makes for a psychological Fifth Column right at home. For that reason, the confrontation with the Soviet Union is merely epiphenomenal. Far more important is to confront the enemy at home, to do battle against those "anxieties which drive people in free society to become traitors to freedom."[23]

How is one to make war against these traitors who reside within the "psychological economy" of the American psyche? As with Tocqueville before him, Schlesinger recommends that we fight against the forces of internal anxiety that threaten us with the loss of will and purpose by mobilizing against fear. In order to do battle against fear, however, we must first develop a fear of ourselves. Schlesinger openly argues that most Americans do not experience anxiety or, if they do, they are not aware of it. Most Americans "linger over the familiar milkshake in the bright drugstore." They "forget the nightmare in the resurgence of warmth and comfort." They do not consciously feel any fear. "Anxiety is something we hear about. It is not yet part of our lives—*not enough of our lives, anyway.*"[24] If people are to protect and exercise their freedom, fear must be made a part of their lives. They must learn to fear—they must develop a fear of their own unacknowledged desire for submission—if they are to be free.

Schlesinger goes one step further, however, by openly suggesting that though the enemy is internal, we are best served by fighting its external symbol, that is, the Soviet Union and the American Communist Party. "The fact that the contest between the USA and the USSR is not the source of the contemporary crisis does not, however, alter the fact that the crisis must be met in terms of this contest."[25] Unfocused existential anxiety, which is the central problem of our time, can only be resolved by fighting against a clear and certain enemy. As he writes, we "can strike at the dilemma of history," by which he means the anxiety of modernity, "only in terms of the problem" between the United States and the Soviet Union, and in terms of the conflict between the liberal tradition and the Communist Party.[26]

Even though the communist menace is merely a symbolic manifestation of a deeper psychological problem, a political symptom of an emotional anxiety, Schlesinger is confident that confronting it at the political level will provide a structure for resolving the emotional dilemma. A life of political struggle and conflict against the forces of anxiety is the solution to the threats of despair and anxiety; it will produce a new, willful self, brimming with its sense of freedom and power. The only way to generate such a warlike attitude, however, is for the American people to acknowledge their anxiety, to learn to fear it, and then to use that fear as a stimulus to willful action.

Schlesinger's voice was not an isolated cry in the wilderness. His construction of the radical menace as preying upon a weak, anxious self was repeated throughout the Cold War. It was articulated among highbrow intellectuals, in the journals of academic social science, in the literature of communist disillusionment, and in the halls of Congress. All of these forces joined together against communism because they assumed a dangerous symbiosis between communism and the weak ego. Wherever this notion was promulgated, the message was clear: Beware of yourself. Harry Gold—the infamous spy who served as the courier between Klaus Fuchs and David Greenglass (who was the brother of Ethel Rosenberg)—testified in 1956 before the Senate Internal Security subcommittee. He claimed that in working for the cause of world communism he had lost his "identity and . . . desire to be an individual." Relying on the classic trope of the true believer, he claimed, "I had completely lost my free will; I had actually turned over my complete personality, my complete soul, and everything."[27] What allegedly attracted the communist to the cause was not any analysis of economic power in modern society, nor was it a vision of justice for the working class. It was the all-encompassing unity and discipline of the movement, the promise of freeing oneself of the burdens of freedom. Precisely because that was a desire embedded in the democratic psyche, everyone had to guard against it in themselves. As John Dewey wrote:

> The serious threat to our democracy is not the existence of foreign totalitarian states. It is the existence within our own personal attitudes and within our own institutions of conditions that have given a victory to external authority, discipline, uniformity, and dependence upon the leader in foreign countries. The battlefield is also accordingly here—within ourselves and our institutions.[28]

George Kennan was more succinct. Totalitarianism is "a state into which any great national entity can relapse, if it doesn't watch its step."[29]

In discussing the Rosenbergs and their espionage, the literary critic Leslie Fiedler claimed that their execution by the United States government was merely a symbolic act. After all, by joining the Communist Party, the Rosenbergs had ceded their freedom, their individual identities, and hence their humanity, long ago. Having participated in a radical movement, the Rosenbergs no longer existed as individuals. With a stunning coldness, Fiedler asked, "What was there left to die?"[30] For Fiedler, as for so many others, the most frightening fact about the Rosenbergs was that they were not extraordinary. They were artifacts of egalitarian mass culture, living a humdrum life in Knickerbocker Village, a low-income Manhattan housing complex with "identical dwelling units" that embodied the pathological sameness of democratic life. Unfortunately, that sameness was only "the visible manifestation of the Stalinized, petty-bourgeois mind."[31] For liberal intellectuals like Fiedler, there was a direct link between the symbols of the democratic welfare state and the radical menace, and it lay within the anxious soul of the democratic self.

Conclusion: Portrait of an Enemy

Underlying this near hysteria among intellectuals about individuals handing over their freedom to external authorities is an ambivalence about the idea of freedom itself, particularly as it is equated with the notion of autonomy. Since the Enlightenment, liberal intellectuals have been inspired by the ideal of autonomy. This ideal has generated a vision of the individual as particularly susceptible to subtle forms of manipulation and control. Although the ideal of autonomy has inspired a hopeful politics of progressive action, it has also inspired a politics based on fear—of radical movements and democratic mass culture in general.

Autonomy depends to a great degree on a particularly robust notion of the will. It envisions the individual as a self-legislator, as one who can establish the reasons for personal conduct and the principles of moral life. Autonomy places a moral premium on the ability of individuals to fashion for themselves their own individual values and idiosyncratic identities. The autonomous being, claimed Kant, "must regard itself as the author of its principles, independently of foreign influences."[32]

The problem with the idea of autonomy is that, by emphasizing the importance of the self-legislating will, theorists of autonomy often claim that the will's autonomy is threatened not by external forms of coercion but by the individual's desire not to exercise the will. In other words, the main threat to freedom is individual weakness and failure. It would be one thing if autonomy were jeopardized only by the coercive weapons of tyrants, the state, the rich, and the powerful. Autonomy, however, raises the stakes of freedom, placing a moral premium on a kind of independence for which the individual is particularly responsible. While it is true that physical coercion can compromise one's autonomy, many political theorists have been far more nervous about the tendency of the *individual* to compromise his or her own autonomy. In this regard, I would argue, modern intellectuals of all political stripes have led us astray. They inadvertently have shifted our attention away from the instruments of coercion belonging to the state and the powerful to the realm of internal psychology. We are not to fear the state; we are asked us to fear ourselves.

Merely consider in this regard two great figures from the liberal pantheon, Kant and J. S. Mill. In Kant's essay on enlightenment, he claims that individuals often do not make use of their own understanding and autonomy but rely instead on the judgment of another. He claims that this betrayal of their autonomy is due to laziness and fear. Laziness is clearly a product of the individual's own character. As Kant writes, "If I have a book to have understanding in place of me, a spiritual adviser to have a conscience for me, a doctor to judge my diet for me, and so on, I need not make any efforts at all."[33] One is entirely responsible for one's own laziness. Fear, however, is also the fault of the individual. True, he assigns a certain degree of blame to the "guardians," those self-appointed experts who constantly warn individuals of the perils of making their own way. Yet Kant believes that the guardians only can inspire fear because the individual lives in a state of immaturity. Fear is thus a product of ignorance and underdevelopment, even though that ignorance has been fostered by the guardian class. It is not the product of coercion or threatening power from elites but of a "lack of resolution and courage to use [one's rationality] without the guidance of other." While revolution may overthrow the fearful power of the despots and autocrats, it will not release people completely from fear because fear is "self-incurred."[34]

In Mill's analysis, this focus on the individual as the originating source of oppression is even greater. In the modern era, claims Mill, individual autonomy is not chiefly threatened by political restraint or coercion. In fact, such a view of tyranny is only "vulgarly" held among those who believe that modern forms of power emanate from "political functionaries."[35] Instead, he writes, it is society that exercises tyrannical power, but it is able to do so because of the particular weaknesses and foibles of democratic individuals. It is individual people who allow themselves to be controlled by others. "For in proportion to a man's want of confidence in his own solitary judgment, does he usually repose with implicit trust, on the infallibility of 'the world' in general" (21). Elsewhere, Mill writes of that individual "who lets the world, or his own portion of it, choose his plan of life for him." That individual, writes Mill, "has no need of any other faculty than the ape-like one of imitation" (59). If individuals can hold on to their own values and tastes, then no amount of tyrannical power can compromise their autonomy. What is truly despotic is not coercive power so much as situations where individuals do not establish for themselves the values of their own existence. "Even despotism does not produce its worst effects, so long as 'individuality' exists under it; and whatever crushes individuality is despotism" (64).

The unintended consequence of the idea of autonomy, an idea meant to liberate individuals from fear, has been to heighten fear. Modern political theorists and intellectuals have created a veritable moral panic about the tendency of the self to compromise individual freedom. One need only consider some of the basic works of twentieth-century social thought to see how pervasive this fear of ourselves has been.[36] This fear of the self has been intimately linked to the perceived rise of mass democracy. For it is in the context of mass movements, mass society, and mass culture that intellectuals have imagined the self abandoning its autonomy most completely. And in having reviewed the extent to which autonomy has generated a fear of the self and a fear of mass movements, I inevitably wonder whether it has generated more fear than it has freedom.

Notes

1. Thucydides, *The Peloponessian War*, trans. Richard Crawley (New York: Modern Library, 1982), 1.75–76.

2. Aristotle, *Nicomachean Ethics*, trans. Martin Ostwald (New York: Macmillan, 1962), 1107a35–1107b3, 1108b19–1109a19, 1115a6–1117b21.

3. Niccolo Machiavelli, *The Prince*, in *The Portable Machiavelli*, ed. Peter Bondanella and Mark Musa (New York: Penguin Books, 1979), 131.

4. *The Complete Essays of Montaigne*, trans. Donald M. Frame (Stanford, Calif.: Stanford University Press, 1957), 52–53.

5. Thomas Hobbes, *De Cive*, in *Man and Citizen*, ed. Bernard Gert (Indianapolis, Ind.: Hackett, 1991), chap. 1, sec. 2, p. 113.

6. Immanuel Kant, "An Answer to the Question: 'What is Enlightenment?' " in *Political Writings*, ed. Hans Reiss (1970; reprint, New York: Cambridge University Press, 1991), 54.

7. Henry Sidgwick, *The Elements of Politics* (London: Macmillan, 1891), 41.

8. Judith Shklar, "The Liberalism of Fear," in *Liberalism and the Moral Life*, ed. Nancy L. Rosenblum (Cambridge, Mass.: Harvard University Press, 1989), 29.

9. John Locke, *An Essay Concerning Human Understanding*, ed. Alexander Campbell Fraser (New York: Dover Publications, 1959), book 2, chap. 21, sec. 15, p. 320. All subsequent citations are from book 2 of the *Essay* and will appear parenthetically in my text. Locke offers a second definition of liberty in the *Essay* (which I will not analyze here), when he claims that individuals have the ability to examine their desires before choosing to act upon them. This capacity to "*suspend* the execution and satisfaction" of desire in order to assess whether acting upon that desire would lead to ultimate human happiness is the "liberty man has" (chap. 21, sec. 48, p. 345).

10. Edmund Burke, *A Philosophical Enquiry into the Origin of Our Ideas of the Sublime and the Beautiful*, ed. Adam Phillips (New York: Oxford University Press, 1990), 30. Subsequent citations will be from this edition and appear parenthetically in my text.

11. Alexis de Tocqueville, *Democracy in America*, trans. George Lawrence, ed. J. P. Mayer (New York: Harper and Row, 1969), 507. Subsequent citations will be from this edition and appear parenthetically in my text.

12. Tocqueville, *Democracy*, 436, 520, 643–45.

13. Tocqueville, *Democracy*, 515–16, 539–40, 668–81, 692–93.

14. Melvin Richter, "Tocqueville, Napoleon, and Bonapartism," in *Reconsidering Tocqueville's Democracy in America*, ed. Abraham S. Eisenstadt (New Brunswick, N.J.: Rutgers University Press, 1988), 110–45.

15. Tocqueville, *Democracy*, 313, 643.

16. Roger Boesche, *The Strange Liberalism of Alexis de Tocqueville* (Ithaca, N.Y.: Cornell University Press, 1987), 63ff, 173ff.

17. *Selected Letters on Politics and Society*, ed. Roger Boesche, trans. James Toupin and Roger Boesche (Berkeley and Los Angeles: University of California Press, 1985), 143. Subsequent citations will be from this edition and appear parenthetically in my text.

18. *The Recollections of Alexis de Tocqueville*, ed. J. P. Mayer, trans. Alexander Teixeira de Mattos (New York: Columbia University Press, 1949), 87–92.

19. Jean-Claude Lamberti, *Tocqueville and the Two Democracies*, trans. Arthur Goldhammer (Cambridge, Mass.: Harvard University Press, 1989), 204–5, 223; Mayer, ed., *Recollections*, 54–55.

20. Mayer, ed., *Recollections*, 99.

21. Arthur M. Schlesinger, Jr., *The Vital Center: The Politics of Freedom* (1949; reprint, New York: DaCapo Press, 1988), 1, 3, 5, 51–52, 53.

22. Schlesinger, *Vital Center*, 54, 105, 104, 120 (emphases in original).

23. Schlesinger, *Vital Center*, 244, 250, 247.

24. Schlesinger, *Vital Center*, 2; emphasis added.

25. Schlesinger, *Vital Center*, 6.

26. Schlesinger, *Vital Center*, 7.

27. Walter and Miriam Schneir, *Invitation to an Inquest* (1965; reprint, New York: Pantheon, 1983), 365.

28. John Dewey, *Freedom and Culture* (New York: G. P. Putnam's Sons, 1939), 49. Dewey was referring here to Nazism and Fascism, but in the Cold War era, his analysis was taken up as a critique of the communist threat, which, it was argued, had penetrated much deeper into the American psyche than had Nazism.

29. George F. Kennan, "Totalitarianism in the Modern World," in *Totalitarianism*, ed. Carl J. Friedrich (New York: Grosset and Dunlap, 1954), 24.

30. Leslie Fielder, *An End to Innocence* (New York: Stein and Day, 1971), 45.

31. Fiedler, *End to Innocence*, 26. Fiedler's obsession with the Rosenbergs' domicile has led one scholar to quip that they were the first spies ever to be convicted on the basis of "guilt by housing." Andrew Ross, *No Respect: Intellectuals and Popular Culture* (New York: Routledge, Chapman and Hall, 1989), 15.

32. Immanuel Kant, *Foundations of the Metaphysics of Morals*, trans. Lewis White Beck (Indianapolis, Ind.: Bobbs-Merrill, 1959), 67.

22

33. Kant, "What is Enlightenment?" 54.

34. Kant, "What is Enlightenment?" 55.

35. J. S. Mill, *On Liberty*, ed. Stefan Collini (New York: Cambridge University Press, 1989), 8. Subsequent citations will be from this edition and noted parenthetically in my text.

36. Cf. Talcott Parsons, *The Structure of Social Action*, 2d ed. (Glencoe, Ill.: Free Press, 1949); Erich Fromm, *The Fear of Freedom* (1942; reprint, London: Ark Paperbacks, 1984); T. W. Adorno, *The Authoritarian Personality* (1950; reprint, New York: W. W. Norton, 1982); David Riesman et al., *The Lonely Crowd* (Garden City, N.Y.: Doubleday Anchor Books, 1950); Erving Goffman, *The Presentation of Self in Everyday Life* (Garden City, N.Y.: Doubleday, 1959); Seymour Martin Lipset, *Political Man* (Garden City, N.Y.: Anchor Books, 1960); Herbert Marcuse, *One-Dimensional Man* (Boston, Mass.: Beacon Press, 1964); Stanley Milgram, *Obedience to Authority* (New York: Harper and Row, 1969); Christopher Lasch, *The Culture of Narcissism* (New York: W. W. Norton, 1978).

"A Plague of Paranoia"
Theories of Conspiracy Theory
since the 1960s

Peter Knight

> "You one of these right-wing nut outfits?" inquired the
> diplomatic Metzger.
> Fallopian twinkled. "They accuse *us* of being paranoids."
> "They?" inquired Metzger, twinkling also.
> "Us?" asked Oedipa.
>
> —Thomas Pynchon, *The Crying of Lot 49*

Promoting her new book *Hystories* during the spring and summer of
1997, Elaine Showalter encountered seemingly unexpected resistance
to her analysis of "Hysterical Epidemics and Modern Culture."[1] Her
argument is that "contemporary hysterical patients blame external
sources—a virus, chemical warfare, satanic conspiracy, alien infiltration—for psychic problems."[2] In the book Showalter is keen to point out
that she doesn't "wish to offend" and that she does not "disparage the
suffering of patients" whose "symptoms are genuine."[3] She argues that
what makes it so hard for people to accept responsibility for their symptoms—and their sources in "unacceptable" sexual desires—is that in
our culture mental illness is seen as a moral failing and not really illness
at all. Many reviewers were prepared to accept the account in *Hystories*
of satanic ritual abuse and alien abduction as outbreaks of hysteria, but
drew the line at Showalter's charge that Gulf War Syndrome (GWS)
and Chronic Fatigue Syndrome (CFS) are just two more examples of the
contemporary "plague of paranoia."[4] Belief in widespread satanic worship and alien infiltration might indeed be the effects of fevered millennial imaginations, it was argued, but for most people the jury is still out
in the case of GWS and CFS. With all we have learned about the abuses
of power in the last two decades, for many commentators it would come
as no surprise to learn that the military is refusing to investigate properly—if not actually covering up the truth about—the appalling catalogue of illnesses associated with the war in the Persian Gulf, illnesses

quite conceivably caused by either careless or deliberate exposure of soldiers to unknown risk, be it pesticides, cocktails of anti-nerve gas drugs, or (in one conspiracy theory) uranium-enriched missile casings.[5]

In significant ways Showalter's analysis follows Richard Hofstadter's classic 1964 essay "The Paranoid Style in American Politics"—and Showalter indeed quotes sections from Hofstadter's piece. Both argue that American culture has a "propensity to paranoia," and that outbursts of hysterical thinking can be extremely damaging for the victims of scapegoating.[6] However, the hostile reception that met Showalter on television and radio talk shows points to a significant shift in attitudes to conspiracy and paranoia since Hofstadter's analysis was first presented in a lecture at Oxford just before the Kennedy assassination in November 1963. One indication would be that whereas Hofstadter could safely assume that most believers in conspiracy theories were right-wing nuts, the reaction to Showalter suggests that, in cases like Gulf War Syndrome, the smart money is on a government conspiracy and cover-up. In this essay I want to explore some of the developments in what might be termed conspiracy culture over the last three and a half decades, and to argue that these changes mean that we can no longer wheel out Hofstadter's analysis of the "paranoid style" and feed in new examples from our own times. Of course, there are many continuities with previous eras of conspiracy culture in the United States, and it is depressing how often the same old racist, homophobic, and anti-Semitic litanies are repeated.[7] There are, however, some significant new developments that require a rethinking of the traditional approaches to the discourse of conspiracy.

The Paranoid Style

Hofstadter identifies the "paranoid style" as an "old and recurrent mode of expression in our public life," but one which is "the preferred style only of minority movements."[8] His conviction that only the fringe (especially on the right) of American politics suffers from a conspiratorial imagination needs to be understood in part as a reaction to the excesses of McCarthyism (and, as the revised version of the essay makes clear in a footnote, to the perceived excesses of the conspiracy-obsessed reaction to the Kennedy assassination by European writers). Hofstadter's stance is that of a cosmopolitan intellectual denouncing the small-minded backwater politics of right-wing hate groups. Trying to reassure himself that the fundamental stability of the American political system will remain unharmed by these isolated episodes of extremist scare-mongering, he asserts that the paranoid fails to see "social conflict as something to be mediated and compromised." The "paranoid style" is the last resort of those who are marginal to the centers of power and whose "ultimate scheme of values" cannot be accommodated by "bargain and compromise."[9] Hofstadter reads countersubversive literature as a failure by various minorities to solve conflict through "the usual methods of give-and-take"; who fail, in effect, to understand the exceptionalist doctrine of American politics, which stipulates that the social and economic mobility of American society meant that it would not follow European models of violent upheaval on the basis of fundamental conflicts of class, race, gender, and sexuality.[10]

Hofstadter's insistence that the "paranoid style" is a minority phenomenon made some political sense in the tense atmosphere in America before the publication of the Warren Commission Report. Now such a claim is no longer plausible. Conspiracy theory has become not only popular, but also symptomatic, frequently pointing to the major conflicts in American society. With the Kennedy assassination as a measure of the popularity of the "paranoid style" (since it is perhaps the central event in any conspiracy-minded version of recent American history), opinion polls indicate that, after the Warren Commission published its findings in late 1964, 87 percent of the American public believed the commission's version that the president had been killed by a lone gunman; by 1993 roughly 80 percent of Americans—including even President Clinton and Vice President Gore—believed in some form of conspiracy theory about the assassination.[11] Other polls, for example, claim that a third of African-Americans believe that the government is responsible for the spread of crack cocaine in the ghetto and deliberately introduced HIV/AIDS into the black community as either an experiment or an attempt at genocide; and that three quarters of African-Americans are convinced that O. J. Simpson was framed by the LAPD.[12] Both the reaction to Showalter on Gulf War Syndrome and these opinion polls—however exaggerated—suggest that in terms of sheer numbers conspiracy theory is no longer confined to a small percentage of Americans on the political fringe.

To be fair, Hofstadter defined the "paranoid style" not so much as a tendency to "see conspiracies here or there in American history," as a belief in "a 'vast' or 'gigantic' conspiracy as *the motive force* in historical events."[13] But this caveat in itself points to a further significant difference between Hofstadter's anatomy of American paranoia and more recent forms of conspiracy culture. His examples are mainly single-issue nativist movements—such as anti-Catholicism—for which a particular demonological view helped forge a sense of group identity. By contrast, many people today—even those not enlisted in a militia—approach conspiracy theories in an eclectic and often contradictory manner, as part entertainment, part speculation, and part accusation. So although many more Americans today believe in conspiracy theories than in Hofstadter's historical snapshots, conversely there is perhaps less evidence of the "paranoid style," in the sense of an inflexible belief in a single, rigid doctrine of scapegoating, since people engage with conspiracy culture in temporary and unpredictable ways.

The increase in conspiracy theories can be explained in part by the diversification of "alternative" information sources over the last three decades: the spread of underground presses during the sixties; the growth of talk radio and local cable shows in the seventies; the emergence of fax networks and home publishing in the eighties; and, most important of all, the use of the Internet in the nineties, with its possibilities for infinite connectedness. With so many sources of information, conspiracy theorists argue, it is impossible for "Them" to monitor every last cable channel and every transaction over the Internet—despite fears about the government's attempt to ensure a back door into every computer with the "clipper chip," or rumors that make the rounds on newsgroups like alt.conspiracy of a supercomputer that records and interprets all telephone calls. A common urban legend in UFO circles has it that a local cable channel reports an alien crash-landing on its late-night newscast, only for the item to have been removed by the following morning. The ease and speed with which conspiracy theories multiply and mutate on the Internet produces whole new possibilities for conspiracy culture. Within hours, many public events generate conspiratorial interpretations that feed off one another: for example, the remarkable spread of conspiracy theories about TWA flight 800 became caught up in a spiraling feedback loop when Kennedy's former press secretary, Pierre Salinger, reported to the mainstream press what he had gleaned from the net, producing a new confirmation to those "facts," which then circulated around the net once more.

Perhaps a more significant contribution to the visibility of conspiracy theory than "the gossip of the global village" is the increasing centrality of conspiratorial themes and forms to both high literature and popular culture.[14] Postwar American literature is saturated with conspiratorial images and plots, and the work of Pynchon, Burroughs, DeLillo, Heller, Mailer, Kesey, and others feeds off and feeds into popular genres, leading to crossover texts like cyberpunk that are similarly shot through with the "paranoid style."[15] American film over the last three decades has produced not just explicitly conspiratorial films such as *Three Days of the Condor*, *The Parallax View*, or *Capricorn One*, but also a vast number of Hollywood thrillers whose plot depends on the discov-

ery of a hidden enemy, be it political, financial, or corporeal.[16] The ubiquity of conspiracy culture has now reached a new level with the phenomenal success of *The X-Files* and its clones. Where Hofstadter found
examples of the "paranoid style" in newspaper editorials, political pamphlets, and government speeches, an updated survey would also have to
take into account the variety of *fictional* engagements with notions of
conspiracy. I think it is far from clear what it would mean to believe in
a conspiracy theory outlined in a fictional text: is it possible to separate
the "message" from the narrative structures in which it is embedded?
can a fictional text promote factual theories?[17] Moreover, the increasingly hazy dividing line between the literal and the metaphorical in conspiracy culture means that audiences begin to read the kind of factual
allegations explored by Hofstadter *as if* they were fictional (and, conversely, with notorious hoaxes in the tradition of the *Protocols of the Elders of Zion* such as *Report from Iron Mountain*, the Torbitt Document,
and Alternative-III, *as if* they were factual).[18]

In short, if there is now a greater variety in the production of conspiracy theories, then there is also a greater diversity and complexity
in their consumption. While at first sight the profusion of conspiracy
theories in tabloids, talk radio, and television would seem to corrobo-
rate Showalter's fears of a "plague of paranoia," I think we need to consider how these stories are consumed by their different, and overlapping,
audiences. Although no doubt some viewers regard a show like *The X-
Files* as a straight-up revelation of What's Really Going On, many others tap into its complex and witty ironies.[19] Similarly, while for some
people every detail of the Kennedy assassination has an aura of sacred
inviolability, others revel in the camp aesthetic of the case, from bootleg
copies of the Zapruder footage intercut with hardcore porn circulating
in avant-garde New York film circles in the 1970s, to the "I'm just a
patsy!" buttons once rumored to be available at the otherwise restrained
Sixth Floor Museum in Dallas.[20] Like *The X-Files*, the Kennedy assassination produces its own diverse subcultures that do not fit neatly into
Hofstadter's model of the "paranoid style" as the last refuge of narrow-
minded rednecks intent on scape-goating already victimized minorities.
Indeed, the picture of the duped masses unthinkingly falling for every
last hokum story television beams at them itself (re)produces the well-
worn conspiracy theory of mass culture. Showalter is of course right
to point out the frequently harmful consequences of conspiratorial beliefs (such as the bitter court actions against family members in cases of
alleged satanic ritual abuse), but it is also important to recognize that
the proliferation of these stories does not necessarily indicate the recru-
descence of a paranoia "virus" whose victims unthinkingly fall prey to

bouts of hysterical demonology. If cultural studies has taught us any-thing over the last three decades, it is that the meanings people attach—both consciously and unconsciously—to the culture they consume are never simple.

Perhaps more important than the mere increase in the amount of conspiracy culture in circulation is the way in which interest in conspir-acy has moved from the fringe to the mainstream of American political and cultural life since the appearance of Hofstadter's essay. No longer can the consumption of conspiracy narratives be understood simply as evidence of a paranoid mentality. It is not so much that the "plague of paranoia" has become pandemic, as that the abnormal has become nor-mal; or, more accurately, that the division between the reasonable and the offbeat has eroded. I think we can identify three main reasons for this shift.

First, as the reaction of BBC Radio Four's Melvyn Bragg (and other such "high-culture" pundits) to Showalter on the Gulf War Syndrome issue demonstrates, a willingness to entertain at least some conspiracy theories about the malfeasance of the government has become common currency for cosmopolitan, left-liberal intellectuals. No longer is the "paranoid style" confined to inarticulate right-wing provincials with obscure grudges and a poor grasp of historiography. A "hermeneutic of suspicion" has become standard operating procedure in much work in the humanities in recent years; as Eve Kosofsky Sedgwick comments, "in a world where no one need be delusional to find evidence of system-atic oppression, to theorize out of anything but a paranoid critical stance has come to seem naive or complaisant."[21] Or, as William Bur-roughs once observed, "the paranoid is the person in possession of all the facts."[22] Conspiratorial thinking has played a crucial role in shaping many of the key social and intellectual movements emerging from the sixties, which have mounted diverse challenges not only to the "official version of events," but also to the legitimacy of authority itself.

For many on the left (but also on the right), the three "lone nut" assassinations of that decade became the cornerstone of a skepticism toward government that was firmly cemented into place by Watergate and the subsequent revelations during the seventies about the activities of the security agencies. The canon of conspiracy theories now reads as an alternative version of recent history; as the tag line of the television show *Dark Skies* puts it, "History as we know it is a lie." Conspiracy culture produces a litany of acronyms, codenames and trebled names, a credo of distrust: JFK, RFK, MLK, Malcolm X, Marilyn Monroe, MK-ULTRA, Operation Paperclip, Phoenix, Mongoose, Majestic-12, COINTELPRO, Lee Harvey Oswald, James Earl Ray, Sirhan Sirhan,

Arthur Herman Bremer, Mark David Chapman, John Hinckley, Jr., MIA, LSD, CIA, FBI, NSA, DIA, Octopus, Gemstone, Roswell, Area 51, Jonestown, Chappaquiddick, Waco, Oklahoma, Watergate, Iraqgate, Iran-Contra, October Surprise, Savings & Loan, BCCI, Whitewater, Lockerbie, TWA flight 800, Ebola, AIDS, crack cocaine, military-industrial complex, grassy knoll, magic bullet, lone nut.[23] With suspicious episodes like Gulf War Syndrome, the assumption for many Americans is that the government is not only responsible but also covering up its culpability. In the light of the revelations about the Tuskegee Institute syphilis studies, and the testing of nuclear radiation, LSD, and Agent Orange on unsuspecting army personnel and civilians, it would come as no surprise, the argument goes, that the government would have conducted similarly callous experiments during the Gulf War.

The second factor in explaining the normalization of conspiratorial thinking is the restructuring of the labor market over the last three decades, which has meant that insecurity and resentment have become an everyday reality for many Americans. Under the pressures of globalization, the security of a job for life and all its attendant benefits has eroded: whereas in the 1950s GM was the nation's largest employer, by the mid-1990s Manpower Inc. occupied that symbolic slot. Facing international competition, companies—whose loyalty is no longer to the nation but to the global constituency of shareholders—downsize, outsource, and relocate without warning. The advertising slogan of the 1950s does not ring true any more: what is good for GM is no longer necessarily good for America. The suburban ideal of the safe nuclear family has gradually faded since the fifties, with the increasing Third-worldization of the domestic economy, producing a narrowing of economic horizons for the many, and the fantasy of a "postindustrial" lifestyle for the few. Globalization for some has meant increasing localization for others. The acceptance of structural unemployment, coupled with the erosion of the welfare state, has led to an increasing feeling of alienation from the political process and the American ideal.

The grand irony is that the final achievement of America's manifest destiny with the seeming triumph of free-market capitalism across the globe has brought with it the fragmentation and decline of a traditionally American sense of identity. What does it mean to be American when the idea of America has spread everywhere, but the actual economic influence of the United States is on the decline and "American" jobs are exported south of the border? In a postfordist economy that has neither the financial leeway nor the political will to maintain affirmative-action programs, the increasing competition for diminishing social resources among "multicultural" groups leads to mutual suspicions among the disinherited. Hofstadter sought to reassure himself and his readers that the "paranoid style" was a last resort of those on the fringes of American politics unable or unwilling to participate in the process of "bargain and compromise" of liberal democratic politics. But "the usual methods of give-and-take" can only work in times of general prosperity needed to cushion the real clash of interests. The coincident outbreak, on the one hand, of the culture wars (with the attendant conspiracy theories about tenured radicals and minorities plotting to overthrow the legacy of academia and America) and, on the other hand, the rise of the patriot movement (with its conspiracy theories about a United Nations takeover of the sovereignty of the United States) points to a profound economic and social restructuring of the American mainstream by the mid-1980s. Whereas Hofstadter sought reassurance that, since the paranoid style" was confined to the fringes of American politics, the mainstream was therefore immune, it is now arguable that the erosion of the traditional mainstream has meant that the rhetoric of conspiracy has become far more widespread in American political and cultural life; or, to put it another way, the mainstream has now become an arena of competing and mutually suspicious "extremist" interest groups (many of whom claim to represent the "mainstream"), no longer certain of the identities of "Them" and "Us." Moreover, whereas for Hofstadter the proponents of the "paranoid style" failed to understand the workings of American consensus politics, I would argue that the "paranoid style" now indicates an implicit understanding of the failure of the idealized consensus.

Finally, the rhetoric of conspiracy is spoken not just by the liberal-left and the fragmented center-right mainstream, but has become, if not a new consensus, then certainly a common language between the two, producing what Michael Kelly in a *New Yorker* article calls "fusion paranoia":

> What Fletcher [spokesman for the Militia of Michigan] believes is nothing but an extreme manifestation of views that have long been shared by the far right and the far left, and that in recent years have come together, in a weird meeting of the minds, to become one, and to permeate the mainstream of American politics and popular culture. You could call it fusion paranoia.[24]

Trying to work out the politics of conspiracy theories has become increasingly difficult. Seemingly right-wing scare-mongering rants about Bush's supposed plan for a new world order are perhaps not so far from what we might normally think of as leftist commentary. For example,

Pat Robertson's anti-Semitic accusations about what he calls the "Manhattan Money Power" placing the control of the American economy in private hands are, except for the anti-Semitism, not so far from left-wing analyses of "the growing concentration of power in the hands of the IMF and the World Bank."[25] And militia rants about UN black helicopters over America might be read together with one of the radical left's *Open Magazine Pamphlets*, which argues (I must admit more convincingly) that "with massive budget cuts in the UN agencies for social and economic development and increases for 'peacekeeping,' the United Nations itself threatens to become a military instrument of corporate power."[26]

What is often striking is the fusing together of seemingly incompatible sources and ideas. Chomsky is cited in militia publications, and compendia of conspiracy research such as *Popular Alienation*, the aptly titled collection put out by Steamshovel Press, contain articles on topics as diverse as the Kennedy assassination, alien abductions, the Trilateral Commission, mind control, Wilhelm Reich, the Rosicrucians, computer encryption, the Turin Shroud, Bill Clinton's mentor Carroll Quigley, vampire deities, Abbie Hoffman's death, Holocaust revisionism, Nazi anti-gravity research appropriated by the CIA—and so on. Sorting out left from right—and plausible from implausible—becomes virtually impossible. With the reconfiguration of the American mainstream, Hofstadter's safe ground of critique of the "paranoid style" is no longer viable.

The common element in this pick 'n' mix of apparently incongruous stories is the growing loss of faith in the legitimacy of authority, marked by a distrust of official and expert knowledge, be it medical, legal, historical, or scientific.[27] The sense of delegitimation indicates a further significant shift in the culture of conspiracy since Hofstadter's classic survey. Many of the conspiracy theories presented in the latter's essay (and represented by extracts in David Brion Davis's 1972 collection *The Fear of Conspiracy: Images of Un-American Subversion from the Revolution to the Present*) decry occasional irruptions by alleged subversives in the normal workings of American politics. More recently, however, many conspiracies theories suggest not so much an invasive threat to the natural order of American life, as that the natural order itself presents a pervasive threat to its citizens. In its extreme form on the libertarian right this fear speaks to people like Timothy McVeigh, for whom the Federal building in Oklahoma City represented the enemy, but the "crisis of legitimacy" spreads beyond the confines of the hardcore militia. In addition, a sense of the pervasiveness of complex conspiring forces has also helped shape the new social movements arising from the New Left in the sixties, namely the counterculture, feminism, gay liberation, and black activism. Whereas most previous conspiracy theories—most obviously with McCarthyism—posited a threat to the American way of life and politics by subversive minorities, since the 1960s these new forms of oppositional conspiracy culture have been based on the assumption that the American way of life is itself a threat to so-called minorities.

The erosion of consensus politics has brought with it not just a proliferation of conspiracy theories but also—in all probability—a growth in conspiracy as an operating principle of politics that is taken for granted. If a government's plans (or those of its intelligence agencies) are now less likely to gain popular and congressional acceptance through "the usual methods of give-and-take," then behind-the-scenes black budget operations become increasingly important. The investigations into political assassinations during the 1970s (particularly the Rockefeller Commission and the Church Committee of 1975), in addition to the Watergate and Iran-Contra hearings, revealed the extent of black budget operations by the intelligence agencies that were not publicly accountable. As sixties radical and Kennedy assassination investigator Carl Oglesby comments, "conspiracy is the normal continuation of normal politics by normal means."[28] With the rise of the national security state since World War II, then, conspiracy theories have become more widespread and acceptable not least because conspiracy has become more widespread and acceptable. Moreover, a feedback loop emerges, in which intelligence agents tap into the popular perception of conspiracy as the normal mode of politics to legitimate their own policies which, when uncovered, serve to multiply existing fears—and so on. A culture *of* conspiracy (secrecy as the normal mode of politics and business) symbiotically feeds off and feeds into a culture *about* conspiracy (the normalization of paranoia), producing the combined force field which I have been calling "conspiracy culture."

Deniable Plausibility

The increasing plausibility of conspiracy theories in the explanation of American politics creates severe problems for the two standard approaches to American conspiracy culture. On the one hand, there is the analysis put forward by Hofstadter (and adapted by Davis and Showalter), which seeks to understand the political and psychological needs that are satisfied by demonizing a particular enemy.

On the other hand, the origins of an alternative approach to the "paranoid style" analysis can be found in work of the progressive historians, writing mainly in the first quarter of the century. They argued that many outbursts of what Hofstadter and others would later term the "paranoid style" were in fact deliberately orchestrated moral panics which enabled those in power to pursue their own repressive policies. According to this view, which was revived by radical historians in the 1960s, the "red Scares" of the 1920s and '30s were thus not the spontaneous and natural expression of real (albeit greatly exaggerated) anxieties about national identity, but public outbursts which were conveniently manufactured and exacerbated by those in power to justify their own policies such as antilabor legislation. According to this model, the elite are not in the grip of a pathological delusion, but ruthlessly rational in their manipulation of public sentiment.[29]

In many ways the two theories of conspiracy theory are talking about different things. As Michael Rogin points out in his analysis of the two positions, "studies of political repression looked at economic and political power; studies of the paranoid style investigated symbols, subcultures, and status anxieties."[30] Whereas Hofstadter, for example, viewed the rise of McCarthyism as a product of small-minded, back-water populist prejudice run riot, Rogin, in an early work on *The Intellectuals and McCarthy* (1955), argues that Hofstadter and others failed to take into account how elitist factions of the Republican Party latched onto McCarthyism to further their own political ends. The Progressive historians focused on the often suppressed ideological conflicts—principally class and race—at the center of American society; by contrast, the consensus historians of the 1950s concentrated on ethnic and religious disagreement, seen as "social conflicts that involve ultimate schemes of values and that bring fundamental fears and hatreds, rather than negotiable interests, into political action."[31]

Although there might be significant differences between the two positions, they both assume that the claims of particular conspiracy theories need not be taken seriously. The task of the historian of demonology has been to explain why people have been drawn to such mistaken beliefs; the "paranoid style" theory focuses on the psychological and political needs that such a belief satisfies, while the elitist theory concentrates on the material interests that are advanced by the promotion of such beliefs. Each approach in effect brackets off the content of a particular accusation. In both cases it is assumed that conspiracy theories are exaggerated and distorted—if not entirely false—representations of history. There is, however, often a recognition that there might be a kernel of truth to at least some of the conspiracy theories. Hofstadter acknowledges that "paranoid writing begins with certain defensible judgements"; for example, there was, he admits, "something to be said for the anti-Masons." But what distinguishes the "paranoid style" from more orthodox scholarship, Hofstadter continues, is the "rather curious leap in imagination that is always made at some critical point in the recital of events." In the final analysis, then, the paranoid style must be taken as a sign of "distorted judgement," and so Hofstadter confesses that the term inevitably is "pejorative."[32] However, in the postwar period, we can no longer afford to take it for granted that conspiracy theories are without foundation, at best cynically manufactured by the elite and at worst entirely delusional. If 1950s fears about fluoridation (leading to the contamination of American "precious bodily fluids") as a socialist plot could famously be satirized in Stanley Kubrick's 1964 film *Dr Strangelove,* then by the 1990s, in a climate of ecological suspicion, body panic once again came to be taken with a hesitant seriousness in films such as Todd Haynes's *Safe* (1995).

The methodological difficulties of both the moral panic and "paranoid style" approaches result from not only the growing possibility that some conspiracy theories might well be true, but also the burgeoning difficulty of distinguishing true from false accusations, hastened by the increasing similarity and intertextual connections between fictional and factual materials. The dilemma is furthermore a result of the restricted access to information, leading to conspiracy theories which point to the lack of democratic accountability of supposedly civilian and public organizations such as NASA: did NASA stage the moon landing, and, if so, was it merely because it could not risk public failure, or—so the theory continues—because so much money had been lost to fraudulent defense industry contractors, or because the whole organization is in fact a CIA front to generate massive income that can then be siphoned off for black budget operations?

Often lack of evidence itself is taken as evidence of a cover-up: why, some conspiracy researchers ask, are there no recordings or transcripts of the interrogation by Dallas police of Oswald—is it because he offered conclusive evidence that he was indeed a patsy? When the possibility of deliberate misinformation is introduced, the epistemological stakes are raised in the game of paranoia: if I uncover a piece of evidence, how can I be sure that They did not deliberately plant it in order to keep me from discovering a far more sinister truth? *The X-Files* abounds with such skeptical conundrums: are They letting us believe in alien-human hybridization so as to hide the far more sinister truth that They are conducting their own genetic experiments—or vice versa?

In other cases, however, there is not so much a lack of available evidence as an abundance. Amateur researchers into the Kennedy assassination soon discover that there is an excess of information, meaning not only that is it virtually impossible for any individual to assimilate all the data from such a wide variety of discourses (law, forensic medicine, acoustics, ballistics, political history, biography, psychology, etc.), but also that the overwhelming mass of often contradictory evidence refuses to coalesce into a single watertight case. What are we to do with "facts" like Nixon's attendance of a Pepsi convention in Dallas on the day of the assassination, or an FBI memo dated 23 November 1963 that surfaced in 1988 suggesting that "Mr. George Bush of the CIA" had been debriefed about the event—and why are Nixon and Bush the only two Americans apparently unable to remember where they were on that fateful day? And what would constitute final and definitive proof of a conspiracy in that most scrutinized of cases: a deathbed confession by one of the hired hitmen on the grassy knoll—to put alongside all the other deathbed confessions already in existence? Or a document which showed conclusively that the Mafia/CIA/Texas oilmen/Cuban exiles were behind it, to add to all the other seemingly conclusive documents? Or more "computer enhancements" of the Zapruder footage or new witnesses to add to the already confused eyewitness account of the shooting? Each item of evidence can be endlessly recontextualized; for instance, in *Oswald's Tale* (1995), Norman Mailer's monumental study of the alleged lone gunman, he interviews those Russians (including KGB officers) who knew Oswald during his time in the Soviet Union. In one interview Mailer will uncover an important new piece of evidence, but then must conduct further interviews and recount more life histories in order to establish the veracity of the original interlocutor, and so potentially onward and backward ad infinitum.

However, this is not to claim, in a grand postmodernist gesture of rejection, that there is no such thing as Truth any more. I am merely suggesting that the production and consumption of information in contemporary America makes the idea of "common sense" extremely problematic; as *The X-Files* logo puts it: The Truth Is Out There™. I would therefore argue that the much discussed self-reflexive skepticism about the status of Truth in postmodern novelists such as Pynchon, Burroughs, and DeLillo needs to be seen not so much as the result of a spontaneous loss of faith in old epistemological certainties as a particular response to the monopolized condition of knowledge in the postwar political scene dominated by suspicion and secrecy. In Pynchon's *The Crying of Lot 49* (1966), Oedipa's four-way hermeneutic dilemma of paranoia—is there really a conspiracy, or is she going mad? are They deliberately making her believe that there is a conspiracy, or that she is mad?—is less a recognition of the uncertain nature of Truth as such than a reaction to her problematic engagement with experts, be they lawyers, literary critics, or philatelists.

If it has become difficult to read conspiracy culture symptomatically as the product of a paranoid imagination, because we can no longer be entirely certain the stories are untrue, then it has also become more difficult to maintain a diagnostic analysis because those accused of resorting to conspiratorial explanations are often fully aware of the logic of such accusations and build that awareness into their theories. Since the sixties the very notion of a conspiracy theory as a form of historical explanation and an indicator of a pathological political sensibility has been recognized, theorized, discussed, parodied, and finally incorporated into common currency: think only of the joke, "I may be paranoid, but that doesn't mean that They're not out to get me." If in the past the political charge of a conspiracy allegation could be defused in advance by diagnosing its proponents as paranoid (or unwittingly in the service of the elite), then in more recent decades there has been an increasing familiarity with the language of symptomology (and ideological analysis) *within* popular conspiracy culture. "Paranoid" narratives have thus begun to internalize the modes of reading traditionally brought to bear upon them, to anticipate and disarm the authority of expert criticism.[33] In the Kennedy case, those who believe in conspiracy theories are accused of being paranoid; Oswald is diagnosed as paranoid; the CIA subculture of secrecy is labeled paranoid; and even those who refuse to believe in conspiracy theories are themselves psychologized. But many assassination critics, aware that they will be deemed paranoid, are quick to point out that Stalin used the same tactic of labeling any opponents insane in order to discredit them. All sides become caught in a game of hermeneutic one-upmanship in which the critical language of symptomatic diagnosis is at stake.

The final round comes when those accused of being paranoid turn the spotlight back on their accusers by asking whose interests are served by such symptomatic interpretations. Where Showalter, for example, is keen to point out that a belief in conspiracy theories about Oklahoma only serves to prolong the suffering of relatives whose relief is to be found in counseling and not inquiries into the possibility of a conspiracy, some might contend that Showalter's analysis itself might play into the hands of those keen to cover up secret malfeasance by forces from the government or otherwise. What better way, a high-level military official might be wondering, to divert attention from the awkward details that are gradually emerging of incompetence or concerted wrongdoing in the Gulf War than a well-respected academic telling everyone that none of it is true, and what's more, that you're a touch hysterical if you believe it? A passage in Pynchon's *Gravity's Rainbow* captures this possibility nicely. Towards the end of the novel the narrator begins to discuss the (apparently true) urban legend of the conspiratorial suppression (in the novel by a tycoon called Lyle Bland) of an energy-saving carburetor in the 1930s:

> By way of the Bland institute and the Bland Foundation, the man has had his meathooks well into the American day-to-day since 1919. Who do you think sat on top of that 100-miles-per-gallon carburetor, eh? Sure you've heard that story—maybe even snickered along with paid anthropologists who called it the Automotive Age Myth or some shit—well, turns out the item was real, all right, and it was Lyle Bland who sprang for those academic hookers doing the snickering and the credentialed lying.[34]

Even if—shock! horror!—respected academics such as Hofstadter and Showalter are not working either knowingly or unwittingly for the CIA (though, the determined conspiracy theorist will point out, many were in the 1950s), the incorporation of such theories into conspiracy lore can be seen as part of an attempt to reconfigure the balance of power between the expert critic and the naive exponent of the "paranoid style." Turning the tables, the conspiracy theorist might now wonder whether Hofstadter is not a little paranoid about the threat of the "paranoid style" to the stability of American politics, and whether Showalter is not a little hysterical at finding examples of the "epidemic of hysteria" everywhere.

Poor Person's Cognitive Mapping

Diagnosing conspiracy theorists as paranoid therefore begins to lose its critical edge. What sense is there to the notion of paranoia as a pathological worldview if vast numbers of Americans are deemed to be suffering from it—if, in effect, you now have to be paranoid to stay sane? To be fair, Showalter, for example, insists first that hysterical symptoms and paranoid beliefs are not necessarily signs of madness, and second that the symptoms of mental illness are neither imaginary nor a sign of weakness. Similarly, Hofstadter is at pains to point out that he does not mean the term in any clinical sense, arguing instead that

> there is a vital difference between the paranoid spokesman in politics and the clinical paranoiac: although they both tend to be overheated, oversuspicious, overaggressive, grandiose, and apocalyptic in expression, the clinical paranoid sees the hostile and conspira-

torial world in which he feels himself to be living is directed specifically *against him;* whereas the spokesman of the paranoid style
finds it directed against a nation, a culture, a way of life whose fate
affects not himself alone but millions of others.[35]

Yet the diagnosis of paranoia, even if it is not individual but collective,
still carries with it the suggestion that the victim is not simply misguided but suffering from an illness that should be pitied and, if possible, cured. What critical work does the concept of paranoia perform in
such analyses? If it is a descriptive analogy, it is virtually tautological,
with the claim that those who believe in conspiracy theories are paranoid, mirrored by the wisdom that the paranoid is someone who believes
in conspiracy theories. If it is an explanation, it is hard to see what analytical function it performs in answering the question why paranoid
people see the world as they do. For clinical paranoia, it might be possible to present a case for a physiological origin to the illness with an account of chemical imbalance in the brain (the hardcore conspiracy theorist would of course have a tale to tell about the source of that chemical
imbalance). Even though this hypothesis might have some validity in
individual cases, it is hard to see how such an explanation could be
transferred to the idea of collective paranoia. The alternative is a psy-
choanalytic account, such as Freud's, which theorizes the mechanism of
paranoia as the inversion and projection of repressed homosexual desires. This model is implicitly at work in the analyses of Hofstadter and
Davis, who point to psychological mechanisms of projection in conjunction with sexual fantasies in the operation of the "paranoid style": "The
sexual freedom attributed to him [the enemy], his lack of moral inhibi-
tion, his possession of especially effective techniques for fulfilling his
desires, give exponents of the paranoid style an opportunity to project
and freely express unacceptable aspects of their own minds."[36] (And,
though not tied explicitly to Freud's model of paranoia, Showalter's
analysis nevertheless maintains a Freudian position, with her reading of
hysterical symptoms as the transformed manifestation of repressed or
unacceptable sexual desires.) I would agree, however, with Eve Sedgwick
who points out that "a chain of powerful, against-the-grain responses
to Freud's argument . . . has [recently] established the paranoid stance
as a uniquely privileged one for understanding not—as in the Freudian
tradition—homosexuality itself, but rather precisely the mechanisms of
homophobic and heterosexist enforcement against it."[37] Accordingly, I
would suggest, for example, that we need to read William Burroughs's
fictions of body horror not as an inverted projection of repressed homosexual desire, but as a series of strategic and fantastical materializations

of straight society's worst fears about same-sex desire, drug addiction, and disease that reverse the emphasis from a psychology of conspiracy to a conspiracy theory of the institutions of psychology.

If the explanatory force of a symptomatic reading of conspiracy culture in terms of paranoia lies in the notion of projected desires or anxieties, however conceived, then the "paranoid style" approach is open to a further, crucial objection. Showalter, for example, reads alien abduction narratives as an expression of repressed sexual desire, told by women unable to accept responsibility for feelings which both they and the culture at large find intolerable, such that "these desires for touch, gazing, penetration have to come from very very far away, even outer space."[38] In effect Showalter seeks to understand such narratives as an unconscious commentary on aspects of the self, and particularly the sexual self. While I would agree with her analysis in many cases, I think it is also important to read some contemporary conspiracy theories not as—or, not merely as—unconscious symptoms of the self (or even the collective self of the culture) projected onto the world, but as symbolic and sometimes conscious expressions about society, culture and history. Where Showalter reads narratives about hidden enemies as an "external solution to conflicts which go very deep" inside the self, I would claim that we need instead—or, in addition—to read some recent conspiracy narratives as symbolic resolutions to conflicts which go very deep in the culture.[39]

Although it doesn't take much to see normally leftish conspiracy theories such as those about NASA or the CIA as expressions not of personal difficulties but of a populist distrust of unaccountable power, what are we to make of militia-style rants? How are we to read stories about black helicopters, alien-human genetic hybrid experiments, the government secretly colluding with gray aliens, personal information being stored in the magnetic strip on driving licenses or in chips implanted during alien abductions (or the CIA using the story of alien abductions to mask its own program of mind control experiments), or the markings on the back of road signs to guide the invading United Nations forces massing just over the border? Although it might be possible to read some of the details of these stories in terms of a paranoid psychosexual dynamic, I think it is (also) necessary to read the stories, if not literally as true revelations, then as a poignant metaphorical commentary on recent history. As I suggested earlier, the idea of a United Nations invasion might be far-fetched, but what if it is read as an expression of distrust that the U.S. government has knowingly collaborated with "alien" powers in the GATT and NAFTA negotiations to hand over the nation's economic destiny to unelected, shadowy groups like the IMF? Such stories thus point to one of the key political questions in the 1990s: if the federal government is betraying its role as protector of national economic welfare (by conspiring with aliens), and if, after the end of the Cold War, there was no longer a role for the government as protector of its citizens against an "evil empire," then what is government for?[40] "The American Dream of the middle class has all but disappeared," one commentator has noted, "substituted with people struggling just to buy next week's groceries." He continues:

> What is it going to take to open the eyes of our elected officials? AMERICA IS IN SERIOUS DECLINE. We have no proverbial tea to dump; should we instead sink a ship full of Japanese imports? Is a civil war imminent? Do we have to shed blood to reform the current system? I hope it doesn't come to that, but it might.[41]

That commentator was Timothy McVeigh. Conspiracy theories about the activities of government agencies (like the BATF at Waco) express the growing sense of the illegitimacy of federal powers, which, the reasoning would continue, can only justify their existence by making their daily presence more noticeable (and supposedly more necessary) by intrusive surveillance.

The above list of conspiracy theories can perhaps be divided into two types of narrative. On the one hand there are stories like the implanted bio-surveillance chips and data strips in driving licenses which speak of fears about increased government interference and control in daily life. Conspiracy theories about a United Nations or alien takeover, on the other hand, express fears about a *lack* of government control in the face of aggressive world—or other-worldly—competition. Often these two seemingly contradictory views (and more besides) are combined into a single all-encompassing conspiracy metanarrative, a Grand Unified Theory of Everything. The narrative integration of the two positions provides a form of symbolic resolution that operates in the same way as the ideological fix used to justify the financial policies of the 1980s and '90s: the ideology of dynamic deregulation (of the labor market, the banking industry, industries and services) could paradoxically make governments look proactive just when Western governments were beginning to realize that global economic processes were not only uncontrolled but uncontrollable. In effect the rhetoric of Reaganite economics served to speed up and make a political virtue out of what increasingly began to seem a historical necessity, namely the eroded possibility of Keynesian intervention in a postfordist economy. The coupling of two different types of conspiracy theory into an elaborate all-encompassing plot thus provides a form of narrative explanation of the seeming paradox that greater government control could lead to a loss of government control. In short, where Hofstadter and Showalter would read such conspiracy theories as externalizing psychic anxieties about individual or collective identity, I see them as internalizing—and giving narrative shape to—some of the perplexing contradictions in the relationship between citizen and government in the era of globalization.

It might be argued, however, that such conspiracy theories are in fact the last defense against the recognition that the "American way" of unfettered capitalism is not what must be preserved, but the cause of the problems. For many middle-income Americans at the end of the millennium the only way to explain, after two of the supposedly most prosperous decades of the century, why their economic prospects were for the first time worse than those of their parents, was to blame anything other than "the system" (of deregulated market capitalism): be it aliens, the United Nations, the federal government, or even a grand conspiracy of all of the above in cahoots with the Illuminati, the Trilateral Commission, and the Council on Foreign Relations. Yet, I would suggest, the very extravagance of conspiracy theories needed to prop up a belief in the legitimacy of the normal order of things in itself indicates that a traditional faith in the American dream no longer comes naturally.

In two of his essays on postmodernism, Fredric Jameson offers— almost in passing—a useful formulation of the relationship between conspiracy narratives and the contemporary social and economic situation. "Conspiracy," writes Jameson, "is the poor person's cognitive mapping in the postmodern age; it is a degraded figure of the total logic of late capital, a desperate attempt to represent the latter's system, whose failure is marked by its slippage into sheer theme and content."[42] According to this view, conspiracy theories attempt to "think the impossible totality of the contemporary world system."[43] I would argue that such a formulation opens up the possibility for replacing Hofstadter's and Showalter's psychological and individual analysis of the functions of conspiratorial discourse with a materialist and collective analysis. I am suspicious, however, that Jameson's approach, predicated on a conviction that the mode of production is (in his borrowing of Althusser's phrase) "the ultimately determining instance," merely substitutes economics for Showalter's sexuality as the fundamental source of fears and fantasies.

Strategic Plotting

What is perhaps more significant, however, is Jameson's barely disguised disdain for conspiratorial thinking as a garish, degraded, desperate failure. Such rhetoric is shared by other commentators on conspiracy theory who similarly regard it as a "failure" of one kind or another. For Showalter, as we have seen, conspiracy theories are guilty of "distracting us from the real problems" by "blam[ing] external sources . . . for psychic problems." In Hofstadter's view a conspiracy theory is a sign of sloppy thinking, evidence of vulgar taste: "a distorted style is, then, a possible signal that may alert us to a distorted judgement, just as in art an ugly style is a cue to fundamental defects of taste." The very term "paranoid style" is, Hofstadter recognizes, "pejorative," and "it is meant to be."[44] One exception to this uniform vilification is suggested in an important article by Gordon S. Wood. Having pointed out the ubiquity of the "paranoid style" not only in America but throughout Europe during the latter half of the eighteenth century, Wood argues that the widespread belief in conspiracy theories was not a sign of irrationality but the response of every reasonable person at the time. It is not so much that many conspiracy theories of the period were accurate as that the paranoid style relied on notions of causality and moral responsibility which were central to eighteenth-century thought. But Wood goes on to argue that, with the rise in the nineteenth century of the social sciences, which viewed history as the effect of abstract forces rather than individual conspiring agents, conspiratorial interpretations of events "now seemed increasingly primitive and quaint." The persistence of conspiracy theories into the twentieth century can, he continues, indeed only be explained "as mental aberrations, as a paranoid style symptomatic of psychological disturbance" favored by the marginal and powerless. Wood concludes—and I think he voices the opinion of many structural historians—that as "modern social science emerged," attributing events to conspiracy theories became "more and more simplistic":

> In our post-industrial, scientifically saturated society, those who continue to attribute combinations of events to deliberate human design may well be peculiar sorts of persons—marginal people, perhaps, removed from the centers of power, unable to grasp the conceptions of complicated causal linkages offered by sophisticated social scientists, and unwilling to abandon the desire to make simple and clear moral judgements of events.[45]

In effect, Wood's conclusion is that conspiracy theorists just don't understand how history works, and indeed the designation of an argument as a conspiracy theory is often enough to end discussion.[46]

While agreeing that conspiracy culture is indeed often misguided and harmful, I would argue that the discourse of conspiracy is not necessarily a "failure." I have been arguing that it produces a form of representation that is at times insightful and forceful, if not always in its investigative accuracy, then in its narrative resonances, formal resolutions, and expressive possibilities. Conspiratorial thinking, as we have seen, has played a crucial role in mounting populist challenges to the legitimacy of authority on both the left and right in American politics. This is not to deny the perhaps inevitable complicity of this antiauthoritarian resistance. Just as New Age challenges to the legitimacy of orthodox science have relied upon the methods and language of that science, so too does conspiracy theory continue to call upon—albeit in an exaggerated fashion—the protocols of evidence in standard historiography: think only of the obsessive reliance on naive notions of evidence in Kennedy assassination studies.

If conspiracy is the poor person's cognitive mapping, then what, we might ask, would the rich person's cognitive mapping look like? Presumably for Jameson it would be the "science" of Marxist economic analysis which would uncover not the interlocking and contradictory networks of power outlined in contemporary conspiracy plots, but the totalizing "single vast unfinished plot" of class struggle.[47] Yet in the article on "Cognitive Mapping" he also asserts that the only hope of mapping the "impossible totality" of late multinational capitalism lies in the formal aesthetic complexities of an as yet undiscovered postmodernist art form. Though conspiracy culture doubtless falls short of this rigorous requirement, I would suggest that the popularity of many recent forms of conspiracy culture, with their outlandishly inventive and integrative meta-narratives that weave together all kinds of fears and fantasies into a contradictory mixture of plausibility and baroque exaggeration, relies as much upon the ideologically saturated pleasures of complex narrative as it does on the political content of the accusations.[48] Or, to put the point another way, is an ideologically compromised attempt at providing narrative resolution to the complexities and contradictions of globalization perhaps better than no mapping at all? In the same way that the images of Earth taken from space contributed to a popular awareness of ecology without necessarily advancing an understanding of its finer points, so recent forms of conspiracy culture enable a popular engagement, however inaccurate in the small print, with notions of global connectedness. It comes as no surprise that the discourses of both ecology and conspiracy, which each attempt to map out connections previously invisible and in many ways unthinkable under the maxim that Everything Is Connected, began to gain popular credence towards the end of the 1960s as the postmodernization of the world (in ecological, cultural and economic terms) began to take effect.

Though it might be possible to reclaim some versions of conspiracy theory for a progressive agenda in this way, Jameson makes a further complaint against the contemporary influence of the "paranoid style." The effect of the self-replicating overload of paranoia in both postmodern fiction and theory, he suggests, is to convince readers of their powerlessness:

> What happens is that the more powerful the vision of some increasingly total system or logic—the Foucault of the prisons book is the obvious example—the more powerless the reader comes to feel. Insofar as the theorist wins, therefore, by constructing an increasingly closed and terrifying machine, to that very degree he loses, since the critical capacity of his work is thereby paralyzed, and the impulses of negation and revolt, not to speak of those of social transformation, are increasingly perceived as vain and trivial in face of the model itself.[49]

Jameson's complaint is thus not so much about the actual content of paranoid depictions of panoptical society, as it is about their tendency to undermine the desire for action. In a similar fashion, Andrew Ross spells out clearly the argument that an excessively conspiratorial mapping of the postmodern surveillance state ends up leaving people resigned to their fate:

> What I have been describing are some of the features of that critical left position—sometimes referred to as the "paranoid" position—on information technology which imagines or constructs a totalizing, monolithic picture of systematic domination. Whilst this story is often characterized as a conspiracy theory, its targets—technorationality, bureaucratic capitalism—are usually too abstract to fit the picture of a social order planned and shaped by a small, conspiring group of centralized power elites.[50]

Ross is dubious about conspiracy always being the best story to tell, for it recreates precisely the mentality and conditions that it warns us against. He too advocates what amounts to a strategic non-deployment of conspiracy metaphors in order to write oneself out of the victim's slot. "The critical habit of finding unrelieved domination everywhere," Ross continues, "has certain consequences, one of which is to create a siege mentality, reinforcing the inertia, helplessness and despair that such critiques set out to oppose in the first place."

Yet I think the same argument can be made *in favor* of conspiracy culture. Precisely because technorationality and bureaucratic capitalism are too "abstract" and "total" and "terrifying," it becomes necessary to imagine their operation in the control of conspiring agents, if only to maintain a strategic fiction that contemporary history is controllable—albeit by the enemy. The ruthlessly efficient notion of agency deployed by conspiracy theories, which conceive of all events as the product of someone's will, paradoxically produces a form of social determinism, since all events are perceived to be shaped by forces (human or alien) beyond "our" control. The idea of a conspiracy thus offers a halfway house between the undiluted faith that, in Showalter's words, we are "free and responsible beings" and the unmitigated assertion that everything is determined by abstract social and economic processes. The proliferation of a popular culture of paranoia needs to be understood not so much as an intellectually impoverished rejection of the complexity of sociological explanation as an attempt to rethink it, to combine a sense of the systematic nature of oppression with a commitment to holding somebody responsible.[51] In the political movements that have arisen since the 1960s, the personal is connected to the political, and isolated individual experiences are linked up to larger narratives of oppression. In short, I'm not entirely certain whether it's better to believe that everything is shaped by discourse, or by the Trilateral Commission.

The very outrageousness of conspiracy theories can also function strategically to call into question forms of historical explanation and notions of agency. For example, in Ira Levin's *The Stepford Wives* (1972) the women exhibit signs of increasing domesticity not because they buy into the ideology of suburban domesticity but because the Men's Association is literally replacing them with obedient automata. In Stepford, housewives behave like inhabitants of advertising fantasies *because* there is a conspiracy to bring it about; but in the real world outside the novel (or "outside" similar conspiracy theories), how else can we explain what looks like a conspiracy, when we tend to think there isn't a literal conspiracy to force women into domesticity and submissiveness? Like so many recent conspiracy theories, Levin's novel operates in the increasingly blurred territory between the literal and the metaphorical, the plausible and the fantastic, challenging what constitutes a reasonable explanation of current events. Contemporary conspiracy culture can thus give narrative shape to suspicions that a host of social processes, ranging from patriarchy to homophobia to globalization, *amount to* a conspiracy, even if we know that there is—probably—not a literal small group of men conspiring in a smoke-filled room.[52] If we are to avoid a knee-jerk dismissal of the popular pleasures of conspiracy culture as a delusional failure, a "plague of paranoia," or part of the dumbing down of America, we need to develop, I have tried to suggest, modes of reading that are responsive to the multiple functions and meanings of these increasingly visible narratives. In effect, we need to learn the perhaps impossible talent of reading both symptomatically and sympathetically.

Notes

I would like to thank my co-conspirator Alasdair Spark for collaboration on this project.

1. For a summary of the hostile popular reception to Showalter's book—including an assassination threat at a book signing—see Jason Cowley, "Hysteria and Gulf War Syndrome," *Times* (London), 22 May 1997; and Wray Herbert, "The Hysteria over *Hystories*," *U.S. News & World Report*, 19 May 1997, 14.

2. Elaine Showalter, *Hystories: Hysterical Epidemics and Modern Culture* (New York: Columbia University Press, 1997), 8.

3. Showalter, *Hystories*, 8, 116–17.

4. Showalter, *Hystories*, 143.

5. For an example of a typical review that praised the book on the whole but took issue with Showalter's analysis of GWS and CWS, see Melissa Ben, "Out of Control?" *New Statesman*, 13 June 1997, 48.

6. Showalter, *Hystories*, 206.

7. For example, in an article in the *New York Review of Books* (February 2 1995, 68–70), Jacob Heilbrun traces the sources of Pat Robertson's brand of anti-Semitism to the books of Nesta Webster in the 1920s.

8. Richard Hofstadter, *The Paranoid Style in American Politics and Other Essays* (New York: Alfred A. Knopf, 1965), 6, 7.

9. Hofstadter, *Paranoid Style*, 31, 29.

10. In the afterword to *"Ronald Reagan, The Movie"; and Other Episodes in Political Demonology* (Berkeley and Los Angeles: University of California Press, 1987), a wide-ranging and perceptive survey of the history of demonological studies, Michael Rogin locates Hofstadter's analysis of provincial status politics in relation to Hofstadter's (and his own) problematic status as a Jewish cosmopolitan intellectual. Rogin also provides a more detailed analysis of Hofstadter's implicit liberal exceptionalism.

11. These statistics are taken from "The Death of a President," *Economist*, 9 October 1993, 133; and Bob Callahan, *Who Shot JFK? A Guide to the Major Conspiracy Theories* (New York: Simon & Schuster, 1993).

12. For a summary of these opinion polls see Wim Roefs, "They're all in it together," *New Statesman & Society*, 29 September 1995, 32–35; on conspiracy theories in African-American culture, see Theodore Sasson, "Afri-

can American Conspiracy Theories and the Social Construction of Crime," *Sociological Inquiry* 65 (1995): 265–85.

13. Hofstadter, *Paranoid Style,* 29.

14. The comment on conspiracy theories as the gossip of the global village is from Robin Ramsay, *Of Conspiracies and Conspiracy Theories: The Truth Buried by the Fantasies,* Political Notes no.128 (London: Libertarian Alliance, 1995).

15. For discussions of paranoia in American literature see: Tony Tanner, *City of Words: American Fiction 1950–1970* (London: Jonathan Cape, 1971); Brian McHale, *Constructing Postmodernism* (London: Routledge, 1992); Tony Hilfer, *American Fiction Since 1940* (London: Longman, 1992).

16. On conspiracy films see: Michael Ryan and Douglas Kellner, *Camera Politica: The Politics and Ideology of Contemporary Hollywood Film* (Bloomington and Indianapolis: Indiana University Press, 1988); Fredric Jameson, *The Geopolitical Aesthetic: Cinema and Space in the World System* (Bloomington and Indianapolis: Indiana University Press; London: BFI, 1992); John Orr, "Paranoid Fictions: Conspiracy Theory, JFK and Nightmare on Elm Street Continued," *Edinburgh Working Papers in Sociology,* no.1 (Edinburgh: Edinburgh University Press, 1995). In *Rational Fears: American Horror in the 1950s* (Manchester: Manchester University Press, 1997), Mark Jancovich argues convincingly that 1950s horror films need be read in the context of technorationalization, marking the first emergence of a postfordist economy and its attendant anxieties during that decade.

17. Showalter draws attention to the feedback loops between fictional stories and factual accounts, with, for example, the imagery and plot structures in certain novels about alien abductions being incorporated into abductees' own narratives (189–201).

18. Robert Lewin's *Report from Iron Mountain* (New York: Dial Press, 1967) supposedly (but satirically) reveals the government planning to maintain the country on a permanent war economy while claiming it to be at peace; the pseudonymous William Torbitt's 1970 photocopied manuscript "Nomenclature of an Assassination Cabal" purportedly shows that former Nazi rocket scientists working for NASA were involved with Hoover and Johnson in the assassination of President Kennedy; and Alternative-III was allegedly a plan to build moon bases, using "abductees" as slave labor, in order to house Earth's elite once the planet self-destructed through ecological disasters. For more on the latter two see Kenn Thomas, ed., *NASA, Nazis & JFK: The Torbitt Document and the JFK Assassination* (Kempton, Ill.: Adventures Unlimited Press, 1996), and Jim Keith, *Casebook on Alternative 3* (Lilburn, Ga.: IllumiNet Press, 1994).

19. The extremely complex narrative structure of *The X-Files* makes it very difficult to "extract" a pure conspiracy theory; the episode guide by Cornell et al. makes a reasonable attempt at piecing together the show's "conspiracy arc," but the different narrative strands just don't tie up. On the

different audiences of *The X-Files*, see David Lavery et al., eds., *Deny All Knowledge: Reading "The X-Files"* (London: Faber and Faber, 1996); and Constance Penley, *NASA/TREK: Popular Science and Sex in America* (London: Verso, 1997).

20. For a discussion of the Zapruder footage see Art Simon, *Dangerous Knowledge: The JFK Assassination in Art and Film* (Philadelphia, Pa.: Temple University Press, 1996).

21. Eve Kosofsky Sedgwick, "Introduction: Queerer than Fiction," *Studies in the Novel* 28 (1996): 277.

22. Quoted in Eric Mottram, *William Burroughs: The Algebra of Need* (London: Calder & Boyars, 1977), p.159.

23. For the lowdown on most of these stories, check out Jonathan Vankin and John Whale, *50 Greatest Conspiracy Theories of All Time* (New York: Citadel Press, 1996); and Doug Moench's cartoon compendium *The Big Book of Conspiracies* (New York: Paradox Press, 1995).

24. Michael Kelly, "The Road to Paranoia," *The New Yorker*, 19 June 1995, 62.

25. Pat Robertson, *The New World Order* (Dallas, Tex.: Word Publishing, 1991); Jeremy Brecher, "Global Village or Global Pillage? Resistance to Top-Down Globalization," in Greg Ruggiero and Stuart Sahulka, eds., *The New American Crisis: Radical Analyses of the Problems Facing America Today* (New York: The New Press, 1996), 86.

26. Kristin Dawkins, "NAFTA, GATT, and the World Trade Organization: The New Rules for Coporate Conquest," in Ruggiero and Sahulka, eds., *The New American Crisis*, 75.

27. In an article in the *New York Review of Books* (10 August 1995, 50–55), Gary Wills develops the observation that "the suspicion that the government has become the enemy of freedom, not its protector, crosses ideological lines" (50).

28. Carl Oglesby, *The Yankee and Cowboy War: Conspiracies from Dallas to Watergate* (Kansas City, Kans.: Sheed Andrews and McMeel, 1976), 15.

29. For further discussion of this approach, see Rogin, *"Ronald Reagan"*; and Eric Goode and Nachman Ben-Yehuda, *Moral Panics: The Social Construction of Deviance* (Oxford: Blackwell, 1994).

30. Rogin, *"Ronald Reagan,"* 273.

31. Hofstadter, *Paranoid Style*, 39.

32. Hofstadter, *Paranoid Style*, 36–37, 5.

33. In *Constructing Postmodernism*, McHale discusses the epistemological paradoxes resulting from the emergence of what he terms "metaparanoia" in postmodernist fiction (171–72).

34. Pynchon, *Gravity's Rainbow* (New York: Viking, 1973), 581.

35. Hofstadter, *Paranoid Style*, 4.

36. Hofstadter, *Paranoid Style*, 34.

37. Sedgwick, "Queerer than Fiction," 277.

38. Showalter, *Hystories*, 196.

39. For an exemplary demonstration of such an analysis, see Robert S. Levine, *Conspiracy and Romance: Studies in Brockden Brown, Cooper, Hawthorne and Melville* (Cambridge: Cambridge University Press, 1989); and for a detailed and convincing analysis of how conspiracy theories cohere with larger discursive formations, see Geoffrey Cubitt, *The Jesuit Myth: Conspiracy Theory and Politics in Nineteenth-Century France* (Oxford: Clarendon Press, 1993).

40. In his article in *The New York Review*, Wills puts this position across forcefully.

41. Letter written by Timothy McVeigh, quoted on Panorama, BBC 1 television documentary, 5 May 1995.

42. Jameson, "Cognitive Mapping," in Cary Nelson and Lawrence Grossberg, eds., *Marxism and the Interpretation of Culture* (Basingstoke: Macmillan, 1988), 355.

43. Jameson, "Postmodernism, or, The Cultural Logic of Late Capitalism," *New Left Review* 146 (1984): 80.

44. Hofstadter, *Paranoid Style*, 6, 5.

45. Gordon S. Wood, "Conspiracy and the Paranoid Style: Causality and Deceit in the Eighteenth Century," *The William and Mary Quarterly* 39 (1982): 441.

46. Karl Popper, in several articles collected in *Conjectures and Refutations* (London: Routledge & Kegan Paul, 1963), lends his considerable intellectual weight to the refutation of what he terms the Conspiracy Theory of Society. Popper's "refutation" has itself been disputed in a recent article: Charles Pidgen, "Popper Revisited, or What Is Wrong with Conspiracy Theories," *Philosophy of the Social Sciences* 25 (1995): 3–34.

47. Jameson, *The Political Unconscious: Narrative as a Socially Symbolic Act* (London: Methuen, 1981), 20.

48. Examples of all-encompassing conspiracy constructs would include Danny Casolaro's Octopus investigation, outlined in Jim Keith, ed., *Secret and Suppressed: Banned Ideas and Hidden History* (Portland, Oreg.: Feral House, 1993); William Cooper's *Behold a Pale Horse* (Sedona, Ariz.: Light Technology Publishing, 1991); and Robert Anton Wilson's extravagantly fictional *Illuminatus! Trilogy* (1975). Although I take issue with Showalter's conclusion that "we must look into our own psyches rather than invisible enemies, devils or alien invaders" (*Hystories*, 207), I would agree with her that attention to narrative structures and literary conventions is one of the most fruitful ways to approach conspiracy culture: "literature spreads hysteria," she writes, "but it can also help us understand it" (*Hystories*, 99).

49. Jameson, "Postmodernism," 86.

50. Andrew Ross, *Strange Weather: Culture, Science and Technology in the Age of Limits* (London: Verso, 1991), 96.

51. Here we might adapt Anthony Giddens' point that the faceless bureaucratic institutions of modernity require personalized "access points" that "provide the link between personal and system trust"; if the maintenance of trust requires a symbolic human face at the point of interaction, so might the operation of distrust need to personalize the otherwise anonymous and secret abuses of power. Giddens, *The Consequences of Modernity* (Cambridge: Polity Press, 1991), 115.

52. For a fuller discussion of the engagement with notions of conspiracy in popular American feminism, see my "Naming the Problem: Feminism and the Figuration of Conspiracy," *Cultural Studies* 11 (1997): 40–63.

PART II

ROOTED FEARS IN AMERICAN CULTURE

"That Epithet of Praying"

The Vilification of Praying Indians
during King Philip's War

Kristina Bross

In 1677, William Hubbard, a pastor at Ipswich, Massachusetts, published *A Narrative of the Troubles with the Indians in New-England,* an account of the recent hostilities between English colonists and coastal Indians, a conflict that would later be called King Philip's War. Benjamin Tompson penned a dedicatory poem to this publication in which he recites a litany of genres that make up the literature of English-Indian contact. Beginning with exploration and conquest writings, this litany proceeds, briefly, to evangelical and linguistic descriptions before culminating in the literature of war history. Tompson writes,

> Former Adventurers did at best beguile,
> About these Natives Rise (obscure as *Nile*)
> Their grand Apostle writes of their Return,
> *William's* their Language; *Hubbard* how they burn,
> Rob, kill and Roast, Lead Captive, slay, blaspheme.[1]

Although Tompson makes note of earlier accounts of English-Indian encounter, he places the rhetorical weight of his litany on war histories, which, from his perspective, provide the most accurate representation of English-Indian relations and perhaps act as correctives to accounts that, since the outbreak of King Philip's War, seem inaccurate, or at least naive. Despite the differences between war histories and earlier genres, his description of Hubbard's history hints at an important connection between wartime representations of Indians and previous depictions. English chroniclers of the war identified demonic or barbaric qualities that led Indians to rob and burn English settlements and to kill and

53

roast the English themselves. However, only a mission-inculcated familiarity with Puritan religious faith itself enabled Indians to blaspheme the English God. Scholars have noted the racist, demonized representations of Wampanoag and other coastal Indians in King Philip's War literature, but their discussions have largely ignored a startling feature: the vilification of Christian Indian converts.[2]

Beginning in 1646, Puritan missionaries published an image of a convert whose adaptation of "English" traits served as evidence of ongoing cultural and spiritual transformation. Citing the scriptural charge to make "new creatures" in Christ, missionaries proclaimed that they had a twofold task, to make Indians "men" as well as "Christians." They asserted that the reformation of a convert's external appearance and behavior corresponded to internal regeneration of the soul. Thus they lauded Indian converts who spoke imperfect English, adapted English clothing to their own dress, and gathered in Puritan worship. These characteristics assured English observers that converted Indians, whom they called "Praying Indians," were "progressing" toward an Anglicized Christian ideal, but that they had not yet arrived, necessitating continued infusions of prayer and money. The figure of the Praying Indian was popular among elite New England writers, who recognized the importance of Indian evangelism to New England's transatlantic identity. Mission publications sold well in Old England. One bookseller's catalogue names the mission tract *Tears of Repentance* in his list of "most vendible books" of the late 1650s.[3]

Such was the power and influence of this image that the Praying Indian became a normative figure of English-Indian relations between 1646 and 1675.[4] On the eve of King Philip's War in 1674, Daniel Gookin, an English civil official in the Praying Indian communities, did not hesitate to assert an absolute, identifiable difference between Praying Indians, who lived within colonial bounds and were subject to colonial laws, and unconverted Indians. Converts were distinguished from others, he wrote, "by their short hair, and wearing English fashioned apparel."[5] Moreover, he had great hopes for the conversion of the sachem Philip, whom he described as "a person of good understanding and knowledge in the best things." Gookin reported that he himself heard Philip "speak very good words, arguing that his conscience is convicted."[6]

Such optimism about Indian evangelism came to an abrupt end in June of 1675 when war broke out between English colonists and Indian forces allied under the leadership of Philip, the same sachem whom Gookin had praised a short time earlier. Praying Indians took part on both sides of the conflict, but their presence among the enemy received

the most attention by English authors. Their very identification as
Christians acted as camouflage, or so observed some writers. Mary Pray,
a resident of Providence, wrote to James Oliver, a merchant and military
man in Boston about reports that "those Indians that are caled praying
Indians never sh[oo]t at the other Indians, but up into the tops of the
trees or into the ground; and when they make shew of going first into
the swamp they comonly give the Indians noatis how to escape the English."[7] Other observers seconded her testimony, and the survivors of
the attacks on outlying colonial towns swore that men identified as Praying Indians fought directly against them.

The association of converts with depredations caused many colonists
to meet the phrase "praying Indian" with rage and fear, and prompted
those friendly to converts to advise them to disassociate themselves from
the name. Daniel Gookin reported that "some wise and principal men
did advise some that were concerned with them, to forbear giving that
epithet of praying."[8] Those writers less interested in preserving the
reputations and lives of Indian converts began to associate characteristics typical of Praying Indians with cruelty, betrayal, and hypocrisy.

In 1675, N. S., a "merchant of Boston," wrote his report on the first
months of the conflict. Published under the title *The Present State of
New England*, the account describes the role that many New Englanders
believed Praying Indians played in the war and endorses actions taken
by colonial authorities:

> Care now is taken to satisfie the (reasonable) desires of the Com-
> monalty, concerning Mr. Elliot's Indians, and Capt. Guggin's In-
> dians. They that wear the Name of Praying Indians, but rather . . .
> they have made Preys of much English Blood, but now they are all
> reduced to their several Confinements; which is much to a general
> Satisfaction in that Respect.[9]

This play on words, the transformation of "Praying Indians" to "Preying Indians" is more than an example of linguistic wit. By transforming the "praying Indian" of evangelistic literature into an Indian who
preyed on English blood, the author of the tract signaled a widespread
re-evaluation of the mission figure. Whereas bobbed hair, psalm sing-
ing, and broken English were presented by missionaries as evidence of
the Praying Indians' transformation into Christians, chroniclers of the
war cited the same signs as evidence of intrinsic deception, blasphemy,
and stupidity made all the more despicable by evangelists' earlier promises of acculturation. In much the same way that Puritan anagramma-
tists probed names to uncover truths about the life and faith of the recently deceased, this punning reversal revealed, to the Puritan reader,

the whole truth of a no longer viable Indian identity. It reflects fears that true Indian conversions were impossible, that Indian converts were Christian in name only, and that they used the identity as a cover from which to launch bloody assaults on the English.

The discredited figure of the Praying Indian appears in reports by royal commissioners, in accounts penned by colonial merchants and published in the *London Gazette,* as well as in letters sent from religious dissidents to friends in England. It is possible that these observers, antagonistic to Boston magistrates, extended that hostility to Praying Indians, the fruit of Massachusetts evangelism. If these writers alone had vilified Praying Indians, the discursive reversal could be attributed to their partisanship. However, even William Hubbard, a prominent New England divine who was, in principle, supportive of missionizing, expressed his misgivings about the converts. In his history of the war, he cites Scripture to characterize his sense of betrayal by Indians who were long supposed friends: "in them is made good what is said in the *Psalm,* That *though their Words were smoother then Oil, yet were they drawn Swords.*"[10] Throughout New England, observers concluded that Indian converts were not to be trusted and their previous professions of friendship had been attempts to lull their English neighbors into complacency.

Before the war, missionaries had pointed to a "civilized" appearance as a sign of Indians' inward reformation. In the war literature itself, physical transformation becomes an enemy Indian's disguise rather than an external manifestation of inward grace. William Hubbard, for instance, reports that "a Lad keeping Sheep, was shot at by an *Indian* that wore a Sign, as if he had been a Friend: the *Indian* was supposed to belong to the *Hassanemesit Indians,* at that Time confined to *Malberough,* where they had Liberty to dwell in a Kind of Fort."[11] The desire for English clothing, attributed by missionaries to their converts, becomes a lust for booty rather than the reward for pious Indian converts. In Tompson's poem *New England's Crisis,* clothing heads the list of promises Philip makes to induce warriors to join him: "Now if you'll fight I'll get you English coats, / And wine to drink out of their captains' throats. / The richest merchants' houses shall be ours, / We'll lie no more on mats or dwell in bowers."[12] Philip's promises replaced the mission tradition of gifting Praying Indians with English goods and clothing in hopes of encouraging conversions.

In terms of linguistic rather than physical representation, we witness in the narratives and poems written during and just after the war a radical shift in the representation of Indian speech. Roger Williams, John Eliot, and other missionaries who transcribed their converts' "broken English" in earlier writings did so within a context of "brokenheartedness" and "plain speech." In their publications, dialect was meant to connote authentic expression as well as to invoke the reader's sympathy for the Indians' lost state. By contrast, war writers aimed for the ironic effect of "King Philip" speaking a degraded English or a Praying Indian exhibiting only partial civility. The result is an extreme "broken English" linked to Indian barbarism.

The appropriation and revaluation of mission linguistic representation is especially clear in Hubbard's account of Benjamin Church's battlefield "converts." These were Indians who had fought against the English and upon capture had been persuaded to join Church's troops. Upon approaching an Indian village, one such former enemy pointed to a dwelling and told Church,

> that was *his Father's Wigwam* and ask'd if he must now go and *kill his Father?* No saith Captain *Church*, do but shew me where he is and I will deal with him; do you fall upon some others: to which the said Indian only replyed in broken English. *That very good speak.*[13]

Hubbard here first explicitly identifies the Indian's expression as broken English, then goes on to gloss it with his understanding of the moment's deeper signification:

> whereby their natural Perfidiousness even to their nearest Relations may be observed, which makes their Treachery towards us their Foreign Neighbours, the less to be wondred at. And therefore till they be reduced to more Civility, some wise Men are ready to fear Religion will not take much Place amongst the Body of them.[14]

Hubbard, in effect, denies any association of broken English with a proper brokenheartedness. As a positive marker of cultural or religious transformation, English language skills were, in this sense, apparently meaningless. Hubbard's particular care in noting the Indian's mode of expression thus creates a contrast between the profound betrayal of his father and notions of Christian civility.

The Present State of New England presents the most extreme examples of broken English recorded in the war literature. The tract demonstrates the assumption of the author (identified only as "N. S.") that both allied and enemy Indians spoke or understood English, and it contradicts missionaries' earlier assertions that Indians who spoke English (however imperfectly) were closer to regeneracy than those who did not. When, as N. S. reports, in the heat of battle Captain Samuel Mosely took off his wig, the Indians "fell a Howling and Yelling most hideously, and said, *Umh, Umh me no stawmerre fight Engismon, Engismon got two Hed, Engismon got two Hed; if me cut off un Hed, he got noder, a put on beder as dis;* with such like Words in broken English."[15] N. S. intends more than a faithful transcription of the Indians' actual language; he draws attention to its pidginized form—the Indians spoke "such like words." Even more important, he conveys a sense of the Indians' linguistic inadequacy: broken English is of a piece with "howling" and hideous "yelling." Furthermore, the Indians' astonishment at the sight of such a common English item as Mosely's wig underscores their ignorance of "civilized" norms and contradicts the evangelists' assertions that Anglicized Indians were familiar with and valued English apparel.

English observers in New England and in Old England alike assumed that the Indians' exposure to English missionaries and Puritan doctrine had not prompted regeneracy but, instead, had provoked a hatred of the English and their ways which was violently expressed.[16] Writers from across the cultural landscape noted incidents in which that violence was directed in particular toward symbols or representatives of Christianity. Even writers who favored Indian evangelism, such as Increase Mather or Daniel Gookin, believed that some Indians' anti-Christian sentiments contributed to the conflict. They pointed out that pious Praying Indians were the primary objects of heathen rage and attributed John Sausamon's death, which for the English marked the opening of hostilities, to the enemy's hatred of Christianity. Gookin calls Sausamon the "first Christian martyr of the Indians," a description upon which Mather elaborates:

> No doubt but one reason why the Indians murthered *John Sausaman,* was out of hatred against him for his Religion, for he was Christianized and baptiz'd, and was a Preacher amongst the Indians, being of very excellent parts, he translated some part of the bible into the Indian language, and was wont to curb those Indians that knew not God on the account of their debaucheryes.[17]

In this passage from *Brief History,* Sausamon is a full-fledged missionary figure martyred for preaching the gospel.

Writers indifferent to missions slight Sausamon's death, but in nearly every account they report that other symbols of Christianity receive similarly violent treatment from Indians: Bibles are torn and scattered "in Hatred of our Religion therein revealed."[18] The unnamed author of *News from New England* reports that "these devillish Enemies of Religion seeing a man, woman, and their Children, going out towards a meeting house, Slew them (as they said) because they thought they Intended to go thither."[19] Likewise, these writers understand the abduction of Mary Rowlandson, a minister's wife captured in an attack on Lancaster, as an assault on her husband, the Reverend Joseph Rowlandson. *News from New England* reports Rowlandson's captivity, chiefly so that the readers "shall understand the Damnable antipathy [Indians] have to Religion and Piety."[20] Rowlandson's captivity is also reported by N. S. in *A New and Further Narrative* "that you may perceive the malicious Hatred these Infidels have to Religion and Piety."[21] These interpretations of the captivity, however, suppose the Indians' knowledge of Mary Rowlandson's importance (or that of her husband) in terms of religious authority or New England's social hierarchy. Indians with this understanding must have had an intimate knowledge of English customs and religion—a familiarity heretofore ascribed to Praying Indians.

Tellingly, Indians in war literature are knowledgeable enough of English prayers and piety to outrage English sensibilities, not just by their capture of Rowlandson, but also by the manner in which they repeatedly attempt to undermine English morale. Mather reports that upon burning the house of worship in Groton, which Indians singled out for destruction, they taunted the Reverend Willard, pastor of the congregation there: *"What will you do for a house to pray in now we have burnt your Meeting-house?"*[22] In battle, they hear and understand the English commanders' shouts of encouragement to their own men, yelling back that "God is against them, and for the *Indians.*"[23] Thomas Wheeler reports that when Captain Simon Davis encouraged his men with the assurance "That *God is with us, and fights for us, and will deliver us,*" the Indians *"shouted and scoffed saying:* now see how *your God delivers you.*"[24] *A Farther Brief and True Narration* reports that "Our Enemies proudly exult over us and Blaspheme the name of our Blessed God; Saying, *Where is your O God?* taunting at the Poor Wretches, which . . . they cruelly Torture to Death."[25] The syntax here indicates an imperfect command of the language, suggesting that the Indians are calling out in English and the tract's author is not silently substituting a translation.

More revealing than the battlefield cries that echo the English themselves or make a general reference to God are those moments when enemy Indians specifically parody prayer. The author of *A True Account* notes that an Indian, upon capturing an "elderly Englishman," offered up an "insulting" prayer: *"Come Lord Jesus, save this poor English man if thou canst, whom I am now about to Kill."*[26] Similarly, Hubbard suggests that near the end of the war, when the Indians must have been aware of impending defeat, they may have "pensively" considered their condition: "whether it were by any Dread that the Almighty set upon their execrable Blasphemies which 'tis said they used in the torturing of some of their poor Captives (bidding *Jesus* come and deliver them out

of their Hands from Death if he could) we leave as uncertain."[27] The
Indian understanding of English religious expression and practices extended to public forms of Christian worship. Wheeler notes a fascinating moment in the siege of Brookfield when the attacking Indians, in
perfect parody of approved Praying Indian behavior, act out a Christian
worship service:

> The next day being *August 3d*, they continued *shooting & shouting,*
> *&* proceeded in their *former wickedness blaspheming the Name of*
> *the Lord*, and *reproaching* us *his Afflicted Servants*, scoffing at our
> *prayers* as they were sending in their shot upon all quarters of
> the house And many of them went to the Towns *meeting house*
> (which was within *twenty Rods* of the house in which we were)
> who mocked saying, *Come and pray, & sing Psalms, &* in Con-
> tempt made an hideous noise *somewhat resembling singing.*[28]

Although mission tracts described Indian worship in which psalms in
an Indian language were matched to English meter, here Indian speech
degenerates into nonsense, a hideous and empty noise "somewhat re-
sembling" human expression.

The Indians may have knowingly occupied the role of devilish
tempter, challenging their captives and Jesus to prove the power of the
Christian God in words that echo gospel accounts of the crucifixion.[29]
However Indians put their gospel knowledge to use, whatever the veracity of these reports, the English writers themselves clearly saw white
captives as Christian martyrs and their Praying Indian enemies as tor-
mentors who put their knowledge of Christianity to evil blaspheming
purposes.

The treacherous Indian convert appears prominently in what was
(and continues to be) the best known publication to emerge from King
Philip's War: Mary Rowlandson's narrative of her captivity and redemption, *The Sovereignty and Goodness of God*. Rowlandson was captured during a February attack on her home in Lancaster and traveled
with her captors for eleven weeks. Her account of the ordeal was first
published in 1682, although she probably wrote it fairly soon after her
ransom.[30] Appearing in several editions in both Boston and London, it
has been considered the primogenitor of the captivity genre in America,
and a primary influence on American literary expression as a whole.[31]
Her understanding and representation of Indian conversion and cultural
hybridity, then, has farther-reaching effects than any other wartime
publication. Her narrative registers the permanent impression of mission writings on the Indian discourse in seventeenth-century writings,

and the re-evaluation of the missionaries' normative "Praying Indian" figure.

Rowlandson's narrative is structured by "removes"—successive geographic and temporal displacements that lead her away from and then back toward her home. Early in Rowlandson's captivity narrative, during the first remove, she introduces the topic that troubled other wartime chroniclers: the presence of converted Indians in the ranks of the heathen enemy:

> Little do many think what is the savageness and brutishness of this barbarous Enemy, even those that seem to profess more than others among them, when the *English* have fallen into their hands.[32]

In Rowlandson's narrative, she repeatedly singles out Praying Indians—those who "profess more than others"—for description and judgment.

Rowlandson is careful to note the participation by Praying Indians in attacks against the English. She remarks about an earlier attack on her town of Lancaster: "Those seven that were killed at Lancaster the summer before, upon a Sabbath day, and the one that was afterward killed upon a week day, were slain and mangled in a barbarous manner by one-eyed John, and Marlberough's Praying *Indians*."[33] Note that Rowlandson carefully distinguishes between Sabbath and week-day killings. In conjunction with her identification of Praying Indians as the culprits, her statement points to the special nature of their crimes. Not only do "professing" Indians kill, but they also intensify the horror of the crime by killing on the day they know they must honor.

Missionaries had repeatedly assured white New Englanders that Praying Indians loved them, that their adaptation of English customs and dress reflected their desire to Anglicize and Christianize not only their external appearances, but their hearts as well. In Rowlandson's account, transculturated appearances come under scrutiny and suspicion. Unlike mission writers who praised their converts' English dress, Rowlandson finds the ease of Indian transformation through attire and the subsequent unreadability of appearance threatening:

> In that time came a company of *Indians* to us, near thirty, all on Horse back. My heart skipt within me, thinking they had been *English-men* at the first sight of them; for they were dressed in *English* Apparel, with Hats, white Neckcloths, and Sashes about their waists, and Ribbons upon their shoulders; but, when they came near, there was a vast difference between the lovely Faces of *Christians*, and the foul looks of those *Heathens*.[34]

Although, as one critic has suggested, Rowlandson's distress may be caused by an assumption that the English clothes had been stripped from English dead, these men are not dressed haphazardly with trophies, but carefully and completely. Immediately before this description of the Indian company, Rowlandson discusses the first letters that Massachusetts authorities and her captors exchanged to negotiate her release. Those letters, together with the appearance of this company, suggest that she thought these were her English redeemers, and it is the newly dislocating experience of Indian bodies inhabiting English clothing (however the clothes were acquired) that makes the moment notable.[35]

Rowlandson, like missionary writers before her, distinguishes between the categories of heathen and Christian, but contrary to missionary claims, she links the term "Christian" to a particular racial identity: only the English are Christian. Even the two converts who successfully negotiate her release are identified simply as Indians with whom she has some fellow feeling, rather than as Praying Indians. Rowlandson accordingly redefines a mission binary of heathen or Christian. She asserts that Praying Indians are not Christians, no matter how much they might appear to be so. Indeed, she argues that they are even worse than the heathen enemy because their mission education enables them to perform unusual acts of treachery.

English missionaries were committed to teaching their converts to read and write and to understand Scripture. They believed that the best second-generation missionaries to the Indians would be drawn from the ranks of the converts themselves. In 1671, John Eliot—the foremost evangelist in Massachusetts—published his *Indian Dialogues,* in which he imagines three conversations that such Praying Indian proselytizers might have with their non-praying brethren. He even includes a fictionalized version of the sachem Philip as one of the interested, but unconverted Indian characters.[36]

Against this backdrop, Rowlandson describes her experience with such mission-educated and scripturally literate Praying Indians in terms that argue that putative converts pervert their education for their own ends. She describes a kind of mission dialogue:

There was another Praying *Indian,* who told me, that he had a Brother that would not eat Horse; his Conscience was so tender and scrupulous, (though as large as Hell for the destruction of poor *Christians.*) Then he said, he read that Scripture to him. . . . *There was a famine in* Samaria, *and behold they besieged it, until an Ass's head was sold for four-score pieces of silver, and the fourth part of a Kab of doves dung for five pieces of silver*. He expounded this place to his Brother, and shewed him that it was lawful to eat that in a Famine, which is not at another time. And now, says he, he will eat Horse with any *Indian* of them all.[37]

This passage describes a Christian dialogue with exactly the form encouraged and exemplified in John Eliot's *Indian Dialogues*. One Indian raises an objection to a desired belief or behavior, another convinces him of the "right" path by citing and interpreting Scripture.

Such an appropriation of Christian conventions overturns missionaries' characterizations of Indian piety. What could be more blasphemous than an enemy Indian quoting and expounding scriptural text for his own evil purpose? Rather than leading one Indian on the path to "civil" English transformation, this dialogue makes the tender-hearted brother *more* Indian in that he accedes to his community's dietary necessities. The "preacher" here uses his scriptural knowledge to aid and comfort the enemy. By citing chapter and verse, he saves his brother from starvation, possibly to fight another day.

The discursive shift that I have been sketching in Rowlandson's narrative and in other chronicles of the war was accompanied by real human consequences; one of the saddest was the persecution of faithful converts by angry and fearful white colonists. Missionaries in the years preceding the conflict had insisted that their converts could readily be distinguished from non-Christian Indians by their appearance and by their conversation. Daniel Gookin and John Eliot specifically identified Philip—the supposed leader of the anti-English forces—as a sachem inclining toward Christian conversion. When events of the war proved that appearances could deceive, the middle ground between English and Indian, always precarious, became untenable. The very name "Praying Indian" became a liability for a beleaguered people who were incarcerated, attacked, and killed by the white New Englanders, for whom the image had originally been constructed.

In his postwar history of the Praying Indians, *An Historical Account of the Doings and Sufferings of the Christian Indians*, Daniel Gookin quotes Joseph Tuckapowaillin, pastor at Hasananesit, a praying town:

The English have taken away some of my estate, my corn, cattle, my plough, cart, chain, and other goods. The enemy Indians have also taken a part of what I had; and the wicked Indians mock and scoff at me, saying "Now what is become of your praying to God?" The English also censure me, and say I am a hypocrite.[38]

For faithful Praying Indians, the war resulted in white suspicion accompanied by official colonial legislation restricting their movement. A few months after the start of the war, it meant the exile of men, women, and children to Deer Island in the Boston harbor, a place destitute of adequate food or shelter in the winter, since the Indians were enjoined from cutting live wood or killing any sheep among the island's herds. Even then, relocated and incarcerated as they were, Praying Indians were subjected to more threats. Gookin reports that after enemy Indians burned the town of Medfield, some colonists called for mob vengeance, crying "Oh, come, let us go down to Deer Island, and kill all the praying Indians."[39] Colonial authorities took these feelings of the general populace seriously, and the General Court considered what measures they should take against the new residents of Deer Island. They included in their deliberations the possibilities of destroying or enslaving them.[40]

Eventually, colonial authorities realized that Praying Indians could be usefully integrated into their war effort. Converts Tom Neppanit and Peter Conway negotiated Mary Rowlandson's release from captivity. Job Kattenanit and James Quamapokit served as spies among the enemy. Other converts acted as scouts or fought alongside English troops. Their service did much to blunt English rage against them. But this recovery of a few individuals' reputations did not translate to a more general recuperation of the image. The positive possibilities that missionaries had constructed around Indians who displayed a measure of Anglicization ended. The writings produced during King Philip's War established a literary legacy in which Indians who were in some measure transculturated dangerously blurred the boundaries between English and Indian. Indian inhabitants of a middle ground, no matter what their allegiances, were ridiculed, suspected, and finally feared more than those quickly and easily identified as an enemy.

Notes

1. B[enjamin] T[ompson], "Upon the Elaborate Survey of New-Englands Passions from the Natives, By the Impartial Pen of that Worthy Divine Mr. William Hubbard" in William Hubbard, *The History of the Indian Wars in New-England from the First Settlement to the Termination of the War with King Philip in 1677,* ed. Samuel Drake (Roxbury, Mass.: Printed for W. E. Woodward, 1865), 1:24.

2. For an account of the English treatment of Praying Indians during the war, see Jenny Hale Pulsipher, "Massacre at Hurtleberry Hill: Christian Indi-

ans and English Authority in Metacom's War," *William and Mary Quarterly*, 3d ser., no. 53 (July 1966): 459–86. Studies that discuss the representation of Native Americans after the war include Louise Barnett, *The Ignoble Savage: American Literary Racism, 1790–1890* (Westport, Conn.: Greenwood Press, 1975); Robert F. Berkofer, *The White Man's Indian: Images of the American Indians from Columbus to the Present* (New York: Vintage Books, 1979); Francis Jennings *Invasion of America: Indians, Colonialism and the Cant of Conquest* (Chapel Hill: University of North Carolina Press, 1975); Roy Harvey Pearce *Savagism and Civilization: A Study of the Indian and the American Mind*, rev. ed. (Berkeley and Los Angeles: University of California Press, 1988); Raymond William Stedman, *Shadows of the Indian: Stereotypes in American Culture* (Norman: University of Oklahoma Press, 1982).

3. William London, *A Catalogue of the Most Vendible Books in England* (1660; reprint, London: Gregg Press, 1965).

4. I have discussed at length the invention and evolution of the Praying Indian figure in my doctoral dissertation, " 'That Epithet of Praying': The Praying Indian in Early New England Literature" (Ph.D. diss., University of Chicago, 1997). Other pertinent scholarship on the Puritan missions and Praying Indians is extensive; an exhaustive list is impossible here. Alden Vaughan's *New England Frontier: Puritans and Indians 1620–1675*, 3rd ed. (Norman: University of Oklahoma Press, 1995) is the most frequently cited pro-Puritan treatment of missions. Jennings, *Invasion of America*, and Neal Salisbury, *Manitou and Providence* (New York: Oxford University Press, 1982), document the many ways that Puritan missionaries were complicit in the invasion of the "New World." George Tinker, in his *Missionary Conquest: The Gospel and Native American Cultural Genocide* (Minneapolis, Minn.: Fortress Press, 1993), denounces the ongoing "canonization" of Puritan missionaries. For investigations of Indian responses to missionizing, see James Axtell, *The Invasion Within* (New York: Oxford University Press, 1985); Charles Cohen, "Conversion among Puritans and Amerindians: A Theological and Cultural Perspective," in Francis J. Bremer, ed., *Puritanism: Transatlantic Perspectives on a Seventeenth-Century Anglo-American Faith* (Boston: Massachusetts Historical Society, 1993); Dane Morrison: *A Praying People: Massachusetts Acculturation and the Failure of the Puritan Mission, 1600–1690* (New York: Peter Lang, 1995); James Ronda, " 'We Are Well as We Are': An Indian Critique of Seventeenth Century Christian Missions," *William and Mary Quarterly*, 3rd ser., 31 (January 1974): 27–54; Harold Van Lonkhuyzen, "A Reappraisal of the Praying Indians: Acculturation, Conversion, and Identity at Natick, Massachusetts, 1646–1730," *New England Quarterly* 62 (1990): 396–428.

5. Daniel Gookin, *Historical Collections of the Indians in New England*, Massachusetts Historical Society, *Collections*, 1st ser., 1 (1792): 165.

6. Gookin, *Historical Collections*, 200. Morrison defines "sachem" as a "tribal overlord" (*Praying People*, 242).

7. "The Winthrop Papers," Massachusetts Historical Society, *Collections*, 5th ser., 6:106.

8. Daniel Gookin, *An Historical Account of the Doings and Sufferings of the Christian Indians in New England, in the Years 1675, 1676, 1677*, American Antiquarian Society, *Archaeologia Americana, Transactions and Collection* 2 (1836; reprint, New York: Arno Press, 1972): 449.

9. N. S., *The Present State of New England*, in *Narratives of the Indian Wars, 1675–1699*, ed. Charles Lincoln (New York: C. Scribner's Sons, 1913), 49.

10. Hubbard, *History of the Indian Wars*, 1:123.

11. Ibid., 1:95.

12. Benjamin Tompson, "New Englands Crisis," in *So Dreadfull a Judgement: Puritan Responses to King Philip's War, 1676–1677*, ed. Richard Slotkin and James K. Folsom (Middletown, Conn.: Wesleyan University Press, 1978), 218.

13. Hubbard, *History of the Indian Wars*, 2:276.

14. Ibid.

15. N. S., *Present State*, 39.

16. For a discussion of the London reception of reports on the war, see Stephen Saunders Webb, *1676: The End of American Independence* (New York: Alfred A. Knopf, 1984), 221–44.

17. Gookin, *An Historical Account*, 441; Increase Mather, *A Brief History of the Wars with the Indians in Newe England*, in *So Dreadfull a Judgement*, 87.

18. Hubbard, *History of the Indian Wars*, 1:71.

19. *News from New-England, Being a True and Last Account of the Present Bloody Wars* (London, 1676), 5.

20. Ibid., 3.

21. N. S., *A New and Further Narrative of the State of New-England*, in *Narratives of the Indian Wars*, 83.

22. Mather, *Brief History*, 113.

23. *New England's Present Sufferings, under Their Cruel Neighbouring Indians* (London, 1675), 4. In Benjamin Church's memoir of his war adventures, he remembers a desperate moment in which he and his forces were hemmed in by the enemy on one side and a river on the other. A boat approached them, "Which some of Mr. Churches Men perceiving, began to cry out, *For God's sake to take them off, for their Ammunition was spent* &c. Mr. *Church* being sensible of the danger of the Enemies hearing their Complaints, and being made acquainted with the weakness and scantiness of their Ammunition, fiercely called to the Boats-master, and bid either send his Canoo a-shore, or else begone presently, or he would fire upon him"; see *Entertaining Passages*, in *So Dreadfull a Judgment*, 408. Church's response to his men's fear indicates that he believed the enemy could understand English.

24. Thomas Wheeler, *A Thankfull Remembrance of Gods Mercy*, in *So Dreadfull a Judgment*, 247.

25. *A Farther Brief and True Narration of the Late Wars Risen in New-England* (London, 1676), 4.

26. *A True Account of the Most Considerable Occurances*, in *King Philip's War Narratives*, March of America Facsimile Series, no. 29 (1676; reprint, Ann Arbor, Mich.: University Microfilms, 1966), 2.

27. Hubbard, *History of the Indian Wars*, 1:213.

28. Wheeler, *Thankfull Remembrance*, 248.

29. See Matthew 27:43: "He trusted in God; let him deliver him now, if he will have him"; Luke 23:35: "He saved others, let him save himself, if he be Christ, the chosen of God"; Luke 23:37: "If thou be king of the Jews, save thyself." And in Luke 23:39, the thief taunts Jesus: "If thou be Christ, save thyself and us."

30. See Kathryn Zabelle Derounian, "The Publication, Promotion, and Distribution of Mary Rowlandson's Indian Captivity Narrative in the Seventeenth Century," *Early American Literature* 23 (1988): 240. *The Sovereignty and Goodness of God* is the title of her narrative's New England edition. In England it appeared under the title *A True History of the Captivity and Restoration of Mrs. Mary Rowlandson*. See Amy Lang's introduction to Rowlandson's narrative in *Journey's in New Worlds: Early American Women's Narratives*, ed. Amy Lang and William L. Andrews (Madison: University of Wisconsin Press, 1990), 19.

31. Editors Richard Slotkin and James K. Folsom write that Rowlandson's account is "to be taken not only as the creation of a Puritan myth, but as the starting point of a cultural myth affecting America as a whole. Gradually, 'the captivity' became part of the basic vocabulary of American writers and historians, offering a symbolic key to the drama of American history" (*So Dreadfull a Judgment*, 302).

32. Mary Rowlandson, *The True History of the Captivity and Restoration of Mrs. Mary Rowlandson*, in *Journeys in New Worlds*, 34.

33. Ibid.

34. Ibid., 51.

35. The suggestion of war trophies is Michelle Burnham's in "The Journey Between: Liminality and Dialogism in Mary White Rowlandson's Captivity Narrative," *Early American Literature* 28, no.1 (1993): 69.

36. *John Eliot's Indian Dialogues: A Study in Cultural Interaction*, ed. Henry W. Bowden and James P. Ronda (Westport, Conn.: Greenwood Press, 1981).

37. Rowlandson, *True History*, 54.

38. Gookin, *Historical Account*, 504.

39. Ibid., 494.

40. Ibid., 497.

"Satan among the Sons of God"

The Creation of the Loyalist Enemy, 1774–84

J. L. Walsh

By 1774 the royal governor of New Hampshire, John Wentworth, had lost control of the mechanisms of the provincial government allowing for a nearly unopposed rebel takeover. The rebels, however, were not a majority of the population of New Hampshire. In order to solidify their position, the rebel leaders needed to secure the support of the people, or at least their acquiescence to a new state of affairs.

Though many New Hampshire loyalists left their province to serve in the British army or in provincial units, none of them saw action near home the way the loyalists of New York or Pennsylvania did. The rebellion in New Hampshire was a peaceful one, which made the experience of New Hampshire's loyalists unique. Around New Hampshire a shooting war raged; men bled and died on both sides of an armed conflict, the aim of which was to determine the political destiny of a continent. Within that war swirled another, perhaps more important struggle, the battle that had spawned the rebellion: a cultural conflict which split the residents of British North America at the local, provincial, and, later, national levels.

This essay places the rebellion in New Hampshire squarely within the definition of a culture war: an ideological clash between two opposing camps, both absolutely convinced of the righteousness of their cause.[1] A culture war was, and is, carried out publicly, primarily through the available media of public discourse, but the struggle may extend into the realm of actual physical conflict, as it did during the American Revolution.

The rebel faction was led by, and consisted of, wealthy merchants and landowners, magistrates, militia officers, and assemblymen, some of the best men in the colony.[2] It was their belief that the time had come to redefine the nature of the provincial community. The leaders of the rebel faction understood the need for popular support of their cause. They recognized that a small minority could not effectively control the province by coercion alone, even though the faction had a monopoly on the threat of force. At least in New Hampshire, argument replaced bullets as the means to an effective revolution, just as discourse replaced the battlefield as the arena in which the rebellion would be fought.

Wentworth's departure in August 1775 marked a major shift in the intensity and direction of the culture war in New Hampshire. The division between rebels and loyalists had not been as clear when the writings filling the newspapers were devoted to the constitutional questions of taxation and representation or the other issues which slowly divided the self-proclaimed Whigs from the so-called Tories. Those pieces continued to illuminate the thinking of the reading public, but a considerable number of rebel writers began to construct a new reality for the reading public, one designed to draw the reader into the fold of the convinced rebels and, at the same time, to discredit totally the position of the ideological enemy, the Tories.[3]

The goal of the rebel campaign in New Hampshire was the reformation of provincial society into a new and significantly different one than had existed prior to the middle of 1775. To accomplish that end the rebels created a new government, the legitimacy of which rested on the relatively new and untried Enlightenment concept of popular sovereignty, the idea that the power to rule was derived from the consent of the ruled. Once a new government, however unstable, was in place, it became possible for the rebels to utilize both existing methods of political persuasion: discourse and force.[4]

The threat of force overshadowed all of the residents of the province, not just loyalists. The example of mobbed or beaten loyalists must surely have had some effect on the majority of men and women who were unsure which way the conflict would go and thus had not committed themselves to either side. But the rebels needed commitment from the majority in order for the rebellion to succeed. Money had to be raised, men had to be enlisted, and supplies had to be gathered.

Rebel writers were aware that a great deal of convincing needed to be done. They were also aware that they dominated the only source for the dissemination of ideas, the *New Hampshire Gazette,* founded in 1756 by Daniel Fowle. Thus they began the creation of a new myth, a myth which could be used to elevate the patriotic Whigs to nearly legendary status in the minds of their readers. The rebels created a new way of looking at the present by adopting a special way of viewing the past.[5] The rebel writers also created the myth of the legendary ancestors, those people who had originally colonized the province and given for all posterity their example of heroic stature: "Brothers! Let us think of our heroic ancestors who fought and bled and died for this country. Let us think of our aged fathers and mothers, think of our wives and children, let us look forward to posterity . . . in this great day of conquest."[6]

The myths perpetuated by the rebel writers had to be powerful constructs which could inform a new reality in ways both agreeable and persuasive to their audience.[7] This discourse itself was full of language designed to convey a sense of greatness to the rebels' "glorious cause" and was infused with descriptive phrases that advanced self-justification: the righteousness of the rebellion, the virtue of the rebels, and the connection between the present and the heroic past. No sacrifice was too great, and everyone in the province must be in agreement. Rebel writers argued that "it appears to be the general sentiment that the man is unworthy the name of an English American who would hesitate one moment to prefer death to the slavish subjection demanded by the ministry and parliament of Great Britain" (*NHG*, 2 June 1774).

The first salvo in the discursive battle was the newspaper account of a seemingly innocuous incident. In December 1774 a story appeared in the *Gazette* that began the campaign to create an internal enemy. At first the letter from Stephen Boardman seemed to be merely an attack on a single loyalist. Hardly apologizing for his hand in the affair, Boardman wrote to explain a situation that attracted attention and aroused concern among the people of Portsmouth and the New Hampshire coastal region in general. Boardman recounted that William Pottle of Stratham had entered the town on private business and that as he approached the state house, a group of approximately one hundred men were gathered there. At that point someone shouted "There is a Tory . . . there is an enemy to his country . . . see how he looks . . . behold him, how he looks!" "Upon this," Boardman reported, "knowing the said Pottle had conducted in a manner inimical to his country, and thinking this a suitable time to intimidate and humble him, I said 'Gentlemen this villain has appeared an open enemy of his country.' " The crowd then advanced on Pottle and physically assaulted him. How badly Pottle was handled is unclear. Boardman concluded by adding: "though I abhor all illegal mobs and assemblies and would have no man's person or property injured I think everyone who is a friend to America is in duty bound to condemn such a man and have no connection or dealings with him 'till repentance and reformation entitle him to forgiveness"[8] (*NHG*, 30 Dec. 1774).

Boardman's letter elicited a pair of responses within a couple of weeks. The first was a lengthy letter condemning all mob actions of the kind Boardman seemed so proud:

> At a time when the reins of government are evidently slackened, when the sacred name of liberty is so villainously prostituted to the most licentious purposes, when nothing more is wanting to pull down the ungovernable rage of a furious mob on the head of an honest and worthy citizen than for some malicious disappointed wretch falsely to represent him as an enemy to the constitutional rights of his country, I say, at such a time as this the public ought to be exceedingly cautious how they listen to any reports that may in the least tend to inflame the minds of the people against any person whatever, whether these reports and insinuations come dressed up in the sly garb of a Horse Jockey, the hypocritical cant of a Saint, or the still more detested authority of a Trading Justice, they are equally despicable and unworthy of notice. Every honest, well-disposed man is to be respected especially such as have faithfully served their country in public stations and employments and even such of these as have been so unfortunate as not to have had the advantages of education, are much more to be honored and valued than some who with all their boasted literature will remain stupid puppies to their life's end. (*NHG*, 20 Jan. 1775)

The letter, signed "A Lover of Peace," was from the town of Greenland and appeared in the same number of the *Gazette* as William Pottle's own reply. Though some of "A Lover's" allusions might be difficult to trace, his purpose was clear: to attack the rebel tendency to accuse individuals of inimical acts without any clear or evidential basis, as well as without any pretense at due process. The signs were clear to "A Lover" that such continued behavior would be injurious not just to real loyalists, but to others, who had no political convictions, and could be publicly attainted and attacked with potentially serious consequences. Pottle himself began by observing, "See Reader, what lengths enthusiastical zeal may lead a man under the notion of duty." He then listed and denied three charges that had been leveled against him, including holding a mock meeting in competition with an important local meeting. Pottle next suggested that Boardman was really motivated by personal animosity, and strongly asserted that a deacon (Pottle chose to ignore Boardman's identification of himself as a member of the committee of inspection, and rather pointed out that Boardman was a deacon of the church in Stratham) ought to behave in a much more Christian manner toward others.

Boardman replied within a month, still insisting that Pottle was an enemy to his country and that there was no truth to the idea that he (Boardman) held some grudge concerning his seat as deacon (*NHG*, 17 Feb. 1775). Pottle's response to this charge was a month in coming but to the point. Boardman, he said, was unchristian and jealous and had lied when he suggested that Pottle's father had attempted to oust him from the deacon's place. The real root of his attack, Pottle countered, had nothing to do with his own conduct, but that Boardman was seeking to revenge himself upon Pottle because of a land dispute that Pottle had won through arbitration in the recent past (*NHG*, 31 March 1775).

Public disputes such as the Boardman-Pottle battle served a purpose in the discursive arena of the cultural clash in New Hampshire. From the rebel perspective, the tale of Pottle's fate at the hands of the Portsmouth mob served as a warning to others to amend their behavior or face a similar fate. Pottle's responses to Boardman's accusations were the efforts of an individual intent upon defending himself personally. To the rebels those letters were nothing but the squirming protestations of a traitor. To the loyalists they were the reasonable explanations of a man falsely accused of a crime which was no crime. The entire situation pointed up one of the principal contentions of loyalist discourse, that the attacks on individuals as enemies of liberty really had nothing to do with the current political crisis. Rather they emanated from personal enmity and petty grudges that small and dangerous men could now air out by falsely accusing any old foe and exacting vengeance for old scores real or imagined. This sort of public allegation also served another purpose in the rebel strategy. By publishing attacks on loyalists, either specific or general, they hoped to elicit responses which would render the identity and counsels of the enemy open to public scrutiny.

The rebel mythmakers continued their attempt to create a sense of righteousness among the people they hoped to count among their number. "An American" suggested that recent events proved that God was on America's side and that ultimate victory was at hand (*NHG*, 11 July 1775). The rebel writers also began to create another myth, a counterweight to the glorious crusade of liberty-loving Americans. They began to attack the image of Great Britain, its inhabitants, rulers, and supporters in America. Another correspondent to the *Gazette*, "Americanus," began the campaign by suggesting that anyone who opposed the cause or did it any harm ought to "quit the country and his personal estate seized for so much as may be thought his proportion of the public debt, and if found insufficient then his real estate to be incumbent for the same" (*NHG*, 1 Aug. 1775). A perfect example of the evil which lurked in the heart of every "Tory" was provided by Matthew Christian of Antigua. Christian, who had taken refuge aboard *H.M.S. Scarborough*, anchored in Portsmouth harbor, allegedly wished "the small pox in all our borders and especially in the damned rebel army 'round Boston." Safe aboard a British warship, Christian was untouchable. Regardless, the committee of safety in Portsmouth voted to exile him from all ports "in the known world" (*NHG*, 8 Aug. 1775).[9]

During the middle of 1776 the *New Hampshire Gazette* increased the number of opinion pieces as its campaign against loyalists intensified. First came a scathing attack reprinted from the *Providence Gazette*. The authors, "Amicus Patriae" and "Filius Libertatis," desired that the government "seize and confine within the narrow circuit of a jail or prison the sons of this infernal monster." They alleged that "as our saviour was betrayed by one of his disciples, so is our country by her pretended friends." Their central theme included the idea that the wealthy were not to be trusted because they either did not support liberty or put personal interest before the general good (*NHG*, 8 June 1776).

Another writer, "Orthodoxus," supplied weekly pieces during July in support of independence and the liberty of America and ended the month with another piece of negative propaganda. On 27 July "Orthodoxus" described the British as "our cruel oppressors . . . who come armed with fire and sword to waste and destroy our country robbing us of our lives, exposing to the greatest danger and distress men, women, and children, and cowardly butchering even the helpless and unarmed." "Orthodoxus" was followed the next week by "Amicus Reipublica," who claimed that "America . . . is attacked by unnatural enemies without and still more wicked wretches within who are aiming to destroy her, may they fall into those very pits themselves they have digged for her and like Haman be hanged on the very gallows they have erected for others" (*NHG*, 3 Aug. 1776).

Those two pieces and another in January 1777 typify the invective used by the rebel writers to create an image, an identity, in the minds of their readers. "An Enemy to Tories" contended that "there are many such shameful wretches among us at this late hour that would sell their God, their country, their wives, their children, and all that is near and dear to them." The writers had a dual purpose, first to destroy the loyalists totally in the eyes of their neighbors by implicitly connecting them with the British enemy. The second goal was to rid the land of the scourge of enemies within: "Upon the whole, what ought to be done in order to rid us of such vermin? . . . provide some kind of a bark and after putting on board some provisions, set them adrift and make it death for any of them ever to land on any part of the American shore that is inhabited by free men" (*NHG*, 14 Jan. 1777).

The language of the Whig/rebels is complex and full of resonances with other places and times. Their objective was to make of the British a race of monsters, so infernal and frightening that there could be no hope of compromise. In late 1776 and throughout 1777 their cause was not as sure as the rebel leaders would have liked. A sizeable number of the inhabitants of the province were as yet unhappy with the precipitous nature of the Declaration of Independence, and many were equally unhappy with the state of provincial government. Some of the same arguments used against John Wentworth were still in use in attacks against the rebel assembly. In response, the rebel writers tried diligently to create an enemy so fearsome that it would drive the divisive issues from the minds of their readers. While Gage and Burgoyne issued proclamations and pardons to those who would once more pledge their loyalty to the crown, the rebels identified the loyalists with the devil incarnate.

The passions of the readers continued to be inflamed by the steady publication of news pieces such as "An Account of the Inhumane Cruelties to Prisoners in New York," which told of starvation and disease, of torture and the introduction of smallpox by deliberate act (*NHG*, 22 March 1777).

This trend continued through 1777 and 1778. This type of writing became familiar as the victory at Saratoga brought renewed confidence and the king's commissioners seeking to make an early peace without the grant of independence. But it was too late for reconciliation with the loyalists as far as General Livingston of New York was concerned. Writing to the Continental Congress in response to the suggested act offering pardon to and reconciliation with them, Livingston lamented: "Alas, how many lives had been saved and what scene of inexpressible misery prevented had we from the beginning treated our bosom traitors with proper severity and inflicted the law of retaliation upon an enemy too savage to be humanized by any other argument." He continued calling the loyalists "a race of murderers before unequalled" who "waged an infernal war against their dearest connections." Furthermore, they were "apostates from reason . . . whose very presence among the genuine sons of freedom would seem as unnatural as that of Satan among the sons of God" (*NHG*, 7 July 1778). Livingston's words might well be understood, since in New York the war between loyalists and rebels had become as savage a civil war as had ever been fought. But the inclusion of this piece in the *New Hampshire Gazette* had another reason than a need to fill space.

The *Gazette* was by then reflecting a distinct sense of optimism. Most of the news of the war was good, especially the surrender of Burgoyne at Saratoga. Problems still remained, however, particularly those involving money. The battle still raged between shopkeepers and farmers over who was raising prices faster, and why. Counterfeiting was having a serious effect on the provincial and continental currency, a crime that was, rightly or not, attributed primarily to loyalists.

In fact the loyalists were being blamed for the entire war: "to our internal foes are we indebted in a great measure for the present war, the immense expense incurred and the devastation, ravage, and ruin suffered by us" (*NHG*, 23 Aug. 1777). The rebel writers were attempting to convince the populace that no war would have ensued had it not been for the loyalists. The thrust of their contention arose from the idea that it was the loyalist plea for protection of their interest that impelled George III to embark on war in the first place. By the end of the war that idea was prevalent. As late as 1781, just three weeks after the news of Yorktown had arrived in New Hampshire, a satirical piece was printed purporting to be a conversation between Prince William Henry, the heir to the British throne, and Sir Henry Clinton, British commander in New York. The prince, upon being told of the real situation in America, cried, "Damn the loyalists, all this comes from listening to their tales. They teased my father into this cursed war. I wish he may hang Galloway at the yard arm of a seventy-four. . . . I will be revenged on your vile loyalists who have divided the British empire and brought this ruin upon my father's family" (*NHG*, 17 Nov. 1781).

The rebels' intentions were multiple. First, in 1777, they were yet afraid of invasion, even in New Hampshire. The Canadian threat seemed quite real especially as Burgoyne approached the province through upper New York. American victories at Bennington and Saratoga, however, went a long way to assuage those fears. At that point a secondary objective came into focus, the conversion of loyalist property into funds the province desperately needed. To accomplish that end, the enemy needed to be clearly identified and made to look as though he were a minion of the devil himself. The reports of loyalist and British atrocities from the other colonies provided the only clear means of demonstrating the danger from within to which even New Hampshire might fall prey. Despite the successes of 1777 the rebels needed the apparition of "Britons, Hessians, Savages, and more savage tories" (*NHG*, 25 May 1779). That was especially true in New Hampshire where a substantial body of the unconverted, residing in Portsmouth, remained relatively unmolested.

The state of affairs there was, from the perspective of one writer, terribly dangerous. "M' Namora" wrote that "It's astonishing to see daily the insults offered by the Tories and unnoticed by the Committee." This writer alleged that the loyalists had a sophisticated network of intelligence agents who gathered reports for the British in New York, and were able to learn of the outcomes of battles elsewhere even before the rebel authorities. Thus these Tories were able to disappoint and delude the public by making claims of British victories, exaggerating rebel losses and minimizing their victories. "Namora" further stated that these traitors continued to have dinners and drink toasts, and that they gave each other secret signs in the streets through eye contact and nods of the head, and that something ought to be done about it (*NHG*, 21 Sept. 1776).

A reply appeared the following week in the *Gazette*. The writer appealed to the pride of an "unprejudiced impartial printer" to get his letter printed. Signed, "I Am What You Will," the loyalist writer mocked "Namora's" paranoia:

Well done Namora, you talk sense, you preach liberty, real genuine liberty, downright alamode liberty, by God. I must observe however that I was at first a good deal alarmed on discovering your design of abolishing looks and nods, those dear conveyors of our secret meaning, but when I found you only meant significant ones, and that out of the abundance of your great goodness and impartiality you had confined it to tories, I was immediately reconciled to it and discovered by the help of certain political microscopic glasses, that it tended to the public good. . . . 'Tis a disgrace to the state to allow such significant looks and nods and if the legislative body of these states have not in their great wisdom already provided a punishment adequate to the diabolical nature of so black a crime (which hardly admits of a doubt) I think the honorable committee of this town, if they desire that the trumpet of fame should sound their praises to after ages cannot have a fairer opportunity of immortalizing their names, that by enacting laws against such treasonable and unheard of practices which would at once discover their patriotic zeal for their country, their wise and godlike penetration into the nature and cause of things, and their unerring knowledge of mankind who carry on daily the most villainous conspiracies in no other language than looks and nods. . . . I humbly think a significant look ought to be punished by a burning out of the optics, and a nod by severing off the offending head from the unoffending body. (*NHG*, 28 Sept. 1776)

The humor of "What You Will" was lost on some like "A. B.," who responded by saying "we have some among us who not only refuse to submit to the authority by which we are governed, but in the most insolent and unprovoked manner, ridicule those by whom we consent to be governed" (*NHG*, 12 Oct. 1776).

By 1779 the war appeared lost to the loyalists who were endeavoring to ameliorate the impact that a rebel victory might have on them and their absent friends. The Acts of Proscription and Confiscation had attainted absentees as traitors and given the government power to seize loyalist property. So, when a town meeting was convened in Portsmouth in March 1779, a petition was introduced for the purpose of repealing a portion of the confiscation act. The supporters of the petition desired that the town meeting endorse their effort and transmit it to the legislature for approval. According to "A. Z.," who wrote to the *Gazette* to protest this meeting, which, he contended, was hastily called, the whole thing was a plan fomented by "those kind of beings called tories, together with great numbers of a worse character (if possible), I mean the two-faced go-between gentry whose conduct is regulated by our good or ill success" (*NHG*, 30 March 1779). "A. Z." further claimed that the meeting was dominated by that group and their friends.

The following week a response was printed, signed "Veritas," that vehemently denied the presence of Tories and their sympathizers at the meeting but suggested instead that many of the foremost men of the town had been there, including a former representative of the state to the Continental Congress, and several members of the state assembly. "Veritas" explained that the petition was concerned only with the point that the loyalist estates were confiscated without due process. In the same number, "A Freeholder" added, "No one can detest a tory more than myself, nor do I think any punishment too severe for such as have malignantly deserted their country or took up arms against it, but I can never consent that even one of them or any other person for any crime whatsoever should be punished without a trial" (*NHG*, 6 Apr. 1779). The author concluded by castigating a government more tyrannical than that which the country was fighting against.

A reply from "A. Z." was swift and scathing. In the 13 April edition of the *Gazette*, "A. Z." responded with vitriol, calling "Veritas" a liar in no uncertain terms and at length, and then contended that the petition was a Tory contrivance. After blasting "Veritas" and Tories in general, "A. Z." advised "A Freeholder" to be very careful "in [the] future about calling the present government 'the mock liberties of a boasted American constitution' as it is apprehended he will be indicted for high

treason if he should persist therein." As if threats and vilification were
not enough, beneath the letter "A. Z." included a poem entitled "To
Veritas," which read:

> Poor misguided Veritas, how couldest thou
> in a fit so mad prostitute thy pen
> to such ignoble use? Sure some demon
> invaded then thy melancholy mind
> and in that gloomy hour didst it turn all
> thy noble flights of fancy to ——
> and abuse to please but a wretched few
> Harpies and Parricides that daily suck
> the vital blood from this wounded country. . . .
>   (*NHG*, 13 Apr. 1779)

The next edition saw a reply from "Veritas" that was full of name-
calling but little else. "A Freeholder," threatened in the 13 April letter
from "Veritas," fought back by saying he was not afraid to contend
against "crafty and designing men [that] thrust themselves into legislative power, who to satisfy their own selfish purposes or indulge a malicious disposition should subvert our happy constitution, abolish our
most valuable privileges and in their stead substitute the most arbitrary
acts of violence and oppression, then truly every honest man will have
sufficient cause not only to be cautious but to fear that instead of being
mocked with the formality of an indictment he may find himself fet-
tered in the dreary apartments of an Inquisition" (*NHG*, 20 Apr. 1779).
The exchange of letters ended with that piece, but the feeling that Tories represented a threat to the peace and security of the state persisted.
Those fears were fueled by the rebel writers who consistently portrayed
loyalists as "savage tories."

Nor was the reading public allowed to forget the kinds of atrocities
practiced by the British and the Tories, crimes all the more heinous in
rebel eyes because they were committed by former neighbors, by brothers. "A. Z." 's use of the word "parricides"[10] was not a conceit based on
classical allusion but a reference to a civil struggle which in other provinces actually saw brothers slaying each other. The rebel writers complained that "among the many errors America has been guilty of during
her contest with Great Britain few have been greater or attended with
more fatal consequences to these states than her lenity to the tories"
(*NHG*, 7 Sept. 1779).[11] Despite the efforts of the rebel writers and the
printer who filled the pages of the *New Hampshire Gazette* with their
words, the loyalists still residing in New Hampshire remained relatively

unmolested. Indeed it might be that very situation which provoked even more concern among the locals.

It became a pronounced fear among the rebels that loyalists would somehow insinuate their way into a place where they could assume responsible positions in the government. For that reason Fowle copied a warning from "A Whig" reminding his readers that the cause was not yet won, nor would it be if the community relaxed its vigilance. "Rouse America, your danger is great from a quarter where you least expect it, the tories. The tories will yet be the ruin of you" (*NHG*, 7 Sept. 1779).[12] In September 1779 assembly elections loomed large in the minds of the populace, and with the threat of imminent invasion nearly gone, the electorate was in danger of sliding into a sense of complacency that the ardent rebels found dangerous. Thus their need to remind the readers, indeed to enlarge upon the theme that the Tories were responsible solely for the conditions of fear and economic disturbance through which the province had suffered since 1775. "[W]ho were the occasion of the war?" asked "A Whig." "The tories. Who persuaded the tyrant of Britain to prosecute it in a manner before unknown to civilized nations and shocking even to barbarians? The tories." The rebels would convince the voters that the loyalists were completely responsible for the war, and still in a position to affect its outcome. The solution offered was difficult but necessary: " 'tis time my countrymen to rid ourselves of these bosom vipers. . . . Think of these things betimes, my countrymen, before it be too late and your posterity forever have reason to repent your lenity to the tories" (*NHG*, 7 Sept. 1779).[13] The campaign against loyalists continued with another warning from "A Whig." "Beware of those who have not been firm and unshaken from the beginning of the contest to the present time; beware of those who, under the mask of Whigism, are now hand in glove with persons strongly suspected to be enimical to our cause" (*NHG*, 23 Nov. 1779). The attacks of "A Whig" went unchallenged. Remaining loyalists prudently chose to keep silent. The rebel position was reiterated the following year by "A Farmer" who again asserted the rebel myth of "insinuating traitors, who at this time employ every engine and pursue every probable method to discourage a virtuous people bravely struggling for their freedom and who would gladly wallow in the blood of those whom under a veil of friendship they wish to deceive and ruin. The various artful measures adopted by these cruel parricides are too numerous to relate" (*NHG*, 5 Aug. 1779).

The *New Hampshire Gazette* of Portsmouth became the primary vehicle by which the culture war was fought in New Hampshire. Such a struggle was necessitated by conditions peculiar to the rebellion in New Hampshire, but present in different forms in the other provinces as well. The rebel faction in New Hampshire was neither large nor particularly powerful at the outset of the contest. Indeed, one writer has concluded that the revolt in New Hampshire may have been more influenced by the Massachusetts model than it was by the incendiary leadership of rebellious elite.[14] Yet the faction was faced with the task of converting a significant portion of the populace to its viewpoint as quickly as possible, while also struggling with the potential of invasion and actual fighting. The rebellion in New Hampshire was not fought by military means but as a contest for the "hearts and minds" of its inhabitants. From the rebel perspective nothing less than total victory would suffice. Failure would mean disgrace, destitution, and perhaps the gallows. By gaining the upper hand in the paper wars, the rebels helped to create a new identity for the community. The threat of force implicit in the militia and the sophisticated surveillance network encompassed of town committees could not meet that need through coercion alone. Victory was achieved through the conversion of the populace in thought as well as action.[15]

The rebel strategy required more than mere acquiescence to a change in status. Military means were inadequate to convince or compel the populace to embrace the "glorious cause." It was necessary to recast the colonial identity into a new American identity, one based upon but superior to that identity which had defined society for two centuries and more. In the course of doing so, the rebels created the myth of the evil Briton and the even more despicable Tory, casting the enemies of the people into stark terms of good and evil. By creating the dichotomy of righteous "patriot" versus diabolical "tory" and Briton, the rebels accomplished a means of control and conquest far more effective and lasting than any which could have come about merely through military occupation. The rebellion in New Hampshire was won by effecting the change of allegiance among the people from the mother country to the province, by shifting the commitment of the hearts of the people to the new polity.[16] No amount of force could effect that change in identity, only a victory in a war of persuasion, a war for which the loyalists were unprepared at the outset, and in which they never succeeded in recouping their initial losses. The revolution in New Hampshire was accomplished before the first shots were fired.

Notes

This essay is part of a much larger study of the loyalist identity, J. L. Walsh, "Friend of Government or Damned Tory: The Creation of the Loyalist Identity, 1774–1784" (Ph.D. diss., University of New Hampshire, 1996).

1. On that clash, see James Davison Hunter, *Culture Wars: The Struggle to Define America* (New York: Basic Books, 1991); Gordon S. Wood, *The Radicalism of the American Revolution* (New York: W. W. Norton, 1991).

2. On the makeup of the faction's leadership, see, for example, Paul W. Wilderson, *Governor John Wentworth & the American Revolution: The English Connection* (Hanover, N.H.: University Press of New England, 1994), 250.

3. Throughout the struggle, the rebel writers referred to themselves consistently as Whigs. Even the word "patriot" is noticeably absent. In the original sources the word Whig is used almost exclusively when referring to the rebel faction. For the purpose of clarity I will continue to use the term rebel when referring to the leaders of the radical faction or the usurped government, and when referring to the writers who adopted the appellation whig. Hunter describes the strategy of adversaries engaged in a discursive struggle, arguing that two forms of argument are used: positive and negative. "The positive face of moral conflict is expressed through constructive moral reasoning and debate . . . the negative face of moral conflict [is] the deliberate, systematic effort to discredit the opposition" (*Culture Wars*, 136).

4. Bruce Lincoln comments that "Together, discourse and force are the chief means whereby social borders, hierarchies, institutional formations, and habituated patterns of behavior are both maintained and modified." Force "is regularly employed by those who hold official power to compel obedience and suppress deviance" (*Discourse and the Construction of Society, Comparative Studies of Myth, Ritual, and Classification* [New York: Oxford University Press, 1989], 3).

5. Lincoln defines this kind of myth as "a form of meta-language in which preexisting signs are appropriated and stripped of their original context, history, and signification only to be infused with new and mystificatory conceptual content of particular use to the bourgeoisie. Myth, Barthes argued, 'has the task of giving an historical intention a natural justification, and making contingency appear eternal' " (*Discourse and the Construction of Society*, 23).

6. "An American," in *New Hampshire Gazette*, 20 May 1774. Subsequent citations will be noted parenthetically by the acronym *NHG* and the date.

7. According to Lincoln, myths are "that small class of stories that possess both credibility and authority . . . a narrative possessed of authority is one for which successful claims are made not only to the status of truth, but what is more to the status of paradigmatic truth" (*Discourse and the Construction of Society*, 24).

8. December 1774 also marked the effective end of royal authority in New Hampshire. The crowd Boardman referred to in his letter was the standing mob of Portsmouth, the same group in all likelihood which took part in the assault on Fort William and Mary.

9. Exactly how that was to be accomplished is unclear, though the plan did call for letters to be sent to officials throughout the area with which Portsmouth could correspond.

10. *The Concise Oxford Dictionary* defines parricide as "One who murders his father or near relative or one whose person is held sacred; person guilty of treason against his country."

11. Quoted from the *Pennsylvania Packet*, 5 August 1779.

12. Quoted from the *Pennsylvania Packet*, 5 August 1779.

13. Quoted from the *Pennsylvania Packet*, 5 August 1779.

14. Richard Francis Upton, *Revolutionary New Hampshire: An Account of the Social and Political Forces Underlying the Transition from Royal Province to American Commonwealth* (New York: Octagon Books, 1971), 16.

15. As Lincoln put it, "such a radical recasting of collective identity, which amounts to the deconstruction of a previously significant sociopolitical border and the corollary construction of a new, encompassing sociopolitical aggregate, can hardly be accomplished through force alone." (*Discourse and the Construction of Society*, 4).

16. "Ultimately," writes Lincoln, "that which either holds society together or takes it apart is sentiment, and the chief instrument with which such sentiment may be aroused, manipulated, and rendered dormant is discourse" (*Discourse and the Construction of Society*, 11).

"These Worms Will Cut the Root of Our Independence"

Fears of a State Church among the Anti-mission Baptists of the Nineteenth Century

Jeffrey W. Taylor

Background: The Rise of the Religious Societies

From 1796 to 1830 many groups in America organized societies to promote missions, Bible distribution, tract publication, Sunday school, Sabbath practice, and so on. These bodies were national organizations in both structure and intent, though most were Eastern in terms of leadership and support. Specifically, the leadership tended to be of New England origin. The reforming values that prompted these new organizations have been linked with the modernizing ethos associated with Yankee Protestantism. The motivation behind the formation of these societies has been characterized as optimistic vitality in response to the new American situation or, conversely, as fear of this same situation. Whatever the causes may be, as these societies spread their message and culture, the traditional religious landscape changed.[1]

For no group were these changes more of a challenge to tradition than the Baptists. The first national organization of Baptists in America met 18 May 1814 in Philadelphia. Thirty-three delegates formed the General Missionary Convention of the Baptist Denomination in the United States for Foreign Missions. The focus was foreign missions, especially the work of Adoniram Judson, whose major promoter was Luther Rice. The work of the Triennial Convention, as it was known, expanded in 1817 with the organization of a "Domestic Missionary" effort. Rice and John Mason Peck provided the impetus. Peck and James Welch were sent to Saint Louis the same year to begin mission work. Perhaps the newness of organized mission work for Baptists in America is best illustrated by the fact that Rice and Peck were former Congregationalists.[2]

It would be difficult to overemphasize the magnitude of change in Baptist life as a result of the organized missionary effort. Prior to 1814 there had been no national organization. As Leon McBeth has noted, "out of foreign missions arose the women's movement, home missions, theological education, and even, to some extent, the Sunday School Movement."[3] Restless ferment indeed.

Historiography

The work of the new religious societies, and their very existence, were opposed from among the churches themselves. Based on his work with early-nineteenth-century periodicals and the "anti-missionary movement in the United States," Gaylord Albaugh found opposition to have occurred among a wide variety of groups, including Universalists, Unitarians, Christian Connection, "Reformed Methodists," Hicksite Quakers, "Free Thinkers," and Baptists. In his analysis, these groups were all united by a single "basic cause" of opposition:

> The basic cause was a deep-running fear of the consequences of the early [nineteenth] century tendency toward centralization of religious authority. . . . [These societies were seen to be a] danger to religious liberty. A single denomination or group of denominations might conceivably become so powerful as to effect a practical union of Church and State despite constitutional guarantees to the contrary.[4]

Albaugh has characterized the concerns specific to each group as "subsidiary props to support this basic fear."

Byron Cecil Lambert built on Albaugh's work in his 1957 dissertation entitled "The Rise of the Anti-Mission Baptists: Sources and Leaders, 1800-1840 (A Study in American Religious Individualism.)" Close to half of Lambert's work is devoted to non-Baptist antimission society groups. He understood the fears of a state church expressed by the early Baptist opposition leader John Leland to have originated in his controversy with the established churches of Massachusetts and Virginia, fears strengthened by Leland's political attachment to Jeffersonian individualism and theological understanding of a separated church.[5] Lambert is unclear, however, as to the extent, function, and role of this fear among the other prominent leaders—John Taylor, Daniel Parker, and Alexander Campbell—or among the early founders of the Primitive Baptist movement.

Lambert saw as a deeper motive a religious individualism resistant to centralizing tendencies. My reading of the relevant Baptist material of the period would challenge this analysis. Most Baptist leaders in opposition to missions were working with the older definition of liberty rather than with individualism: their thinking was more in terms of communities and classes of society.[6] In this respect, Bertram Wyatt-Brown's attention to issues of class and of regionalism in his 1970 analysis of the Baptist antimission movement in the Jacksonian South is more convincing. Wyatt-Brown, however, did not include fears of a state church as an essential part of his analysis.[7]

Returning now to the more narrowly focused topic of this essay, I intend to sketch the map I am beginning to draw of this fear. I am especially interested in examining Albaugh's claim that the fear of a state church was the basic cause of opposition to the new societies with other concerns only acting as "props" to this basic cause. My questions include: Does Albaugh's analysis accurately portray the antimission Baptists? Can fear of a state church be traced subsequent to Leland? Can it be traced in other prominent leaders? For how long? What role did it play in the life of the institutionalized Baptist opposition, the Primitive Baptists, also called Old School Baptists?

Fears of a State Church

One of the strengths of Lambert's work is his attention to Baptist preacher John Leland (1754–1841) in his role as opposition leader to the new societies. Wasting no time, Leland had traveled to Philadelphia in April 1814 to preach against the new national organization of Baptists as it was being formed. He saw it as disobedience to God's pattern for the church. Leland wrote prolifically concerning both politics and religion. The two were joined in his activities on behalf of religious liberty. The great enemy, in his eyes, was the established clergy, who after disestablishment formed religious societies to regain the control they had lost. Therefore, when his fellow Baptists also adopted similar structures, he regarded this development as both a sin against God and a danger to religious liberty.[8] This point of view is seen, for example, in an 1832 article printed in the periodical *Signs of the Times*. The concluding paragraph states:

There are a number of religious denominations in the United
States so equally balanced, that no one of them can tyrannize over
all the rest: the present scheme seems to be, for each society to
sacrifice its peculiar characteristics, and all unite to form a *Christian Phalanx*, to be established by Congress as the religion of the
United States. If my painful fears, on this head are ever realized,
the glory of America will depart—and the asylum for the distressed turned to a prison and an inquisition.[9]

For Leland the fear of a state church was certainly a basic cause of
his opposition. There were other concerns, just as basic, such as faithfulness to God's plan for the church as seen in a reading of the New
Testament, a reading that did not see any instruction for mission societies. While Albaugh did not mention Leland by name, he did list John
Taylor, Daniel Parker, and Alexander Campbell as Baptist opposition
leaders. In the writings of these men, though, the fear of a state church
does not appear to occupy a prominent place, let alone function as
the basic cause. The other motivating factors of opposition—scriptural
faithfulness, faithfulness to the Baptist heritage, the greed of the new
societies, and their danger to congregational independence—are often
expressed without a church/state connection.

Leland's concerns were echoed, however, by another leader of the
1820s and 1830s, Baptist preacher Joshua Lawrence of North Carolina
(1778-1843.) Though not mentioned by Albaugh, Lawrence was one of
the organizers of the Primitive Baptist movement as a distinct group
within Baptist life. Concerned over the greed he perceived in the society system, along with its favoring of the rich, he grounded his objections in an understanding that an explicit New Testament command or
example was necessary for any church practice and that significant departure from traditional Baptist practice must of necessity be heretical.[10] In these views he is in step with the leaders already mentioned.
Yet, again and again he returned to the dangers of a state church in
language similar to Leland's.

In the 1825 pamphlet *The American Telescope,* Lawrence expressed his
apprehension over the possible combination of religion and money with
civil power. He argued that church history showed what a terror this
mixture was to the true church. With money-hungry mission clergy on
the loose, Lawrence was thankful that all clergymen were prohibited
from civil office by the North Carolina Constitution. He also saw danger in the mission's clergy "fawn[ing]" over civil authorities in search
of money: they "are endeavoring to bring together church and state."
This fear was also expressed in the "Declaration of the Reformed Bap-

tist Churches in the State of North Carolina," put before the Kehukee Association in 1826 and adopted in 1827. *The North Carolina Whig's Apology for the Kehukee Association,* an 1830 pamphlet, reminded its readers that the moneyed clergy of Massachusetts and other states had persecuted Baptists, Methodists, and Quakers. But it was the "Patriotic Discourse" of 1830 that sounded the shrillest alarm. Originally a Fourth of July Oration delivered in Tarborough, it was reprinted as a pamphlet and widely distributed.[11]

In the "Discourse," Lawrence wrote that "civil and religious liberty must live and die together." Such liberty was now in danger from "tyrannical priests" who invaded the "rights of conscience." The times were seen to be threatening:

> Oh, that I had a voice like thunder, I would speak to every American to stop, pause and think—think what theological schools, priestly influence, and law religion have brought other nations to. . . . [he then compared modern clergy efforts at influence to the slow and gentle training of oxen to the yoke.] . . . they are coaxing, persuading, begging, and putting on the yoke and cart, by large sums of money, theological and Sunday schools, combined with the press and priestly influence. And I tell you, these worms will cut the root of our independence.[12]

The new society system showed its true nature, wrote Lawrence, through its organized petition of Congress to "help to maintain the sanctity of the Sabbath" by stopping Sunday mail transport. These societies wanted the power of civil law to promote their own religious ends. Their desire for power, Lawrence thought, would lead to the day when "Sunday School Unions force out of schools all books but those approved by the priests and their party." The society clergy had a desire for control that propelled them to disregard Scripture, forbidding drink in the name of "Temperance." If the missionaries got law on their side, warned Lawrence, then there would be persecution of the sort that old New England and Virginia experienced. And if the people were to "suffer the priest by law to ride on your back, you will soon I assure you, have to carry a king behind him." Then the revolution would be undone.[13]

Lawrence was still of the same opinion in 1836. Writing in the new periodical *The Primitive Baptist,* he compared missionary clergy to legally established clergy in Europe and in America before the revolution. Both wanted to fetter religion. Fortunately, he wrote, in present-day America missionary societies were limited to "dunning" the people and promising heaven as a reward. Missionary clergy, however, could not be content to stop there, according to Lawrence. In "Froggery," a series of articles that interpreted human history providentially through the book of Revelation, the side of God was characterized by civil liberty and religious liberty and that of the devil by tyranny and priestcraft. These sides were seen to be in perpetual warfare until the time of God's victory. According to Lawrence's analysis, since the missionary system was on the devil's side, it must promote tyranny and priestcraft, thereby constituting a continuing danger to the nation. By 1840 Lawrence had not mellowed: missionary societies and the desire for power and wealth were linked, he wrote, as demonstrated by British imperial expansion in India.[14]

Certainly for Lawrence the fear of a state church was a basic cause of his opposition to the new religious societies. He termed himself a "Whig." Like a good eighteenth-century republican, as sketched by Bailyn in *The Ideological Origins of the American Revolution*, he perceived a conspiracy against the operations of liberty. He and Leland also shared the republican understanding that power in human hands necessarily attempts to expand at the expense of liberty. By placing this conspiracy into an overarching religious/historical framework, Lawrence allowed his fear to occupy a place at the core of his worldview. He thus recalls the Dissenting tradition and its rhetorical practices as charted by Clark in *The Language of Liberty*. Both Leland and Lawrence can be understood as traditional Baptist preachers seeking to maintain an earlier Baptist position on religious liberty in the midst of what Edwin Gausted has termed "the tensions within the citizenry" over the degree and the exact form of the separation of church and state.[15]

Lawrence's fear of a state church can also be seen to function as a means of defining both his ministry and the movement he helped lead, as a boundary marker between his group and the opposition, and as a characterization of the other side as necessarily evil. In other words, it helped to establish group identity and shape the necessary propaganda. Fear of a state church, however, was not the sole idea at the core of Lawrence's understanding. The image of greedy society clergy occupied a similar and related role.[16]

Lawrence himself was a slaveholder, and the readership of *The Primitive Baptist* was primarily Southern.[17] Lawrence and others also saw a link between the new societies and the abolitionists. The growing tensions between North and South were increasingly reflected in this periodical through the 1830s–1860s, a development that additionally explains the fear of church and state collusion.[18]

Albaugh wrote that fears of a state church waned after 1840. While I have not yet examined *The Signs of the Times*, and therefore cannot address the issue of "waning influence," my reading of *The Primitive Baptist* certainly indicates that fears of a state church continued past 1840. For example, in 1860, a proposed change in the North Carolina Constitution to make ministers eligible to serve in the legislature drew fire from the editor of *The Primitive Baptist*, who complained that this was a move "to unite Church and State." As a warning example of the consequences of such a change, the reader's attention was directed "to the New-England, North and North-Western States." In those areas "fanatical priests" were "fanning the flames of discord and division."[19]

In 1861 the same editor compared proper civil government to proper church government. Both are to operate from a "compact" system. Sovereign states agree to form a union; sovereign congregations agree to form an association. The original sovereignty is not given up. According to the editorial, the devil attacks both systems, hating true churches and true republics. His attacks on the republic have come through the Northern abolitionists, who, in the editor's view, deny the Bible, since they deny slavery. The goal of the devil and of the abolitionist ministers is tyranny in this nation. Another letter writer pointed to the tragedy of the times and wrote that it proved the Primitive Baptists had been right all along—the new religious societies were a danger to church and nation.[20] Lawrence's thought was apparently still exerting its influence. A further area for investigation is how, or whether, the fear of a state church was expressed among antimission Baptists who opposed slavery prior to the war.

A Primitive Baptist periodical, the *Messenger of Peace*, first published in Macon, Missouri, in November 1874, took a positive view of emancipation. Fear of a state church can be seen in this paper to have survived the Civil War and to be operating outside a Southern partisan context. For example, a correspondent from California wrote in 1882: "Our relation to Christ is one thing; our relation to Caesar is another thing." The Church of Christ itself has no direct voice in government, he wrote; only individual members in their capacity as citizens may lobby for such laws as serve the common good. A government may prescribe a rest day, but it cannot prescribe a holy day. An 1890 correspondent maintained that God appointed the idea of government as a protection from evil, but did not appoint any particular form of government or any particular ruler. In the words of the Declaration, government power derives from the consent of the governed. Human beings appoint particular governments and governors. But one thing is a given—church and state must not be mixed. Several writers by 1890 saw the separation of church and state threatened by the religious forces of those who promoted organized missions and Sunday schools. These arms, so the thinking went, sought the establishment of a religious tyranny in the United States. The perceived proof was the push for Sunday as a legally enforced day of rest and the drive for prohibition. One author even viewed as ominous the placing of "In God We Trust" on coins.[21]

In summary, fear of a state church seems to have operated as a basic cause of opposition to the new societies among those Baptists who fought the new measures. This fear was not the only cause; nor can other concerns, such as commitment to traditional Baptist practice, be devalued into mere props. The fear of a state church continued past the original Baptist opposition leaders and formed a part of the worldview of the Primitive Baptist movement throughout the nineteenth century. However, it may have taken specific provocations, such as abolitionism in the antebellum South, as well as the push for Sabbath laws and temperance, for this fear to have resurfaced throughout the century.

Notes

1. Byron Cecil Lambert, "The Rise of the Anti-Mission Baptists: Sources and Leaders, 1800–1840 (A Study in American Religious Individualism)" (Ph.D. diss., University of Chicago, 1957; reprint, New York: Arno Press, 1980), 2–23; James M. McPherson, *Ordeal by Fire: The Civil War and Reconstruction,* 2d ed. (New York: McGraw-Hill, Inc., 1992), 14–21; Charles I. Foster, *An Errand of Mercy: The Evangelical United Front, 1790–1837* (Chapel Hill: University of North Carolina Press, 1960), 3–10, 115–16; Alice Felt Tyler, *Freedom's Ferment: Phases of American Social History from the Colonial Period to the Outbreak of the Civil War* (New York: Harper & Brothers, 1944; Harper Torchbook, 1962), 1, 31–32; Richard Hofstadter, "The Paranoid Style in American Politics," in *The Paranoid Style in American Politics and Other Essays* (New York: Alfred A. Knopf, 1966), 20–21; Edwin S. Gausted, *Neither King nor Prelate: Religion and the New Nation 1776–1826* (Grand Rapids, Mich.: William B. Eerdmans, 1993), 119–24; Anne M. Boylan, *Sunday School: The Formation of an American Institution, 1790–1880* (New Haven, Conn.: Yale University Press, 1988), 1–4.

2. H. Leon McBeth, *The Baptist Heritage: Four Centuries of Baptist Witness* (Nashville, Tenn.: Broadman Press, 1987), 344–53.

3. H. Leon McBeth, ed., *A Sourcebook for Baptist Heritage* (Nashville, Tenn.: Broadman Press, 1990), 232.

4. Gaylord Albaugh, "Anti-missionary Movement in the United States," in *An Encyclopedia of Religion,* ed. Vergilius Ferm (New York: The Philosophical Library, 1945).

5. Lambert, "Rise of the Anti-Mission Baptists, 119–22, 126, 150.

6. See Daniel Parker's *A Public Address to the Baptist Society, and Friends of*

Religion in General. On the Principle and Practice of the Baptist board of Foreign Missions [f]or the United States of America (Indiana: Stout & Osborn, 1820), and John Taylor's *Thoughts on Missions* (Franklin County, Ky.: n.p., 1820), as well as his *A History of Ten Baptist Churches,* 2d ed. (Bloomfield, Ky.: Will. H. Holmes, 1827; reprint, New York: Arno Press, 1980), or any of the work of Joshua Lawrence cited hereafter.

7. Bertram Wyatt-Brown, "The Antimission Movement in the Jacksonian South: A Study in Regional Folk Culture," *The Journal of Southern History* 36 (Nov. 1970): 501–29.

8. Lambert, "Rise of the Anti-Mission Baptists," 126–27; Wyatt-Brown, "Antimission Movement," 514; John Leland, *The Writings of the Late Elder John Leland,* ed. L. F. Greene (New York: G. W. Wood, 1845; reprint, New York: Arno Press & The New York Times, 1969), see especially "Syllabus of a Sermon Preached at Philadelphia, April 17, 1814," "The Rights of Conscience Inalienable," "The Modern Priest," "Speech in the Massachusetts House of Representatives," "Missionary Societies," "King's Evil and Priestcraft," and "Extract of a Letter to Rev. John Taylor."

9. Leland, "Free Thoughts on Times and Things," in *Writings,* 670.

10. See, for example, Lawrence's *The American Telescope, By a Clodhopper, Of North Carolina* (Philadelphia, Pa.: Printed for the Author, 1825).

11. Lawrence, *Telescope,* 17, 22–23; idem, "The Declaration of the Reformed Baptist Churches in the State of North Carolina (written by Joshua Lawrence in 1826)," *The Primitive Baptist* 7, no. 9 (14 May 1842): 130; idem, *The North Carolina Whig's Apology, for the Kehukee Association* (Tarborough: North Carolina Free Pr[ess], 1830), 17–18; idem, "A Patriotic Discourse Delivered by the Rev. Joshua Lawrence, at the Old Church in Tarboro, N.C. (at the request of the Committee of Arrangements appointed by the citizens) on Sunday, the 4th of July, 1830," *The Primitive Baptist* 7, no. 18 (1842): 273–80, no. 19: 289–95, no. 20: 305–12; the "Patriotic Discourse" was printed as the pamphlet *Missionary Craft* (N.p., n.d. [1831?]).

12. Lawrence, "Discourse," 280.

13. Ibid., 294, 306, 305–6, 311.

14. Lawrence, "Remarks on Missionaries," *The Primitive Baptist* 1, no. 3 (1836): 34; idem, "Froggery," *The Primitive Baptist* 1, no. 17 (1836): 259; idem, "For the Primitive Baptist," *The Primitive Baptist* 5, no. 13 (11 July 1840): 203.

15. Bernard Bailyn, *The Ideological Origins of the American Revolution* (Cambridge: The Belknap Press of Harvard University, 1967); J. C. D. Clark, *The Language of Liberty, 1660–1832: Political Discourse and Social Dynamics in the Anglo-American World* (Cambridge: Cambridge University Press, 1994); Gausted, *Neither King nor Prelate,* 113–18.

16. See, for example, *The American Telescope,* 6–10, and *Apology,* 3.

17. The *Primitive Baptist* periodical published in the North was the previously mentioned *Signs of the Times*.

18. Leland had opposed slavery, so these tensions represent a shift.

19. Burwell Temple, "A Warning to the People!" *The Primitive Baptist* 24, no. 20 (27 Oct 1860): 313.

20. Burwell Temple, "Dearly Beloved Brethren and Sisters of the 'Primitive Baptist,' " *The Primitive Baptist* 25, no. 1 (12 Jan. 1861): 12; J. B. Miller, "For the Primitive Baptist," *The Primitive Baptist* 25, no. 14 (27 July 1861): 217–19.

21. All citations are from the *Messenger of Peace* (Macon, Missouri): 9, no. 2 (1 Dec. 1882): 4–5; 16, no. 5 (15 Jan. 1890): 33; 16, no. 6 (1 Feb. 1890): 43; 16, no. 8 (1 Mar. 1890): 57; 16, no. 9 (15 Mar. 1890): 65; 16, no. 12 (1 May 1890): 89–90; 16, no. 14 (1 June 1890): 106–7; 18, no. 7 (15 Feb. 1892): 49–50.

"There Are No Ranks among Us"

The Ursuline Convent Riot and the Attack on Sister Mary Ursula Moffatt

John Regan

To celebrate the first anniversary of the infamous 1834 burning of the Ursuline convent in Charlestown, Massachusetts, a group of townspeople planned to march through the streets and burn in effigy a well-known Catholic leader. Surprisingly, the target of the group's wrath was not the Pope, the usual symbolic target of anti-Catholic agitation, or even Bishop Benedict Fenwick, the head of Boston's Catholic diocese, but Sister Mary Ursula Moffatt, the Lady Superior of the destroyed convent.[1] Although town officials put a stop to the march, this planned demonstration suggests that Moffatt, the victimized leader of a vanquished community, stands out as the most vilified figure in the aftermath of the riot. Why exactly did she arouse such intense hatred?

I contend that the answer lies beyond simply her religious affiliation to encompass the implications of her dual roles as an aristocratic educator and Catholic nun, "Lady" *and* "Superior." The Ursuline convent doubled as an elite boarding school for the daughters of wealthy Protestants, and while previous readings of the riot have thoroughly documented antebellum fears about Catholic convents, elite female boarding schools were also a site of cultural contestation in Jacksonian America. Critics charged that elite boarding schools, like convents, were institutional threats to democratic ideals. The Ursuline convent's coupling of these institutional identities exacerbated male economic and sexual tensions regarding the physical and cultural accessibility of adolescent females. Furthermore, this coupling underscored the lack of educational access available to a working class deeply anxious about such barriers. Thus, as head of a genteel school and a Catholic convent—

93

positions of authority further complicated by her gender—the Superior embodied a combustible combination of institutions. By examining the rhetorical attacks on the elite boarding school and the Superior, the educational institution and the individual educator, this essay will explore how the collision of antebellum conceptions of class and gender informs a reading of the Ursuline convent riot.

On 11 August 1834 a group of between fifty and a hundred men stormed and destroyed the Ursuline Convent, driving ten nuns, three domestic helpers, and forty-seven girls into the night as a crowd of between one and two thousand people looked on. The furious destruction of the convent stunned Boston residents, shattering a view of the Hub as a civilized place immune to the social unrest sweeping Jacksonian America. Before the convent burning, with labor riots in Philadelphia and anti-abolitionist agitation in New York City, a Boston writer smugly noted, "They [the instigators of riots] may labor as diligently as they please, they cannot make Mob Law triumphant in the good city of Boston. Our population is too orderly, well-educated, and intelligent."[2] After the riot, however, the paradigm of Boston as an unassailable fortress of social tranquillity was challenged if not shattered, hitting Bostonians, as a committee investigated the event reported, "like the shock of an earthquake."[3] With changes in print and transportation technologies allowing for the more rapid production and distribution of printed materials, the subject of the riot generated an astonishing discursive response in the form of speeches, sermons, letters, essays, newspaper and magazine articles, books, novels, eyewitness accounts, trial documents, and even book-length compilations of the above. Although published opinion about the riot almost universally condemned the perpetrators, the character of the Catholic victims rather than the rioters became the focus of discussion. Twentieth-century scholars such as Ray Allen Billington and Jenny Franchot have ably examined this discourse in the context of antebellum conceptions of Catholic convents, but less developed are the implications of the Ursuline convent's other institutional identity as an elite boarding school for wealthy Protestant girls. Thus, while Franchot points out that many New Englanders were bothered by the "institutional ambiguity" of the Ursuline convent, what really troubled them was its institutional duplicity.[4]

While a late-eighteenth-century novel like Hannah Foster's *The Boarding School* (1798) could reasonably argue that a boarding-school education was superior to that of home or day schooling, by the 1830s boarding schools were clearly on the defensive, attacked in popular and professional discourse as partly to blame for the breakdown in the social and cultural fabric. As Linda Kerber points out, from the time of the American Revolution the education of children was a primary duty of republican women.[5] While mothers who sent daughters away to school were at times criticized for abdicating their responsibility, the elite female boarding school emerged in the 1830s as a site deemed antithetical to the needs of the new republic. Critics contended that an elite boarding-school education removed the female from the home, which limited her ability to hone her domestic skills, and thus promoted social aspirations through the acquisition of "uncommon" accomplishments, abilities incompatible with the needs of the common man. As Richard B. Thomas, the editor and publisher of the popular *New England Farmer's Almanack* charged, "The fashion of keeping a girl at school all the time is a miserable one; for the preceptress, or school dame, is generally a despiser of common sense, and would think it degrading in a lady to know how to cook a dinner of pot luck."[6]

Even more dangerous than not knowing how to cook was a woman's inability to care for her children. The dangers of an inattentive or ignorant mother echo throughout educational discourse of the 1830s. Numerous essays in William Woodbridge's *Annals of Education,* the preeminent professional journal of the times, cite examples (usually from fiction) of children who became criminals or other social deviants due to maternal neglect. While these essays often followed traditional late-eighteenth- and early-nineteenth-century arguments that the lack of female education was responsible for maternal negligence and ignorance, they also discovered a new source of blame—the elite boarding school. For example, one essayist in the *Annals of Education* suggests that poorly educated women contribute to infant mortality, but his definition of what constitutes an inferior education and what class receives such an education is revealing: a woman whose wealthy parents died was left enough money to afford "what is called a good education at a 'fashionable' boarding school."[7] After her first child is born, and "never having lived where there were infants in the family, she had no opportunity of learning *by experience,* how to rear such tender plants."[8] Her inexperience in dealing with infants leads to the child's death.

Perhaps no other cultural artifact underscores the perceived liabilities of a boarding-school education more dramatically than Susanna Rowson's *Charlotte Temple.* Still popular in the 1830s, the novel chronicles Charlotte's experiences at Madame Dupont's popular boarding school. The school's popularity, however, poses a problem: "Madame Dupont was a woman well-calculated to take the care of young ladies, had that care entirely devolved on herself, but it was impossible to

attend to the education of a numerous school without proper assistants."[9] One of Dupont's assistants is Mademoiselle La Rue, a woman
of "a liberal education" who was recommended to the unsuspecting
Dupont by a lady whose "humanity overstepped the bounds of discre-
tion."[10] Madame Dupont was unaware that La Rue had run away from
a Catholic convent with a young officer and then had lived openly with
several different lovers. Having "too much spirit of intrigue not to be
without adventure,"[11] La Rue plots with Lieutenant Montroville to facilitate his access to Charlotte. For example, when Montroville sends
Charlotte a letter and she refuses to read it because her mother told her
she should never read a letter given by a young man without consulting
her first, La Rue intercedes: "Lord bless you, my dear girl, . . . have you
a mind to be in leading strings all your lifetime. Prithee, open the letter,
and judge for yourself."[12] Charlotte follows her teacher's advice, a decision that leads to seduction and death. Because a proper moral authority
figure, such as Charlotte's mother or Madame Dupont, is not present to
read the letter from Montroville, the association with La Rue proves
fatal.

In its promotional materials the Ursuline convent school addressed
the concerns of wary parents by marketing itself as providing intensive
security and surveillance. To appeal to its upscale clientele, the school
distributed a prospectus that included a lavish drawing of the building
and grounds as well as general information about the school and its cur-
riculum. Catholic roles and ranks are converted into forms more palat-
able to Boston Protestants; the nuns are given the genteel appellation of
"the ladies" who "spare no pains to adorn [the students'] minds with
useful knowledge, and to form their hearts to virtue."[13] And, the prospectus insists, no pains are spared to monitor and record the movements of the students, who are always "under the immediate supervision
of one or more of the Ladies."[14] Suggesting that parents are "anxious to
know even the smallest details of what concerns" their children, the
prospectus promises a meticulous record of the pupils' "health, the extent of their applications, and their progress of study."[15] To this end, the
ladies issue report cards, a rarity for educational institutions at this
time; students were assessed not only on subject matter and deportment, but also "Care of Books," a facet that underscores the degree of
surveillance.[16] Such surveillance also extended to letter writing; the ladies insisted that the students would write their parents once a week,
implying the type of supervision over letter writing and reading that
might have saved Charlotte Temple.

But convent critics charged that the meticulous attention paid to each
Ursuline pupil was evidence of a fascination with the Protestant female.

In a recent study of antebellum anticonvent discourse, Susan M. Griffin suggests that "the Protestant press evokes the image of a vulnerable daughter in need of strong paternal protection and control" in an effort to limit female access to religious choice during the period of the feminization of American Protestantism.[17] While Griffin's point is revealing, it is also important to consider the class conflict inherent in gestures of paternal control, and here the value of foregrounding the convent's other institutional identity as an elite boarding school is apparent. To convent critics the Ursuline's interest in the education of the Protestant female education suggested Catholic collusion with moneyed elites to insulate "impressionable" students physically from contact with "dangerous" classes and inculcate in them an aristocratic education that would maintain this separation on a cultural and social level. The fear of losing access to women, either physically behind convent walls or socially through aristocratic education, permeates anticonvent discourse. As one convent critic reasons, "The next step may be, that whenever a young girl, thus educated, is crossed in love, or disappointed in securing a fashionable establishment in marriage, she will turn Nun, and take the vows of the Ursuline order, and wealthy parents, who have more daughters that they can portion in the style that they have been brought up, may find it convenient to persuade the least beautiful to take the veil."[18] This passage hints at a deep male economic and sexual anxiety over the availability of women at a time when land was increasingly scarce and young men were forced to migrate westward: women would then have not only an alternative to marriage, but also access to an aristocratic education that could leave them dissatisfied with husbands who faced reduced material circumstances, the less than "fashionable establishments."

Convent critics further asserted that the patrons of elite institutions like the Ursuline school considered working-class Protestant schoolgirls unworthy associates, potential bad influences, for their daughters. This claim took on a special resonance given contemporaneous debates about educational reform. While professional educators repeatedly called for the sons of the rich and the sons of factory workers to sit side by side in the classroom, arguing that the beneficial influence of the higher-class students would filter down to the lower ones and make them responsible and productive citizens (and no deleterious effects would find their way upward), no such arguments were promoted regarding girls, who were deemed too impressionable and too unpredictable for such a trickle-down theory of emulation. In a popular address first given in Charlestown in 1832, union activist and Charlestown native Seth Luther responded to the hypocrisy of these gendered arguments for educational reform. Observing that ruling-class rhetoric about universal education, however laudable in theory, could not be put into practice unless the classes were willing to share the classroom, Luther scathingly proclaims that equal access could never be achieved because "the wives and daughters of the rich manufacturers would no more associate with a 'factory girl' than they would a Negro slave."[19] Perched majestically on a hill overlooking Charlestown, the Ursuline convent and its lavish grounds symbolized to the town's large working-class populace the denial of educational opportunity at the expense of reinforcing class inequity.

Simultaneously embodying Catholic nun and aristocratic educator, renunciation and sophistication, Lady Superior Moffatt fused these highly contested ideals in the person of a formidable female authority figure who evoked radically divergent reactions. The Brahmin *New England Magazine* praised her as "a lady of rare accomplishments," with "elegance of person, amenity of manners, and dignity of deportment."[20] A critic of the convent, however, pointed out that "there is no more likeness between Protestant and Catholic female institutions than there is a similitude between Hannah More [the beloved educator and textbook author], and the superior of the Ursuline convent in Charlestown," an analogy that conflates institution and individual as well as assumes the reader's familiarity with and pejorative opinion of the Superior.[21]

The first rhetorical attack on the Superior occurred even before the attack on the convent. Orally circulating throughout the town for several months and published shortly after the trial of the convent rioters, Rebecca Reed's *Six Months in a Convent* (1835) documents unusual institutional practices among the Ursulines. Why Reed, a Charlestown native, spent some time during 1832 in the convent, as well as everything else she claimed, was open to dispute. She contended that devious Catholics had induced her to become a nun and that the Mother Superior was secretly plotting to send her to another convent. (In a book-length response to these charges, the Superior countered that Reed was not recruited to become a nun, or even a Catholic, but that "our design in admitting her was to enable her to obtain sufficient education to keep a small school, whereby she might have a moderate salary for her own support."[22]) Reed further details how the Superior manipulated the circulation of information to control the convent community. Like Mademoiselle La Rue, the Superior, according to Reed, knowingly perverts her responsibilities as an educator for her own devious ends. Reed discovers that the Superior uses letter writing and reading to maintain power: those who enter the convent are read letters from home in which their families say how happy they are that their daughter has entered a Catholic convent; meanwhile, the families receive letters from their daughter saying how happy she is in the convent.[23] Reed's book, along with rumors of an escaped and recaptured nun and a series of fiery anti-Catholic sermons by Lyman Beecher, was influential in turning many Charlestown residents decidedly against the convent.

In the aftermath of the riot the Superior's character became a focal point in the trial of John Buzzell, one of the riot's ringleaders. The defense attorneys questioned the veracity of prosecution witnesses, suggesting that the jurors would hear two kinds of testimony: truthful and Catholic. Moreover, they sought to demonstrate that the Superior provoked the rioters with threats of revenge at the hands of an Irish mob, a charge she denied, although she did admit that she may have voiced a similar threat to a neighbor earlier in the day. And just as Reed had accused the Superior of manipulating the circulation of information, in his opening argument defense attorney Samuel Farley declared that the Superior tried to emotionally blackmail the escaped nun by sending a note saying that she would commit suicide if the nun did not return, although evidence to back up this charge was never produced. And during a lengthy cross-examination, Farley, who was relatively restrained while questioning the Bishop and the other nuns, treated the Superior with brazen contempt, going so far as to ask her whether two nuns ever slept in the same bed, an outrageously indecorous question to be asked a woman in a public setting. In his closing remarks, he openly mocked her character and appearance: "To call her the Lady Superior is ridiculous. There are no ranks among us, but those obtained by integrity or virtue. Dress yourself as you please, deform the beauty of the human person by an uncouth garb, and put a cross around your neck, this will not add to your credibility."[24] Buzzell was acquitted to the thunderous approval of the packed courtroom gallery.

While the facts that Reed was defending her tale and Farley his client call into question the veracity of their charges against the Superior, the most compelling rhetorical attack comes from one of the Protestant students at the convent, Louisa Whitney. In a recollection of the riot written over forty years after the event, Whitney presents a withering portrait of an arrogant and self-centered Superior. According to Whitney, when the Charlestown selectmen came to the convent before the riot, the Superior "gloried in her haughty reception of them" and afterwards called them "vulgarians, plebeians, shop-keepers, and what-not."[25] From an upstairs window some of the students also teased the Selectmen during their arrival and departure, an incident noted at the trial of the rioters as evidence of the Superior's inability to control the students in her care. Whitney recalls the Superior's interaction with the mob on the fateful Monday night in August, contending that not only did her actions fail to quell the riot, but also may have helped to precipitate it. At dusk between sixty and one hundred men gathered outside the convent, ripped up the fences, started a bonfire, and demanded to see the imprisoned nun. When the Superior came to the top of the front entrance, she was greeted with shouts of "Down with the Convent" and called "a figurehead made of brass," an immediate indication that her authority was a source of contention. Furthermore, her appearance above the crowd and her attempt to address it enacted a volatile dynamic. As Sandra Gustafson points out regarding antebellum female speakers, "When a woman mounted a platform, she staged a high civil drama representing persons and values excluded from the American political realm," a drama here intensified because the working-class listeners and their values were also largely ignored in the political realm.[26] Whitney recalls the Superior's address to the mob:

> Curiosity as to what she would say caused a sudden silence to fall on the rioters, and it is possible that had she known how to address them she might have prevailed with them and persuaded them to disperse. For they seemed at first by no means determined to commit violence, in spite of their savage threats to that effect. [However,] the Superior addressed that listening crowd in language as violent as their own, delivered with the utmost arrogance and imperviousness of manner. I never knew what her words really were, with the exception of one threat, which I myself heard her boast of having made; and if she uttered it to the mob with half the angry vehemence that she used in repeating it afterwards, I do not wonder that she excited violent indignation. "Disperse immediately," she said to the rioters; "for if you don't, the Bishop has twenty thousand Irishmen at his command in Boston, and they will whip you all into the sea!" Think of the effect of such a speech as that on a body of American Truckmen and mechanics!"[27]

Here the "elevated" Superior "speaks down" to the mob, responding in an aggressive, condescending language, whereas Whitney implies that a gentler, more submissive tone would have been more effective. In Whitney's view, the Superior's transgression of social boundaries for women is not only an indecorous display, like the public speeches of Angelina Grimke or the "scribblings" of Hawthorne's "damned mob" of women writers, but also the inexcusably reckless act of a negligent mother who endangers the lives of the children in her care. In her recollection of the hours immediately after the attack, Whitney reinforces her view of the Superior as antimaternal. She writes that when concerned parents arrived at the farmhouse where the children and nuns took refuge, "The Superior took very little notice of us [children], and seemed not to care whether we stayed or went. She was talking volubly to the [fathers of some of the students] about the treatment to which she had been subjected and the losses she had been made to suffer. The gentlemen, who would have sympathized with her keenly at any other time, were just then too anxious about their daughters' safety to think of anything else, and they left her abruptly."[28]

Whitney's scathing portrait of the Superior is echoed in twentieth-century readings of the riot. For example, James J. Kenneally draws heavily from Whitney's account to advance his argument that the mob's actions were in part a response to the Superior's personality and conduct. Contending that the Superior's masculine, aggressive demeanor contradicted the ideals of genteel womanhood, Kenneally concludes that the "[d]estruction of the convent by working-class males was not a rejection of the societal image of 'ladies' and could even be interpreted as supportive of that concept."[29] While Kenneally's argument is intriguing, it is difficult to see the mob's violence as reaffirming gentility; in fact, their furious destruction of the convent's pianos, paintings, books, and other symbols of refinement suggests the opposite. Moreover, as I have shown, representations of the Superior by Reed, Whitney, and others repeatedly critique her aloofness and condescending pretentiousness, a rhetorical posture that seems designed to emphasize the dangers of genteel extremes.

The pejorative representations of the Superior—manipulating information, exacerbating class tensions, endangering the safety of the children in her care—appear less grounded in a critique of "ladyism" than in a desire to position her as an antimaternal threat to the social order. Such representations serve an important ideological function. Informed by Mark Kahn's *On the Man Question: Gender and Civic Virtue in America*, Jane Rose discusses how "an ideal of womanhood was formulated through the rhetoric of Republican Motherhood and encouraged by a fear of unmanageable, passionate, untrustworthy women perceived as threats to social order."[30] According to Kahn, women in late-eighteenth-century America "were not born with natural rights" and could not be "granted rights until their passions were subdued and their informal [influences in town meetings and courts] powers were constrained."[31] Once subdued and constrained, the pious, nurturing mother was a suitable model of womanhood that counteracted the subversive woman, a catalyst to social disorder. Given this ideological dynamic, we can see why representations of the Superior go to great lengths to pin-point her transgressions, her refusals to be subdued or constrained, as the source, not the effect, of social unrest.

But defenders of the Superior offered a different view. While they refuted most of the charges against her, they did not deny her assertive-ness in dealing with the rioters, a point demonstrating that the tenets of the Cult of True Womanhood—here passivity and domesticity—were not always compatible. Consider the recollection of the events of the night of the riot by another student eyewitness, Lucy Thaxter. Thaxter recalls that after the Superior addressed the mob "one of the lay sisters went out to [them], beseeching them "not to molest farther a parcel of helpless women and children, who had no one to protect them." "Ah! Ah!" cried one of the men, "that's all we wanted to know, now we can go ahead," or some similar expression, intimating that all that had restrained them so far had been the fear that we had some concealed means of defense. The Superior's bold and fearless demeanor, had prob-ably given them this idea."[32] Interpreting ostensibly the same events as Whitney, Thaxter suggests that the Superior's aggressive attitude held the rioters at bay and only a display of weakness on the part of one of the lay sisters undermined her success. In this version, the Superior's unflinching attitude was both effective and appropriate, the actions of a brave, decisive woman doing everything in her power to protect the children in her charge. Thaxter also commends the selflessness of the Superior, who did not exit the building until she was sure that all of the children were safely out; she was the last to leave through a back door as the rioters poured through the front entrance. Just as Thaxter's defense of the Superior seems predicated on an expanded conception of the social roles for women in antebellum America, the public statements of Lydia Smith Russell, a mother of one of the students, demonstrate a similar awareness. Russell states that the Superior demonstrated "the merit which has so eminently qualified her for the responsible station that she holds there," a rebuke to those who questioned a women's right to a position of public authority.[33]

Yet public opinion was decidedly against the Superior. Shortly after the trial of Buzzell, she permanently relocated to Canada. Although the individual who was so vilified by a large segment of the Boston populace departed, a few remaining Ursuline sisters reopened a scaled-down ver-sion of the school in West Roxbury. However, even their most ardent supporters were unwilling to risk the safety of their daughters and send them to live with the besieged nuns. The school quickly closed, thus ending the life of an institution whose dual identities sparked a complex dynamic of fear and violence.

Notes

1. Ray Allen Billington, *The Origins of Nativism in the United States 1800–1844* (New York: Arno, 1974), 168. While most contemporary scholars of antebellum nativism consult Billington's *The Protestant Crusade, 1800–1860: A Study of the Origins of American Nativism* (New York: Macmillan, 1938), *The Origins*, a 1933 Harvard dissertation that evolved into the 1938 classic, provides a more detailed discussion of many aspects of 1830s' anti-Catholicism including the Ursuline convent riot. For a more recent examination of the Ursuline convent riot, see Nancy Lusignan Schultz, "Burning Down the House: The Ursuline Convent Riot, Charlestown, Massachusetts, 1834," *Sextant, The Journal of Salem State College* 4, no. 2 (1993): 24–29.

2. Quoted in Wilfred J. Bisson, *Countdown to Violence: The Charlestown Convent Riot of 1834* (New York: Garland, 1970), 107.

3. Quoted in *The Charlestown Convent; Its Destruction by a Mob, on the Night of August 11th, 1834* (Boston: Patrick Donahoe, 1870), 28.

4. Jenny Franchot, *Roads to Rome: The Antebellum Protestant Encounter with Catholicism* (Berkeley and Los Angeles: University of California Press, 1994), 149.

5. See Linda Kerber, *Women of the Republic: Intellect and Ideology in Revolutionary America* (Chapel Hill: University of North Carolina Press, 1980).

6. Quoted in Richard D. Brown, *Knowledge Is Power: The Diffusion of Information in Early America, 1700–1865* (New York: Oxford University Press, 1989), 194.

7. "Review of George Combe's Lectures on Popular Education," *Annals of Education* (September 1834), 398. Edited by noted educator and textbook author William Woodbridge, *The Annals of Education* (1831–39) was the most influential education journal during this seminal time in educational reform.

8. Ibid., 398.

9. Susanna Rowson, *Charlotte Temple* (1794; reprint, New York: Viking Penguin, 1986), 28.

10. Ibid., 26.

11. Ibid., 26.

12. Ibid., 31.

13. "Prospectus of the Ursuline School, 1834," reprinted in George Hill Evans, *The Burning of the Mount Benedict Ursuline Community House* (Somerville, Mass.: Somerville Public Library, 1934), 19–22.

14. Ibid., 21.

15. Ibid., 19.

16. Report Card from the Ursuline School, 1834, reprinted in Evans, *Burning*, 16–17.

17. Susan M. Griffin, "Awful Disclosures: Women's Evidence in the Escaped Nun's Tale," *PMLA* 111, no. 1 (Jan. 1996), 104.

18. "Some Prefatory Remarks for Candid Readers," in *Six Months in a Convent and Supplement* (1835; reprint, New York: Arno, 1969), 7.

19. Seth Luther, *An Address to the Working-Men of New England, On the State of Education, and On the Conditions of the Producing Classes in Europe and America* (Charlestown, Mass.: Published by the Author, 1834), 19.

20. "The Ursuline Community," *New England Magazine* 8 (May 1825): 397.

21. Mr. De Potter, "Introduction to *Female Convents. Secrets of Nunneries Disclosed*," Scipio de Ricci (New York, 1834), xx. This work is an example of how in the wake of the convent riot American publishers repackaged well-known European anti-Catholic texts with introductions that aimed to situate the work in an American context.

22. Mary Ursula Moffatt, *An Answer to Six Months in a Convent Exposing Its Falsehoods and Manifold Absurdities by the Lady Superior* (Boston, Mass.: J. K. Eastburn, 1835), 3.

23. Rebecca Reed, *Six Months in a Convent, Or, The Narrative of Rebecca Theresa Reed* (1835; reprint, New York: Arno, 1977).

24. *Trial of John R. Buzzell before the Supreme Judicial Court of Massachusetts for the Arson and Burglary in the Ursuline Convent at Charlestown* (Boston, Mass.: Russell, Odiorne, and Metcalf, 1834), 70.

25. Louisa Goddard Whitney, *The Burning of the Convent: A Narrative of the Destruction, by a Mob, of the Ursuline School on Mount Benedict, Charlestown, as Remembered by One of Her Pupils* (1877; reprint, New York: Arno, 1969), 61.

26. Sandra Gustafason, "Choosing a Medium: Margaret Fuller and the Forms of Sentiment," *American Quarterly* 47, no. 4 (March 1995): 41.

27. Whitney, *Burning of the Convent*, 86–87.

28. Ibid., 129.

29. James J. Kenneally, "The Burning of the Ursuline Convent: A Different View," *Records of the American Catholic Historical Society of Philadelphia* 90, no. 14 (1979): 16.

30. Jane Rose, "Conduct Books for Women, 1830–1860: A Rationale for Women's Conduct and Domestic Role in America," in *Nineteenth Century Women Learn to Write*, ed. Catherine Hobbs (Charlottesville: University of Virginia Press, 1995), 44.

31. Ibid., 44.

32. Lucy Thaxter, "Letter to the Editor," *The Boston Transcript* (4 Feb. 1843), 2.

33. Lydia Smith Russell, "Letter to Richard S. Fay," in *An Answer to Six Months in a Convent Exposing Its Falsehoods and Manifold Absurdities by the Lady Superior* (Boston, Mass.: J. K. Eastburn, 1835), 47.

"A Very Deep Design at the Bottom"

The Shaker Threat, 1780–1860

Elizabeth A. De Wolfe

For more than two hundred years, Shakerism has provided a mirror for American society. While today America looks upon the Shakers with admiration for their classic furniture and dedication to a religious life, in the first decades of Shaker history the public scorned the sect. In gazing at it, opponents saw a fearsome vision—of the future, one that would turn society upside-down. In this future, self-appointed leaders would, with unbridled power at their disposal, delude followers into practices that destroyed their bodies, their families, and their nation. To many converts in the period 1780 to 1860, Shakerism appeared at first glance to be exactly as promised, heaven on earth, the welcome return of Christ's spirit in the person of founder Ann Lee. "But," a disillusioned apostate later wrote, "on a nearer inspection of their character and sentiments, it is at once evident that their principles and conduct are . . . subversive of Christian *morality* . . . [and] detrimental to the *well-being* of *society*."[1]

From 1780 to 1860 roughly thirty anti-Shaker authors (many of them seceders from the Shaker faith) sought to reveal to the public the "very deep design at the bottom" of Shakerism.[2] Motivated by revenge, the prospect of money, or genuine fear, anti-Shaker authors addressed through their published works fears that went beyond the threat from a curious religious sect. Their writings reveal the tenuous relationship between Shakers and the dominant culture. While anti-Shaker sentiment was consistent throughout the early American and antebellum eras, and anti-Shaker authors found numerous and diverse reasons to attack, three periods of activity emerge in which anti-Shaker authors reveal distinct foci for their fears. In the earliest anti-Shaker publications, published in the immediate post-Revolutionary era, authors feared Shaker leadership and social organization as a threat to the newly emerging American nation. Concerned with the Shaker elders' kinglike autocratic power, anti-Shaker authors warned fellow citizens to be wary of the Shaker threat to liberty. A second period of anti-Shaker activity occurred between 1810 and the early 1830s. While the elders' destructive power was still a significant concern, the ultimate effect of such power was now focused on the family. When the Shakers destroyed families through conversion, society suffered. In the final wave of anti-Shakerism, roughly the late 1830s to 1860, the public focused attention on individual Shakers members who, subject to the elders' continuing use of power, were in danger of destroying their minds and physical bodies. In each period, when the public looked in the Shaker mirror, they saw a vision of what was feared in society—they saw a Shaker "Other," and, in isolating this Other, anti-Shaker writers identified key components of the American self.

In the late eighteenth century, five authors published anti-Shaker tracts. In this early period (1780–1800), few references to the Shakers existed in print. An occasional newspaper article mentioned the Shakers, but for the most part, word of mouth spread rumors about this new religion. These first authors set the parameters of what would become a devastating way to attack the Shakers—print culture. The Shakers as Other took on those qualities society feared, including an autocratic government, social disorder, and a Popish pagan faith. In the first apostate works noise and movement stigmatized the Shakers' unique religious practice. Authors compared the quiet, ordered, Protestant services of the day with the ecstatic Shaker worship and used the striking differences as evidence that the Shakers were not Protestant, or even Christian. Citing alleged similarities to Tahitians, Egyptians, and Babylonians, authors linked the Shakers to groups distant in geographic space and chronological time to imply that Shakerism was a contemporary version of an ancient pagan faith. In the context of the American Revolution, the Shakers' British origins singled them out for suspicion. Finally, a female leader prompted further derisive attacks. In the eighteenth century, the first apostate authors portrayed the Shakers as a threat to the fabric of the newly emerging American society, a subversive element whose presence and blasphemy destroyed democracy, patriarchy, and Protestantism—the foundation of American society. If left unchecked, Shakerism would doom the future of the nation.

The earliest anti-Shaker texts were published as pamphlets, the distinctive literary form of the Revolutionary period. Flexible in length and format, the pamphlet permitted anti-Shaker authors a wide latitude in the construction of their argument and the ability to disseminate their words relatively inexpensively and quickly. Valentine Rathbun offered the first published apostate account, *An Account of the Matter, Form, and Manner of a New and Strange Religion* (1781). His eyewitness account of the Shakers was republished in several editions between 1781 and 1783 with slight variations in text and title. The first section of the pamphlet described the Shaker leaders and their distinctive manner of speech. The central section concerned theology mixed with descriptions of doctrine and Shaker worship. Rathbun focused on the conversion of new members, based on his own experience as a former Shaker. This emphasis on personal experience marked the unique feature of apostate literature and made it the most authoritative form of anti-Shaker writing. Rathbun concluded his pamphlet with an analysis of Shakerism, supporting his conclusions with scriptural references. Using his own "sorrowful experience" as a model, Rathbun warned fellow ministers and the public to avoid the Shakers.

Anti-Shaker authors focused on the elders' considerable power over their followers. Amos Taylor, for example, claimed that the Shakers controlled two thousand people "with no will of their own."[3] Apostate attacks on Shaker power reflected a prevalent fear of conspiracies, particularly rampant during the Revolutionary era and during periods of rapid cultural change. Revolutionary-era rhetoric decried the unchecked use of power and feared unbridled power as the root cause of social decay. In the hands of men, power had the potential to corrupt liberty, its "natural prey."[4] Anti-Shaker authors argued that the Shaker elders were part of a larger scheme to destroy American liberty.

Who was behind this very deep design? Anti-Shaker authors imagined a conspiracy led variously by the Catholic Church, the British monarchy, or the Devil. Benjamin West concluded that "as to [Shaker] doctrine, it is well known to all who are acquainted with the several branches of it and are also acquainted with the doctrine of the church of Rome, that there is no essential difference."[5] Valentine Rathbun asserted that Shaker "doctrines in general exactly agree with the doctrines of the Church of Rome" and asserted his authority as a Shaker apostate and "having been in the Romish Dominions, and seen and heard for myself."[6] Daniel Rathbun, in his 1785 treatise, devoted a considerable amount of space to a comparison of the Shakers and Catholics, highlighting the elders' popelike autocratic power.[7] Comparisons between the Shakers and the Roman Catholic Church drew on decades of Protestant-Catholic antipathy. In the Revolutionary era, Catholicism represented not only an erroneous belief, but a tyrannical, anti-enlightenment power that enslaved its followers by deception and repressed its members by suppressing knowledge. Catholicism was both an age-old enemy and a threat to liberty. Tying together the autocratic power of the Pope and the King, colonists feared a conspiracy where the British leaders would plant Catholics in the colonies to do their bidding and halt the progress of liberty. With Catholics in Canada, the fears of conspiracy, tyranny, and loss of liberty were heightened. Apostate authors tapped into anti-Catholic fear and prejudice in connecting Shakerism and Catholicism.

In addition to the concern with secrecy and the misuse of power, critics found the very practice of Shakerism alarming. "Shaker" was a pejorative term for the United Society of Believers. The term itself derived from the ecstatic dance and song that marked Shakerism's early period. Observers and opponents seized upon the worship service as evidence that Shakerism was folly, not true faith. Valentine Rathbun described a Shaker meeting:

> Some will be singing, each one his own tune; some without words, in an Indian tone, some sing jigg tunes, some tunes of their own making, in an unknown mutter, which they call new tongues; some will be dancing, and others stand laughing, heartily and loudly; others will be drumming on the floor with their feet, as though a pair of drumsticks were beating a ruff on a drum head; others will be agonizing, as though they were in great pain; others jumping up and down; others fluttering over some body, and talking to them, others will be shooing and hissing evil spirits out of the house till the different tunes, groaning, jumping, dancing, drumming, laughing, talking and fluttering, shooing and hissing, makes a perfect bedlam; this they call the worship of God.[8]

The chaotic worship paralleled the social chaos detractors feared would result from a religion with a female founder and female leaders. Apostate Benjamin West argued that Shakerism forced husbands to disown wives and children, and wives to disown natural affection for their husbands. "Thus women become monsters and men worse than infidels in this new and strange religion."[9] This faith, feared its critics, turned the social order upside-down and led individuals to turn away from the nation. Valentine Rathbun argued that Shakerism led those who professed it to throw down their arms and

> appear the most obstinate against all the proceedings of the country . . . the effect of this scheme is such that men and their wives

have parted, children ran away from their parents, and society entirely broken up in neighborhoods.[10]

Amos Taylor, like many anti-Shaker authors, was highly critical of the strict hierarchical structure of the faith, beginning with a woman at the top of the earthly hierarchy: Ann Lee obeyed God, the elders obeyed Lee, American laborers followed the elders, and the common man formed the base. At issue was the flagrant contradiction of Saint Paul's admonition that women should remain silent in worship. Following the death of Ann Lee and two subsequent male leaders, the emerging Shaker hierarchy and the ministration of Lucy Wright as sole Shaker leader were too much for many outsiders (and Shakers) to bear. Angell Matthewson made his feelings clear in a letter to his brother that "women are fools and that men who are willing to have a woman rule over them, are fools also." Matthewson railed against following "every old whim imagined up by women or elders ruled by women" and eventually left the Shakers.[11]

By the 1820s Shakerism had grown to seventeen communities with over two thousand members. Tenuously accepted as part of the American landscape, established Shaker communities continued to attract converts. In this period (roughly 1810–1830) anti-Shaker critique once again became highly visible. This time the critics argued that Shakerism destroyed families. James Smith raised the argument in 1810 when he related, on behalf of his daughter-in-law, how the Shakers destroyed his son's family.[12] Anti-Shaker authors Eunice Chapman and Mary Marshall Dyer honed this argument and stirred up a frenzy of public sympathy for the anti-Shaker cause. They argued that a communal village with celibate women was hardly a proper home for tender, impressionable children. In a period of rapidly changing roles for women and new ideas about the nature of childhood, Dyer and Chapman's anti-Shaker critique played to a public already anxious over the proper roles for wives, mothers, fathers, and families. Like their eighteenth-century predecessors, early nineteenth-century anti-Shaker authors feared a future where Shakerism predominated. The cost would be the family.[13]

The paired publications of Mary and Joseph Dyer captured the tension surrounding changing gender roles and relations in this period. The Dyers joined the Enfield, New Hampshire, Shakers with their five children and several neighbors in 1813. Mary tired of the faith and left in 1815, but Joseph stayed on with the five Dyer children, who had been legally indentured to the Shakers.[14] Mary Dyer's argument to the public and to officials who could restore her children to her focused on the dangerous nature of the Shaker communal family. In print and in testimony to the New Hampshire legislature, Dyer charged the Shakers with the destruction of her family and the denial of her rights as a mother. In her publications, she continued the eighteenth-century theme of the elders' abuse of power when she argued that the Shaker elders had deluded her husband who then forced Mary to join the Shakers or suffer abandonment. Once at the Shaker village, the Shakers separated her family. Mary Dyer argued she remained with the sect only to protect her children. Once she realized she had little access to them, she fled for outside assistance.

The Shakers countered Mary Dyer's publications with Joseph Dyer's *A Compendious Narrative* (1818).[15] It was not the Shakers, Joseph wrote, that destroyed his family. In Joseph's account, Mary destroyed the Dyer family long before they ever learned of Shakerism. Joseph alleged that Mary, who longed to preach, focused on indulgent self-interests to the neglect of child rearing. Accusations flew back and forth between the opposing sides: Mary charged that the Shakers were deviant because of their doctrine of celibacy. She further claimed that the Shaker elder hypocritically seduced young naive Shaker sisters. The Shakers countered and offered affidavits to charge Mary with shameless flirtation with a Shaker elder in her own selfish bid for a leadership role. Mary appealed to the public and the legislature to retrieve her children. She combined first-person narrative and affidavits to present herself as a faithful, religious wife and a loving, child-focused mother while at the same time portraying the Shakers as everything a mother was not: deceptive, immoral, and unable to care for children. Drawing on the icon of Mother, Mary Dyer based her claim on emotions and potent cultural symbols.

Joseph Dyer was explicit in his claim that he had "the first and exclusive right with regard to the protection and well being of my children, vested in me not only by the laws of man, but by the creator."[16] He would determine the structure of his family and decided that a communal village was better for his children than life with Mary. The Dyers' dispute revealed different interpretations and understandings of marital relationships in a period of change. Mary's position reflected a newer, more flexible definition of marriage as a partnership of differing but equally important roles. Joseph, however, favored the more traditional pattern with its rigid, hierarchical family structure. Although Joseph and Mary were locked in a bitter dispute, they agreed on one point: both wished to alter the structure of their family.[17]

The nineteenth-century public, their curiosity piqued, devoured the pamphlets, newspaper articles, books, and broadsides that Mary, Joseph, and the Shakers printed throughout the 1820s. Unlike any previous, or later, anti-Shaker attack, Mary Dyer's campaign generated a tremendous public response. Newspaper editors across New England offered editorials and citizens recorded their impressions in diaries, letters to friends, and the margins of both Dyer's publications. The Shakers, too, rebutted each of her publications with texts of their own. The titillating tales of life within a Shaker village and the details of a marriage falling apart gave grist for public mills about the role of women and the shape of the family both within and outside the Shaker community. Much of the discussion focused on Mary's veracity, morality, and motives. She sought a traditional goal—to be a mother to her children—but her unconventional methods of public speaking, authorship, and itinerant bookselling placed her under intense scrutiny. Her aggressive public attempt to retrieve her children undercut her own argument that she was at heart a traditional mother. Joseph argued that this public persona was the true Mary; Mary argued the Shakers forced her into this abhorrent role. Mary's accusations, Joseph Dyer's counterattack, and the public discussion made clear that the threat to the nation was not from peculiar religious beliefs per se, but from women who stepped out of their role as mothers and from families that failed to match the norm.

By the end of the 1820s public perceptions of orderly Shaker villages and superior agricultural products contradicted Mary Dyer's complaints that the Shakers presented a threat to American society. The Shakers had become a hallmark of quality and purity, and although the public still found their religious ideas misguided, for the most part it no longer felt as threatened by a Shaker presence. James Fenimore Cooper, writing in 1828, praised Shakers as "an orderly, industrious sect, and models of decency, cleanliness, and of morality, too" with "villages so neat, and so perfectly beautiful, as to order and arrangement."[18] Curiosity about Shakerism stimulated a flood of visitors to the communal settlements. A glut of fiction, nonfictional accounts, and apostate texts provided written information on Shaker life and addressed the public's wonder. These printed sources shared a concern with the physical appearance of Shaker villages and the physical health of individual Shakers.

"Shaker Girl," a short story published in *Godey's Lady's Book* (1839), provided a typical description of Shaker women who wore "garments as peculiar and unbecoming" as the men's garments were "ancient." The author described in sickly terms the physical features of Shaker women with their "chill and ghost-like attire . . . the phantasmagoria of a dream, so pale and unearthly did they seem."[19] "Shaker Girl" featured a frequently considered plot—love within a Shaker village. In story after story, authors used near-death images to suggest that without love, there was no life. Ghostly Shaker women, without the role of wife and mother, simply wasted away and died.

In addition to fiction, non-fictional visitor's accounts appeared in newspapers and magazines. As in fiction, the appearance of the Shaker body provided information. Just as phrenologists read bumps on the head, the physical form and clothing of Shakers revealed their cloistered life. Nathaniel Hawthorne, who visited the Harvard (Mass.) Shakers with Ralph Waldo Emerson, found the women "pale" and "none of the men had a jolly aspect."[20] Charles Dickens described a "grim old Shaker, with eyes as hard, and dull, and cold, as the great round metal buttons on his coat and waistcoat: a sort of calm goblin."[21] Humorist Artemus Ward visited a New York Shaker community and later described a Shaker woman as "a solum female, lookin sumwhat like last year's beanpole stuck into a long meal bag."[22]

Public curiosity increased during the late 1830s and through the 1840s when Shakerism underwent an internal revival known today as the Era of Manifestations. This period, lasting roughly a decade, manifested itself in unpredicted gifts from heavenly sources. Beginning in 1837 in western Massachusetts, young Shaker girls claimed to be the instruments for inspired messages from departed Shaker leaders (such as founder Ann Lee), from notable historical figures (such as Washington or Lafayette), or from a wide variety of cross-cultural and cross-temporal personalities, including Native Americans, aboriginal peoples, and "French ladies." The instruments delivered messages inscribed in beautiful "gift drawings," sung as inspired songs, spoken aloud in meeting, or offered as physical directives such as spinning, laughing, or stomping. Verbal and written messages connected past and present Shakers. These communications contained uplifting personal messages as well as more general admonitions for behavior and instructions for daily Shaker life. As Mother's Work spread from one Shaker community to the next, both males and females acted as instruments for an increasing host of gifts such as the "sweeping gift," which directed an entire community of Shakers to walk through the village sweeping with what, to outsiders, appeared to be invisible brooms. Worship services included a cacophony of songs, glossolalia, and Shakers barking like dogs, crying, or hooting—a scenario reminiscent of Rathbun's eighteenth-century description.

The public seized on the opportunity to witness the bizarre displays of religiosity. Many viewed the worship services as entertainment and hundreds flocked to Shaker villages to take in a show. In fact a number of Shaker communities, distressed at the disrespect for their sacred beliefs, closed their formerly open religious services to mocking eyes. Apostate authors emphasized the meeting's lack of control and structure. Sixty years earlier Valentine Rathbun interpreted the frenzied meetings as a threat to the stability of American society. In the 1840s, anti-Shakers interpreted the physically strenuous worship as a threat to individual thought (an old theme) and the physical self (a new theme), as they reported on injured participants or rough treatment received at the hands of Shakers in response to a gift. In addition to the contrast between the pristine appearance of Shaker buildings and the sickly appearance of Shakers, a new contradiction motivated public curiosity— the tension between the neat, ordered setting and the disorder and bodily chaos of the Shakers in worship.

Physical autonomy, the right and the desire to be firmly in control of one's own body, formed the crux of complaints regarding both children and adults, and anti-Shaker authors in the period 1830–60 borrowed themes of power, temperance, and abolition in their drive for legislation against the Shakers. Again power formed the heart of the debate, the power of elders to delude and control the innocent converts' minds and bodies. An especially rich source of information on this period comes from testimony to the New Hampshire legislature session of 1848; 498 individuals filed four group petitions to protest the treatment Shakers gave to individual members. Testimony featured vivid descriptions of chaotic worship services and incidents of alleged child abuse. The Shakers believed that during worship God worked through the physical body of the instrument. The apostates argued that the elders controlled the members through mesmerism or an "extraordinary and invisible influence."[23] The anti-Shaker complaints of corporal punishment of children, unusual illnesses of adults, the mesmeric power of the elders, and the strange actions of those under inspiration were elements of the larger argument that Shakerism destroyed individual physical autonomy. Former Shaker Theresa Willard described how her sister whirled and whirled during inspiration and when she failed to stop at an elder's command, was thrown down a flight of stairs. Willard's sister, still a Shaker, rebutted the testimony and explained that the power of God threw her down the stairs, not the elders, and because of the divine source she had not been injured.

The case of George Emery was vital to the petitioners's charges. Five-year-old Emery had lived at the Canterbury, New Hampshire, Shaker village. He died after falling and striking his head against a rock. Anti-Shakers alleged that his death was no accident—they claimed the Shaker children's caretaker had beaten Emery to death. The cross-examination exposed much of the apostate testimony as hearsay. For example, although Theresa Willard had testified that the Shakers whipped and beat the children in their care, she admitted under cross-examination by the Shaker attorney, future president Franklin Pierce, that although she had heard of some maltreatment, she was "always treated well *myself*."[24] Another witness for the petitioners revealed that in fact the Shakers had recognized a problem with the children's caretaker and had promptly removed him from the position before harm could be done. Many witnesses who were present at Emery's open-casket funeral testified that his face was black and blue, but none, however, had actually witnessed the accident, his medical treatment, or his subsequent death.

Several physicians took the stand. The discussion during the testimony strongly suggested that it was not Emery's injury that caused his unfortunate death, but inappropriate medical treatment from a young, inexperienced physician. Physicians also testified that the Shakers were as healthy as other rural farmers. Shakers suffered no higher rates of cancer, insanity, or other diseases than the general population. The body of Shakers worked hard, ate simply, and lived strictly, but they suffered no unusual physical effects as a result of their religious choice. Emery's death was ruled an accident and the petitioners's quest for repressive legislation was unsuccessful. As Pierce argued in his three-hour summary, Shaker villages were admired for their clean order and superior agricultural products. As the reasoning went, an ordered physical plant reflected an ordered, civilized, and moral society. Shaker works outweighed anti-Shaker words.

Formal, organized opposition to Shakerism after the Civil War was minimal. After nearly one hundred years, the public interpreted Shakerism not as a novel threat on the landscape, but as a curious anachronistic throwback to "simpler" times—religiously fervent, agricultural, and dressed in the fashion of a previous century. Shakerism embodied that which society praised and felt was lacking in the rapidly, industrializing world. By the century mark of Shakerism (1874), writers saw the Shakers in a nostalgic light. The apostate authors changed their tone a decade earlier, finding much to praise in the Shaker experiment. Hervey Elkins, for example, stressed that any fault with the Shakers lay within the individual member, not with the faith as a whole. Even apostate Mary Dyer whose campaign against the Shakers lasted nearly fifty years argued that Shakerism would be acceptable if they would only abandon celibacy, then "they would be fathers and mothers, sons and daughters, instead of taskmasters, task-mistresses, servants and slaves."[25] Although Mary Dyer tied celibacy to immorality, most critics focused on the practical effect of the belief, not as a threat to the nation, the family, or the individual, but as a threat to the Shaker movement which, experiencing a rapid decline in membership, the public believed was on the wane due to its own tragic belief.

In the first century of Shakerism, anti-Shaker sentiment was a consistent presence. Spread widely via print culture, anti-Shaker texts portrayed Shakerism at various times as a danger to the individual, the family, or the nation. Anti-Shaker authors varied widely in their critiques. In fact they critiqued each other in their quest to be the authoritative voice of the Shaker experience. Several authors took issue with Mary Dyer's attack and critiqued her assault even within their own anti-Shaker publications. Nonetheless, several persistent themes appear in the corpus of anti-Shaker writing including the creation of the Shaker Other, the elders' abuse of power, the deception of the mass of Shaker adherents, and the allusions to Catholicism, and, later, masonry. The Shaker Other took on those qualities the rest of society feared. Like contemporary portrayals of cults, the Shaker mirror reflected an image of a system of beliefs and practices and a family organization that did not match the mainstream norm. Threatened by this alternative vision, anti-Shakers attacked the Other while simultaneously defining self. Today, the Shakers stimulate not fear but admiration. Their furniture and products are highly collectible and former and current Shaker villages remain popular tourist destinations. Praised for their simple life, peaceful existence, and devotion to the philosophy of "hands to work and hearts to God," Shakers today mirror not what the nation fears it might become, but rather what many fear the nation has left behind.

Notes

1. Mary M. Dyer, *A Portraiture of Shakerism* . . . [Haverhill, N.H.]: [Printed by Sylvester Goss], 1822), v.

2. Amos Taylor, *A Narrative of the Strange Principles, Conduct, and Character of the People Known By the Name of Shakers* . . . (Worcester, Mass.: [Printed by Isaiah Thomas], 1782), 3. Shakerism is a Protestant sectarian faith first brought to the American colonies in 1774 by founder Ann Lee. From the 1790s on, Shakers lived in communal villages separate from the dominant surrounding culture. Espousing celibacy, communalism, and confession of sin, the Shakers presented an alternative form of social organization that attracted, at its peak in the 1840s, more than 4,000 followers. One small community of Shakers remains today in Maine. On Shaker history see Stephen Stein, *The Shaker Experience in America* (New Haven, Conn.: Yale University Press, 1992).

3. Taylor, *A Narrative*, 3.

4. Bernard Bailyn, *The Ideological Origins of the American Revolution* (Cambridge, Mass.: The Belknap Press of Harvard University Press, 1967), 57. See also Homer L. Caulkin, "Pamphlets and Public Opinion during the American Revolution," *The Pennsylvania Magazine of History and Biography* 64 (1940).

5. Benjamin West, *Scriptural Cautions against Embracing a Religious Scheme . . .* (Hartford, Conn.: Printed and Sold by Bavil Webster, 1783), 14.

6. Valentine Rathbun, *An Account of the Matter, Form, and Manner of a New and Strange Religion . . .* (Providence, R.I.: Printed and Sold by Bennett Wheeler, 1781), 4.

7. Daniel Rathbun, *A Letter from Daniel Rathbun, of Richmond in the County of Berkshire, to James Whittacor, Chief Elder of the Church, Called Shakers* (Springfield, Mass., 1785).

8. V. Rathbun, *An Account*, 11–12.

9. West, *Scriptural Cautions*, 14.

10. V. Rathbun, *An Account*, 20–21.

11. Angell Mathewson, Reminiscences, Letter 24, 1 May 1799, Shaker Collection, New York Public Library. Opposed to female leadership and resistant to increasing strict regulations in the faith, once-faithful members seceded, and the rate of apostasy in New Lebanon soared from 2.4 percent between 1787 and 1790 to 19.9 percent in the following decade. On rates of New Lebanon apostasy, see table A.2, appendix A in Priscilla Brewer, *Shaker Communities, Shaker Lives* (Hanover, N.H.: University Press of New England, 1986). On the difficulties with female Shaker leadership, see Jean Humez, " 'Weary of Petticoat Government': The Spectre of Female Rule in Early Nineteenth-Century Shaker Politics," *Communal Societies* 11(1991): 1–17.

12. James Smith, *Remarkable Occurences Lately Discovered among the People Called Shakers; Of a Treasonous and Barbarous Nature, or Shakerism Developed* (Carthage, Tenn.: Printed by William Moore, 1810); and *Shakerism Detected, Their Erroneous and Treasonous Proceedings, and False Publications . . .* (Paris, Ky.: Printed by Joel R. Lyle, 1810). The Shakers responded to Smith's allegations in Richard McNemar, *"Shakerism Detected, &c" Examined and Refuted, in Five Propositions . . .* (Lexington, Ky.: Printed by Thomas Smith, 1811).

13. In her attempt to retrieve her Shaker-held children, Eunice Chapman published two pamphlets: *An Account of Conduct of the People called Shakers: In the Case of Eunice Chapman and Her Children, since Her Husband Became Acquainted with That People, and Joined Their Society* (Albany, N.Y.: Printed for the Authoress, 1817); and *No 2 Being the Additional Account of the Conduct of the Shakers, in the Case of Eunice Chapman and Her Children with Their Religious Creed . . .* (Albany, N.Y.: Printed by I. W. Clark, 1818). Mary Dyer published five major works detailing her experiences among

the Shakers: *A Brief Statement of the Sufferings of Mary Dyer* (Concord, N.H., 1818), *A Portraiture of Shakerism* (Haverhill, N.H., 1822), *Reply to the Shakers' Statements* (Concord, N.H., 1824), *The Rise and Progress of the Serpent* (Concord, N.H., 1847), and *Shakerism Exposed* (Hanover, N.H., ca. 1852). On Dyer's lifelong anti-Shaker campaign, see Elizabeth A. De Wolfe, "Erroneous Principles, Base Deceptions and Pious Frauds: Anti-Shaker Writing, Mary Marshall Dyer, and the Public Theater of Apostasy" (Ph.D. diss., Boston University, 1996).

14. It was common practice for parents to indenture their children to the Shakers when they joined or, frequently, in situations where a family could not afford to feed and clothe the children. The Shakers agreed to house, clothe, feed, educate, and train in some trade each indentured child until the age of majority, at which time the child was free to leave or to join the Shaker community. In exchange, parents gave up all rights to their children and promised not to reclaim them. As long as the indenture was executed properly, courts supported the Shakers' practice.

15. Joseph Dyer, *A Compendious Narrative* . . . (Concord, N.H., 1818). A second edition was published in 1826 (Pittsfield, Mass.). Shaker Richard McNemar responded to the complaints of Eunice Chapman, Mary Dyer, and others in *The Other Side of the Question* . . . (Cincinnati, Ohio: Looker, Reynolds, and Co., 1819).

16. J. Dyer, *A Compendious Narrative,* 32.

17. Joseph's and Mary's different interpretations of marriage led both of them, willingly, to Shakerism. The possibility of holding a leadership position appealed to Mary's ambitious, charismatic personality. Joseph saw in the Shakers the hierarchy, order, and discipline missing in his troubled marriage.

18. James Fenimore Cooper, *Notions of the Americans: Picked Up by a Travelling Bachelor* (1828), quoted in Flo Morse, *The Shakers and the World's People* (New York: Dodd, Mead, and Company, 1980), 85–86.

19. Caroline Lee Hentz, "Shaker Girl," *Godey's Lady's Book,* 1839, 49–58. For a chronological listing of works of fiction with Shaker settings and visitors' accounts of the Shakers, see Morse, *The Shakers and the World's People,* 360–71. The development of Shaker-related fiction produced several stereotyped Shaker characters, such as the licentious elder, the naive young Shaker girl, and the old, bitter Shakeress. See Ruth McAdams, "The Shakers in American Fiction" (Ph.D. diss., Texas Christian University, 1985).

20. Hawthorne, *American Notebooks* (1832), in Morse, *Shakers and the World's People,* 184–85.

21. Charles Dickens, *American Notes for General Circulation* (1842), in Morse, *Shakers and the Worlds' People,* 184–85.

22. Artemus Ward, *Vanity Fair* (23 February 1861), in Morse, *The Shakers and the World's People,* 202.

23. Hervey Elkins, *Fifteen Years in the Senior Order of the Shakers* (Hanover, N.H.: Dartmouth Press, 1853), 36.

24. *Report of the Examination of the Shakers of Canterbury and Enfield before the New Hampshire Legislature at the November Session, 1848* (Concord, N.H.: Ervin B. Tripp, 1849), n.p.

25. M. Dyer, *Shakerism Exposed*, 27–28.

PART III

FEAR OF THE DARK

Miscegenation, "Melaleukation," and Public Reception

Eve Allegra Raimon

The press scandal that erupted during the 1996 U.S. presidential campaign over the appearance of the anonymous political novel *Primary Colors* was tame compared to a singular publishing event in 1864, another election year, this time between the incumbent President Lincoln and his Democratic challenger, General George B. McClellan.[1] In the winter of that year, between military campaigns, notices began to appear about an anonymous pamphlet with the provocative title *Miscegenation: the Theory of the Blending of the Races, Applied to the American White Man and Negro.* The intimation that such "blending" might be desirable was incendiary enough unto itself, but the mysterious author had also substituted the familiar—and disparaging—term "amalgamation" with the wholly novel—and distinctly approving—"miscegenation."[2]

While the word itself has become part of the contemporary idiom of U.S. race relations, the circumstances surrounding its appearance in the language have strangely been almost lost to history. This act of historical forgetting is particularly curious in that it obscures one of the most outrageous acts of partisan chicanery in the history of U.S. race politics. The authors of the tract, it turned out, were not radical abolitionists at all; they were political journalists. Sympathetic to conservative Copperhead Democrats, they had issued the pro-miscegenation treatise as polemical bait to garner abolitionist approval and, in the process, embarrass the Republican party in order to thwart Lincoln's re-election campaign. Given the episode's political flamboyance, its originary linguistic importance, its central place in the history of U.S. interraciality, and its relevance to the ensuing Jim Crow era, its relative obscurity is

121

all the more puzzling. Though I leave speculation about the reasons for this historical omission to others, I want to help correct the record by revisiting the incident and re-examining its significance in the context of fear in American culture.

Of course, the episode has not been entirely overlooked. At least two extended studies have appeared about *Miscegenation* and the events surrounding it, but they were published in the '40s and '50s, well before the civil rights movement got fully under way. In "The Miscegenation Issue in the Election of 1864" (1949), Sidney Kaplan for the first time exposed the role of an editor at the antiabolitionist *New York World,* David Goodman Croly, as the instigator and primary agent of the hoax. Kaplan provides a detailed and thorough historical investigation of the matter and concludes that, as a piece of political sabotage, the document "had done its work—and well." That is, Croly and George Wakeman, a reporter at the *World,* had succeeded in making the subject of miscegenation a central issue in the presidential campaign and a liability for the Republicans: "Throughout the land, in sharp polemic, right up to the November balloting . . . the national press would bandy word and issue about in an unending saturnalia of editorial, caricature, and verse."[3] Kaplan's study was followed in 1958 by a little-known volume, *Miscegenation, Melaleukation, and Mr. Lincoln's Dog* (a reference to a political cartoon about the incident). Like its predecessor, the forty-eight-page monograph recounts the facts of the case, but unlike Kaplan, J. M. Bloch speculates about the wider cultural implications surrounding the publication and reception of the controversial booklet: "The *Miscegenation* controversy," Bloch concludes, "represents an episode in the history of the white race deeply absorbed in soul-searching on the race question."[4]

Such soul-searching was furthered by the anonymous nature of the treatise. The absence of a fixed authorial identity attracted a wider readership than would otherwise have been the case. But more important, the very lack of knowledge surrounding the writer enticed readers to entertain the question as to whether *Miscegenation* was a parody—a "burlesque," as columnists sometimes called it—or a serious brief for interracial acceptance. The publication, then, was a political scandal and a literary mystery in one and, as such, functioned in 1864 as a vehicle through which the popular press could give voice to the public's greatest fear and greatest fantasy: the prospect of a mixed-race *union*—in both senses of the word.

The term "miscegenation" itself, the author explains in a glossary of "New Words Used in This Book," is a compromise from the more precise "melaleukation," Greek for "black and white." Still more accurate, according to the writer, would be the unwieldy "melamigleukation," from the Greek "mignumi," to mix, but, he acknowledges, such a construction, "aside from its difficulty of pronunciation," would be "ill adapted for popular use."[5] In any event, the twenty-five-cent booklet begins with solemn, almost biblical gravity:

> The word is spoken at last. It is Miscegenation—the blending of the various races of men—the practical recognition of all the children of the common father. While the sublime inspirations of Christianity have taught this doctrine, Christians so-called have ignored it in denying social equality to the colored man; while democracy is founded upon the idea that all men are equal, democrats have shrunk from the logic of their own creed, and refused to fraternize with the people of all nations.[6]

Thus, the democratic ideals of the *Declaration* combine with nineteenth-century "scientific" theories of monogenesis and other contemporaneous notions of racial hybridity to produce the anonymous author's extraordinary thesis:

> Whatever of power and vitality there is in the American race is derived, not from its Anglo-Saxon progenitors, but from all the different nationalities which go to make up this people. All that is needed to make us the finest race on earth is to engraft upon our stock the negro element which providence has placed by our side on this continent. Of all the rich treasures of blood vouchsafed to us, that of the negro is the most precious, because it is the most unlike any other that enters into the composition of our national life.[7]

Here, then, the writer appears to turn on its head generations-old social and legal doctrine about the threat of black contamination of Anglo-Saxon genetic stock. In its place he asserts that only an amalgam of the most disparate races possible—blacks and whites—will achieve the most auspicious genetic mixture. The great wars of modern Europe, the text proclaims, have already produced an intermixing of "different bloods and complexions," but it is up to the union to complete the process by adding "the Mongolian and African" to this "rich blending of blood."

Such calls for racial hybridity were scandalous enough. Yet perhaps the most compelling—and inflammatory—contention in the document is the affirmation of mixed-race marriage:

It is idle to maintain that this present war is not a war for the negro. It is a war for the negro. Not simply for his personal rights or his physical freedom—it is a war if you please, of amalgamation, so called—a war looking, as its final fruit, to the blending of the white and black. . . . Let it go on until church, and state, and society recognize not only the propriety but the necessity of the fusion of the white and black—in short, until the great truth shall be declared in our public documents and announced in the messages of our Presidents, that it is desirable the white man should marry the black woman and the white woman the black man—that the race should become melaleuketic before it becomes miscegenetic.[8]

Of course, this piece was not the first political tract to discuss the inevitability of intermarriage among whites and blacks, or the first to argue for that freedom—Lydia Maria Child's *An Appeal in Favor of That Class of Americans Called Africans*, published in 1833, constitutes one such important precursor.[9] Indeed, Child was ostracized from the Boston literati for her defense of interracial marriage. Yet it is the recurrent emphasis on the "desirab[ility]"—indeed, the "necessity"—of such unions and the contention that a more perfect union will result from such racial "fusion" that made the anonymous document so scandalous. On its face, at least, *Miscegenation* argues for nothing less than interracial sex as recommended domestic public policy. The booklet's chapter headings do nothing to moderate the radical intent of its purported program. They include such titles as "All Religions Derived from the Dark Races"; "Love of the Blonde for the Black"; "How the Anglo-American May Become Strong and Comely"; "The Miscegenetic Ideal of Beauty in Women"; and "The Future—No White, No Black."

Advertisements for the brochure appeared most prominently in antislavery publications, where editorial reaction was largely favorable. The *National Antislavery Standard*, for example, suggested that "It is in the highest degree improbable that [God] has placed a repugnance between any two families of his children. . . . The probability is that there will be a progressive intermingling, and that the nation will be benefited by it."[10] Such endorsements helped propel the issue into the political arena, where it erupted during debate over the bill establishing the Freedmen's Bureau. According to Bloch, Samuel Sullivan Cox, a Democrat from Ohio, began his floor speech by objecting to the bill on constitutional grounds, but concluded with an impassioned attack on the anonymous publication. Alluding to the prospect of widespread intermarriage, Cox denounced abolitionist proponents of the idea and proclaimed, "[N]o system so repugnant to the nature of our race can save the negro."[11]

Political Cartoon satirizing "Miscegenation or the Millennium of Abolitionism." Artist and source unknown. Courtesy of the American Antiquarian Society.

Republicans countered that it was the slaveholding Democrats who were already, in fact, the true "miscegenators."

The press in turn responded to the congressional uproar with a second round of editorials, including perhaps the most influential commentary on *Miscegenation*, Theodore Tilton's "The Union of the Races." Writing in the *Independent*, the abolitionist editor wondered aloud whether the document was a ploy, but agreed that the Republic did indeed comprise "an unparalleled amalgamation of races." However, Tilton argued, interracial mixing should occur "by natural affinity between individuals" rather than as the result of a concerted political program, as the anonymous treatise advised: "[W]e do not believe in any forecasted scheme or humanly-planned union of races; nor that the next Presidential election . . . should have anything to do with Miscegenation," Tilton declared. At the same time, he predicted that "The Negro of the South, growing paler with every generation, will at last completely hide his face under the snow."[12]

The intensity of public sentiment about the issue can be measured by the increasingly sensationalist tenor of the press commentary. For instance, the *New York Tribune* renewed the charge of Democratic hypocrisy for expressing outrage at the prospect of interracial sex. In an editorial defending the pamphlet against its critics, the paper proclaimed: "[T]he affected Democratic horror of 'Miscegenation' is, of the cants of this canting age, the most notoriously impudent."[13] In response, the *New York World* labeled Horace Greeley's *Tribune* an "unblushing advocate of 'miscegenation,' " and noted astutely that the document itself was less important than "the strongly developed tendencies of abolition public opinion which [it] has brought out in bold relief."[14] Indeed, the anonymous treatise functioned as an impetus to galvanize political opinion on both sides of the issue.

More than that, it served as a medium through which the public could express its fears and desires about the matter that was most profoundly at stake in the war—the nature of black-white relations in a nation whose future was inescapably multiracial. That the pamphlet's author was unknown only accentuated its role as an index of public sentiment, and encouraged commentary such as the following from the *New York Times*, which anxiously lamented the extravagant attention paid to a tract "all about the possibility of the whites of this continent losing their admiration for their own women, repudiating the standard of beauty furnished them by natural instinct, and intermarrying with Negroes."[15] The unknown authors had thus managed to excavate deeply buried fears—and fantasies—about the cultural consequences of a practice that had of course been occurring on a large scale in the South since well before the Founding.

Although the revelation of the authorship of *Miscegenation* brought a degree of closure to the press scandal, as with any good sensationalist affair, questions lingered about the intentions of the instigators and the wider cultural effects the incident generated. The secret was first disclosed by the London press, which broke the story three days prior to the 1864 presidential election, too late for the news to reach the United States and influence the election outcome. *The London Reader* announced that

> The Miscegenation question turns out to have been a hoax of two gentlemen of New York, who little thought when they started it that learned professors and doctors, anthropologists and ethnologists, and all the class who groping about in the dark believing themselves the only true lights of science, would have given Miscegenation a literature of its own. The pamphlet itself was set forth merely as a clever bit of electioneering jugglery to damage a faction.[16]

Soon afterwards, a banner headline appeared in the *World* announcing: "THE GREAT HOAX OF THE DAY / THE GREAT MISCEGENATION PAMPHLET EXPOSED / THE 'MOON HOAX' IN THE SHADE." The paper went on to describe the writers as "two young gentlemen connected with the newspaper press of New York, both of whom are obstinate Democrats in politics." The purpose of the scheme, the *World* explained, was to prompt the Republican party to defend the beliefs the document espoused, including "the complete social equality, by marriage, of the white and the black races," thereby causing the party to come into conflict "with the strong anti-negro prejudice existing in the North."[17]

Though accounts years after the fact continued to treat the pamphlet as a sincere polemic, both Kaplan and Bloch conclude that Croly and Wakeman, the "two young gentlemen connected with the newspaper press of New York," did in fact hatch the scheme to embarrass the Republican party by parodying its radical stand on racial intermixing and goading abolitionists to advocate pro-miscegenation views. In our contemporary idiom, that is, the pair were playing a certain skewed mid-century version of the "race card," the object of which was to scandalize moderate voters into turning away from Lincoln at the polls. The booklet's persuasiveness depended on a combination of abolitionist theory, political polemic, biblical references, and, most effective, extended parodies of current "scientific" theories of evolution and racial difference. *Miscegenation*'s most important source in this regard is John William Draper's 1858 study, *Human Physiology, Statical and Dynamic or the Conditions and Course of the Life of Man.* For example, the pamphlet quotes Draper as asserting that

> The ideal or type man of the future will blend in himself all that is passionate and emotional in the darker races, all that is imaginative and spiritual in the Asiatic races, and all that is intellectual and perceptive in the white races. He will also be composite as regards color. . . . [T]he extremes of humanity, which are represented by a prognathous aspect, and by a complexion either very dark or very fair, are equally unfavorable to intellect, which reaches its greatest perfection in the intermediate phase.[18]

In addition, Croly and Wakeman aggravated existing class and race antagonisms between working-class Irish and Northern Blacks by declaring that "Wherever there is a poor community of Irish in the North, they naturally herd with the poor negroes." Further, they project derisively that "The blending of the Irish in this country with the negro will be a positive gain to the former" and appeal to the Irish to "set aside the prejudice which is the result of unfortunate education, and proclaim, both by word and by the practice of intermarriage, their true relations with the negro." Finally, in a transparently cynical political gesture, the pair call on the Republican party to adopt their radical miscegenation doctrine as part of its platform. The authors charge that "the Party will not perform its whole mission till it throws aloft the standard of (so-called) Amalgamation."[19]

Though Kaplan is convinced that such hyperbole did its job of appalling readers with the prospect of the "beiging" of the Republic, it is also entirely possible that, for some, the tract in fact did its job *too* well. While the object of *Miscegenation*'s wide circulation was to undermine progress toward emancipation, it may unwittingly have abetted the abolitionist cause and Lincoln's re-election. That is to say, its caricatures of pro-miscegenation doctrine were so successful they may have provoked readers to question the legitimacy of prevailing race theory *altogether*— including notions of black inferiority based on conjecture about craniometry, physiognomy, and polygenesis.[20] Unintentionally, then, the journalists' satire of abolitionist philosophy may also have revealed the dubious nature of racialist "science" as "proof" of blacks' anatomical or evolutionary retrogression.[21]

Such a result is especially credible given the cynical tone of much of the press commentary. The *Tribune* and the *World* carried on a satirical

interchange about whether "those who are neither physiologists, eth-
nologists, historians, theologians, nor economists" were qualified to "issue conclusive dogmas upon a topic so important."[22] Comparing the
issue to incest, the conservative *World* goaded its readers to reject
the abolitionist *Tribune*'s appeal to specialized knowledge, asserting sarcastically that

> [I]f only great clerks and famous savants are competent to have
> an opinion on such subjects, it logically follows that the unlearned
> multitude ought to hold their minds in candid suspense on the in-
> cest question until they shall have mastered half the sciences in the
> encyclopedia.[23]

Clearly, if the main target here was the Republican party, another one
was lofty scientific theories from self-professed specialists of whatever
political stripe.

In a similarly sardonic editorial, the *New York Times* alluded to the
political motivations it suspected were behind the *Miscegenation* publication and its reception in the Democratic press:

> We were fast approaching the conclusion that, right or wrong, the
> notions of the Caucasian race, and particularly of the Anglo-Saxon
> branch of it, on the subject of personal beauty during the last
> 2,000 years were so set, that it was not at all likely they would un-
> dergo any material change during the approaching Presidential
> campaign. We find, however, from an article in the *World*, that we
> were mistaken, and that there is strong reason to believe that all
> unmarried Republicans of both sexes will marry negroes and
> negresses immediately after the meeting of the convention next
> Summer.[24]

Given the derisive tenor of the commentary on both sides, then, the
issue with respect to which political faction was ultimately the victor
from Croly and Wakeman's burlesque of abolitionist philosophy is open
to genuine debate.

Indeed, the possibility that the volume performed such multifari-
ous and diverse cultural operations coextensively is suggested in a letter
written in 1900 by Jane Cunningham Croly, the editor's widow:

> [T]ho it was written partly in the spirit of joke, it was not a hoax,
> and was not palmed off upon the public as one . . . you can rely
> upon the absolute truth of what I say. Both Mr. Croly and Mr.
> Wakeman have passed away; but I remember the episode perfectly,

and the half joking, half earnest spirit in which the pamphlet was written.[25]

Regardless of the extent to which the spirit of *Miscegenation* was in jest or in earnest, or had unintended consequences, there is no doubt that press sensation attendant upon its release reflected a republic deeply ambivalent about the future course of its race relations. Indeed, the document itself powerfully enacted such ambivalence and anxiety. "Passing" as a radical abolitionist tract, the work was eventually "exposed" as a "fraud," an act of political artifice. That is, it dramatized discursively the act of racial "passing"; indeed, we can say that the very term "miscegenation" slipped into our discourse "in disguise." Such linguistic duplicity staged for white readers the very act of deceit involved in racial "passing" itself. In so doing, it heightened whites' already acute uncertainty about racial divisions. Thus, the history of the volume's authorship and reception documents its essential role in compelling the nation to confront its most profound fear and its most urgent challenge in 1864—the potential for a truly interracial union.[26] The fact that the United States failed to meet that challenge and Jim Crow segregation followed Reconstruction makes it all the more imperative that now, when the population of multiracial citizens is exploding, we attend more closely to such signal events in the history of U.S. interraciality if we are to avoid the political reversals of the past.[27]

Notes

1. The scandal persisted for much of the election season—well after the identity of the author, *Newsweek* columnist Joe Klein, was finally revealed. The novel is Klein's fictionalized account of the 1992 presidential race. See *Primary Colors: A Novel of Politics* (New York: Random House, 1996).

2. [David Goodman Croly], *Miscegenation: The Theory of the Blending of the Races, Applied to the American White Man and Negro* (New York: H. Dexter, Hamilton & Co, 1864).

3. Sidney Kaplan, "The Miscegenation Issue in the Election of 1864," *Journal of Negro History* 34 (July 1949): 273–343; reprinted in *American Studies in Black and White: Selected Essays*, ed. Allan D. Austin (Amherst: University of Massachusetts Press, 1991), 67. I quote from this edition.

4. J. M. Bloch, *Miscegenation, Melaleukation, and Mr. Lincoln's Dog* (New York: Schaum, 1958). It is particularly odd that the episode under study here does not appear in more recent work on miscegenation. See, for example, its omission from Joel Williamson's *New People: Miscegenation and*

Mulattoes in the United States (New York: New York University Press, 1984), an otherwise excellent examination of the history of U.S. interraciality. A brief discussion occurs in Aaron Daniel, "The 'Inky Curse': Miscegenation in the White Literary Imagination," *Social Sciences Information* 22, no. 1 (1983): 169–90.

5. Croly, *Miscegenation*, 9.

6. Ibid., 1.

7. Ibid., 11.

8. Ibid., 19.

9. Lydia Maria Child, *An Appeal in Favor of That Class of Americans Called Africans* (Boston, 1833; reprint, New York: Arno, 1968).

10. *National Anti-Slavery Standard*, 30 Jan., 1864, 7.

11. Quoted in Bloch, *Miscegenation, Melaleukation*, 8.

12. "The Union of the Races," *The Independent*, 25 Feb., 186; reprinted in *The National Antislavery Standard*, Feb. 29, 1864, n.p. Tilton's article, together with the congressional debate and the widespread press commentary, created sufficient demand for the printing of a second edition of the *Miscegenation* pamphlet in March 1864.

13. *New York Times*, 16 March 1864, 4.

14. *New York World*, 17 March 1864, 2.

15. "The Waste of Pro-Slavery Twaddle," *New York Times*, 3 April 1864, 4.

16. Quoted in Bloch, *Miscegenation, Melaleukation*, 34.

17. *The World*, Friday, 18 Nov. 1864, 1. The article explains that the "Moon Hoax" refers to the fact that the *Miscegenation* scandal eclipsed another hoax, perpetrated by J. Locke "immediately after the completion of Lord Ross's great telescope." The story was reprinted from the *London Morning Herald* by its "New York correspondent." Given the level of detail described in the execution of the hoax, it is likely that Croly himself is the author. At several points, the writer can barely contain his glee over the success of his achievement. He asserts, for example, that the booklet "was constructed with so much tack [sic] and cleverness that it 'swindled' everybody." The article is followed by a reprinting of the endorsements the tract received from numerous leading abolitionists, including Horace Greeley, Henry Ward Beecher, Parker Pillsbury, Sarah M. Grimke, William Wells Brown, and many others. The anonymous authors had solicited the endorsements prior to the pamphlet's public distribution.

18. Croly, *Miscegenation*, 25–26. Cf. Jon William Draper, *Human Physiology, Statical and Dynamic or the Conditions and Course of the Life of Man*, 2nd ed. (New York, 1858).

19. Croly, *Miscegenation*, 31–32, 49.

20. For a discussion of race theory and racialist science in the nineteenth

century, see Stephen Jay Gould, *The Mismeasure of Man* (New York: W. W. Norton & Co., 1981).

21. Bloch is apparently the first to note that *Miscegenation* "paradoxically held up to ridicule the similar but widely accepted 'reasoning' of the believers in Negro anatomical and physiological inferiority" (*Miscegenation, Melaleukation*, 47).

22. *New York Tribune*, 16 March 1864; reprinted in the *World*, 17 March 1864, 2.

23. *World*, 17 March 1864, 2.

24. *New York Times*, 21 March 1864, 4.

25. MS letter from Jane Cunningham Croly, Boston Athenaeum, 15 December 1900, quoted in Kaplan, *American Studies*, 82. Since Kaplan views the events surrounding the publication of *Miscegenation* as narrow partisan politics, his interpretation of Mrs. Croly's letter is as a strictly cynical gesture: "Her apology is pitiful and guilty; for the facts challenge it." Kaplan also notes that "to his dying day . . . Croly never admitted authorship or mentioned the word miscegenation in any of his voluminous writings" (82, 81).

26. In a wider sense, the ambiguity inscribed in *Miscegenation* represents a culmination of the radical ambivalence and uncertainty surrounding the overlapping categories of race and nationalism with which the United States had been grappling since its inception. The volume's appearance during wartime—when the very future of American nationhood *and* black selfhood were most at risk—can be no accident. See Raimon, "(S)tra(te)gic Mulattoes: Nationalism, Interraciality, and the Figure of the 'Tragic Mulatto' in Nineteenth-Century American Reform Fiction" (Ph.D. diss., Brandeis University, 1995).

27. For a discussion of contemporary biracial identity, see Lise Funderburg, *Black, White, Other* (New York: William Morrow, 1994). For considerations of the increasingly multiracial U.S. population and the controversy over the 2000 census, see Nathan Glazer, "The Hard Questions: Race for the Cure," *The New Republic*, 7 Oct. 1996, 29; John Leland and Gregory Beals, "In Living Colors: Tiger Woods Is the Exception That Rules. For His Multiracial Generation, Hip Isn't Just Black and White," *Newsweek*, 5 May 1997, 58–61; Hannah Beech, "Don't You Dare List Them as 'Other,'" *U.S. News & World Report*, 8 April 1996, 56.

"A Shameless Prostitute and a Negro"

Miscegenation Fears in the Election of 1872

Amanda Frisken

"Free-Lovers Convention," the tabloids screamed in the spring of 1872: "Victoria Woodhull Nominated for President of the United States—Frederick Douglass for Vice President."[1] During Reconstruction, the birth of the enduring mythology of the black male rapist and his pure white female victim confronted a very different interracial alliance posed by the Equal Rights Party (ERP) in 1872. Delegates to this new-found party, representing a broad spectrum of political, social, and economic reform groups, united briefly at New York City's Apollo Hall to nominate sex radical Victoria Woodhull and black statesman Frederick Douglass for the respective offices of president and vice president of the United States. The controversy surrounding this convention reveals the role of the press in generating, as well as reflecting, popular ideas about the future of racial and sexual equality. This symbolic coupling of one of the century's most disreputable white women with one of its most respectable black men in the popular press posed a volatile and ulti-mately unstable alternative to the emergent black rapist/white victim narrative.[2] The convention ultimately contributed to the containment of reform at the turning point of Reconstruction.

The staged Woodhull/Douglass nomination and subsequent "campaign" was purely symbolic. Woodhull was, by virtue of her sex and age (only thirty-four years old at the time), unqualified to run for the office of president; Douglass (who had not been consulted beforehand) never seriously considered the nomination. Transient and marginal, the Woodhull-Douglass nomination nevertheless played an important role in the cultural politics of 1872, a role that has not yet been fully exam-

133

ined. The convention's egalitarian message was lost to contemporaries amidst its raucous reception in the press, and Woodhull's later racism in her eugenics work in the 1890s has come to overshadow the latent idealism behind the joint nomination. Without ignoring or denying Woodhull's later views, we can still view the convention as a dramatic attempt by a group of radical reformers to engage in the most controversial social question of Reconstruction—namely, miscegenation.

1872 was a pivotal year in Reconstruction politics. Andrew Johnson's vacillating Presidential Reconstruction having failed by the late 1860s, the radical Republican Congress passed sweeping legislation that conferred civil and legal rights upon the freed slaves, in the form of the Fourteenth and Fifteenth Amendments, the Civil Rights Act, the Force Act, and the Ku Klux Klan Act, to protect the newly enfranchised black (male) citizens. By 1872, however, such measures had lost popular support. This important presidential election ironically pitted the incumbent Republican president and war hero, Ulysses S. Grant, against the longtime abolitionist, liberal Republican champion, and Democratic party candidate, Horace Greeley. Greeley represented a short-lived "fusion strategy" of the Democratic party, which sought to moderate its image as the party of slavery, and attract black votes by forming an alliance with disaffected "liberal" Republicans. These liberal Republicans sheared off from their radical counterparts, decrying the expanded role of the federal state amid reported widespread corruption and questions about the need for even the Ku Klux Klan Act.[3] Despised by the "straight out" (conservative) Southern Democrats and denounced by most northern Republicans, Greeley stood little chance of winning, and indeed Grant would win an enormous popular majority that November. The Greeley defeat marked the death of the Democratic strategy of compromise; after the election the party balance shifted back to favor a conservative, white-supremacist strategy that would ultimately destroy the principles of Reconstruction.[4]

The election of 1872 came during a brief hiatus in Southern racial violence brought about by the successful (albeit temporary) enforcement of the KKK Act.[5] The success of the KKK Act in deterring political lynching apparently conveyed to white supremacists the notion that only social crimes (rape, for example) could be safely punished through extralegal violence. Lynching a man for exercising political rights risked Northern anger; a lynching justified as "protection for women" avoided this response. Pitting the unassailable character of white womanhood against the "bestial" nature of the black man, Southern racists thus created a new rationale for lynching, and a powerful mechanism for social, and *political*, control. While there is some evidence that not every white woman was protected from rape (or vindicated through violence against the alleged perpetrator) during Reconstruction, the era also set into motion the democratization of the pure white womanhood ideal.[6]

The political use of miscegenation fears predated the Civil War by several decades. Abolitionists in the 1830s were frequently accused of sponsoring the "mongrelization" of the American people.[7] White women, in turn, who spoke out for abolition had been labeled sexual exhibitionists and advocates of interracial sex.[8] The specter of Emancipation stepped up the miscegenation scare. Northern Democrats had invented the term "miscegenation," which first appeared in an anonymous pamphlet that circulated in the final months of the Civil War as part of a (largely successful) attempt to discredit the Republican party.[9] But the figure of the black male rapist was a cultural product of Reconstruction, easing long-standing miscegenation fears: by casting the rapist as a black man, Southerners denied a long tradition of white men's rape of black women and simultaneously justified violent retribution.

The conflicting interests of race and sex, heightened by the miscegenation scare of the early 1860s, precipitated the disintegration of more than thirty years of collaboration among white women suffragists and black freed women and men in the debate over the Fourteenth and Fifteenth Amendments. The issue first came to a head in Kansas in 1867 over the question of suffrage in the new state's constitution. In this case, a faction of the territorial Republican party hostile to black suffrage introduced the measure, but it was linked to woman suffrage; as a result, both propositions were defeated.[10] The "black scare" abated as the 1870s progressed because of not only the transfer of political power back to the white supremacists (that is, home rule and redemption) but also the spread of miscegenation fears from the limited arena of "legitimate" politics and legislation into the realm of popular culture on a national scale.[11]

In the summer of 1872, Frederick Douglass was the national spokesperson for "social equality," namely the application of civil rights to public spaces, including transportation, schooling, churches, cemeteries, and juries. He was, in the eyes of the press, a "representative black man."[12] The cornerstone of the social equality or civil-rights debate during the campaign spring of 1872 was the public-school system, which raised the controversial question of mixed schooling. One of the main reasons *cited* for rejecting Reconstruction and public education was taxation, but it is clear that miscegenation fears were critical in the debate. Mixed schools existed in some state constitutions (for example, Louisiana),[13] but more often in law than in practice. Under pressure from the freeborn black elites, the radical senator Charles Sumner reintroduced his Civil Rights Bill (with its federal provision for national mixed schooling) late in 1871, and the issue was hotly debated in the Senate in April and May 1872. Because most states practiced de facto segregation of schools, and white taxpayers would not tolerate mixed schools in most states, this bill threatened an upheaval of a particularly personal kind, an upheaval that even most white Republicans did not welcome.[14]

Douglass was particularly outspoken and adamant on the subject of mixed schooling. He spoke on the subject to large audiences as the Senate debated that May. "Educate the poor white children and the colored children together," Douglass insisted. "[L]et them grow up to know that color makes no difference as to the rights of a man; that both the black and the white man are at home; that the country is as much the country of one as of the other, and that both together must make it a valuable country." The *New York Republican,* a moderate party organ, rebuked Douglass's support of mixed schooling in no uncertain terms: "we do not believe in mingling the black and the white children in one school. We do not think the mingling is good for either race. God intended that the negro should be with the negro in society, as He intended the white should be with white." The irony of this statement was not lost on Douglass, and the *New National Era* responded:

> We do favor the 'mingling' of white and black children in common schools as affording the best means for a common education. The 'mingling' of colored and white, to which the *Republican* objects, has been a fact for generations in this country. . . . Abundant evidence [in the form of "colored people of mixed blood"] exists in our midst of the desire on the part of whites to mingle with the blacks.

White men had, in other words, through force and other exertions of power, frequently mixed their blood with that of black women during slavery.[15] Despite such eloquent protests, mixed schooling would eventually be dropped from the Radical Reconstruction program, in no small part because Democrats convinced many Northern Republicans of its potential for promoting miscegenation.[16] For all his diligence in explaining and clarifying the concept, white supremacists had made Douglass's idea of "social equality" synonymous with interracial sex.

Victoria Woodhull, on the other hand, was the national spokesperson for "social freedom" (or *free love*), and was the press's favored "representative" leader of the women's suffrage campaign. Woodhull had spent two years shocking New York and the nation with her willingness to bear the standard for unpopular causes: she had opened a stock brokerage firm on Wall Street to demonstrate women's ability to run a business, spoken in Congress on behalf of woman's suffrage, marched with the International Workingmen's Association in honor of the executed leadership of the Paris Commune, publicly defended prostitution, and publicly advocated free love. During the six months previous to the Woodhull/Douglass nomination, Woodhull had brought the free-love cause to national attention in a series of speeches, particularly "The Principles of Social Freedom."[17] As a woman who defied convention and sought to revolutionize the social and sexual realms, Woodhull was the ideal target for Democratic scorn during the 1872 campaign summer.

Social equality (civil rights) and social freedom (sexual rights) collided amid the Senate debate over mixed schooling at the ERP convention, where Woodhull and Douglass were nominated for president and vice president respectively. Under such headlines as "The Free Lovers Convention," highly sexualized descriptions of the proceedings received front-page coverage in such high-circulation commercial papers as the *New York Herald, World,* and tabloids such as *The Days' Doings.* The controversial convention proceedings reported in these Eastern presses soon crossed state lines and migrated into all regions of the country, where they generated a national debate over the question of equal rights, to which the concept of miscegenation was by now firmly linked.

The ERP delegates meeting at Apollo Hall spent the day of 10 May 1872 engaged in a series of speeches, debates, and committee sessions. Banners hung on all sides of the hall, which boldly linked the propositions of social welfare (including government "protection and provision from the Cradle to the Grave" and public employment as "the Remedy for Strikes"), populism ("The Laws must be Submitted to the People"), and Christian socialism ("Neither said any that what he possessed was his own, but they held all things in common. *Acts V*"). Because the platform based on these principles failed to pass during the afternoon sessions (due, according to the *World,* to "strong opposition"), the divided convention recessed until 8 P.M. That evening Woodhull took the stage and gave an hour-long speech, advocating revolution as the solution to the social problems that this new party had been designed to remedy.[18] Following this speech, which the audience received (by all accounts) with great enthusiasm, Judge W. Carter (an associate of Woodhull's) nominated Woodhull for president. At this point, all newspapers agreed, the audience went wild. As the *Tribune* reported, "Instantly a scene of the wildest confusion ensued. Almost all sprang to their feet, and cheers, shouts, and roars of laughter shook the building, the more enthusiastic waving hats, handkerchiefs, shawls and other articles." Or, as the tabloid *The Days' Doings* described, "the whole audience rose to its feet, and for fully five minutes cheer after cheer rent the air. Women waved their handkerchiefs and wept, men shouted themselves hoarse, and perfect confusion reigned."[19]

When the excitement had partially subsided, Moses Hull (another Woodhull associate and fellow spiritualist) moved that "as the Convention had seen fit to nominate a representative of the sex comprising one-half the nation, and the half which was in servitude, for the high position of President, now let us further the good work by nominating a man out of the race lately in bondage, and give me the honor of naming Frederick Douglass, of Rochester." The *Tribune* quoted Hull more specifically as saying "that true friend of human liberty, Frederick Douglass." This vice-presidential nomination immediately sparked a heated debate on the convention floor over the cultural meaning of the ticket. Many papers, for example, noted the anger of one delegate who "made himself heard above the tumult, shouting 'I move the nomination of Spotted Tail. Indians ought to have a voice here before the niggers.' " The *Tribune* more moderately reported that "another indignant auditor, who appeared intensely disgusted at the turn affairs had taken, shouted 'I move that we nominate Spotted Tail for Vice President, as the Indians had possession of this country before the negroes.' Shrieks of laughter followed." After some heated debate over whether Douglass would actually accept (given his public support of President Grant's reelection), "A delegate moved, in case Mr. Douglass did not accept, that some colored man be substituted in his place," which suggestion brought forth "cries of 'Heathen Chinee [sic],' 'Spotted Tail,' 'Ku Klux,' etc." As captured by the press, the convention was simultaneously a parade of race prejudice under the banner of reform, and a throwback to utopian abolitionist ideals of universal humanism.[20] Both interpretations mocked the issues presented there.

The role of the press in reconstructing this convention is even more evident in the editorial commentary that followed. A highly amused *Herald* editorial (the highest-circulation newspaper in the country at the time) ran under the headline "The Highly Colored Human Ticket for the Presidency—the Free Love Communist Candidates in the Field":

The first place on its ticket is devoted (*place aux dames!*) to the fair sex, and, to make the contrast more forcible, the second fiddle is handed, to draw it mildly, to a male brunette. Considerable doubt was expressed in the Convention as to whether the venerable and colored Fred Douglass could stand on the platform beside the young and painted creature in petticoats. . . . It may be objected that Victoria Woodhull had long ago nominated herself for the Presidency, and her endorsement for the candidature might be considered as a "put-up job"; but with regard to the Vice President, expectant or desired, the case is different. There can be little doubt that the position has been thrust upon him, and it remains to be seen how the representative black man will act under the circumstances.

As the *New York World* put it, Douglass was "very well qualified to be the ideal 'respected fellow-townsman' whom the convention agreed in chiefly hating. We really do not see why a convention in behalf of chaos should spoil its work and make a distinction in disfavor of Mr. DOUGLASS, as it is clear that it did make that distinction solely on the grounds of his race and his color."[21] That this symbolic goal was, in fact, a legitimate objective for the ERP convention escaped almost every editorial assessment of the event.[22]

The ratification meeting in early June underscored the egalitarian mission of the nominations in its campaign song:

> If you nominate a woman
> In the month of May
> Dare you face what Mrs. Grundy
> And her set will say?
>
> How they'll jeer and frown and slander
> Chattering night and day
> Oh, did you dream of Mrs. Grundy
> In the month of May.
>
> If you nominate a Negro
> In the month of May
> Dare you face what Mr. Grundy
> And his chums will say?
>
> Yes, Victoria we've selected
> For our chosen head;
> With Fred Douglass on the ticket
> We will raise the dead.
>
> Then round them let us rally
> Without fear or dread
> And next March we'll put the Grundys
> In their little bed.[23]

"The Grundys," those representatives of social inertia, proved resourceful. The press used ridicule and distortion to contain the revolutionary potential of this mixed-race political alliance between the "immoral" Woodhull and the respectable Douglass.

Douglass, with his impeccable credentials as speaker and editor, was an unlikely "brutish rapist." The press instead used his nomination as second fiddle to Woodhull to feminize Douglass. The *Herald,* for example, labeled him a "male brunette." Perhaps more tellingly, the racist *Pomeroy's Democrat* satirically accused the women suffragists (collectively, via Woodhull) of committing an "outrage" (common parlance for rape) upon Douglass by putting him behind a woman.[24] This comic reversal of the paper's standard black/white rape scenario easily reduced the convention to the ridiculous. A later issue elaborated on the comic aspect of the Woodhull/Douglass pairing with a woodcut image of Woodhull and Douglass in the garb of minstrel performers, complete with stage-prop horses (worn about the waist), with large booted feet showing below. These costumes were suggestive, for they raised the possibility that Woodhull was not really a woman, and that Douglass was not really a black man, but rather that they were white men in disguise, seeking only to entertain. Finally, many papers used the convention to put Woodhull firmly and finally beyond the pale of acceptable social behavior. Western newspapers, for example, dismissed the candidates as "A Shameless Prostitute and a Negro."[25]

In spite of, or perhaps in response to, the hilarity in Democratic papers over the Woodhull/Douglass nominations, black presses ignored the convention entirely, distancing themselves from Woodhull and reaffirming their commitment to Grant and the Republican party. The *New National Era,* for example (the only nationally circulated black press in 1872), was conspicuously silent on the nomination of its former editor, Douglass, by the ERP convention. Only once, in late October and on the eve of the election, did the *Era* refer to Woodhull, and then it was in sarcastic reference to the association of the "virtuous Mrs. Woodhull" with the Greeley campaign.[26] Other prominent Black presses likewise observed this silence on the Equal Rights Party convention (perhaps as an oblique response): the Hampton Institute's *Southern Workman* ignored the convention, pointedly praising instead the virtues of domesticity; the *Louisianian* of New Orleans filled the relevant issue with advice columns for girls on how to influence men from the hearth; the San Francisco *Elevator,* a passionate advocate of mixed schooling, was equally silent on the convention. Only after some urging from old abolitionist allies, who warned him that ignoring the convention would only fuel Democratic abuses, did Douglass publicly reject the nomination.[27]

The extent to which the ERP convention influenced the election of 1872 is difficult to determine—what is clear, however, is that it deliberately engaged in and reflected the cultural politics of that summer. The reverberations of the convention in the presidential campaign demonstrate just how disruptive such an interracial male/female political and cultural alliance could appear. The Democratic *New York World*, for example, linked Woodhull to Grant in their small headline (buried on page 5) "DOUGLASS OBJECTS: He does not Care to Keep Company with Woodhull—*Grant Favors woman Suffrage.*"[28] The Republicans, on the other hand, used a "colored professor" (in the shape of a blackface performer at campaign stops) to lampoon Greeley by linking him to Woodhull. This satirical monologue was simultaneously replete with an inaccurate, but extensive, vocabulary and the ironic "Black" dialect so dear to the blackface tradition. "I'se 'peared afore you to-night to 'cuss Mrs. Woodhull," the 'professor' began, "an' de new an' strange ideaths which dat ar' much married critter am tryin' to obfusecate de 'stablish doctrines." In this one parody, the Republican party distanced itself not only from Woodhull and woman suffrage, but also from the cause of black civil rights: this representative "colored professor" was hardly meant as an exemplar of an educated black man.[29] Not fitting the emerging mold for interracial pairings (that is, rape), the Woodhull/Douglass nomination became a parody, through which the aspirations of woman suffrage and black civil rights could be distorted, contained, and dismissed.

The mixed-school question, "social equality" for freed men and women, suffrage for women, and indeed the notion of suffrage as an inalienable "right," were all casualties of the failure of Reconstruction ideals to maintain widespread popular support.[30] In part this was a failure of the Republicans to overcome the miscegenation controversy thrust upon them by the Democrats. The abstract ideal of "social equality" had become indistinct from the more concrete (and feared) notion of "social freedom" that implied race-mixing and interracial sex. Douglass did not appear in *The Days' Doings* in coverage of the nomination, in its ratification the next month, or in his rejection of the nomination.[31] The respectable black man had no place in the tabloid forum. *The Days' Doings'* subsequent issue instead sported a headline describing a "Bloody Affray" in which "A Frenzied Negro Coachman Attempts an Outrage" upon a white woman. The fact that this coachman worked for Commodore Vanderbilt, who had set Woodhull and her sister up in the brokerage business two years previously, implicitly linked the two stories. Although it developed in court that the woman had been his willing companion, and that the coachman was himself the victim of police brutality, rather than the reverse (as the arresting officers had claimed), the tabloid used the story as a suggestive sequel to the Woodhull/Douglass alliance.[32]

To counteract the deliberately overblown threat of black male/white female alliances, Democrats and allied presses painted all women suffragists as "bad" women like Woodhull, and all black men as potential rapists, a myth with remarkable staying power. Between 1882 and 1892, according to Ida B. Wells, the leading justification for the lynching of black men was rape (or at least the accusation of rape), eclipsing even murder, with robbery a distant third. As Wells wrote in 1892, "The Southern white man says that it is impossible for a voluntary alliance to exist between a white woman and a colored man, and therefore, the fact of an alliance is a proof of force."[33] In 1914, a white-supremacist South Carolina Senator wrote, "Amalgamation is the hope and ultimate purpose of the Negroes, the obliteration of the colored line; and many whites, too many, oblivious to their duty to their race and caste, are voluntary criminals in this regard, while, thank God, our white women prefer death to such a fate."[34] As recently as the late 1980s, cultural theorist bell hooks has warned that the press's myth of the black male rapist and virtuous white woman victim—with its implicit denial of historic or contemporary rape of black women by white men—retains its cultural power to confuse and divide reform coalitions.[35] As Eva Saks puts it, miscegenation fears continue to play a powerful, "symbolic part in maintaining the alienated status of American blacks."[36] The Equal Rights Party's idealistic attempt to put forth Woodhull and Douglass as a symbol of voluntary interracial alliance did not have the requisite social or cultural capital to challenge the more politically useful rape mythology. Woodhull's sexual radicalism and Douglass's social respectability, moreover, exaggerated the incomprehensibility of the nomination. The Woodhull/Douglass nomination contradicted, but could not supplant, the rapist/victim dyad that continues to define black male/white female pairings in the popular press to this day.

Notes

1. *The Days' Doings* (New York), June 1, 1872.
2. Lynching would become the dominant social mechanism for policing the race/sex boundary. For a discussion of the four necessary figures in the

lynching ritual, namely the black "beast," his pure white "victim," the white "avenger," and the black "prostitute," see Sandra Gunning, *Race, Rape, and Lynching* (New York: Oxford University Press, 1996). On the lasting stereotype of the immoral black woman and its implicit justification for her sexual assault by white men, see for example, Patricia Morton, *Disfigured Images: The Historical Assault on Afro-American Women* (New York: Greenwood Press, 1991). Jacquelyn Dowd Hall refers to lynching as a "ritualistic affirmation of white unity," and discusses the rape of African-American women by white men as a political weapon; see Hall, *Revolt against Chivalry: Jessie Daniel Ames and the Women's Campaign against Lynching* (New York : Columbia University Press, 1993), 141. See also Annecka Marshall, "From Sexual Denigration to Self-Respect: Resisting Images of Black Female Sexuality," in Delia Jarrett-Macauley, ed. *Reconstructing Womanhood, Reconstructing Feminism: Writings on Black Women* (London: Routledge, 1996).

3. The passage of this act in April 1871 enabled federal enforcement of civil crimes, namely, those acts of violence or intimidation that prevented citizens from the exercise of their rights, especially voting rights.

4. The Democratic party's "divisive search for a secure electoral base," evident in its brief merger with Liberal Republicans, coincided with the Republican party's moderation and ultimate abandonment of Radical Reconstruction. After this "New Departure" failed with the Greeley rout, the Democrats became more conservative, the Republicans more "Black": the distinction between parties on a national and local level increasingly became one of race, with the Democrats running open white supremacy campaigns; see Michael Perman, *The Road to Redemption: Southern Politics, 1869–1879* (Chapel Hill: University of North Carolina Press, 1984), 77–78, 106, 108, 136–37, 170. See also George Frederickson, *The Inner Civil War: Northern Intellectuals and the Crisis of the Union* (New York: Harper & Row, 1965), 193, 198; and Eric Foner, *Reconstruction: America's Unfinished Revolution, 1863–1877* (New York: Harper & Row, 1988), 503.

5. Foner, *Reconstruction*, 545–59.

6. In South Carolina, at least, there is evidence that during Reconstruction white elites were not overly concerned about the rapes of poor white women, even if the aggressor was black. See Laura Edwards, *Gendered Strife and Confusion: The Political Culture of Reconstruction* (Urbana: University of Illinois Press, 1997), 198–210.

7. As early as 1836, the spectacle of mixed marriage became a central organizing symbol in an election campaign and was at issue during the Lincoln-Douglass debates of 1858. See for example, Thomas Brown, "The Miscegenation of Richard Mentor Johnson as an Issue in the national Election Campaign of 1835–36," *Civil War History* 39 (1993): 5–30.

8. See Jean Yellin, *Women and Sisters: The Antislavery Feminists in American Culture* (New Haven, Conn.: Yale University Press, 1989), 45–50.

9. David Goodman Croly, *Miscegenation* (1864; reprint, Upper Saddle River, N.J.: Literature House, 1970). The term previously used, in a more general sense, was "amalgamation." According to Forrest Wood, "After 1863, those who sought an abusive word used 'miscegenation,' which instantly acquired all sorts of salacious and derisive connotations"; see Forrest Wood, *Black Scare: The Racist Response to Emancipation and Reconstruction* (Berkeley and Los Angeles: University of California Press, 1968), 54, 129–30, 143–46. See also James Kinney, *Amalgamation: Race, Sex, and Rhetoric in the Nineteenth-Century American Novel* (Westport, Conn.: Greenwood Press, 1985). On the fear of miscegenation as a justification for social inequality for blacks, see Charles E. Wynes, "Social Acceptance and Unacceptance," in Joel Williamson, ed., *The Origins of Segregation* (Boston, Mass.: D. C. Heath, 1968), 20, 29. See also Joel Williamson, "The Separation of Races," in Williamson, ed., *The Origins of Segregation*, 11, 13, 40.

10. Ellen DuBois, *Feminism and Suffrage: The Emergence of an Independent Women's Movement in America, 1848–1869* (Ithaca, N.Y.: Cornell University Press, 1978), 86–89. See also Andrea Moore Kerr, "White Women's Rights, Black Men's Wrongs," in Marjorie Spruill Wheeler, ed., *One Woman, One Vote: Rediscovering the Woman Suffrage Movement* (Troutdale, Oreg.: NewSage Press, 1995), 66, 68, 76–77. Forrest Wood agrees that by linking female suffrage to black suffrage in 1867 Kansas united the two issues in the public mind, making black suffrage less likely. The "white womanhood symbol" became the "extremist's ultimate weapon in the miscegenation and social equality controversies [and] found a place . . . in the resistance to Negro suffrage" (Wood, *Black Scare*, 95). Note that Stanton spoke in 1868 on the dangers of the exclusion of women from the Fifteenth Amendment: "With judges and jurors of negroes, remembering the generations of wrong and injustice their daughters have suffered at the white man's hands, how will Saxon girls fare in their courts for crimes like this" (a remark on the case of a girl tried for murder—i.e., infanticide—of a child following rape by a black man; while this statement can be interpreted as racist, it also reflects her awareness of the particular burdens for black women under slavery); Stanton speech quoted in Ellen Carol DuBois, ed., *The Elizabeth Cady Stanton, Susan B. Anthony Reader: Correspondence, Writings, Speeches* (Boston, Mass.: Northeastern University Press, 1992), 123.

11. Forrest Wood argues that Southern whites deliberately exaggerated the incidence of black men's rape of white women for political effect. "The favorite tool in the racist's bag of tricks was the idea of a brutish black man and a delicate white woman engaged in the unthinkable act—interracial copulation." Beyond the pale of any discussion of interracial sexuality was the idea of a "willing white woman." Wood claims that "the Negro rapist was essentially a product of the Reconstruction period" and notes that even the accusation of rape could result in lynching by the early 1870s; see Wood, *Black Scare*, 65, 73–87.

12. *New York Herald,* 12 May 1872.

13. The Reconstruction experiment of mixed schooling in Louisiana, which included measures to fine white families boycotting the public schools, collapsed in rioting and legitimized a persistent resistance among whites to the idea of public schooling; see William Preston Vaughn, *Schools for All: The Blacks & Public Education in the South, 1865–1877* (Lexington: University Press of Kentucky, 1974), 78–94, 127–28; and James D. Anderson, *The Education of Blacks in the South, 1860–1935* (Chapel Hill: University of North Carolina Press, 1988), 80–81.

14. Social segregation of blacks and whites in public spaces was typically enforced by extralegal means. For example, "jostling" by black men of white women on crowded walkways could lead to "beatings, shootings or lynchings." This kind of social enforcement clearly required the complicity of the white women who had a stake in protecting their own honor and class status. See Vernon Lane Wharton, "Jim Crow Laws and Miscegenation," in Williamson, ed., *Origins of Segregation,* 18. The mechanisms of segregation, North and South, were complex and have been the subject of scholarly controversy. Joel Williamson claims that Emancipation precipitated "an immediate and revolutionary separation of races"; see Joel Williamson, Introduction, in Williamson, ed., *Origins of Segregation,* vi. While disputing the assertion of legal segregation during Reconstruction, C. Vann Woodward concurs that some voluntary and involuntary separation and withdrawal of the races occurred during the 1870s, and a coinciding "state of mind bordering on hysteria among Southern white people" emerged; see C. Vann Woodward, *The Strange Career of Jim Crow,* 3rd ed. (New York: Oxford University Press, 1974), xiii, 23, 25.

15. Douglass and New York *Republican* quoted in *New National Era,* 16 May 1872. The term "miscegentation" was used almost exclusively to denote black male/white female sexual pairings. This reading, as Neil McMillen argues, effectively silenced "the reality of white male exploitation of black women." Despite anti-miscegenation laws, sanctions were rarely taken against white men in relationships with black women; see Neil McMillen, *Dark Journey: Black Mississippians in the Age of Jim Crow* (Urbana: University of Illinois Press, 1989), 14–16. As Catherine Clinton argues, during Reconstruction a kind of "sexual terrorism" took the place of the slave system: "White women's bodies became sacred territory over which ex-Confederates organized and battled, refighting the war and re-exerting regional and race pride. Black women's bodies were just as critical. For too long shame and silence cloaked their sexual violation"; see Catherine Clinton, "Bloody Terrain: Freedwomen, Sexuality and Violence during Reconstruction," in Catherine Clinton, ed. *Half-sisters of History: Southern Women and the American Past* (Durham, N.C.: Duke University Press, 1994), 149. On Northern responses to racial "mingling," see David H. Fowler, *Northern Attitudes towards Interracial Marriage: Legislation and Public Opinion in the Middle Atlantic and the States of the Old Northwest,*

1780–1930 (New York: Garland Publishing, 1987), 238–40. On lynching and rape, see also Glenda Elizabeth Gilmore, *Gender and Jim Crow: Women and the Politics of White Supremacy in North Carolina, 1896–1920* (Chapel Hill: University of North Carolina Press, 1996), 67–71 and chapter 4.

16. As W. E. B. Du Bois commented, the "propaganda of race hatred made [mixed schooling] eventually impossible, and the separate school system so increased the cost of public education in the South" that it became untenable; see W. E. B. Du Bois, *Black Reconstruction in America; An Essay toward a History of the Part Which Black Folk Played in the Attempt to Reconstruct Democracy in America, 1860–1880* (1935; reprint, New York: Russell & Russell, 1966), 657–63. For conservatives, interracial marriage and mixed schooling became indistinguishable issues; see Foner, *Reconstruction,* 321. See also Vaughn, *Schools for All,* 76–77. Identical concerns about mixed schooling and miscegenation resurfaced during the 1950s amidst the controversy over *Brown v. Board of Ed.* See Renee Romano, "Sex at the Schoolhouse Door: Fears of 'Amalgamation' in the Southern Response to *Brown v. Board of Education,*" unpublished paper presented at the One Hundred and Eleventh Annual Meeting of the American Historical Association (New York, 1997).

17. Full text of this speech, "The Principles of Social Freedom," is reprinted in Madeleine Stern, ed., *The Victoria Woodhull Reader* (Boston, Mass: M&S Press, 1974). Woodhull continues to elude comprehensive historical analysis. On her impact on the Woman Suffrage movement, see Ellen Carol DuBois, *The Elizabeth Cady Stanton, Susan B. Anthony Reader,* and also her "Taking the Law into Our Own Hands," in Nancy A. Hewitt and Suzanne Lebsock, eds. *Visible Women: New Essays on American Activism* (Urbana: University of Illinois Press, 1993). See also Kerr, "White Women's Rights, Black Men's Wrongs." The best biography of Woodhull's life is Lois Beachy Underhill, *The Woman Who Ran for President: The Many Lives of Victoria Woodhull* (Bridgehampton, N.Y.: Bridge Works Press, 1996).

18. The convention received wide, if disparaging, coverage. See, for example, the *New York World,* 11, 12 May 1872.

19. *New York Tribune,* 11 May 1872. *The Days' Doings,* 1 June 1872.

20. *New York Tribune,* 11 May 1872. *The Days' Doings,* 1 June 1872. Spotted Tail was the leader of the Brulé Sioux tribe who had recently negotiated a treaty with the U.S. Government.

21. *New York Herald,* 12 May 1872. *New York World,* 12 May 1872.

22. *The Tribune* (whose coverage was the most moderate, going so far as to include a full description of the party platform) is a possible exception: as Greeley's campaign organ (despite his protestations to the contrary), the paper was probably anxious not to offend the various reform groups col-

147

lecting under the rubric of the ERP, as many were potential supporters of the Greeley ticket if the ERP failed.

23. Campaign song quoted in Johanna Johnston, *Mrs. Satan: the Incredible Saga of Victoria C. Woodhull* (New York: G. P. Putnam's Sons, 1967), 149–50.

24. *New York Herald,* 12 May 1872.

25. *Pomeroy's Democrat,* 18 May 1872, 25 May 1872. Unidentified Portland, Oregon, press report published in the feminist *New Northwest,* 31 May 1872.

26. *New National Era,* October 1872. Greeley and Woodhull were connected through Theodore Tilton, a reform editor who had, for reasons disputed by historians, published a biography of Victoria Woodhull the previous November. He was Greeley's campaign manager throughout the campaign. He is also the Tilton whose wife, Woodhull alleged in November 1872, had an affair with the popular minister of Plymouth Church, Henry Ward Beecher.

27. *The Southern Workman* (Hampton, Virginia), June 1872. *The Weekly Louisianian* (New Orleans), 11, 18 May 1872. *The Elevator* (San Francisco), 4, 18 May; 1, 15 June 1872. On Douglass's rejection of the nomination, see "Douglass Objects: He Does Not Keep Company with Woodhull," *New York World,* 24 June 1872. See also Philip Foner, *Frederick Douglass: Selections from His Writings* (1945; reprint, New York: International Publishers, 1964), 302.

28. *New York World,* 24 June 1872, emphasis added.

29. "A Colored Professor 'Cussin' de Free Lub," in *The 'All Among the Hay' Songster: Full of the Jolliest Lot of Songs and Ballads That Have Ever Been Printed* (New York: R. M. DeWitt, 1872). Robert Toll argues that women's rights activists were "consistently ridiculed and condemned" by minstrel and blackface shows; see Robert Toll, *Blacking Up: The Minstrel Show in Nineteenth Century America* (New York: Oxford University Press, 1974), 163. On the minstrel show as a political force of containment, see Eric Lott, *Love and Theft: Blackface Minstrelsy and the American Working Class* (New York: Oxford University Press, 1993), 234.

30. See, for example, F. James Davis, *Who Is Black? One Nation's Definition* (University Park: Pennsylvania State University Press, 1991), 52–53.

31. The ERP ratified the nomination on 5 June 1872. See, for example, *New York Tribune,* 7 June 1872.

32. *The Days' Doings,* 15 June 1872. Because the tabloid adhered to the practice of many weekly papers of postdating their news, it is not clear whether the incident had yet made it to court. The court hearing is described in detail, including testimony from Vanderbilt and his brother-in-law, which

clearly documents the brutality of the two arresting officers; see *Herald*, 7 June 1872.

33. Wells-Barnett insisted that lynchings implicitly denied the possibility that white women could desire black men, and simultaneously ignored the very real sexual terrorism practiced on black women by white men during the same time period. Ida B. Wells-Barnett, *On Lynchings: Southern Horrors, A Red Record, Mob Rule in New Orleans* (New York: Arno Press, 1969). See also Trudier Harris, ed., *Selected Works of Ida B. Wells-Barnett* (New York: Oxford University Press, 1991). As Laura Edwards argues "Emancipation did not invert the social hierarchy: white men were not reduced to abject powerlessness, nor were their womenfolk exposed to sexually predatory black men. . . . If anything, emancipation heightened the vulnerability of African American women to violence at the hands of white men, who used rape and other ritualized forms of sexual abuse to limit black women's freedom and to reinscribe antebellum racial hierarchies"; see Edwards, *Gendered Strife and Confusion*, 199.

34. South Carolina Senator Pitchfork Ben Tillman, quoted in Jeffrey Crow, "An Apartheid for the South: Clarence Poe's Crusade for Rural Segregation" (Jeffrey Crow, Paul Escott and Charles Flynn, Jr., eds. *Race, Class, and Politics in Southern History: Essays in Honor of Robert F. Durden* [Baton Rouge: Louisiana State University Press, 1989], 240).

35. Reflecting on the exaggerated media attention given to the Central Park Jogger rape in the late 1980s, hooks describes a "story, invented by white men, . . . about the overwhelming desperate longing black men have to sexually violate the bodies of white women. The central character in this story is the black male rapist. . . . As the story goes, this desire is not based on longing for sexual pleasure. It is a story of revenge, rape as the weapon by which black men, the dominated, reverse their circumstance, regain power over white men"; see bell hooks, *Yearning: Race, Gender and Cultural Politics* (Boston, Mass.: South End Press, 1990), 58, 61.

36. Eva Saks, "Representing Miscegenation Laws," *Raritan* 8 (Fall 1988): 44.

"Absolute Whiteness"

Mudsills and Menaces in the World of Madison Grant

Matthew Guterl

When you are actually in America, America hurts, because
it has a powerful disintegrative influence upon the white
psyche. It is full of grinning, unappeased aboriginal demons . . . and it persecutes the white men . . . until the
white men give up their absolute whiteness.
        —D. H. Lawrence, *Studies in Classic American Literature*

Writing of Madison Grant after his death, the eminent paleontologist
Fairfield Osborn distilled the general character of Grant's life this way:
"[a] man of distinguished appearance, over six feet tall and of very upright carriage, a meticulous dresser, he had a great self assurance, was
formidable in discussion or debate, and had great tenacity in carrying
through any project or idea."[1] Grant's tenacity is, I think, less important than his earnest desire for order—or for meticulousness—reflected
in his always perfectly trimmed mustache and his stiff, precise "upright
carriage." Grant's warped Mendelian eugenics, made famous during the
Great War, was similarly designed to impose order on a chaotic and unruly world through the construction of a simple racial taxonomy. This
project—the grandest public manifestation of Grant's inner character—
received its most famous expression in his algebraic assertion that "the
result of the mixture of two races . . . gives us a race reverting to the
more ancient, generalized and lower type . . . [thus] . . . [t]he cross between a white man and an Indian is an Indian; the cross between a white
man and a negro is a negro . . . the cross between any of the three European races and a Jew is a Jew."[2]

In discussing the world of Madison Grant, historians have generally
reduced his life to his racism, depicting him as an unchanging "archetype" or as the "father" or "prophet" of American racism. Grant's remarkable popularity in the 1910s and 1920s and his penchant for hyper-
bolically connecting the end of America to presumed "alien menaces"

make him the perfect foil for those who wish rightly to celebrate the agency of the various ethnic and racial groups he so despised. In those few instances where Grant's life has been discussed directly and with some small amount of detail, he is inevitably cast as the embodiment of racism. When, for instance, historian John Higham discusses Grant in the context of nativism, he does so finally to introduce "racism" into the history of the urban North. With an almost audible sigh of relief, Higham marks *The Passing of the Great Race* as, "at last," racism.[3] This reductive understanding of Grant's life adds little to our understanding of *fin-de-siècle* America, and most certainly does not explain either his popularity or his passion for order.

To understand why Grant is historically important, we need to grapple with the connections between that popular zeal for "race" in the 1920s, which West Indian émigré Hubert Harrison termed "the New Race-Consciousness," and the sense of world history, science, and economics that was ubiquitous in the 1910s and 1920s.[4] In short, we need to connect the "macrolevel" of world economics and geo-politics to the level of everyday experience. Theorizing these connections becomes essential to my reading of Madison Grant's work, for Grant's own use of an economic idiom to discuss race relations was representative of larger, subtly coercive hegemonic culture whose outlines became clear at the point where transforming world events and structures met American lives and culture, producing a whole new set of representations, concepts, and culture wrapped around "race."[5] Part of what made the "New Race-Consciousness" so new, in other words, was its use of the language of economics and science—twin discourses which emerged from the debates over international socialism and communism in particular and out of the Progressive Era more generally and which reflected some profound changes in the culture of world capitalism.

The new economic culture that emerged in America during the 1910s and 1920s used a worldly economic idiom to organize culture around "race." That confusion of racial and economic discourses reflected the combination of several factors, including several drastic demographic shifts, the emergence of a media-driven national popular culture, and a growing sense of the world as an organic economic system. Americans immersed in this new economic culture and in the discourse of the "new race-consciousness" grew increasingly aware of the proper geopolitical and world cultural hierarchies for races, and this understanding, in turn, bore heavily on the way racial difference was thereafter spoken and symbolized. For someone with Grant's desire for order and hierarchy, such a culture could also increase the awareness of the dangers posed by distant events and change the definition of what was dangerous. Indeed, the evolution and origins of Grant's taxonomy of racial threats (and races) become clearest when both his well-known *The Passing of the Great Race* and *The Conquest of a Continent,* his lesser-known later work, are placed in the context of this emergent American culture.

Before attempting to place Madison Grant and Progressive America in a world context, however, I want to undertake a brief critical dissection of his life and scientific work.[6] Nowhere was the self-persecuting, angst-ridden Protestant elite more entrenched and more defensive of its privileges and authority than on the tiny island of Manhattan. Grant, representing one segment of the generation born after the Civil War, embodied Richard Hofstadter's classic description of the Progressives as conservative anti-Semites, paranoid fascists, and zealous rivals of the upstart robber barons.[7] After some early efforts at reform, Grant became involved in the great Progressive Era tradition of institution-building— colored, of course, by his patrician "race-consciousness." As historian Donna Haraway has suggested, the growth of cultural institutions in the early twentieth century was an integral part of patrician efforts to resolidify cultural authority and social status. By attempting to control public representations of nature, for instance, Carl Akeley's dioramas at the American Museum of Natural History were part of a larger, concerted effort to dictate the rules of social relations through subtler means.[8] Grant's work on genetics and his steadfast refusal to allow amateur photographers into what later became the Bronx Zoo were underwritten by a similar sense of order and authority. As a founding member of the New York Zoological Society, among other institutions, Grant's cultural authority was strong enough to overcome his lack of professional credentials when it came to the general American sense of "race." Given the enormous prestige accorded to science beginning in the 1910s and throughout the 1920s, Grant's position on the boards of several well-endowed institutions, while somewhat surprising, nevertheless lent additional weight to his earnest scientific discussions of the need for a resurgence of "race-consciousness" in the urban North.[9]

The Passing of the Great Race, published in 1916, captured Grant's angst in language and symbols designed to resonate with all of white America. Pressed deeply into the blue cover of the book, an irregular golden hexagon drew for its prospective readers a frightening analogy between the lost "racial civilizations" of the past and the endangered American civilization built by men like Grant's father, to whom the book was dedicated. Appearing after the hysteric conclusions of the Dillingham Commission and in the midst of a national craze for scientific precision and expert knowledge, *Passing* became an instant bestseller of great and lasting cultural importance. The zeal and passion of

Passing's prose lent the work a sermonesque quality—a quality that masked the cunning, authoritarian undertones of Grant's scientific practice.

"Race-consciousness," for Grant, entailed the celebration of biological and cultural heritage, as well as an acceptance of social authority. The "Nordic" race, Grant suggested, was physically perfect, as well as "domineering, individualistic, self-reliant and jealous of their personal freedom. . . . .Chivalry and knighthood . . . are peculiarly Nordic traits."[10] More important, Grant, like sociologist William Ripley, believed that genetic material alone—not world-historical spirit, religion, language, or nationality—was constitutive of race. The pure white Nordic race, qualitatively superior to the terrible and dusky Alpine and Mediterranean races found in eastern and southern Europe, could be found throughout the world in positions of power and influence. In contrast to those Europeans who continued to measure heads attempting to determine once and for all who was an Anglo-Saxon and who was a Prussian, Grant spoke lovingly of "absolute whiteness"—to borrow D. H. Lawrence's perfect phrase—in a singular, or more global and inclusive sense, and thus to consider racial identity as far larger than national or regional identity.[11] As one of many global races, the Nordic, with its physical and psychological perfection, ruled with an authority derived from a conflation of race and class. The biological, technological, cultural, and economic superiority of the Nordic world, however, was ultimately assured only by that shared and heightened sense of "race-consciousness" as class consciousness; as Grant later put it, "all is race."[12]

The brutal violence of the Great War and the perceived absence of that all-important race consciousness in the urban Northeast motivated Grant to write *The Passing of the Great Race*. Disaster appeared to be at hand, for Nordics were killing Nordics in the Old World. "From a race point of view," Grant huffed, "the present European conflict is essentially a civil war and nearly all of the officers and a large proportion of the men on both sides are members of [the Nordic] race."[13] Ironically, the same physical and psychological traits which Grant so admired in Nordic men made them ideally suited for warfare, thus making the First World War an exercise in "race suicide." European Nordics, overly obsessed with their national origins, were betraying "race" for nation.

Grant's peculiar pacifist eugenics also drew strength from public discontent with the slaughter of the war in Europe and the dread of American involvement. In direct contrast to those who argued for the centrality of struggle in weeding out the unfit, Grant argued—as Fairfield Osborn put it—that "war is in the highest sense dysgenic. . . . It is destructive of the best strains, spiritually, morally, and physically."[14] Indeed, the dysgenic nature of war was all the more dangerous, Grant suggested, now that the ill-conceived civilizing mission had broken down the process of natural selection in backward lands around the world. Members of the Nordic race, if they hoped to secure their tenuous grasp on world domination and genetic magnificence, needed to recognize the global nature of their racial identity—thus regaining their race consciousness—and organize professionally and scientifically to order their world. Science, taxonomy, and classification were, for Grant, the logical tools with which to resolidify Nordic cultural authority and thus to restore a sense of racial order throughout the world, or at least in America.

In an interesting and important twist, the two groups whose status formed the bedrock of American racial discourse in the nineteenth century were not prominently represented in *Passing of the Great Race*.[15] The increasingly powerful (and assimilated) Irish in America found themselves subsumed—somewhat unwillingly—into the folds of Nordicism, with Irish-American nationalism understood to be a sort of false "race-consciousness." Only the Irish in the far west of Ireland were of the "middle Paolithic race."[16] African-Americans were regarded with little, if any fear. Blacks, Grant suggested, seemed fixed in their "place" in the South, and so long as they remained there on rural segregated farms, they would be welcome in America.[17] Indeed, Grant attributed the enviable fluorescence of race consciousness in the South directly to the physical presence of African-Americans. The inclusion of the Irish into Nordicism and the reluctance to consider "the Negro" in Africa or in the American South as a threat mark Grant's work as decidedly different in tone and content from the "negrophobic" works of Thomas Dixon and D. W. Griffith. *Passing of the Great Race* also testifies to the continued disjunction between the political economy of "race" in the North and in the South in 1916.[18] Casting about for a Northern equivalent of "the Negro," Grant established clear and immutable boundaries between Nordicism and the newly arrived "Mediterraneans" or "Jews." The return of popular race consciousness in the North might, he believed, help to secure the passage of national legislation which would end the influx of undesirables and protect the white working classes from competition with these purportedly fecund races.

With the passage in 1924 of the National Origins Act and Virginia's Racial Integrity Law, the differing racial dynamics of the North and South intersected as Grant's popular importance reached its apex. In the North, the paranoid, resurgent superpatriotism of the postwar era proved fertile ground for the seeds of restriction and order which Grant had sown in 1916. Encouraged by the widespread popularity of racial thinking, a cadre of eugenicists and legislators submitted and passed legislation linking immigration quotas to "national origins," legislation based on the work of Grant and others.[19] Grant's remarkable personal prestige also helped to secure passage of Virginia's Racial Integrity Law, which replaced older classifications of "white" (resting on an ancestry $^{15}/_{16}$ "white") to ones in which any nonwhite blood rendered one, quite simply, not white at all.[20] In both cases, Grant also worked hard behind the scenes in determining the language of the legislation and consolidating public support.[21]

The differences between the respective pieces of legislation—the Virginia law geared towards black/white relations, the federal legislation aimed at southern and eastern European and Asian immigrants—are, I think, as important as Grant's role in securing the passage of both. Through the mid-1920s, Grant continued to see significant differences in the racial dynamics of the industrialized North and agricultural South, with the former burdened with an influx of undesirable labor brought into the republic at the behest of the robber barons, with the latter needing only legislation to protect against miscegenation with "Negroes." While there was an increasing national convergence of economic, cultural, and demographic factors in the 1920s, regionally different racial dynamics continued, in Grant's mind, to require radically different responses—responses commonly understood as either nativist or racist. At some point, however, the blending of regional issues would erase the razor-thin line between nativism and racism—between the political and symbolic economies of race in the North and the South.

That crucial juncture was reached, in Grant's mind, in the late 1920s. As late as 1927, Grant had urged Lothrop Stoddard to attend to the problems of China because "the Negro," as he put it, was not then a "live issue."[22] By 1930, however, Grant's traditional Northern nativist animus towards Mediterraneans, Jews, and the Chinese had been rather quickly replaced with a dread fear of "the Negro." This new terror of "the Negro" appeared in its most sophisticated form in what Grant considered the crowning achievement of his life, the high-school history textbook entitled *The Conquest of a Continent* (1933). "Among the various outland elements now in the United States which threaten in different degrees our national unity," Grant bellowed in it, "the most important is the Negro."[23] Social dynamics of recent vintage had, Grant believed, undermined the basis for the separation of the races in the South, converting "the Negro problem" into a national problem; "one race," he concluded, "must drive out the other or be destroyed . . . unless some remedy is found the nation is doomed to mongrelism."[24]

On the surface, Grant's new fear of "the Negro" reflected his recognition that the National Origins Act had failed to restrict immigration from the Americas. The influx of dark-skinned and predominantly Catholic peoples from Latin and South America—lands traditionally understood as historically miscegenetic and presumably peopled by swarthy, inferior races—led Grant to reflect upon the dangers posed by even the smallest amount of Negro blood to the urban North. A "mulatto menace," he had come to believe, threatened to undo all the gains achieved in 1924. "[W]e have facing us," Grant warned,

> a serious Negro problem with an ever-increasing number of quadroon and octoroon types which often pass for Cubans, South Americans, Portuguese or Italians, and it is by no means certain that the percentage of individuals with Negro blood in their veins is not increasing relatively to the pure Whites in spite of all statements to the contrary.[25]

Continued immigration restriction, then, served a twofold purpose—denying inferior stock admission to the United States while simultaneously denying anyone with even the smallest amount of Negro blood the ability to pass surreptitiously for a dingy white.[26] The smallest drop of Negro blood would destroy the absolute whiteness of the Nordic male and bring about the end of America; this was negrophobia tempered, or complicated, by nativism.

The distance between *The Passing of the Great Race* and *The Conquest of a Continent*—or between the "alien menace" of 1916 and the "mulatto menace" of the 1930s—can also be tied to several jolting changes in American life. First, the emergence of a sophisticated consumer culture brought with it a species of national popular culture founded largely on race, more particularly on more inclusive notions of whiteness and blackness. As David Nasaw has suggested, this national popular culture masked (or even erased) older divisions between ethnic groups—divisions which had formed the basis of much of nativism—in favor of a white-over-black racial calculus.[27] Widespread representations of "the African" and "Africa" in film, fairs, and novels lent precious strength to connections between the presumed servility and technological inferiority of "the Negro" and white dominance of the dark continent.[28] Through the first thirty years of this century, then, the growth of a homogenized visual culture lent strength to a symbolic economy of race in which whiteness and blackness had little space for ambiguity—in which, for instance, it was increasingly difficult for the Irish to be positioned "between" Anglo-Saxondom and whiteness. The use of "the African" or "the Negro" as a psychological mudsill for absolute white-

Matthew Guterl

ness was buttressed, of course, by the growth of internationally minded national media chains which encouraged the growth of those "empires of the mind" pervading the new national culture.[29]

In addition to the emergence of a national, racialized popular culture, demographic changes linked to industrialization may also have encouraged Grant suddenly to fear "the Negro." Severe crop failures, the rigors of life under Jim Crow, and the lure of higher paying work elsewhere encouraged tens of thousands of African-Americans to flee Dixie and head North.[30] Many of these ambitious "Negroes," as Grant well knew, had some corrupted Nordic blood in them and were thus capable of "passing" for "white." The outmigration of poorer Southern whites to the urban North also risked inflaming racial sentiments further. While the pace of black migration did slow in the early 1920s, the flooding of the Mississippi in 1927 was responsible for a renewed dispersion of African-Americans to the North that lasted for several years.[31]

The biological or genetic threat posed by light-skinned blacks was accompanied by the dangers of political and social intercourse, dangers which multiplied when presumably radical Caribbean blacks arrived in Harlem, reawakening memories of Toussaint L'Ouverture.[32] The presence of African-Americans in Manhattan was accompanied by assertive political and cultural behavior. In politics, the newly emergent African-American leadership class exerted "decisive" influence in municipal elections through group voting, which the dingy white city machines recognized.[33] Moreover, this formal political behavior was accompanied by the widely publicized and remarkably stylish New Negro Movement, which engendered several proto-political organizations—such as the UNIA, the NAACP, or the provocatively named African Blood Brotherhood.[34]

Madison Grant's negrophobia of the 1930s suggests that the most interesting byproduct of the transformations of the 1910s and 1920s may be the psychological impact of an altogether out-of-place black presence in the North: "[t]here are," Grant intoned apocalyptically in 1933, "now swarms of [Negroes] in the Harlem District of New York."[35] The proliferation of Northern race riots, the brief national resurgence of the second Ku Klux Klan, and Grant's increasing fear of African-Americans reflect an ironic and unanticipated consequence of the Great Migration, underwritten, in part, by the emergence of a racialized national popular culture. This return to, and appropriation of, Southern—and in some cases colonial—racial discourse engendered a crystallization of the ever-widening categories of whiteness and blackness and the "hypnotic division," to borrow Jean Toomer's phrase, of increasing numbers of Americans into those two classifications.[36] Whites and blacks—or Nordics and Negroes—were becoming prominent in each other's minds and in the urban geography of the North. It was, in part, the aftereffects of this symbolic and real penetration of "the Negro" into the Nordic world of urban, northeastern America that encouraged Grant (among others) to reorganize his thoughts on "race" in accordance with what he termed the "Southern way," and to "sympathize," as he wrote, "with the firm resolve of the handful of white men in South Africa."[37]

The mudsill of Southern society, out of place as it was, had rendered Grant's precious taxonomy unstable. It is not surprising that the growing presence of "the Negro" in the North began to effect subtle changes in the way Americans spoke and symbolized race. Grant's racial histories, his work on immigration reform, and his advocacy of eugenics were wrapped around a deeper desire to foreclose the potential for ambiguity in American racial discourse. In early 1920, Grant sent a copy of Stoddard's *The Rising Tide of Color* to Charles Davenport, another nationally recognized figure in the eugenics movement. Davenport's reply, I think, is illustrative of the success of this aspect of Grant's project. "Can we build," Davenport wrote,

> a wall high enough around this country, so as to keep out these cheaper races, or will it only be a feeble dam which will make the flood all the worse when it breaks, or should we admit the 4 millions picks and shovels which Mr. Coleman, du Pont, and other capitalists are urging Congress to admit in order to secure what wealth we can for the moment, leaving it to our descendants to abandon the country to the blacks, browns, and yellows and seek an asylum in New Zealand?[38]

What is most important about this passage is its complete lack of ambiguity—the clear sense that racial identity was an immutable conflation of color, class, and genetic material—which resulted from the cross-fertilization of economic culture and race on a global level. A Chinese laborer in America was out of place in exactly the same sense that the transplanted Negro in the North was. Grant, of course, worked out this intersection of race, class, and color from a particular vantage point, but others, with political agendas and social positions far different from Grant's, spoke of race in strikingly similar terms. Here we can begin to see that the lines of racial classification were drawn wider in the '20s and '30s through the use of economic language. The many white and black celebrants of this new race consciousness managed—to paraphrase Davenport's letter—to build a "wall high enough" around the concepts of whiteness and blackness to make those racial classifications impregnable and nearly uncomplicated by the 1930s.

In addition to an emergent racialized popular culture and the psychological aftereffects of demographic shifts, there is, then, a third factor behind the emergence of this new symbolic economy of race. Grant's taxonomy was grounded in an economic culture in which the representations of races corresponded to classes in a global economy; his angst grew not from a purely domestic set of changes, but from the "menace" of brown or black races out of place in the capitalist and colonial order of things. Grant's eugenicist following worked hard to undo the damage done to Nordic world supremacy by unregenerate capitalist robber barons and more restrained "large policy" advocates such as Teddy Roosevelt; all three groups, however, found themselves speaking of race and race problems in the same economic idiom during the 1920s. Like many Progressive Americans, Grant believed that the supposedly future-oriented and presumably well-organized economic cultures of Europe and America marked off "the West" from Africa, Asia, and India. With socialism and the then current debate over communism electrifying American political culture, a new racial map of the world was crystallizing; Grant may have disagreed with both the means and ends of white dominance as understood by Roosevelt, McKinley, and others, but he most certainly used the same language of race to air his grievances against them.

For the Grants, Roosevelts, and Du Ponts of America, this sense of Western superiority rested upon a fervent belief in the rightful supremacy of the "dark red blood of the capitalist superman" in a racialized world economic culture.[39] The resulting congruence of race, class, and place marked the geopolitical and world economic positions of both the West and "the darker nations" with the former invariably cast in the role of metropolitan entrepreneur and innovator and the latter as backward peasant.[40] Africa and Africans were seemingly always already at the bottom of the list. Thus the picture of Africa as "a land of enormous potential wealth . . . raw materials, and foodstuffs" drawn by Grant's protégé, Lothrop Stoddard, went hand in hand with the suggestion that black Africans—at home and abroad—were a natural, perfectly exploitable workforce.[41] More important, this organic world economy rested upon a deep and fervent belief that economic, intellectual, technological, and cultural capital all resided in the West—and in American more particularly. This concentration of capital (very broadly conceived) could then be exported in one fashion or another to Haiti, the Philippines, and the American South. The resulting conflation of race, class, and color on a global scale served inevitably to justify the singularly

American experiences in, for example, Haiti, where blackness and whiteness were further entwined in a paternalist colonial setting. Thus the occupation of Haiti was marked by a desperate need to better the infrastructure of Haiti—building railroads, improving roads—in order to facilitate the inroads made by big business as well as to demonstrate the technological, cultural, and intellectual superiority of white Nordic America.[42]

The sense of the world economy as an organic, racialized entity found its clearest expression after the war devastated Europe, and after the Russian Revolution threatened to turn the world upside-down. If race, class, and color were synonymous on the world stage—and if the resultant racial divisions rendered the world economy both organized and functional—then Bolshevism was a very serious threat to the proper economic relationship of the races. "The menace of Bolshevism," thundered Lothrop Stoddard,

> is simply incalculable. Bolshevism is a peril in some ways unprecedented in the world's history. It is not merely a war against our civilization; it is a war of the hand against the brain. For the first time since man was man there is a definite schism between the hand and the head. Every principle which mankind has thus evolved: community of interest, the solidarity of civilization, the dignity of labor, or muscle, of brawn, dominated and illumined by intellect and spirit—all these Bolshevism howls down and tramples in the mud. . . . Bolshevism has vowed the proletarianization of the world . . . [and] seeks to enlist the colored races in its grand assault on civilization.[43]

This remarkable sense of the world as a living, hierarchical, economic system endangered by Bolshevism led directly to the Red Scare of 1919, to the anti-Communist racial violence of the New South, and to Madison Grant's—and America's—negrophobia. Grant's *Conquest of a Continent*, we must remember, was published just five years after the Sixth World Congress of the Communist International suggested that blacks in the American South constituted an oppressed nation deserving of communist support and organization. Fearing an organized Communist menace in America, Grant trembled in *Conquest* at the thought of Jews, Italians, and Negroes breeding Communist mulatto children in Harlem.[44]

This idiom of race and economics emerged from the unprecedented growth of capitalism and its culture during the first thirty years of the twentieth century. The attendant elements and causal factors of this new culture were widespread and of central importance: the explosion of U.S. economic productivity before and after the Great War, America's rapid entry into overseas imperialism as market expansionists, the triumph of Fordism and pervasive faith in business and technology, the widespread idealism of Wilsonian internationalism, the growing sense that the distances that separated cultures around the world were somehow shrinking, and the emergence of multinational business empires.[45] This new economic culture did not merely reflect the deeper, wholly structural changes in the American economy—namely industrialization, the problems of overproduction, and the subsequent celebration of an export economy—for in some sense those structural changes were both productive of this new culture of capitalism and produced by its attendant ideologies as well. In short, America's vibrant and growing economic culture had begun to envision itself as an integral part of a world economy that was organic, racial, and systematic, and most Americans of Grant's generation understood that system using the lingua franca of "race."

In considering Madison Grant's work on race as an integral part of this multileveled history of American capitalism, we can better see the relationship between the ascendancy of a global modern economic culture and the emergence of race (meaning a conflation of color, class, and genetics) as the key "metalanguage" of difference in America. Grant thus becomes far more than "the last Brahmin racist"—he becomes a synecdoche for the new order of things, and his corpus of "musty ethnological ideas" becomes a striking representative of the emergent hegemony of race in the culture of big business in America.[46] For Grant, this new economic culture produced one sweat-drenched nightmare after another. The changed American culture could make threats appear nearer and more dangerous; the "alien menace" of 1916 was replaced—after the National Origins Act, the rise of Bolshevism, and the birth of an unstable peace in a tattered Europe—with a fear of mulattoes posing as Latins and "showing a tendency toward Communism" in Harlem.[47] The Great Migration and the proliferation of a national culture racialized at its bedrock were, of course, central to the emergence of the modern American culture, but the conflation of race, class, and color on a global scale and the concomitant growth of modern capitalism provided an additional impetus to the reordering of American racial discourse. These three factors, then, are of profound importance if we are to understand how we get from 1916 to 1933, from *Passing* to *Conquest*, from nativism to widespread negrophobia in American culture, and towards absolute boundaries between whiteness and blackness. It is no coincidence that these factors also help us recognize the deeper historical importance of Madison Grant.

Notes

This essay has benefited from the comments of the audience of the "Fear of Miscegenation" panel of the NEASA conference, as well as from the criticisms of Michael Adas, John Aveni, William Cobb, Rosanne Currarino, Finis Dunaway, David Levering Lewis, Khalil Muhammad, Neil Miller, Nancy Schultz, and Todd Uhlman.

1. Fairfield Osborn, "Grant, Madison," in *Dictionary of American Biography*, ed. Allen Johnson and Dumas Malone; corrected reprint, ed. Robert Livingston Schuyler and Edward T. James, vol. 22, supplement 2 (New York: Charles Scribner's Sons, 1958), 256.

2. Madison Grant, *The Passing of the Great Race, or, the Racial Basis of European History* (New York: Charles Scribner's Sons, 1916), 16.

3. John Higham, *Strangers in the Land: Patterns of American Nativism, 1860–1925* (1963; reprint, New York: Athenaeum, 1975), 157. The origins of the Grant-as-archetype school of thought can be found in Gunnar Myrdal, *An American Dilemma: The Negro Problem and Modern Democracy* (New York: Harper and Row, 1944), 114; see also Charles C. Alexander, "Prophet of American Racism: Madison Grant and the Nordic Myth," *Phylon* 23, no. 1 (spring 1962): 73–90; and Digby Baltzell, *The Protestant Establishment: Aristocracy & Caste in America* (New York: Random House, 1964), 96–98. In his edited collection of documents on immigration, Oscar Handlin lists Grant—and Grant alone—under the heading "racism"; see *Immigration as a Factor in American History*, ed. Oscar Handlin (Englewood Cliffs, N.J.: Prentice Hall, 1959), ix, 183–85.

4. Hubert Harrison, *When Africa Awakes: The "Inside Story" of the Stirrings and Strivings of the New Negro in the Western World* (1921; reprint, Chesapeake, Md.: ECA Associates Press, 1991), 76–83.

5. Michael Adas and Thomas Holt have suggested that historians should integrate discussions of representation, language, and discourse within the critical exploration of global capitalism, giving rise to a more complex understanding of culture in which race, gender, and class play key roles in both a particular context and a broader socioeconomic medium. See Michael Adas, "Bringing Ideas Back In: Representation and the Comparative Approach to World History," in Philip Pomper, ed., *World Histories: Ideologies, Structures, Identities* (Oxford: Basil Blackwell, 1998), 74–104; Thomas Holt, "Marking: Race, Race-making, and the Writing of History," *American Historical Review* 100 (February 1995): 1–20.

6. For fuller portraits, see Osborn, "Grant, Madison"; Alexander, "Prophet of American Racism"; *The New York Times*, 31 May 1936; John F. Reiger, *American Sportsmen and the Origins of Conservation* (Norman: University of Oklahoma Press, 1986), 114–41; Richard Slotkin, *Gunfighter Nation: The Myth of the Frontier in Twentieth Century America* (New York: Harper Collins, 1992), 29–62, 198–200.

7. Hofstadter, *Age of Reform: From Bryan to FDR* (New York: Knopf, 1955). Hofstadter's work has been criticized as reductive and ahistorical. Progressivism is now understood to be a complex, multifaceted movement, which contained contradictory elements. Grant, however, continued to speak in the terms Hofstadter describes well into the 1920s, and we would do well to understand immigration reform in the 1920s as the embodiment of the version of Progressivism that Hofstadter describes. For implicit and explicit criticisms of Hofstadter, see Gabriel Kolko, *The Triumph of Conservatism: A Reinterpretation of American History, 1900–1916* (New York: Free Press, 1963); David Thelen, "Social Tensions and the Origins of Progressivism," *Journal of American History* 56 (September 1969): 323–47.

8. Haraway, "Teddy Bear Patriarchy: Taxidermy in the Garden of Eden, New York City, 1908–1936," in *Cultures of United States Imperialism,* ed. Amy Kaplan and Donald Pease (Durham, N.C.: Duke University Press, 1993), 237–91. For another intriguing treatment of the role of institutions in defining social relations in terms of "race" and "nation," see the chapter titled "Census, Map, Museum," in Benedict Anderson, *Imagined Communities: Reflections on the Origin and Spread of Nationalism,* rev. ed. (London: Verso, 1991), 163–85.

9. In addition to serving as chairman of the New York Zoological Society for many years, Grant was an esteemed member of the Immigration Restriction League, the Society for the Preservation of the Fauna of the British Empire, the Eugenics Research Association, the American Geographical Society, the Galton Society, the American Museum of Natural History, and the Boone and Crockett Club.

10. Grant, *Passing of the Great Race,* 227, 29, 20, 228.

11. D. H. Lawrence, *Studies in Classic American Literature* (1923; reprint, New York: Viking Press, 1964), 51. It is precisely the sense that race loyalty had become, in Grant's work, more important than any other group loyalty that, John Higham feels, marks *Passing* as "racism." Such an argument rests on an unfortunate conflation of Anglo-Saxonism with nationalism and not racism, thus absurdly relieving that form of chauvinistic thinking from any charges of racism. See Higham, *Strangers in the Land,* 157.

12. Grant, "Restriction of Immigration: Racial Aspects," *Journal of the National Institute of Social Sciences* 7 (1 August 1921): 54.

13. Grant, *Passing of the Great Race,* 230.

14. Osborn, Preface, *The Passing of the Great Race, or, the Racial Basis of European History,* 2nd ed. (New York: Scribner's, 1917), xiii.

15. For works which argue for the centrality of these two groups for the nineteenth century, see David Roediger, *Wages of Whiteness* (London: Verso, 1991); Noel Ignatiev, *How the Irish Became White* (New York: Routledge, 1996); and Eric Lott, *Love and Theft* (New York: Oxford University Press, 1993).

16. Thomas Gossett depicts Grant's work as an attempt to popularize Anglo-

Saxon notions of "civilization" through the inclusion of the Irish. See Gossett, *Race: The History of an Idea in America* (Dallas, Tex.: Southern Methodist University Press, 1963), 361; Grant, *Passing of the Great Race*, 53–58, 182, 183, and the chart facing 123. For another example of the widespread and ultimately final inclusion of the Irish as absolutely white, see Sinclair Kennedy, *The Pan-Angles: A Consideration of the Federation of the Seven English-Speaking Nations* (New York: Longmans, Green, 1914), 140. For a suggestive treatment of the ambiguities of "race" in the 1890s and 1900s, see Matthew Frye Jacobson, "Between Whiteness and Anglo-Saxondom: Irish-American Nationalism and the Crosscurrents of 'Race,' " unpublished manuscript, 1995. See also Jacobson, *Special Sorrows: The Diasporic Imaginations of Irish, Polish, and Jewish Immigrants in the United States* (Cambridge, Mass.: Harvard University Press, 1995), 177–216.

17. Grant, *Passing of the Great Race*, 88.

18. Michael Rogin, " 'The Sword Became a Flashing Vision,' " in *Ronald Reagan, the Movie* (Berkeley and Los Angeles: University of California Press, 1987).

19. The best discussion of the general fervor of postwar superpatriotism is still Higham, *Strangers in the Land;* see also Alan Kraut, *Silent Travelers: Germs, Genes, and the "Immigrant Menace"* (New York: Basic Books, 1994). On the widespread national popularity of "race-consciousness," see Nancy MacLean, *Behind the Mask of Chivalry* (New York: Oxford University Press, 1991).

20. Interestingly, the Virginia legislation deliberately evaded evidence of miscegenation between native Americans and white Southerners, a fact Grant found quite amusing; see Grant to Charles Davenport, 8 April 1924, Correspondence Files—Madison Grant, Folder 4, Charles Davenport Papers, American Philosophical Society (hereafter CDAPS).

21. For evidence of Grant's involvement, see the various correspondence in "Grant, Madison," CDAPS, folder 4.

22. Grant to Maxwell Perkins, 3 May 1927, Author File—Madison Grant, Charles Scribner's Sons Archives, Princeton University, box 67, file 1 (hereafter SA).

23. Grant, *The Conquest of a Continent, or, the Expansion of the Races in America* (New York: Scribner's, 1933), 281.

24. Grant, publicity comment on pamphlet promoting a second edition of Earnest Sevier Cox's *White America*, no date, SA, 67:63. Grant had tried to convince Scribner's to publish the original edition of *White America* in 1924 to no avail; Grant to Perkins, 7 November 1924, SA, 67:3.

25. Grant, "Closing the Floodgates," in *The Alien in Our Midst, or, "Selling Our Birthright for a Mess of Pottage,"* ed. Madison Grant and Charles Stewart Davidson (New York: Galton Publishing Co, 1930), 23.

26. In articulating a fear of a "mulatto menace," Grant was giving voice to a crucial aspect of American racial thought. For a clever and speculative

history of thoughts on "the mulatto," see Joel Williamson, *New People: Miscegenation and Mulattoes in the United States* (1980; reprint, Baton Rouge: Louisiana State University Press, 1995), esp. 61–186.

27. David Nasaw, *Going Out: The Rise and Fall of Public Amusements* (New York: Basic Books, 1993).

28. See, for example, the immensely popular Edgar Rice Burroughs, *Tarzan of the Apes* (New York: A. L. Burt, 1914).

29. The phrase is from a speech by Teddy Roosevelt. In addition to Nasaw, see Robert Rydell, *All the World's a Fair: Visions of Empire at American International Expositions, 1876–1916* (Chicago, Ill.: University of Chicago Press, 1984); Rydell, "The Culture of Imperial Abundance: World's Fairs in the Making of American Culture," in *Consuming Visions: Accumulation and Display of Goods in America, 1880–1920,* ed. Simon Bronner (New York: W. W. Norton, 1989), 191–216; and Jackson Lears, "Beyond Veblen: Rethinking Consumer Culture in America," in *Consuming Visions,* 91–96.

30. Between 1910 and 1920, Chicago's black population exploded by 50,000. The black population in Manhattan increased 80 percent between 1910 and 1920, as over 315,000 African-Americans migrated to the Northeast and Mid-Atlantic states alone. In Chicago, where the population more than doubled to 109,458 in 1920, the summer of 1919 proved to be the moment that racial tensions boiled over as white "ethnics" and blacks fought what amounted to guerrilla warfare in that city; see Louise Venable Kennedy, *The Negro Peasant Turns Cityward: Effects of Recent Migration to Northern Centers* (New York: Columbia University Press, 1930), 23–40, esp. 34, 37; Daniel M. Johnson and Rex R. Campbell, eds., *Black Migration in America: A Social Demographic History* (Durham, N. C.: Duke University Press, 1981), 75–77. On the Chicago race riot in the context of black migration, see William M. Tuttle Jr., *Race Riot: Chicago in the Red Summer of 1919* (New York: Athenaeum, 1970), esp. 32, 49, 60, 257. On the general characteristics of black migration leading up to and during the war years, see Robert Higgs, *Competition and Coercion: Blacks in the American Economy* (Cambridge, Mass.: Harvard University Press, 1977); Florette Henry, *Black Migration: Movement North, 1900–1920* (New York: Anchor Books, 1975); and Darlene Clark Hine, "Black Migration to the Urban Midwest: The Gender Dimension, 1915–1945," in *The Great Migration in Historical Perspective: New Dimensions of Race, Class, and Gender,* ed. Joe William Trotter (Bloomington: Indiana University Press, 1991), 127–46.

31. John M. Barry, *Rising Tide: The Great Mississippi Flood of 1927 and How It Changed America* (New York: Simon and Schuster, 1997), 412–22.

32. Stoddard had written with great fear of the impact of the French Revolution in the Caribbean, and the general impression among racists was that West Indian blacks were politically dangerous. See Stoddard, *The French Revolution in San Domingo* (New York: Scribner's, 1910). On the migration of Caribbean immigrants and the resultant tensions, see Emma Watkins-

Owens, *Blood Relations: Caribbean Immigrants and the Harlem Community, 1900–1930* (Bloomington: Indiana University Press, 1996).

33. Spear, *Black Chicago*, 71–89, quote on p. 208; see also St. Claire Drake and Horace Cayton, *Black Metropolis: A Study of Negro Life in a Northern City* (1945; reprint, Chicago, Ill.: University of Chicago Press, 1993), 78–83.

34. In 1928, Al Smith—an Irish Catholic "wet"—secretly courted the African-American vote in Manhattan, and in 1932, the year in which Grant was writing *The Conquest of a Continent*, an astounding 50 percent of African-Americans living in Grant's Manhattan—a larger percentage than any other northern city—voted Democratic; see Nancy Weiss, *Farewell to the Party of Lincoln: Black Politics in the Age of FDR* (Princeton, N.J.: Princeton University Press, 1983), 3–32, 180–208; Harold F. Gosnell, *Negro Politicians: The Rise of Negro Politics in Chicago* (1935; reprint, Chicago, Ill.: University of Chicago Press, 1967).

35. Grant, *Conquest of a Continent*, 349.

36. The remarkable phrase "hypnotic divisions" is taken from novelist Jean Toomer. See Toomer to Suzanne La Follete, 22 September 1930, Jean Toomer Papers, Beineke Rare Book and Manuscript Library, Yale University, box 6: folder 191.

37. Grant, *Conquest of a Continent*, 353.

38. Davenport to Grant, 3 January 1920, CDAPS, folder 3.

39. I am borrowing this clever phrase from Bram Dijkstra, *Evil Sisters: The Threat of Female Sexuality and the Cult of Manhood* (New York: Knopf, 1996), 248.

40. See Adas, "Bringing Ideas Back In"; Adas, *Machines as the Measure of Men: Science, Technology, and Ideologies of Western Dominance* (Ithaca, N.Y.: Cornell University Press, 1989), 199–265, 292–342, 402–18.

41. Stoddard, *Rising Tide of Color against White World Supremacy* (New York: Scribner's, 1920), 90–93.

42. Hans Schmidt, *The United States Occupation of Haiti, 1915–1934* (New Brunswick, N.J.: Rutgers University Press, 1971). For a sense of how this "modernization" impulse could, in turn, buttress notions of racial superiority, see Adas, *Machines*, 402–18.

43. Stoddard, *Rising Tide of Color*, 220.

44. *Conquest of a Continent*, 283. For the rapid growth of black communism, see Mark Naison, *Communists in Harlem during the Depression* (Urbana: University of Illinois Press, 1983); Robin D. G. Kelley, *Hammer and How: Alabama Communists during the Great Depression* (Chapel Hill: University of North Carolina Press, 1990).

45. For a discussion of these issues, see Alfred D. Chandler, *The Visible Hand: The Managerial Revolution in American Business* (Cambridge, Mass.: Harvard University Press, 1977); Terry Smith, *Making the Modern: Industry, Art, and Design in America* (Chicago, Ill.: University of Chicago Press,

1993); Mira Wilkins, *The Maturing of Multinational Enterprise: American Business Abroad from 1914 to 1970* (Cambridge, Mass.: Harvard University Press, 1974), 3–63; Slotkin, *Gunfighter Nation.*

46. Baltzell, *Protestant Establishment*, 96; Harrison, *When Africa Awakes*, 142.
47. Grant, *Conquest of a Continent*, 283.

Re-gendering the Enemy
Orientalist Discourse and National Character Studies during World War II

Mari Yoshihara

World War II prompted Americans to refine their understanding of Asians as an undifferentiated mass of an alien race. After the attack on Pearl Harbor in 1941, it became imperative for Americans to be able to distinguish between the "evil" Japanese and the Chinese "heroes risen" against the Japanese.[1] The public media put out sensational and propagandistic calls for distinction between the two groups, exemplified by articles such as "How to Tell Your Friends from the Japs."[2] On a more strategic level, government agencies and the military mobilized academics to study and analyze enemy behavior for the purposes of military planning, psychological warfare, and policy-making for the postwar period. The projects of these specialists—mostly anthropologists, sociologists, and psychiatrists—in developing what later came to be called "culture and personality studies" or "national character studies" differed from earlier American efforts at understanding Asia in that these purported to be "scientific" in their findings, although wartime circumstances and political objectives inevitably shaped the nature of these studies.[3] It was also significant that this first institutionalized attempt to understand a modern culture—as opposed to the dominant anthropological tradition of studying "primitive" cultures—emerged out of wartime imperatives.

The Chrysanthemum and the Sword, a study of Japanese national character by the prominent anthropologist Ruth Benedict, was the most influential product of this wartime project.[4] The publication of *The Chrysanthemum and the Sword* in 1946 came at a critical moment in the history of U.S.-Japan relations. Before the book first came out, studies on Japanese character were scarce in the United States. Aside from more specialized books and articles written for an academic or intellectual audience, there were few writings about Japanese culture available to the general American reader. The awareness about and interest in the Japanese psyche were heightened by the war and created a receptive audience for Benedict's work. In an accessible language and style, *The Chrysanthemum and the Sword* explained aspects of Japan that were foreign to American readers, such as the role of the emperor in nationalist ideology and daily life, structures of interpersonal relations, and moral codes and methods of social control. In the final chapter, Benedict offered suggestions for the treatment of postwar Japan under occupation.

This essay examines Benedict's interventions in the gendered discourse of American Orientalism by looking at the process by which Benedict constructed her model of Japanese national character and the theoretical framework on race, culture, and gender shared by Benedict and her contemporary anthropologists. I will demonstrate that *The Chrysanthemum and the Sword* reinforced the dominant Western notion of Japan as emasculated and feminized through a rather different process from the preceding approaches to Japan which focused on the feminine. First, I argue that Benedict "feminized" Japanese culture not by looking at women and the feminine spheres of life, but by looking at the masculine. Second, I demonstrate that Benedict, like her peer scholars of national character, used the paradigm of "culture" to explain Japanese gender relations and sexuality. Although Benedict's uses of the concepts of culture and gender differed from the approaches taken by many other American Orientalists, her paradigm of culture and the place she assigned to gender within that paradigm validated and naturalized the existing association between Japanese culture and particular notions of gender and sexuality. As a consequence, the anthropologists' replacement of racial determinism with the culture paradigm brought about the familiar result of gendering the Other.

The Gendering of Japan in
The Chrysanthemum and the Sword

The title of the book, *The Chrysanthemum and the Sword*, epitomizes what Benedict considered to be most symbolic of Japanese culture. For someone who has some familiarity with Japanese history and culture, it is easy to guess what the metaphors of the chrysanthemum and the sword signify. The chrysanthemum is the symbol of the Japanese imperial family, and the sword represents the feudal system of *samurai* and the ethics and aesthetics of the *samurai* way of life. They are also gendered metaphors. The chrysanthemum is associated with femininity, fragility, and delicacy, the sword with masculinity, strength, and aggressiveness. In many ways, the content of the book proves that these are apt metaphors for symbolizing different—and seemingly contradictory—aspects of Japanese culture, and that the gendered associations with the two symbols are appropriate. However, when one pays closer attention to the way in which Benedict unfolds these metaphors and their function in the overall scheme of the book, it becomes clear that the gendered meanings inherent in the title are more complex than a simple binary between femininity and masculinity.

Benedict refers to the metaphors of the chrysanthemum and the sword only toward the end of the book. She brings up the chrysanthemum metaphor in her discussion of an autobiography of a Japanese woman. A daughter of a prestigious *samurai* family is sent to learn English at a mission school in Tokyo, where her teacher allows each girl to have a plot of wild ground and any seeds she asks for. The plant-as-you-please garden gives her a "wholly new feeling of personal right," and she decides to plant potatoes while all other girls plant flowers. She juxtaposes this "sense of reckless freedom which this absurd act gave [her]" with the carefully calculated and tamed aesthetic of the Japanese garden, in which the chrysanthemum is grown in pots with tiny wire racks inserted in the living flower.[5] In Benedict's account, the chrysanthemum stands for the meticulous constraints and rules governing Japanese life and its lack of freedom and naturalness. In prescribing new norms of freedom for Japanese society, Benedict advises that "chrysanthemums can be beautiful without wire racks and such drastic pruning."[6] Thus, the chrysanthemum is not simply a symbol of delicate and fragile femininity associated with the Japanese woman author of the autobiography, but also represents the intensely rigid and drastic forms of discipline and social order which constitute, as I will show later, the masculinist ideal/ideology and the male spheres of Japanese life. In its way, the chrysanthemum is also the ultimate masculinist symbol in that it represents the epitome of Japan's "old" order, the imperial family. By seeing the emperor as the "father symbol" of the Japanese nation, Benedict and other scholars understood the chrysanthemum to stand for the man who represents and governs the nation. However, her prescription ultimately curtails Japan's aggressive masculinist symbol. At the end of the book, she legitimizes the maintenance of the emperor in postwar Japan under the tutelage of the United States administration. By using the symbol of the chrysanthemum to suggest that Japan's masculinist ideology of imperialism will be defeated by the American notion of freedom and democracy, Benedict not only feminizes Japan but also feminizes the *masculine* Japan.

The metaphor of the sword also carries complex gendered meanings. Benedict argues that the Japanese virtue of self-responsibility, symbolized by the owner's maintenance of the sword's shining brilliance, can help the Japanese maintain an even keel as they make the transition to a greater freedom:

> As the wearer of a sword is responsible for its shining brilliancy, so each man must accept responsibility for the outcome of his acts. He must acknowledge and accept all natural consequences of his weakness, his lack of persistence, his ineffectualness. Self-responsibility is far more drastically interpreted in Japan than in free America. In this Japanese sense the sword becomes, not a symbol of aggression, but a simile of ideal and self-responsible man. . . . Today the Japanese have proposed 'to lay aside the sword' in the Western sense. In their Japanese sense, they have an abiding strength in their concern with keeping an inner sword free from the rust which always threatens it. In their phraseology of virtue the sword is a symbol they can keep in a freer and more peaceful world.[7]

On the one hand, Benedict here validates Japan's masculinist ethos of self-responsibility associated with the sword. But on the other hand, Japan's postwar decision (made by the Americans) "to lay aside the sword"—that is, to demilitarize—is taken as an act of emasculation. By allowing Japan to keep its masculinist symbol of the sword as "not a symbol of aggression but a simile of ideal and self-responsible man," Benedict makes demilitarization less demeaning to the Japanese and gives a new meaning to the masculinist symbol.

Thus, Benedict genders and re-genders Japan in several different ways. She affirms existing notions of Japan's femininity and hypermasculinity with the metaphor of the chrysanthemum and the sword, but she also shows that they do not form a simple, parallel binary. She emasculates and feminizes Japan, first by suggesting that Japan's masculinist ideology will surrender in the face of the Western spirit of freedom, democracy, and independence; and then by taking away Japan's masculine symbol. She assigns new meaning to both the chrysanthemum and the sword by allowing Japan to retain the emperor and to govern itself under the U.S. administration. An examination of Benedict's purposes, sources, methodology, and analysis offers further insight into the process of gendering and re-gendering epitomized by her book's symbolic title.

"Assignment—Japan": Benedict's Project in the Office of War Information

The writing of *The Chrysanthemum and the Sword* came relatively late in Benedict's career, when she was already known as a prominent anthropologist in the United States. Benedict's involvement in the study of Japanese character was part of her job at the Office of War Information (OWI), where she worked from 1943 to 1945. The OWI was established by executive order in June 1942 for the purpose of disseminating news about the war on the homefront and spreading propaganda overseas to help with the war effort.[8] Benedict was recruited to be the head analyst in the Cultural Analysis and Research Division of the Bureau of Overseas Intelligence. In June 1944, she was assigned to the study of Japan in the Foreign Morale Analysis Division (FMAD), which brought together about thirty staff members, including anthropologists, psychologists, psychiatrists, sociologists, political scientists, and Japan specialists.[9] Benedict, who was *not* an Asian specialist and had no background or training in either Japanese studies or language, would have less than a year to research the Japanese before their final surrender.

Wartime circumstances severely restricted the sources and methods Benedict could use for her study; to be sure, the nature of her sources and the ways in which she treated them greatly influenced her analysis. She used three types of evidence in researching and understanding Japanese culture. First, she conducted interviews of so-called "native informants," or Japanese who were currently in the United States, Japanese Americans, or non-Japanese people who had lived in Japan. Second, she studied several dozen films written and produced in Japan. Finally, she reviewed various writings from and about Japan, written by both Japanese and Westerners. Each of these sources had its strengths and limitations as anthropological evidence; while Benedict was aware of some of these features, she was not aware of all of them.

The most critical, although certainly not the most extensive, of Benedict's sources were the interviews she and her colleagues had with Japanese informants. As her following remarks in *The Chrysanthemum and the Sword* demonstrate, Benedict considered these interviews a crucial aspect of her research, which validated it as scholarly anthropological work:

> As a cultural anthropologist, in spite of these major difficulties, I had confidence in certain techniques and postulates which could be used. At least I did not have to forego the anthropologist's great reliance upon face-to-face contact with the people he is studying.

There were plenty of Japanese in this country who had been reared
in Japan and I could ask them about the concrete facts of their own
experiences, find out how they judged them, fill in from their descriptions many gaps in our knowledge which as an anthropologist
I believed were essential in understanding any culture. Other social scientists who were studying Japan were using libraries, ana-
lyzing past events or statistics, following developments in the written or spoken word of Japanese propaganda. I had confidence that
many of these answers they sought were embedded in the rules and
values of Japanese culture and could be found more satisfactorily
by exploring that culture with people who had really lived it.[10]

Although it is unclear from the documents how many of these interviews Benedict actually conducted herself and how many came second-
hand to her as reports that her colleagues had submitted, Benedict's
handwritten notes suggest that she did conduct a number of interviews
herself in 1944 and 1945, and the experience provided her with professional confidence and scholarly credibility.[11] While she acknowledges the
limited access she had to the object of her study, she does not spell out
what exactly she meant by "people who had really lived [Japanese cul-
ture]." Benedict shows no concern with the sampling of the interviewees, although her informants were varied in their positions and relationships to Japanese culture. Some were Japanese prisoners of war, some
were Japanese or Japanese Americans who worked for the OWI, and
some were Americans who had previously lived in Japan. Benedict does
not differentiate among these interviewees' social, political, and ideological positions or comment on their mental state at the time of the interviews. Furthermore, she does not theorize the relationship between the
"concrete facts of their own experiences" and "how they judged them."
She seems to assume that the "face-to-face contact with the people
[she] is studying" leads her to see the "rules and values of Japanese
culture" and validates the anthropological credibility of her project.

Another group of sources available to Benedict were films produced
in Japan. Although one would expect that the visual images presented
in the films would have given her a sense of Japanese life unavailable
from literature and interviews, Benedict does not comment on any aspect of their visual content. Rather, the narratives and themes of the
films concerned her more. Describing how she discussed the films with
Japanese friends who "saw the hero and the heroine and the villain as
the Japanese see them, not as [she] saw them," Benedict says:

When I was at sea, it was clear that they were not. The plots, the
motivations were not as I saw them, but they made sense in terms
of the way the movie was constructed. As with the novels, there

was much more difference than met the eye between what they meant to me and what they meant to the Japanese-reared. Some of these Japanese were quick to come to the defense of Japanese conventions and some hated everything Japanese. It is hard to say from which group I learned most. In the intimate picture they gave of how one regulates one's life in Japan they agreed, whether they accepted it gladly or rejected it with bitterness.[12]

During Benedict's research, the Office of Strategic Services surveyed twenty Japanese films, and Benedict studied the report of the survey. The researchers' concern with Japanese wartime mentality and the films' propaganda value shaped the ways in which the films were classified and described. The films' "basic themes" were categorized as the "dominant theme," which is "the spirit of sacrifice or the subjection of self to pattern"; "theme of filial piety," "theme of the faithful wife," "theme of patriotism," and "theme of Japan's role in Greater East Asia." The "psychological content" was divided into "attitude towards life," "attitude towards love," "attitude towards fatherland and Emperor," "attitude towards war," "attitude towards death," and "attitude towards religion."[13] In addition to such a politically charged approach to the films, Benedict's interest in "how one regulates one's life in Japan" also shaped her reading of the films in her own research.

The most extensive group of sources Benedict relied upon in her unique anthropological project was the literature of and about Japan. Anthropology was still considered to be primarily a study of "primitive" cultures, many of which had no written language. Studying a culture like Japan—which had had a written tradition for more than a thousand years and whose history, literature, art, and politics had been written about by hundreds of Westerners—was a relatively new project not only for Benedict but for anthropology as a discipline. Benedict says in *The Chrysanthemum and the Sword* that "[t]he vast literature on the Japanese and the great number of good Occidental observers who have lived in Japan gave me an advantage which no anthropologist has when he goes to the Amazon headwaters or the New Guinea highlands to study a non-literate tribe."[14] Benedict studied an amazingly wide range of literature, written mostly between the turn of the century and the 1940s, including travel narratives, histories of Japanese religion, novels, myths and folklore, sociological studies, military and strategic analyses, and psychological studies of sexual behavior.[15]

While the wide-ranging literature she sampled greatly informed Benedict's study, her use of written materials as a resource had a basic limitation: the language. Benedict did not read Japanese; therefore her reading was restricted either to works written in English or to Japanese works that had been translated into English. This limitation made Benedict a direct heir of existing Western discourse about Japan. The English-language sources included, although were not limited to, works by male intellectual "authorities" on Japan, such as William Griffis, Lafcadio Hearn, Percival Lowell, Ernest Fenollosa, Ezra Pound, and George Sansom. Recent sociological, historical, or strategic studies of Japanese society had been written by scholars such as E. H. Norman, Hugh Borton, Miriam Farley, Sidney Gulick, Harley Farnsworth Mac-Nair, and Lt. Col. Paul W. Thompson. The available Japanese literature that had been translated into English and was deemed classically and authentically Japanese by Westerners included mostly works by canonical male writers and intellectuals, such as Natsume Soseki, Kikuchi Kan, Nitobe Inazo, Tanizaki Junïchiro, and Watsuji Tetsuro. Benedict's inability to reach beyond the existing English-language sources prevented her from breaking free of the dominant discourse about Japan.

These limitations on Benedict's sources and methods significantly affected her analysis of Japanese culture. Later critics have pointed out and critiqued these methodological problems that undermined the validity and credibility of Benedict's accounts.[16] Practically every work that discusses *The Chrysanthemum and the Sword,* even the ones that give a more tempered and favorable view of Benedict's work, notes that it was a "study of culture at a distance," and that Benedict lacked both the experience of doing fieldwork in Japan and Japanese language skills. Many critics have also been concerned with the so-called "accuracy" and "authenticity" question. They argue that Benedict's representation of Japan is inaccurate, skewed, or dated and thus lacks validity as an account of contemporary Japanese culture. Japanese scholars and intellectuals, who were invested in the "accurate" portrayal of Japan in the eyes of the foreigners, raised most of these criticisms.[17] Still, these critiques miss the point. As a prominent American anthropologist, Benedict had a specific "assignment" to fulfill, and, mindful of that goal, she took the best advantage she could of the sources and tools to which she had access. Thus, rather than criticize Benedict for not using the sources and methods she had no access to, one should assess the context in which the specific sources became available to her, the discourse in which such sources were embedded, her treatment of the sources, and her processes of theorizing Japanese culture.

Feminizing Japan by Looking
at the Masculine

The purpose of Benedict's study, along with her sources and methods, resulted in a narrative that was full of gendered meanings and symbolisms, as the title of the book implies. What was unique about Benedict's study, however, was not that she produced a gendered narrative about Japanese culture—gendered narratives about Japanese culture existed long before Benedict's—but that she took a rather different path from the one taken by many other Orientalists to reach the same conclusions about the feminized Japan. Rather than feminizing Japan by focusing on women, gender relations, or the domestic sphere in Japan, she feminized Japan by looking at the masculine. She constructed her model of the normative Japanese character based on male figures and mapped her pattern of Japanese social order based on male, public spheres of life; she then characterized them as deviant from Western norms of masculinity, which are associated with individualism, democracy, and freedom. Benedict feminized Japan by diagnosing the Japanese male as insufficiently masculine.

Benedict's construction of the normative Japanese character based on male figures largely resulted from the gendered nature of her evidence, which was most apparent in the gender composition of her "native informants." Of the existing documents on these interviews, all but one (which is a report of an interview with a Japanese couple) record interviews with men. Of this informant pool, particularly important were the Japanese soldiers who either became prisoners of war or deserted their troops. Although Benedict by no means drew all of her arguments from these interviews, it would be safe to say that the gender composition and social position of her informant pool significantly affected her narrative about Japanese culture, particularly with regard to Japan's nationalist/imperialist ideology and the Japanese attitude toward the emperor.

To supplement the limited number of interviews she conducted, Benedict also consulted the "community analyses" written by anthropologists working in Japanese internment camps. Under the auspices of the War Relocation Authority, a group of anthropologists investigated social structures and behavior patterns of the Japanese in relocation camps on the West Coast. This Japanese American Evacuation and Resettlement Study (JAERS), under the directorship of sociologist Dorothy S. Thomas, produced several important works on Japanese culture, the most notable of which was Weston La Barre's "Some Observations on Character Structure in the Orient: The Japanese."[18] Whereas La Barre's study lacks self-reflexivity and consideration of the specific circumstances under which the research was conducted, Alexander Leighton, who conducted a community analysis at the Poston Japanese Relocation Center in the Colorado River Valley, produced a more contextualized study which shows sensitivity to the political and social situation of the camps.[19] In addition to the tensions in the camps which situated the community analysts in a particular social position, Leighton raises the issue of gender, which also affected the contours of his project. He mentions that while the anthropologists involved in the Poston project included women, such as Laura Thompson and Elisabeth Colson, the Japanese evacuee staff, trained to penetrate the community in a manner impossible for white project members, included only two women.[20] Although there is no record documenting that Benedict visited the Japanese internment camps and/or interviewed the internees herself, she did rely on the WRA's community analysis surveys as a substitute for fieldwork, and the gendered nature of these surveys certainly affected her analysis.

But the gendering of Japanese character in Benedict's model was also a result of the theoretical assumptions and analytical processes shared by the contemporary scholars of national character. The most illustrative example of such assumptions and processes can be seen in Geoffrey Gorer's manuscript, "Japanese Character Structure," which was the single most influential analysis of Japanese national character presented before Benedict's study. Gorer's study was "a first attempt to give a systematic and dynamic description of the average Japanese character structure, with the aim of giving direction to future propaganda programmes by radio, insofar as these may be addressed to the Japanese."[21]

Gorer's theoretical assumptions reveal the gendered way in which national character studies, including Benedict's work, constructed the "average," "normative" Japanese character. First of all, Gorer saw the "typical" Japanese as being male. In the beginning of the manuscript, he justifies this model by arguing that

> Owing to the very considerable political and social subordination of women, men are the predominant formers of opinion and carriers of the culture. To a very large degree, Japan can be considered a "male culture." The contrast in typical character between men and women is very strong; it is above all the men's character which is desirable to understand in the present situation.[22]

The "political and social subordination of women" and the social and cultural divisions according to gender were certainly a visible reality in Japan. However, differential social norms for men and women, gender divisions of labor, and sexism in Japanese society themselves do not validate Gorer's conclusion that the portrayal of the typical Japanese should be based on a male character. Gorer's model of Japanese character is based on the premise that the objective of the study is to outline the characters of the male Japanese who shaped and embodied the ideologies of the public sphere. Such a premise was passed on to the next cohort of scholars of national character, including Benedict.

Gorer not only used a male figure as the normative Japanese individual, but also based his analysis of Japanese social order upon male social relations. Reflecting Freudian psychoanalysis and child-development theories which dominated national character studies in this period, Gorer describes the ways in which Japanese boys are disciplined, rewarded, and punished, and argues that

> The male universe gives assurance and safety, but little indulgence; it administers the heavy punishments for deviance, controls the sanctions and all the secondary rewards. One must be compliant (fit oneself in) with the patterns of the male universe. Resistance and aggression are dangerous.[23]

He then goes on to portray the female world in Japan as the one which is controlled or dominated by male aggression. According to Gorer, the female world is sentimentally loved, ill-treated, and despised—so despised that no male wishes to identify himself with it.[24] Based upon this premise of the sexual division of character and the assumption that social institutions and political organizations are explicable through the psychology of the individual, Gorer attributes the reasons for the Japanese aggression in war to "every Japanese man['s] urge to *control the environment.*"[25]

In addition to constructing the normative model of Japanese national character out of the male figure and the male sphere of social order, Gorer uses a highly gendered and sexualized perspective and language in his argumentation as well. He makes his most interesting point in his account of Japan's characterization of other races and societies in sexual terms. Rather than ascribing gendered and sexualized meaning to Japanese culture, Gorer turns the model around and claims that "to the contemporary Japanese other races and societies are viewed as either male or female; as groups to be followed and obeyed implicitly, or as groups to be forced to yield by aggression or threats of aggression." In the nineteenth century, according to Gorer, Japan saw England and America as indubitably male, and therefore yielded to and copied them as much as possible; but that since the turn of the century, with the defeat of the Russians and subsequent developments in international relations, the Japanese called into question the "virility" of the whites. Japan perceived that "the Anglo-Saxons showed all the female characteristics," and finally, with the attack on Pearl Harbor, the virility of the Anglo-Saxons as a group was definitely undermined.[26] Gorer's account of the Japanese "sexing" of races and nations obscured the fact that Americans and Europeans used the same gendered and sexualized frameworks and stereotypes in talking about Japan, and that Gorer himself was doing precisely that. Attributing such modes of sexualized categorization solely to the Japanese allowed him to officially justify American characterization of the Japanese in sexualized terms:

> Only military defeat at the hands of the Anglo Saxons will convince the Japanese that their "sexing" of the nations was incorrect; but if we wish for decent treatment of prisoners during the war, and a cooperative population in defeated Japan after, it is essential that by every symbolic means possible we should attempt to reestablish ourselves in male roles. This means the complete abandonment of threats, cajolery and appeals to pity, which all indicate the female; and adopting instead the calm certainty of obedience, sanctioned by mockery, which indicated the male.[27]

By calling for the retrieval of western masculinity, Gorer can prescribe and legitimize American military and political domination over Japan. While he critiques the gendered and sexualized characterization of races and nations by the Japanese, Gorer himself assigns explicitly gendered and sexualized meanings not only to individual behavior and interpersonal relations but also to U.S.-Japan relations. His agenda here is to reassert American masculinity and to reestablish the feminine—and thus subordinate—position of the Japanese.

Although Benedict's relationship to the psychoanalytical and developmental approaches was somewhat ambivalent, she was part of the contemporary discourse on Japan in which such gendered perspectives and language were prevalent. Benedict used similarly gendered assumptions and argumentations in her account of Japanese culture, and constructed its model based on a male figure and male sphere of life. Furthermore, by stressing the undemocratic, anti-individualist aspects of Japanese male culture, Benedict implicitly suggests that Japanese culture deviates from Western notions of masculinity.

At the core of Benedict's "pattern" of Japanese culture was an intricate social structure of hierarchy, in which individuals have their "proper place" and act according to their differential "obligations" to other members of the social matrix. Benedict saw this hierarchical social arrangement as the most Japanese element of Japanese culture, and interpreted personal behavior, the cultural ethos, social structures, and historical development through this lens. Early in her book, Benedict states that

For a long, long time Japan will necessarily keep some of her in-
bred attitudes and one of the most important of these is her faith
and confidence in hierarchy. It is alien to equality-loving Americans but it is nevertheless necessary for us to understand what Japan meant by hierarchy and what advantages she has learned to
connect with it.[28]

With each example—ranging from bowing practices to filial piety, from
emperor worship to Japan's military aggression in Asia—Benedict constructed a Japanese "pattern" of hierarchy.

Her interest in the Japanese system of hierarchy, compounded by the
book's purpose of studying wartime ideology and individual mentality,
led her attention particularly to the most hierarchical and most masculinist sphere of Japanese life: men in military service and their attitude toward the emperor. In the chapter outlining Japanese behavior
during the war, she describes how the Japanese prioritize spirit over
material circumstances, providing a rather extreme example that "[i]n
battle, spirit surmounted even the physical fact of death." She describes
the tale of a hero-pilot: he had been fatally shot in his chest and had
been dead for quite some time, yet his spirit drove him to report to the
Commanding Officer at Headquarters, and he dropped to the ground as
soon as he made the report.[29] Much of the chapter is also devoted to the
discussion of the Japanese attitude toward the emperor. Using anecdotal
examples of military and civilian men who willingly died in the name
of the emperor, Benedict depicts how the emperor "was all things to
all men," and that the emperor was "inseparable from Japan."[30] This
unconditional and unrestricted loyalty to the emperor, which seemed
to Westerners to be conspicuously at odds with Japanese criticisms of
all other persons and groups, epitomized Benedict's view of Japanese
culture.

Benedict constructed her model of normative Japanese character and
mentality based upon a figure of the soldier ready to die for the emperor
or male civilians who were equally loyal to the emperor and the nation-
alist/imperialist ideology. The archetype is most vividly manifested
through the interview records of Suetsugu Shoji.[31] A twenty-six-year-
old single man from Hokkaido who had not graduated from upper gram-
mar school and had been a welder, Suetsugu had been in service for four
years in China, Malay, and Burma, where he was captured in May 1944.
Suetsugu's answers to the interrogations show what was to become
Benedict's normative Japanese attitude toward the war. He regarded the
capture as "a discredit to the Emperor." "*And* he was also shamed," the

reporter stressed, "because his captors were the inferior Chinese." He maintained his faith in victory, the purposes of the war, the reliability of news and the production front. He said that he had never considered surrendering; he had never heard of a Japanese surrendering. He did not wish to return to live in Japan, fearing that he would be punished if he did, and intended to "live alone in mountains of Burma till the war [was] over and then start a new life in Asia."[32]

Benedict's emphasis on the stories told by soldiers notwithstanding, Japanese women, as well as men, were mobilized into wartime nationalist ideology. Japanese women embraced the imperial doctrines, assisted wartime economy, and supported the nationalist goals on the home front. Just as Western women were complicit in the masculinist project of Western imperialism and Orientalism, Japanese women were also an integral part of Japanese imperialism. Still, men in uniform had a different relationship to the nationalist and imperialist ideology than women did. Men enacted Japan's imperialist ideology not just militarily but in the practice of conducting daily affairs within the rigid hierarchy of the military that governed surveillance, interactions with and violence against the natives, and sexual violence against native women. Furthermore, trained under the no-surrender policy, they were expected and willing to give their lives in the name of the emperor. Their interviews informed and shaped Benedict's view on "official" wartime Japanese morale, including the soldiers' faith in the purpose of the war, devotion to the emperor, and attitude toward death.[33]

Thus, based on the male figure and male spheres of life epitomized by the military, Benedict constructed a model of Japanese national character that heavily focused on the system of hierarchy and social order. And in characterizing Japanese culture as rigid, unindividualized, and undemocratic, she implicitly suggested that Japanese masculinity—represented by the male figure and male sphere of life—was lacking in what is considered to be masculine qualities by Western norms. As a consequence, Benedict's narrative at once emasculated and feminized the masculine Japan.

Gender in the "Culture" Paradigm

The fact that Benedict constructed—and naturalized—a model of Japanese character based on a male figure and male social relations did not mean that she failed to pay attention to Japanese women or deal with the issue of gender: they were not, as she saw, exempt from the Japanese system of hierarchy or the "official" nationalist/imperialist ideology. Their lives were in fact as—or even more—embedded within hierarchical systems, the most obvious of which was patriarchy. Benedict supplemented her own limited knowledge of Japanese women by reading works such as Alice Mabel Bacon's *Japanese Girls and Women* (1902), Mishima Sumie's *My Narrow Isle* (1941), and Sugimoto Etsu Inagaki's *A Daughter of the Samurai* (1926).[34]

What was unique about Benedict's approach to the issue of gender was that she used the paradigm of "culture" to explain gender. Instead of foregrounding gender as a category of analysis in explaining women's experiences, she placed gender under the larger cultural pattern of hierarchy and saw gender relations themselves as a symptom or an effect of culture. Whereas many other Western Orientalists used "gender" to explain "culture," Benedict and the anthropological discourse that she used employed "culture" to explain "gender."[35] But while the two approaches to, and narrativizations of, gender were quite different from one another, they ultimately had the same effect of reinforcing the link between culture and gender and validating the association between Japan and particular types of gender and sexuality.

Benedict treats gender as a subcategory of the larger hierarchical patterns that promote the virtue of "taking one's proper station" in Japanese life and describes gender inequality and patriarchal ideology this way:

> Whatever one's age, one's position in the hierarchy depends on whether one is male or female. The Japanese woman walks behind her husband and has a lower status. Even women who on occasions when they wear American clothes walk alongside and precede him through a door, again fall to the rear when they have donned their kimonos. The Japanese daughter of the family must get along as best she can while the presents, the attentions, and the money for education go to her brothers. Even when higher schools were established for young women the prescribed courses were heavily loaded with instruction in etiquette and bodily movement. Serious intellectual training was not on a par with boys', and one principal of such a school, advocating for his upper middle class students some instruction in European languages, based his recommendation on the desirability of their being able to put their husband's books back in the bookcase right side up after they had dusted them.[36]

While she thus calls attention to the strict gender inequality in Japanese society, Benedict also mentions that Japanese women still have greater freedom than women in most other Asian countries, as they can walk around the town, are responsible for the household finances, have a great say in their children's marriages, and run the household once they become mothers-in-law. But rather than using gender as a category or analytical category, Benedict treats gender inequality and patriarchal ideology as one manifestation of Japan's hierarchical cultural pattern and thus naturalizes it as being "Japanese."

Benedict also explains Japanese family structure and domestic relations within the context of hierarchy. She illustrates a case where a mother forces her pregnant young daughter-in-law to leave her husband. When the child is born, the mother-in-law comes accompanied by her silent and submissive son to claim the baby, and disposes of it immediately to a foster home. Rather than discussing the gender relations (either patriarchy or matriarchy) implicit in this case, Benedict explains it in terms of filial piety and the payment of indebtedness:

> All this is on occasion included in filial piety, and is proper payment of indebtedness to parents. In the United States all such stories are taken as instances of outside interference with an individual's right to happiness. Japan cannot consider this interference as "outside" because of her postulate of indebtedness. Such stories in Japan, like our stories of honest men who pay off their creditors by incredible personal hardships, are tales of the truly virtuous, of persons who have earned their right to respect themselves, who have proved themselves strong enough to accept proper personal frustrations. Such frustrations, however virtuous, may naturally leave a residue of resentment and it is well worth noting that the Asiatic proverb about the Hateful Things, which in Burma, for instance, lists "fire, water, thieves, governors and malicious men," in Japan itemizes "earthquake, thunder, and the Old Man (head of the house; the father)."[37]

This account of filial piety and payment of indebtedness to parents is entirely based on the son's point of view and does not allow any discussion of the status of the bride. The schematized pattern of hierarchy and obligation, of which filial piety is a part, undermines gender as a category of analysis. Here, too, Benedict uses Japanese "culture" to explain gender relations.

Along with the issues of gender relations and patriarchy, sexuality is also embedded within Benedict's larger mapping of the Japanese social order. For example, she cites a letter sent to the advice column of a journal of psychoanalysis in her discussion of the forms of payment for one's debt to others. An elderly widowed man confesses that after his wife died he had dallied with a young prostitute, bought her freedom and took her to his home, taught her etiquette, and kept her as a maid. His children and children-in-law look down on him for this act and treat him as a stranger. The girl's parents, whom he thinks are not after his money, promise to consider the girl as dead and agree that she may continue in the situation. Although the girl herself wants to remain by his side until his death, he sometimes considers sending her home, because the girl is his daughter's age. With a chronic illness and probably only a few more years to live, he asks for advice on what course to take. The doctor makes a judgmental diagnosis on the man's character, obfuscates the interrelated issues of obligations and expectations between parent and children, sexual desire, financial interests involved in the arrangement, and the man's aging. Therefore, while it is reasonable that Benedict sees the advice as "hardly Freudian," it is important that she considers it "thoroughly Japanese." According to Benedict, "the doctor regards this as a clear case of the old man's having put too heavy an *on* [obligation] upon his children."[38] Her focus on the issue of obligation and her characterization of the case and the advice given as "Japanese" exemplify the ways in which Benedict used the paradigm of culture to account for issues such as gender relations, sexuality, and patriarchy.

When Benedict more explicitly and directly discusses the issues of sexuality, it is also within the context of "proper station." In the chapter on "The Circle of Human Feelings," she describes various physical pleasures in which the Japanese indulge and argues that

> The Japanese do not condemn self-gratification. They are not Puritans. They consider physical pleasures good and worthy of cultivation. They are sought and valued. Nevertheless, they have to be kept in their place. They must not intrude upon the serious affairs of life.[39]

Benedict goes on to explain why the Japanese are not moralistic as Americans are regarding erotic pleasure. According to her, "Sex, like any other 'human feeling,' they regard as thoroughly good in its minor place in life. There is nothing evil about 'human feelings' and therefore no need to be moralistic about sex pleasures."[40] She argues that whereas Americans consider love and marriage as one and the same thing, for the Japanese love and erotic pleasure are fenced off from one another as separate provinces, not by the division between the public and the surreptitious, but by the division between a man's major obligations and his minor relaxation. She thus accounts for the accepted practice of upperclass men keeping a mistress or a more general custom of men visiting *geishas* or prostitutes as activities falling within the latter domain. Pointing out the difference between such practices and "the whole Oriental arrangement of polygamy," Benedict states that "the Japanese keep family obligations and 'human feelings' even spatially apart."[41] Benedict renders the explanation through the male point of view, and apart from a cursory remark that a man's search for erotic pleasure outside of the home is openly acknowledged by his wife and that "[s]he may be unhappy about it but that is her own affair,"[42] she does not delve into the cultural meanings or social arrangements of sexuality for Japanese women. For Benedict, the question of sexuality was no more or less than one piece of evidence for her thesis that the Japanese kept everything in its proper place. Thus, Benedict herself kept the issue of sexuality in its "proper" place within her larger picture of Japanese culture.

Benedict thus used the pattern of Japanese culture she mapped in order to explain gender relations, patriarchy, domestic life, and sexuality, subsuming them under the general rubric of the hierarchical order in Japanese life. While the relationship between "culture" and "gender" that she depicted was different from the approaches taken by some of the other producers of American discourse about Asia, Benedict's analysis produced the same effect as those which preceded her study. Whether gender or culture was at the top, the link drawn between culture and gender resulted in affirming the association between Asia and particular types of gender relations (patriarchy) and sexuality (licentious, extramarital).

Race, Culture, and Gender in Anthropological Discourse

Benedict's treatment of gender in relation to culture was an outcome of the paradigmatic context of the contemporary anthropological discourse in which she worked. *The Chrysanthemum and the Sword* was part of a larger scholarly approach—commonly called "Culture and Personality studies" or "national character studies"—which brought together the methodologies of applied behavioral and social sciences such as anthropology, sociology, psychology, and psychiatry. Leading intellectuals in these fields—such as Ruth Benedict, Margaret Mead, and Gregory Bateson—joined in an effort to study and understand the characters of other cultures systematically.[43]

At the core of their pursuits was the commitment to revising the concept of "race" and to foregrounding "culture" as the determining factor in people's behaviors. As disciples of Franz Boas, the scholars who came to be associated with Culture and Personality studies repudiated theories of biologically engendered superiority or inferiority in intellect or character that dominated nineteenth-century American racial thinking. Race, they argued, was not a determining factor in behavior. Rather, integrated cultural patterns, the unconscious logic of sentiments and assumptions, and the processes of enculturation were the keys to understanding people's behaviors. Culture was inherited from the past, but it had to be learned by each generation and was capable of being altered. In many ways, the scholars who formulated Culture and Personality studies simply replaced "race" with "culture" as a paradigm for understanding human behavior.[44]

Benedict's work in anthropology emerged out of this "culture" paradigm. As a pioneer in the field and approach, she explicated the theory and demonstrated the methods of this paradigm in her earlier work, most notably *Patterns of Culture*. Based on the assumption that individual behaviors, beliefs, and customs are always interconnected and constitute a piece of a holistic culture, Benedict maintained that individual behaviors are always defined and constrained by culture. Her study of Japanese culture in *The Chrysanthemum and the Sword* applied this general theoretical and methodological approach to culture as well, as the book's subtitle, *Patterns of Japanese Culture*, suggests. According to Benedict, the book "examines Japanese assumptions about the conduct of life," and "describes these assumptions as they have manifested themselves whatever the activity in hand. It is about what makes Japan a nation of Japanese."[45]

The anthropologists' foregrounding of "culture" over "race" had a highly significant impact on the discourse about race and racism in the United States and contributed much to repudiating biological determinism. Benedict's development and use of the "culture" paradigm offered a lens through which to see a culture holistically and from a relativist perspective, as she carefully avoided Eurocentric judgments on other cultures. However, the anthropologists' replacement of "race" with "culture" brought about the same consequence as many of the preceding approaches and discourses about the racial Other in terms of gendering. By making gender a symptom or effect of culture, Benedict's culture paradigm naturalized certain forms of gender relations or sexuality as constitutive elements of Japanese culture and society. As a result, it not only reinforced the link between gender and culture, but "scientifically" validated the association between particular types of gender relations and sexuality in Japan. Ironically enough, Benedict's work in scientific antiracism and the use of the culture paradigm resulted in re-gendering Japan as the racial Other.

Notes

1. Harold Isaacs, *Scratches on Our Minds: American Images of China and India* (New York: J. Day Co., 1958), 164–76.

2. "How to Tell Your Friends from the Japs," *Time*, 22 Dec. 1941, 33; "How to Tell the Japs from the Chinese," *Life*, 22 Dec. 1941, 7.

3. John W. Dower, *War without Mercy: Race and Power in the Pacific War* (New York: Pantheon Books, 1986), 119.

4. Ruth Benedict, *The Chrysanthemum and the Sword: Patterns of Japanese Culture* (1946; reprint, Boston: Houghton Mifflin, 1989).

5. Sugimoto Etsu Inagaki, *Daughter of a Samurai* (New York: Doubleday, 1926), 136; quoted in Benedict, *Chrysanthemum*, 294.

6. Benedict, *Chrysanthemum*, 296.

7. Ibid., 296.

8. Allan M. Winkler, *The Politics of Propaganda: The Office of War Information, 1942-1945* (New Haven, Conn.: Yale University Press, 1978).

9. Dr. Katherine Spencer, The Development of the Research Methods of the Foreign Morale Analysis Division [OWI], Interim International Information Service, report no. 29 (30 Nov. 1945), 223-25; Alexander L. Leighton, *Human Relations in a Changing World: Observations on the Use of the Social Sciences* (New York: E. P. Dutton and Co., 1949), appendix D.

10. Benedict, *Chrysanthemum*, 6.

11. Miscellaneous records of interviews with Robert Hashima (OWI staff); record of interview with Mr. and Mrs. Shirahata (conducted by H. C. Hu, March 1945); record of interview with Mr. Okami (OWI, New York); record of interview with Mr. Bergher (OWI, New York, July 6, 1945). Ruth Benedict Papers, Vassar College Library, Poughkeepsie, N.Y.

12. Benedict, *Chrysanthemum*, 8.

13. Office of Strategic Services, Research and Analysis Branch, "Japanese Films: A Phase of Psychological Warfare, An analysis of the themes, psychological content, technical quality, and propaganda value of twenty recent Japanese films," report no. 1307 (March 1944).

14. Benedict, *Chrysanthemum*, 6.

15. Pauline Kent has compiled an extensive bibliography of sources used by Benedict. See "Ruth Benedict and Her Wartime Studies: Primary Materials and References," 1995-nendo Monbusho Kagaku Kenkyu-hi Hojokin Shourei Kenkyu (A) Kenkyu Seika Houkokusho, 07710166 ([Tokyo]: Monbusho, 1996), 235-42.

16. For example, see Alfred R. Lindsmith and Anselm L. Strauss, "A Critique of Culture-Personality Writings," *American Sociological Review* 15, no. 5 (October 1950): 587-600; John Bennet and Michio Nagai, "The Japanese Critique of the Methodology of Benedict's *Chrysanthemum and the Sword*," *American Anthropologist* 55, no. 3 (August 1953): 404-11; Richard H. Minear, "Cross-Cultural Perception and WWII: American Japanists of the 1940s and Their Images of Japan," *International Studies Quarterly* 24, no. 4 (December 1980): 555-80; Richard Minear, "The Wartime Studies of Japanese National Character," *Japan Interpreter* (summer 1980): 36-59;

Peter T. Suzuki, "Anthropologists in the Wartime Camps for Japanese Americans: A Documentary Study," *Dialectical Anthropology* 6, no. 1 (August 1981): 23–60; Peter T. Suzuki, "A Retrospective Analysis of a Wartime 'National Character' Study," *Dialectical Anthropology* 5, no. 1 (May 1980): 33–46. See also John W. Dower, *War without Mercy*, chaps. 5–6.

17. The most extreme example of such critique is by Watsuji Tetsuro, an eminent Japanese ethnologist; see "Kagaku-teki Kachi ni taisuru Gimon [Questions as to the Scientific Value]," *Minzokugaku Kenkyu* 14, no. 4 (1950): 23–27.

18. Weston La Barre, "Some Observations on Character Structure in the Orient: The Japanese," *Psychiatry: Journal of Biology and the Pathology of Interpersonal Relations* 8, no. 3 (August 1945): 319–42.

19. Alexander H. Leighton, *The Governing of Men: General Principles and Recommendations Based on Experience at a Japanese Relocation Camp* (Princeton, N.J.: Princeton University Press, 1945); Dorothy S. Thomas, *The Salvage* (Berkeley and Los Angeles: University of California Press, 1952); Dorothy S. Thomas and Richard S. Nishimoto, *The Spoilage* (Berkeley and Los Angeles: University of California Press, 1946); U.S. Department of Interior, War Relocation Authority, *Impounded People: Japanese Americans in the Relocation Centers* (Washington, D.C.: Government Printing Office, 1946). For the details of these studies in the internment camps, see Yuji Ichioka ed., *Views from Within: The Japanese American Evacuation and Resettlement Study* (Los Angeles: UCLA Asian American Studies Center, 1989).

20. Leighton, *Governing of Men*, 376.

21. Geoffrey Gorer, *Japanese Character Structure*, 2nd ed. (New York: Distributed by the Institute for Intercultural Studies, 1942), 1.

22. Ibid., 4.

23. Ibid., 17.

24. Ibid., 18.

25. As later scholars such as Richard Minear have rightly criticized, such a model grossly undermines the historical context for what was happening in international relations; they see the analysis of Japanese national character as an *explanation* of Japanese history, an answer to such questions as why Japan invaded China and why Japan attacked the United States. See Minear, "Wartime Studies," 37.

26. Gorer, *Japanese Character*, 18.

27. Ibid., 19.

28. Benedict, *Chrysanthemum*, 22.

29. Ibid., 25.

30. Ibid., 31–32.

31. OWI interview records. "Suetsugu Shoji." Ruth Benedict Papers, Vassar College Library.

32. For a similar story, also see OWI interview notes on "POW Masuda," June 30, 1944. Ruth Benedict Papers, Vassar College Library, Poughkeepsie, N.Y.

33. The FMAD's "Morale Handbook," which outlines the questions to be asked during the interviews and how to record the answers, shows that in addition to factual information about the interviewee's background, military affiliation, and circumstances of capture, the interviewers were instructed to assess the informants' attitude toward capture (divided into seventeen categories, such as "indifference," "disgrace," "fear of future punishment in Japan," "antagonistic," "requests or desired to be executed or killed," "glad to be prisoner and out of war," etc.). [FMAD], "Morale Handbook," (n.d.) Ruth Benedict Papers, Vassar College Library, Poughkeepsie, N.Y.

34. Alice Mabel Bacon, *Japanese Girls and Women* (Boston, Mass.: Houghton Mifflin, 1902); Mishima Sumie Seo, *My Narrow Isle: The Story of a Modern Woman in Japan* (New York: J. Day, 1941); Sugimoto, *Daughter of a Samurai*. Benedict also consulted a manuscript put together by Baroness Ishimoto on biographical sketches of diverse Japanese women including ancient mythological figures, writers, educators, social workers, and political activists.

35. On uses of gender by some of the so-called American Orientalists, see Mari Yoshihara, "Women's Asia: American Women and the Gendering of American Orientalism, 1870s-WWII," (Ph.D. diss., Brown University, 1997).

36. Benedict, *Chrysanthemum*, 53–54.

37. Ibid., 121–22.

38. Ibid., 109–10.

39. Ibid., 177.

40. Ibid., 183.

41. Ibid., 185.

42. Ibid., 186.

43. George W. Stocking, Jr., *The Ethnographer's Magic and Other Essays in the History of Anthropology* (Madison: University of Wisconsin Press, 1992), 165–68; John Embree, "Applied Anthropology and Its Relation to Anthropology," *American Anthropologist* 47 (1945): 516–39; Laura Thompson, "Some Perspectives on Applied Anthropology," *Applied Anthropology* 3 (1944): 12.

44. For a critique of the "culture" paradigm in anthropology, see Christopher Shannon, "A World Made Safe for Differences: Ruth Benedict's *The Chrysanthemum and the Sword*," *American Quarterly* 47, no. 4 (December 1995): 659–80.

45. Benedict, *Chrysanthemum*, 13.

PART IV
LITERARY FEARS

American Agoraphobia
Moby-Dick and the
Mid-Nineteenth-Century
Rhetoric of Size

Anne Baker

Early in Melville's third novel, *Mardi* (1849), a becalmed sailor confronts the terrifyingly blank and seemingly endless space of the open sea. The experience "revolutionizes his abdomen" and "unsettles his mind," and he begins to lose faith in mapping conventions such as the intersecting lines marking longitude and latitude.[1] Though the passage clearly emerges out of Melville's experience as a sailor, it is no mere anecdote of life at sea. In fact, it epitomizes a kind of agoraphobia that recurs throughout mid-nineteenth-century American culture alongside the better-known optimism about national expansion typified by "manifest destiny."

The belief that the survival of the United States (or at least its democratic political system) depended on the capacity of the nation to retain its manageable size appears repeatedly in antebellum American writings of all kinds. Explorer Zebulon Pike, for example, writing in 1810, was relieved to find the Western prairies unsuitable (so he believed) for habitation by a settled farming people, reasoning that "restriction of our population to some certain limits" would ensure "a continuation of the Union."[2] During the middle of the nineteenth century, however, as territorial expansion reached fever pitch, an insistent anxiety about boundlessness manifested itself in a variety of ways. Clergyman William Ellery Channing, for example, arguing against the annexation of Texas, worried that "The moment we plant our authority on Texas, the boundaries of those two countries [Texas and Mexico] will become nominal, will be . . . little more than lines on the sand of the sea-shore."[3] Even many pro-expansionists felt uneasy as they confronted the nation's rapidly increasing size and the arbitrary nature of its national boundaries. In a rhetorical move that some historians have called "geographical predestination," they assuaged their anxiety by declaring successive geographical barriers (the Mississippi, the Rockies, and finally the Pacific) to be the natural, God-given boundaries of the nation.[4]

This fear of boundlessness and the desire for reassuringly enclosed national space were expressed not only in literature and political rhetoric, but in material culture as well. From the 1840s to the 1860s, the practice of erecting fences or stone curbs around family cemetery plots became so popular that the influential landscape gardener Andrew Jackson Downing, in his campaign to discourage such fences, referred to the trend as "fencing mania." Not until the 1880s, when the anxious sense of spatial formlessness expressed in the period's literature and political rhetoric subsided, did the idea of naturalistic, parklike cemeteries take hold and the widespread removal of fences and curbs begin.[5]

Concern about the nation's size during this period is reflected in pervasive and innovative nation-as-body metaphors that are used not, as in the traditional body-politic metaphor, to convey an organic wholeness, but to express attitudes about expansion. Thoreau, for example, in *Walden* (1854) writes that "The gross feeder is a man in the larva state; and there are whole nations in that condition, nations without fancy or imagination, whose vast abdomens betray them."[6] In a like view, Margaret Fuller expresses hope that American youth will "help to give soul" to the "huge, over fed, too hastily grown-up body" of the United States.[7] The similarity between these statements—their shared vision of the nation as an unhealthily large, voracious body—reflects a widespread fear among Northeastern intellectuals of the consequences of annexation.

But anxiety about the nation's astonishingly rapid growth also manifested itself in representations of the literal human body. A number of visual and literary artistic productions portray human beings dwarfed by their surroundings. The becalmed sailor of *Mardi*, for example, understands his agoraphobic experience in terms of an *Alice in Wonderland*-like change in his own size: his voice begins to feel "in him like something swallowed too big for the esophagus," and he imagines his ship speaking to him like "the old beldam" to "the little dwarf."[8] Other artists, on the other hand, attempt to dispel fears that the acquisition of uncharted territory will destroy or diminish the acquirer by depicting Westerners as monstrously large.

Cooper's *Leatherstocking Tales*, his epic of Westward expansion, provide the most obvious examples of the nineteenth-century rhetoric of size. In these novels the forester, settler, or woodchopper whose presence in the wilderness presages its later destruction is always gigantic. In *The Prairie* (1827), for example, Ishmael Bush's "frame" is "vast, and in reality of prodigious power . . . like the slumbering and unwieldy, but terrible strength of the elephant."[9] His brawny eldest son regards a tree that he plans to cut down "with that sort of contempt with which a giant might be supposed to contemplate the puny resistance of a dwarf."[10] Cooper likewise describes Hurry Harry, the "forester" of *The Deerslayer* (1841) as "a man of gigantic mould," adding that he "exceeded six feet four, and being unusually well proportioned, his strength fully realized the idea created by his gigantic frame."[11]

Images of large Westerners appear regularly in the work of other writers as well. In *Moby-Dick* (1851) Bulkington's "fine stature" immediately convinces Ishmael that he must be "one of those tall mountaineers from the Alleghanian Ridge."[12] And Whitman, in *Leaves of Grass* (1855), refers to himself as "comrade of free North-Westerners, (loving their big proportions)."[13]

Visual art of the period, particularly in its more popular forms, demonstrates the same association of Western settlers with exaggeratedly large body size. An anonymous 1852 banknote engraving depicts a massive wood-chopping settler who is entirely out of proportion to the trees, log cabin, and covered wagon in the background (see fig. 1). Emanuel Leutze's mural *Westward the Course of Empire Takes Its Way* (1862), painted for the west wall of the Capitol building, portrays a Westerner (identifiable by his coonskin cap) who is literally twice the size of the two women he shelters (see fig. 2). A popular print taken from John Gast's painting *American Progress* (1878) represents "Progress" as a massive toga-clad woman who floats, stringing telegraph wire behind her, above westward-moving travelers (see fig. 3). In this case, vastness is not embodied by the settlers themselves, but is displaced onto a mythical figure who accompanies them.

This nineteenth-century obsession with size has a telling antecedent in the eighteenth-century debate between the French naturalist Buffon and Thomas Jefferson. The cornerstone of Buffon's comparison of the animal species of the Old and New Worlds is his assertion that all animals are "considerably smaller in America than in Europe."[14] While he has to acknowledge that Indians are about the same height as Europeans, he claims that they have smaller "organs of generation" and "no ardor for the female."[15] Buffon's belief in the greater size and, by his own logic, the greater stability and maturity of European animals reflects a Eurocentric bias typical of the period, as various commentators have

Figure 1. Anonymous banknote engraving, Rawdon, Wright, Hatch, and Edson 1852. Prints and Photographs Division, Library of Congress, Washington, D.C.

Figure 2. Emanuel Leutze, *Westward the Course of Empire Takes Its Way,* 1862. United States Capitol Art Collection, Washington, D.C. Reproduced Courtesy of the Architect of the Capitol.

Figure 3. John Gast, *American Progress*, engraving, 1878.

pointed out.[16] But Buffon's writings on American fauna also reveal an uneasiness about what he sees as the overpowering qualities of American space, a fearful sense that the American continent, untamed by humankind, has the capacity to overwhelm and diminish its inhabitants. In Europe, according to Buffon, "the great seeds . . . have received their fullest form, their most complete extension." In America, on the other hand, they are "reduced, shrunken beneath this ungenerous sky and in this empty land, where man, scarce in number, was thinly spread, a wanderer, where far from making himself master of this territory as his own domain, he ruled over nothing."[17]

Thomas Jefferson, who devotes over one-eighth of his *Notes on the State of Virginia* (1781) to a vociferous refutation of Buffon's theory, catalogs the size of numerous American animals in his effort to prove Buffon wrong. He even argues, on the basis of Indian legend, that the mammoth may still exist west of the Mississippi, in "[t]hose parts still . . . in their aboriginal state, unexplored and undisturbed by us."[18] Thus where Buffon sees "this empty land" as capable of shrinking animals and human male "organs of generation," Jefferson imagines the unsettled and unexplored regions of North America as capable of harboring immense animals long extinct in other parts of the world. Where Buffon sees a threat, Jefferson imagines the potential for a remarkable exception. Buffon differs from Jefferson primarily in that he believes the size of the continent's inhabitants to be *inversely* proportional to the size of the continent itself. In both cases, however, the mystery of American continent inspires obsessive interest in the size of its inhabitants and a sense that the latter should somehow correspond with the former.

Like both Buffon's theory and Jefferson's refutation of it, antebellum representations of large Westerners suggest a direct correlation between body size and environment. The nineteenth-century rhetoric of size, however, unlike that of the eighteenth-century one, reflects a cultural need to see Westerners as adequate to the task of subduing newly incorporated territory. The "vast" frames of Cooper's frontiersmen indicate their physical capacity to impose their will on the landscape. Unlike small, terrified Pip, who in *Moby-Dick* goes insane after his "ringed horizon [begins] to expand around him," men like Ishmael Bush and the oversized figures in the period's popular art *should* be able to handle, and indeed thrive on, what Melville calls the "intense concentration of self in the middle of such a heartless immensity (453). But writers and orators also raise the possibility that Americans won't measure up. Whitman, in the 1855 Preface to *Leaves of Grass*, warns that "The largeness of nature or the nation were monstrous without a corresponding largeness and generosity of the spirit of the citizen, while Daniel Webster rather desperately pleads: "let our comprehension be as broad as the country for which we act, . . . let us not be pigmies in a case that calls for men."[19]

Melville's *Moby-Dick*

Readers of *Moby-Dick* have long commented on the size of Melville's most famous novel. One of the most recent to do so is Edward Said, who, in his introduction to the Library of America edition, addresses the question of the novel's size head-on: "But why, finally, such bulk, such almost gargantuan mass for what is after all a work of fiction?"[20] He arrives at two answers to his own question. First, that Melville is "an irrepressible enthusiast," and second, that "*Moby-Dick* is . . . a book about going too far, pressing too hard, overstepping limits." Both of these answers are fine as far as they go, but they beg further questions. Why should Melville have chosen to *thematize* size in his gargantuan book? And what is the significance of the meditations on size and art within the novel? Both of Said's responses to his own questions imply that *Moby-Dick*'s size is exclusively the result of Melville's temperament and private obsessions. Although Said acknowledges that in *Moby-Dick* "Melville has very accurately caught something of the imperial motif that runs consistently through United States history and culture," he seems not to take into account the possibility that Melville, in writing a massive book about a huge whale—a book in which he evokes vast open space and pays careful attention to the size of various human characters—was responding to the proliferation of size imagery circulating in the mid-nineteenth-century United States.

In *Moby-Dick*, Melville reveals himself to have been keenly aware of, and indeed inspired by, the nineteenth-century rhetoric of size, as well as conscious of its origins in the fear of vast open space. Melville scholars have long acknowledged that political allegory plays an important role in the novel and have seen the *Pequod* as an American ship of state in pursuit of further territory, represented by the whale.[21] What I argue, building on this scholarship, is that Melville portrays various crew members of this ship of state engaging in self-enlarging maneuvers that parody the self-enlarging rhetoric of the period. At the same time, through the character Pip, Melville explores the consequences of failing to participate in such self-inflating strategies. My point, then, is that *Moby-Dick* is not simply a critique of American imperialism, as many readings of the novel as political allegory have suggested, but is also, and more importantly, a comic exploration of the cultural mechanisms by which expansion was justified or made to seem reasonable. The tension between Melville's sense that the rhetoric of size was ludicrous and his attraction to the self-enlarging impulses it quite literally *embodied* is in fact part of what generates the power of the novel.

In "The Castaway" chapter, Pip, the small, perpetually frightened black cabin-boy of the *Pequod*, is temporarily abandoned on the open sea. There, overwhelmed by "the intense concentration of self in the middle of such a heartless immensity," Pip goes insane. This episode clearly reflects a link between the representation of space in *Moby-Dick* and the politics of annexation. Just as the sectional conflict brought on by expansion and annexation leads to the Fugitive Slave Law (1850), which required that escaped slaves be sent back to their masters, so, after the horizon "expand[s] around him," Pip speaks of himself in the third person in the language of handbills advertising escaped slaves: "Reward for Pip! One hundred pounds of clay—five feet high—looks cowardly" (567) and "have ye seen one Pip?—a little negro lad, five feet high, hang-dog look, and cowardly!" (581). In both examples, Pip's size and fearfulness identify him, the repeated juxtaposition of the two qualities reinforcing their connectedness within the logic of the narrative.

Pip's cowardice and small size acquire meaning in relation to the foolhardy courage and inflated belief their own powers possessed by other members of the crew. In "The Cassock" chapter, the sailors gain a sense of invincibility by wearing the skin of the whale's phallus, which Ishmael describes as "longer than a Kentuckian is tall, nigh a foot in diameter at the base, and jet-black as Yojo, the ebony idol of Queequeg" (459). Michael Paul Rogin—who reads this chapter as being primarily about the commodification of the natural world, the transformation of the whale's body into oil—observes quite rightly that the "phallus-skin armor" that the mincer wears is an image of "a borrowed, self-preserving, masculine aggression," adding that "the cassock aggrandizes its wearer" and "allows the mincer to produce sperm."[22] It should be added that the episode is a send-up of the oversized figures in the period's literature and art, an astute commentary on the comical futility of such cultural work.

Small Pip's most significant foil among the crew is Flask, the diminutive third mate of the *Pequod*, to whom "the wondrous whale was but a species of magnified mouse, or at least water-rat" (129). Flask's inability or unwillingness to acknowledge the whale's true size is, rather obviously, a compensatory measure that enables him to suppress all fear of the whale and to assume a swaggering bravado.

Just as the sailors enlarge themselves by wearing the "cassock," Flask enlarges himself by standing on the shoulders of his gigantic African harpooneer Daggoo, a maneuver that symbolizes America's willingness to use the physical labor of other races, particularly the slave power of Africans, to fuel its expansion. The loggerhead, Flask's original lookout point, is "not more spacious than the palm of a man's hand" (240) and rises only two feet above the level of the whale boat. By standing on Daggoo's shoulders, Flask can see, and thus symbolically possess, a much greater area. No longer believing himself in danger of being overwhelmed by the vast space around him, he becomes master of all he surveys.

Though Pip's inability to participate in such enlarging practices causes him to go insane, his vulnerability also enables him honestly to confront the ocean's vastness, and so to acquire a kind of costly truth to which the sailors, encased in the whale's phallus, have no access: after his experience alone at sea, he plays the part of wise fool to Ahab. And ultimately, of course, neither "the cassock" nor Flask's elevated position on Daggoo's shoulders can protect the whalers from the power of the massive white whale. In the apocalypse of *Moby-Dick*'s final chapter, the self-inflating practices of the sailors, already shown to be comical, are exposed as utterly ineffectual as well.

In portraying such practices as useless, Melville indicts the self-aggrandizing rhetoric of his age. The destruction of the *Pequod* foreshadows the fate of a nation too caught up in the thrill of its own expansiveness to acknowledge that such rhetoric offers no protection against forces unleashed by annexation. Though Melville parodies the rhetoric of size through various characters in *Moby-Dick*, he is too keenly aware of the appeal of self-enlargement to allow his narrator any sense of superiority to these characters. In fact, *Moby-Dick* itself can be seen as a conscious exercise in exuberant self-enlargement.

Ishmael points to the significance of size in aesthetic projects several times over the course of his odyssey, at first merely raising the issue of size and proportion, but later deliberately engaging on a verbal level in the kind of self-magnification that he simultaneously laughs at. In "The Lee Shore," at the beginning of the novel, he directs the reader's attention to the small size of the chapter at hand in relation to the figure it memorializes, a figure whose very name suggests his magnitude: "this six-inch chapter is the stoneless grave of Bulkington" (116).

In "Of the Monstrous Pictures of Whales," Ishmael again reinforces the obsession with size that shapes the novel when he critiques an illustration "purporting to be a 'Picture of a . . . Spermaceti whale, drawn to scale'": "it has an eye which applied, according to the accompanying scale, to a full grown sperm whale, would make the eye of that whale a bow-window some five feet long" (287). Ishmael clearly intends to poke fun at this representation of the whale, in particular its outlandishly oversized eye. But in his final rhetorical question, "Ah my gallant captain, why did ye not give us Jonah looking out of that eye!" Ishmael also hints at the modus operandi of *Moby-Dick:* disproportion taken to imaginative extremes.

In "The Town-Ho's Story," Ishmael portrays himself at an earlier period participating in the worship of largeness that accompanied the expansionism of the mid-nineteenth century. When Ishmael wants to swear to the truth of the story he has just told, he asks Don Sebastian to "be particular in procuring the largest sized Evangelists you can" (284). Ishmael seems to believe that swearing on a larger Bible will make a greater impression on his listeners or make his story seem more truthful. But if the purpose of the Bible is to lend credence to Ishmael's story, then readers are surely meant to respond by protesting mentally that biblical size should make no difference. Its sanctity, rather than its size, makes the Bible proof of the storyteller's truth. If we see the entire small episode as being *about* storytelling, truth, and size, then the request should be read as Melville's ironic, self-deprecating comment on the size of his own book *Moby-Dick*.

Ishmael again addresses the issue of size and artistic effect when he remarks in chapter 104 ("The Fossil Whale") that "it now remains to magnify [the whale] in an archaeological, fossiliferous, and antediluvian point of view" (496). He feels called upon to justify his language, and notes:

> Applied to any other creature than the Leviathan—to an ant or flea—such portly terms might justly be deemed unwarrantably grandiloquent. But when Leviathan is the text, the case is altered. Fain am I to stagger to this emprise under the weightiest words in the dictionary. And here be it said, that whenever it has been convenient to consult one in the course of these dissertations, I have invariably used a huge quarto edition of Johnson, expressly purchased for that purpose; because that famous lexicographer's uncommon personal bulk more fitted him to compile a lexicon to be used by a whale author like me (496).

Here, as in his call for an extra-large Bible in "The Town-Ho's Story," Ishmael pokes fun at the rhetoric of size. Again, however, *Moby-Dick*'s own conspicuous size calls attention to itself. Melville satirizes love of largeness, but finds it irresistible nonetheless.

In *Moby-Dick*, then, Melville participates in his culture's obsession with size, and at the same time is able to stand back and comment perceptively on its absurdity. What's most interesting, ultimately, about Melville's complex relationship to this cultural phenomenon is the way it precipitates formal innovation. By incorporating various genres—the sermon, the tall tale, treatises on etymology and cetology—into *Moby-Dick*, Melville stretches the limits of the novel form. Deeply aware of the folly of aggressive territorial expansion, he nevertheless felt an imperative to redraw the boundaries of the novel.

Notes

1. Herman Melville, *Mardi,* Northwestern-Newberry ed., Harrison Hayford, Hershel Parker, and G. Thomas Tanselle, eds. (Evanston and Chicago, Ill.: Northwestern University Press and the Newberry Library, 1970), 9–10.

2. Zebulon Pike, *The Expeditions of Zebulon Montgomery Pike, to the Headwaters of the Mississippi River, through Louisiana Territory, and in New Spain, during the Years 1805-6-7,* quoted in William H. Goetzmann, *Exploration and Empire: The Explorer and the Scientist in the Winning of the American West* (New York: Alfred A. Knopf, 1966), 51.

3. Channing to Henry Clay, 1837, in *The Works of William E. Channing* (Boston, Mass., 1848), 2:184–248, quoted in Norman A. Graebner, ed., *Manifest Destiny* (Indianapolis, Ind.: The Bobbs-Merrill Company, Inc., 1968), 48.

4. The term "geographical predestination" was coined by Albert K. Weinberg in *Manifest Destiny: A Study of Nationalist Expansionism in American History* (Baltimore, Md.: Johns Hopkins University Press, 1935). For more on the anxiety underlying mid-nineteenth-century expansion, see Thomas R. Hietala, *Manifest Design: Anxious Aggrandizement in Late Jacksonian America* (Ithaca, N.Y.: Cornell University Press, 1985).

5. Historians have offered various explanations for this trend. Stanley French believes it was "symbolic of the national trait of possessive individualism"; see Stanley French, "The Cemetery as Cultural Institution: the Establishment of Mt. Auburn and the Rural Cemetery Movement," *American Quarterly* 26 (1974): 37–59. Blanche Linden-Ward disagrees, arguing that the craze for elaborate iron fences arose out of a desire to imitate the fences found at the Père LaChaise cemetery in Paris, along with improvements in metalworking technology; see Blanche Linden-Ward, " 'The Fencing Mania': The Rise and Fall of Nineteenth-Century Funerary Enclosures," *Markers* 7 (1990): 35–58. But why should the "fencing mania" have occurred in the 1840s and 50s when illustrated books on Père LaChaise appeared in the 1820s? Linden-Ward's explanation also fails to account for the appeal of stone curbs. She suggests that "lot owners associated their funerary property with domestic space, . . . a place to be personalized and defined as private, albeit in a quasi-public landscape" (47). No doubt this is true. But why should such a need have arisen at this particular historical moment? In the context of the anxious sense of boundlessness and spatial formlessness expressed in the period's literature and political rhetoric, it may be more profitable to see the "fencing mania" of the late 1840s and 1850s, as well as the subsequent replacement of fences with stone curbs, as symptomatic of a midcentury need for solid boundaries—a way of producing finite space.

6. Henry David Thoreau, *Walden* (New York: Norton, 1992), 144.

7. Margaret Fuller, *"These Sad but Glorious Days"*: *Dispatches from Europe, 1846–1850,* ed. Larry J. Reynolds and Susan Belasco Smith (New Haven, Conn.: Yale University Press, 1992), 166.

8. Melville, *Mardi,* 10.

9. James Fenimore Cooper, *The Leatherstocking Tales* (New York: Library of America, 1985), 1:890.

10. Ibid., 898.

11. Cooper, *The Leatherstocking Tales,* 2:497–98.

12. Herman Melville, *Moby-Dick, or, The Whale* (New York: Penguin, 1992), 17. Hereafter cited parenthetically from this edition.

13. Walt Whitman, *Leaves of Grass* (New York: Library of America, 1992), 202.

14. George Louis Leclerc, Comte de Buffon, *Œuvres complètes de Buffon* (Paris: Baudoin Frères, 1824–28), 15:444, quoted in Antonello Gerbi, *The Dispute of the New World: The History of a Polemic, 1750–1900,* rev. and enlarged

ed., trans. Jeremy Moyle (Pittsburgh, Pa.: University of Pittsburgh Press, 1973), 5.

15. Gerbi, *Dispute of the New World*, 6.

16. For more on eighteenth-century European views of America, including the belief that American animals were smaller and feebler than European animals, see Henry Steele Commager and Elmo Giordanetti, *Was America a Mistake: An Eighteenth-Century Controversy* (New York: Harper & Row, 1967).

17. Gerbi, *Dispute of the New World*, 5.

18. *The Portable Thomas Jefferson*, ed. Merrill D. Peterson (New York: Penguin, 1977), 86.

19. Quoted in Kenneth E. Shewmaker, ed., *Daniel Webster "The Completest Man"* (Hanover, N.H.: University Press of New England, 1990), 129.

20. Edward Said, introduction to *Moby-Dick*, by Herman Melville (New York: Library of America, 1991), xxv.

21. The seminal work on *Moby-Dick* as political allegory is Alan Heimert, "*Moby-Dick* and American Political Symbolism," *American Quarterly* 15 (winter 1963): 498–543. See also James Duban, *Melville's Major Fiction: Politics, Theology, and Imagination* (DeKalb: Northern Illinois University Press, 1983).

22. Michael Paul Rogin, *Subversive Genealogy: The Politics and Art of Herman Melville* (New York: Alfred A. Knopf, 1983), 113, 114.

Fear of Seduction

The Allure of Alcohol in Late-Nineteenth-Century Temperance Thought

Elaine Frantz Parsons

It is not new to suggest that late-nineteenth-century temperance thinkers were afraid. Scholars have posited an extensive list of fears as motivations for the temperance movement. While some have claimed that temperance reformers were natives reacting against threatening cultural traditions and institutions introduced by immigrants, others have seen them as the middle class holding out desperately against the upper and lower classes, or as manufacturers afraid that the drinking of their workers would threaten efficiency and profitability. Still others have presented them as ruralites struggling against urban encroachment.[1] For all the diversity within these analyses, there is a common strain: temperance reformers were inspired by the desire to control the behavior of some group other than their own. Any reading of temperance newspapers, speeches, minutes, or pamphlets provides ample evidence that all of these fears were significant within the movement.

Turning from nonfictional sources to fictional ones, such as temperance novels, plays, and poems, changes this picture, however. American temperance fiction, which emerged in the 1830s with the writings of the prolific Lucius Manlius Sargent and grew in popularity through the antebellum period, came into its own in the 1870s through the 1890s. In these decades, temperance, religious, and popular presses published thousands of temperance novels, short stories, and plays.[2] Publication of temperance fiction would abate after the turn of the century, and such fiction would be much less significant by the beginning of national prohibition. But at its peak, in the Gilded Age, it was widespread enough that pamphleteers and the popular press felt comfortable alluding to it and parodying it in their pages without background explanation.[3] Dramatic renditions of novels such as *Ten Nights in a Barroom* were staples of traveling acting troupes; cheap paperbound scripts of hundreds of other temperance plays and pageants were made available to church groups, temperance societies, schools, and lodges; temperance short stories and poems were published in a wide array of popular magazines and newspapers; and temperance novels and stories, some by such august figures as Harriet Beecher Stowe, Walt Whitman, and Louisa May Alcott, went through multiple editions.[4]

Those who produced and consumed fictional temperance literature ought not to be understood as inhabiting an entirely separate place within the movement than those producing and consuming nonfictional sources. The two types of sources were understood to be absolutely interdependent. Temperance novelists would frequently interweave lengthy statistic-filled speeches into their works, and temperance speakers and pamphleteers would often attempt to gain their audiences' attention through a heart-rending tale or two, perhaps presented as "true stories" but certainly employing the generic conventions of temperance fiction. The major organ of the Woman's Christian Temperance Union, the *Union Signal*, like most other temperance papers of the day, promiscuously intermixed temperance stories and poems with statistics, news items, and committee reports in its pages. To talk about the fictional component in temperance writings is, in short, to identify an element essential to the movement as a whole.

By their nature, "fictional" genres leave room for some level of ambiguity and invite a sort of introspection that would seem out of place in a speech or pamphlet. Perhaps because of this difference, temperance novels, short stories, and poems reveal a different kind of fear from that most evident in nonfictional sources. Whereas the latter focus on a fear that some other group's drinking will disrupt the society inhabited by the reformer, the former reveal the fear that reformers themselves, or those close to them, will be seduced into the world of drink.[5] As these sources suggest, fear was central to reformers' motivation: not only a fear of the other but also a fear of the weakness of the self in the face of the other's seductions. It was as if temperance reformers had to destroy drink because they knew that it was too tempting to resist.[6]

Temperance writers' seemingly paradoxical tendency to glamorize alcohol in their literature was noted by some of their more astute contemporary critics. Kansas newspaperman and novelist Edgar Watson Howe, for instance, charged that temperance rhetoric made drink, the saloon, and even the drinker, appear exciting and dangerous, when in fact they were simply degraded:

> mistaken people also talk too much about the allurements and pleasure of drink: of the gilded palaces where drink is sold, and of its pleasing effects . . . [in reality] whiskey is man's enemy in every particular and his friend in nothing; . . . the "gilded palaces" in which it is sold are low dens kept by men whose company is not desirable; . . . the reputed pleasure in the cup is a myth, . . . drinking is an evidence of depravity as plainly marked as idleness and viciousness.[7]

Howe perceived an incongruity in a group of professed opponents of alcohol dwelling at great length upon alcohol's attractions. In his own novels, he regularly created hypocritical reformers who in fact participated, either in the very vices they condemned, or in others much worse.[8] But how widespread among temperance reformers was the tendency to glamorize the world of the saloon? And if it was widespread, can we, along with Howe, read this tendency as a sign of hypocrisy?

Though there is a good deal of diversity within the body of temperance fiction, there is also enough thematic unity that readers could know, within certain limits, what to expect when they picked up a piece of this fiction. The most common narrative in temperance fiction begins with a young male on the brink of manhood who, in longing to exercise the privileges of adulthood and yearning for excitement, allows himself to be lured, usually by a "fast" young man, into a saloon. The entry into the saloon, and the subsequent "fatal first drink" launch him into the downward spiral of the chronic inebriate. After the first drink, the story often drops off and is picked up a few years later, when the young man is well along the road to ruin. His young wife and children are suffering from hunger, cold, and his abuse. His parents have often gone to an early grave out of sorrow. He has drunk and gambled away everything that he has accumulated, and everything that had been built up by ancestors and passed along to his family. Ultimately, after a dramatic bout of delirium tremens, the drunkard usually either dies or is reformed through some external power or the sudden shock of having caused the death of a loved one.[9]

Temperance writers did not think of themselves as extolling the attractions of the saloon. But as Edgar Watson Howe pointed out, they ventured into that territory often enough that we can reconstruct what they found compelling about drink. Of course they had to concede a certain attractiveness to the saloon to make their own narratives plausible. A goal of temperance literature was to create or reinforce the conviction that alcohol was dangerous and ought to be prohibited or, at the very least, consumed far less. On the other hand, since the future drunkard was usually portrayed as an appealing and sympathetic figure, the author needed to give credibility to his decision to take that fatal first glass. That is, temperance writers needed to make drink and the saloon attractive enough to have lured a good young man from the path of virtue without making them so attractive that the reader would want to follow him. Temperance writers generally confronted this dilemma by acknowledging liquor's initial attractiveness, but then going on to expose this attractiveness as a mask behind which lurked the horrifying true consequences of drink.[10]

In describing the allure of the saloon, however, temperance writers seemed to go beyond the requirements of their narratives. When they explicitly addressed the issue of alcohol's attractiveness, they employed powerful images, such as jewels, bright lights, gilding, music, warmth, and mirrors to signal sensual attractiveness.[11] The rather implausible description of a working-class saloon from "The Drunkard's Wife" serves as a good example:

Ah, soon they beheld the door opened wide
That led to a tapestried palace inside,
Where chandeliers shone like jewels ablaze
And electric lights flashed like the sun's bright rays.
How bewitching the sight! Grand mirrors were there,
Bright pictures adorning the walls everywhere
And the noted works of sculpture and art
Were gleaming with beauty to ravish the heart.[12]

Through such lavish description, temperance authors opened themselves to Howe's criticism that they unnecessarily glorified alcohol. Not only did they associate saloons with sensual enjoyment, they also went an important step further by, bits and pieces, presenting drink and temperance as inhabiting separate and nonintersecting worlds and proceeding to construct a strikingly thorough and consistent set of dichotomies between these worlds. It was this set of dichotomies which betrayed how troubled their attitude toward drink was.

Gradually and unsystematically, temperance narratives separated drink, the drinker, and the saloon, on the one hand, from temperance, the sober citizen, and the home, on the other. As was noted above, the realm of the drink was associated with luxury, glitter, and brightness; the realm of sobriety was associated with simplicity and plainness. Similarly, whereas the realm of drink was associated with dreaming, illusion, fastness, the present, modernity, the city, chance, ambition, change, fantasy, and the pursuit of wealth with minimal labor, the realm of sobriety was associated with acceptance, nature, slowness, the past, tradition, the farm, virtue, resignation, stability, contentment, and the pursuit of moderate compensation through hard work.[13]

Temperance narratives stressed that these realms were entirely separate, that to pass the inevitable opaque screen, which at once blocked the view of the saloon's interior from the street and of the street from the interior of the saloon, was an irreversible act. One could not be a permanent resident of both worlds. In fact, descriptions of the interiors of saloons often took on the character of "travel narratives" for those who presumably had never crossed, and would never cross, the screen themselves, though they might encounter visitors from the world of drink among ubiquitous drunkards. Particularly for respectable women, who were absolutely forbidden to view the inside of the saloon, its interior was as inaccessible and distant as the Orient.

Just as the encounter with the foreign or the fantastic in the English literature of this period often served as a means to come to terms with social evils and terrible realities within English culture, things too frightening to be addressed directly, temperance writers imagined the world of the saloon as separate from their own world, and portrayed terrors there that they hesitated to acknowledge in their own world.[14] In this roundabout way, they placed the saloon in the midst of two great nineteenth-century discourses: moral responsibility and social mobility. In temperance fiction, the saloon served at once as the place where the morally upright, through one small, instantaneous, and heavily coerced choice, gave themselves over to a lifetime of sin, and where those young people who dreamed of better, easier, more splendid lives were led to their destruction.

During the last decades of the nineteenth century, the question of moral responsibility had come to the fore in social thought. These were the years during which social reform gave birth to social science disciplines, such as sociology and economics. Social reformers of all stripes, such as Jane Addams of Hull House and Frances Willard of the Women's Christian Temperance Union, became increasingly interested in collecting statistics relating individuals' criminal or antisocial activities to their parentage, environment, and education. Though statistics themselves could not predict the course of any given individual's life, their use allowed more certainty about the collective future of groups from the same area and background. These ideas challenged the notion of free will, so important in Christian thought; the rise of the social gospel, with its concept of collective salvation and of the necessity of social improvement to the propagation of Christianity served in large part to address this deeply troubling issue.[15]

The question of drink figured prominently into the debate over free will. Temperance advocates, in both fictional and nonfictional sources, asked how men should be expected not to drink when society provided licenses for enticing saloons to line his path as he walked home from work. Furthermore, the drunkard often served as "Exhibit A" for those who argued that a man could lose his free will, becoming a "slave to drink" or a mere pawn in the hands of the saloon keeper.[16] A number of state legislatures in the late nineteenth century passed "dramshop" or "civil damage" acts, shifting the civil responsibility for damage caused by the actions of a drunken man from the drunken man himself to the saloon keeper who had provided drink. In so doing, these legislators and the courts that interpreted their laws sometimes stated explicitly that the drunkard's acts, not being willful ones, did not supersede the saloon keeper's act of serving the alcohol as a proximate cause of injury.[17] In depicting the moment of the "fatal first drink" and in exploring the relationship of the drinker to his drink and to the saloon keeper, temperance writers participated in the wider cultural discussion about the nature of free will, as well as of moral responsibility for antisocial acts. Temperance novels should be considered alongside the many works of late Victorian fiction that attempted to express and explore that moment at which a person was transformed from an average man or woman into a social monster.[18] In imagining the saloon as a place where a good man, through one momentary lapse of moral vigilance, could be transformed into a drunkard who would deprive and brutalize his once-adored family, temperance writers explored the terrifying implications of loss of free will.

Much as writers of early American seduction narratives depicted the seduced as innocent or nearly innocent victims of the seducer's wiles, so temperance writers held saloon keepers and devious "fast friends" chiefly, or even solely, responsible for the drinker's downfall.[19] Taking advantage of the potential drunkard's weaknesses—his dream of achieving a more exciting and rewarding life than the one he knew, and his tendency to trust those who claimed to be working for his interest—these men and women convinced him that drink would bring him closer to his fantasy world of wealth, comfort, leisure, beauty, excitement, and elegance. Saloon keepers, in this literature, filled their establishments with gaudy mirrors, bright lights, and suggestive statuary and wore diamond stick pins and fast new suits.[20] Young women offering drink were always beautiful and always "bejeweled." Seduced by this promise of luxury and beauty that the victim had dared to hope would one day supplant his plain and "plodding" life, he took his first drink. The first drink often surpassed expectation. In Mary Chellis's *From Father to Son,* for instance, Casper, a young art merchant, takes his first drink, which gives him "a feeling of exhilaration" that would soon bring him back for a second.[21]

Temperance writers made it clear, however, that while a young man's curiosity and desire for excitement or change brought him to take his first glass, the violence and degradation that followed were out of his control. Significantly, given the contemporary debate about the importance of environmental and hereditary factors in determining criminal behavior, temperance writers went to great lengths to depict the drunkard's progress not as a sin or failing on his part, but rather as a seduction and enslavement by liquor itself.

Once a young man had entered the space of the saloon and had taken that fatal first drink he was, in the logic of temperance fiction, absolutely powerless to resist future drink. Sometimes a saloon keeper would covertly pour strong liquor in what was purportedly only small beer, or drug a customer's glass of liquor, or even serve liquor to a customer who thought he was drinking only soda water.[22] One fictional saloon keeper actually imprisoned a drunkard attempting to escape his clutches, fed him nothing but salt herring, and would allow him to drink nothing but beer. Another temperance novel went so far as to depict three of a town's four saloon keepers chasing a drinker-turned-reformer down the town's main street in broad daylight and ultimately gunning him down.[23]

One of the most obvious ways in which temperance writers manifested their anxiety about free will was in their tortured defenses of it. In works prior to the 1880s, many temperance writers asserted, often against the apparent logic of their own stories, that the drunkard was not entirely devoid of free will. Chellis's *From Father to Son* is perhaps the most strained of these attempts. Although this story of a moderate drinker's six sons—the older three of whom become drunkards, and the younger three of whom are saved only by the moral exertions of their father's new child-bride—seems to point the finger of blame for inebriety primarily at the habits of drunkards' ancestors and secondly at their parents' moral instruction, it still insists upon individual moral responsibility. In an argument between son Caspar, the art merchant-turned-drunkard whom we encountered earlier taking his "fatal first drink," and his temperate brother, the latter insists, "There are no chances in life, Caspar. What a man sows, that shall he also reap." When Caspar (who, according to Chellis, had "the power to will, without the strength to perform") bitterly asserts, "But parents sow for their children," the temperate brother rejoins, "That is true. Yet a man or woman with will, principle, and God's help, may break up fallow ground, and cast in seed which shall ripen and bear fruit in old age."[24] Yet, a mere seven pages after this reassuring discussion, the book ends with the brothers' father, a moderate drinker, looking, "with fast flowing tears" over another of his drunkard sons, beseeching God to "lay not my sin to his charge!"[25]

If the first horror of the temperance fiction saloon was the specter of the loss of free will, the second and equally ghastly horror was the impossibility of upward social mobility. It is at first counterintuitive to associate temperance with the *lack* of social mobility. Temperance, of course, had been closely associated with upward mobility since the early years of the movement, and fictional and nonfictional sources alike continued to tout the relationship between prosperity and total abstinence.[26] A young man who wanted to establish a reputation as a reliable business associate could advance his cause by "signing the pledge." But even in those early years, temperance fiction told another story about the relationship between social advancement and drink, one that worked alongside and undermined the first. After the first drink of the drunkard in one of the very first works of American temperance fiction, Lucius Manlius Sargent's short story, "My Mother's Gold Ring," the drinker "came home in wonderful spirits, and told [his wife] he meant to have [her] and the children better dressed, and, as neighbor Barton talked of selling his horse and chaise, he thought of buying them both."[27] Similarly, in Walt Whitman's early temperance novel, *Franklin Evans*, Franklin is made vulnerable to the seduction of drink through his ambition to leave his hard and thankless farming lifestyle for the risky opportunity to succeed in New York.[28]

From very early on, drink was closely associated in temperance literature with a dangerous desire for social advancement. Ambition served as both a warning sign that a man was likely to become a drunkard and, as in "My Mother's Gold Ring," a result of drink itself. This early association between drink and ambition continued alongside the association of temperance and social mobility through the late nineteenth century.

In the dichotomy between the realm of the sober and the realm of the saloon in temperance fiction, imagination and ambition were associated with drink, while contentment and resignation were associated with sobriety. Imaginative and ambitious young men were thought to be particularly susceptible to drink's seductive powers. Finding their day-to-day existence boring and unfulfilling, they imagined the possibility of better lives and tried to make their dreams realities.[29] Therefore, they were willing to take risks by drinking or engaging in other activities associated in this literature with drinking—moving to the city, speculating, or gambling. To step into a saloon was to enter a world of luxury and fellowship and, apparently, to travel in more exalted circles. It was also a world of constant transformation, where a man could be judged by his present appearance and behavior rather than by his family's station or his own past reputation. At the heart of the temperance writer's message was the age-old republican warning that once individuals placed themselves in the hands of chance, they would ultimately meet their destruction.[30]

Side by side with the temperance writer's advocacy of sobriety as the road to prosperity was the clear warning that the desire to prosper was a dangerous one, and that the young man with too much ambition was destined to fall prey to the saloon, lead a drunkard's life, and lose even that with which he had started. Prosperous sober characters in temperance fiction often made much of the fact that their prosperity came without conscious pursuit through their conscientious and steady hard work. A young man consulting a piece of temperance fiction for practical advice on "getting ahead" might well have found it more troubling than enlightening.

The ambitious man's attempt to improve his lot, his willingness to abandon his secure position in the real world in favor of the opportunity to create his own realities, placed him squarely within the realm of drink. In temperance fiction, only by preferring the natural to the artificial could a man be safe from the horrors of drunkenness. In the opening pages of *The Worst Foe*, for instance, the home of the temperate Denesmores comes complete with "a bubbling spring," contented cows, and beautiful flowers: a fine example of how "[m]an's intelligence, co-operating with nature, can make what was once beautiful more beautiful still. Nature is thus guided and aided by human intelligence, and the rugged grandeur softened and made pleasing to the eye."[31] The intemperate Day's house is in "marked contrast . . . farther up town and far more aristocratic than Mr. Denesmore's, more elegantly finished and furnished. Grand and proud as the home of some lord, it stands in the center of a large glass plot without tree or shrub, enclosed by stone wall and reached by a flight of broad stone steps."[32]

Outside of the realm of the saloon, appearances reflected either pure nature or nature enhanced by man's gentle and respectful improvements—whether the nature of objects or of individuals' social positions or intentions—whereas the realm of drink was removed from nature, a realm of pure construction: saloon fixtures appeared costly but were actually only base materials covered with thin layers of gilding; the stranger at the bar appeared to be a businessman just passing through town, but in fact was a professional gamester; the smiling barman appeared to be a generous host, but in fact was overcharging his customers and taking a cut of the gamester's profits.[33] The liquor served over the bar itself appeared to be pure, but in fact was an admixture of ingredients, each more vile than the next.[34] Directly upon entering into the realm of illusion, the drinker imagined himself to be entering the world of the prosperous, comfortable, and well-respected, when in fact he was on the road to ruin.[35]

In stepping into this unnatural world of drink, the ambitious young man-turned-drinker inevitably forgot the real world outside of the saloon. To quote again from "The Drunkard's Wife," when a drinking husband and father saw the saloon:

> Forgetting the darkness, the gloom the night;
> Forgetting his children so hungry and cold;
> Forgetting his wife with her heart of gold;
> Forgetting the ruin, the snare and the sin,
> He tore loose from her grasp and entered within.[36]

As the drinker's family became progressively poorer, as his house became shoddier, as he was finally unable to give any pretense of working, as his wife's pleas became more pathetic, as his friends fell away and his children began to die from want and abuse, he would spend more and more of his time escaping reality in this illusory world of the saloon. By crossing from the realm where things and people were as they seemed to one in which they were not, the drinker discovered that his formerly secure ties to the outside world had corroded.

The drunkard's progress was ultimately not only a progress from health to sickness, from comfort to want, but also, and perhaps most significant, from the realm of nature to the realm of illusion. That this progress was much in the mind of temperance writers is indicated by their frequent use of the delirium tremens scene as the emotional climax of temperance narratives. In the late nineteenth century it became almost unthinkable to present the story of a drunkard's decline without a good, melodramatic bout of delirium tremens toward its end. In a sense, delirium tremens was the quintessential illusion. Whereas the young man susceptible to the allure of drink imagined the possibility of a different life, and the confirmed drinker forgot his real life by entering into the fantasy space of the saloon, the man suffering through delirium tremens lost the use of his senses. That is, even when out of the saloon and in his own home (scenes of delirium tremens were usually set in the drinker's home), surrounded by his own family, he was unable to recognize the real through the layer of illusion created by his use of liquor.

The moment of this triumph of illusion was significantly also the moment of terror in temperance fiction. It was almost exclusively in the delirium tremens scenes that temperance fiction characters experienced fear. Even domestic abuse excited surprisingly little fear in temperance fiction: children killed by drunkard fathers were generally caught by surprise; wives beaten by drunkard husbands had attitudes of Christian resignation. In a fit of delirium tremens, however, the drunkard was described as alive with terror. Satan came for him, snakes and "enormous spider[s]" persecuted him, his eyes were wild, his face white. He clung to his children for protection against the demons. The terror delirium tremens inspired even in observers was considerable. In one temperance play a man who witnessed delirium tremens awoke the next morning to find that his hair had turned white overnight.[37]

Ultimately, the temperance-fiction saloon is the location where those young men (the ambitious, the dreamers) who have not learned to accept the "harsh realities of life" represented by tradition, the family, hard work, and sobriety, imagine they can remake themselves but are instead abjectly destroyed. Temperance writers seem to be sending a strong message: "escape is futile," they suggest, and it is folly to believe in radical self-determination. One had best to accept one's lot, "plodding" and "coarse" as it may be.

If the saloon served to house the social fears that temperance thinkers shrunk from directly confronting, how can one understand their tendency to emphasize the attractiveness of that same saloon? One important clue is found in the identification of temperance fiction writers with the figure of the drunkard. One might expect that the drunkard, lured into a world where neither social mobility nor free will is possible, would be a sort of "other" differentiated from the author. In an obvious way, he is. While temperance fiction drunkards were almost exclusively men, a clear majority of temperance writers were women. Although temperance writers were clearly aware of the existence of female drunkards, they generally made appearances as minor characters in a number of writings and only rarely took center stage. When they did, they were treated very differently, often with much less sympathy than were male drunkards.[38] Aside from this one very significant difference (to which we shall return in a moment), the typical temperance fiction drunkard—white, Anglo-Saxon, Protestant, and middle-class—closely resembled the typical temperance-fiction writer. Nor was he the dregs of white middle-class manhood. He was particularly handsome, particularly affable, even particularly "good" before his decline. The only failings commonly ascribed to men who would become drunkards were the possession of "too trusting natures," overactive imaginations, and ambitions too strong to transcend their station in life.

In Grace Strong's *The Worst Foe*, for instance, future drunkard Guy Denesmore is described as

> all a fond parent might ask. He was obedient, kind, with no ignoble qualities, and enough ambition to stimulate him to action, yet not enough to trample under foot the rights of others. Guy was a merry, unselfish lad, who, if he possessed any fault, was an overweening confidence in his friends and a tendency to have his actions directed by their desires. This weakness, if it was a weakness, was more the outpouring of a generous heart than a real fault.[39]

These traits, the potential drunkard's "fatal flaws," intriguingly enough were more commonly understood in American fictional tradition to be associated with women. The future drunkard's vulnerability to suggestion, indulgence in romantic notions, and willingness to leave home ties behind in pursuit of these notions, placed the drunkard squarely in the tradition of seduced heroines, such as Charlotte Temple.[40]

In fact, temperance writers commonly did depict the drunkard as "unmanned." The most obvious origin for the association between drinking and loss of manhood was, of course, the adverse effects of alcohol on male sexual performance. The association must have been particularly satisfying to temperance men and women so often characterized by their prosaloon opponents as "unsexed women and emasculated men."[41] However it originated, this relationship was commented upon and glossed incessantly in temperance novels, plays, poems, and songs: the drink competed with the wife, and the homosociality of the saloon was her other rival. In the language of temperance fiction, to behold a drunkard was to behold "manhood shorn of its manliness."[42]

Edgar Watson Howe suggested that temperance activists made it tempting to be a drunkard, for a drunkard, instead of having a multitude of character failings, was thought to have been perfect before taking the fatal first drink.[43] In fact, the science of the day gave authority to temperance writers' depictions of drinkers as superior beings: medical experts identified chronic inebriety as one possible manifestation of neurasthenia, a disease to which only those with particularly refined constitutions were susceptible.[44] Frequently, temperance authors chose the drunkards themselves to deliver their most concentrated temperance messages.[45] Even as the drunkard drank, he cursed the saloon keeper who took his money and the government that failed to prohibit saloons and remove him from the temptation he was unable to resist.[46] If the votes of temperance-novel drunkards' decided local option elections, the saloons would be long gone.[47] In these senses, then, the drunkard stands as a figure for the author rather than as some alien and threatening other.

Temperance authors created drunkards ethnically, socioeconomically, and religiously like themselves, suggesting that they were superior within their circles, and speaking their temperance messages through them. They seem to have wanted the reader to sympathize, even identify, with the drinker. Because of the gender difference between the drunkard and the writer and reader, however, this identification could not be a simple one. Though a significant number of women in the late nineteenth century suffered from addictions either to laudanum or to liquor-laden patent medicine, middle-class women, such as the writers of temperance fiction, were highly unlikely to encounter the public saloon directly. The protagonists of these narratives were not, then, properly homologous with the group of female reformers who produced them—but neither, given the ambiguity of their gender positions, were they simply opposed to their creators. Rather, it seems as if they were a displacement of the author.[48]

Reimagining temperance writers and readers—who formed a significant body within the temperance movement—as fearing liquor's seductive power, or a seductive power of which liquor was the emblem, rather than fearing the drinking "other," provokes a new set of questions. Rather than exploring what temperance activists found so disturbing about liquor and the saloon in which it was served, we need to turn the question on its head, asking what, precisely, temperance writers understood to be so dangerously attractive about drink and about the saloon.

The dangerous allure of the saloon to temperance writers was precisely its deceptive promise of self-transformation. The drinker believed that he could radically better his lot through an exertion of his will. He was willing to leave behind the comfort, protection, and tradition of the home in favor of the promises of the realm of drink. He desired—and temperance writers absolutely understood his desire—to pass into a forbidden realm, a realm of glitter, wealth, and risk, in which an individual could construct himself as one apart from the ties of family and community. But the reward was not worth the sacrifice—the exhilaration promised by the saloon proved momentary, the value of the domestic sphere was often realized too late.

Earlier I mentioned that temperance fiction served in the capacity of the travel narrative, since no respectable middle-class woman could ever hope to actually see the inside of the saloon. This is not precisely true. Temperance women could enter saloons as missionaries from the outside world during temperance crusades. By the turn of the century, most notoriously in the case of Carrie Nation, some few went so far as to enter these drinking establishments as invading warriors. Because of the temperance movement, in other words, women were increasingly moving into formerly male realms. This penetration had potentially troubling implications: perhaps temperance women were entering male spaces only to destroy them, but there they stood, side by side with the drunkard, in the very space that had so successfully seduced and ruined him.

The warning leveled in temperance fiction against the drunkard could easily be read as a warning against certain tendencies within the temperance movement itself. Clearly, there was a considerable overlap between those women involved in the temperance movement and those in the women's suffrage movement. The significance of the connection between these two movements is, however, still far from obvious, because temperance reformers have often been understood as the conservative troops only reluctantly amassed under the banner of women's suffrage. It is often suggested that their grudging acceptance of prosuffrage politics came about largely through three factors: the immense charisma and manipulative rhetoric of Frances Willard; the realization that suffrage, though distasteful, was the most effective means to achieve temperance; and the inevitable march of progress as women reformers' gradual inroads into the public sphere opened their eyes and whetted their appetites for more integrated forms of engagement.

Not enough attention, however, has been paid to the ways in which the content of the two movements related to one another. Was there something about the message of temperance that made it more effective in mobilizing traditionalist women for the suffrage cause than the countless other reforms of the late nineteenth century? The most obvious sympathies between the two causes were that the figure of the drunken father could easily be made to stand for the arbitrary and faulty nature of patriarchal authority in general—that, given the late-nineteenth-century notion that the drunkard had lost his will power, the problem seemed to call for a political rather than a personal solution, and that the problem was particularly amenable to portrayal as a "home protection" issue. All of these aspects of the temperance message worked to "bridge the gap" between domestic and the political. Perhaps equally important to temperance's effectiveness in mobilizing the reluctant, however, was its success in incorporating the fears of these women into the movement itself. The story of the drunkard, the central narrative of the movement, not only took these fears seriously, but in fact was built entirely around them.

If the drunkard served as a representation of the temperance writer, and if the narrative of the drunkard was an illustration of the dire consequences of his decision to leave home—to risk all in pursuit of the saloon's glittering promises of novelty and transformation—temperance fiction provided a cultural space for traditionalist women to express and work through their fears as they advanced into men's sphere. Because temperance, to a much greater extent than the suffrage movement, provided such a central space for these fears, temperance women were much less likely to be perceived by traditionalists as mannish, radical, or antifamily. Rather, a traditionalist woman encountering the movement would see a number of women sharing her fears, not embracing change and novelty eagerly, but stepping into new roles reluctantly—essentially out of duty and necessity. It was precisely in acknowledging and validating women's fears of moving into the public sphere that the temperance movement provided a space in which they could attempt such a move.

Notes

I have been extremely fortunate to have benefited from the skill and generosity of Ronald Walters, John Higham, Walter Michaels, Jotham Parsons, and Dorothy Ross, all of whom read this essay in draft form and gave valuable criticism. This paper is also the richer for numerous conversations with JoAnne Brown. I would also like to thank the participants in the NEASA conference for their thought-provoking feedback.

1. See, for instance, Norman H. Clark, *The Dry Years: Prohibition and Social Change in Washington* (Seattle: University of Washington Press, 1965), 68, 74; Joseph R. Gusfield, *Symbolic Crusade: Status Politics and the American Temperance Movement* (Urbana: University of Illinois Press, 1963); Also, see Andrew Sinclair's text and the introduction by Richard Hofstadter in *Age of Excess: A Social History of the Prohibition Movement* (1962; reprint, New York: Harper and Row, 1964); Barbara Lee Epstein, *The Politics of Domesticity: Women, Evangelism, and Temperance in Nineteenth-Century America* (Middletown, Conn.: Wesleyan University Press, 1981), 3-4; Harry Levine, introduction to *Profits, Power, and Prohibition: Alcohol Reform and the Industrialization of America, 1800-1930* by John Rumbarger (New York: State University of New York Press, 1989); Roy Rosenzweig, *Eight Hours for What We Will: Workers and Leisure in an Industrial City,*

1870–1920 (Cambridge: Cambridge University Press, 1983); Suzanne M. Marilley, "Frances Willard and the Feminism of Fear," *Feminist Studies* 19 (1993): 123–46.

2. This is a somewhat impressionistic account based on temperance fiction catalogued at the Library of Congress and on the Worldcat database, and on my own experience in other libraries and archives. Since I wrote this essay, an important collection of essays on temperance literature has appeared: David S. Reynold and Debra J. Rosenthal, eds., *The Serpent in the Cup: Temperance in American Literature* (Amherst: University of Massachusetts Press, 1997). Still, American temperance fiction awaits a comprehensive history.

3. See Charles Willsie, *The Eye-Opener or The Evil Fruits of the Prohibitory Law in Kansas* (Wellington, Kans.: n. p., 1890) [Kansas State Archives, Topeka, Kansas, Prohibition Pamphlets, vol. 2]; George Melville Baker, *A Little More Cider* (Boston, Mass.: Lee and Sheppard, 1870); and idem, "We're All Teetotalers" (Boston, Mass.: W. H. Baker 1876). Also see Edgar Watson Howe, *Story of a Country Town* (Atchison, Kans.: Howe and Company, 1888), 89–90.

4. Timothy Shay Arthur, *Ten Nights in a Bar-room, and What I Saw There* (Philadelphia, Pa.: J. W. Bradley, 1854); Louisa May Alcott, *Rose in Bloom: A Sequel to "Eight Cousins"* (Boston, Mass.: Roberts Brothers, 1876); Harriet Beecher Stowe, "Betty's Bright Idea," in *Betty's Bright Idea: also, Dean Pitkin's Farm; and the First Christmas in New England* (New York: Ford, 1875); Louisa May Alcott, "Silver Pitchers," in *"Silver Pitchers" and "Independence: A Centennial Love Story"* (Boston, Mass.: Roberts, 1876); Walt Whitman, *Franklin Evans, or The Inebriate: A Tale of the Times* (1842; reprint, New York: Random House, 1929).

5. Jack S. Blocker, Jr., *"Give to the Winds Thy Fears": The Women's Temperance Crusade, 1873–1874* (Westport, Conn.: Greenwood Press, 1985), shows that many women involved in the crusade were directly related to men who had been arrested for drunkenness or who were known drunkards (62, 85–88, 116). Blocker also argues forcefully against the notion that class and ethnic difference between crusaders and drinkers was the primary motivation for crusaders; Norman Clark, in his *Deliver Us from Evil: An Interpretation of American Prohibition* (New York: W. W. Norton & Co., 1976), also understands temperance advocates to be looking inward when he argues convincingly that temperance was a struggle for the buttressing of the "bourgeois interior" against the seemingly chaotic forces of rapid mobility and social change that assailed it. As early as the 1950s, Richard Hofstadter had recognized the importance of self-reformation to the progressives, but he excluded the prohibitionists from the ranks of progressivism; see Hofstadter, *Age of Reform* (1955; reprint, New York: Vintage Books, 1960). Jed Dannenbaum, in his *Drink and Disorder: Temperance Reform in Cincinnati from the Washingtonian Revival to the WCTU* (Urbana: University of Illinois Press, 1984), also suggests that the temperance reformers were not

only interested in controlling others, but also in reinforcing their own self-control (10, 219).

6. For a theoretical discussion of destruction and seduction, see Jean Baudrillard, *Seduction*, trans. Brian Singer (New York: St. Martin's Press, 1990).

7. Howe, *Story of a Country Town*, 98.

8. Howe, *A Moonlight Boy* (Boston, Mass.: Ticknor and Co., 1886), 182; idem, *Story of a Country Town*, 30, 111.

9. A. H. Griffith, *The Drunkard's Home: or The Curse of Rum* (Springfield, Ohio: Advertiser Printing Co., 1869), 19.

10. Grace Strong, *The Worst Foe* (Columbus, Ohio: W. G. Hubbard, 1885), 67, describes a saloon as a "gilded *hell.*" In Mary Dwinell Chellis, *All for Money* (New York: National Temperance Society and Publication House, 1876), it is asserted that saloon keepers are paid in "Glittering coin, whose baseness they fail to recognize" (211).

11. In T. S. Arthur, *Three Years in a Mantrap* (Philadelphia, Pa.: J. M. Stoddard and Company, 1872), the narrator's saloon is described as "shiny as a new pin" and as "done . . . up elegantly" (87, 96). In Emma Pow Bauder, *Ruth and Marie: A Fascinating Story of the Nineteenth Century* (L. W. Walter, 1895) (later published as *Anarchy*), Marie entices her future husband to drink "with jeweled hand" (57); in Mrs. Nellie H. Bradley's *The First Glass: or, The Power of Woman's Influence* (Washington, D.C.: Society of Temperance, 1867), before Frank West succumbs to the seductions of Mollie Mason, "Often ha[d] the ruby wine been proffered by the hand of beauty only to be refused" (7).

12. Mrs. Martha E. Whitten, "The Drunkard's Wife" (Austin, Tex.: Hutchins Printing House, 1887).

13. This constellation of qualities was attributed not only to the drinker but to the saloon keeper, who not infrequently would become a drinker towards the novel's end. For instance, in Chellis, *All for Money*, saloon keeper Wyatt "got enough of farm-work before [he] was twenty-one. [He wanted] to make money faster than [he could] by raising corn and potatoes" (204). He had become involved in the liquor trade after his attempt to open his own business had failed due to the periodic shifts of the market, to which he had made himself particularly vulnerable by leaving the farm. Also see the conclusion of T. Trask Woodward, *The Social Glass, or Victims of the Bottle: The Great Sensational Temperance Drama in Five Acts* (New York: Samuel French and Son, 1887).

14. See, for instance, Martin Tropp, *Images of Fear: How Horror Stories Helped Shape Modern Culture (1818–1918)* (Jefferson, N.C.: McFarland & Co, 1990); Elaine Showalter, "The Apocalyptic Fables of H. G. Wells," in John Stokes, ed., *Fin de Siècle/Fin du Globe: Fears and Fantasies of the Late Nineteenth Century* (New York: St. Martin's Press, 1992), 69–84; and Linda Cole, "The Rhetoric of Reform in Stoker's *Dracula:* Depravity, Decline, and the Fin-de-Siècle 'Residuum,' " *Criticism* 37 (1995): 85–108.

15. Dorothy Ross, *The Origins of American Social Science* (Cambridge: Cambridge University Press, 1991); and Paul T. Phillips, *A Kingdom on Earth: Anglo-American Social Christianity, 1880–1940* (University Park: Pennsylvania State University Press, 1996).

16. See a treatment of this theme in John W. Crowley, "Slaves to the Bottle," in *The Serpent in the Cup*, 115–35. In Laura M. Johns, "An Appeal to Kansas Teachers in Behalf of Temperance, Health, and Moral Purity" (Topeka: Kansas Publishing House, 1889), Johns asserts both that "Alcohol and tobacco paralyze the highest powers and aspirations and enslave the will" and "The origin of the evil [social impurity] is a long, sad way back. To cure a person of this ill the doctoring should begin some two or three hundred years before his birth. Holmes says: 'Every man is an omnibus in which ride all his ancestors' " (23).

   Though the language of slavery was pervasive throughout late-nineteenth-century temperance literature, perhaps the most striking example of the fictional depiction of drink as a form of slavery is Miss Jane Collins, *Free at Last* (Pittsburgh, Pa.: Press of Murdoch, Kerr & Co., 1896). This work tells the story of a temperate young freed slave who travels about spreading temperance ideas and is re-enslaved by the rum power. Other such examples abound. For instance, in Colfax Burgoyne Harman, *Redeemed by Love: A Temperance Play in Two Acts* (Oskaloosa, Kans.: n.p., n.d.] [Kansas State Archives, Topeka], the drinker holds the cup to his lips: "Thy will, not mine is holding sway / Thou dost command, I must obey." His wife enters and remonstrates with him and he decides that he does have will after all: "Drink alcohol—become a slave / For ever more with madness rave / Throw off the yoke and break the chain/Stand forth a conscient [*sic*] man again. / Make firm resolve—assert your will / Virtue enthrone! honor instill!"; also see Strong, *Worst Foe*, 151; Woodward, *Social Glass*, 32.

17. Blocker, *Give to the Winds*, 124.

18. I would like to thank Walter Michaels for this insight. Two of the most obvious examples are Robert Louis Stevenson, *Strange Case of Dr. Jekyll and Mr. Hyde* (New York: Charles Scribner's Sons, 1886); and Bram Stoker, *Dracula* (New York: Modern Library, 1897).

19. Jan Lewis, "The Republican Wife: Virtue and Seduction in the Early Republic," *William and Mary Quarterly*, ser. 3, 44 (1987): 717; Lewis A. Erenberg, *Steppin' Out: New York Nightlife and the Transformation of American Culture, 1890–1930* (Westport, Conn.: Greenwood Press, 1981), 79, 84; Dannenbaum, *Drink and Disorder*, also notes that late-nineteenth-century temperance advocates tended to place the blame for inebriety on the shoulders of the saloon keepers and drink manufacturers rather than on those of the drinker (81–83). Also see Epstein, *Politics of Domesticity*, 104.

20. Arthur, *Three Years*, 87, 96; Strong, *Worst Foe*, 66.

21. Mary Dwinell Chellis, *From Father to Son* (New York: National Temperance Society and Publication House, 1879), 218.

22. A.D. Milne, *Uncle Sam's Farm Fence* (New York: C. Shepard & Co., 1854); Woodward, *Social Glass*, 9.

23. B. G. McFall, *Among the Moon-Shiners, or A Drunkard's Legacy: A Temperance Drama in Three Acts* (Clyde, Ohio: Ames Publishing Company, 1897), 17; Mrs. W. S. (Ivy) Blackburn, *In the Toils of Slavery* (Chicago, Ill.: American Baptist Publishing Society, 1903).

24. Chellis, *From Father to Son,* 404, 405.

25. Ibid., 412. In the same novel, the father has a discussion with the temperate minister. He confesses that he "can't see why folks are any to blame for the way they are made up. It is the natural disposition of some folks to be cross, and ugly, and stingy. They show it when they ain't much more than babies, and they certainly don't know any better, do they?" (133).

26. For a discussion of antebellum temperance as a path to social mobility, see Ronald G. Walters, *American Reformers, 1815–1960* (New York: Hill and Wang, 1978), 141. See also Brian Harrison, *Drink and the Victorians: The Temperance Question in England, 1815–1872* (Pittsburgh, Pa.: University of Pittsburgh Press, 1971), for a treatment of the theme in the English context.

27. Lucius Manlius Sargent, "My Mother's Gold Ring: Founded on Fact" (Boston, Mass.: Ford and Damrell, 1833). Similarly, in A. H. Griffith's *A Drunkard's Home: or The Curse of Rum* [From Lynde Palmer's *Little Captain*] (Springfield, Ohio: Advertiser Printing Company, 1869), the father comes home from the saloon to tell his wife "we shall yet ride in our own carriage, we will move from these suburbs down into the city, you shall have servants, fine dresses and everything your want" (5).

28. Whitman, *Franklin Evans*, 45.

29. Similarly, an overly ambitious or dreamy young woman risked becoming a drunkard's wife: scorning the plodding farm boy, she chose the dashing young man headed for the city; see I. A. Sites, *Ned Hampden, or, The Ravages of Intemperance: With a Plea for Prohibition of the Liquor Traffic* (Reading, Pa.: D. Miller, 1893).

30. Karen Halttunen, in *Confidence Men and Painted Women: A Study of Middle-Class Culture in America, 1830–1870* (New Haven, Conn.: Yale University Press 1982), discusses the "cult of sincerity" in the mid-nineteenth century and explores the relationship between public drinking places and deception in nineteenth-century thought. For the classic discussion of the conflict between virtue and fortune in the history of Western culture, see J. G. A. Pocock, *The Machiavellian Moment: Florentine Political Thought and the Atlantic Republican Tradition* (Princeton, N.J.: Princeton University Press, 1975). For examples of this temperance literature suggesting that chance ultimately leads to destruction, see Arthur, *Three Years,* 52; and

"King Bibbler's Army," Words and Music by Henry C. Work (Cincinnati, Ohio: John Church and Company, 1877) [in the Lester Levy Sheet Music Collection, Johns Hopkins University Special Collections].

31. Strong, *Worst Foe*, 6.

32. Ibid., 17. Similarly, in Bauder's *Ruth and Marie*, "Nature had done much for" pro-drink heiress Marie Earnestine, "her brilliancy was in her diamonds; and the rouge upon her cheek was there instead of the healthful glow that might have been hers had she taken proper exercise" (3).

33. McFall, *Among the Moonshiners;* Woodward, *Social Glass;* Blackburn, *In the Toils.* Also in Whitman, *Franklin Evans,* Franklin admires a fashionable gentleman and a beautiful actress from afar. Upon closer inspection, they are revealed to be a waiter in an oyster bar and a "course," "sickly," and "masculine" woman (67–68).

34. Chellis, *All for Money*, 142.

35. Strong, *Worst Foe*, 68. In McFall, *Among the Moonshiners*, this focus on deception leads to the development of an early detective figure who appears in various disguises throughout the play. The goal of subverting the illusion of the saloon, and of making visible the truth beneath the illusion, was at the very heart of the project of temperance. Toward this end, temperance writers, when *they* fantasized, not infrequently imagined the possibility of such visibility. For instance, in an early piece of temperance fiction, George Barrell Cheever, "The True History of Deacon Giles' Distillery: Reported for the Benefit of Posterity" (New York: n.p., 1844), demons write warnings about the true consequences of drink in a sort of fiery invisible ink on liquor containers, to glow when the liquor is poured. The same dynamic is at work when temperance fiction drunkards look into their glasses and see demons or hellfire.

36. Whitten, "Drunkard's Wife."

37. Woodward, *Social Glass*, 30; Metta Victoria Fuller Victor, *The Senator's Son, or, the Maine Law: A Last Refuge; A Story Dedicated to the Law Makers* (Cleveland, Ohio: Tooker and Gatchell, 1853), 235; M. F. Carey, *Adela Lincoln: A Tale of the Wine Cup* (Philadelphia, Pa.: See, Peters, 1854), 235–36; Chellis, *From Father to Son*, 104; Rev. A. C. Gallahue, *Rumseller's Remorse: His Singular and Terrific Dream, His Desperation, Attempted Suicide, and Reformation* (New York: Wilbur B. Ketcham, 1891), 3; Blackburn, *In the Toils.*

38. Mrs. Nellie H. Bradley, *Wine as a Medicine: or Abbie's Experience* (Rockland, Maine: Z. Pope Vose, 1873); Mary Dwinell Chellis, *Wealth and Wine* (New York: National Temperance Society and Publication House, 1874); Chellis, *All for Money*, 297.

39. Strong, *Worst Foe*, 13; see also the description in Mrs. Nellie H. Bradley, *Reclaimed: or the Danger of Moderate Drinking* (Rockland, Maine: Z. Pope Vose, 1868), of drunkard George Stanley, "so proud and ambitious, pos-

sessing a cultivated mind and more than ordinary talent" (4). According to one character, in fact, "a firmer, stronger, nobler mind and clearer intellect than George Stanley's was never given to man" (6).

40. Mrs. [Susanna] Rowson, *Charlotte Temple: A Tale of Truth* (Philadelphia, Pa.: Printed for Matthew Carey, by Stephen C. Ustick, 1797).

41. Blocker, *Give to the Winds*, 75, cited from the *St. Louis Dispatch*.

42. Woodward, *Social Glass*, 19; Milne, *Farm Fence* (New York: C. Shepard & Co., 1854), 69; Strong, *Worst Foe*, 119. I would like to thank JoAnne Brown for reminding me not to neglect the physical effects of alcohol on male sexual performance.

43. Howe, *Country Town*, 97.

44. George M. Beard, *Sexual Neurasthenia: Its Hygiene, Causes, Symptoms, and Treatment* (New York: Arno Press, 1972); Norman Kerr, "Study of Inebriety and Its Relationship to the Temperance Movement," *Quarterly Journal of Inebriety* 12 (1890): 137.

45. Elizabeth Avery Meriweather, *The Devil's Dance: A Play for the Times* (St. Louis, Mo.: Hailman Brothers, 1886), 51; Robert M. Peace, *A Drunkard's Wife: A Drama in Four Acts* (Plainview, Tex.: Robert M. Peace, 1911), 15–17; Woodward, *Social Glass*, 14.

46. McFall, *Among the Moonshiners*, 3, 21–22; Milne, *Farm Fence*, 50; Chellis, *Out of the Fire*, 236.

47. In this connection, it is fascinating to read Jack London's autobiographical work, *John Barleycorn* (New York: Macmillan, 1913), which begins with London's announcement that he voted for women's suffrage in the hopes that women would close the saloons that were destroying him.

48. There are some exceptions to this generalization, of course. In Bauder, *Ruth and Marie*, Polly Hopkins is brought into a peripheral role in the story as a public drunkard. She had been made to drink her first glass by the heroine's father and was eventually discharged. Whereas the story required the redemption of the heroine's husband, to whom she had given the first glass, the end of the story found Hopkins, the female drunkard, still out on the streets (217, 248, 261–62).

Anxious Dwellings
The Rhetoric of Residential Fear in American Realism

Adam W. Sweeting

Dwellings and terror go hand in hand in early-nineteenth-century American fiction. From the decaying Gothic villas depicted by Charles Brockden Brown to the "putrefying fungi" that eats away at Roderick Usher's house, psychological distress often accompanies architectural decay. As several scholars have recognized, text and dwelling function as doubles in these works: readers enter into the claustrophobic house of Usher only to watch and even participate in the mental undoing of both the narrator and the protagonist.[1] As the house goes, so goes the tale. Drawing on well-established Gothic tradition, Brown and Poe use architectural space to locate spatially and symbolically their investigations of terror. The spatial figures as the psychological in their works.

We might call this strain in our fiction "architectural anxiety."[2] Such anxiety is not limited to the antebellum period, however; nor does it continue to manifest itself primarily through psychological terrors. Indeed, with the rise of realism in the late nineteenth century, the pattern of fears that I am calling architectural anxiety underwent a dramatic transformation. By unfolding itself from the individual house, the later variant of architectural anxiety soon embraced entire neighborhoods in cities. Whereas Brown located the terrors of *Wieland* within a house far removed from the urban community, the spatial fears of the realist novel derive from the very presence of the city and its people. In Howells and James the part of town where characters live assumes a new importance. Less frequently presented as zones of terror than their earlier counterparts, homes and neighborhoods in canonical realist texts instead become places to situate oneself within the rapidly changing cityscape.

There are of course exceptions. Charlotte Perkins Gilman's "The Yellow Wallpaper," for example, employs an architecture of terror reminiscent of earlier works. Henry James's ghost stories also draw on earlier modes of spatial fear. But when we look at the body of novels traditionally grouped under the rubric of nineteenth-century realism, we encounter a form of architectural anxiety that finds fear in urban geography.[3] This essay explores why this is the case.

Although much of my discussion documents specific examples of architectural anxiety, I am more interested in the role this anxiety played in the development of realistic fiction. By mapping the relationship between fear and architecture, I will argue, we can better understand both realism and late-nineteenth-century residential space. Of course, all definitions of realism remain notoriously slippery. In the aftermath of the new historicist projects of Amy Kaplan and Walter Benn Michaels we can no longer identify a body of work with a coherent definition for either realism, reality, or the real.[4] Rather, we must look to the social, economic, and literary practice of the writers we conventionally label realists. Realism emerges from such an analysis less as a fictional mode that purports to re-present the material world and more as a debate over what it means to represent anything at all. What follows draws on new historicist critics, particularly Kaplan and Michaels, to clarify the function of fear in the allocation and selection of residential space. As I hope to make clear, the genesis of these fears informs discussion of both literature and architecture. The two art forms, I will argue, contribute equally to the late-nineteenth-century psychology of fear.

Architectural anxiety usually represents itself as the fear of being misplaced. Not misplaced in the conventional sense of lost keys or wallets, but mis-placed—the state of occupying space that conflicts with one's sense of self. One's location within the urban pattern of streets and neighborhoods becomes an issue in the realistic novel, particularly in the novels published by Howells and James in the 1880s. Quite literally—and oxymoronically—characters in these works *find* themselves misplaced, a discovery that leads to no small amount of anxiety. In works such as *The Rise of Silas Lapham, Washington Square,* and *The Bostonians,* we encounter narrative voices acutely aware of the division between acceptable and unacceptable parts of town. These same narrators are equally aware of the social anxieties inspired by individual houses. Caught on the wrong end of social, cultural, and economic change, the Silas Laphams of the period struggle to place themselves more appropriately.

The anxiety fueled by architectural space has counterparts in other genres. The theater historian Una Chaudhuri, for example, recently coined the term "geopathology" to refer to "the problem of place" in early modern drama. With the emergence of realist drama in the late nineteenth century, tension-ridden residential spaces increasingly preoccupied playwrights. In Ibsen, Chekhov, and Strindberg, home functions as "a discursive field" in which characters reveal "a certain psychological homelessness." Indeed, works such as Ibsen's *A Doll's House* and O'Neill's *A Long Day's Journey into Night* derive much of their dramatic energy from characters who are in some sense misplaced within their homes. In *A Doll's House* the "previously given factualness of where one is" becomes "a matter of where one finds oneself." For Nora Helmer, this transformation leads to questions of "where one should be and where one belongs." Similarly, O'Neill's claustrophobic depiction of a family coming apart at the seams depends on characters who "occupy spaces without inhabiting them."[5]

Despite sharing traits with the geopathology of characters from Ibsen, Chekhov, and O'Neill, the architectural anxiety experienced by characters in American realist fiction contains far greater spatial specificity than its dramatic counterparts. Rather than feeling generally misplaced, characters in Howells and James novels associate particular locations or buildings with mounting feelings of anxiety. Unlike the dramatists, whose subject seems to be home-life itself, realist novelists focus on the spatial location of the home. In *A Doll's House,* for example, Nora feels misplaced not because she lives in particular section of town but because her husband treats her like a child. In *The Rise of Silas Lapham,* however, the title character believes himself misplaced because of the social implications of urban geography. Silas convinces himself that continued residence in Boston's South End will place a stain on his social standing while preventing his daughters from entering into better circles. "If the girls are going to keep on living in Boston and marry here," he claims, "we ought to try to get them into society."[6] Such a goal, Silas believes, can be attained only by moving to the right part of town. Howells, of course, also dissects the ethics of Gilded Age business practice, but in *Silas* he draws upon his knowledge of changing Boston demographics and residential patterns to chart a geography of morals. Where one is situated in the city is almost as important as how one behaves. Indeed, the two usually function in tandem.

Howells develops the business plot and love triangle that informs most discussion of the book by paying close attention to the moral geography of Gilded Age Boston. Set in 1875, the novel charts the efforts of Silas, a newcomer to wealth, to force his way into Brahmin society. The Laphams live in the South End, a once fashionable neighborhood that has recently fallen into decay. Wealthy families have either left for the newly opened Back Bay district or returned to the parlors of Beacon Hill.[7] Silas consistently finds himself on the wrong end of the social/geographic ladder. He had purchased his house in 1863 from a "terrified gentleman of good extraction who discovered too late that the South End was not the thing.[8] Still, the Laphams do not recognize the undesirability of their address until the summer before the start of the narrative. Once they become entangled with the Coreys, an old Brahmin family residing in proper Beacon Hill, Silas convinces his reluctant wife that their place of residence will prevent the children from entering the higher precincts of Boston life. Geography matters, they conclude.

Despite his vast wealth, Silas remains socially and spatially separate from the likes of the Coreys, a family whose diminished economic circumstances have not lessened its status. Nothing more brings home the Laphams isolation than Mrs. Corey's casual statement that she lost her way trying to find the Lapham's street. Fearing future similar embarrassments, Silas decides to build a new house in the Back Bay, where presumably the more prestigious location will lead to greater access to the elite. Nothing, of course, is further from the truth; Silas's new house goes up in flames before the family moves in. That a newcomer to money like Silas would ever be granted access to equal status in Brahmin Boston is revealed as a cruel hoax, a hoax utterly dependent upon the anxieties engendered by neighborhood exclusivity.

Howells again presented the specter of living in the wrong neighborhood during the famous search for an apartment in the 1890 *A Hazard of New Fortunes*. Here the city is New York rather than Boston, but the rapid social and economic change of late-nineteenth-century New York only accentuates the fears experienced by Silas in comparatively genteel Boston. In the later novel Howells devotes several chapters to the efforts of a young couple—the Marches—to find an apartment in a neighborhood that appropriately reflects their status. Mrs. March, who had been reluctant to leave Boston for New York, insists that her new home "was not to be above Twentieth Street nor below Washington Square." Change occurs so quickly, however, that areas of town only recently considered desirable have become off-limits to anyone with aspirations to residential grandeur. The search for an apartment takes the Marches through the gamut of New York neighborhoods. Forced to confront one unsightly scene after another, they learn the boundaries of respectable living. Struck by the disparities in cleanliness and cost, the Marches impose onto the Manhattan grid a new grid separating the barely tolerable from the beyond the pale. Mrs. March in particular understands the social meaning of streets. While her "husband was still stuck in the superstition that you could live anywhere you like in New York," Mrs.

March "found that there was an east and west line beyond which they could not go if they wished to keep their self respect."[9]

The apartment search is occasionally comic as the Marches traipse across the cityscape and lose track of the number of places they have seen. They even examine some apartments twice, forgetting their visits from the day before. Far less comic is the extent to which the house hunt also underscores the disparity between rich and poor in the metropolis.[10] Wholesale subscribers to middle-class aspirations of comfort, the Marches find in New York a series of neighborhoods that provoke either envy or disgust. One downtown street particularly unnerves them. Filled with trash and ash barrels and peopled by peddlers and drunks, the street's appearance advertised "a poverty as hopeless as any in the world." While earlier they might have found the view "picturesque," in the wake of the exhausting house search they find it "disgusting."[11] True, their hunt leads to an important understanding of the spatial and economic logic of the city, but their understanding pales before the fear that pockets of urban squalor inspire. Quite simply, the Marches are afraid; they fear becoming misplaced in a city whose regular, numeric street pattern would seemingly render misplacement impossible. But misplaced they are, scuttling from one block to another, wondering on which side of the line—acceptable or not—they will land.[12]

Although the Marches are well intentioned, their view of the city and its dwellings is mediated by the economic and cultural distance they place between themselves and their surroundings. They watch but do not fully understand the lives of poorer New Yorkers, a fact underscored during their ride on the Third Avenue El. While speeding past second floor apartments, Basil March claims that elevated transport was "better than the theater" because it enables riders to enjoy glimpses into urban domestic life. "What suggestion! What drama! What infinite interest!"[13] Theater, as Basil no doubt understands, implies a watcher and a watched, a physical and psychological split that inheres in performance. Like Jacob Riis, whose 1890 *How the Other Half Lives* offered middle-class viewers voyeuristic glances into tenement districts, Howells presents the range of social classes from the seemingly detached perspective of an outside observer. But whether in the theater or the views described by Howells and Riis, observers always stand apart; they enter into the place of performance but do not participate in the performance itself.

Such a rhetorical move informed much literary and artistic work aspiring toward "realistic" depictions of city life, even when the depicted scenes appeared less threatening than the poor of Howells and Riis. Students of American painting have identified a detached gaze in the urban canvasses of artists such as John Sloan. In *Sunday, Girls Drying Their Hair,* for example, Sloan positions the viewer just above the slightly erotic view of three women relaxing on a Manhattan rooftop. But while we are invited to the edge of the women's world, our view remains outside and above the scene. As with Riis's camera, the painting catches us staring. Sloan understood the voyeuristic aspect of his art, although he was at pains to distinguish his painterly gaze from its salacious counterpart. In a 1911 diary entry, he claimed that "I peep through real interest, not being observed myself." Less subtle ways of watching, he continued, reveals "evidence of real vulgarity." Elsewhere, Sloan berated friends who stared too intently into the windows of neighboring apartments.[14] Still, for Sloan and similarly inclined artists and writers the seemingly detached glance toward others remains central to their work. We might even call it the essential gesture of realism.

Alan Trachtenberg identifies this kind of view as a "touristic device" of the middle class, "wherein the worlds of the subject and the observer remain separate and distinct."[15] By bringing viewers to the edges of tenement life, Riis defined a social space that respectable people should not enter. The Marches' search for the line defining residential respectability follows a similar aesthetic dynamic. Like Riis's camera, they gaze at but remain slightly aloof from squalid living quarters. Of course, the motivations of Riis and the Marches are quite different. Riis seeks to alter living conditions while the Marches are content just to gaze. Both, however, remain epistemologically separate from their subjects.[16] The lives of the poor can be shown, but never fully known. As a result, an absolute psychological line divides places to inhabit from places to avoid. The visible presence of poverty, however, always threatens to blur that line. Moreover, the logic of the realist stare potentially works both ways; one can just as easily become the object of such a gaze. With everything and everyone a stared-at object, we can hardly wonder that the Marches' search for living space occurs in a climate of fear.

Henry James also diagnosed the fear of being misplaced in the wrong neighborhood, although not with the same detail Howells employed. James, of course, used architectural metaphors more frequently than any other figure in American letters, giving rise in turn to a rich hermeneutical tradition of houses in his work.[17] His remark that "the house of fiction has in short not one window, but a million" has led readers to see in his work a pattern of spatial metaphors that associates the construction of consciousness with the building of a house.[18] Less remarked upon is the spatial specificity of Jamesian architectural anxiety. Like his friend Howells, James charts his characters' movements through cities with an eye toward locating them in appropriate spaces. Early in

Washington Square, for example, the narrator offers a "topographical parenthesis" to describe the neighborhood of the heroine, Catherine Sloper. Catherine's father had moved to the north side of Washington Square in 1835, considerably after New York's leading families had fled his former neighborhood near City Hall. By the time the Slopers had moved, the "murmur of trade" and "the base use of commerce" had rendered their downtown location undesirable. Unfortunately for the Slopers, Washington Square had already lost some of its luster when they settled there in the 1830s. Catherine's favorite aunt had set up house "in an embryonic street with a large number," a region, the narrator remarks, "where the extension of the city began to assume a theoretical air." The move of society uptown leaves the narrator forlorn. James fills the page-long parenthesis with regrets that Washington Square had been left behind. The area has "a riper, richer, more honorable look than any of the upper ramifications" of New York. The narrator remarks that here, some thirty years after the events described in the novel, one could comfortably have a "social life."[19]

The social history of changing neighborhoods also informs James's 1883 novel, *The Bostonians*. As Janet Wolf Bowen has claimed in her study of architectural envy in *The Bostonians*, the novel "incessantly fluctuates between the appeal of being housed and unappealing houses."[20] While the principal characters may temporarily occupy a house, they shuttle from room to room, from street to street, and even from city to city in an unending quest for stability. Olive Chancellor, for example, lives at the foot of seemingly stable Beacon Hill, but she and others are led to several neighborhoods where demographic fluctuation turns the hope for residential stability into a never obtained dream. On one such occasion, Olive and her cousin Basil Ransom travel by coach to the South End, the very neighborhood from which Silas had fled. They arrive at a house caught between eras; it has "a peculiar look of being both new and faded—a kind of modern fatigue," the narrator suggests. The house itself is a center of activity, but its many residents are transients, "among whom there prevailed much vagueness of boundary."[21] The word "boundary" is important in this context. Unlike the proper middle-class March family—which masters the line between acceptable and unacceptable neighborhoods—the artists, activists, and hangers-on in James's South End remain unaware of that line. The transient nature of the neighborhood makes it difficult to determine one's proper place.

The difficulty of developing feelings of home within the transient rental economy contributes to the realist sense that geography occasions fear. In *The Rise of Silas Lapham*, for example, the newspaper man Bartley Hubbard sheepishly confesses that occupying rented space is analogous to residential death. When Silas asks the young man where he resides, Hubbard responds, "we don't live; we board." He quickly adds, however, that he will "soon be under a roof of [his] own," assuming that Silas will applaud the move toward ownership.[22] Lily Bart in *The House of Mirth* also finds herself abandoned to the vagaries of the rental market. Unlike Hubbard, her renter's death functions as more than a simple metaphor. Throughout the novel she visits the homes of others, but never has one of her own. Out of money and seemingly out of options, she eventually takes her life in a rented flat far downtown. Her friends are troubled by the turn of events, so much so that Rosedale, her occasional suitor, can barely disguise his disgust while escorting her home. Acutely aware of the ramshackle appearance of her street, "Lily felt that Rosedale was taking contemptuous note of the neighborhood."[23]

Because neighborhood fluctuation and the transience of renting could inspire such anxiety, individual houses functioned as indices of order. Consequently, the appearance of one's house could itself turn into the cause of nervousness. Once again, Howells's *The Rise of Silas Lapham* provides perhaps the clearest example. Once Silas decides to move from one part of town to another he must overcome the fear of architectural embarrassment, which he attempts to do by peering through the windows of homes in the Back Bay. Adopting the spectatorial gaze characteristic of realism, Silas stares into and attempts to replicate the living conditions of other wealthy men. Unfortunately, the fear of embarrassment and his own "crude taste in architecture" leads to building decisions that he does not understand and cannot afford. Primarily concerned with the exterior appearance of his house, Silas envisions a house with "a brownstone front, four stories high, and a French roof with air chamber above." To avoid catastrophe, the Laphams hire an architect, Seymour, whose homophonic name suggests a heightened ability to observe. One by one Silas's assumptions are shattered, as Seymour persuades his client to forego most of his initial plans. The high entrance is replaced with a low ceiling. Silas's hoped-for fancy cornices become Seymour's "effect of amplitude and space." The former's dream for walnut walls stained with black succumbs to the latter's insistence on exposed wood. At the end of their conversation, Silas stands befuddled, unable to prevent any of Seymour's transformations. Once he recovers from the "complete upheaval of his pre-conceived notions," Silas announces that he "swears by the architect."[24] Whatever oath he utters, however, grows out of his initial fear of embarrassment.

Walter Benn Michaels's discussion of the function of commodities in late-nineteenth-century fiction applies to Silas and his house. Michaels identifies a commodity as "an example of a thing whose identity is something more than its physical qualities."[25] For all of his bluster, Silas recognizes that domestic space had entered into just such an economy. Like all houses, the one Silas hopes to build embodies a system of value exchanges. As it is designed, constructed, and eventually destroyed, the house assumes new aesthetic, economic, and cultural values. Silas stands in a speculative relationship to his house. He gambles that the residence within its walls will elevate his social standing within the city. But like all exchanges, this one works in more than one direction. The economic and cultural value of Silas's new residence must be negotiated within the context of the broader urban community. Silas's abdication to Seymour thus makes perfect sense. With the stakes so high, entrance into the economy crafted by an expert such as an architect is a necessary step for anyone hoping to participate in modern urban culture. Indeed, given Silas's nervousness and fear, his willingness to turn all decisions over to an expert seems the only logical solution.

The question remains, however, as to why residential location and neighborhoods became so problematic with the rise of realism? Or, to phrase the question slightly differently, why does realism lend itself to this particular form of spatial anxiety? One reason no doubt grows out of a long-standing American belief that physical space and character are intimately related. Jefferson relied on this connection when he platted a nation of orderly towns divided into equal sections that marched across the country. His 1785 plan for future settlement was as much a moral document as it was a vision of space. In a much different context that nonetheless relied on a similar faith, antebellum architects such as Andrew Jackson Downing viewed domestic spaces in distinctly moral terms.[26] But the fear of being embarrassed by one's home represented a new twist in our literature. Surely publications such as Charles Lock Eastlake's 1878 *Hints on Household Taste* fueled the fear of embarrassment.[27] But just as surely, these publications entered into the marketplace precisely because of widespread architectural unease.

A second reason for the appearance of architectural anxiety stems from the dramatic changes in urban space during the last decades of the nineteenth century. Advances in street transportation, electricity, and steel construction allowed for an unprecedented reorganization of urban space. In Boston, entire neighborhoods were created on land reclaimed from the swamp known as the Back Bay. In New York, city space vaulted skyward with the advent of skyscrapers. At the same time, the first apartment buildings created zones of privacy within the new regions of vertical space. Howells himself was a committed apartment dweller, first at the Chelsea Hotel, then on East 17th Street, and later in a studio on East 57th.[28] Even if we assume that the realist project has aims other than mere verisimilitude—and we should—an author setting fictional works in the modern city would have to account for the disruptions of usual patterns caused by the new cityscape. Architectural anxiety was also clearly a manifestation of the social and spatial distinctions wrought by the economic roller coaster of the Gilded Age. With fortunes to be made and lost, the physical trappings of wealth assume a larger importance. Such is clearly the case in *The Rise of Silas Lapham*.

But realism leads to architectural anxiety for reasons other than verisimilitude and social climbing. As Amy Kaplan has argued, "realism" occupies a cultural space between competing forms of representation. It mediates between different strategies to present "the real."[29] An author such as Howells positioned his "reality" against the supposedly documentary reality of daily newspapers. Silas himself questions his portrayal in a newspaper profile written by Bartley Hubbard. But rather than judge realism for the success or failure of its representation, Kaplan argues that we should instead view this form as an attempt to understand and describe social forces that to many seemed increasingly "unreal." In this view, realism tries to "tame" the unreal by bringing it into representation. Architectural anxiety fits this model, particularly in Howells, whose houses and streets find meaning in the efforts of characters to use the urban built environment to solidify their place within the community. Unfortunately, Silas and his literary brethren forever play catch-up with a system that refuses to set permanent value on anything, least of all a house.

Although not specifically residential space, commercial pleasure zones, such as department stores and hotels, mediate between the individual house anxiety of Silas and the neighborhood nervousness of the Marches. For in such places the distinction between interior and exterior spaces lessens, a blurring that can help us understand both architectural anxiety and realist fiction. As the geographer Mona Domosh has noted, new department stores and other commercial spaces unfolded previously private areas such as bedrooms and dressing rooms into public view. Grand window displays in 1880s department stores, such as Lord & Taylors' and A. T. Stewart's, presented apparently private scenes in an unabashedly public manner.[30] The ethic of consumption represented by these architectural spaces could lead one to wonder what was public and what was private. While realist fiction depends on a seemingly private consciousness observing a public spectacle, department store windows simultaneously emphasized and negated the distinction between the two realms. Separated from the objects by a wall of glass, public crowds gazed into the private world. In doing so, however, they called into question the notion that there existed any discernible difference between them. Like Sloan's women—whose intimate private moments became public—the presence of clothes, furniture, and appliances in store windows turned apparently private purchasing decisions into the subject of public scrutiny. The private had become entirely public, a transformation made possible and apparently natural by the power of architectural space.

Given the ever present sense that the inside flowed out, the emphasis on the appearance of doors in Edith Wharton's *The Decoration of Houses* should hardly cause wonder.[31] Doors exist within a peculiar architectural and private space; they separate the inside from the out, but also allow passage from one zone to the next. What can be said of doors can also be said of the architectural spaces that interest Howells, for in these spaces we encounter the operation of both public and private consciousness. Whether we are in Silas's Boston or in the Marches' New York, a neighborhood is both a private place to live and the subject of public commentary. Similarly, a house houses private individuals, but it also faces public thoroughfares. It is worth remembering that Silas Lapham was particularly interested in the exterior of his house, the place where his individual aspirations would be tested by community standards of taste. For Silas and all other house builders the walls of a house create the line where the public and private converge. Any embarrassment projected outward from these walls simultaneously projects inward to the residents.

A brief but telling passage in Henry James's *The American Scene* exemplifies the anxiety engendered by the confusion between public and private space. While sitting in the restaurant of the Waldorf-Astoria Hotel, James finds himself misplaced amid the public spectacle. During his twenty-year absence from New York, the private act of eating had become a highly decorous act, replete with its own codes and potential pitfalls. Sitting in the restaurant of a hotel, a structure that carves private rooms out of its larger public space, James wondered at the "immense promiscuity" of his setting.[32] He yearned for an experience of privacy that this new public space essentially precluded. Like Howells and Wharton, James recognized that one's place in space was challenged by the new urban form. Location mattered profoundly, but space had implications even more complex than location. It is in this context of confusion over public and private that we can best understand the new architecture of anxiety.

Notes

1. Marilyn R. Chandler, *Dwelling in the Text: Houses in American Fiction* (Berkeley and Los Angeles: University of California Press, 1991), 3–5.

2. Janet Wolf Bowen uses the phrase "architectural envy" to describe a related reaction to architectural form: "Architectural Envy: A 'Figure Is Nothing without a Setting' in Henry James's *The Bostonians*," *New England Quarterly* 65 (March 1992), 3–23. While anxiety certainly may include a degree of envy, I am more interested in the overall patterns of fear inspired by the urban built environment. Bowen's analysis, however, is cogent.

3. The geographer Yi-Fu Tuan discusses the varieties of fear experienced in cities in *Landscapes of Fear* (Minneapolis: University of Minnesota Press, 1979), 145–74.

4. Amy Kaplan, *The Social Construction of American Realism* (Chicago, Ill.: University of Chicago Press, 1988); Walter Benn Michaels, *The Gold Standard and the Logic of Naturalism: American Literature at the Turn of the Century* (Berkeley and Los Angeles: University of California Press, 1987).

5. Una Chaudhuri, *Staging Place: The Geography of Modern Drama* (Ann Arbor: University of Michigan Press, 1995), 11, 53, 56–63.

6. William Dean Howells, *The Rise of Silas Lapham* (New York: Signet Classic, 1963), 29.

7. Walter Muir Whitehill discusses the transformation of the South End in *Boston: A Topographical History* (Cambridge, Mass.: The Belknap Press of Harvard University Press, 1968), 119–40.

8. Howells, *Rise of Silas Lapham*, 24.

9. William Dean Howells, *A Hazard of New Fortunes* (New York: New American Library, 1965), 67, 51.

10. Da Zheng, *Moral Economy and American Realistic Novels* (New York: Peter Lang, 1996), 56.

11. Howells, *Hazard of New Fortunes*, 56. Peter Conrad discusses Howells's use of picturesque vocabulary in *The Art of the City: Views and Versions of New York* (New York: Oxford University Press, 1984), 67.

12. The best discussion of the apartment search occurs in Kaplan, *Social Construction*, 44–55. Kaplan is particularly good in discussing the importance of lines between neighborhoods.

13. Howells, *Hazard of New Fortunes*, 66.

14. Quoted in Patricia Hills, "John Sloan's Images of Working-Class Women: A Case Study of the Roles and Interrelationships of Politics, Personality, and Patrons in the Development of Sloan's Art, 1905–16," *Prospects* 5 (1980): 178. For discussion of Sloan's rebuking others for not knowing how to stare, see John Loughery, *John Sloan: Painter and Rebel* (New York: Henry Holt & Co., 1995), 153–54. Both Loughery and Hills take issue with arguments that Sloan displayed overly voyeuristic tendencies.

15. Alan Trachtenberg, "Stephen Crane's City Sketches," *American Realism, New Essays*, ed. Eric J. Sundquist (Baltimore, Md.: The Johns Hopkins University Press, 1982), 144.

16. For discussion of the importance of staring in Riis's work, see Conrad, *Art of the City*, 155–57.

17. For James's use of architecture, see Elizabeth Sabiston, "Isabel Archer: The Architecture of Consciousness and the International Theme," *The Henry James Review* 7 (winter–spring 1986), 29–47; and R. W. Stallman, "Some Rooms from the Houses That James Built," *Twentieth-Century Interpretations of* The Portrait of a Lady," ed. Peter Buitenhuis (Englewood Cliffs, N.J.: Prentice Hall, 1968), 37–44. Marilyn Chandler's chapter on James in *Dwelling in the Text* offers an excellent discussion of architecture as metaphor.

18. Henry James, Preface to the New York Edition, *The Portrait of a Lady* by Henry James (New York: Charles Scribner's Sons, 1980), x.

19. Henry James, *Washington Square* (New York: New American Library, 1964), 16–17.

20. Bowen, "Architectural Envy," 7. Bowen's discussion of urban space in *The Bostonians* is the most comprehensive to date.

21. Henry James, *The Bostonians* (London: Penguin Books, 1986), 54, 57.

22. Howells, *Rise of Silas Lapham*, 15.

23. Edith Wharton, *The House of Mirth* (New York: Alfred A. Knopf, 1991), 308.

24. Howells, *Rise of Silas Lapham*, 38–39, 41.

25. Michaels, *Gold Standard*, 21. My reading of Silas's sense of his house has been greatly influenced by Michaels's description of the function of commodities in late-nineteenth-century fiction.

26. I discuss the importance of moral imagery in early American architecture in *Reading Houses and Building Books: Andrew Jackson Downing and the Architecture of Popular Antebellum Literature, 1835–1855* (Hanover, N.H.: University Press of New England, 1996), 93–121.

27. Chandler, *Dwelling in the Text*, 154.

28. Elizabeth Hawes, *New York, New York: How the Apartment House Transformed the Life of the American City (1869–1930)* (New York: Alfred A. Knopf, 1993), 113–28.

29. Kaplan, *Social Construction*, 12–13.

30. Mona Domosh, *Invented Cities: The Creation of Landscape in Nineteenth-Century New York and Boston* (New Haven, Conn.: Yale University Press, 1996), 63.

31. An excellent discussion of the importance that Wharton assigned to doors is in Sarah Luria, "The Architecture of Manners: Henry James, Edith Wharton, and the Mount," *American Quarterly* 49 (June 1997): 298–327.

32. Henry James, *The American Scene* (New York: St. Martin's Press, 1987), 74.

Terrorism as Terrorific Mimesis in Floyd Salas's *State of Emergency* (1996)

María DeGuzmán

> my torturers would hold a mirror to my face
> —Floyd Salas, *State of Emergency*

Self-termed "Spaniard/Spic/Hispanic" writer and ex-boxer Floyd Salas's work is well-acquainted with fear.[1] From Salas's first three novels, *Tattoo the Wicked Cross* (1967), *What Now My Love* (1969/1994), and *Lay My Body on the Line* (1978), through the more recent *Buffalo Nickel: A Memoir* (1992), *State of Emergency* (1996) and his book of poems *Color of My Living Heart* (1996), so well acquainted with fear is his work that fear might be said to function as a "familiar." Fear operates in guises ranging from constant companion to inquisitorial accuser, a cross between Diogenes' faithful dog and a menacing shadow. Fear is ever present, inspiring mistrust, vigilance, and a kind of perpetual Kierkegaardian anguish turned sociopolitically specific along Dostoevskian lines. In Salas's work, one finds fear of incarceration and degradation; of the adolescent "reform" system; of Death Row and capital punishment; of blatant injustice and futility; of physical and psychological abuse; of betrayal by family, friends, and lovers; of selling out and prostituting oneself; of the tyranny of an "overdeveloped, technological police state society"; of narcotics agents, the FBI, and cops, especially plainclothes policemen; of police brutality; and of right-wingers and a right-wing coup.[2]

All these specific sociopolitical fears in Salas's work may be classified as fear of fascism. This fear of fascism is most concisely articulated in the 1978 novel *Lay My Body on the Line,* the prelude to the 1996 novel *State of Emergency* with which this essay is principally concerned. Roger Leon, the main protagonist of both *Lay My Body on the Line* and *State of Emergency,* thinks to himself:

The most important thing of all is to have the freedom to fight the
fascists of whatever color, flag, nationality or ideology, the MVD
or the FBI, Beria or J. Edgar Hoover, the Rockefellers or the party
bureaucrats, all the oppressive enemies of freedom. Freedom, that
is the issue, that is what is at stake. Political freedom. Economic
freedom. Spiritual freedom. Freedom is the key to progress and
unfettered evolution, the end result of a genuine peoples' revolution.[3]

While "fascism" and "freedom" remain somewhat undefined or abstract, two things are clear. "Fascism" is opposed to "freedom" and
"freedom" is linked to self-determination and individual liberty conceived of in a collectivist, not individualist, sense—hence, the phrase "a
genuine peoples' revolution." Freedom for the Salas of *Lay My Body on
the Line* is synonymous with "true democracy," which he terms "a blend
of Marx and the Bill of Rights."[4] While "fascism" is not equated exclusively with the United States, *Lay My Body on the Line* hardly exempts
the United States from its grip—from either its institutional formations
or its restructuring of subjectivity, by which I mean the effect of an
internalized ideology on a person's conceptions, interpretive and analytical abilities, judgment, feelings, and behavior. As *Lay My Body on
the Line* unequivocally conveys through Roger Leon's reflections on his
trials and tribulations as a Berkeley Bay Area activist in the political
movements of the 1960s, "the State can break the love of any human
being on earth, except for those few rare people willing to die first."[5]
Salas's novels construe "the State" as meaning more than the "government" per se in order to signify that apparatus by which society regulates, channels, circumscribes, and invades the dreams, desires, and actions of its citizens. "The State" includes prisons, mental hospitals,
schools, media and campaign bureaus, and numerous other sites and
sources of so-called authority, expertise, and information. Through this
figuration of the State as an intimate and familiar agent of fear, Salas's
novel endeavors to dissolve the Cold-War boundary between the United
States and Stalinist Russia. In short, fear of fascism in Salas's novels
brings fascism home, not in the sense of creating fascism where none
existed before, but in the sense of endeavoring to retrace the grounds of
its existence in U.S. culture—especially in the reaction formation of
authorities to the civil rights and student peace movements of the 1960s.
  Both Salas's presumably nonfictional memoir *Buffalo Nickel* (1992)
and an 1989 interview with Gerald Haslam have encouraged readers
and critics to see fear of fascism as more than an abstraction, a groundless anxiety, but instead as having a basis in actual lived experience. In

Buffalo Nickel sentences, passages, people, and situations reappear which first emerged in the supposedly "fictional" novel *Lay My Body on the Line*, published fourteen years earlier. A reader may well wonder whether Roger Leon is not Salas's "persona" and, furthermore, his alias. In the interview with Haslam, Salas declares, "Roger Leon's behavior in *Lay My Body on the Line* was an objective correlative of paranoia. But his paranoia came from his perception and experience. Where there's smoke there's fire."[6] Here, the writer seems to be prompting readers toward an identification of himself with his protagonist and of fascism with actual "perception" and "experience." With the stated exception of *Tattoo the Wicked Cross* (1967), Salas's novels are in fact more or less autobiographical.[7] That is to say, they are thinly veiled fictional reenactments of real-life experiences and are characterized by a bittersweet tone, by almost embarrassing disclosures, as well as by a tendency toward self-justification and the sometimes facile judgment of other people/characters.

The biggest difference between *State of Emergency* and the other novels, including *Lay My Body on the Line*, is its emphasis on the effects rather than the causes of fear, particularly fear of fascism. *State of Emergency* presents fascism as state-sanctioned terrorism and vice versa. However, this latest novel suggests that the fear of fascism is implicated in terrorism and fear is symptomatic—as a warning sign against the social disease of fascism and as an indication of the damage to individual subjectivity by the internalization of such a totalizingly guarded view of things. *Lay My Body on the Line* began this exploration of the effects of fear of fascism. Referring to this novel, Salas himself tells his interviewer Gerald Haslam:

> It drives him [Roger Leon] nuts, makes him bitter and destroys the good impulses he started with. I think that very characterization could be applied to Abu Nidal, the renegade Palestinian terrorist. I meant to show that Roger is now on the edge himself to becoming just that sort of terrorist if things don't change."[8]

Fear, the catalyst to change, can backfire and turn attempted revolution into terrorism and an idealist into a terrorist. But in *State of Emergency* Roger Leon does not become a terrorist. This novel moves away from the clichéd Cold-War scenario of enmity between the United States and the Soviet Union and takes up where Ernest Hemingway left off and uses the relatively unexamined alliance between the Franco regime in Spain and the Nixon administration in the United States.[9] In this way, the novel avoids the conventions of many contemporary international espionage and terrorism thrillers. That is, *State of Emergency* refrains from

the reification of sociopolitical conflict into incidents and mere plot—
for example, terroristic acts—and also refuses the epistemological certainty typically brought in to resolve disturbing puzzles. A novel of consciousness, *State of Emergency* is manifestly a complication of novels of
the thriller genre, as well as of Salas's earlier work—both his memoir
and other three novels which rely more heavily on incident and action.

State of Emergency reconceptualizes terrorism from social or political
event to psycho-social *effect* of a fearful sameness, what I call terrorific
mimesis. The novel itself is an epic tale of fear—an odyssey of surveillance and paranoia. It revisits the years 1968–1969, Richard Nixon's
election to the presidency, as well as student rebellions against the Vietnam War and "the war machine" of the U.S. military-industrial complex.[10] The novel is divided into eleven episodes about the odyssey of
a radical professor Roger Leon, his former student turned girlfriend,
Penelope Lawson, and his false friend, undercover agent George Leary.
This odyssey extends from London to Bilbao and Madrid through some
of Spain's Balearic and Canary islands, to Northern Africa, then to
Paris (site of the '68 student uprising), and finally back to the United
States. "[A]lienated from America,"[11] Roger is trying to write a novel-
istic exposé of U.S. government and military endeavors to annihilate
not only dissidents like himself, but any dissent at all. He finds himself
constantly on the move because he dreads being tailed and arrested by
agents of a state-sanctioned terrorism carried out by the U.S. government, including the CIA and the FBI, who plot to sabotage, in the name
of a just war of law and order against the "forces of Communism,"[12] the
civil rights promised to U.S. citizens under "democracy." His more immediate and less heroic reason for fearing arrest is his habit of trans-
porting small amounts of dope across various national borders. In
Spain, Roger thinks that he is being followed by CIA- and FBI-like
agents of Franco's *Brigada Social de Investigación* established to arrest,
jail, and, so it is rumored, torture and kill political opposition. Roger,
who believes that Nixon and Franco are co-conspirators against all
forms of dissent, thinks Franco's regime has defined him as a political
dissident:

> [I]t was all related to the State of Emergency decreed by Franco
> and Nixon's inauguration and their just finished Chiefs of State
> meeting. . . . Now he knew why Nixon came to Spain right after
> becoming President, why there'd been a State of Emergency and
> why they had tried to harass him [Roger] out of the village and
> drive him from Spain![13]

With regard to an actual declaration of a "State of Emergency" in 1969 by the Franco regime, Salas, to convey Roger's state of mind, has deliberately exaggerated the involvement of President Nixon with such a declaration. For two months between 24 January and 22 March 1969, when labor unrest and nationalist agitation occurred in the Basque provinces along with continued student rebellion, a "State of Exception"—to be distinguished from the more serious "State of Alarm" and "State of War"—was declared.[14] This "State of Exception" had no direct connection with any visit from President Nixon in the late 1960s. Nevertheless, according to historian Stanley Payne, "the relationship with the United States remained the cornerstone of Spain's foreign policy."[15] The United States in turn was interested in minimizing the chances for social revolution or upheaval during the transition from Franco's regime to a democratic monarchy. From the point of view of the United States, such uprisings might have resulted in a socialist or communist government, which would have been inconvenient to the maintenance of U.S. air bases and other investments in Spain. Thus, in 1970, the United States and Spain signed the five-year Agreement of Friendship and Cooperation, and Nixon made a brief visit to Madrid during his European tour. Shortly thereafter, General Vernon A. Walters, deputy chief of the CIA, made a follow-up visit.[16] Some historians, including Payne, argue that by the late 1960s Franco's regime had grown more moderate, that censorship officially ended in 1966, and that a general liberalization and expansion of the press followed. However, the regime still disciplined and punished opposition, jailed activists, fined and censored liberal and leftist papers, and doled out the death penalty to certain communist leaders and various members of anti-Franco terrorist groups. Rising opposition to the regime by university students, progressivist priests, and industrial workers characterized the second half of the 1960s. Those who opposed the regime put their lives and livelihoods at risk, with the harshest treatment reserved for defecting priests and workers.

State of Emergency, despite its historical references, is not a historical novel of social protest. Rather it reads like a cross between a disturbing memoir of the times disguised as third-person fiction and Pynchon-esque parody along the lines of *Gravity's Rainbow* (1973) of a male protagonist on a mission who cannot achieve the distance from himself that the text maintains. Although the paranoia that Roger feels is never explicitly dismissed as the effect of unfounded conspiracy theory induced by hallucinogens or hallucinogenic cannabis, he allows his every action to be governed by a fear of the government agents who are supposedly dogging him, bugging his rented rooms, tailing him in the streets, and, above all, staring at him in various guises. His '60s countercultural idealism, manifested by his professed adherence to truth, justice, free love, and hashish, is framed by bitterness and suspicion born out of the fear of being undermined or betrayed by those closest to him, as well as by "plants," some of them highly seductive, such as Anne Marie, "the beautiful blonde with the bare brown midriff and the white hot pants swaying back and forth."[17] His state of vigilance comes to mirror that of a government agent. Roger begins to imitate the at-war mentality of his enemies, from both the United States and Spain. As if acting out a common meaning of his first name, "Roger," he receives and internalizes messages from a remote source and replies in kind: "*They* were giving him a signal through the invisible wall they had wrapped around him."[18] This "Roger" is implicated even on the level of his name in the reduplication of the terroristic effects of the state. Despite the apparent authorial corroboration in the first episode of *State of Emergency* that George Leary does exist independent of Roger's state of mind and that Leary is in fact "a security agent" who goes wherever Roger goes, Leary drops out of the narrative after this initial episode to reappear briefly, almost apparitionally, under the alias of "Fuzz" (slang for policeman or detective) in the fifth, six, tenth, and eleventh episodes, leaving the reader with a lingering uncertainty as to whether Roger is fighting a "real" enemy or merely shadowboxing.[19]

Salas's *State of Emergency* recycles the well-worn Anglo-American trope (as old as the Puritans and inherited by them from England) of Spain as primarily an inquisitorial "state of emergency" where an alienated "American" can experience the full brunt of persecution. However, unlike the many Anglo and even non-Anglo narratives that present Spain as tyrannical "Other," Salas's novel represents its Spanish scenario as altogether familiar, as parallel to that of the United States. It is precisely this sameness, this mirror-like mimetic relation between the United States and Spain, that defines danger, persecution, and psychic pain as draconian, bilateral state-sanctioned terrorism. *State of Emergency* does not locate terrorism in a particular country and/or city. Terrorism is not merely the punishing gaze of one government on its dissident citizens, but the punishing gaze of two or more governments configured in parallel complicity with each other's intentions and aims—in Salas's novel, Franco's regime and Nixon's administration, Spain and the United States.

One could argue for a connection between *State of Emergency*'s "parallax view" (to borrow the title of the 1974 film) of the late 1960s' diplomatic relationship between Spain and the United States and the sense of being doubly "colonized" and besieged. Significantly, Roger Leon, from whose point of view most of the novel is narrated, is descended from Spaniards and Native Americans.[20] In other words, like the writer Floyd Salas himself, he is a "Hispanic" whose ancestors are neither wholly from Spain nor from the Americas and whose "home," if under such continual persecution he may be said to have one, is in the United States. This United States is assumed to be dominated by Anglos, the hitherto hegemonic ethnic group of that nation. The hegemony of this ethnic group is not so much numerical as socioeconomic, political, and ideological. It was this ethnic group, which through warfare, land-grabbing, slavery, educational institutions reproducing the sociocultural order, and the rhetorical reiteration of stories (historically based and otherwise) favorable to themselves, that managed to extend its English language, its varieties of Protestantism, and its ethos, systems of belief and representation, over a large part of North America and even over other parts of the world.[21] As the dominant cultural group, Anglos are not counted as "ethnics" and generally do not subject themselves to either of the frequently marginalizing categories "ethnic" or "minority." Rather, to be "Anglo" is to be "American," no questions asked. The Americas, however, were colonized by the Spaniards before the Anglos ever set foot on Plymouth Rock. *State of Emergency* gestures toward a different version of "American" history by using the Spaniards, not the Anglos, to gauge the antiquity of Roger's Native American ancestors: "The other branches [of Roger Leon's family] have supposedly been in the United States since Ponce de León came."[22] Nevertheless, implicit in the use of the Spaniards rather than Anglos is a critique of colonization by either Anglos or Spaniards.

Within the odyssey of returning "home," Floyd Salas's *State of Emergency* deploys the trope of Spain as a familiar pain toward an ending without closure. Spain is a "familiar" pain in two senses of the word "familiar," one marking a kinship relation (Roger's ancestors) and the other denoting that which is well-known or recognizable. From a cultural standpoint, the idea of Spain as a place of suffering and possible death is more than a trope. It is a cliché. *State of Emergency* repeats this cliché to simultaneously shock (making good on "emergency") and inspire a certain amount of skepticism. This skepticism creates an ironic distance which feeds into the text's distance effect on the main protagonist, Roger Leon. The text's more fundamental distance effect is achieved through the tension produced by the technique of narrating from Roger's point of view, but as told through the third person. The reader is never certain whether Leon is really being followed, hounded to death, or is just suffering paranoid delusions from inhaling too much hashish. The most disturbing and disorienting possibility is that he is being followed and the drugs have simply magnified or expanded legitimate concerns. The distance effect—brought about through reliance on a trope so familiar as to be cliché, as well as through the manipulation of perspective—plays a paradoxical role. It lends a suspenseful edge both to the mimetic codes of the book (evident in the mention of historical events such as the Kennedy and King assassinations, the Vietnam War, FBI and CIA infiltrations into the student movement, Nixon's inauguration, Franco's regime) and to the dynamic of terrorific mimesis.

Doubts, fears, and suspicions that state-sanctioned terrorism is undermining the civil rights of citizens, rather than playing themselves out on the page, are gradually internalized by the reader. More than discrediting Roger, the lack of solid evidence produces a festering anxiety denied the catharsis of proof or resolution. A terrorific mimesis rules not only international relations between Spain and the United States but also Roger—and, potentially, the reader caught in the text's spectral hall of mirrors. The effect of the novel as that of a funhouse hall of mirrors is quite literally crystallized in the scene in which Roger joins the French intellectual Pierre in a Paris café:

> Pierre led them down the stairs and out onto the winding street a couple of doors to a cafe. They all walked through to a back room with big, black, soft-leather booths and walls lined with mirrors. Roger, in spite of the pleasure of having James Jones' phone number in his pocket, felt instantaneously uncomfortable. There was almost no place he could look without seeing himself. He noticed, though, that Hans and Beverly both looked full at themselves, then at him before and after they sat down, and a horrible feeling came over him. Everywhere he looked he saw himself reflected in mirrors. He had to stare straight at a person to keep from looking into his own face. He felt as if he were in the nuthouse and everyone was looking at him, watching him, trying to see how he'd react.[23]

This passage is a *mise-en-abyme*—a recessed replication in miniature—of the form and concerns of the novel as a whole and thus of the psychological effects of state-sanctioned terrorism, which invades all spaces of private or intimate communication between people and the very constitution of subjectivity.

Although set almost thirty years back in the past, the novel cannily manipulates the contemporary reader's sense of an enigmatic or elusive legacy (who indeed was responsible for the killing of King and both Kennedy brothers?) to create a textual "state of emergency," a radical uncertainty about so-called "American democracy." In this respect, the book is not retro, but entirely postmodern. There is no sure center around which to rally or mourn, only the "symbolic symbols" with which the secret agent Leary, alias Fuzz, obliquely threatens Roger.[24] What remains in this scenario of surveillance and fear is a proliferating network of shadowy signs "disappearing" the political.[25] In such a universe, terrorism—state-sanctioned terrorism included—is, as Jean Baudrillard has theorized, not merely a set of particular acts or events. It is a hyperreal "state" of fear in which orientation (national, international, and the like) through differentiation is impossible and a displacing sameness reigns supreme, one that threatens to exhaust action and numb passion, to produce a massive burnout. State-sanctioned terrorism in particular strips its citizens of the very features of their citizenship: the desire to act, forums in which to constitute themselves, write, and speak out, and the right to be both public and private persons. It is an enervating nervous exhaustion induced by the disruptions of being tracked and surveilled and the fear of further persecution. Penny expresses this kind of exhaustion on her return "home" from Spain, where she and Roger were never really "away" but were instead wandering around small islands (Mallorca, Formentera, Ibiza, the Canaries, the Spanish mainland itself) rather than a large one (the United States): "I just want to live a normal life. I can't take this constant suffering."[26] *State of Emergency* suggests that the Balearic islands and the United States are all the same kind of place, Panopticons of perpetual surveillance.[27] Penny, whose name suggests another famous Penny—Penelope, Odysseus's long-suffering wife—is not alone in her desire for refuge, for the presumed safety of a private life in which she hopes to avoid the pain of feeling like a suspect and of suspecting everything. On more than one occasion, the continually voyaging Roger fantasizes about committing suicide as a solitary way "out" of the unrelenting pressure of his predicament as a persecuted radical:

> He [Roger] stopped at the next landing and looked over the banister. There was room for a body to drop straight down to the white tile floor of the foyer. It would be quick and easy. *Just a few seconds of fear* [my italics] and one good swan dive. That's all. Then falling, knowing it was too late. The gaping hole had a magnetic pull, like a promise that would end all his troubles. He had to push himself away from the banister and make himself turn to start down the stairs again.[28]

Like the death-wish fantasy picture of nuclear war as lasting "just a few seconds," Roger's picture of suicide presents him with the temptation of exchanging a life of fear for "a few seconds of fear," but he manages to resist and continue his embattled endeavor to write his exposé. He writes so as not to die, so as not to commit suicide, so as not to use "the only weapon left against a totalitarian state when there's no avenue for hope."[29] Writing for Roger is his weapon of preference and he writes both to stave off the last resort and, like an unvanquished idealist, "make a better world."[30]

While the novel's effects may be terrorifically presentist they are also poignantly, even embarrassingly, nostalgic. Renato Rosaldo, in his article "Imperialist Nostalgia" (1989), connects the historical invention of the word with domination:

> Far from being eternal, the term *nostalgia* (from the Greek *nostos,* "to return home," and *algia,* "a painful condition") dates from the late seventeenth century when it was coined to describe a medical condition. The term described, for example, a pathological home-sickness among Swiss mercenaries who were fighting far from their homeland. (Even in its origins, the term appears to have been associated with processes of domination.)[31]

Rosaldo defines nostalgia as both the painful yearning to return home from somewhere else and a mourning for or longing to return to the traditional/primitive society whose passing/demise one has brought about. He views nostalgia as complicitous with processes of domination, the colonizer's desire to see the colonized culture as it was when the colonizer first encountered it—hence, imperialist nostalgia.[32] More recent articles on nostalgia—for instance, Stuart Tannock's "Nostalgia Critique" (1995)—have questioned the blanket association of nostalgia with dominator culture or reactionary forces. Borrowing Raymond Williams's phrase for nostalgia—a "structure of feeling"—Tannock's article argues that "nostalgia is a valuable way of approaching the past, important to all social groups" and that it can be liberating or merely palliative, progressive or reactionary, remindful or amnesiac, activist or escapist, an inspiration for challenging the status quo or merely a mystification of the processes of domination, a safety valve of misplaced feeling restricting action.[33]

In *State of Emergency,* nostalgia manifests itself as a desire to go home—to the United States—by way of a familiar pain, Spain, located in the past, as it so often is in cultural representations. The devices of recession in time (the 1990s to the 1960s) and perspective (the funhouse hall of mirrors of terrific mimesis) are deployed toward an ending without closure. The nostalgic, elegiac move of *State of Emergency*—its purposely failing revivification of the struggle for agency of the counterculture of the late 1960s and its journey "home" through Franco's Spain as a familiar pain—manages to prevent nostalgia from functioning as the usual antidote to fear of the contemporary scene, in this case, the 1990s. Instead of delivering an "all's well that ends well" finale or permitting the reader to escape either through a violent blow-up or an emotional resolution, *State of Emergency* provides no such cathartic exit from the imperial, border-crossing, globetrotting, co-opting "State of Emergency," which, through nightmarish figurations of Spain, the novel suggests "America" has become. The implication would seem to be that nothing short of a *collective* existential crisis will change the present course of things accelerating, the novel suggests, toward a terrifying sameness.

Flying into Kennedy airport on the return trip to the United States, Roger thinks to himself, "He was approaching the fascist fist of the state on Independence Day!"[34] In other words, "Independence Day," the high holiday of democracy in the "American" way, appears in conjunction with "the fascist fist of the state" or totalitarianism. Independence Day nostalgically functions as the occasion of prospective hope for the continuation of "democracy" within a militantly patriotic retrospective celebration of its founding. *State of Emergency* transmutes this holiday into a prospective mirror image of democracy's proverbial Other—of fascism. Earlier in the story, Roger had remarked about the United States, "We're still a partial democracy, not a total corporate fascist state yet![35] At the novel's conclusion, for Roger, anyway, the "still" has departed and the "yet" has arrived. And, because of the superpower status of the United States, this "now"—the novel's 1969 prefiguring of things to come—is more fearful than Franco's so-called fascism, which Roger has left behind in Spain and its little islands.

Notes

Portions of this essay appear in the conclusion of my dissertation, " 'American' In Dependence: Figures of Spain in Anglo-American Culture." For their comments and suggestions, I wish to thank Nancy Schultz, Betti and Luis de Guzmán, and especially Jill Casid. This essay is dedicated to the memory of Rafael Gasti.

1. Salas's self-construction as "Spaniard/Spic/Hispanic" would constitute fighting words to many self-identified Chicanos for whom Spain and the Spanish empire in the New World represent a legacy of oppression no less than that of the Anglo colonization and Anglo-American hegemony in the United States. However, Salas positions himself ambivalently, attempting to claim for "Hispanic" an original heritage not only rivaling but also preceding that of the Anglos while at the same time identifying both as

centrally, representatively "American," as well as the oppressed underdog. In calling himself a "Spic," a derogatory Anglo epithet for, among other Spanish-speaking people, Spaniards, Salas claims the mythic heritage and original status of the "proud Dons" and "Anglo pioneers," but also—and this is equally important for his project—he places himself alongside those who are marginalized and reviled. Written across all of Salas's work is the desire to be at once the "American" pioneer and the repulsed underdog. With regard to Salas's self-positioning, see Gerald Haslam, "A *MELUS* Interview: Floyd Salas," *MELUS: The Journal of the Society for the Study of Multi-Ethnic Literature of the United States* 19, no. 1 (spring 1993): 97–109. On the history and politics of ethnic identification on the part of Latinos in the United States, see Suzanne Oboler, *Ethnic Labels, Latino Lives: Identity and the Politics of (Re)Presentation in the United States* (Minneapolis: University of Minnesota Press, 1995).

2. Floyd Salas, *Lay My Body on the Line: A Novel* (Berkeley, Calif.: Y'Bird, 1978), 54.

3. Ibid., 22.

4. Ibid., 24.

5. Ibid., 54.

6. Haslam, "Interview," 108.

7. "*Tattoo the Wicked Cross,* my first novel, was not an autobiographical novel. I never experienced any of the experiences of the protagonist, Aaron d'Aragon" (Haslam, "Interview," 103).

8. Ibid., 108.

9. Stanley G. Payne (*The Franco Regime, 1936–1975* [Madison: University of Wisconsin Press, 1987]) argues that this alliance was a continuation of the "strategic rehabilitation" (417) of Spain, ostracized during the 1940s as a "fascist beast," to the position of "sentinel of the Occident," Mediterranean gatekeeper against the forces of Communism (397). This revindication was sealed during the Eisenhower and Franco regimes with the signing on 26 September 1953 of the Pact of Madrid, a bilateral agreement pledging and arranging for military, economic, and cultural cooperation between Spain and the United States. Specifically, the pact involved the establishment of three air bases (at Rota, Torrejon, and near Zaragoza), a surveillance station in Mallorca, a naval base, a branch of Radio Liberty managed by the CIA near Barcelona, and an underground oil pipe beginning at Rota, running to Seville, then to Jerez de la Frontera, subsequently to Madrid, and finally to Zaragoza in order to provide the three bases with a continuous, uninterrupted supply of fuel. As Payne points out, "[t]hough the fact was denied, it was widely suspected that the pact contained additional secret clauses" permitting, among other things, the potential storage of atomic bombs in Spain (419).

10. Floyd Salas, *State of Emergency* (Houston, Tex.: Arte Público Press, 1996), 19–21.

11. Ibid., 150.

12. Ibid., 18.

13. Ibid., 199–200.

14. Payne, *Franco Regime*, 511–20.

15. Ibid., 572.

16. Ibid., 573.

17. Salas, *State of Emergency*, 79.

18. Ibid., 330–31.

19. Ibid., 18, 12.

20. Ibid., 11.

21. María DeGuzmán, " 'American' In Dependence: Figures of Spain in Anglo-American Culture" (Ph.D. diss., Harvard University, 1997), 1–2.

22. Salas, *State of Emergency*, 11.

23. Ibid., 317.

24. Ibid., 395.

25. In *The Transparency of Evil: Essays on Extreme Phenomena,* trans. James Benedict (New York: Verso, 1993), 75–80, Jean Baudrillard discusses this form of disappearance.

26. Salas, *State of Emergency*, 394.

27. See Michel Foucault, "Panopticism," in *Discipline & Punish: The Birth of the Prison,* trans. Alan Sheridan (New York: Vintage Books, 1979), 195–228.

28. Salas, *State of Emergency*, 111.

29. Ibid., 277.

30. Ibid., 366.

31. Renato Rosaldo, "Imperialist Nostalgia," *Representations* 26 (spring 1989): 108–9.

32. Ibid., 107.

33. The phrase "structure of feeling" is to be found in Raymond Williams's *Marxism and Literature* (Oxford: Oxford University Press, 1977). See also Stuart Tannock, "Nostalgia Critique," *Cultural Studies* 9, no. 3 (October 1995): 453–64.

34. Salas, *State of Emergency*, 389.

35. Ibid., 104.

PART V

COLD WAR ANXIETIES

"Unlucky" Luciano
Fear of Crime during the Cold War

Lee Bernstein

What did it take to become the man in the gray flannel suit? Tom Rath (Gregory Peck), the protagonist in the film of that name, commuted every day between his Manhattan job and a family in the Connecticut suburbs. One day, the man who often sat next to him on the train told him that there was an opening in public relations at United Broadcasting, where he worked. Rath knew nothing about P.R., but his companion asked: "Who does? You got a clean shirt, you bathe every day, that's all there is to it."[1] In the cynical response he offered, clothing and hygiene seemed enough to become typically middle class in the postwar United States. Rath eventually took the job, and the film quickly became a lesson in responsibility to family and the virtues of honesty and integrity. As Betsy Rath (Jennifer Jones) explained to her husband, "for a decent man, there's never any peace of mind without honesty." Tom Rath's honesty, rather than ambition, made him the man in the gray flannel suit.

Clean shirts, the movie assured its viewers, did not immediately connote decency. Far from it, one influential criminologist of the time argued, white collars were increasingly the uniform of criminals. Edwin H. Sutherland reminded readers, in his 1949 *White Collar Crime*, of Thorstein Veblen's comparison of the "ideal pecuniary man" to the "ideal delinquent": "The ideal pecuniary man is like the ideal delinquent in his unscrupulous conversion of goods and persons to his own ends, and in callous disregard of the feelings and wishes of others and of the remoter effects of his actions, but he is unlike him in possessing a keener sense of status and in working more far-sightedly to a remoter end."[2] Sutherland went further: his study showed that the criminality of corporations was characterized by high rates of recidivism, were largely hidden, and were organized. Most important, Sutherland overturned the widely held assumption that crime rates were higher among the majority of the population with low incomes and lower among the few with high incomes.[3] You could no longer tell a criminal by the way he or she looked, dressed, or smelled.

The changing shape of fears of crime during the late 1940s and early 1950s revealed the convergence of Cold-War anxieties present in attacks on domestic and foreign communists. Where Cold-War anticommunists dramatized these threats with a series of inquiries, trials, deportations, and executions so well known that they need not be enumerated here, Cold-War crimebusters similarly focused attention on their crusade through a series of inquiries, trials, and deportations. The first of these, beginning in the late 1940s and extending into the mid-1950s, involved federal crime-fighting agencies joining the mass media in locating the source of virtually all illegal drugs as Italian-American deportee Lucky Luciano. Widely perceived as the CEO of a multinational vice industry, Luciano became the focus of newspaper stories, popular nonfiction, Senate inquiries, and constant attention from the Federal Bureau of Narcotics.

The volume of public attention directed at Lucky Luciano smacks of the anti-Italian prejudice that had been in place since media outlets, social reformers, and police agencies first shouted "Mafia" in the late nineteenth century. However, this case was not merely another chapter in the scapegoating of Italian-Americans for the failures of the criminal-justice system. Italian-Americans remained a largely working-class population in the 1940s and 1950s, but, as for other white ethnic groups, the many success stories allowed some observers to describe an increasingly class-stratified Italian-America.[4] Reflecting this change was another Italian-American whose role of "ideal pecuniary man" stood in contrast to Luciano's "ideal delinquency." His name was Charles Siragusa, and as the Federal Bureau of Narcotics' (FBN) chief European agent, he pursued Luciano by donning not gray flannel but a pinstriped suit and going undercover.

Scholarly treatments of Cold-War U.S. culture typically explain the ways multiple forces created and reinforced an ideological consensus across demographic differences. The process of lionizing Siragusa and demonizing Luciano did in part contribute to this phenomenon. However, the forging of a Cold-War consensus was a dual process consisting of attempts to impose uniformity while celebrating the notion that the United States could absorb all comers. From this perspective, the celebrated investigations into crime and communism appear more complex than purges of all dissenters. Law enforcement bureaucrats and the mass media did not try to *eliminate* the differences within U.S. borders. They *employed* them. As two Italian-Americans on opposite sides of the law, Luciano and Siragusa revealed that the attempt to build a postwar consensus relied on choices between "good" differences and "bad" differences. These two Italian-Americans living in Italy—one portrayed as earning money from exporting heroin to the United States, the other portrayed as protecting the United States from that trade—provided the terms under which the United States would accept the children of Italian immigrants. Just as Luciano served as the epitome of inappropriate behavior in his role as "the mastermind of the whole racket," Siragusa was the ideal foil because he "rendered differences useful" while conforming to the middle-class ideal of the 1950s.[5]

Siragusa turned his scholastic success and Italian heritage into jobs with the Immigration and Naturalization Service, wartime espionage, and, later the Federal Bureau of Narcotics. Because Siragusa could pass as an underworld gangster in service of U.S. espionage, he would earn the Exceptional Civilian Service Medal. He later explained that "At first I was based in the United States, posing as a hoodlum in my pinstripe suit with the wide lapels and the fancy shoes. Because of my Sicilian ancestry and face, I was able to infiltrate successfully into Mafia-controlled gangs and to finger, time and time again, the drug pusher, the peddler, the small-time dope overlord." Siragusa's Sicilian heritage made him a useful agent because he was able to gather evidence otherwise unavailable to the FBN. While Eliot Ness and Al Capone personified a polarity between the native born "good" and a foreign born "evil" for an earlier generation, Siragusa drew his power from his ethnic similarity to the gangsters. According to the *Saturday Evening Post*, Siragusa's Sicilian origins showed that he "knew what he was talking about when he talked about the Maffia, and he knew what he was up against now—not a string of cheap dope peddlers but some of the most tightly organized criminals in the world."[6] Many observers in the United States saw drug smuggling as being of Italian origin, but they also saw using Italian-American government agents as the best antidrug tactic. No longer basing their assumptions of criminal pathology wholly on ethnic origins, the FBN, like the larger U.S. culture, defined the terms under which the children and grandchildren of European immigrants could show patriotic loyalty.

Siragusa's undercover work earned him promotions and awards, but Luciano did some undercover work of his own. His earnings from the illegal sale of alcohol during Prohibition financed an undercover operation in a world closed to most Italian-Americans at the time—an expensive wardrobe and a suite at New York's exclusive Waldorf-Astoria under the name "Charles Ross." Toward the end of his life, Luciano recalled that "around 1925, I had a take of at least twelve million dollars from booze alone for the year." After the repeal of Prohibition, Luciano and his associates operated illegal gambling clubs, supplemented by the hijacking and reselling of legal merchandise. In 1936 he became the target of Thomas Dewey, the special prosecutor for the City of New York with grand political ambitions. Luciano was ultimately convicted of sixty-two counts of compulsory prostitution, extortion, and racketeering in 1936. Luciano's thirty-to-fifty-year term was unprecedented.[7]

His years in prison coincided with World War II and the election of Thomas Dewey to New York's governorship. There were rumors, later substantiated, of Luciano's participation in the Navy's "Operation Underworld," which followed an unexplained fire aboard the French luxury liner *Normandie* in New York Harbor in 1942. On 8 May 1945, V-E Day, attorney Moses Polakoff requested executive clemency for his client based both on Luciano's unusually long sentence and war service. Governor Dewey commuted his sentence on the condition that Luciano be deported to Italy. Partisan questions about this commutation arose almost immediately. The pro-Dewey *New York Daily Mirror* routinely featured what *Newsweek* columnist John Lardner called "the Luciano war legend," while the *New York Post*, then owned by the prominent Democrat Dorothy Schiff and edited by James Wechsler, routinely made insinuations that Dewey accepted bribes. In any case, Dewey claimed that rumors of Luciano's wartime assistance justified the commutation. Dewey's political opponents claimed that he had been paid off by Luciano and constructed the war service story as a cover.[8] After his deportation, Luciano briefly fell into obscurity. His going-away party aboard the *SS Laura Keene* received some media attention, followed by an unremarkable first year of exile. However, in 1947 Luciano turned up in a chic Havana suburb and Walter Winchell's syndicated column. On the heels of Winchell, articles in *True, Newsweek, Time,* countless major newspapers, and two popular nonfiction books catapulted Luciano simultaneously into the media limelight and drug enforcement searchlight. According to these sources, Luciano was suddenly "the most important drug smuggler in the world." The FBN reacted swiftly to this news. The bureau prevented the shipment of all medicinal narcotics to Cuba pending the deportation of Luciano. Because Luciano also had visas for Bolivia, Venezuela, and Columbia, Commissioner of Narcotics Harry Anslinger threatened the governments of those countries with similar action should they admit Luciano. Cuba's interior minister arrested Luciano in February 1947 and sent the newly dubbed "Unlucky" Luciano to Genoa.[9]

Anslinger was by that time obsessed with Lucky Luciano, obsessed enough to write an unpublished biography of the figure called "The Boss." He was convinced that Luciano was the largest exporter of heroin and other narcotics into the United States. At times, Anslinger intimated that Luciano, in collusion with communist countries, was the sole sources of illegal drugs in the United States. And, when interviewed, he rarely failed to point to Luciano as the greatest menace in U.S. drug smuggling history. *True* was one of the first popular magazines to feature his Luciano theory: "Take it from Commissioner Harry Anslinger. . . . Lucky is the largest single figure in the traffic in this contraband in America today." Shortly after Luciano's return to Italy, his name emerged in virtually every major smuggling seizure.[10]

When investigations resulted in the arrest of large-scale smugglers, the press remarked that they were "aides of Luciano" or "a former associate of Luciano in the policy racket." When a major heroin ring was broken up in San Francisco in 1952, the FBN argued that "Luciano was behind it" and was "controlling all drug smuggling from Italy." In another case, the bureau joined forces with the Royal Canadian Mounted Police to stop a group of Montreal restauranteurs from smuggling heroin. The chief of the Mounties' Criminal Investigation Department, James R. Lemieux, told one reporter that "the syndicate 'definitely' was linked with an international narcotics cartel headed by deported vice overlord Charles (Lucky) Luciano." In response to an FBN request, Italian police officials detained Luciano in July 1949 after New Yorker Vincent Trupia was arrested in Rome in possession of half a million dollars worth of cocaine. While an uncharged Luciano was released one week later, he was barred from Rome for the remainder of his life.[11]

In addition, prosecutors urged drug dealers to name Luciano as their source in exchange for lighter sentences. When they did not, they felt the consequences. For example, in 1956 two heroin dealers, Ralph "Sunny Cheeks" Zanfardino and George Palmieri, were arrested with $400,000 worth of heroin and were sentenced to 6 to 12 years and 7 to 15 years, respectively. The prosecutor felt justified in asking for these then unusually long sentences. Assistant District Attorney Murphy "had asked severe sentences for the two, who as first offenders might have been given a two-year minimum sentence. He held that their lack of cooperation had thwarted attempts of federal authorities to track down the suspected chief of an international dope syndicate," a clear reference to Luciano.[12] Many factors, most notably H.R. 3490 (1951), known as the Boggs Act, made possible these draconian sentences (by 1950s standards). Prior to 1951 the maximum penalty for these crimes would have been ten years in prison. As first offenders, Palmieri and Zanfardino would likely have received far shorter sentences. In addition, the association of this heroin with one of its points of origin, Communist China, made their crime particularly vulnerable to aggressive prosecution.[13] By the time Zanfardino and Palmieri faced prosecution, the pieces were in place. As Italian-Americans selling relatively large quantities of heroin, they fit cleanly into a framework of crime, pathology, and demonization developed around Lucky Luciano during the 1950s.

Proof that Luciano ran a smuggling ring consisted of a belief that the increase of drug smuggling "has been coincidental with Luciano's deportation from the United States to Italy" and that Luciano had an unexplainable source of revenue. In fact, while total arrests for smuggling had gone up between 1948 and 1949, the total amount of illegal narcotics seized had actually gone down—a trend that continued in 1950. Some within the Bureau of Narcotics attributed this drop to the smugglers' tactical shift to "trying numerous small shipments, instead of risking large supplies on single ventures." In addition, while the number of arrests had been going up since the war, prewar figures resembled those of the 1950s. Thus, rather than a sudden increase after the war, the lack of available merchant ships and stepped-up military patrols created an unusually low figure during the war. Finally, while heroin and opium originating in the Middle East and Asia did often move through southern France and Italy, the Bureau of Narcotics acknowledged that the two most popular illegal drugs—cocaine and marijuana—came principally from Peru and Mexico, respectively.[14]

Luciano attributed FBN charges against him to "an old-style frame-up" and disingenuously feared that they were "spoiling my reputation."[15] Central to this frame-up would not be a smoking gun with Luciano's fingerprints or a packet of heroin stashed in the unsuspecting deportee's luggage. Rather, as in *The Man in the Gray Flannel Suit*, this frame-up centered on public relations. The bureau relied on cultivating relationships with writers and favorable press reports, as well as closing off those who worked against its interests. It used Luciano, along with the more general myth of the Mafia, to stress the criminal elements of drug use, a position that conflicted with the medical and sociostructural focus that many doctors, sociologists, and social workers emphasized in their research on drug use.

According to his published writings, private memos, and professional correspondence, Anslinger was reluctant to authorize any portrayal of drug addicts. The commissioner thought that even negative portrayals would result in an upsurge of drug use. Not only would it show the curious how to use drugs, but it also risked making prosecutors, judges, and juries feel sympathetic to the plight of "sick" drug abusers. In fact, Anslinger hypothesized to his district supervisors that "irresponsible and uninformed propaganda" was the reason for drug use.[16]

From this perspective, all portrayals of drug use—whether positive or negative—constituted propaganda that would result in shorter sentences and more drug addicts. Those who sought to treat drug addiction as a sickness rather than as evidence of a global conspiracy were actively discredited by the bureau. Anslinger conducted investigations of criminologists, writers and editors, doctors, community activists, and police officers who dared offer medical explanations or solutions to the illegal use of narcotics. In addition, he cultivated relationships with so-called "friendly writers," including the editor of *Reader's Digest*, best-selling author and columnist Lee Mortimer, and *True* magazine's Michael Stern. *Life* magazine cooperated with the FBN from the thirties until at least the 1970s. In most cases, Anslinger traded information about bureau cases for final copy approval.[17]

Many of the articles already discussed here, including a *Saturday Evening Post* feature on Siragusa, were written with Anslinger's approval and suggestions. By 1957, Siragusa was a crime fighting celebrity featured in the *Saturday Evening Post* as he "squires Marlene Dietrich at a Rome cocktail party." Anslinger wanted Siragusa to serve as poster boy for FBN efforts to stop the flow of drugs originating in Italy. He was clearly sensitive to charges that the bureau was unjustifiably targeting Italian-Americans for the problem of drug traffic and hoped public relations would help. Generoso Pope, Jr., publisher of *Il Progresso Italiano*, argued that the Mafia was a myth created by the "reds" to throw U.S. crime fighters off the track. In addition, the Sons of Italy argued that the "Mafia" stereotype represented evidence of anti-Italian prejudice in the bureau. Thus, the story on Siragusa highlighted his Italian-American heritage.[18]

This coverage helped Anslinger achieve his policy objectives. In addition to a desired growth in the size of his bureau, the Narcotic Control Act of 1956 increased penalties for violations of existing narcotic and marijuana laws and provided funds for a training school for state and local officers.[19] This legislation was a turning point for the bureau, but the result of the attention on Luciano and Siragusa went beyond their usefulness in stimulating legislation or expanding the Federal Bureau of

Narcotics. While Anslinger's interest in "framing" Luciano lay in his organizational and ideological goals, why it took hold with such strength calls for explanation.

To answer this question, I shall return to *The Man in the Gray Flannel Suit*. Early in the film, Mr. Hopkins, Rath's boss and mentor, describes the difference between the kind of man who builds a company and the nine-to-five man who lives off of it. Hopkins is clearly a company builder who, as we learn, sacrifices his personal life for the greatness of the corporate machine. After viewers see how Hopkins has destroyed his family in building the company, Rath's decision to become a nine-to-fiver redefines heroism in bureaucratic terms.

The emerging middle-class sensibility that *The Man in the Gray Flannel Suit* reflects can be characterized by its heterosexual nuclear families, suburban living, whiteness, corporate work for men and housework for women, and consumption for all. This age of strict roles, however, was rife with anxiety over what to do about the multitudes that did not conform, either because they were corporate leaders like Mr. Hopkins, gays and lesbians, juvenile delinquents, or gangsters. Did Lucky Luciano fail to conform because he disapproved of middle-class mores or because he was excluded by prejudice? If he could not conform, was it because of job discrimination or because he was physically and culturally unable to do so? Popular attention paid to Luciano showed that all reasons could be applied, depending on the context. In one popular true crime book, Luciano was simultaneously a "sleek beetle-browed mobster" whose crimes pointed to his Sicilian heritage and the head of a "far-flung narcotics organization already submerging the United States," which pointed to a decision he had made to break the law for personal profit alone.[20]

This construction of Luciano as both atavistic throwback and cunning manipulator of global economies elucidated a wider anxiety over increased corporatization within the mass mediated culture. U.S. culture turned gangsters into the ultimate "organization men," diverting anxieties over societal changes by locating them in figures everyone could fear and hate. Racketeering, drug smuggling, prostitution, gambling, and the other crimes targeted by police and investigative agencies were, after all, *organized* crime. During the 1950s, popular critics both in and out of universities offered damning appraisals of this corporatization of U.S. life. In particular, many scholars saw the shift from "rugged individuals" to bureaucratic drones as a threat to traditional (albeit stereotypical) masculine roles. C. Wright Mills saw these "white collar" men as cloaking their base greed in the mechanized routine of daily life: "The men are cogs in a business machinery that has routinized greed and made aggression an impersonal principle of organization." Others, including David Riesman and William H. Whyte, also documented the change and offered warnings to men who worked within larger organizations. To Riesman, who called white-collar workers "other-directed," it was unfortunate that conformity was seen as virtuous by the culture at large: "Modern popular culture stresses the dangers of aloneness and, by contrast, the virtues of group mindedness." Sociologist E. Franklin Frazier argued that conformity by African-Americans to a middle-class standard was an effort to make oneself over " 'in the image of the white man:' The black bourgeoisie exhibits most strikingly the inferiority complex of those who would escape their racial identification." Criminologists like Edwin Sutherland began exploring the newly dubbed "white-collar crime" as evidence that the middle-class ideal was inherently tainted by privileging economic gain regardless of the means of obtainment. Within this context, gangsters were no aberration. A quest for status via conforming to a masculinized white middle-class standard, these sociologists argued, evidenced sick—even criminal—minds.[21]

But countless others celebrated conformity as a sign of maturity. Norman Podhoretz criticized anyone who thought it chic to rebel: "There was great beauty, profound significance in a man's struggle to achieve freedom *through* submission to conditions. . . . The trick, then, was to stop carping at life like a petulant adolescent and to get down to the business of adult living as quickly as possible [and strike the] perfect attitude of the civilized adult: poised, sober, judicious, prudent." Daniel Bell, Edward Shils, and Seymour Martin Lipset, among others, celebrated a society able to absorb all comers into a consensual middle class.[22] Lucky Luciano and Charles Siragusa became enmeshed in this disagreement over the value of conformity. By constructing, denouncing, and sometimes celebrating people who did not—or could not—conform to a white middle-class ideal, consumers both questioned and reaffirmed "submission to conditions."

Thus, Luciano was caught in a contradiction. While his organization stood in for more general fears of the loss of social freedom within bureaucratic organizations, he could also be targeted for not conforming. Those outraged by drug use saw its connection to all forms of nonconformity as threatening. Charles Siragusa not only was out to get the Mafia, but he also battled nonconformity. He asked readers of his memoir to "consider the person who becomes dependent on heroin. In a great majority of cases he is definitely not normal. . . . He may be contemptuous of his fellow men or a guy who thinks it is fashionable to be a nonconformist. Nonconformity in his case means shooting heroin into his veins." In addition, many commentators linked the nonconformity of drug use to sexual promiscuity; one cleverly evil case argued that drug use by white women in jazz clubs owned by gay men led to sex with African-American musicians. In addition, while drug use was believed to enhance the sexual urges of white women, some believed that it decreased sexual desire in white men. This powerful linkage of sex, drugs, and nonconformity was compounded by fears that foreign-born men could harness and exploit native-born female sexuality by addicting women to heroin while simultaneously depriving white "American" men of their sex drive.[23]

In 1962, the year Anslinger retired, Luciano died of natural causes. Luciano collapsed on the afternoon of 26 January while picking up American movie producer Martin Gosch at Naples' Capodichino Airport. The two men were tailed by a U.S. Bureau of Narcotics agent collecting evidence to tie Luciano into an international heroin smuggling ring recently uncovered in New York City. Appropriately, his death was shared by two representatives of the institutions that watched him and shaped his image since his deportation in 1946: the media and the Bureau of Narcotics. After returning to the States in 1958, Charles Siragusa continued his rise within the Bureau of Narcotics, moving from field supervisor to assistant director, working as FBN liaison to Attorney General Robert F. Kennedy's aggressive Organized Crime and Racketeering Section. He later became head of the Illinois Crime Commission and kept in close contact with the bureau.

While Luciano's death and Anslinger's retirement in the same year marked the ending of one chapter in the history of the Bureau of Narcotics, that year's inquiry into a new conspiracy theory marked the beginning of another. A Senate subcommittee looked into Communist involvement in drug traffic, with particular attention paid to Cuba. The committee's star witness, Charles Siragusa, testified that "cocaine came from Cuba and that the sudden influx of narcotics was 'definitely a Communist project' aimed at raising money, demoralizing Americans, and discrediting Cuban exiles in Miami." He added that "the cocaine trafficking had been insignificant before the Fidel Castro regime came to power in 1959." The specter of Lucky Luciano served as a shorthand target for those hoping to end illegal drug use. Similarly, his nemesis became the "ideal pecuniary man" because he valued conformity at the same time that he served as false proof of the ability of the U.S. middle class to absorb all. These fears that centered on Lucky Luciano and cultivated by Anslinger limited the range and results of U.S. drug policy. The fears held because Luciano's image could contain the multiple paradigms of Cold-War crime-fighting and media representation and serve the legislative agenda of the Bureau of Narcotics, making Luciano into an unlucky "ideal delinquent."[24]

Notes

I am grateful for helpful comments from Lisa Collins, Carol Miller, David Roediger, Nancy Schultz, and Rudy Vecoli.

1. Nunnally Johnson, *The Man in the Gray Flannel Suit* (Twentieth Century Fox, 1956); from the Sloan Wilson novel (New York: Simon and Schuster, 1955).

2. Thorstein Veblen, *Theory of the Leisure Class* (New York: Macmillan, 1899), 237.

3. Edwin Sutherland, *White Collar Crime* (New York: Holt, Rinehart and Winston, 1949), 217–33, 3.

4. Charles Siragusa as told to Robert Wiedrich, *The Trail of the Poppy: Behind the Mask of the Mafia* (Englewood Cliffs, N.J.: Prentice-Hall, 1966).

5. Foucault described this as "rendering differences useful by fitting them on to another"; see Michel Foucault, *Discipline and Punish: The Birth of the Prison* (New York: Vintage, 1979), 184; Toni Howard, "Dope Is His Business," *Saturday Evening Post*, 27 April 1957, 38.

6. Howard, "Dope Is His Business," 39, 147; Siragusa and Wiedrich, *The Trail of the Poppy*, x–xi.

7. Martin Gosch and Richard Hammer, *The Last Testament of Lucky Luciano* (Boston, Mass.: Little, Brown, 1974), 73–74; while largely beyond the scope of this essay, the history and politics of the Dewey-Luciano trial are the subject of a recent book by Mary Stolberg. Stolberg argues that the prosecution of Luciano (and organized crime figures more generally) was intentionally overstated to further the political ambitions of Dewey. Several key witnesses, including the only witnesses to link Luciano to prostitution—Nancy Presser and Flo Brown—said Dewey's assistants threatened them with jail sentences if they did not testify, and paid them $200 in exchange for their testimony. See Mary M. Stolberg, *Fighting Organized Crime: Politics, Justice and the Legacy of Thomas E. Dewey* (Boston, Mass.: Northeastern University Press, 1995), 152, 158.

8. John Lardner, "How Lucky Won the War," *Newsweek*, 31 January 1955, 66; Max Lerner, "Payoff Blues," *New York Post*, 18 October 1950, 48; "Luciano Seized in Cuba, Will Be Shipped to Italy," *New York Daily Mirror*, 23 February 1947, 3. During the Kefauver crime hearings several years later, George White wrote to Harry Anslinger: " 'Gene' told me yesterday the parole fix on Luciano was arranged by Costello thru James Bruno, Republican ex-Deputy Com. of NY State Athletic Com, now believed to be

a clerk in NY Supreme court. The Haffenden stuff was only 'window-dressing' because they had to have something on which to hang their hat.—GAW. I told Halley about this and they will probably question Bruno and Costello in this regard eventually." Letter from "GAW" [George White] to Harry Anslinger, 1 November 1950, Record Group 170, Papers of the Federal Bureau of Narcotics, National Archives and Records Administration, College Park, Md.; Gosch and Hammer, *Last Testament,* 255–56, 268.

9. Rodney Campbell, *The Luciano Project: The Secret Wartime Collaboration of the Mafia and the U.S. Navy* (New York: McGraw-Hill, 1977), 193–212; Walter Winchell, *New York Mirror,* 11 February 1947; *New York Times,* 22 February 1947, 1; "People: Unlucky Lucky," *Newsweek,* 3 March 1947, 20–21; "Cuba: Hoodlum on the Wing," *Time,* 3 March 1947, 36–37; Michael Stern, *No Innocence Abroad* (1947; reprint, New York: Random House, 1953); Sid Feder and Joachim Joesten, *The Luciano Story* (New York: David McKay, 1954); "Luciano Seized in Cuba," 3. "Unlucky Lucky," 20–21; Dean Jennings, *We Only Kill Each Other: The Life and Bad Times of Bugsy Siegel* (Englewood Cliffs, N.J.: Prentice-Hall, 1968), 170.

10. Anslinger Papers, Pennsylvania State University; discussed in John C. McWilliams, *The Protectors: Harry J. Anslinger and the Federal Bureau of Narcotics, 1930–1962* (Newark: University of Delaware Press, 1990), 140; Stern, *No Innocence Abroad,* 33. John C. McWilliams and Alan A. Block argue that Stern was one of the primary outlets for the FBN's misinformation campaign. See below for discussion. "All the Commissioner's Men: The Federal Bureau of Narcotics and the Dewey-Luciano Affair, 1947–54," *Intelligence and National Security* 5 (1990): 171–92; "US Reports 'Lead' in Narcotics Haul," *New York Times,* 9 January 1949, 56; "Five in Ring Convicted," *New York Times,* 3 March 1951, 28; "Narcotics Air Courier Ring Broken; 5 in New York–Canada Cartel Held," *New York Times,* 5 August 1951, 1; Camille M. Cianfarra, "Luciano Detained by Italian Police; Deported Vice King Is Held for Questioning on Any Link to Smuggling of Cocaine," *New York Times,* 9 July 1949, 28.

11. "U.S. Reports 'Lead,'" 56; "Five in Ring Convicted," 28; "Narcotics Air Courier Ring Broken," 1.

12. "2 Get Long Terms in 400G Dope Raid; Heroin Peddler, Aide Off to Prison Today," *New York Post,* 11 May 1956, 1.

13. In the early 1970s, Alfred McCoy found evidence that opium was cultivated not by Chinese Communists, but by Nationalists who used sales to finance guerrilla campaigns. In addition, U.S. military and intelligence forces encouraged opium and heroin use in Southeast Asia in the 1940s and 1950s to "hedge the growth of popular liberation movements." See Alfred McCoy, *The Politics of Heroin in Southeast Asia* (New York: Harper and Row, 1972), 8; McWilliams, *Protectors,* 152.

14. Total narcotic and marijuana arrests were 2,855 for 1947; 3,180 for 1948;

5,851 for 1950; and 4,874 for 1951 (United States Treasury Department Information Service, Press Release, 15 August 1948, Papers of the Federal Bureau of Narcotics, Record Group 170, National Archives and Records Administration, College Park, Md. [hereafter, FBN Papers]). Narcotics were primarily opiates. Seizures included opium and various forms: 7,894 ounces in 1947, 4,990 ounces in 1948; cocaine: 36 ounces in 1947, 175 ounces in 1948; marijuana: 27,314 ounces in 1947, 48,822 ounces in 1948 (United States Treasury Department Press Release, 5 March 1949, FBN Papers); the *New York Times* reported slightly different figures for 1948 and 1949 (3,895 and 5,273, respectively) ("Narcotics Arrests Show Sharp Rise; New York Leads All Districts in US," *New York Times*, 5 March 1950, 17; "Narcotics Unit Cites Lure to Teen-Agers," *New York Times*, 2 March 1951, 19).

15. "Luciano Cries 'Frame-Up' " *New York Times*, 9 January 1949, 56; "Luciano Says He'll Talk," *New York Times*, 5 August 1951, 53.

16. Harry J. Anslinger, Memorandum to all District Supervisors, 10 March 1950, FBN Papers, Box 46.

17. FBN Papers, Box 10; Lee Mortimer, "New York Confidential," *New York Mirror*, 8 August 1960; "Ever stop to think that the pennies, dimes and dollars from lottery and bookmaking provide the capital to buy the junk from the Reds? (Smart work by U.S. Narcotics Commissioner Anslinger and his smart boys has proved that time and again)." Lee Mortimer, "New York Confidential," *New York Mirror*, 22 August 1960.

18. Harry Anslinger to Charles Siragusa, 7 February 1957, FBN Papers, Box 10; Howard, *Dope Is His Business*, 38; Anslinger's statement to this effect was leaked to columnist Drew Pearson in October 1950. Similar efforts were made to appease criticism from Jewish American and Chinese American groups who felt unduly charged. The Concord, New Hampshire ADL contacted Senator Charles Tobey, a member of the Kefauver Committee, who wrote in outrage to Anslinger. Senator Herbert Lehman wrote to the Secretary of the Treasury. Anslinger discussed the matter with Herman Edelsberg, director of the ADL, on 19 October 1950, denying that any reference to people of Jewish faith was mentioned. Secretary of the treasury to Senator Herbert H. Lehman, no date. FBN Papers; Gon Sam Mue with William J. Slocum, "They Haven't Killed Me Yet," *Saturday Evening Post*, 16 August 1952. The article says that he was the first Chinese-American to serve a federal police function. At times, Mortimer refers to as "Sam Gon," a name that Gon also used. Jack Lait and Lee Mortimer, *U.S.A. Confidential* (New York: Crown, 1952), 146. On the Sons of Italy, see Lee Bernstein, "The Greatest Menace: Organized Crime in U.S. Culture and Politics, 1946–1961" (Ph.D. diss., University of Minnesota, 1997).

19. Federal Bureau of Narcotics, Bureau Organization. History, 1960, FBN Papers, Box 49.

20. Feder and Joesten, *Luciano Story*, 7, 234.

21. Robert Warshow, "The Gangster as Tragic Hero," *Partisan Review* 15 (1948): 240; C. Wright Mills, *White Collar* (New York: Oxford University Press, 1953), 109; David Riesman with Nathan Glazer and Reuel Denney, *The Lonely Crowd: A Study of the Changing American Character* (Garden City, N.Y.: Doubleday, 1953), 183; E. Franklin Frazier, *Black Bourgeoisie: The Rise of a New Middle Class in the United States* (1957; reprint, New York: Collier Books, 1962), 112; Edwin Sutherland, *White Collar Crime* (New York: Holt, Rinehart and Winston, 1949); Robert Lindner called the conformist male "a psychopath," points out Barbara Ehrenreich, *The Hearts of Men: American Dreams and the Flight from Commitment* (Garden City, N.Y.: Anchor Press/ Doubleday, 1983), 30.

22. Podhoretz quoted in James Wechsler, *Confessions of an Angry Middle-Aged Editor* (New York: Random House, 1960), 21–22; Daniel Bell, *The End of Ideology: On the Exhaustion of Political Ideas in the Fifties* (Glencoe, Ill.: Free Press, 1960); Edward Shils, "The End of Ideology?" *Encounter* 5 (November 1955): 52–58; Seymour Martin Lipset, *Political Man* (Garden City, N.Y.: Doubleday, 1959). For a discussion of these and other postwar sociologists, see Wini Breines, *Young, White, and Miserable: Growing Up Female in the Fifties* (Boston, Mass.: Beacon Press, 1992), 25–46; Terence Ball, "The Politics of Social Science in Postwar America," and Lary May, introduction, in *Recasting America: Culture and Politics in the Age of Cold War,* ed. Lary May (Chicago, Ill.: University of Chicago Press, 1989).

23. Siragusa and Wiedrich, *Trail of the Poppy,* 205–6; Jack Lait and Lee Mortimer, *Washington Confidential* (New York: Crown, 1952); Tibor Koeves, "Lucky Luciano vs. the United Nations," *United Nations World* 3 (August 1949): 35.

24. "Unlucky at Last," 28; "Cuba Said to Push Opium Sales in US," *New York Times,* 15 March 1962, 9; Arnold H. Lubasch, "Cuba Is Accused of Cocaine Plot," *New York Times,* 14 April 1962, 3. Anslinger influenced the focus of U.S. drug policy long after his retirement by arguing that discrete cartels of foreign origin were responsible for the postwar influx of narcotics. The ongoing effects of this policy can hardly be overstated. As recently as this past February, General Barry R. McCaffrey, President Clinton's drug-policy advisor, and Attorney General Janet Reno sought to discredit medical applications for drug use. "The Drug War," as it is commonly called, clearly owes much to the criminalization of the problem by Anslinger's FBN; see David E. Rosenbaum, "I.R.S. Bans Deducting Medical Cost of Marijuana," *New York Times,* 23 February 1997, 19.

The Cold War Comes to Erie
Repression and Resistance, 1946–1954

James A. Young

A specter haunted right-wing circles as World War II drew to a close. That specter was the continuation of the New Deal. The New Deal coalesced middle-of-the-road, liberal, socialist, and other progressive forces of the 1930s and continued into the 1940s as an alliance opposed to fascism and supportive of the social and economic policies of the welfare state. In practice, then, the coalition included most of labor, many farmers, professionals, small businessmen, and others in the Popular Front. Against this alignment stood opponents of the nascent welfare state and the newly assertive labor and civil-rights forces freed by the New Deal from the "belated feudalism" of U.S. society. Therefore, many Manufacturers' Association members, resentful white-collar workers, integralist Catholics, some Protestant traditionalists, Ku Kluxers, and others who saw in the innovations of the New Deal the beginning of a Soviet America—all rallied in a growing coalition of Cold-War warriors. For, despite its origins under a nominally liberal and prolabor Truman Administration, the Cold War soon became the launch pad for right-wing missiles aimed at destroying the remnants of the Popular Front, rolling back the New Deal, and containing the labor movement.[1] In Erie, Pennsylvania—an almost quintessentially American town—the struggle invaded the churches, obsessed the media, and divided communities. In the end, a weakened liberal-labor coalition survived, and the lines of future struggles were formed.

In Erie, unions affiliated with the Congress of Industrial Organizations (CIO) provided the lead for the New Deal and for progressive causes generally. Chief among Erie's CIO unions ranked the United

Electrical, Radio, and Machine Workers of America (UE), which, in 1947, contained over 50 percent of the county's 22,000 CIO members in a half-dozen locals. The largest of the UE locals, Local 506 of the General Electric Corporation's Erie Works, accounted for half of that UE total with production workers in suburban Lawrence Park, GE's stratified company town.[2] The UE, then, bulked large in the Erie Industrial Union Council, and GE moved forcefully in local business circles. During the war, little conflict arose in Erie between pro– and anti–New Deal forces such as these. Work stoppages and other job actions did occur, but, for the most part, a truce held in industrial and political arenas.[3]

Erie's largest circulation newspaper, the *Daily Times*, also upheld Popular Front sentiment and the antifascist alliance. In doing so, the *Times* scolded the British in the summer of 1945 for their attack upon Greek leftists who rebelled against their country's right-wing monarch: "What Are the Allies Fighting For?" an editorial questioned. Similarly, the Erie daily found pleasure in the apparent discomfort of Spanish fascist Generalissimo Francisco Franco as the war's end neared.[4] Yet, cracks in the Front soon appeared.

The *Times* published the syndicated column of Westbrook Pegler, champion of the Spanish dictatorship. And, the war over, vacationing publisher John J. Mead turned over his column early in 1946 to Rev. W. Lawrence Franklin, editor of the diocesan weekly *Lake Shore Visitor*, who supported Franco against his "pink" journalistic critics, as Franklin characterized them.[5] Mead provided the same guest column to Dr. Elmer Hess, whose essay opposing national health insurance boiled down to: "Do we Americans wish to have our country controlled by the Russian philosophy?"[6]

If anyone in Erie led the way in assaulting the remnants of the Popular Front it was Franklin, his weekly, and Catholic Bishop John Mark Gannon, for whom the *Visitor* spoke. In keeping with the "gloves off" policy of the church towards the left after the war, Franklin and the paper sustained that integralist Catholic worldview captured so well in Carl Marzani's description of Italian and Vatican politics.[7] For Franklin, the enemy consisted of the entire rationalist tradition as received from the Enlightenment. The Erie priest stood squarely with Pius IX and the Syllabus of Errors, inveighing against modernism, liberalism, and socialism, among which communism was only the most recent abomination. Gannon stated his basic agreement with this Manichaean view in a 1947 speech before the Catholic Daughters: "The world is too small for Christian democracy and atheistic communism to live side by side, and we are not going to get off."[8]

It is not surprising, then, that the *Lake Shore Visitor* pioneered the

Cold War in the Erie area, initially among its 20,000 subscribers and those who listened to Franklin's weekly newscast over WLEU radio. A serial sample of ten issues of the *Daily Times* and of the *Visitor* in 1945, for example, reveals a stark contrast. Whereas the *Times* printed only one editorial and one page-two article critical of the Soviet Union, and no such pieces on page one or on page-one local, a *Visitor* sample of ten turns up an editorial, three page-one articles, four page-two articles, and five pieces on the first page of section 2—all on the Soviet threat. Moreover, the *Visitor* added two articles on the communist threat in other countries; and, most important to this study, the *Visitor* alluded to links between militant trade unionists at home and the Red Menace from abroad.[9] On the strength of that linkage would stand the forces that were not only to persecute real and imagined communists but also to bludgeon progressives and labor for years to come.

The corporate community also promoted the labor-Red Menace connection. Still reeling from the massive strike wave of 1945–46, Charles E. Wilson, president of General Electric, proclaimed in October 1946 that "The problems of the United States can be captiously summed up in two words: Russia abroad, labor at home," a mild echo of the declaration of Pennsylvania Manufacturers' Association president G. Mason Owlett in 1945 that the New Deal was a "disaster-bound communist trend."[10] Wilson then sent a team into the field to learn why the company had lost the 1946 struggle with UE and to devise antidotes to labor's apparent hold on the good will of various communities such as Erie in which GE operated.[11]

The striking CIO workers of 1946 had won broad support in the Erie area. The Strike Relief Committee headed by Wilbur White raised some $50,000—1946 dollars—through direct solicitations and procured extended credit arrangements from store owners and landlords. Workers unaffected by the strike contributed money, as did small businesses and social clubs. Two predominantly Italian groups, the Nuova Aurora on the near West Side and the East Side's Liberty Club, gave $300 each week.[12] The depth of community support was revealed when Bishop Gannon added $5,000 to the fund. If this gesture reflected more a confidence in the Catholic leadership of the CIO than any shift in the bishop's Cold-War views, the contribution nonetheless lifted strikers' spirits. "We knew we'd won when the bishop came through like that," recalled one striker thirty years later.[13] And so they had.

In Erie as elsewhere, the Manufacturers' Association (NAM) and the Chamber of Commerce led business's counterattack against labor and the New Deal. Raising the specter of subversion, the chamber published and circulated nationally a million copies of the booklet *Communist*

Infiltration in the United States in 1946, demanded a loyalty program for government employees, and insisted upon an investigation of the film industry. In 1947 the chamber followed with *Communists in the Labor Movement* and *Communists in Government;* and, in 1948, came *Program for Community Anti-Communist Action.* In Erie, General Electric complemented such efforts with full-page newspaper ads such as "RAPID WAGE JUMPS HALT LIVING STANDARD RISE," which, in May 1947, questioned the motives of those critical of "the American way," while the Gannon Radio Hour also reinforced the rightist socioeconomic edifice in giving over a May 1948 program to the discussion of "socialized medicine" by three area doctors, including the president of the Erie County Medical Society. In June NAM's new president, Earl Bunting, joined M.I.T. professor Erwin H. Schell in speaking before the Regional Conference on the National Association of Foremen, which was sponsored in nearby Meadville by Allegheny College.[14] Meanwhile, the *Lake Shore Visitor* raised further the pitch of its growing campaign on dangers from the left.

In the year September 1946–September 1947 the *Visitor*'s anticommunist pieces doubled, and they increased again by almost a third in 1948. And, while 1950 saw only a 12 percent rise over 1948, the *Visitor* clearly brought the Cold War home: subversion in the United States now received almost as much coverage as did the Soviet Union. Moreover, the link between subversion and local labor came through forcefully and repeatedly.[15] During the same period the *Daily Times* began to shift decisively to the right. Early in 1948 the paper published the names and addresses of every Erie County resident who had signed a Progressive Party petition to place Henry Wallace's name on the presidential ballot. The editors explained that, although the communists backed Wallace, not *all* of the signatories could be assumed to be communists, but added that those who stated that they had signed the petition mistakenly, or had not signed it at all, could gain a retraction from the paper. By September the paper made banner headlines on unsubstantiated charges that the UE was a communist union.[16]

The *Daily Times* also supported incumbent congressman Carroll Kearns's redbaiting campaign against Democratic challenger Jim Kennedy, the UE 506 business agent. Both the congressman—originally the candidate of Sharon Steel Co. executives—and the newspaper hammered relentlessly with unsubstantiated charges and innuendo against the challenger and his union. Characteristically, the paper's coverage of the reelection of UE international president Albert Fitzgerald began, "Denies He's a Communist." Since no one of the slightest political acumen, even the union's severest critics, had charged Fitzgerald with communist sympathies, the *Times's* provocative splash seems to have been clearly aimed at affecting local attitudes about the UE and its officers, including Kennedy.[17]

Editorially, the *Daily Times* left no question about its view of the UE and the union's officers. Following Kearns's attack on the union's refusal to comply with the so-called "non-communist oath" required by the Taft-Hartley Act—a refusal joined by many CIO unions and by the United Mine Workers (AFL)—the *Times* argued that, if polled, Erie UE members surely would demand that their officers sign the affidavit. "Or," asked the *Times* rhetorically, "would the communist-saturated leadership shun such a referendum?" Later, after having accused President Truman of covering up for communists and having dismissed Wallace's Progressive Party as "the Communist Party stooge" of 1948, the paper went on to support General Electric management's attack upon the UE for its "big government" orientation.[18]

Several days later, the assault continued with an editorial, "How Long Will They Take It?" "They" were UE members and "It" was, of course, communist domination. The UE had been shown "by factual evidence" (none of which was cited) to be "dominated by the Commies." Mead then tried in his own column to link Kennedy to the web of conspiracy. This tactic had been standard Republican campaign fare since 1936; and Mead's candidacy as a Republican presidential elector may explain such behavior by his newspaper. Yet the continuation of such attacks upon the UE and others over the following years begs for further explanation.[19]

In elaborating upon the labor-communist linkage begun earlier by GE's Charles Wilson, and in other aspects of the post-1946 corporate counterattack, the *Daily Times* ranged broadly afield; labor, however, served repeatedly as a chief focus. In expressing alarm about American leaders who "exert tremendous, unstoppable power" that may be exercised at a whim, the *Times* chose to editorialize about Michael Quill of New York City's Transport Workers' Union and James C. Petrillo of the American Federation of Musicians.[20] No corporate leader rated so much as a nod.

The Meads and the Catholic clergy by no means stood alone in attacking labor and the left. General Electric weighed in often during these years with a well-funded advertising campaign that constituted one piece of the effort to win people away from New Deal values and the nascent worker's culture that had grown since the 1930s. During the 1948 campaign, for example, GE published in its own *General Electric Commentator* and in at least one full-page newspaper advertisement a condemnation of both left- and right-wing factions of the

UE as "collectivists" and then lumped *collectivists* together as "Communists, Fascists, Socialist[s], and the like."[21] The daily Erie *Dispatch,* meanwhile, jabbed candidate Kennedy for his reticence on the "paramount issue" of the day, the communist question.[22] Not to be outdone as superpatriots, some Protestant churches also became open supporters of the right, just as religion was employed by secular groups to foster right-wing views.

In what the *Times* reported as a "bristling sermon," the Emmanuel Baptist Church's Rev. E. A. MacDonald lashed out at "statism and Communist" on 12 October 1947. The sermon, one piece of a nation-wide Baptist campaign, also attacked the vices of drinking and gambling, but special attention focused upon the government's "unlimited . . . power to tax in time of peace." This political speech from the pulpit ended with a call for an amendment to the U.S. Constitution "to protect our savings and endowments." This crusade against communism, then, arose really from the fear that the New Deal would soon tax religious institutions in order to fund the nascent welfare state.[23]

Others entered the field, too, especially after the outbreak of war in Korea. In 1953, the Christian Endeavor Society sponsored a Loyalty Day activity in suburban Belle Valley, which was followed a few months later by a "Back to God Day" sponsored by American Legion Post 773 as part of its national effort, and this was in turn praised by the Rev. Fredrick W. Hunt of Lakewood Methodist Church. Millcreek Township supervisors, meanwhile, had proclaimed 1 February 1953 "Back to God Day" in that township.[24] God, clearly, was pro–American and a capitalist.

Not all Erie churchmen joined in the rising Cold-War hysteria. A few even spoke out against the trend, although most of these responded only to a direct threat. An exception was the First Unitarian Society's Rev. Russell Bletzer. Bletzer, whose weekly radio program won the support of CIO leaders, was seen as the only Erie clergyman who was consistently liberal and prolabor.[25]

Clerical opposition to the redbaiting juggernaut increased after Rep. Harold Velde (R–Ill.) suggested in 1953 that his House Committee on un-American Activities (HUAC) might find in U.S. churches a new field for investigation. In Erie, Rabbi Randall Falk replied that "If Moses, Isaiah, and Jesus were alive today, Velde and his ilk would brand them Communists, too," and went on to denounce the "demagoguery of would-be dictators." Similarly, the Rev. Edward Donner of Erie's Christ Methodist Church labeled Velde's suggestion "an outrage": "They're trying to dictate what our consciences should believe," he charged. Yet, when polled, Catholic Auxiliary Bishop Edward P. McManaman replied, "Of course; why not? The churches should be eager to assist in any legitimate undertaking to ensure national security."[26]

The United Electrical Workers continued to serve as a special target of Cold-War warriors. Beginning in 1950 these forces sought to influence GE workers in Erie, as elsewhere, to replace the UE with the new International Union of Electrical, Radio and Machine workers (IUE), a rival union created by the CIO specifically to raid the UE. Nationally, the IUE was led by former UE president James Carey; locally, Dave Crotty headed the challengers. At GE's Erie Works—focal point of the local struggle—IUE received the enthusiastic support of Rev. John Lerhinan, who was an instructor at the diocesan seminary; of labor priest Charles Owen Rice of Allegheny County (financed by CIO President Philip Murray); and, of course, of the *Lake Shore Visitor* and the daily press.[27]

General Electric facilitated the IUE challenge by requesting that the National Labor Relations Board conduct an election on the basis that GE could no longer be certain that UE enjoyed majority support among union employees. Consequently, IUE was spared the requirement of attracting 30 percent of the workers to sign a petition demanding an election, an achievement probably beyond the capability of IUE activists, who had failed to attract significant support as a UE faction in elections of 1949.[28] GE's tactic also supplied the rationale for stalling on contract negotiations and for suspending the collection of UE union dues through the payroll deduction system.[29]

As the 25 May union representation election approached, both sides pulled out the stops. Activists of the Association of Catholic Trade Unionists (ACTU) arrived in Erie from Pittsburgh and elsewhere and were directed by Father Rice in a door-to-door campaign. Priests mounted the pulpits of St. Mark's, St. Patrick's, St. Hedwig's, St. Ann's, and other churches to denounce the "Communist-dominated" UE.[30] And the *Visitor* contributed its share of heat to the battle.

The *Visitor*'s last issue prior to the UE-IUE runoff featured the article "Communism vs. Americanism Issue in the IUE-UE Elections," by Rev. Lerhinan. In his introduction to the article, Rev. Franklin stopped just short of declaring that a vote for the UE would constitute a sinful act. Lerhinan's piece then labeled virtually all leaders of UE 506 as either Stalinists or "front men" for the communists, although the priest offered not a shred of evidence against business agent Jim Kennedy and two others. Only in the case of President Johnny Nelson did the author even try to build a case, and that was very tenuous.[31]

As a result of the highly charged campaign, GE workers could not escape the conflict. One UE member recalls that "Just going to work in the morning was like asking for a punch in the mouth." At parties, at church, on the streets, and in the clubs, the question remained the same: How can you support that commie union? For Tom Rafter, a member of the Knights of Columbus, the answer was simple: The members vote on all-important policies, so if the union were being used for communist purposes, "the members would be the first to know."[32]

Meanwhile, UE leaders returned the fire. Kennedy utilized the *UE 506 Union News* to ridicule the IUE—the Idiotic Union Employees, he dubbed them—and to redbait the redbaiters, as with a reproduction of James Carey's 1945 greeting to "the heroic people of Leningrad."[33] In May UE 506 began a program, "UE on the Air," broadcast over WIKK radio and WICU-TV, the latter of which was owned by Edward Lamb, a liberal Democrat from Toledo, Ohio, who also owned the *Dispatch* newspaper.[34] The union also relied heavily upon traditional lunchtime and evening rallies to reach the members.

In the heady final days of the campaign the *Daily Times* apparently sought to influence GE workers in a peculiar way. The paper's editorial column, letters-to-the-editor section, and page one all were utilized directly or indirectly to mount anti-UE sentiments. A bogus letter to the editor, purporting to support UE for all the wrong reasons, provided icing for the poisoned cake.[35]

Among labor unions, the UE found only one major ally, United Rubber Workers Local 61, which represented 500 workers at the Continental Rubber Company and which—along with a few other local unions—retained membership with the UE in the United Labor Club, which offered the only racially integrated bar in town. Now the URW denounced the "disorganizing, union-busting actions of certain leaders of the CIO," who aimed to "break up an organization which has resisted the dictates of the CIO both economically and politically" in a struggle which had nothing to do with communism. In so doing, Local 61 charged, the CIO leaders gave "aid and comfort to the company."[36]

The final decision rested with Erie's GE workers, and their choice was clear. On 25 May UE won a resounding victory, 6608 to 4378—a 60.1 percent showing for UE 506. The jubilation which followed was tempered, however, by the office workers' vote to join the IUE. That they would return to the UE fold by a five-to-one vote in 1952 did not mask the fact that the culture of repression exerted great influence in the Erie area.[37]

The survival of the community's largest progressive union local did little to abate the virulence of the enemies of the left. If, as historian Robert Zieger suggests, corporations had redoubled efforts following the stunning defeat in the elections of 1948, the outbreak of war in Korea reinvigorated the right once again. And, in the connection, Erie newspapers—especially the *Daily Times*—rushed into editorial abandon during the summer of 1950.

The renewed offensive opened with an apparently innocent interview of local communist leader Sam Reed in early August. Reed may have assisted his own victimization by exaggerating his party's local strength, for, he reportedly told *Daily Times* journalist Paul Haney, "There are a lot more Communists in Erie than the government authorities know about. We're doing all right!" Reed thus challenged the government's assessment that 21 communists and about 250 fellow travelers lived in greater Erie when, in fact, those figures were quite accurate. Reed's further efforts to play down the communist's reliance upon violence and revolution failed to placate his adversaries.[38]

A low point in Erie journalism followed the Reed interview and revolved around a proposed ordinance before city council that would require that communist residents and visitors register with the city police. Mayor Clarence Pulling's administration, which had swept to victory over Tom Flatley and the Democrats in 1949 in a campaign highlighted by redbaiting, proved a likely sponsor of such legislation, which also won the support of the *Daily Times* and the *Dispatch*.

When Reed and Benjamin Caruthers, a black communist from Pittsburgh, appeared at a city council meeting and urged that the council would better spend its time enacting laws against racial discrimination in employment than passing laws in restraint of civil liberties, the *Times*'s headline shouted "COMMUNISTS SEEK TO IMPOSE SOVIET 'GAG' ON CITY COUNCIL." Besides, noted the text of an accompanying article, the director of the Erie Manufacturers' Association had assured those attending the council meeting that he knew of no racial discrimination in Erie. Demonstrations protesting the refusal of the Woolworth and the Kresge's department stores to serve blacks at their lunch counters would soon belie such smooth assurances. Yet, the reds—real and imagined—continued to enthrall the media.[39]

Next to the *Times*'s front-page lead, an editorial screamed: "AN INSULT TO ERIE!" The paper proclaimed that: "When Communists get to the point of telling our city officials what legislation to enact and what not to adopt, it is time for a showdown—immediately!" And, of Sam Reed and his "slimy cohorts," the *Times* urged that "It is time these enemies of our government were caught up short—registered, jailed, and otherwise controlled. Finally, and consistent with sentiments voiced within the FBI during its campaign against the communists, the

Times held that "the hundreds of fellow-travellers" of the area should also be rounded up. The author did not specify just how such persons were to be identified.[40]

For his part, *Times* publisher John Mead thought that prison might not suffice. In yet another column, Mead expressed agreement with former governor James Duff of Pennsylvania, who had told the American Legion that "Instead of putting these guys in jail for five years, they ought to be hanged."[41]

The Erie *Dispatch* failed to match the venomous tone of its rival, but the Reed-Caruthers appearance received sensationalist coverage here, too. "REDS 'INVADE' COUNCIL CHAMBER," announced page one. In an editorial on the following day, the *Dispatch* advocated that these "filthiest kind of conspirators" be subjected to laws "to shut them up and put them where they can do Erie no harm—which is outside the city limits."[42]

At least until the UE's split from the CIO in 1949, the CIO provided something of an antidote to the right in Erie. The CIO's *People's Press*, edited in the early postwar years by Marlin Allen, reached 15,000 Erie County families through subscriptions, and another 5,000 copies were usually sold by other means.[43] In circulation, then, the CIO organ compared favorably with the *Lake Shore Visitor*, whose 20,000 subscribers spread across the entire diocese of northwestern Pennsylvania, as both papers reached many of the same working families.

The *People's Press* served for a time as a forceful champion of the spirit of the Popular Front. Couched frequently in the vocabulary of the moral economy, that is, the traditional notion that a society's economy should operate for the benefit of ordinary people and in accordance with customary norms of fairness, the *Press* consistently promoted the extension of New Deal reformism and, implicitly, the continuation of the Popular Front. Jim Kennedy, whose "Kennedy Komments" appeared each week, took the early lead in exposing the antilabor bias which lay at the heart of redbaiting, and Allen promoted a similar view. A content survey of articles reveals Kennedy's preference for words such as "greedy" and "security," concepts of "full employment" and "adequate wage." Together with the Labor Press Association columnist who wrote under the name Ben Dor, Allen and Kennedy leaned heavily on the themes of corporate profits, depression, and monopoly. In 1948 the paper—no longer edited by Allen—gave Kennedy a warm endorsement for U.S. Congress, despite growing tension between the UE and the CIO's national leadership.[44] In all, the *People's Press* provided something of a counter to other papers.

In addition to the *People's Press*, Erie labor in general and the UE in particular maintained a high profile in the media. Until 1950 the UE sponsored the radio news commentary of Arthur Gaeth, who reached Erie listeners over WERC radio with a progressive, prolabor reading of contemporary affairs. Following the break with the CIO, UE 506's own paper, noted earlier, reached thousands of members and others. The *UE 506 Union News* maintained the populist thrust of the *People's Press* under Allen; but this trend declined under Allen's successor, Wavil See, owing in part to the loss of UE subscriptions, which in time forced the paper to become a semi-weekly. It ceased publication in the mid-1950s.[45]

In the 1950s the UE made further headway in the electronic media. Radio and television scripts supplied by the international office aired over WIKK radio and WICU-TV long after the 1950 UE-IUE election. From such self-serving programs as "A Report on UE-GE Negotiations" and "UE: Greater Security for GE Workers," the programs included "Labor's Fight for a Shorter Work Week" and an annual "Roosevelt Memorial." In "The Changing Tide" the union took on Senator Joseph McCarthy and his redbaiting campaign directly.[46] Together with Rev. Bletzer's weekly program, the UE effort guaranteed that progressive voices continued to reach the community.

Labor's media presence could not match that of the corporations, however, which advertised heavily—often with conservative political and economic messages—and received the lion's share of commercial news coverage. Like UE, General Electric published a substantial in-house organ, the *General Electric News*. This weekly published articles of almost every description, from general business conditions to technological advances, labor negotiations, features, and publicity campaigns. On 31 December 1953, the *News* reported GE's sponsorship of Bing Crosby's first television show; and, in the same space a month later, the GE paper defended Cordiner Policy 20.4, whereby employees such as 506 president Johnny Nelson could be fired without due process for allegedly holding communist beliefs or for invoking their Fifth Amendment rights regarding current or past membership in the Communist Party. GE also produced a pamphlet on communism in the unions, specifically the UE.[47]

In its ability to draw upon the talents and prestige of the "outside expert," corporate Erie enjoyed an additional advantage over labor and progressive forces. Labor and liberals could bring to town a Labour member of the British parliament, A. Emil Davies, to discuss the merits of the mixed economy at the Erie Educational Forum; but business's views poured forth in a steady stream of celebrities and other notables sponsored by the Manufacturers' Association, the Chamber of Commerce, and other institutions.[48]

Hard on the heels of Davies came Earl Bunting, president of O'Sullivan Rubber and chairman of the National Association of Manufacturers. In opposing economic controls then sought by labor and other progressives, Bunting charged that "Our domestic collectivists have done a comprehensive job of propaganda which is apparently determined to make our economy an organ of Washington [just] as Stalin is to make the economy of Europe an organ of Moscow."[49]

When occasion called for someone other than a corporate spokesperson to communicate the corporate and/or Cold-War view to the public, willing voices could be found. Sometimes, as with the director of the Erie Labor-Management Institute, the Rev. Henry Paul, the clergy served to urge the repudiation of militant union leaders such as Kennedy and Nelson: "all members of Local 506 who are real Americans," intoned the priest at a St. Mary's communion breakfast, "must do all in their power to prevent the re-election of these officers."[50] And, by the time that anticommunism became a big business, celebrated experts could be summoned to Erie through an appropriate front organization.

Such an organization emerged from the Chamber of Commerce and was known as Penn-Erie. The Penn-Erie Club recruited members from outside the business community in a classic case of a dominant group's effort to deepen its hegemony by expanding its public (or civic) role. Admitted to Penn-Erie for a ten-dollar fee were doctors, lawyers, and educators. Dr. Elmer Hess, who had equated national health insurance with the Sovietization of the United States in a *Times* column in 1946, was its president. From the southernmost reaches of the county came officials from Edinboro State Teachers' College, which supplied a large portion of the region's teachers.[51] With the image of a civic-minded organization as camouflage, then, Penn-Erie sponsored the appearances of celebrities whose hostility to progressive forces and ideas had attained almost legendary dimensions. Late in 1953, for example, the club brought to Erie both Victor Riesel, the redbaiting syndicated columnist, and Senator McCarthy's chief counsel, Roy Cohen; and the Erie newspapers heralded their coming and covered their appearances with all due attentiveness.[52]

Corporate spokesmen who rode the propaganda circuit urged greater freedom for trade and capital and a stronger foreign policy to protect its interests abroad. When GE board chairman Phillip D. Reed argued this case in Erie late in 1953, he failed to forewarn his audience that GE would utilize the loosening of restrictions on capital outflow to build sixty-one plants in foreign countries in the years 1957-67.[53] Nor did the American Petroleum Institute chairman, P. C. Spencer, project the country's dependence upon foreign oil in conveying the corporate message two weeks later. The theme of the hour was Pax Americana and profits: a Cold War, then, fit the bill. And a Cold War continued to justify the repression of dissenters.[54]

In 1954 a deep wrinkle formed in the press's nearly uniform support of repressive politics when Edward Lamb, owner of the *Dispatch*, WICU-TV, and WLEU radio, found himself a victim of the witch hunt. The future of Lamb's FCC license was threatened as he fell under attack for having been associated with communists in the past, during his Popular Front era support of the Spanish Loyalists and of the National Lawyers Guild. The charges appeared crudely political: Lamb refused to allow an accusation against anyone by Senator Joseph McCarthy to be broadcast over his several electronic media outlets unless and until a reply by the accused could be arranged. Moreover, Lamb had signed a *Dispatch* editorial, "Can Sen. McCarthy Be Libeled?" some years earlier. The fact that the *Dispatch* seemed otherwise to subscribe largely to the Cold-War journalistic norm of the day could not save him from this ordeal, which the *Daily Times* chronicled with attendant banner headlines.[55]

Lamb, of course, possessed many more resources for counterattack than did most other victims of the American inquisition. While memories of the electronic media's role remain vague, Lamb's *Dispatch* clearly changed its posture toward the Red Scare in 1954. Not only did the paper defend Lamb by publishing his offer of $10,000 to anyone who could prove false his many affidavits averring his noncommunism and other specialized articles on his case, but the *Dispatch* also attacked the redbaiting behemoth itself with new vigor. McCarthy, as the best-known adversary, received most of the force of Lamb's counterattack, as on April 10, when the front page featured both "McCarthy Denounced by Bishop" and "State AFL Blasts McCarthy," as well as "Lamb Files Brief to Charges by FCC." Two days later, "Editor to Seek Joe's Indictment" and (U.S. attorney general) "Brownell Opposes Banning Red Party" continued a line of direct and indirect commentary that was to extend in the *Dispatch* for months.[56] The paper did miss an opportunity to broaden its critique of the witch hunt, however, in the case of Ted Buczek, a labor organizer and World War II veteran who embarrassed the feared House Committee on un-American Activities.

When another UE-IUE representation election loomed early in 1954, HUAC summoned Buczek to a hearing, in keeping with the committee's pattern of intervention in such contests. Unlike many such HUAC efforts around the country, this effort backfired. Buczek seized upon the false testimony of a federal witness to lecture the committee on "the Nazi-like Walter-McCarran Act" and on the sanctity of the Fifth Amendment's protections. "I fought where the fighting was hardest, on the front lines, for this privilege," Buczek reminded the committee, "I bled for this privilege in my country." After denouncing his accuser as "a trained seal," Buczek dismissed HUAC as "a bunch of small-minded men."[57] His triumph circulated chiefly by word of mouth, however, because the *Daily Times* reported only that he had invoked the Fifth Amendment when asked about possible communist associations, and the *Dispatch* failed to report the event at all.[58] Yet, the halcyon days of the century's second red scare were near the end.

In Erie, another IUE bid to ride anticommunism into power among GE workers fared no better than the first, and the *Dispatch* made a small contribution to that end. On the day before the election a *Dispatch* editorial, "Painful and Costly," lay responsibility for the "strife" and "the painful and costly by-product effects" of the situation squarely at the door of the IUE. The vote was 3,847–2,794 for the UE. "We just didn't get anywhere," remembered Msgr. Rice of Erie's GE workers many years later. To which Kate Buczek offered something like an answer, also long after the fact: "It was almost like a nationalism, that loyalty. Like patriotism."[59]

Many forces worked both in Erie and nationwide to deflect and, later, to repudiate the worst abuses of the McCarthy Era. The role of certain labor organizations, especially the United Electrical Workers, in sustaining democratic and liberal alternatives to corporate and rightist worldviews can hardly be exaggerated. Moreover, the case of Edward Lamb and his counterattack played something of the same role in Erie that Senator McCarthy's attack upon the Army played at the national level; for, in attacking the powerful, the right overreached itself and became the object of widespread criticism and even ridicule. The left, though weakened, could not be exterminated in Erie any more than nationally, and the culture of repression fell short of the aims of its most extreme proponents. Yet the weight of that era remains heavy even today.[60]

Notes

1. On the New Deal coalition and its antagonists, see James MacGregor Burns, *Roosevelt: The Lion and the Fox* (New York: Harcourt, Brace, Jovanovich, 1956), chap. 14 and 350–51. See also his *Roosevelt: The Soldier of Freedom* (New York: Harcourt, Brace, Jovanovich, 1970), 524–28; and

Art Preis, *Labor's Giant Step* (New York: Pathfinder Press, 1972), 46–49. On opponents in Pennsylvania, see Philip Jenkins, *Hoods and Shirts: The Extreme Right in Pennsylvania, 1925–1950* (Chapel Hill: University of North Carolina Press, 1997), 34–61. See also Karen Orren, *Belated Feudalism: Labor, the Law, and Liberal Development in the United States* (New York: Cambridge University Press, 1991), on the United States' "belated feudalism."

2. Interview with Marlin Allen, notes in the author's possession, 7 August 1980. See also Marlin Allen, "Ten Years of Growth," *The People's Press*, 28 August 1947; and "Labor Day Greetings," ibid., regarding numbers.

3. One the wartime truce, see David Milton, *The Politics of U.S. Labor* (New York: Monthly Review Press, 1982), 139–53; and Robert H. Zieger, *The CIO, 1935–1955* (Chapel Hill: University of North Carolina Press, 1995), 147–77. In Erie, union activists were warned by managers that "things will be different after the war" (author's interview with John Savelli and Wilbur White, 1 April 1981). For the European situation, see Patricia Cayo Sexton, *The War on Labor and the Left* (Boulder, Colo.: Westview Press, 1991), 157ff.

4. Erie *Daily Times*, 2 January, 30 July 1945.

5. Ibid., 24 January 1946.

6. Ibid., 6 February 1946.

7. Carl Marzani, *The Promise of Eurocommunism* (Westport, Conn.: Lawrence Hill, 1980). See Steve Rosswurm, "The Catholic Church and the Left-Led Unions," in *The CIO's Left-Led Unions*, ed. Steve Rosswurm (New Brunswick, N.J.: Rutgers University Press, 1992), 119–20.

8. Quoted from a 1946 speech in *Lake Shore Visitor*, 28 February 1947.

9. I chose a September-to-September calendar to avoid the 1946 strike wave.

10. Quoted in Richard O. Boyer and Herbert Morais, *Labor's Untold Story* (New York: Cameron Associates, 1955), 344; and Jenkins, *Hoods and Shirts*, 48, respectively. Wilson and Owlett did not simply act as individuals, as similar statements by Charles E. Wilson of General Motors and others make clear. James B. Atelson, *Values and Assumptions in American Labor Law* (Amherst: University of Massachusetts Press, 1983), 148. For the general sweep, see Elizabeth Fones-Wolf, *Selling Free Enterprise: The Business Assault on Labor and Liberalism, 1945–1960* (Urbana: University of Illinois Press, 1994), 5–6, 15, chap. 2.

11. Boyer and Morais, *Labor's Untold Story*, 344. See also Robert H. Zieger, review article, *Labor History* 37, no. 4 (fall 1996): 574–75.

12. Erie *Daily Times*, 15, 16, 22, 26 January, 2, 6, 7, 15 February 1946. Interview with Kate Buczek, 29 October 1997. Buczek noted that UE 506 officers belonged to the Liberty Club.

13. Marlin Allen interview; also, Wilbur White interview, 1, tapes and notes in the author's possession, 30 April 1980.

14. Alex Carey, *Taking the Risk Out of Democracy*, ed. Andrew Lohrey (Urbana: University of Illinois Press, 1997), 29. Lawrence S. Wittner, *Cold War America* (New York: Praeger Publishers, 1974), 88. David Caute, *The Great Fear* (New York: Simon and Schuster, 1978), 350. Fones-Wolf, *Selling Free Enterprise*, 37–38.

15. I included *all* issues in my survey.

16. On Wallace and Wallaceites, see Erie *Daily Times*, 1 March, 16, 22, 24 April 1948.

17. "Erie Man Called in Probe of Reds in U.E.W.," ibid., 2 September 1948. Also, "Erie UE Official Accuses Kearns of 'Political Move,' " ibid., 3 September 1948. On Kearns, Edward Doll interview, 2 February 1982. Doll was a long-time officer of the Erie Manufacturers' Association. Erie *Daily Times*, 9, 30 September, 1–2 October 1948.

18. Ibid., 4 September 1948. On the refusal of the Mine Workers, the Typographical Union, and others to take the oath, see *People's Press*, 10 July 1947; and Zieger, *CIO*, 279.

19. Editorials, Erie *Daily Times*, 6, 7, 29 September, 2, 11 October.

20. Ibid., 26 January 1946.

21. Ibid., 28 September 1948. On GE's two-step dance through business politics see Fones-Wolf, *Selling Free Enterprise*, 8. Fifty-one congressional supporters of the Taft-Hartley Act lost bids for reelection in 1948. *Harrisburg Telegraph*, 3 November 1948.

22. Erie *Dispatch*, 21 October 1948.

23. "Erie Pastor Cites Perils to Freedom," ibid., 13 October 1947.

24. "Loyalty Meeting Slated for Belle Valley," Erie *Daily Times*, 7 December 1952; and "Our Sunday Sermon," ibid., 1 February 1953.

25. Marlin Allen interview. In 1948 Allen was elected the Typographical Union's delegate to the AFL's Erie Central Labor Union.

26. "Clerics Flay 'Red Hunt' in Churches," Erie *Daily Times*, 10 March 1953.

27. Interview with Msgr. Charles Owen Rice, tapes and notes in the author's possession, December–January 1981/82.

28. *UE 506 Union News*, 17 October 1949. On the GE intervention, see James Matles and James Higgins, *Them and Us* (Boston, Mass.: Beacon Press, 1974), 198.

29. Interview with Tom Brown, Tom Rafter, and Gus Conti, notes and tapes in the author's possession, 27 December 1979.

30. Ibid.

31. *Lake Shore Visitor*, 19 May 1950.

32. Interview with Charles Curlie, 2 December 1980. Also, Brown-Rafter-Conti interview.

33. *UE 506 News*, 9, 23 March 1950.

34. Ibid., 4 May 1950.

35. Erie *Daily Times*, 23, 24, 25 May 1950. See also the issues of 4, 11, 18 May and 27 April 1950. The *Dispatch* betrayed no such bias at this juncture.

36. Erie *Daily Times* and Erie *Dispatch*, 24 May 1950.

37. Erie *Daily Times* and Erie *Dispatch*, 26 May 1950. Also, *UE 506 Union News*, 2 June 1950. One the 1952 vote, see Erie *Daily Times*, 17 December 1952.

38. See Zieger, review article, concerning the rebound from 1948. For the Reed interview, see Paul Haney, "Reed Claims That Reds Gain at GE," Erie *Daily Times*, 8 August 1950. On the membership and sympathizer numbers, see Wilbur White interview, 1. White, who was secretary of the party at that time, held that the Steelworkers constituted a larger bloc than GE workers did.

39. Erie *Daily Times*, 22 August 1950. On the civil-rights demonstrations, see interview with Catherine Buczek, notes in the author's possession, 4 April 1997. Buczek was an NAACP activist.

40. Gil Green (*Cold War Fugitive* [New York: International Publishers, 1984], 26) quotes extensively from D. M. Ladd, director of Domestic Intelligence, on such matters in documents from 1948.

41. Erie *Daily Times*, 14, 22 August 1950.

42. Erie *Dispatch*, 22, 23 August 1950.

43. Marlin Allen interview.

44. *People's Press*, 6 May 1948.

45. Marlin Allen interview.

46. Copies of the program manuscripts in the author's possession.

47. *General Electric News*, 31 December 1953, 29 January 1954.

48. "UN Official Says Britain Chief Communism Defense," Erie *Daily Times*, 1 March 1948.

49. "Stalin Must Beat U.S. to Make Grabs Safe," ibid., 14 April 1948.

50. "UE Members Called to Support CIO Policy," Erie *Dispatch*, 15 March 1949.

51. Ibid., 3 November 1953.

52. "Riesel Hits Commies in Erie Speech," ibid., 18 November 1953. Riesel's was one of a few pro-McCarthy labor columns in the U.S.; see Edwin R. Boyley, *Joe McCarthy and the Press* (Madison: University of Wisconsin Press, 1981), 59.

53. "GE Engine Market Good," Erie *Dispatch*, 6 November 1953. On the overseas construction, see Richard Barnet and Ronald E. Muller, *Global Reach* (New York: Simon and Schuster, 1974), 41.

54. "Anti-Trust Laws Hit by Speaker," Erie *Dispatch*, 15 November 1953.

55. Lamb's radio and television policy regarding redbaiting was recalled in Andrew Pressman's interview with Lamb on WCCK-FM on 6 May 1981. See also Edward Lamb, "Can Sen. McCarthy Be Libeled?" Erie *Dispatch*, 17

April 1950; and Stephen Feeley, "FCC Hearing Hinges on Lamb's Answer" and "U.S. Probes Edward Lamb," Erie *Daily Times,* 13, 14 March 1954. Lamb's Popular Front activities were also recalled in part of Catherine Buczek interview.

56. Erie *Dispatch,* 10, 12 April 1954. See also Saul Pett, "The McCarthy Story: 'Young Many in a Hurry,' " and "Getting to know Joe," ibid., 11 April, 4 May 1954, as well as "Put Up or Shut Up," ibid., 6 May 1954.

57. U.S., House Committee on un-American Activities, *Hearings, Investigation of Communist Activities in the Albany, N.Y., Area* (Washington, D.C.: U.S. Government Printing Office, 1954), 344–52. Also interview with Ted and Catherine Buczek, notes in the author's possession, 20 November 1980. See also Emanuel Fried, *The Un-American* (Buffalo, N.Y.: Springhouse Editions, 1992), 222–25, for a spirited account of Buczek's testimony (as Bill Kosciusko).

58. Erie *Daily Times,* 10 April 1954.

59. Erie *Dispatch,* 15 December 1954; Erie *Daily Times,* 15 December 1954; *UE 506 Union News,* 17 December 1954. Interview with Msgr. Charles Owen Rice. Interview with Ted and Kate Buczek.

60. Fones-Wolf, *Selling Free Enterprise,* chap. 9. Zieger, *CIO,* 351–56. Harry Kelber, *My 60 Years as a Labor Activist* (New York: A. G. Publishing, 1996), 109–10. Dorothy Sue Cobble, "Zieger's CIO: 'A Modest Defense,' " *Labor History* 37, no. 4 (fall 1996): 603–7. P. C. Sexton, *War on Labor,* chap. 16. "GOP Harmony Overdue," Erie *Daily Times,* 12 December 1954, demonstrates the paper's continued support of McCarthy even after his censure by the U.S. Senate. Also, interview with Charles Patrick Sheldon, notes in the author's possession, 16 March 1981, which indicates a continued hostility to labor unions as "red" among diocesan teachers into the late 1960s.

Incredible/Shrinking Men

Masculinity and Atomic Anxiety in American Postwar Science-Fiction Film

Anna Creadick

On 7 August 1945, Harry Truman issued a press statement which helped shape the way Americans would interpret the bombing of Hiroshima and Nagasaki.[1] By calling the bomb "the greatest achievement of organized science in history," the president allowed Americans to feel a sense of "innocence" and "progress" about atomic technology. By 1951, however, Americans already revealed their sense of "fear and foreboding" about atomic power.[2] What would atomic power look like if it got out of control? How would we handle an atomic emergency psychologically? How would institutions, organizations, and individuals respond? Who or what would save us?

The fear of atomic or nuclear disaster seems to have been a particular paranoia for American postwar audiences and filmmakers (Japan's early *Godzilla* films notwithstanding). While most of us are familiar with the "alien invasion" movies and "creature features" of the immediate postwar period, many science-fiction films of the time invoked the atomic *explicitly*. These are the films I want to analyze here, as they have something to tell us about postwar atomic anxiety and the ways it was—and wasn't—"contained."

The Cold-War foreign policy of "containment," as enunciated by George Kennan in 1946, has in the last decade become one of the dominant ways of understanding the *culture* of the postwar period.[3] Although I employ the term frequently in this essay for descriptive purposes, I also want to suggest that the "containment thesis," as it is applied to postwar culture, needs to be rethought. Just as "containment" could fail as a foreign policy, the idea of the "containment" of culture sets up an either/or dynamic that fails to allow for the subtle forms of critique, rebellion, and resistance that took place in the postwar period. Reading 1950s sci-fi films for their metaphors of "containment" (of women, of excess masculinity, or of disaster, for example) does provide some insights into cultural coercion, but it can also create a blindness to the films' politically charged *critiques* of women's "place," of men's gender identity, and of U.S. experimentation with the atomic.

For this project I considered how masculinity becomes connected to atomic fear in four early Cold War-era films: *The Day the Earth Stood Still* (1951), *Them!* (1954), *The Incredible Shrinking Man* (1957), and *The Amazing Colossal Man* (1957). Between 1951 and 1957, the period these films span, atomic fear on film intensifies, subsides, and then re-intensifies. Cold-War audiences' atomic anxiety was likely both fed and soothed by these film fantasies, in which danger is not always controlled. Questions of masculinity became connected to fear when male characters' authority was tested in the face of an atomic emergency.

Contrary to some commentators' readings of Cold-War sci-fi as illustrations (or fantasies) of male military, governmental, and scientific competence, I want to argue that these particular films actually critique military-government-scientific competence, as well as acknowledge the vulnerability of white middle-class males in a postwar atomic culture. I close by positioning this argument in its relevant scholarly context in order to suggest that these film representations of fear constitute a cultural critique of the atomic age—from within the atomic age—a critique that scholars have yet to appreciate.

Inscribing Fear:
The Day the Earth Stood Still (1951)

Dr. Barnhardt: Tell me, Hilda, does all this frighten you? Does it make you feel insecure?
Hilda (his secretary): Yes sir, it certainly does.
Dr. Barnhardt: Good. I'm glad.[4]

In this climactic scene in *The Day the Earth Stood Still,* the alien visitor Klaatu (played by Michael Rennie) and the Einstein-type intellectual Dr. Barnhardt (Sam Jaffe) have orchestrated a scare tactic, shutting off the world's electricity for half an hour in order to make international leaders listen to Klaatu's important message about the dangers of atomic power. As the world "stands still," Dr. Barnhardt cruelly baits his female secretary Hilda (Marjorie Grossland), apparently enjoying the power he and Klaatu are able to wield over her and the world at large.

Such a scare tactic was necessary because, contrary to dominant readings of '50s sci-fi, none of our earthly "institutions" have been able to respond to the crisis. The government, as represented by the secretary of state and other top Washington officials, is ineffectual, too wrapped up in stubborn Cold-War politics to come together even under the threat of global annihilation. True, the army is an extremely organized and effective machine—but too effective for its own good. Trained for combat, it is incapable of dealing with a crisis in any peaceful way. On the Mall, the highest-ranking army generals and "metallurgical experts" have tried to blowtorch Klaatu's robot bodyguard and break into the spaceship, but have failed. In the hospital, where Klaatu is first sent, renowned doctors and scientists have tried to understand Klaatu's physiology—and failed. "He was nice about it, but he made me feel like a third class witch doctor," one says, lighting a cigarette. Another wails, "I don't know whether to get drunk or just give up the practice of medicine." For these men of the military and medical establishments, what "worked" during the war no longer works in the postwar world. The transition from World War II uniformed masculinity to a (so-called) peacetime uniform of the "gray-flannel suit" parallels a transition from wartime aggression and force to a peacetime need for negotiation and cooperation. But these American men are still in uniform, still building weapons, still trying to be heroes.

Ironically, after effortlessly escaping the authorities, the alien Klaatu—who is perfectly humanoid in appearance, as played by the "charmingly suave and cosmopolitan" Rennie[5]—spends the rest of the film "passing" as Mr. Carpenter, a mild-mannered businessman. Despite being (alien)ated and outcast, this debonair outer-space "man in a gray flannel suit" is more of a man than any other. He is a classier boyfriend for the pretty widow Helen (Patricia Neal), a better father figure for her little son Bobby (Billy Gray), and a better mathematician than Dr. Barnhardt, the world's smartest professor. This "alien" has thrown off the balance of masculinity and the gender-defined hierarchies of knowledge and power in this postwar militarized culture.

By the film's end, a news conference announces to a still-frightened public that martial law has been declared in Washington, D.C.: "Stay in your homes," the newscasters say—a phrase which will become a mantra in these films (returning yet again in the 1996 blockbuster *Independence Day*). This directive advises the public that the safest space from which to face fear is the (feminized) domestic one, a place to receive information and instruction from radios and televisions. When the international leaders have finally gathered, Klaatu relays his message. The use of atomic weapons and the escalating threat of Cold-War military activity have become a risk that the rest of the intergalactic nations will not tolerate. "Your choice is simple," Klaatu tells them. "Join us and live in peace, or pursue your present course and face obliteration. . . . The decision rests with you." The film ends there.

As early as 1951, then, the fear connected to the atomic was potent enough to allow for a critical look at the unchecked development of atomic technology. From the start, control over atomic fear is linked to a certain kind of *masculine* power: the cool, white, male competence of Klaatu and Dr. Barnhardt in the face of danger. In *The Day the Earth Stood Still*, the men in charge—an alien visitor and a genius mathematician—must create fear in order to "contain" the possibility of future destruction. By making the world "stand still," the film operates as a metaphor for the logic of the use of the bomb at the end of World War II. By his example, however, Klaatu also shows American men their military, scientific, and even interpersonal inadequacies in a new age. By threatening to take away atomic weapons, the culture's greatest toy, Klaatu has effectively threatened America's very manhood.

Naming Fear: *Them!* (1954)

Dr. Medford: Tell me, in what area was the atomic bomb exploded? I mean the first one, back in 1945.
FBI Agent Graham: Right here in the same general area, White Sands.
Dr. Medford (looking at his daughter, also a scientist): That's nine years ago. . . . Yes, genetically it's certainly possible.[6]

In the 1954 film *Them!* a small collection of scientists, local police, and FBI agents work together to try and explain the disappearance of a young couple vacationing in New Mexico. "Robert Graham, from the FBI office in Alamogordo," attempts to take the lead in the investigation. Played by the cowboyish James Arness, Graham is not unlike Klaatu: handsome, unmarried, and a bit of a maverick. Soon, however, Graham must defer to the authority of two U.S. Department of Agriculture scientists flown in to help. Doctors Medford—Patricia (Joan Weldon), the pretty daughter, and her elderly father, Harold (Edmund Gwenn)—soon discover that the desert menace is a colony of irradiated ants, twelve feet tall and carnivorous. "A fantastic mutation!" the elder Dr. Medford gasps. "Probably caused by radiation from the first atomic bomb." Immediately, his tone changes: "We may be witnesses to a Biblical prophecy come true: 'And there shall be destruction, and darkness come over the nation, and the beasts shall rule over the earth.' " Here, as in the scene that heads this section, Dr. Medford "names" the fear by going to its historical source, locating the danger in a domestic context, and then "imagining" its apocalyptic possibilities. While in *The Day the Earth Stood Still* the alien messenger was feared more than the antiatomic message he brought, the carnivorous "creatures" in *Them!* are simply by-products of another, more permanent danger in the recent past: the human error of experimenting with atomic technology before we completely understood its power.

Where complete power over the atomic isn't possible, these films often console men with the possibility of continued power over women. Such gender concessions occur early on in *Them!* as the FBI agent Graham (Arness) pulls the lady doctor Patricia Medford aside to try and get some information: "Look, Miss—uh—*Doctor*," he stumbles. "If the 'Doctor' bothers you, well, why don't you call me *Pat*," she coos. Apparently sensing his insecurity, "Pat" elects to reinforce Graham's masculinity at her own expense: she must deny her professional identity as a scientist in order to establish her femininity in his eyes. Later, however, as they all set out on a carefully planned, secretive, search-and-destroy mission Pat firmly reestablishes her authority. Graham at first objects to her coming along: "There's one thing for sure, it's no place for you or any other woman!" But Pat is insistent, arguing that they need someone with scientific knowledge, and that her father is too "feeble" to go: "Look, Bob, there's no time to give you a course in insect pathology, so let's stop all the talk and get on with it." In a sense, this woman inhabits the postwar world more comfortably, and with more competence, than the men in authority who surround her. As they enter and investigate a giant anthill, for example, the female scientist remains calm and interested, while the local male cop, Sgt. Peterson, is terribly anxious: "Look," Pat notes, pointing at the walls, "—held together with saliva." "Yeah, spit's all that's holding me together, too," Sgt. Peterson replies, bashfully.

While plenty of cool and collected male scientists appear in postwar sci-fi films (William Hopper in 1957's *Deadly Mantis*[7] is a good example), the fact that the scientists here are represented by a *woman* and an *elderly* (and again, Einstein-ish) man suggests—even more overtly than the Klaatu-Barnhardt duo did—that middle-aged, middle-class postwar men are less capable of operating with authority than they were in wartime. Also important is the fact that the FBI man Graham does not "get the girl" in the end. The tensions between him and Dr. Patricia

Medford have been resolved, not romantically, but professionally. She has established her authority as a scientist, and he has had to recognize her in that role—which is more than can be said for the *New York Times* film reviewer who declared that the female entomologist, "played by Joan Weldon, is pretty but hardly the academic type."[8]

Midway through the film, we cut to Washington, where men in suits sit around a huge table, smoking and looking at reports. They agree to keep the New Mexico crisis "hush-hush," and the elder Dr. Medford shows them a quick ant documentary film to "edify" them. "Ants are the only creatures on earth other than man that make war," Dr. Medford observes. "That, gentlemen, is why you are here. To consider this problem, and I hope solve it. Because unless you solve it, . . . man, as the dominant species of life on earth, will probably be extinct within—a year." Putting the crisis into language of secrecy, combat, and dominance, the scientist taps into the government's Cold-War logic of problem solving. The very fate of the species is in the hands of these men.

Eventually the plan does work, and the "authorities"—speeding through the L.A. sewers in jeeps with flame throwers and with the two scientists along for expert advice—destroy the last two queen ants and their colonies, saving two little freckle-faced boys in the process. But the FBI man Graham wonders whether other species will show effects of the atomic bomb in the future. The elder scientist replies solemnly, "Nobody knows, Robert. When man entered into the atomic age, he opened a door into a new world. What we eventually find in that new world, nobody can predict." *The End.*

The audience is left to ponder a paradoxical message: the immediate danger has been eradicated, but the future remains frighteningly unpredictable. The film walks a fine line, then, implicating the military's atomic experiments as the source of unnatural horror, present and future danger, panic, and fear, but also constructing the men (and one woman) in charge as calm and capable of solving the problem, at least when they work together. Unfortunately, we see that they are only *barely* able to save us, and so the film ends not with a sense of security, but with fear—or at best paranoia—renewed.

In the "post-Hiroshima world," according to Joe de Bolt and John Pfeiffer, "Science Fiction made emotional sense." They describe the 1950s as a "golden age for [sci-fi]" writing.[9] According to film scholar Phil Hardy, the restructuring of Hollywood's studio system gave independent motion picture companies new opportunities to produce films, and the identification of teenagers as the major cinema-going audience gave filmmakers a financial base. Economically viable and emotionally relevant, science-fiction film emerged for the first time in the '50s "as a genre in its own right."[10] In his preface to *The Creature Features Movie Guide,* sci-fi writer Fritz Leiber argues that such films could appeal to "our imagination and our cowardice":

> Take the Geiger counter, whose ominous clicking signals the presence of radioactivity. In the 1950s when the atomic bomb was the deepest dread of most of us, most monsters became radioactive too.[11]

What frightened the sci-fi film audiences of the '50s was not the bomb or radioactivity per se, but the *uncontrolled* power they represented. To watch a representation of this uncontrolled power, however, was both to confront and avoid it. Postwar audiences could confront the subject of the atomic indirectly by watching men battle, say, irradiated ants on-screen. At the same time, they might avoid the atomic by "containing" it within that fictional context, rather than contemplating the "real world" atomic of Hiroshima, Nagasaki, Alamogordo, or Cold-War militarization. In all four of the films I have examined, however, the fear or danger is *always* grounded in some reference to a "real-world" atomic context.

Reviews of *Them!* called it "terrifying," "fascinating to watch," and "taut science-fiction." The real stars, according to the *New York Times,* were the "horrible hymenoptera"—those enormous, man-eating ants, whose White Sands origins were "surprisingly enough, somewhat convincing." Referring repeatedly to the film's implication of the 1945 New Mexico atomic tests, reviewers seemed genuinely disturbed by the film's "unadorned and seemingly factual approach."[12] What seems to us the campiest of giant-insect films, then, was tempered in its own time by its real-world atomic underpinnings. While *The Day the Earth Stood Still* invoked the postwar escalation of atomic weapons, *Them!* locates the atomic historically and geographically around the original White Sands test site. The last two films I discuss point to radioactive fallout and military weapons testing as the sources of danger for their incredible shrinking men.

The *Incredible Shrinking Man* and *The Amazing Colossal Man* (both released in 1957) differ from the first two films in that "the atomic" is applied not to alien outsiders or to insects, but to the male body itself. Significantly, in June 1956, the National Academy of Sciences released the first results of a study of the potential effects of atomic radiation on *man.* The report warned that

> atomic radiation is harmful to the person exposed to it and to all of his descendants. This is true . . . no matter how small the amount

of the radiation and regardless of its source—from bombs, nuclear reactors, X-rays or the natural environment. [A]ny radiation which reaches the reproductive cells causes mutations. . . . Human gene mutations which produce observable effects are believed to be universally harmful.[13]

While both *The Incredible Shrinking Man* and *The Amazing Colossal Man* seem to address this real-world concern, the fates of the two "atomic men" transmit different messages about fear, danger, and the American male's ability to face both of these in his postwar context. While the shrinking male protagonist learns to control his environment and conquer his own fears, the colossal man is victimized by his environment and destroyed by fear.

Conquering Fear:
The Incredible Shrinking Man (1957)

Scott Carrey (in voice-over): So I resolved, as man had dominated the world of the sun, so I would dominate my world.[14]

The Incredible Shrinking Man opens with the protagonist, ad exec Scott Carrey (played by Grant Williams), aboard a small boat with his wife, Louise (Randy Stuart). While Louise is below deck, a mysterious fog floats off the ocean water towards and around Scott, leaving him disoriented and covered with glittery dust. A week later, he starts shrinking. It seems the combination of exposure to lawn chemicals in his own neighborhood and the mysterious cloud of atomic fallout (apparently from an underwater test) have created a physiological reaction which even the best scientists and medical experts cannot understand or solve. In this film—with no aliens, Einstein-intellectuals, or female scientists to save him—the male postwar protagonist is left to conquer his own fears.

As Scott's body shrinks, so does his sense of his own manhood. He immediately thinks bitterly of the sexual implications: "Louise," he tells his wife, "I want you to start thinking about us . . . our marriage. . . . Some awful things might happen. There's a limit to your obligation." Of course Louise remains devoted, but Scott becomes crueler to his wife as his own condition worsens. He says, again in voice-over:

[Despite] my desperate need for her . . . I felt puny and absurd. A ludicrous midget. . . . I loathed myself. Our home, the caricature my life with Lou had become—. . . . Every day it was worse. Every day a little smaller. And every day I became more tyrannical, more monstrous in my domination of Louise.

This tortured man/victim must establish domination over someone in the face of his own increasing insignificance. In her discussion of this film, Tania Modeleski argues that "women . . . are made to bear, as always, the burdens of masculine ambivalence about the body."[15] But it is important that Scott describes his "domination" of Louise with self-disgust; he sees his own behavior as cowardly—a "tyrannical . . . monstrous" way to react. As a white middle-class "organization man," he had been the epitome of postwar normalcy. Now, Scott has become different from everyone else, and from that position of difference, he begins to question the meaning of "normal": "Sometimes I begin to think that it's the *world* that's changed, that *I'm* the normal one," he remarks. But for the Shrinking Man, unlike the Colossal Man, there is regeneration in store.

Attacked by the family house cat and accidentally trapped in his own cellar, Scott turns into Tarzan, Lord of the Basement, wrapping himself in burlap, carrying a straight pin as a sword, and relying on his strength and ingenuity to survive. "As man had dominated the world of the sun," he resolves, "so I would dominate my world." Scott scales wooden boxes with needle and thread, drinks giant drops from a leaky water heater, and climbs table legs to fight an enormous spider for cake crumbs. With each act of bravery, Scott's manhood is reestablished, even in excess, despite the continued shrinking of his body.

In the end, though Scott's wife and brother fail to find him, he "finds" himself. He stabs the mammoth spider with the needle, and escapes into the moonlit yard, still shrinking, but feeling existential, talking metaphysical:

> I felt my body dwindling, melting, becoming nothing. My fears melted away, and in their place came—acceptance. All this vast majesty of creation, it had to mean something, and then I meant something. . . . To God, there is no zero. I still exist!

Church bells ring, music swells, and Scott disappears into grass and leaves as the camera pulls back through underbrush and trees, and then outward toward the stars. The scene clearly presents an existential epiphany for this corporate male, a sense of acceptance despite "becoming nothing." But the gendered nature of this existentialism also emerges as we recall Scott's wife, Louise, packing up her belongings, abandoning their home, and driving away to move in with Scott's brother and his wife: "In relation to others, I still exist!" she might have concluded.

In terms of masculinity and the atomic age, *The Incredible Shrinking Man* constitutes another indictment of atomic and other modern technologies as dangerous to all; and in this case, dangerous to the white middle-class businessman in particular. What happens to Scott could be read as a metaphor for what was happening for many corporate men at the time, an increasing sense of smallness, of insignificance as an anonymous part of a larger "organization." Given the way he interacts with women and the way he reverts to a Cro-Magnon existence in the basement, this corporate male allows us to see that masculinity itself is at risk. In this film, the basement world becomes a place to confront fear, a place where an individual's skills matter again, where a man can use his body, however small, to survive, kill, and dominate.

The conclusion of *The Incredible Shrinking Man* presents Scott's simultaneous death and re-birth. He has narrated his own story in voice-over from the beginning, so he truly must "still exist." In fact, Scott becomes *atom-ic* by the end, dissolved/atomized into a cosmic order. He understands his size as a metaphor for *man's* place in the universe, *man*-kind's existential condition. He does not die a "freak" or a "creature," feared by others. He lives on, without fear: tiny and alone in the universe, but cognizant and accepting of his place in it.

Re-inscribing Fear:
The Amazing Colossal Man (1957)

Mr. Klingman (nuclear expert): The fact that Glenn Manning lived after the blast, and that new skin replaced the burned, dead tissue in a matter of hours, means only one conclusion: something out there is beyond the limits of our knowledge.[16]

A "colossal man" might be expected to embody the opposite gender image of a "shrinking man," but in fact the two characters are remarkably similar. *The Amazing Colossal Man* (released only six months after *Incredible Shrinking Man*, and widely considered a low-budget knock-off) takes place almost entirely within the organization of the U.S. Army, as the action moves from a Nevada plutonium-bomb test site, to an army hospital, to an isolated army research center, to a final climactic contest between the military and the man/monster atop the Hoover Dam.

The film opens with Colonel Glenn Manning (played by Glenn Langan) and dozens of other soldiers crouching in trenches at a Nevada test site, ready to be exposed to a plutonium blast (from a safe distance, we are told). The bomb blast is delayed because of a malfunctioning timer, and the soldiers must stay in the trenches to wait it out. When a civilian plane accidentally enters the airspace above the test site and crash lands, Colonel Manning heroically—and foolishly—disobeys orders and leaves the trench to try to save the man in the plane. The plutonium bomb suddenly explodes in Manning's face with a flash, blasting away his shirt, the heat beginning to burn and melt his chest as his arms shield his face in quite a graphic image. Later, when Manning awakes in the army hospital to find his exposure has made him "colossal," he speaks his first words, in horror: "What sin . . . could a man have committed in a single life, to bring this upon himself?" What sin, indeed?

Even immediately after Hiroshima, the atomic bomb did not represent "progress" to everyone. To a few people, James Farrell argues, the bomb represented

> something radically unfamiliar in the American cultural experience: a sense of sin. . . . Yet in 1945 the words and images which might reinforce this countercultural view were few and far between in the American press. Images of burnt and irradiated corpses, of individual human suffering, for example, were invisible to American eyes.[17]

By 1957, apparently, "sin" was a more familiar sense, and "Images of burnt and irradiated" bodies and "individual human suffering" were becoming visible to American eyes. The violent blast-exposure images— repeated a total of three times in *The Amazing Colossal Man*—are not, of course, representations of the *real* bomb victims, the people of Hiroshima and Nagasaki, but the image is emphasized, nonetheless. And in a late-1950s xenophobic context, the bomb-blast damage done to the body of this white, American male soldier/hero may have had an even stronger effect.

Manning's skin regenerates the next morning, but when the "cellular process" will not stop he becomes "colossal." He is moved to an isolated army research center where he's kept in a circus tent, since—at twenty-two feet—he is outgrowing the buildings. Although exposure to plutonium has made Colonel Manning's body monstrous, he seems most affected mentally. Slowly, his state of mind degenerates, and when science fails, Manning, just like the Shrinking Man, takes out his fury and frustration on his loyal and pliant fiancée Carol (Cathy Downs), who has disobeyed the military's orders and followed him to the center.

The gender tensions become highly ironic: as Manning grows more and more colossal, he feels less and less a man. He too is tortured by the ridiculous and horrible image of a sexual future with Carol, and repeatedly tries to manipulate her emotionally into leaving him. Of course, she doesn't. Again, part of the masculinity message promoted by these films seems to be an assurance that if all else fails, at least women will remain loyal, and against them, these protagonists can remain "men." But at the same time, the female characters are subtly represented as more capable of handling the crises of the postwar world. The women in these films are not often hysterical or in need of consolation; instead, they seem to be sources of stability, support, and comfort for the incredible/shrinking men.

Again, a frightened public is told to find safety in the domestic space of home, and put their problems into the capable hands of police, doctors, and the military. In Las Vegas a newscaster repeats nearly the same message we have heard in *Them!* and in *The Day the Earth Stood Still:* "Police Chief Benson has asked me to tell you to stay in your homes. *Stay in your homes!* The army is rushing two doctors to Las Vegas by helicopter. They apparently know what to do with the giant." Described now as a "giant," Colonel Manning has lost his status as a man. His exposure to the atomic has erased his humanity, creating an interesting parallel to the Hiroshima/Nagasaki victim's "invisibility"—and an opposition to the Shrinking Man's increased humanity. Although the physical effects of the atomic have simply caused an exaggeration of his body, Colonel Manning is now perceived as a "monster" to be destroyed. The doctors find Manning and try to give him a giant hypodermic full of serum, but they are too late. His mental state has worsened, and in a rage, he stabs one doctor with the huge syringe, grabs Carol, and heads for the Hoover Dam. The remaining doctor convinces the confused Colossal Man to release his squiggling fiancée just before the military blows him away with their bazookas and rifles, in a scene reminiscent of *King Kong.* The film ends with the camera looking down into the pulsing water at this man/monster who, like Kong, seems to have been "more sinned against than sinning."[18]

That image leaves us with a turning tide. It is pause for thought when eloquent spacemen make threats about atomic bombs. It is creepy when atomic radiation creates giant bugs. But when the atomic starts affecting the American male—his mind, his body, his character, his love life—and doctors and the military are not able to keep one step ahead of this "atomic" man, things get, well, *personal.* At the end of this film, the military kills the giant, but we are not so relieved. This was a man—a hero, in fact—who earlier left the (relative) safety of the trench to try to save another man. Again, wartime heroics fail to transfer into a postwar context: Glen Manning seems an ironic victim of the same atomic technology he was helping to test on behalf of the military "organization." Even though Manning grows colossal, the viewer, like his fiancée, Carol, is reluctant to see him as a monster. Glen Manning is a human being, not a giant irradiated ant. The death of "us" is not as easy to watch as the death of *Them!*

Conclusions

I am uncomfortable with arguments which collapse all giant insect/space invader/human mutation films of the 1950s together as apolitical aesthetic experiences or allegories—a reading that likely began with Susan Sontag's 1966 essay, "The Imagination of Disaster." While Sontag posits that "There is absolutely no social criticism, of even the most implicit kind, in science fiction films,"[19] a closer look at these films reveals otherwise. Produced in an era of increasing space research and discovery, "alien invader" films may have spoken to a real fear of the extra-terrestrial unknown. "Creature features" surely spoke to an anxiety about science's perhaps "unnatural" success in destroying or altering the natural world with technology. Closer attention to the particular kinds of anxiety-producing technology being portrayed—weapons, chemicals, and bombs in these four films—reveals more pointed cultural critiques than Sontag and others have seen. Ultimately, reducing these sci-fi films to metaphor makes arguments about repression, consensus, and complicity in the postwar years too easy to prove.

Peter Biskind locates American film critiques of Cold War institutions squarely in the 1960s, epitomized by the 1964 political satire *Dr. Strangelove.*[20] The '60s, Biskind argues, gave us the critique of the arms race, government, atomic energy, and paranoid anti-communism that "would have been unimaginable in the fifties."[21] My reading of these four 1950s films shows that filmmakers of the '60s did not invent such critique. Criticism of the atomic was clearly bolder and more sophisticated in such 1960s films as *Dr. Strangelove,* but it certainly was not "unimaginable" in the '50s: *The Day the Earth Stood Still* condemns the arms race; *Them!* points to the White Sands test site as the beginning of an age of uncertainty; *The Incredible Shrinking Man* warns us about radioactive fallout and the dangerous chemical materials even within domestic spaces; and *The Amazing Colossal Man* critiques military bomb testing—and perhaps, obliquely, the original use of the bomb—by showing the fallibility of these tests, the effects of exposure on the body, and the risks of experimentation with "something . . . beyond the limits of our knowledge."

All of these films are set in the postwar present, suggesting that both filmmakers and their audiences—52 percent of whom were teenagers by 1957[22]—were concerned with how to live in the current atomic age. While the atomic emerges as an central object of fear and anxiety for these audiences, the way fear is played out regularly hinges on questions of male gender identity. The science-fiction films that represent the atomic explicitly do *not* tend to leave that danger "contained." Similarly, the "men in charge" are not fully in control, but full of contradictions. Some—such as the G-men and doctors in *The Day the Earth Stood Still* or the "expert" scientists in *The Incredible Shrinking Man* and *The Amazing Colossal Man*—are utterly ineffectual. Others—such as the scientists in *The Day the Earth Stood Still* and *Them!* or the military men in *The Amazing Colossal Man*—can solve pressing problems in an immediate sense, but are unable to assuage larger fears about the future.

There are significant differences among the men in these films, especially in terms of "masculinity": business men do not pack bazookas; military men don't have to understand atomic physics, medicine, or ant physiology to get in there and shoot; and doctors, scientists, and intellectuals cannot seem to operate helicopter radios, follow protocol, or protect themselves from a Colossal Man's fury. The white, male protagonists in each film—Klaatu/Mr. Carpenter, Robert Graham, Scott Carrey, and Glenn Manning—could all be seen as postwar "organization men." Whether working for science, the government, business, or the military, the "organization man" virtually *embodied* Cold-War ideological tensions: he is at once pressured to be a self-interested individual and a small cog in a wheel. His interactions with women often illustrate his growing sense of insignificance. But interestingly, in the majority of these films, the isolated man becomes a victim, while the corporate male, or the one who works as part of a group, finds solutions.

Research which aims to historicize (and thus denaturalize) masculinity is uncommon, tentative, and, in the case of the postwar period, still nearly nonexistent. Gender roles are always more visible in the caricatured spectacles produced for a big screen, but those performances do not simply mirror or construct the gendered identities of the "real" men of the time. If we consider that gender is always to some extent a performance, then the way men "wore" their gender identities must have been influenced by these images that surrounded them. And the fact that such a large percentage of the movie-going audience was made up of teenagers at this time further suggests that a younger generation was interested in seeing both what frightened them and who might—or might not—be able to save them.

In the 1951–57 films I have presented, white middle-class men create atomic power, test it, and contain it, but they also fall victim to it, fail to control it, and fear it. None of these films leaves the audience with a clear sense of resolution. The reinscription of fear, coupled with the ambiguity of the male characters' authority, may well correspond to a growing sense of conflict over whether *men* were indeed the ones who could "save us" in a postwar world.

Notes

I am grateful to Kevin Dunn and Barton Byg for reading drafts of this essay.

1. James M. Farrell, "Making (Common) Sense of the Bomb in the First Nuclear War," *American Studies* 36 (fall 1995): 5–41.

2. Ibid., 34–35.

3. Contemporary examples of scholarly use of the "containment" thesis range from Elaine Tyler May's 1988 *Homeward Bound* (New York: Basic Books) to Alan Nadel's 1995 *Containment Culture* (Durham, N.C.: Duke University Press).

4. Robert Wise, *The Day the Earth Stood Still*, screenplay Edmund H. North (20th Century Fox, 1951).

5. Bosley Crowther, "Emissary from Planet Visits Mayfair Theatre in 'Day the Earth Stood Still,' " review of *The Day the Earth Stood Still*, *New York Times*, 19 September 1951, 37.

6. Gordon Douglas, *Them!* (Warner Bros./First Pictures, 1954).

7. Nathan Juran, *Deadly Mantis* (Universal-International, 1957).

8. A. W. review of *Them! New York Times*, 17 June 1954, 36–37.

9. Joe de Bolt and John Pfeiffer, "The Modern Period, 1948–1975," *Anatomy of Wonder: Science Fiction*, ed. Neil Barron (New York: R. R. Bowker Co., 1976), 121.

10. Phil Hardy, ed., introduction to *Science Fiction: The Overlook Film Encyclopedia* (Woodstock, N.Y.: Overlook, 1995), xv.

11. Fritz Leiber, introduction to *The Creature Features Movie Guide*, by John Stanley (Pacifica, Calif.: Creatures at Large, 1981), 6–7. See also Tom Weaver, *They Fought in the Creature Features: Interviews with 23 Classic Horror, Science Fiction and Serial Stars* (Jefferson, N.C.: McFarland, 1995).

12. A. W., review of *Them!* 37. See also Brog., review of *Them! Variety Film Reviews*, 14 April 1954, ix.

13. Harry Hansen, *The World Almanac and Book of Facts for 1957* (New York: New York World-Telegram/The Sun Corp., 1957), 376.

14. Jack Arnold, *The Incredible Shrinking Man* (Universal Pictures, 1957).

15. Tania Modeleski, "The Incredible Shrinking He(r)man: Male Regression, the Male Body, and Film," *Differences* 2, no. 2 (1990): 55–75. Thanks to T. J. Boisseau for suggesting this source.

16. Bert I. Gordon, *The Amazing Colossal Man* (American International Pictures, 1957).

17. Farrell, "Making (Common) Sense," 35 (emphasis added).

18. This parallel to *King Kong* was noted by Andrew Dowdy in the chapter "My God! It's a 50-Foot Woman!" in *The Films of the Fifties* (New York: Morrow, 1973), 168.

19. Susan Sontag, "The Imagination of Disaster," *Against Interpretation* (New York: Farrar, Straus & Giroux, 1966), 223.

20. Stanley Kubrick, *Dr. Strangelove, or How I Learned to Stop Worrying and Love the Bomb* (Columbia Pictures, 1964).

21. Peter Biskind, *Seeing Is Believing: How Hollywood Taught Us to Stop Worrying and Love the Fifties* (London: Pluto Press, 1984), 344.

22. Garth Jowett, "Audience Age during WWII," H-Media Listserve, 9 Mar. 1995. Also found in appendices for his *Film: The Democratic Art* (Boston, Mass.: Little, Brown, 1976).

PART VI

ANXIETIES OF THE MODERN AGE

Witch-hunting during America's First War on Drugs

Richmond Pearson Hobson and "Narcotic Education"

Mark C. Smith

In 1987, Dr. David Musto, physician, Yale professor of history, and the dean of cultural historians of drugs, looked back to 1973 and the writing of his classic *The American Disease: Origins of Narcotic Control*. He worried that "the fear of drugs will again translate into a simple fear of the drug user and will be accompanied by draconian sentences and specious links between certain drugs and distrusted groups within society."[1] In short, the war on drugs would become a war against the drug user. In 1990 Darryl Gates, then Los Angeles chief of police, advised a Senate subcommittee that "casual drug users should be taken out and shot" for committing "treason."[2] At approximately the same time, America's best-known drug-policy advisor, William Bennett, an individual who has since risen to the role of national moral arbiter, advocated the beheading of drug dealers on *Larry King Live*.[3] Bennett's reasoning behind such an apparently extreme view was that drugs were illegal and therefore by definition immoral. In his estimation, the nation was going through a "crisis in authority," which was his duty to remedy. He would have been willing to base his campaign on abortion, teen pregnancy, or any other issue that dealt with matters of "character." As one of his chief aides declared, "Drugs are the hill we are fighting over at the moment, but the war is much bigger than that."[4] The current war on drugs has become, in the estimation of many, a witch-hunt driven by fear of the unknown in which ostracized individuals serve as convenient scapegoats for feared social change.

While the definition and classification of witch-hunts may differ, a common theme in all of them is the presence of scapegoats and attacks upon them and their defenders. About the literal witch-hunts of New England, John Putnam Demos has noted how conflicted communities labeled one or two economically and psychologically marginal women beyond the age of menopause as witches and used their persecution for cathartic purposes.[5] Paul Boyer and Stephen Nissenbaum somewhat similarly attribute the "major panic" of Salem to the Salem villagers who scapegoated economically and geographically mobile individuals associated with prosperous Salem Town.[6] Particularly in Salem, individuals who courageously defended their neighbors or kin or questioned proceedings often found themselves accused of witchcraft as well. The evolution of American attitudes toward drug users provides a useful case study of the development of just such a witch-hunt, and the career of the antidrug propagandist Richmond Pearson Hobson reflects this process of scapegoating.

While most Americans unthinkingly believe that the federal government banned such drugs as opiates when they were first introduced in the United States, this assumption is not correct. Physicians referred to morphine, upon its introduction in America in the early part of the nineteenth century, as "God's own medicine"; by 1834 it was the single most prescribed item in the American pharmacopoeia.[7] Individuals soon became addicted, but almost all did iatrogenically—that is, through prescription by physicians. These patients tended to be overwhelmingly middle- and upper-class women whose physicians had prescribed morphine for mysterious "women's problems." According to different surveys, the percentage of female opiate addicts in the late nineteenth century ranged from between 61 and 72 percent of all addicts.[8] A few upper-class women turned to morphine as an alternative to liquor, which was much more stigmatized; one women reported that "Morphine makes life possible . . . without professions, without beliefs."[9] Many physicians shared their patients' addiction; observers estimated that from 6 to 10 percent of physicians in the late nineteenth century were addicted to morphine. Use peaked during the 1890s. The best estimate we have is that about 4.59 individuals per thousand used opiates regularly during this time.[10] That is one of the highest, if not the highest, percentage of opiate users in American history. Still, while drug addiction was condemned, Americans overwhelmingly perceived it as a private vice, a tragedy perhaps to the individual and her family, but one, unlike alcoholism, that did not affect society negatively.

Ironically, as iatrogenically addicted patients died and rates of addiction decreased, the pressure for criminalization of drugs increased. This development came about due to the changing nature of the addict population—first, with the entrance of opium-smoking Chinese laborers into the country; and second, with the adoption of morphine and later heroin by young urban toughs. The first federal law to prohibit drug use targeted smoking opium and, by extension, the Chinese. Even with the passage of the Harrison Act in 1914, many localities attempted to deal with their addicted populations humanely. In contrast to Prohibition, during which no provisions were made for alcoholics cut off from their drug, many towns and states set up narcotic clinics to provide maintenance doses of morphine and heroin to already addicted individuals. Although these clinics suffered from mismanagement and harassment from the Narcotics Bureau of the Treasury Department, some, such as the efficient Shreveport, Louisiana, hospital, operated until 1923. Indeed, throughout the 1920s various politicians sent addicted constituents to the Narcotic Division of the Prohibition Department, which then referred them to U.S. Public Health Service physicians for possible maintenance. The papers of Dr. Lawrence Kolb, a Public Health Service physician, psychiatrist, and narcotics expert assigned to Washington during the 1920s, contain hundreds of such referrals from a six-state area. In all but one case, Kolb arranged for continued prescription of opiates. In one representative letter, Kolb referred to a patient as "a good moral, hard working citizen who had ample reason for becoming an addict and who is now in such a state of health that cure would be of no benefit to him even if it could be effected. . . . He would probably not be able to work again if morphine was taken from him."[11]

Gradually public opinion toward addicts changed. Obviously, the different composition of the addict population had an impact. Medical and psychological views toward addiction also changed, from physiological to environmental explanations of causation, with Freudian-influenced psychiatrists referring to all addicts as "psychopaths" who freely chose their addiction because of character defects. The key role in attitudinal change, however, was played by publicists and propagandists who reported to the American public that narcotics use was reaching epidemic proportions and constituted a national emergency. By all accounts the most important of these figures was Richmond Pearson Hobson, a Spanish-American War hero, ex-Alabama congressman, and leading Prohibitionist. Hobson's career and personality, his conception of "narcotic education," and his attacks upon people like Kolb who opposed him represent, I believe, a revealing case of an American witch-hunt based upon groundless fears that helped establish the misguided pattern for our continuing war on drugs and their users.

Although almost totally unknown today, Hobson was a conspicuous figure from the 1890s through the 1930s. Born in Greensboro, Alabama, to a prominent family, he attended a small college in his hometown and later transferred to the U.S. Naval Academy. There he demonstrated the moral fervor and self-righteousness that would characterize his career. Obeying the academy code to the letter, he religiously informed on all his classmates, winning for himself their enmity and silent treatment. Glorying in their hatred and graduating at the top of his class, he became a naval engineer specializing in the construction of warships. While serving aboard the flagship of the American fleet during the Spanish American War, he volunteered to take a small ship into the narrow channel of Cuba's Santiago Harbor and sink her, thus effectively bottling up the Spanish fleet. While failing to carry out this mission completely because of inadequate equipment, he and his seven-man crew acted courageously and after a brief imprisonment in Cuba returned to a hero's welcome. Indeed, he was the first of the many American heroes of the war and was sent on a goodwill tour to drum up support for the ongoing conflict. At a Chicago welcome he spotted a cousin with whom he exchanged a decorous kiss. Other women demanded similar attention, a ritual repeated on subsequent stops. The handsome Hobson quickly became, according to the newspapers, "the most kissed man in America," and a quick-thinking confectioner hustled "Hobson's Kisses" to the market, gaining a quick fortune for himself and adding to Hobson's national reputation.

Retiring from the navy several years later, he defeated a powerful Alabama incumbent congressman in 1906 and served four terms. In 1909 he became a leader of Alabama's strong Prohibition movement and quickly became one of the leading spokesmen of the national Anti-Saloon League. In 1914 Hobson, with a 150-foot scroll containing six million signatures hanging from the gallery to the floor behind him, introduced the national prohibition amendment into Congress. Although it failed in Congress that year, it would pass during the next session. In 1914 Hobson narrowly lost election to the U.S. Senate to Oscar Underwood, speaker of the house, later Senate majority leader, two-time serious candidate for the Democratic nomination for president, and probably the most powerful national southern politician since John Calhoun. In addition to national prohibition, Hobson fought for an expanded navy, women's suffrage, federal aid to education, and the end to the electoral college, and against the Japanese, whom he regarded as an "international scourge."

While one scholar correctly described the cold, humorless Hobson as a man of "virtually unlimited moral indignation," such an assessment overlooks his strengths and virtues.[12] While not above criticizing his military superiors, Hobson as an officer was undeniably brave, gracious to his captors, and totally devoted to his men.[13] His support of

Prohibition won him the enmity and financial opposition of the national brewers and wholesale liquor dealers, who launched a national campaign to raise money for Underwood, a crafty conservative Birmingham politician and favorite of Wall Street. In the House of Representatives, Hobson was the lone southern congressman calling for a court of inquiry into the dishonorable discharge of three companies of African-American soldiers thrown out of the army after defending themselves during a race riot in Brownsville, Texas. Hobson not only supported but also spoke in favor of this inquiry, which led to the exoneration of 167 of the servicemen. For his defense and support of these soldiers as well as such actions as his sponsorship of ten Filipinos to Annapolis and West Point, his participation in an integrated women's suffrage parade, and his reference to a Negro minstrel group as "ladies and gentlemen," the Underwood campaign labeled him "unsound."[14] In a later speech before the House, he noted that his views had cost him the election but stated that he preferred his honor.[15] A histrionic speaker, Hobson was the leading Anti-Saloon League publicist and fund-raiser and one of the most popular and best-paid public lecturers in the nation.

Hobson would derive his strategy against narcotics from his earlier prohibition campaigns. Combining his talks on temperance into one speech, "The Great Destroyer," Hobson traveled across the country, giving the speech and using his congressional mailing and printing privileges to send out two and a half million copies of it. Mixing scientific and pseudo-scientific evidence, he referred to alcohol use as "the greatest question in the history of the human species, actually determining more than all other questions combined the perpetuity of any civilization." Juggling his figures, Hobson proved to his supporters that more people had died from alcohol use than in all wars combined and that the current European war death toll could not keep up with the number of Americans dying from alcohol. Drinking destroyed human will, almost guaranteed death or deformity to one's children, and ultimately created sterility in its users. Moderate drinking was "ten times worse than drunkenness" and led automatically to physical and spiritual slavery.[16]

The quick ratification of the Prohibition Amendment by the states and the passage of the Volstead Act left Hobson and the Anti-Saloon League itself searching for a role. No one, not even the ASL, had expected such speedy passage of the bill, but the sense of self-sacrifice created by the commitment to the war effort quickly propelled the amendment through the states. The founders of the Anti-Saloon League had created the league for one purpose and one purpose only: to lobby for the passage of local, state, and national prohibition laws. It lost its mission once it had achieved this purpose and also any reason for the continued employment of a publicist such as Hobson. Although its director of education, Ernest Cherrington, tried to direct the league into educational efforts, he lost out to those who continued to concentrate on electoral politics.[17]

By 1922 Hobson had severed any direct connection to the ASL and in 1923 founded his own organization, the International Narcotic Association, which would be joined by the World Conference on Narcotic Education in 1926 and the World Narcotic Defense Association in 1927. Hobson turned to the connections he had forged during his years as a temperance crusader; church temperance organizations, veterans' groups, the general federation of womens' clubs, and service organizations such as Kiwanis, Moose, the Knights of Columbus, and Masons. He petitioned all of them for financial and political support. Setting a fund-raising goal of one million dollars at first, and then ten million dollars, Hobson promised to obtain information about narcotics and publicize this new threat to America through dissemination of such intelligence through sponsoring groups. For many of these organizations, drugs were a perfect crusade. Everyone could agree on their evil, and their users were perceived as alien and criminal outsiders who represented a threat to American society.

Hobson's facts about drugs mirrored and sometimes even plagiarized his alcohol material. As with alcohol, the United States "had never faced a deadlier peril." The physiological danger of opiates and cocaine was again to the upper brain, where they permeated the physiological source for "the Temple of the Spirit, the seat of altruistic motives, character, and those high Godlike traits." Moreover, as with alcohol, drugs quickly led to sexual impotence and sterility and were a major reason for the rise of the so-called "subnormals" the army had detected during World War I.[18]

Hobson was not willing merely to repeat past assertions, however. According to him, withdrawal from opiates was next to impossible and usually led to death. "Addiction . . . is as uncurable as leprosy . . . far more tragic . . . and probably far more communicable." Indeed, the government's attempts to prevent the importation of drugs was hopeless, since foreign chemists were now manufacturing heroin from coal tar. Opiates were so pervasive in American society that he advised against accepting "headache powders" or, indeed, anything to eat, drink, or smoke when away from home. He also recommended that people analyze their makeup for heroin.[19]

The reason for these precautions came directly from Hobson's differentiation of drug addicts from alcoholics and his depiction of them as totally evil creatures. In his alcohol propaganda, Hobson had carefully differentiated drinkers from saloon owners. The first were helpless creations of the latter, and the proof of their residual humanity lay in their refusal to introduce others to drink. Only the saloon owners, with their desire for profit, would do that.[20] Drug addicts, on the other hand, had "an absolute mania" (a phrase he repeated five times in one ten-page speech) for leading others into addiction to share their pain and constant search for supplies. Pioneering what later Federal Bureau of Narcotics chief Harry Anslinger would refer to as "the gore file," Hobson collected tales, most if not all apocryphal, of mothers addicting their eight-year-old children and adolescents, their baby sisters. Such addicts were, in Hobson's repeated phrase, "the living dead." As he bluntly declared, "Neither can we expect much from salvage [from this] vast army of daring criminal youths in our midst who can not be controlled, who can not be changed, who are capturing others of our youth by the thousands." Hobson stated that he had told his sixteen-year-old son that if he ever went to "a snow party" that he would blow his brains out for his own good.[21] Drug addicts, in Hobson's imagination— or rhetoric—became a nearly omnipotent force attacking the very future of American society. While such demonization certainly aided his incessant fund-raising, it also coincided with his Manichaean view of the world, for his enemies—whether they be cheating cadets, expansionist Japanese, or greedy liquor dealers—were totally evil. He, by contrast, was absolutely righteous. In such a world, one could never expect or show mercy.

Much of the hysteria of this demonization came from Hobson's contention that the number of addicts was growing exponentially. Using numbers from decade-old Treasury reports, unsubstantiated proclamations from ambitious politicians, and at times purely imaginary statistics, Hobson extrapolated the highest figures he could obtain from the New York urban area to the entire nation and wound up with 1,750,000 addicts, or roughly 1.57 percent of the American population.[22] In one of New York City's boroughs, he identified 17,000 addicts in the public schools despite the school board's denial of any addicts whatsoever. This statistical profile clearly constituted a national emergency and called for immediate action.

Since already addicted individuals were as good as dead, the obvious response was "swift education of those not already infected." As before, Hobson's strategy involved the development of a speech with which he barnstormed the country. Hobson gave this talk, "The Peril of Narcotics," thousands of times at various churches, public lectures, and service organizations throughout the nation. Also, by employing the tactics used for his "The Great Destroyer" speech, he arranged for a friendly congressman to introduce legislation providing for the printing and mailing of 50 million copies of the speech, enough for every family and student in the country. Indeed, the speech insisted that it was each individual citizen's civic duty to read the pamphlet aloud to every member of the family and to keep it next to the family Bible for easy reference.[23]

Among those few individuals who dared to disagree publicly with Hobson was Kolb, a U.S. Public Health Service psychiatrist. While Kolb pointed out the mistakes and paranoia of Hobson's speech and Hobson's personal economic interests in his crusade, he concentrated primarily on Hobson's figures, noting exactly how he had manipulated numbers and misquoted authorities to reach his conclusions.[24] After all, even if Hobson was incorrect about makeup and coal tar, any nation that had well over a million addicts had cause for alarm. Coincidentally, Kolb had recently coauthored an article estimating the number of addicts to be between 110,000 and 150,000 and actively declining.[25] When Kolb refused to revise his numbers upward, Hobson attacked him as "adroit, unscrupulous, and unscientific" and demanded that the surgeon general of the United States prevent him from testifying on his bill. According to Hobson, Kolb had "discredited" the Public Health Service and should be removed from office.[26] Soon, letters from Hobson's influential allies flooded the offices of the surgeon general and congressmen. Luckily for Kolb, a parsimonious federal government, a cash-strapped U.S. Printing Office, loyal superiors, and congressmen familiar with Hobson's actions from previous acquaintance combined to defeat Hobson's bill and salvage Kolb's career.

While Kolb would continue to serve as the Public Health Service's resident expert on addiction and support a relatively humane treatment toward addicts for another twenty years, the momentum was with Hobson. His use of pseudoscience, invented statistics, and scapegoated addicts pioneered a new brand of moral crusaders willing to turn fear of dangerous substances into vengeful attacks upon their victims and their sympathizers. Increasingly, drug addicts were seen as alien and even inhuman. During Harry Anslinger's tenure as chief of the Federal Bureau of Narcotics, he refused to allow drug addicts to be shown, even negatively, in films. He publicly attacked sympathetic researchers like Kolb and Indiana sociologist Alfred Lindesmith and sought to prevent their publication and even employment. In 1964, he referred to Marie Nyswander, cofounder of the first program for methadone maintenance, as that "so-called research woman who says that she likes addicts. Can you imagine anyone of such a low moral character as to say that she likes addicts[?]"[27] As it turns out, the patterns established by Hobson have persisted and been embellished by even more powerful figures such as Anslinger, Gates, and Bennett. The financial and personal cost to contemporary America of our draconian drug laws is just another indication of the ongoing price of our fear.

Notes

1. David F. Musto, *The American Disease: Origins of Narcotic Control* (New York: Oxford University Press, 1987), 277.

2. Ronald Ostrow, "Casual Drug Users Should Be Taken Out and Shot, Gates Says," *Los Angeles Times*, 6 September 1990.

3. William John Bennett, *The De-Valuing of America* (New York: Summit Books, 1992), 116.

4. Dan Baum, *Smoke and Mirrors: The War on Drugs and the Politics of Failure* (Boston, Mass.: Little, Brown and Co., 1996), 263.

5. John Putnam Demos, *Entertaining Satan: Witchcraft and the Culture of New England* (New York: Oxford University Press, 1982).

6. Paul Boyer and Stephen Nissenbaum, *Salem Possessed: The Social Origins of Witchcraft* (Cambridge, Mass.: Harvard University Press, 1974).

7. David Courtwright, *Dark Paradise: Opiate Addiction in America before 1940* (Cambridge, Mass.: Harvard University Press, 1982), 36–37.

8. Ibid., 60.

9. Ibid., 41.

10. Ibid., 28.

11. Lawrence Kolb, Narcotics Case Histories Folder, 1924–28, Lawrence Kolb papers, box 7, National Library of Medicine, Bethesda, Md.

12. Edward Jay Epstein, *Agency of Fear: Opiates and Political Power in America* (New York: Putnam, 1977), 25.

13. Richmond Pearson Hobson, *The Sinking of the "Merrimac": A Personal Narrative* (New York: The Century Co., 1899).

14. Evans C. Johnson, *Oscar Underwood: A Political Biography* (Baton Rouge: Louisiana State University Press, 1980), 226–44.

15. Richmond Pearson Hobson, "The Truth about Alcohol: The Speech of Honorable Richmond P. Hobson of Alabama in the House of Representatives, December 22, 1914 (Washington, D.C.: U.S. Printing Office, 1914), 9.

16. Ibid.

17. K. Austin Kerr, *Organized for Prohibition: A New History of the Anti-Saloon League* (New Haven, Conn.: Yale University Press, 1985).

18. Richmond P. Hobson, "The Peril of Narcotics," unpublished paper, 1924, Hobson folder, Kolb papers, box 3.

19. Ibid.

20. Hobson, "Truth about Alcohol," 21–22.

21. Hobson, "Peril of Narcotics."

22. Ibid.

23. Ibid.

24. Dr. Lawrence Kolb to Honorable Bascom Slemp, 15 January 1925, Hobson folder, Kolb papers, box 3.

25. Lawrence Kolb and A. G. DuMez, "Extent and Trend of Drug Addiction in the United States," *Public Health Reports* 39 (23 March 1924), 1179–1204.

26. Richmond Hobson to Captain D. N. Carpenter, 29 June 1925 (Kolb copy); and Hobson to Surgeon General of the United States, 28 October 1924; both Hobson folder, Kolb papers, box 3.

27. David Courtwright, Herman Joseph, and Don Des Jarlais, *Addicts Who Survived: An Oral History of Narcotics Use in America, 1923–1965* (Knoxville: University of Tennessee Press), 312.

The Shadow Meets
the Phantom Public

Jason Loviglio

Beginning in 1937, the Shadow haunted the evening airwaves, battling underworld masters of murder, racketeering, and the occult. The Shadow began each program with a haunting question, "Who knows what evil lurks in the hearts of men?" However, it was the evil lurking just *outside* the boundaries of the national and intimate spheres of American life that figured most centrally in the popular mystery stories of *The Shadow*. As the commercial network radio system helped create and spread the emergent national public culture of the 1930s, *The Shadow* evoked and assuaged fears of a phantom public, a dark and heterogenous urban world marked by uncertain boundaries, a vulnerable citizenry, and a steady stream of "Oriental" national and racial outsiders.

The rise of radio broadcasting in the 1920s and 1930s, along with other dramatic developments in mass media (motion pictures, cheap periodical press, and national advertising) contributed to a popular and scholarly preoccupation with the concept of distinct spheres of public and private life. In its immediacy, intimacy, and ability to reach a national audience, radio was the most powerful of the new media in terms of its ability to blur the boundaries of interpersonal speech and mass communication. The sense of uncertainty it provoked was exacerbated by the dramatic economic and political transformations brought on by the Depression, the threat of an expanding European war, the New Deal, and the rise of a culture of consumption.[1] These developments added to the confusion about the coherence of public and private spheres of autonomy at home and abroad.

In order to speak to a new national audience during this period of heightened concern about the borders, definitions, and meanings of American public life, network radio in the late 1930s had to create a new discursive space, *the intimate public,* that both straddled and redefined the public/private distinction. Network radio performed a paradoxical twin feat. On the one hand, it addressed its vast, indeterminate audience as a unified national public, irrespective of geographical and social boundaries; on the other hand, by dramatically evoking and assuaging fears of foreign invasion, mass-manipulation, and social and political upheaval, it emphasized the importance of maintaining and mobilizing traditional exclusions, hierarchies, and boundaries within the imagined community of America in the 1930s.

The early years of the popular radio serial *The Shadow* illustrate how network radio's discourse of intimate publicity could attract a national mass audience at the same time that it dramatized the dangers that such an audience posed. Following a brief history of the regulatory and political development of the broadcasting industry and some background on *The Shadow*'s origins in radio and pulp fiction, I will closely examine "The Hypnotized Audience," an episode from 1937, the show's first season. In this episode, the mystical threat of "Oriental culture" to white denizens of an urban sphere of popular entertainment becomes the means for dramatizing and resolving the interrelated crises of public space, mass culture, and national/racial outsiders. This episode is significant in the context of American anxiety about Asian immigration, crises at home and abroad, and the cultural changes being wrought by the media of communications and entertainment. I conclude by comparing the world of *The Shadow* with Walter Lippmann's "phantom public," suggesting that the conservatism and pessimism of this conception of mass-mediated democracy during the 1920s became a central feature of the paradigm of radio programming and regulation in the 1930s.

Radio History

Recent studies of the regulatory, economic, and ideological development of the network system of commercial sponsorship have revealed that the first two decades of broadcasting were a period of intense negotiation, struggle, and debate between competing definitions of "the public interest, convenience, and necessity," a phrase taken from public utilities law and applied to broadcasting in the Radio Act of 1927, as well as the Communications Act of 1934.[2] Lizabeth Cohen has demonstrated that network radio's eventual triumph over early radio's role in "promot[ing] ethnic, religious, and working class affiliations" was possible only as part of the broader "triumphs of mass culture, mass consumption, mass unionization and mass politics," which together "hail[ed] a national market of consumers."[3] Robert McChesney has shown that after consolidating the economic and political underpinnings of their preferred system of broadcasting, the networks spent the latter half of the 1930s winning broad ideological and cultural support for it in the arena of public opinion.[4] Shrewdly dubbed "The American Plan," the networks' vision of a national broadcasting system equated "the public" with the consumers of nationally advertised goods—in other words, "the public interest" with market forces.[5] The plan was opposed by advocates for nonprofit stations dedicated to educational, religious, and labor-oriented broadcasts as well as to definitions of the public that embraced to varying degrees the role of the state, civic institutions, and local control.[6] The networks, along with independent, for-profit broadcasters, advertising agencies, and other business interests, sought a system of spectrum allocation that entrusted the public airwaves to the stewardship of private interests, free from congressional interference or rival claims of "public service." Through a series of legislative victories, the American Plan privatized the public airwaves and the concept of the public interest.[7]

In the years that followed, the struggle to sell this system to a national audience, still wary of advertising on the radio, required broadcasters to sell the American Plan as part of an emergent "American Way" superior to foreign schemes of state-owned airwaves.[8] Radio's discourse of intimate publicity could be heard in the emerging accents, modes of address, and aesthetic considerations that developed as part of the ideological process of accommodating an American audience to the idea of private sales talk delivered into the domestic sphere via publicly-owned airwaves.[9] Broadcasters and advertisers addressed their audience as an intimate public, a form of discourse combining familiarity, immediacy, and cultural authority.[10] Reflecting a unified, coherent, and potent national purpose linked to optimism about an imminent business recovery, the American Plan successfully linked its definition of the public to broader definitions of an American plan for solving the political, economic, and cultural crisis facing America in the 1930s.[11]

The Origins of *The Shadow*

The early history of *The Shadow* provides a good example of the web of relationships connecting early episodic radio, other popular culture forms, and the financial interests of their corporate sponsors, who, through their advertising agencies, came to have a larger role in the development and production of radio programming throughout the 1930s.[12] *The Shadow* debuted in 1930 as the omniscient voice of the mysterious narrator for CBS's *Detective Story Hour*, sponsored by Street and Smith, publishers of *Detective Story Magazine*.[13] This early Shadow was created to help promote the magazine, but the popularity of the radio narrator with the mirthless laugh inspired Street and Smith to develop a new magazine around a character named the Shadow who solved mysteries while remaining a bit of one himself.[14]

The Shadow character, complete with alter-ego Lamont Cranston, supporting cast, and a dark urban mise-en-scène was created by Walter Brown Gibson for Street and Smith's *The Shadow Magazine*.[15] Gibson also provided Cranston's origin story: a youthful pilgrimage to the Orient, where he learned "how to cloud men's minds." In the weekly magazine pulp novels, the Shadow inhabited a world of twisting city streets, convoluted plots, and foreign foes. This urban public setting was populated with a diverse cadre of amateur "agents," including a taxi driver, a reformed gambler, a Chinese-American doctor, and many other blue-and white-collar denizens of the city whose loyalty the Shadow had won by having helped them in the past. Together, they formed a shadowy network of cooperation, a counterpublic often at odds with both criminals and the police. Even so, Gibson's pulp novels relied heavily on the theme of threats from the "Orient," frequently pitting the Shadow against the imperialist designs and telepathic powers of the Mongols, Afghans, and Tibetans constantly invading New York City.[16]

The Shadow of the 1937 radio program, by contrast, had little connection to the citizenry, working most often alone or with the help of his "constant aide and companion, Margo Lane." In place of his citizen network, this Lamont Cranston was merely a "wealthy young man about town," who moved in a very narrow circle of elite cultural and official power.[17] This version of *The Shadow*, which aired on Sunday evenings at 5:30 P.M. on the Mutual Radio Network, quickly became one of the most popular programs on the air, maintaining its sponsorship by Blue Coal and high ratings throughout most of its seventeen-year run.[18]

The Hypnotized Audience

Throughout the 1937–38 season, announcer Ken Roberts began each episode with an explanation of the program's purpose: "to demonstrate forcibly to old and young alike that crime does not pay." According to Roberts, the Shadow struck "terror into the hearts of sharpsters, lawbreakers and criminals," a list that may at first seem redundant, though it aptly conveys the program's emphases on a broad taxonomy of outsiders and the Shadow's long reach into every den of iniquity.

In the Shadow's dark urban landscape, where outsiders and foreigners—especially Eastern mystics and Eastern European dissidents—constantly threaten the social order, the public sphere appears precarious, insubstantial, vulnerable—indeed, a phantom. The Shadow confronts hypnotists, telepaths, bombers, poisoners, and snipers, all of whom profess contempt for crowds.[19] Showdowns take place in the city's subway tunnels, streets, arcades, theaters, and nightclubs—the physical and cultural infrastructure of the modern city. The phantom public becomes a symbol for the chronic dangers and confusions of modern urban life and a rationale for the xenophobia and agoraphobia of official and popular forms of discourse in the years leading up to World War II.[20]

Thus it is important that *The Shadow*'s phantom public serves as the site where urban mass entertainments are figured as threats from national/racial outsiders. In "Can the Dead Talk?" (1939), for example, Anton Proscovi, "the famous [Russian] anarchist" turned theatrical performer, reads the minds of an entire audience, discovers the Shadow's secret identity, and then asks the Shadow to join him in a hypnotic/telepathic venture to control the world. In "The Temple Bells of Neban" (1938), the Shadow is nearly swept off his feet by the lovely young Sadi Bel Ada, an "Oriental dancer" whose movements, chants, and bell ringing are in fact components of very powerful spells that she employs in the service of a complicated international heroin and kidnapping ring.

"The Hypnotized Audience" (1937), illustrates the program's conflation of fears of foreigners, mass culture, and the public sphere; it also shows how the Shadow's verbal and technical powers of mind control, surveillance, and persuasion simultaneously mirror and counteract the threats posed by alien forces. In this episode, the Shadow confronts "The Durga Khan," another "oriental dancer," whose mystical chants mesmerize an entire theater full of citizens, including the governor, the commissioner of police, and Margo Lane, effectively and symbolically stopping the entire public and private worlds of Lamont Cranston in their tracks. A full minute of this scene is dedicated to Lamont's attempt to rouse Margo from a deep, and rather sensual, hypnotic stupor caused by Durga Khan's chanting and gyrations. Then, under cover of mass hypnotism, Khan's henchmen kidnap the governor, dragging him from his box in the balcony as Lamont screams, "Wake up everyone! Listen to me! The Governor has been kidnapped!"

At this, the hypnotized audience snaps out of it, erupting in howls of hysterical fear. The careful listener is not surprised by this turn of events, as Lamont has been waxing skeptical about the cultural value of Oriental dancing all evening. During the intermission at the Durga Khan's performance, Lamont bristles with disgust when overhearing a silly-sounding society woman gushing, "I just love Oriental culture." "Everything Oriental is perfect," Lamont responds sarcastically; he then launches into a scathing critique of "Oriental culture," linking Khan to Joseph Hakim, a brutal and notorious murderer scheduled to die that night in the electric chair. "Nobody cheered over *his* display of Oriental culture," Lamont sniffs. Hakim and the Durga Khan "are both the product of the Orient, from the same section and caste," Lamont notes significantly over Margo's blithe objections as he trudges back into the theater, wondering, rather superciliously, *why* the governor has left his office on the night of an execution and, rather ominously, *what* Durga Khan will do for an encore.

Despite yelling kidnap in a crowded theater, Lamont fails to stop Khan's men; he quickly discovers that Durga Khan is in fact the brother of the murderer Joseph Hakim and that the kidnapping is an attempt to get the governor to order a stay of execution. What follows is a fairly virtuoso performance of technical and psychological wizardry, in which the Shadow and Margo use shortwave radios, tap into phone lines, impersonate telephone operators and prison officials, finally turn Khan's sister-in-law against him, and liberate the governor.

After intercepting Durga Khan's phone call to the prison warden, the Shadow outtalks the Durga Khan and persuades Joseph Hakim's widow, Princess Zada, to turn on her brother-in-law instead of shooting Governor Barnes:

The Shadow: Great is Durga Khan! He talks while his brother dies.
Princess Zada: His brother . . . dies?
Durga Khan: My brother lives! I saved him.
The Shadow: Princess Zada, this man, with his dreams of power, has deceived you. He has not saved Joseph Hakim.
Durga Khan: You must be mad.
The Shadow: Even now, your husband is dead.
Durga Khan: Wild talk, Shadow, and false!
The Shadow: You cannot stop the course of justice, by the power of your will. Hakim is dead. Your kidnapping was in vain.
Durga Khan: He lies, Zada. Shoot the Governor.
The Shadow: Princess wait.
Durga Khan: Zada, obey my orders!
The Shadow: Listen Princess! Do you wish to know the truth about your husband

Princess Zada: Yes, O voice!
Durga Khan: Oh, Zada!
The Shadow: Listen! Turn on the radio here. Its time for the news.
Listen, and learn if Joseph Hakim was saved tonight or not. *Listen
Princess!*
(click, sound of radio static)
Radio Announcer: . . . and that is the weather report for tonight.
The Shadow: Listen, Princess.
Radio Announcer: And now we bring you a news flash which just
arrived in the studio. Exactly two minutes ago, Joseph Hakim was
executed at State Prison for murder. Hakim walked to the death
chamber unaided and he . . .
Princess Zada: (gasps)
Durga Khan: There must be some mistake.
Princess Zada: Durga Khan, you faithless one! You of so many
promises! You, the fourth brother! The mistake was in my trusting
you.
The Shadow: That was the mistake, Princess Zada.
Durga Khan: Zada, put that gun down. Zada, Durga Khan speaks!
Princess: Durga Khan speaks for the last time!
(gunshots, sound of body falling) (italics added)

In many ways, "The Hypnotized Audience" is emblematic of the episodes from the early years of the program. Most begin with a threat
to the public order by a national outsider who has mastered some form
of mass mind control; many end with the Shadow persuading his foes
to shoot each other and/or themselves. And in between, most episodes
feature the Shadow's descent into the invisible world of crime, where
he manipulates information through various technical and rhetorical
strategies in order to preserve the public order, if only until the next
episode.[21]

Orientalism

The figure of the foreign, seductive, theatrical mesmerist recurs frequently on this program, perhaps because it is such a powerful symbol
for the fear that the urban public, crammed into public spaces and exposed to foreign influences and new media, was turning into an easily
hypnotized audience. Overflowing theaters, nightclubs, arcades, and city
streets are the most common scenes of public peril in *The Shadow*, providing a symbolic representation of the invisible, abstracted, and frag-

mented radio audience that broadcasters, regulators, and listeners themselves were in the process of imagining. The figure of the Durga Khan provides an ideal foil for the Shadow, whose powers are also a product of "Oriental culture." The Shadow calls their showdown "a battle of wills," but it also represents a struggle over the ambivalently defined turfs of mass culture, national identity, and American public space.

This preoccupation with the "orientalist" myth of the criminally dangerous interloper from the East also speaks to some very specific anxieties circulating though official, popular, and literary discourses in the 1930s. As Edward Said has shown, such discourse has been crucial in the development of a range of Western civilization's literary and popular constructions of itself. Said argues that the interwar era was a particularly charged one for East-West relations, as rising political and economic demands for independence from Asian countries forced the West to rethink the meanings behind the "irreducibly opposed" Occident and Orient.[22] This new version of Orientalism responded to a powerful matrix of fears about cultural distinctions in the modern era: "the apocalypse to be feared was not the destruction of Western civilization but rather the destruction of the barriers that kept East and West from each other."[23]

Historians of immigration and the 1930s have demonstrated that a virulent racist discourse about "Orientals" persisted in popular and official discourses from the 1882 Chinese Exclusion Act, the Immigration Act of 1924, the Tydings-McDuffie Act of 1934, right through to the internment of Japanese-Americans during the Second World War.[24] As Lisa Lowe has argued, these images and policies mark the contradictions surrounding the role that Asian immigrants and Asian-Americans have played in the U.S. workforce, as citizens, and in the national imagination. Lowe suggests that "throughout the twentieth century, the figure of the Asian immigrant" reveals "a series of condensed, complicated anxieties regarding external and internal threats to the mutable coherence of the national body."[25] Jackson Lears observes a similar web of anxieties and anti-immigrant symbolism in the advertising copy of the 1920s and 1930s; in particular, he points to the "obsession with expelling 'alien' filth" in these ads, which captures the "connection between bodily and national purification: the eugenic dream of perfecting Anglo-Saxon racial dominance in the United States through immigration restriction."[26]

Of the twenty-four episodes from the years 1937 to 1941 that I reviewed for this essay, eighteen featured national, racial, or ethnic outsiders as villains. Nine featured a villain with supernatural or advanced scientific powers of telepathy, hypnotism, and/or mass mind control.

The Shadow's weekly battles with national, racial, ethnic, and social outsiders presume a public mind susceptible to foreign, antidemocratic forces *and* unable to discern the crucial distinctions undergirding social and political hierarchies of race, gender, class, and ethnicity. This easily seduced public mind, often figured as feminine, is epitomized in "The Hypnotized Audience," first by the gullibility of the unnamed society woman's love of "Oriental culture" and then by Margo's breathy, moaning, hypnotic surrender to Khan, which Lamont is nearly powerless to overcome.[27] These surrenders echo the governor's failure to estimate the danger of Joseph Hakim's "crime family" and his inability to resist the lure of the exotic theatrical entertainment, which drew him away from his execution-night vigil at the state house. These twin failures, linked in Cranston's intermission attack on "Oriental culture," lead to the governor's kidnapping, torture, and near-death at the hands of Princess Zada. The governor's reduction, first to culture vulture, then to hostage, enacts a symbolic decapitation of state authority in the face of a cultural public sphere marked by heterogeneity, permeable borders, and exoticism.

The particular form the Orientalist menace takes in "The Hypnotized Audience" is also connected to the peculiar features of radio itself, in particular its ability to render invisible the most common (that is, visual) markers of social difference, such as race, gender, national identity. Michele Hilmes calls this "the basic transgressive quality of the medium itself."[28] Susan Douglas and Catherine Covert have pointed out the widespread ambivalence that radio waves inspired in the first decade of broadcasting, emphasizing the commonly expressed fears that radio's unseen words and sounds were the uncanny results of supernatural phenomena penetrating into public and private spheres.[29]

The Shadow's pattern of limning the dark, urban, phantom public frequently plays on these very fears of powerful disembodied voices transgressing important social boundaries. "The Hypnotized Audience" begins with a political, cultural, and personal disturbance at the theater largely brought about through aural means. Khan's hypnotic speech in the darkness of the theater effects the symbolic overthrow of state power and the virtual seduction of Margo Lane, just as it contributes to an atmosphere of urban cultural decadence. "Society of the Living Dead" (1938) begins with the sound of reporters' voices on the telephone and radio circulating news of an international "phony passport and identification ring," the details of which are never explained. The radio announcer's most startling revelation, "Mr. and Mrs. Smith are not citizens" also goes unexplained, and we never hear of the Smiths again. Against this backdrop of anxiety about national identity circulating through the invisible voices of radio, the Shadow confronts a world whose boundaries are so uncertain that the identity, to say nothing of the Americanness, of a "Mr. and Mrs. Smith" is left, figuratively and literally, up in the air.

Hilmes argues that the subversive potential of radio was met with a new preoccupation with articulating the *sounds* of difference. "Radio responded by . . . endlessly circulating and performing structured representations of ethnicity, race, gender, and other concentrated sites of social and cultural norms—all through language, dialect, and carefully selected aural context."[30] On *The Shadow*, racial, national and gender differences are also marked aurally; by conflating foreignness, criminal activity, "feminization," and the occult, the program overdetermines what it means to be an outsider. The suspense of each episode consists in the fact that each of *The Shadow*'s villains possesses mysterious powers of manipulation. Indeed, most episodes conclude, as does "The Hypnotized Audience," with a war of words between the Shadow and some dangerously articulate villain.[31]

By outtalking Durga Khan, the Shadow liberates the governor, restores the power of the state, and defends against the effeminizing, seductive, foreign influences threatening to undermine the cultural public sphere of urban entertainment. The Shadow achieves all this through the expert manipulation of speech and the communication devices designed to enhance its range, effects, and speed. In many episodes, the Shadow's success hinges on his ability to manipulate, understand, and transmit language, crack codes, and influence public opinion. In other episodes from this period, the Shadow employs short-wave radio, reedits the soundtrack on a surveillance film that has been tampered with, taps into a municipal public-address system, manipulates public opinion through the newspapers, and employs a state-of-the-art "headline machine" that flashes messages onto a giant electric light kiosk wrapped around the city's daily newspaper building. He also "speaks" in the secret codes of an underground alliance of the city's homeless; masters the code used by an evil professor to control his deaf-mute henchman; and, as Lamont Cranston, is fluent in the cultural codes of the urban elite, among whom he circulates at all the finest restaurants, theaters, and nightclubs. Again and again, crises of the public sphere involve a loss of control of the means of communication, information, and entertainment, all of which have become hopelessly intertwined by mass-mediated consumer culture. Restoring a provisional order to this encoded, shadowy, noisy world requires nothing less than a technocratic magician, a master performer and communicator.

In the final confrontation scene with Durga Khan and Princess Zada, the Shadow's superior mastery of the power of speech makes the crucial difference between victory and defeat. The life or death struggle boils down to a contest over who can command Princess Zada's attention, who can persuade her to "listen" to the truth, and who can control the direction in which she aims her pistol.[32] It is a contest that the Shadow wins handily, with cool, confident admonitions and the help of a well-timed radio newscast. In contrast, Durga Khan's speech is shrill, imperious, and grandiloquent; the foreignness of his voice, which had previously been so seductive in the theater, now sounds panicky compared to the Shadow's authoritative metallic voice (an authority reinforced by the breezy professional voice of the radio announcer who gives the definitive word that Joseph Hakim has been executed). The Shadow begins the confrontation by ridiculing the fact that Khan impotently "talks" while his brother dies. Durga Khan counters by accusing the Shadow of "wild talk," but it is his voice that seems out of control, interrupting, panicky, and finally, completely powerless. In response to his peremptory, "Zada, Durga Khan speaks!" she answers, "Durga Khan speaks for the last time!" Khan loses his life and the right to speak with one squeeze of the trigger. As in many episodes from this period, the Shadow talks the criminal into a corner and the system of law and order back into a tenuous, temporary equilibrium.

The Phantom Public

In many ways, *The Shadow*'s vision of the modern city reflects the pessimism articulated by a generation of journalists, intellectuals, and bureaucrats between the world wars. In the 1920s, Walter Lippmann, the influential journalist, presidential advisor, and public intellectual, laid out a vision of an American public vexed by an unattainable ideal of civic competence and confused by the mass-mediated shadows of an increasingly complex world. Lippmann draws on Plato's parable of the cave for inspiration, arguing that the "pictures inside our heads" are mere shadows of "the world outside."[33] In what could be read as an allusion to Lippmann, the Shadow of the late 1930s eerily intones, "I see the pictures inside your head" to many a lawbreaker. For Lippmann, the Shadow, and an emerging bureaucratic managerial class, understanding the problems posed by the phantom public begins with the assumption that the public is highly vulnerable to mass-mediated manipulation.[34]

In *Public Opinion*, Lippmann calls for a special knowledge class—an elite, highly specialized cadre of "intelligence workers"—to manage the difficulties posed by modern society.[35] This call was answered by the very forces from which Lippmann seemed to think the public needed protection: advertisers, pollsters, public-relations firms, and a press increasingly cynical about the nature of its audience.[36]

Lippmann's phantom public became a guiding assumption for the FCC's policies of spectrum allocation, programming, and broadcast regulation, all premised on serving "the public interest convenience and necessity," a phrase so vague that the task of interpreting it itself has helped to generate an industry of experts on the subject. This process—turning the public into the special and difficult object of study for experts—reinforced the ideology of the American Plan: radio is best left in the hands of those who truly understand the public, the private, and the inevitable blurring of the two.

The FCC's first chief commissioner, Anning S. Prail, speaking to a national audience on the opening night of Mutual Network's first coast-to-coast broadcast in 1936, hailed radio "as a combination of the schoolhouse, the church, the public rostrum, the newspaper, the theater, the concert hall—in fact all media." He then characterized radio as the most intimate medium in American society, an implicit warning to broadcasters to tread lightly in the 23 million American homes in which it had been invited. An amalgam of all media, and a trustee of the public and private registers of American life, radio was seen by its regulators as a new social space joining intimacy and publicity and unifying the nation even in the face of daunting social and ethnic heterogeneity.[37]

The Shadow is, in many ways, an emissary from this new world of intimate publicity. He represents an idealized version of Lippmann's intelligence worker, bringing psychology, surveillance, and communications technologies to bear on the problematic, invisible, and shadowy public world. And, like the network radio system of which he is a product, the Shadow helped to articulate a powerful prewar sense of an imagined national community, bounded by important hierarchies, exclusions, and fears, which he delivered in the accents of a new American form of speech that was both authoritative and intimate, broadly accessible and yet highly useful for marking and policing multiple forms of social difference.[38]

His clipped, telegraphic speech, his penchant for repeating phrases as if transmitting by Morse code; and the metallic sound of his filtered voice all contribute to the sense that the Shadow speaks in the idiom of electronic communication. An expert in the technologies of communication and the psychology of the "mass mind," the Shadow epitomizes the professional managerial consciousness emerging in the ranks of journalists, public relations counsels, broadcasters, and advertising executives.[39] In his intimate knowledge of the hearts of men and women and the trouble spots of the industrial city, he seems to range over a territory as vast as that which Commissioner Prail claims for radio itself. In short, the Shadow knows.

His double identity represents his broad and flexible knowledge of the public and private worlds whose inevitable collisions must be managed so carefully. Lamont Cranston, "wealthy young man about town," inhabits a small, socially intensive world of face-to-face contacts and known quantities. The Shadow lurks in darkness and mystery, where he encounters foreign foes that are both interchangeable and inexhaustibly present. Cranston, amateur detective, must move back and forth between these two identities in order to protect the civic order from external threats; in that movement back and forth, he defines the borders of these worlds even as he transgresses them—from a crowded theater to a criminal's lair to a guilty conscience.

Some have argued that with the rise of the mass media and a bureaucratic welfare state, the terms public and private have ceased to refer to discrete entities.[40] But the terms continued to have meaning in the Golden Age of radio because of programs like *The Shadow*, which dramatized the dangerous play of outside and inside, foreign and domestic, unknown and known. By the late 1930s, as network radio shored up its ideological flanks against competing definitions of the public and private, *The Shadow*, along with a growing number of daytime, evening, and prime time serial and episodic dramas, helped to trace the contours of a new social space precariously situated in the uncanny borderlands between public and private. The public—perhaps always something of a phantom—became, in the idiom of intimate publicity, a rhetorical tool for policing the borders of national and racial difference and an imaginary landscape endlessly evoking and assuaging fears that radio's early national public was becoming a hypnotized audience.

Notes

I am indebted to Rachel Buff, Riv-Ellen Prell, Nancy Lusignan Schultz, Andrew Seligsohn, Michael Willard, and Anne Wolf for their generous and insightful comments on earlier drafts of this essay.

1. For a discussion of the emergence of a culture of consumption in the 1930s, see Warren Susman, *Culture as History: The Transformation of American Society in the Twentieth Century* (New York: Pantheon, 1984). On the role of the new media during this period, see *Mass Media between the Wars: Perceptions of Cultural Tension, 1918–1941*, ed. Catherine L. Covert and John D. Stephens (Syracuse, N.Y.: Syracuse University Press, 1984).

2. Robert W. McChesney, *Telecommunications, Mass Media, and Democracy:*

326

The Battle for the Control of U.S. Broadcasting, 1928–1935 (New York: Oxford University Press, 1993); Michele Hilmes, *Radio Voices: American Broadcasting, 1922–1952* (Minneapolis: University of Minnesota Press, 1997); Susan Douglas, *Inventing American Broadcasting, 1899–1922* (Baltimore, Md.: Johns Hopkins University Press, 1987); Susan Smulyan, *Selling Radio: The Commercialization of American Broadcasting, 1920–1934* (Washington D.C.: Smithsonian Institution Press, 1994). Eric Barnouw's classic three-volume *A History of Broadcasting in the United States* also provides an important account of the technical, regulatory, economic, and cultural developments in early radio. See volume 1, *A Tower in Babel* (New York: Oxford University Press, 1966) and volume 2, *The Golden Web* (New York: Oxford University Press, 1968). See also Lucas A. Powe, Jr., *American Broadcasting and the First Amendment* (Berkeley and Los Angeles: University of California Press, 1987).

3. Lizabeth Cohen, *Making a New Deal: Industrial Workers in Chicago, 1919–1939* (Cambridge: Cambridge University Press, 1990), 135, 8.

4. McChesney, *Telecommunications, Mass Media, and Democracy*, 226–51.

5. Ibid., 114.

6. Ibid., 92–120. Perhaps the most formidable opponent of commercially funded radio in the 1930s was the press, which lost millions in advertising revenue to the Depression and to radio. See ibid., 163–77.

7. See also Smulyan, *Selling Radio*, 65–92, 125–53.

8. For a discussion of the discovery of the related concepts of public opinion and "the American Way" in the 1930s, see Susman, *Culture as History*, 150–83.

9. For a discussion on the public and official opposition to radio advertising, see McChesney, *Telecommunications, Mass Media, and Democracy*, 115, 123–25, 140–42. For an industry account of its own efforts to regulate this problem, see "Trade Commission Cites Ten Radio Users," *Broadcasting and Broadcast Advertising*, 7, no. 2 (15 July 1934): 5.

10. For a discussion of the rise of "personality" over "character" in this period, see Susman, *Culture as History*, 271–85.

11. For a discussion of the networks' strategy of defending the American Plan by invoking the specter of the socialism in the "British" system of government-owned and -operated radio broadcasting, see McChesney, *Telecommunications, Mass Media, and Democracy*, 226–70; Susan Douglas argues that some of this work had already been accomplished as early as 1922; see *Inventing American Broadcasting*, 315–22. See also Barnouw, *Towel of Babel*, 269–83, and *The Golden Web*, 9–44, 155–81. For a document of this ideological strategy at work, see Hendrik Willen Van Loon, "Man's Mightiest Weapon—For Good or Evil," in *Broadcasting and Broadcast Advertising*, 12, no. 1 (1 January 1937): 13.

12. For more on the relationship between radio programming and other popular cultural forms, see Barnouw, *A Tower in Babel*, 273–83; and Hilmes,

Radio Voices, 82–86. Marshall McLuhan suggests that the "content" of a new medium is "always another medium"; see McLuhan, *Understanding Media: The Extensions of Man* (Cambridge, Mass: MIT Press, 1994), 80–93, 305. For more on the tensions and conflicts surrounding the relationships between networks, sponsors, advertising agencies and a broader public debate over the direction of radio, see Barnouw, *The Golden Web*, 9–44; Hilmes, *Radio Voices*, 97–129; and McChesney, *Telecommunications, Mass Media, and Democracy.*

13. Anthony Tollin, *The Shadow: The Making of a Legend* (New York: Conde Nast Publications, 1996), 4.

14. As the first of radio's mysterious narrators, the Shadow inspired many programs featuring a mysterious, omniscient storyteller with a compelling voice, for example, *The Mysterious Traveler, The Whistler, Inner Sanctum,* and *Suspense.* See Tollin, *The Shadow*, 4–7. As the first crime-fighting superhero with an alter-ego, the Shadow of magazine and pulp novel fame is also an important precursor to, and inspiration for, Superman, Batman, Captain America, etc.

15. Tollin, *The Shadow*, 13–14.

16. In the pulp novels *The Golden Master* (1939) and *Shiwan Khan Returns* (1939), for example, the Shadow confronts an invasion of Oriental foes under the power of a master of mind control. They are descended from Genghis Khan and attempt to pillage New York City for the weaponry Khan needs to take over the world. See Walter Gibson, *The Golden Master* and *Shiwan Khan Returns* (New York: Conde Nast Publications, Inc., 1967).

17. The Shadow of the 1940s and 1950s, in turn, explored an increasingly psychological and sociological landscape of fears, featuring as villains isolated madmen or organized-crime syndicates. For a discussion of the more formulaic nature of the plots and the more dilettantish character of Lamont Cranston in *The Shadow* of the 1940s, see Tollin, *The Shadow*, 32–35.

18. The program hit its peak of popularity in 1942, when it dominated the all-important Hooper Ratings with a 17.2 share, good for 55.6 percent of the listening audience. By the late 1940s, it was heard on nearly 300 stations nationwide, with an unusual split-sponsor setup: Blue Coal in the East, Carey Salt in the Midwest, Balm Barr in the South, and the U.S. Air Force over the Don Lee Pacific Coast network. Blue Coal stopped sponsoring the show in 1950 because of a collapse in the anthracite market, not because of popularity ratings. After that the program had several different sponsors and one season of "sustaining" (i.e. unsponsored) broadcasts. See Tollin, *The Shadow*, 26–54.

19. Many of these episodes feature long soliloquies by villains, revealing the inner workings of their sociopathic minds. A haughty contempt for the American masses is typical, based either on the villains' greater intellectual powers and/or racial/national difference.

20. For a discussion of the ways in which prime-time "prestige" dramas (*The Fall of the City, War of the Worlds*) expressed the domestic and international crises of the 1930s, through stories of the city in peril, see Barnouw, *The Golden Web*, 66–70, 74–89.

21. J. Fred MacDonald has argued that the formulaic plots and quickly resolved crises of radio thrillers "supplied millions of Americans with understandable stories of achievement within a competitive, mass society," thereby providing "a paradigm for social existence." J. Fred MacDonald, *Don't Touch That Dial! Radio Programming in American Life from 1920 to 1960* (Chicago, Ill.: Nelson-Hall, 1979), 159, quoted in Hilmes, *Radio Voices*, 112. Hilmes suggests the form's popularity stems from the twin pleasures of exploring and containing subversive ideas and actions all within the space of a single episode (110–13).

22. Edward Said, *Orientalism* (New York: Pantheon Books, 1978), 248–57.

23. Ibid., 263. Said argues that the discourse of Orientalism is not as prevalent in the United States as in Europe (291–92); however, in "The Hypnotized Audience," "The Temple Bells of Neban, and in the origin story of *The Shadow* (which pops up in other episodes), the Shadow/Cranston epitomizes Said's account of the nineteenth-century Western Pilgrim, attracted to and estranged from the sexual and sensual excesses of Oriental culture (166–97). Orson Welles's aristocratic, vaguely British rendition of Lamont Cranston in the first season emphasizes this association with colonialist tradition that Said describes. And as the twentieth-century Orientalist Said describes, Cranston/Shadow is drawn back to the East as "the origin of European science," yet he is, as Said says of the Western Pilgrim, adamant that it is "a superseded origin" (251). The Shadow/Cranston is also given to making "summational statements" that conflate "one bit of Oriental material" with "the Orient as a whole," when, for example, he links Khan's dancing with Hakim's "butchery" (255).

24. See Lisa Lowe, *Immigrant Acts: On Asian American Cultural Politics* (Durham, N.C.: Duke University Press, 1996). Bill Ong Hing argues that the passage of the Tydings-McDuffie Act of 1934, which granted the Philippines its independence from the United States in the name of a more total exclusion of all Asian immigration, "symboliz[ed] the peak of anti-immigrant power." Bill Ong Hing, *Making and Remaking Asian America through Immigration Policy, 1850–1990* (Stanford, Calif.: Stanford University Press, 1993), 35–36. See also John W. Dower's *War without Mercy: Race and Power in the Pacific War* (New York: Pantheon Books, 1986), 38–45. For a discussion of the ways that radio demagogues such as Father Charles Coughlin exacerbated and articulated nativist fears of immigration; racial, religious, and ethnic outsiders; and international trade, see Alan Brinkley's *Voices of Protest: Huey Long, Father Coughlin, and the Great Depression* (New York: Knopf, 1982); and Donald Warren, *Radio Priest: Charles Coughlin, The Father of Hate Radio* (New York: Free Press, 1996).

25. Lowe, *Immigrant Acts*, 101.

26. Jackson Lears, *Fables of Abundance: A Cultural History of Advertising in America* (New York: Basic Books, 1994), 166. Lears also points out that since the nineteenth century, images of the Orient were linked to sexual rejuvenation, sensual excess, and ambivalent feelings toward the expanding world of consumer goods in general, and luxuries and patent medicines in particular. He argues that the patent medicine peddler, precursor to the professional advertising executive of the 1920s and 1930s, was strongly associated with the mysterious, seductive powers of the Orient (45, 63–88).

27. The suggestion of Margo's sexual surrender to Khan is hard to miss: after nearly a minute of trying to rouse her from her blissful hypnotic state, Lamont scolds, "shame on you, Margo!"

28. Hilmes argues that radio's "ability to escape visual overdetermination had the potential to set off a virtual riot of social signifiers" (*Radio Voices*, 20). While the peculiar effects of radio's aurality have not been studied in much depth, there is a considerable literature on the broader transgressive nature of electronic media, particularly their ability to blur and reorder social hierarchies. For Marshall McLuhan, electronic media create a "tribal" sense of connectedness across boundaries of individual bodies, and geography, by extending the human "sensorium"; see McLuhan, *Understanding Media: The Extensions of Man* (New York: McGraw-Hill, 1964). Similarly for Joshua Meyrowitz, who draws on the work of McLuhan, Harold Innis, and Erving Goffman, these electronic media blur older lines of social distinction and hierarchy based on a fixed "sense of place," ushering in a more egalitarian age in which we are "hunters and gatherers" of information. See Joshua Meyrowitz, *No Sense of Place: The Impact of Electronic Media on Social Behavior* (New York: Oxford University Press, 1985), 131–83, 315–17.

29. See Susan J. Douglas, *Inventing American Broadcasting*, 292–314; and Catherine Covert, "We May Hear Too Much: American Sensibility and the Response to Radio, 1919–1924," in *Mass Media between the Wars*, 199–220.

30. Hilmes cites the centrality of exotic and familiar racial stereotypes in important early network programs such as *Amos 'n' Andy*, *The Cliquot Club Eskimos*, *The A&P Gypsies*, and *The Goldbergs* (*Radio Voices*, 21).

31. In the illustrated pulps, by contrast, stories tend to conclude in a spectacular hail of bullets, knives, and fists. The pulps' less verbal Shadow is also less invisible than his radio counterpart and thus is forced to defend himself physically.

32. The Shadow asks the Princess to "listen" to him five separate times. His success here is a reversal of his first contest with Khan, when, as Lamont Cranston, he struggled to rouse Margo from a hypnotic stupor. In that encounter, he begged Margo to "listen" several times as well, before shouting "Listen to me!" to the entire theater.

33. Walter Lippmann, *Public Opinion* (New York: MacMillan, 1922), 3–32.

34. See Covert, 207–10; and Michael Kirkhorn, "This Curious Existence:

Journalistic Identity in the Interwar Period," in *Mass Media between the Wars*, 127–40.

35. Lippmann, *Public Opinion*, 379–97.

36. Edward L. Bernays's *Crystallizing Public Opinion* (New York: Boni and Liveright, 1923) is often regarded as the first primer on how to be a "public relations counsel" for private interests. Bernays draws extensively on the insights of Lippmann's *Public Opinion*, published the year before.

37. See Covert, "We May Hear Too Much," 199–214; Hilmes, *Radio Voices*, 20.

38. In his analysis of Hollywood films of the 1930s and 1940s, Lary May has argued quite convincingly that the mobilization of a national consensus narrative does not become dominant until World War II. This consensus narrative, May argues, marks a conversion away from the themes of many 1930s' films, including class and ethnic consciousness, New Deal values critical of monopoly capitalism, and support for "an autonomous series of public arenas where men and women of different races mingle." My analysis of *The Shadow*'s transformation from Gibson's magazine stories to the radio program in the years 1937–1941 suggests that perhaps elements of this conversion were already underway in other popular forms just prior to World War II. As Lizabeth Cohen has argued, during the 1930s Americans came to identify with national networks, national brands, and a national mass-mediated culture in general, often at the expense of the locally, class-, and ethnicity-oriented patterns of identity. A more exhaustive analysis of popular radio dramas of the period, paralleling May's analysis of a sample of over 240 films, has not, to my knowledge, been conducted, but would be very useful in exploring this issue in greater depth. See Lary May, "Making the American Consensus: The Narrative of Conversion and Subversion in World War II Films," in *The War in American Culture: Society and Consciousness During World War II*, ed. Lewis A. Ehrenberg and Susan E. Hirsch (Chicago, Ill.: University of Chicago Press, 1996), 71–102.

39. See Kirkhorn, "This Curious Existence," for a discussion of the narrowing gap between journalists' and advertisers' cynical views of the "mass mind" in the interwar period; see Bernays, *Crystallizing Public Opinion*, for a discussion of the emergence of the public relations counsel; and Lears, *Fables of Abundance*, 137–260, on the development of an ethos of managerial-industrial efficiency in the early modern advertising industry.

40. Jürgen Habermas, *The Structural Transformation of the Public Sphere: An Inquiry into a Category of Bourgeois Society* (Cambridge, Mass.: MIT Press, 1989); and Richard Sennett, *The Fall of Public Man* (New York: Knopf, 1977). For an excellent collection of essays that challenge some of the historical and normative assumptions behind this argument, see *The Phantom Public Sphere*, ed. Bruce Robbins (Minneapolis: University of Minnesota Press, 1993).

The Short Life
of a Dark Prophecy
The Rise and Fall of the "Population Bomb" Crisis, 1965–75

Michael Smith

On 17 January 1969 the *Star Trek* episode "The Mark of Gideon" aired for the first time. As in most episodes of the original *Star Trek* series, Captain Kirk succumbs to the twin impulses of his chivalric and libidinous nature and develops a romantic interest in an alien woman, Odona. She, however, has ulterior motives. She wants to become infected with the viral meningitis of which Kirk is a carrier. Kirk has beamed down to the surface of the planet Gideon, literally teeming with people. The "love of life" Odona's species embraces as *its* prime directive has led to the elimination of all the Malthusian checks on population: there is no disease, no famine, no war—only a love ethic, which has produced a society of nearly immortal beings who live overcrowded, meaningless lives. As Odona's father later explains to Kirk, "Births have increased our population until Gideon is encased in a living mass of beings without rest, without peace, without joy."[1]

While confined with Odona in an ersatz *Enterprise,* Kirk hears a muffled pounding, as of the hearts of a million people pressed against the hull of the "ship." He sees a vision of thousands of hooded, impassive faces staring into the view screen. Odona tells him, before her father's plot to introduce disease back into Gideon society is exposed, "All my life I've dreamed of being alone." Where I come from, she says, "there are so many people . . . so many."

There is no place, no street, no house, no garden, no beach, no mountain that is not filled with people. If he could, each one would kill to find a place to be alone. If he could, he would die for it.[2]

Slowly it dawns on Kirk that he is dealing with a society in the final throes of the overpopulation pathogen.

"The Mark of Gideon" marked *Star Trek's* entry into the debate about the "population explosion," which by 1969 had been reaching ever higher levels of stridency in the United States. The Gideon scenario was, in many ways, lifted directly from the contemporary headlines about the tragic apathy of laboratory rats subjected to severe overcrowding and the implications of these tests for humanity.[3] Also imbedded in this tale about the consequences of too much reverence for life was a criticism of the Roman Catholic Church's implacable stand against artificial birth control in the population debate ("we cannot interfere with the creation we love so deeply," pleads Odona's father when Kirk suggests sterilization or birth control as the solution to Gideon's problem).[4] Like many prophesying voices of the late 1960s and early 1970s, the producers of *Star Trek* were warning that humanity faced a most unpleasant future unless measures to reverse population growth were taken immediately. Indeed, the fate of the Gideons was mild compared to the scenarios of war and pestilence conjured by Paul Ehrlich, author of *The Population Bomb* (1968).

This essay will explore this phenomenon of jeremiads foretelling the impending collapse of civilization due to the "population bomb." Beginning in the early 1960s this notion of a population explosion gained ever greater currency, with prophets of doom joining voices in a crescendo that peaked in the early 1970s. I do not propose to write a history of population here, nor do I intend this to be a study of demographics during this period. Rather, I wish to examine the words and rhetoric of writers like Paul Ehrlich, C. P. Snow, John Holdren, as well as a host of journalists and science-fiction writers, to see what their projections and forecasts say about the society in which they lived. It is no coincidence, I contend, that fears of overpopulation reached a peak at the end of one of the most tumultuous decades in American history.[5] Ehrlich's shrill warnings in particular generated a collective consciousness primed for a new crusade. The window of opportunity was, however, small. The liberal spirit of the Great Society and the New Frontier— epitomized by the belief that any problem was solvable by one's willingness to bear burdens and make sacrifices—was almost played out. By the mid-1970s the population crisis was considered one of many insoluble dilemmas about which American society threw up its hands.

Figure 1. "Have You Ever Been Mugged?"

A New Awareness of Crisis

After the Second World War a growing number of scientists and demographers began to note the unprecedented growth of the world's population.[6] Although the discussion for the most part remained fairly sedate, in 1954 a pamphlet published by the Hugh Moore Fund introduced a new phrase into the population crisis lexicon and a new image about the

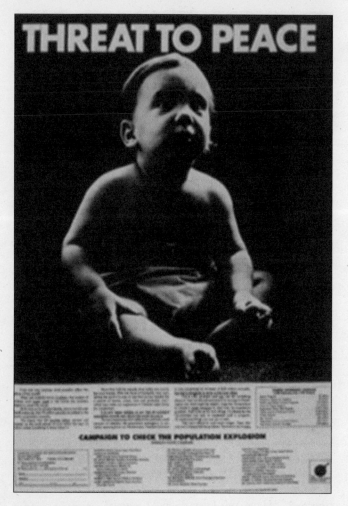

Figure 2. "Threat to Peace"

implications of overpopulation for the future: "The Population Bomb."[7]
It would be more than another decade before this term became common
usage in overwrought prognostications about the future. But the idea
that population was a potential explosive force stuck, consonant as it was
with the rhetoric of the Cold War.

Yet even so eminent a demographer as Kingsley Davis seemed not to
think too much of the potential "explosive force" of population. In 1957
there was no talk of a future of human-lemmings or "eco-catastrophe."

"A runaway inflation of people in the underdeveloped nations is not in our national interest," Kingsley said. The chief danger for the future from a rapidly increasing population was the susceptibility of the young—the largest cohort in an expanding population—to demagogues.[8] Science-fiction writer and scientist Arthur C. Clarke, writing in *Harper*'s a year later, was not so sanguine about the prospects of a billion more youth, communist or otherwise. The population explosion had no realistic solution, argued Clarke, and was, ironically, such a problem because the Cold War had been so successful in helping avert atomic war, which would have checked the population quite adequately. Not far in the future, he figured, humanity would face either some kind of police state (necessary in a crowded world) or will have to contemplate "a complete change in the patterns of human sexual behavior." Clarke did not hold out much hope for future happiness.[9] By decade's end, a CBS documentary called "The Population Explosion" cautioned that an unrestricted birthrate could lead to catastrophe and became the first national television network to air a program containing a frank discussion of contraception.[10]

An article published in the journal *Science* in late 1960 carried the debate into newspapers nationwide with its scientific forecasting of 13 November 2026 as the date when the planet would be one heaving mass of humanity (much like the planet Gideon). The premise of the paper—that our "great-great grandchildren will not starve but will be squeezed to death"—was obviously a jest, but the authors made clear their belief that the time had come to do something about the problem or face the consequences. In subsequent issues of *Science* dozens of letters chastised the authors for being so pessimistic (it was the beginning of the New Frontier, after all) and challenged the data used to "predict the date of crushing." But the main author of the original article offered an eloquent response:

> The real problem today is that we have to prepare each single member of the family of three billion to face soon a decision—namely, either to persist in enjoying his children and to pay for it by having no more than two and remaining mortal, or to reach for individual mortality and remain childless forever. In twenty years, of course, four billion will have to make this decision.

The answer to this vexing question as to whether "[man can] guide his future end more wisely than the blind forces of nature, only the future can reveal; the answer will not be long postponed," wrote another contributor to *Science*.[11]

This discourse in a scientific journal set the tone for the debate and was picked up by the more mainstream media. Science, albeit disputed science, had established that humanity faced a very unpleasant future if current population trends persisted. Nothing, not even the Cold War, threatened the maintenance of a high quality of life (only recently achieved by so many in the United States), as did the specter of over-population. "This is the major problem of our day," wrote a physician in *The New Republic*, "Not Communism, not war, not poverty." Some even began to write of the population bomb in atomic terms, referring to poverty and hunger as "the twin fall-outs of this bomb of humanity." "It is possible," declared the teen magazine *Senior Scholastic*, "that there will never be a nuclear war. But the population of the world *is* explod-ing—and right now." In an ominously titled article, "Danger: Megaton-nage Unknown," *The Nation* said:

> Slowly public opinion is awakening to the fact that the arms race is not the only threat to survival, that the population explosion, though less dramatic, could ultimately prove no less lethal than the multi-megaton bomb.

And in the introduction to the first anthology on overpopulation to ap-pear in the 1960s, Fairfield Osborn, long an influential conservationist, wrote that if public opinion could not be swayed in favor of population control during this transitional period, "man may allow himself to suf-fer atomic devastation or to face ever mounting difficulties due to pres-sures of his own numbers." These alternatives were, for Osborn, fates of the same order of magnitude.[12]

By the mid-1960s, as the war in Vietnam underscored the sense that something was terribly amiss in the world and that the United States seemed out of balance, voices warning of the consequences of un-checked population growth grew louder and more desperate. This in-creasing stridency may be in part attributable to a sense that the public was still ignoring the crisis. A Gallup poll in the fall of 1965 revealed that while 54 percent of Americans were concerned about population growth, they still ranked it beneath international communism, crime, and racism in importance.[13] In order to mobilize the public, students of overpopulation, via opinion essays, books, and advertisements, began to point out that overpopulation subsumed all other fears, including qual-ity-of-life issues, such as crowding, crime, racial tension, and even clean water, which would only worsen under the pressure of population. To make this issue all the more real, population activists read the future in the current generation of children. Former president Eisenhower lent his support to the cause by sending a letter to the first ever Congressional hearing on birth control in mid-1965. Population, he wrote, is "the most critical of the problems facing man today":

> If we ignore now the plight of those unborn generations which, because of our unreadiness to take corrective action in controlling population growth will be denied any expectations beyond abject poverty and suffering, then history will rightly condemn us.[14]

The "dark future" promised in the absence of family planning seemed more believable when the published results of the first tests that measured the effect of crowding on rats appeared. Writing in the popular *Science Digest*, Bruce Frisch observed that unless birth control were widely practiced, the human race faced "climbing infant mortality, sexual perversion [crowding seems to have contributed to homosexuality among the rats], cannibalism, and zombieism" or "lemming-like suicide." Royal Society president Howard Flory agreed with the likelihood of cannibalism, adding that a new Dark Age was imminent. One letter writer to the *New York Times* in fact pleaded: "Unless we slow down the runaway increase our problems of today will seem like child's play for those who live in the world of A.D. 2000." Harrison Brown, a well-respected demographer, opined publicly that he believed population would *cause* a nuclear conflagration in the near future. And in its final issue of 1966, *The Christian Century* invoked the Doomsday Clock of the Atomic Scientists, the wages of the sin of hubris, and two of the four horsemen of the apocalypse:

> In [1970] . . . men will . . . be faced by grim reminders of abysmal human failure. Famine and plague, already stalking the earth, will rebuke man for his failure to control his own rampant reproduction. . . . Modern man has filched the secrets of the atom but he has not yet comprehended the magnitude of the threat manifested in the ascending powers of the number two, the dangers of a propagation that doubles and doubles again. . . . If man continues to multiply at the present accelerating rate, all the wizardry of modern technology . . . will not be able to produce enough food . . . to prevent starvation.[15]

In 1967, this time in *Esquire*, another writer worried that "Perhaps the must disturbing thing about the world population situation . . . is the almost uniformly pessimistic outlook of so many very capable people who have examined the matter closely."[16] What accounted for such a dismal outlook? By the mid-1960s it had become clear that the general social calm that had obtained since the end of the Second World War was being disturbed. The nonviolence of the early civil-rights movement had succumbed to the desperate urban realities of racism in the North, and it seemed that the apocalyptic predictions invoked by Malcolm X and James Baldwin could no longer be discounted. The dire predictions of *Silent Spring* also seemed to have prophetic qualities for the population doomsayers as they observed Lake Erie dying, Los Angeles's air turning sulfuric, and the extinction of animal species accelerating. Moreover, not only did technological developments of the previous twenty years place human existence in jeopardy, but also technology itself offered no solutions to the population problem, other than as a tool for repression. The angst of the era affected even the most apparently dispassionate scientists. The debt incurred from overpopulation, in short, led to a quite fatalistic view of the future.[17]

Prophets of Doom

Among the most fatalistic and certainly the most prominent of the population Jeremiahs who carried the crusade into the late 1960s and early 1970s was Paul Ehrlich. He alone published no fewer than twenty-four articles in periodicals during this period and was cited another forty-seven times.[18] In addition to his prodigious output of articles, Ehrlich wrote or cowrote three books between 1968 and 1972 dealing with the population crisis.[19]

But Ehrlich's was by no means a solitary voice in the late 1960s and early 1970s. Through the sheer magnitude of their publications, a chorus of prophets transformed the issue of overpopulation into *the* crisis of Western civilization for a number of years.[20] In 1970 alone, over one hundred articles were published in periodicals cited in the *Reader's Guide to Periodical Literature.* The *New York Times* printed dozens of stories about the crisis between 1967 and 1973. And between 1967 and 1975 no fewer than twelve collections of essays and/or articles on the population crisis appeared, many of them containing articles that had stirred debate and controversy.[21] The United States government convened commissions and study committees, foremost among them the Commission on Population Growth and the American Future, otherwise known as the Rockefeller Commission (1970). A study committee at Johns Hopkins University in 1971 recognized that "the task [of reducing the world's population growth rate] may well be the most difficult mankind has ever faced, for it involves the most fundamental characteristic of all life—the need to reproduce itself."[22] Moreover, these writings and studies linked all the other social problems of the period to overpopulation to such a degree that the editor of a high school textbook on American problems in 1972 wrote: "problems of war and peace, crime, racism, prejudice, poverty, health care, decaying cities, alienation, drugs, pollution, and social disorder can all be directly related to population size."[23]

By the last three years of the 1960s, outspoken demographers such as Harrison Brown increasingly began to abandon the role of impartial scientific observer for one of advocate. He saw population growth in the industrialized world as an even greater threat to civilization than that occurring in the developing world, as the former compromised "individual freedom of choice and action" and intensified "race problems." By 1970 he was advocating world government as the only way the human race could extricate itself from the crisis of overpopulation.[24]

Also by the late 1960s, the rather staid scientific discourse on population, which only a few years before viewed population itself in terms of a laboratory experiment with a manipulable outcome, had virtually disappeared. In its place appeared the rhetoric of a population out of control. Common to many of the doomsayers was the notion that as a result of uncontrolled population growth since the Second World War, disaster of some kind was both imminent and inevitable. The time for action to avert a catastrophe had passed—mitigation of the disaster was the best that could be hoped for. William and Paul Paddock peppered their 1967 book, *Famine—1975!* with phrases such as "the population-food collision is inevitable: it is foredoomed;" Americans must face the "sad realism" of starvation in many parts of the world; and "before the end of the 1970s the interplay of power politics will be based on who is starving and who is not. . . . Food will be the basis for power."[25] In a series of speeches given at Westminster College in Fulton, Missouri, in November 1968 (much discussed in the popular press in the weeks after), C. P. Snow said that the number of people in the world squash all hope: "The food-population collision *will* occur, the attempts to prevent it, or meliorate it, will be too feeble," he despaired.[26]

Awareness of a population crisis came when, in Leo Marx's words, "postmodern pessimism" was beginning to define the national mood. This pessimism stemmed from the realization that the progressive agenda of limitless growth and improving quality of life for everyone, a product of the Enlightenment itself, was a fool's errand.[27] To many, the population explosion represented the straw that would break the back of civilization. Human agency in the control of something so basic to existence as reproduction and population growth seemed lost; population growth was a problem that defied even technological solutions. Indeed, uncontrolled population growth was the main specter that left Americans "full of guilt and pessimism," according to the *New Yorker*, as it looked in 1969 toward the next millennium. Francis S. L. Williamson explicitly linked "population pollution" to the collapse of civilization, citing studies about psychoses and urban life and speculating that humans would soon deal with these mental problems on a global scale. "Standing room only conditions mean no time for culture," he wrote. And without culture, civilization could not long persist.[28]

The severest critics of Americans' willful ignorance of the crisis pointed the finger not at China or India, as had Snow and the Paddocks, but at Western civilization itself. We, they argued, the wealthiest and most "enlightened" peoples of the world, had sown the seeds of our own destruction. Irresponsible affluence, not sheer numbers of people, would destroy civilization. With our relatively small numbers we had fouled our own nest to a far greater degree than had the so-called developing nations, argued more than one writer. Although India could not be saved, wrote Wayne Davis in his 1970 piece in *The New Republic* characterizing the work of the Paddocks, neither could the United States, which

> will be a desolate tangle of concrete and ticky-tacky, of strip-mined moonscapes and silt-choked reservoirs. The land and water will be so contaminated with . . . hundreds of . . . toxic substances, which have been approaching critical levels of concentration in our environment as a result of *our* numbers and affluence, that it may be unable to sustain human life. . . . Thus as the curtain gets ready to fall on man's civilization let it come as no surprise that it shall first fall on the United States.[29]

Such were the stakes for Paul Ehrlich, the Stanford University biologist whose crusade during the late 1960s and early 1970s (and which continues to this day) is a composite of all the arguments heretofore presented. In part this is so because Ehrlich's own work influenced countless other writers on the subject of overpopulation. His polemical writings appeared in periodicals from the middlebrow *Reader's Digest* to the literary *Saturday Review* to the peer reviewed journal *Bulletin of the Atomic Scientists*. His pronouncements on the "population bomb" were often quoted in the press, as was the case, for example, when he made great fanfare of his own sterilization in 1969.[30] His work that was most influential and had the greatest impact during the period was *The Population Bomb* (1968). Indeed, all the arguments Ehrlich made about overpopulation and the fate of humanity can be found either fully developed or in embryonic form in this book. This crisis at hand, the crisis from which, according to Ehrlich, all other contemporary crises devolved, was made plain on the cover of the first edition of *The Population Bomb*: "Population Control or Race to Oblivion?"[31]

The Population Bomb was a transitional work, and in it one finds all the rhetoric so far discussed, as well as all of the flights of fancy about overpopulation, which I will address in the final section of this essay. In *The Population Bomb* Ehrlich drew on the kinds of biological science debates about crowding and overpopulation that gained attention in the late 1950s and early 1960s: rising birth rates and "doubling times"; declining death rates; the young average age of the world's population.[32] His primary focus was not, however, on the present but on what present behaviors and trends *portended*. Ehrlich believed there was a way to avert the total collapse of civilization: voluntary population control.[33] But unless this course of action were embarked on immediately, Americans and the rest of the world faced (1) draconian population control measures that would constrain individual freedom, (2) a miserable, crowded existence without hope leading to the slow death of civilization, or (3) a rapid extinction of the human species in the near future, brought on by the "death rate" solution to the population explosion. Although certainly not alone in predicting such a dismal future for humanity, Ehrlich's scenarios were among the most colorful of all those printed as "scientific" predictions. Moreover, the three alternative fates awaiting humankind *were* widely fictionalized (even by Ehrlich himself) shortly after the publication of *The Population Bomb*, evidence that the fears of overpopulation ran the entire gamut of the imagination, from forecast to fantasy.[34]

The Population Bomb is from the outset a decidedly pessimist book. Although filled with predictions about the future of civilization, Ehrlich also writes as the emissary of sad news from the future: "The problem [of a massive die-off] could have been avoided by *population control*, in which mankind consciously adjusted the birth rate so that a 'death rate solution' did not have to occur," he writes before describing the tragic future he sees so clearly.[35]

American affluence, moreover, offers no antidote to the problem of overpopulation. In not too many more years, writes Ehrlich, the explosion in American rates of consumption and destruction of its physical landscape—which already has led to a "deteriorating 'psychic environment' " manifested in "riots, rising crime rates, disaffection of youth, and increased drug usage"—will produce a dog-eat-dog society far more vicious than anything seen in the areas of the world most affected by the population "bomb."[36] The destruction of the environment was evidence that there were too many people in the United States, however comparatively uncrowded it seemed. Indeed for Ehrlich, American indifference to environmental destruction augured ill for any meaningful engagement with the problem of overpopulation itself. Moreover,

Ehrlich makes clear, in the global community of the late twentieth century, the losing battle to control population in India and China is a battle lost by everyone, for a lost battle against overpopulation unleashes "three of the four apocalyptic horsemen—war, pestilence, famine," which heed no international boundaries.[37]

One can almost imagine Ehrlich heaving a great sigh as he begins to relate the three scenarios he deems most probable for humanity's future. Taken together, they represent the most extreme predictions about the overpopulation crisis during the period of high interest in the problem and a splendid example of "high" postmodern *Weltschmerz*. In scenario 1, the 1972 flooding in China creates massive famine there, and to distract its starving population, China itself enters the conflict in Southeast Asia, which has now spread into Thailand. In an attempt to stop China, while also attempting to avoid a bloody ground war, the United States launches tactical nuclear strikes against China's troops and a preemptive strike against China's nuclear facilities. Alas, five "dirty" Chinese missiles get through. Result: one hundred million dead Americans—all due to an out-of-control population. Scenario 2 defers the reckoning day until 1979, when, because of prolonged food shortages, much of Asia, Latin America, and China have turned communist. Bubonic plague outbreaks are blamed on biological warfare experiments by the United States, which is subsequently totally isolated internationally. Food and water rationing have been instituted even in the United States. The seas are rising due to global warming. Compulsory restriction of births to one per couple and sterilization of people with IQs under 90 go into effect. "Overkill" pesticides have sterilized much of the United States' best agricultural land. Finally, in 1980, with Chinese and Russian missile bases all over Latin America, the inevitable nuclear conflagration occurs, and by the end of this scenario, "the most intelligent creatures ultimately surviving this period are cockroaches." Scenario 3, the "cheerful" scenario, begins in 1974 and anticipates that the United States cuts off food aid to India, China, and other areas that the United States considers "beyond hope." Sustainable agriculture is mandated in the United States, and the pope endorses birth control and abortion. The United States, Canada, Western Europe, Russian, Japan, and Australia wait for the "major die-back" in the rest of the world to end, then begin "area rehabilitation," which involves "population control, agricultural development, and limited industrialization, to be carried out jointly in selected sections of Asia, Africa, and South America" with the eventual goal of a world population stabilized at 1.5 billion by 2100. At the end of this chapter Ehrlich issues a challenge for the reader to create a more optimistic scenario, then implies that other than by extraterrestrial deliverance, there is no hope for one:

> I will leave you to decide which scenario is more realistic, and I challenge you to create one more optimistic than the last. (I won't accept one that starts, "In early 1972 the first monster space ships from a planet of the star Alpha Centauri arrive bearing CARE packages . . . ")[38]

Although millions read *The Population Bomb,* most decided that none of Ehrlich's scenarios were particularly realistic, especially when the dates of his proposed cataclysms came and went and no one seemed worse for wear, at least in the industrialized world. Ehrlich's book (and his other writings) generated a tremendous amount of interest in the notion that there was a population crisis in progress. Indeed, the Commission on Population Growth and the American Future cited Ehrlich's work as a stimulus for their formation.[39] But Ehrlich's suggested antidotes to the problem required too much sacrifice for the average American to swallow them, as Ehrlich himself conceded: "Americans will do none of these things [driving less, showering less, eating less meat, being more manipulative of the private lives of people in developing countries], you say. Well, I'm inclined to agree."[40] Even though *The Population Bomb* appeared during the twilight of liberalism in the United States, most Americans could not endorse Ehrlich's proposals of spiking foreign food aid with antifertility drugs (never mind that such technology did not yet exist), to say nothing of child lotteries in the United States itself.[41] In short, Paul Ehrlich probably contributed as much to the decline of interest in the population explosion as he contributed to consciousness raising. Both his scenarios and proposed solutions to the problem sounded, in the end, too much like science fiction.

Imagined Destinies

Writers of speculative and science fiction have been addressing the issue of overpopulation since at least the late nineteenth century.[42] Unlike simple forecasts or predictions, which must at least tacitly acknowledge that what is possible must be rooted in some way in current probabilities, science fiction can project without limits. In creating hypothetical societies operating under conditions imagined to emerge from "real" social conditions, the writer can provide quite an enlightening comparative analysis, much in the way the sociologist compares two societies. "Science fiction provides heuristic extrapolations of current trends and contrasting portraits of alternative social arrangements," writes Martin Greenberg in *Social Problems through Science Fiction*.[43] This view is precisely what the writers of speculative fiction about the consequences of unchecked population growth tried to embrace. As social critics they were less constrained by probability than Ehrlich (who, it must be said, seemed not at all constrained at times) and could therefore allow their imaginations to conjure up believable scenarios that could "make more concrete and therefore more understandable the consequences of social trends."[44]

In the postwar era, science-fiction writers began creating futures in which human freedom and quality of life were constrained by overpopulation. In many cases writers took their premises straight from the scientific literature. In 1955 Frederick Pohl and C. M. Kornbluth published their justifiably acclaimed *The Space Merchants*, a satirical account of a universe teeming with consumers and run by advertising executives and a warning about both runaway consumerism and runaway population growth. A few years later Pohl revisited the theme of overpopulation and the measures that might someday be necessary should the growth go unchecked. In "The Census Takers" those age-old quantifiers of population have also become assassins: to reduce population, they must eliminate every three hundreth person they count.[45]

Perhaps the most mature satirical admonition about overpopulation before the great flood of science fiction dealing with the "population bomb" is J. G. Ballard's "Billenium" (1962). In this story set in New York City in the not-so-distant future, Ballard anticipates many of the rhetorical strategies used by population bomb polemicists to stimulate public interest in the issue. In this New York of the near future crowding is so great that human traffic jams leave the protagonist near the Public Library where he works "swaying helplessly on his feet as the jam shifted and heaved," like some undifferentiated mass of gelatin. The unimaginable population density has severed traditional forms of social interaction, sapped initiative, and ended the notion of privacy. Each person is allotted four square meters of living space. Since all rural land is needed for agriculture, the urbanized overpopulation results in what the sixties' demographer Philip Hauser has called the "population implosion."[46] All this congestion was the fault of "a short-sighted nationalism and industrial explosion fifty years ago," laments the protagonist, in a warning to the readers of 1962. The message is clear: Americans must face the loss of social values they formerly embraced—privacy, freedom of movement, individualism—if they do not control population growth.

By the late 1960s science-fiction interpreters of the overpopulation crisis (and the rhetoric of that crisis) had begun to imagine scenarios that both echoed and embellished the doomsday prognostications found in mainstream literature on the subject. Harry Harrison's vision of a New York City in 1999 with 35 million inhabitants has become one of the most familiar science-fiction renderings of an overcrowded future. Later combined into the screenplay for the film *Soylent Green*, Harrison's novel *Make Room! Make Room!* (1966) and short story "Roommates" (1971) provide a troubling look at the twin specters of crowding and food shortages occurring not in some city of the Third World but in New York. Above all, Harrison offers a searing indictment of just the sort of technological enthusiasm Paul Ehrlich warned of in "Eco-Catastrophe!" and *The Population Bomb*.

In Harrison's near future the law of diminishing returns has played itself out: the green revolution has proved to be an ephemeral solution to world hunger; pollution and overexploitation have exhausted the seas as a source of food; air pollution has made New York's air almost unbreathable; and global warming has raised the level of the oceans and transformed the northeastern United States into a subtropical climate. Harrison turns the Pollyannaish optimism of late sixties' and early seventies' population crisis naysayers on its head. Accordingly, population is a quality-of-life problem. But when our technological quick fixes begin to fail, he imagines, we will be driven to meaningless existences fraught with social unrest (Harrison's descriptions of food riots are especially unsettling, with humans portrayed as so many carp seething in the waters toward bits of food), with our enfeebled bodies sustained by protein cannibalized from the dead. Like Paul Ehrlich's and the Paddock brothers' forecasts from the late 1960s of global famine and political upheaval by 1975, Harrison's scenario now seems absurd. But if the now famous final scene of *Soylent Green* (in which Charlton Heston runs wild-eyed from the processing plant screaming like some fourteenth-century flagellant, "It's people! Soylent Green is made out of people!") seems laughable today, it resonated in the early 1970s. A secret government operation for rendering people into food smacked of just the sort of authoritarianism Ehrlich and so many others believed overpopulation would bring.[47]

Harrison was only one of many writers who, through the lens of science fiction, magnified the social problems caused by overpopulation. Some, like Robert Sheckley in "The People Trap" (1968), employed a satirical approach. Though ineptly written, "The People Trap" is worth examining because it jabs right at the heart of the deterioration of the quality of life issue, the appeal of final resort made by Ehrlich and the other neo-Malthusians. In the story sixty men have been selected to race to the Land Grant office in downtown Manhattan. The first ten to arrive will receive a one-acre homestead on a rutted, treeless mountainside, but quite a spread in a world in which the average family lives in a ten-foot-square room. The initial challenge for the competitors is to penetrate the "core crowd" of people not even lucky enough to share a tiny room. They live in the streets, a seething mass of humanity, "composed of slack-jawed men with unfocused eyes—agglutinating hysterophiliacs, in the jargon of the pandemologists. Jammed together sardine fashion, reacting as a single organism, these men were incapable of anything but blind and irrational fury toward anything that tried to penetrate their ranks." The irony, writes Sheckley, is that because "science, with splendid irrationality, continued to work insensately toward the goal of more life for more people," no one has a life worthy of the word.[48]

Loss of freedom due to overcrowding, another central component of Ehrlich's rhetoric, is also a pervasive theme in science fiction of the late 1960s and early 1970s. Maggie Nadler's "The Secret" (1970) is a sinister tale about the extremes of compulsory birth control, set in a society in which sterilization is the supreme patriotic act and sexual behavior is monitored by a bureaucratic regulatory agency. In "East Wind, West Wind" (1970), Frank Robinson conjures a world so polluted and so crowded (Bosnywash is now the only city on the East Coast) that automobiles, that most celebrated symbol of independence and freedom in 1960s America, have been outlawed. Yet even this interdiction has failed; too many people have driven too many cars for too long. Robert Silverberg's "In the Beginning" (1971) portrays a superficially utopian society in which the world's tens of billions have been shoehorned into thousands of skyscrapers, where, although no one goes hungry, people live under constant surveillance and according to the dictates of the government. Perhaps the most extreme example of constrained freedom in an overcrowded future can be found in Philip Jose Farmer's "The Sliced-Crosswise Only-on-Tuesday World" (1971). In this story the world's population has been divided (as usual, by some shadowy, authoritarian bureaucracy) into sevenths: each group lives one day a week, existing in suspended animation the other six. When the protagonist falls in love with a woman from another day, he is out of luck.[49]

Of the many examples of period science fiction that I have examined, not a single piece featuring population growth as its main theme predicted anything other than the collapse of civilization. The promise of renewal that concludes *2001: A Space Odyssey*—otherwise a rather stark warning against technological hubris—and other popular works of late 1960s science fiction does not glimmer at the conclusions of stories about overpopulation. Science-fiction writers who dealt with this issue seem, like Ehrlich and Wayne Davis, exemplars of that postmodern pessimism.

Limits to Receptivity

The Club of Rome's contribution to the debate on population and the general depletion of resources, *The Limits to Growth* (1972) produced the last surge of popular interest in the crisis of overpopulation. *The Limits to Growth* used mathematical models to demonstrate that

> if present trends in world population, industrialization, pollution, food production, and resource depletion continue unchanged, the limits to growth on this planet will be reached sometime within the next one hundred years. The most probable result will be a rather sudden and uncontrollable decline in both population and industrial capacity.[50]

This study also purported to provide empirical evidence that the fate of humanity was going to be much as Paul Ehrlich had imagined it if population and resource consumption trends were not reversed. "The crux of the matter," the authors wrote, "is not only whether the human species will survive, but even more whether it can survive without falling into a state of worthless existence."[51]

There had always been an oppositional position within the debate over overpopulation.[52] But *The Limits to Growth* was greeted with a hail of criticism and rebuttals; a year after it appeared, a group of scientists in England produced a sharp rebuttal of the conclusions drawn by the Club of Rome.[53] Its predictions and proposals, derived though they were from mathematics and computer science rather than the imagination, demanded too much sacrifice for the public to take them seriously.

To be sure, the issue did not simply disappear in the second half of the 1970s. The Ehrlichs, Lester Brown, the Meadows and others continued to warn that humanity was on the road to disaster if population growth and resource consumption were not controlled or even reversed. Despite the fact that the world's population continued to grow exponentially, interest in the crisis in the United States declined steadily after 1973.[54] Several factors account for this fall off. The success of the green revolution in some of the world's population-crisis areas—notably India—gave the illusion that technology had indeed solved the problem of hunger, if not overpopulation itself. The end of the baby boom (coupled with the onset of a "baby bust") in the United States relieved the pressure on social services, especially education, which in 1970 had seemed on the verge of collapse. The collapse—and perceived failure—of liberalism and its can-do optimism in conjunction with the full flowering of a conservative backlash in American politics contributed to a psychological disengagement with difficult global problems like overpopulation. And, of course, the imminent collapse of civilization foretold by Ehrlich and others proved, at least in the short term, chimerical.

With the onset of the energy crisis of 1973–74 Americans were much less receptive to demands that they make sacrifices in order to solve a problem that seemed not to impinge directly on their lives.[55] By 1975, more than one writer was lamenting that population was a forgotten crisis. "[Americans]," wrote Russell W. Peterson, "like to hit problems on the head with our doctorates and our dollars today and see them crumple tomorrow." Since the population crisis did not crumple so easily, he argued, Americans have chosen to forget about it. A writer for *Science* that same year revisited the prediction made in 1960 of standing room only in 2026 and found the world ahead of schedule; however, Americans were also curiously less concerned about the problem than they had been even fifteen years before.[56]

The Rockefeller Commission concluded in its 1972 report that "if this country is in a crisis of spirit . . . then population is part of that crisis." But they acknowledged the difficulty of mobilizing the government and public opinion to face the crisis and noted, almost wistfully, that "unlike other great public issues in the United States, population lacks the dramatic event—the war, the riot, the calamity—that galvanizes attention and action. It is easily overlooked and neglected."[57] Rather than marking the beginning of decisive action against the problem, the Rockefeller Commission's report came at the end of what Anthony Downs, writing in 1972 about the decline in interest in ecological issues, called "the issue attention cycle." First comes the preproblem stage, followed by alarmed discovery and "euphoric enthusiasm to solve the problem in a short time without fundamentally reordering society." Then comes a realization of the cost of the solution and a decline of intense public interest when the reality of difficult and costly solutions becomes too discouraging or threatening. Finally the issue reaches the postproblem stage, "a twilight realm of lesser attention or spasmodic recurrences of interest."[58] The rise and fall of interest in the population crisis fits neatly into Downs's model. In the early 1960s, scientists and demographers identified the problem. Population-control advocates such as Paul Ehrlich certainly embodied the "euphoric enthusiasm" for addressing the problem, but their solutions proved too threatening to the established order, so threatening, in fact, that they became fodder for science-fiction writers.

Observing the collapse of one social movement after another in the

1960s and early 1970s—civil rights, anti-war, New Left, environmental—
Leo Marx has found that the "entrenched institutionalism" that under-
pinned the social problems of that period was remarkably resistant to
propaganda and rhetoric.[59] So many of the writers examined in this essay remind us that civilizations, to say nothing of institutions, eventually buckle under pressure. As Paul Ehrlich continues to remind anyone
who will listen, the pressure of population continues to rise; in the end,
we ignore it at our own peril.

Notes

I wish to thank the students of David Pace's "History of the Future" seminar
at Indiana University, and especially David himself, for many helpful suggestions on drafts of this essay.

1. The dialogue has been taken from the collection of novelized *Star Trek*
   episodes. See James Blish, *The Star Trek Reader III* (New York: Dutton,
   1977), 283.

2. Ibid., 273.

3. One of the most beloved earlier *Star Trek* episodes, "The Trouble with
   Tribbles" (1967), also dealt with the consequences of exponentially expanding population but was more frivolity than social criticism. See Blish,
   The Star Trek Reader II (New York: Dutton, 1977), 131–47. An episode
   from the first season, "The Conscience of the King" (1966), explored the
   totalitarian nature of solving famine through triage. See Blish, *The Star
   Trek Reader I* (New York: Dutton, 1976), 120–38.

4. Blish, *The Star Trek Reader III*, 283.

5. See David Farber, *The Age of Great Dreams: America in the 1960s* (New
   York: Hill and Wang, 1994) and William E. Leuchtenberg, *A Troubled
   Feast: American Society since 1945* (Boston, Mass.: Little, Brown, 1983),
   127–287.

6. See John R. Wilmoth and Patrick Ball, "The Population Debate in American Popular Magazines, 1946–1990," *Population and Development Review*
   18 (December 1992): 631–68. Wilmoth and Ball analyze the number and
   ideological bent of articles about population referenced in the *Reader's
   Guide to Periodical Literature* from 1946 to 1990. Although their study offers an incomplete survey of popular literature concerned with population,
   their findings about the steady growth in interest in the subject from the
   1950s on, as well as their documentation of the decline in interest after the
   mid-1970s, are quite useful.

7. Lawrence Lader, *Breeding Ourselves to Death* (New York: Ballantine, 1972),
   3. Hugh Moore, a tireless advocate of population and birth control, made
   his fortune, ironically, with the Dixie Cup, which with its contribution to

improved public hygiene helped to reduce the incidence of infectious disease and lower the death rate.

8. "Population Explosion," *New York Times Magazine*, 22 September 1957, 79.

9. Arthur C. Clarke, "Standing Room Only," *Harper's*, April 1958, 54–56.

10. The program aired on 11 November 1959. See the review in *New York Times*, 12 November 1959, 71.

11. Heinz von Forester et al., "Doomsday: Friday 13 November, A.D. 2026," *Science* 132 (November 1960): 1291–95; *Science* 133 (24 March 1961): 936–38; *Science* 133 (16 June 1961): 1931–32; and Harold F. Down, "World Population Growth: An International Dilemma," *Science* 135 (26 January 1962): 283–90.

12. L. F. Fenster, "The Population Explosion," *The New Republic*, 18 September 1961, 30–31; "Tomorrow's World—Population: Too Many," *Senior Scholastic*, 27 September 1963, 18–20; "Danger: Megatonnage Unknown," *The Nation*, 12 January 1963, 22; Fairfield Osborn, "Introduction," *Our Crowded Planet: Essays on the Pressures of Population* (New York: Doubleday, 1962), 10–12. Osborn was at the time of this collection's publication the president of the Conservation Foundation and one of the most widely known environmental activists of the early 1960s. It should be noted here that not all articles published in the early 1960s were so pessimistic. But assertions like the one found in the boosterish *American City*, October 1964, 7, that high population density signifies "a strong, vigorous, imaginative urban civilization," were rare. See Wilmoth and Ball, "Population Debate," 635.

13. Quoted in *Science News Letter*, 26 February 1966, 137.

14. The text of Eisenhower's letter is reprinted in *New York Times*, 23 June 1965, 21.

15. Bruce Frisch, "Disaster from Overcrowding," *Science Digest* 58 (July 1965): 69–73; Frisch, interview with Harrison Brown, *New York Times*, 20 January 1966, 33; "Population Clock Approaches Midnight," *The Christian Century*, 28 December 1966, 1592–93.

16. David Lyle, "The Human Race Has, Maybe, Thirty-Five Years Left," *Esquire*, September 1967, 116–18.

17. Ibid., 117–18.

18. Wilmoth and Ball, "Population Debate," 636–37.

19. Paul Ehrlich, *The Population Bomb* (New York: Ballantine, 1968); with Anne H. Ehrlich, *Population, Resources, Environment: Issues in Human Ecology* (San Francisco, Calif.: W. W. Freeman & Co., 1970); with Richard L. Harriman, *How to Be a Survivor* (New York: Ballantine, 1972).

20. Though the problem was global and writers offered varying degrees of sympathy for the crowded and often underfed peoples of Africa, Asia, and

Latin America, the general tenor of the debate was, What did the crisis mean for *America?*

21. *Reader's Guide to Periodical Literature* (Minneapolis: H. W. Wilson Co., 1905–) and Wilmoth and Ball, "Population Debate," 657. *New York Times Index* (New York: New York Times Co., 1913–). A sample of these titles: Harrison Brown and Edward Hutchings, Jr., eds., *Are Our Descendants Doomed? Technological Change and Population Growth* (1970; reprint, New York: Viking, 1972); *Population Control: For and Against* (New York: Hart Publishing Co., Inc., 1973); Daniel O. Price, ed., *The 99th Hour: The Population Crisis in the United States* (Chapel Hill: University of North Carolina Press, 1967); and Michael E. Adelstein and Jean G. Privul, eds., *Ecocide and Population* (New York: St. Martin's Press, 1972).

22. National Academy of Sciences, Office of the Foreign Secretary, *Rapid Population Growth: Consequences and Policy Implications—A Study Committee* (Baltimore, Md.: Johns Hopkins University Press, 1971), 4.

23. Jack L. Nelson, introduction to *Population and Survival: Can We Win the Race?* (Englewood, N.J.: Prentice-Hall, 1972), 4.

24. "If World Population Doubles by the Year 2000—An Interview with Harrison Brown," *U.S. News and World Report*, 9 January 1967, 51–54; "Some Conclusions," in *Are Our Descendants Doomed?* 362–68. Interestingly, Brown invested a great deal of hope in the youth movement's capacity to change attitudes toward consumption and reproduction just as that movement was becoming ever more incoherent; see "After the Population Explosion," *Saturday Review*, 6 June 1971, 11–13.

25. William and Paul Paddock, *Famine!—1975: America's Decision: Who Will Survive* (Boston, Mass.: Little, Brown, 1967), 4, 8, 123. In addition to winning the honor of falling furthest off the mark with their predictions, the Paddocks offered the most paternalistic, if not vaguely racist, assessment of overpopulation in the developing world and what needed to be done about it.

26. Snow's speeches were collected in the volume *The State of Siege* (New York: Scribners, 1968). For a sampling of the commentary on Snow's despairing outlook see "Snow's War," *The Nation*, 9 December 1968, 612; and *New York Times*, 21 November 1968, 24.

27. Leo Marx, "The Idea of Technology and Postmodern Pessimism," in Merritt Roe Smith and Leo Marx, eds., *Does Technology Drive History? The Dilemma of Technological Determinism* (Cambridge, Mass.: MIT Press, 1994), 238–57.

28. "1969–2019," *New Yorker*, 22 February 1969, 29–32; Francis S. L. Williamson, "Population Pollution," *BioScience* 19 (November 1969): 979–83. Williamson is another example of how enduring late-nineteenth-century fears about crowding proved to be. Many late-nineteenth-century social reformers in the United States feared not just the deleterious effects of

densely crowded cities on civil order, but also the collapse of civilization itself as a result of overpopulation. For a good discussion of these fears, see Paul Boyer, *Urban Masses and Moral Order in America, 1820–1920* (Cambridge, Mass.: Harvard University Press, 1978), 220–83.

29. Wayne H. Davis, "Overpopulated America: Our Affluence Rests on a Crumbling Foundation," *The New Republic,* 10 January 1970, 15.

30. See, for example, Paul Ehrlich, "World Population: Is the Battle Lost?" *Reader's Digest,* February 1969, 136–40; with John P. Holden, "The People Problem," *Saturday Review,* 4 July 1970, 42–44; with Holden, "One-Dimensional Ecology Revisited," *Bulletin of the Atomic Scientists* 28 (June 1972): 42–45; Ehrlich, interview in *New York Times,* 25 November 1969, 19.

31. Ehrlich, *The Population Bomb,* front cover.

32. Ibid., 17–29.

33. Ehrlich is quite clear that, for all of its selfish, profligate affluence, *Western* civilization essentially equaled civilization; for Ehrlich, the West's greatest sin was overindustrialization and mindless consumption, somewhat less egregious than the mindless breeding which he condemns as the greatest sin of the rest of the world.

34. I will return to the manifestations of Ehrlich's themes in science fiction in the final section of the paper. Ehrlich's story "Eco-Catastrophe!" (*Ramparts Magazine,* September 1969, 24–28) was essentially a distillation of the most disastrous scenarios contemplated in chap. 2 ("The Ends of the Road") of *The Population Bomb.*

35. *The Population Bomb,* 34–35.

36. Ibid., 63–67.

37. Ibid., 69.

38. Ibid., 69–80.

39. *Population and the American Future, The Report of the Commission on Population Growth and the American Future* (New York: Signet, 1972).

40. Ibid., 154–57.

41. Ibid., chap. 4, "What Needs to Be Done?"

42. See W. Warren Wagar, *Terminal Visions: The Literature of Last Things* (Bloomington: Indiana University Press, 1975), esp. chap. 10; and I. F. Clarke, *The Pattern of Expectation, 1644–2001* (London: Jonathon Cape, 1979), 156–62.

43. Martin Greenberg, introduction to *Social Problems through Science Fiction* (New York: St. Martin's Press, 1975), xiii. See also Judith Merrill, "What Do You Mean: Science? Fiction?" in Thomas Clareson, ed., *Science Fiction: The Other Side of Realism* (Bowling Green, Ohio: Bowling Green University Popular Press, 1971). Speculative fiction, she writes, "makes use of the traditional 'scientific method' . . . to examine some postulated approximation of reality, by introducing a given set of changes—imaginary

or inventive—into the common background of 'known facts,' creating an environment in which the responses and perceptions of the characters will reveal something about the inventions, the characters, or both" (60).

44. Greenberg, *Social Problems*, xiv. Science-fiction writers dealing with the consequences of an unchecked nuclear arms race during the Cold War, especially during the height of the Cold War in the late 1940s and early 1950s, performed an analogous role. Indeed, just as the hype about a population bomb in 1967–1969 produced a wellspring of speculative fiction on the subject, so the "massive retaliation" rhetoric of the mid-1950s generated a huge number of nuclear holocaust tales. See Paul Brians, *Nuclear Holocausts: Atomic War in Fiction, 1895–1984* (Kent, Ohio: Kent State University Press, 1987), 16–21.

45. Frederick Pohl and C. M. Kornbluth, *The Space Merchants* (New York: Ballantine, 1953); for a discussion of "The Census Takers," see Paul A. Carter, *The Creation of Tomorrow: Fifty Years of Magazine Science Fiction* (New York: Columbia University Press, 1977), 266–70.

46. J. G. Ballard, "Billenium," in Greenberg, *Social Problems*. Hauser argued that a population implosion—ever higher concentrations of people in urban areas—was of greater concern than an explosion; see Hauser in Wogaman, 226–36.

47. Harry Harrison, *Make Room! Make Room!* (Garden City, N.Y.: Doubleday, 1966); "Roommates," in Ralph S. Clem et al., eds., *No Room for Man: Population and the Future through Science Fiction* (Totowa, N.J.: Littlefield, Adams, and Co., 1979); Richard Fleischer, *Soylent Green* (Metro-Goldwyn-Mayer, 1972).

48. "The People Trap," in Greenberg, *Social Problems*.

49. Maggie Nadler, "The Secret"; Frank Robinson, "East Wind, West Wind"; Robert Silverberg, "In the Beginning"; and Philip Jose Farmer, "The Sliced-Crosswise Only-On-Tuesday World," in Greenberg, *Social Problems*. The premise of Silverberg's story is almost identical to a tongue-in-cheek scenario about limitless growth written by Harrison Brown the same year. See "After the Population Explosion," *Saturday Review*, 6 June 1971, 11–13.

50. Donella H. Meadows et al., *The Limits to Growth* (New York: Signet, 1972), 29.

51. Ibid., 200.

52. See, for example, Ben Wattenberg, "The Nonsense Explosion," *The New Republic*, 4 April 1970, 18–23; William Peterson, "The Population Explosion: A Conservative Reacts," *National Review*, 12 May 1972; Howard M. Bahr, Bruce A. Chadwick, and Darwin L. Thomas, eds., *Population, Resources, and the Future: Non-Malthusian Perspectives* (Provo, Utah: Brigham Young University Press, 1972).

53. Accounts of the debate sparked by *The Limits to Growth* can be found in the *New York Times*, 27 February 1972, 1; 14 March 1972, 43; and 2 April

1972, sec. 8, 1. The Science Policy Research Unit of Sussex University produced *Thinking about the Future: A Critique of* The Limits to Growth (London: Chatto & Windus, 1973).

54. There was a steady decline in the production of books and magazine and newspaper articles about a population crisis beginning in 1973. See *Reader's Guide to Periodical Literature, 1973–80;* and the *New York Times Index, 1973–80.*

55. Ironically, this was just the sort of national posture the Paddocks had warned would bring about global calamity. They argued that without taking global leadership in the fight to control population, the United States would begin to decay in a state of siege while the population bomb destroyed the world; see *Famine—1975!* 236.

56. Russell W. Peterson, "Population: The Forgotten Crisis," *National Parks and Conservation Magazine,* September 1975, 15–18. James Serria, "Is 'Doomsday' on Target?" *Science,* 11 July 1975, 86–87.

57. *Population and the American Future,* 2.

58. Anthony Downs, "Up and Down with Ecology," *The Public Interest* 28 (summer 1972): 38–50.

59. Leo Marx, "American Institutions and Ecological Ideals," *Science,* 27 November 1970, 945–52.

Diabolical Device
or Protective Pessary?
A Cultural Study of the Diaphragm

Rosanne L. Welker

I want to begin this discussion by conjuring up one of the fundamental fears that lurks around my office at the University of Virginia. I am a scholar of American literature and culture, brought up in various English departments, yet I work in an engineering school, in a division called Technology, Culture, and Communication. Essentially, I try to teach engineering students how to write and speak effectively. And I also try—and perhaps here is where I dream the impossible dream—I try to have my students examine the ethical and social dimensions of their work: Do not just tell me how to build something or describe to me how it works; tell me how it will affect (or "impact," as they like to say) the community.

As I was working on this essay, I received an evaluation form from a real engineering professor. She was a technical advisor for the senior thesis of one of my students. In her evaluation of his work, she had crossed out one of the grading criteria and written in red ink: "I don't think [social and ethical issues] have any place in any engineering thesis." And that statement effectively summarizes the fear at the intersection of engineering and the humanities: admitting that mechanical devices have social consequences will force us to examine our values—in particular, the ways in which we choose to distribute knowledge about and access to those mechanical devices.

In the context of contraceptive and reproductive technology, the fear of examining social implications results in restricted access to information and devices. One example of that cultural restriction is the funneling of gynecological information and practice through professional physicians instead of through midwives or women in general. Many scholars have well demonstrated how the rise of professionalism among physicians depended upon the denigration of lay practitioners—in the context of reproductive knowledge, to the denigration of midwives and other lay sources of women's health information. Indeed, my argument here rests in part upon the premise that professionals in American culture—whether engineers, doctors, or lawyers—are reluctant to talk directly about the social consequences of technology, because any discussion reveals problems about knowledge and power in a democracy. Professionals hold on to specialized knowledge (about, say, reproduction), because by controlling access to this knowledge they can create a social and economic role for themselves.[1] Hence, the power of professionals often comes about by restricting knowledge to patients or clients. Power and knowledge are distributed unequally and any discussion of social consequences quickly reveals this phenomenon. Not surprisingly, professionals would rather not discuss power relations, and so they tend to claim it is "unprofessional" and "unscientific" to debate social consequences.

To my knowledge, no one has yet approached the issue of contraception in America from a technological perspective. I would like to begin that investigation here by arguing that in America at the turn of the twentieth century, the fear of women's sexuality joins with a faith in technology, a faith in professionalism, and probably a lot of other cultural shifts, to create a matrix of social and ethical issues affected by any new technological design. My discussion of the contraceptive diaphragm also builds upon such rich social histories of contraception and abortion as John M. Riddle's *Contraception and Abortion from the Ancient World to the Renaissance (1992)* and Janet Farrell Brodie's *Contraception and Abortion in Nineteenth-Century America* (1994).[2] These texts exhaustively investigate the means by which women in the past actually controlled their fertility, thereby correcting many of our currently held misperceptions. Indeed, one of the more pervasive misperceptions about the history of contraception is that until the 1960s, with the development and marketing of the birth control pill, American women had little access to contraceptives of any kind.[3] As Riddle and Brodie, among others, have well documented, however, women have historically had access to a variety of effective contraceptives and abortifacients, mostly chemical but also some mechanical ones.[4]

What strikes me as interesting about this misperception is that it grounds our commonly remembered history of contraception in the late twentieth century and it grounds it in a legal context. Foreshortening the vast social history of contraception and abortion into this narrow legal history tends to de-emphasize women's control over fertility while it emphasizes fears about women's sexuality. Indeed, throughout the conduct of my research into history of the contraceptive diaphragm, I have detected expressions of that fear again and again. The court cases I have examined consistently avoid even naming or describing the devices and repeatedly express the desire to restrict basic reproductive information, despite the fact that women managed fertility and contraceptive methods for centuries without professional intervention. To place the persistence of this fear in context, recall that as late as 1965, several states still prohibited physicians from giving birth-control information to married women.[5] Indeed, as we approach the end of the twentieth century, many school systems still face controversies over sexuality education.

Diaphragms derive from ancient pessaries, and we have some evidence of their use continually back through ancient Greece. The word "pessary" comes from the Greek for "oval stone," and that word choice reflects the presumably original use of the pessary: an oval, flat stone (or similar object) inserted into the vagina to secure in place a prolapsed uterus (a prolapsed uterus partially or fully descends into the vagina; it occurs after significant weakening of the pelvic floor muscles, so it can result from a difficult labor, a large baby, and/or many pregnancies). Obviously, not every nineteenth-century American woman suffered from a prolapsed uterus, but given that the average birth rate in 1800 in America has been calculated at 7.04 children per woman,[6] the incidence of prolapsed uteri was probably high. Today, we find the problem of the prolapsed uterus rather curious, but it was not until the 1930s that surgical procedures to repair prolapsed uteri were perfected.[7]

Still, there is substantial evidence to suggest that not all pessaries were worn for corrective purposes. The word "pessary" was also used to describe contraceptive vaginal suppositories made from various herbs, wool, dung, etc. Depending on the construction materials, these devices had different mechanisms of use and differing rates of efficacy. As agents of contraception, diaphragms are distinguishable within the pessary category because they work as barriers preventing sperm from entering the uterus. Most suppositories, by contrast, worked as chemical spermicides rather than barriers per se. Because diaphragms are mechanical barriers—and thus perhaps appeal to a desire to improve them with good old American know-how—they underwent a design revolution at the turn of the twentieth century, prompted by the vulcanization of rubber in 1844.[8] "Vulcanized rubber provided the first material truly suited for a safe and effective interface between machinery and human organs."[9] Looking at some of the patent applications gathered by Hoag

Levins in *American Sex Machines,* we can see a near obsession with designing better diaphragms. In fact, Levins notes that the first "sex patent" applied for in the United States was in 1788 for a diaphragm, and it was designed by a dentist, the then-guardians of engineering expertise.

Given that women had successfully made and used contraceptive devices well before the turn of the twentieth century, legal responses to contraceptive devices can be read as cultural assessments of how much technological prowess would be accorded to women. These cases take place against the backdrop of the 1873 federal Comstock Act and the state statutes it spawned. Most cases challenged states' statutes rather than the federal act directly.[10] The 1873 Comstock Act, which later became the 1930 Tariff Act, essentially made it a crime to sell, give away, exhibit, display, advertise, mail, or provide any information regarding— or have the intention of doing any of those things—any article or drug that could be used for the purpose of preventing conception or inducing abortion. Many cases challenging state statutes were struck down as the courts repeatedly asserted that it was within the state's police power to "regulate the rights and duties of all persons within its jurisdiction, so as to guard public morals and health and promote the common welfare."[11]

One case, however, brought a very different argument before the court. On 25 October 1916, Margaret Sanger's Brownsville, New York, clinic was shut down by police; although Sanger's sister Ethel Byrne (a registered nurse and the clinic's medical authority) was not present at the clinic that day, she was later arrested.[12] Byrne's case, *People [of NY] v. Ethel Byrne,* came to trial in 1917 and led to her conviction on the grounds that she sold "an article to be used by women, which was designed to prevent conception. . . . In conjunction with the sale the defendant disseminated literature dealing with the question of conception and setting forth the various ways and means by which it could be prevented."[13] Although the published court decision does not specify the name of the device in question, the Brownsville clinic, like many drug stores, did stock the popular Mizpah pessary.[14] That pessary was intended to be prescribed to multiparous, married women with prolapsed uteri, a "disease" condition; but it obviously could be employed contraceptively. Byrne was charged with violating the Comstock laws in two ways: selling a contraceptive device and distributing contraceptive information.[15]

The appellate court made clear its attitude toward educating women about anatomy and reproduction in the first paragraph of its decision:

One of these pamphlets is labeled "What Every Girl Should Know." This contains matters which not only should not be known by every girl, but which perhaps should not be known by any. The distribution of these pamphlets, especially to girls just coming into woman hood, would be a shocking disgrace to the community.[16]

In fact, several courts faced with similar literature responded with the same injunction to ignorance, asserting that knowledge about anatomy and contraception, particularly among adolescents and unmarried people, would encourage sexual behavior. "To remove that fear [of pregnancy and how it occurs] would unquestionably result in an increase in immorality."[17] Ironically, this fear still persists in our own culture: information about, and access to, devices, it is asserted, will directly promote undesirable social behavior and produce the very physical consequence (pregnancy) about which we wish to restrict access to information and preventive devices.

More interesting, however, is Ethel Byrne's unsuccessful argument. She proposed that the Comstock Law was "unconstitutional because it 'interferes with the free exercise of conscience and the pursuit of happiness.' . . . [B]y this statute a 'woman is denied her absolute right of enjoyment of sexual relations.' "[18] Essentially, the defense argued that women had a right to sexual pleasure without fear of pregnancy.

The court, not surprisingly, quashed Byrne's argument, asserting that "each individual's conscience and desire for happiness" were not grounds for determining whether a law is constitutional; if it were, "the same statement could be made with equal force about the statute defining [any other crime]."[19] The court did not even consider the notion that sexual pleasure might not be a crime, that it might just be part of the constitutional right to the pursuit of happiness, that the analogy might fail. By refusing to consider that pregnancy might not be within a given woman's legal rights to control, the justices disregarded the ethical and social implications of denying contraception to women.

Instead of those issues brought to its attention by the defendant, the Byrne court focused on the wider communal consequences of distributing devices and information. The public-health menace posed by sexual intercourse and the preservation of police power controlled the legal discourse. Interestingly, the opinion did not end with the quashing of Byrne's argument, but with the assertion that *physicians may* prescribe and dispense contraceptive devices "to work a cure or prevent a disease." The case closed by ceding technological control to professional physicians.

Yet that decision implies not only that woman cannot manage the moral consequences of diaphragms, but also that they cannot manage the technological demands of diaphragms. Only professional physicians have the expertise to control this technology, according to the Byrne justices. Failing to address the device itself, however, ignores a significant aspect of the debate over who ought to control access to, and knowledge about, a technological device: what is that device and how much expertise is actually required to manage its use. As Arnold Pacey has argued, part of the problem, particularly from a late-twentieth-century perspective, is that the word " 'technology' has become a catchword with a confusion of different meanings."[20] The basic sense of the word itself, the knowledge and application of a craft, seems inadequate to describe the proliferation of sophisticated and complex machinery of, say, a nuclear power plant. Pacey makes the case that processes traditionally controlled by women often lack the label—and the associated professional prestige—of "technology":

> Nearly all women's work, indeed, falls within the usual definition of technology. What excludes it from recognition [as such] is not only the simplicity of the equipment used, but the fact that it implies a different concept of what technology is about. Instead, techniques are applied to the management of natural processes of growth and decay.[21]

While Pacey does not specifically address contraceptive or reproductive technology, his point is well taken here to help illustrate the deceptive simplicity of Byrne's argument.[22] The defense's appeal to a woman's fundamental right to the pursuit of happiness via control over fertility masks a much more complex appeal to a woman's right to practice a craft, to manipulate a (literally) labor-saving device, to control a machine.

Overall, what we see with this 1917 case is a court going out of its way to employ very curious arguments about what is appropriate for virtuous women to read, about what sorts of pleasure are appropriate for women to experience, and about what kinds of reproductive choices women ought (not) to make for themselves. The issue of whether women can or should control the technological devices was not explicitly addressed, although it was arguably the primary problem. Despite the fact that women had used pessaries for thousands of years, without the assistance of professional physicians, to control their childbearing, the courts viewed the technology and knowledge about reproduction as logically and morally belonging to professional physicians rather than to individual women.[23]

This brings us to the 1936 case of *United States v. One Package of 120 Japanese Rubber Pessaries.*[24] This case brought suit against Dr. Hannah Stone, a licensed physician practicing gynecology in the New York area. Margaret Sanger, however, was the original recipient of the pessaries.[25] These devices were initially seized by customs officials. Sanger then requested that the pessaries be reshipped to Dr. Stone, "so as to stage a clear case on medical exemption [to the Comstock Laws]."[26] The case was originally tried in Manhattan, and after a ruling in Stone's favor, the government appealed to the Second Circuit Court. The federal case lists Stone as importing the pessaries from a physician in Japan "for the purpose of trying them in her practice and giving her opinion as to their usefulness."[27] The United States had again seized the pessaries and charged Stone with violating the Tariff Act of 1930. At the original trial, Stone clearly asserted that she prescribed diaphragms for contraceptive purposes when she testified "that she prescribes the use of pessaries in cases where it would not be desirable for a patient to undertake a pregnancy." The suit against Stone was dismissed by both the District Court and the Circuit Court of Appeals; essentially, both courts determined that Stone's experimental purposes did not violate the Comstock laws.

This decision is interesting for a number of reasons, not least of which is that the appellate judges who wrote the opinions—Augustus and Learned Hand—explicitly state that they were reinterpreting the Comstock laws and not strictly construing the legislative language. The majority opinion, written by Augustus Hand, begins to reinterpret Comstock by placing a historical framework around the act:

> It is true that in 1873, when the Comstock Act was passed, information now available as to the evils resulting in many cases from contraception was most limited, and accordingly it is argued that *the language prohibiting the sale of or mailing of contraceptives should be taken literally* and that Congress intended to bar the use of such articles completely.[28]

In his concurring opinion, Learned Hand also grants the prosecution's point regarding the literal interpretation of Comstock:

> There seems to me substantial reason for saying that *contraceptives were meant to be forbidden,* whether or not prescribed by a phy-

sician, and that no lawful use was contemplated. . . . *the act forbids the same conduct now as then.*[29]

Despite this clear expression of the Comstock Act's intention to bar the distribution of contraceptive devices by anyone for any reason, Augustus Hand stands the legislative language on its head:

> Yet we are satisfied that this statute, as well as all the acts we have referred to, embraced only such articles as Congress would have denounced as immoral if it had understood all the conditions under which they were meant to be used. Its design, in our opinion, was not to prevent the importation, sale, or carriage by mail of things *which might be intelligently employed by conscientious and competent physicians* for the purpose of saving life or promoting the well being of their patients.[30]

The court in *One Package* had essentially pronounced that even though the Comstock Act clearly forbids X, it is satisfied that the 1873 Congress did not really mean that, and, in fact, if presented the same bill in 1936, they would modify it to permit physicians to dispense contraceptives as they saw fit.

The impression that the court is arguing illogically is supported by Augustus Hand's acknowledgment of how the language of the original Comstock Act was in fact modified by the 1873 Senate:

> The Comstock Bill, as originally introduced in the Senate, contained the words "except on the prescription of a physician in good standing, given in good faith," but those words were omitted from the bill as it was ultimately passed."[31]

This excerpt from the majority opinion rather perversely recognizes that the 1873 Congress specifically omitted the very language that would have supported Augustus Hand's reading of the act. Hand also notes that Congress did not discuss that linguistic amendment, and he concludes that that omission opened the door for future reinterpretation of the act.

Intuitively, this strategy seems perverse: why attack the Comstock Law on one hand (they did not really mean to omit doctors' power) yet uphold it with the other? Certainly, Hand could not singlehandedly strike down the Comstock Law in its entirety—such relegislation was not within his power as a circuit court judge. Yet his language is not that of a judge simply expanding or stretching the available legislation; instead, he virtually rewrites the act.

Hand's linguistic and legalistic contortions suggest his attempt to bend the Comstock Laws just enough to preserve power for the physicians without breaking the Comstock Laws and thereby allowing anyone—any lay woman—to gain legally sanctioned control over contraceptive knowledge. By the 1930s, of course, the authority of doctors was well established, and the court would be in a difficult spot if it denied doctors the right to pursue scientific medicine. Hand's phrasing neatly acknowledges the physician's authority without ceding control to women over their own bodies. Indeed, the American Medical Association responded to the *One Package* ruling by promoting only professional physicians as proper conduits for contraceptive information.[32]

Early in the opinion, Hand pointedly defines the central question before the court as whether physicians are exempted from the Comstock Act's restrictions.[33] His argument, which ultimately favors the defendant, cites several cases that previously supported the physician's exemption. Yet, the discussion of the Comstock Act itself suggests that even those legal precedents were unsatisfactory, insufficient to justify dismissing the charges against Stone. Hand finally offers medical, not legal, opinion to oppose Comstock as written:

> It seems unreasonable to suppose that the national scheme of legislation involves such inconsistencies and requires the complete suppression of articles, the use of which in many cases is advocated by such a weight of authority in the medical world.[34]

The inconsistency he refers to here is the permission of lawful abortion next to the prohibition of contraception, even though a given woman and her physician may know before conception that any pregnancy would necessitate an abortion. And while I completely agree with this logical, rational attack upon Comstock, I must point out that Hand's arsenal consists of medical, rather than legal, authority. By calling upon medical opinion as the new authority, Augustus Hand could historicize the original Comstock language. He could then reinvent the law, placing the physician instead of the legislator in the position of determining legitimate use of contraception.

Perhaps most striking about the *One Package* case is the disingenuousness of the dismissal itself. The courts, in the end, support Stone's importation of pessaries, specifically "for experimental purposes to determine their usefulness as contraceptives to cure or prevent disease." Some of the more intriguing implications of that grounds for dismissal include: (1) Diaphragms and pessaries had been used since antiquity, so unless Stone were researching efficacy rate, a particular design, or a particular material, the usefulness of diaphragms seems already clear. (2) The notion of pessaries as curing or preventing disease (a) categorizes pregnancy as a sexually transmitted disease (a notion supported by current managed health-care practices of categorizing pregnancy as a disability); (b) sees prolapsed uteri as epidemic; or (c) silently recognizes the barrier method's ability to protect women from infections carried by their husbands. Indeed, Sanger's success in her own Brownsville clinic case rested upon defining pregnancy as a disease.[35]

Contraceptive technology is perhaps the only kind of technology for which a discussion of social and ethical consequences takes precedence over a discussion of function or need. Indeed, as the two court cases highlighted here well illustrate, the devices themselves were hardly discussed; instead, the courts focused on their wider effects on the community. This refusal to focus on the thing itself depends upon a failure to recognize contraception as technology at all. Even court cases about design rather than distribution, such as *Lanteen Laboratories v. Clark* (1938), which addresses a contract dispute over proprietary rights to a diaphragm design, demonstrate this refusal to discuss the thing itself.

And therein lies the linchpin for denying reproductive freedom for women: by mistakenly asserting the newness of contraceptive practices and by focusing on who is the appropriate guardian of information, the courts can ignore the historical evidence that women have already developed and successfully managed such technology without the intervention of professionals. These legal controversies over contraceptive access at the turn of the century mask more ideological concerns over the social status of women, the professional status of physicians, and, I would add, the cultural importance of technological innovation.

Notes

1. For an excellent discussion of professionalism as a cultural phenomenon, see Burton J. Bledstein, *The Culture of Professionalism: The Middle Class and the Development of Higher Education in America* (New York: Norton, 1976), esp. chap. 3, "The Culture of Professionalism" (80–128). See also Arnold Pacey, *The Culture of Technology* (Cambridge, Mass.: MIT Press, 1983).

2. John M. Riddle, *Contraception and Abortion from the Ancient World to the Renaissance* (Cambridge, Mass.: Harvard University Press, 1992); Janet Farrell Brodie, *Contraception and Abortion in Nineteenth-Century America* (Ithaca, N.Y.: Cornell University Press, 1994).

3. In his autobiography, *The Pill, Pygmy Chimps, and Degas' Horse* (New

York: BasicBooks, 1992), chemist Carl Djerassi cites 15 October 1951 as the "birthdate" of the synthesized pill (2) and notes that limited FDA approval was given in 1957 to prescribe the pill to treat menstrual disorders (60). He points out that actual marketing of the pill as a contraceptive agent did not begin until 1962 (63). Similarly, American culture tends to remember the history of abortion as beginning with the *Roe v. Wade* decision.

4. While some scholars have examined the social implications of technology in the realm of contraception, they have focused on different medical theories (such as homeopathy or water cures), the effects of transportation on access, or the effects of telecommunication innovations on political movements. This paper is part of a larger project that investigates the technology of the devices themselves, particularly mechanical devices such as diaphragms and syringes.

5. See the landmark case *Griswold v. Connecticut*, 381 U.S. 479 (1965), which protects the right of married couples to use contraception. C. Thomas Dienes provides an excellent discussion of the case in *Law, Politics, and Birth Control* (Urbana: University of Illinois Press, 1972), 162ff. *Eisenstadt v. Baird*, 405 U.S. 438 (1972) extends that right to unmarried persons.

6. Kristin Luker, *Abortion & the Politics of Motherhood* (Berkeley and Los Angeles: University of California Press, 1984), 15.

7. Hoag Levins, *American Sex Machines: The Hidden History of Sex at the U.S. Patent Office* (Holbrook, Mass.: Adams Media Corporation, 1996), 67.

8. Vern L. Bullough, "A Brief Note on Rubber Technology and Contraception: The Diaphragm and the Condom," *Technology and Culture* 22, no. 1 (January 1981): 104–11.

9. Levins, *American Sex Machines*, 73.

10. For a summary of this legal history, see "Regulating the Sale of Contraceptives," *American Law Reports, Annotated* 113 (1938): 966–75; "Birth Control—Regulations—Validity," *American Law Reports, Annotated*, 2nd series, 96 (1964): 948–69; and *Later Case Service, American Law Reports*, 2nd series, 96 (1993): 220–23.

11. *People [of New York] v. Ethel Byrne*, 163 NYS 682 (1917); 113 ALR 970.

12. For an excellent history of Sanger and the legal system, see Ellen Chesler, *Woman of Valor: Margaret Sanger and the Birth Control Movement in America* (New York: Simon & Schuster, 1992), 150–52.

13. *People v. Ethel Byrne*, 683–84.

14. Chesler, *Woman of Valor*, 151.

15. For further discussion of the legal issues in this case, see Dienes, *Law, Politics, and Birth Control*, 85ff. For the social history surrounding the case, see Chesler, *Woman of Valor*, 150–56.

16. *People v. Ethel Byrne*, 163 NYS 684.

17. *People v. Ethel Byrne*, 686.

18. *People v. Ethel Byrne*, 686–87.

19. *People v. Ethel Byrne*, 687.

20. Pacey, *The Culture of Technology*, 3.

21. Ibid., 104.

22. For a fascinating discussion of the application of technology to natural processes, see Ruth Hubbard, *The Politics of Women's Biology* (New Brunswick, N.J.: Rutgers University Press, 1990).

23. Interestingly, this privileging of physicians over individual women as the appropriate guardians of reproductive power remains in force today. For example, in the current debates over "late-term" abortion, arguments between the pro-choice and anti-choice camps are often phrased as whether decisions about abortion should be made by legislators or collaboratively between individual women and their physicians. "[T]he decision about whether to perform them [late-term abortions] is a medical, not a political, decision"; see Gloria Feldt, President of Planned Parenthood Federation of America, paraphrased in Angela Bonavoglia, "Late-Term Abortion: Separating Fact from Fiction," *Ms.*, May/June 1997, 61.

24. Again, see Dienes, *Law, Politics, and Birth Control*, 109ff., for an excellent discussion of the legal issues in this landmark test case.

25. Chesler, *Woman of Valor*, 372–76.

26. Ibid., 372.

27. *United States v. One Package of 120 Japanese Rubber Pessaries*, 86 F2d 738 (1936).

28. *United States v. One Package*, 739; emphasis added.

29. *United States v. One Package*, 740; emphasis added.

30. *United States v. One Package*, 739; emphasis added.

31. *United States v. One Package*, 740.

32. Chesler, *Woman of Valor*, 374–75.

33. *United States v. One Package*, 738.

34. *United States v. One Package*, 740.

35. *People [of New York] v. Sanger*, 118 N.E. 637–38 (1918).

Representing Roseanne
Working Class Women
in American Popular Culture

Jacqueline Ellis

> I have always been enchanted by the word fuck. I still am.
> It's my favorite word. It's the only word that is a verb and
> a noun and an adverb and everything else. It's beautiful
> and coarse and ugly all at the same time. And it's
> excruciatingly shocking, so of course I had to write it.[1]

In two autobiographies written within five years—*My Life as a Woman*
in 1989 and *My Lives* in 1994—Roseanne Barr Pentland Arnold
Thomas presents herself in a myriad of strongly affirmed, sometimes
mutually exclusive, often contradictory ways. She expresses these identities in language that combines self-defensive humor and self-reflec-
tive autobiography; feminist philosophy and banal psychobabble; arrogant self-promotion and painful self-destruction. She defines herself as
simultaneously a working-class heroine and a millionaire celebrity, as an
active feminist, and as a virulent critic of successful women such as
Meryl Streep and Jodie Foster. She describes herself as a subversive
stand-up comedian while expressing a desire for mainstream commercial success. She has "come out" as a survivor of child abuse while also
confessing she physically and psychologically abused her own children.
She is an all-American patriot, whose mangling of "The Star Spangled
Banner" provoked George Bush to call her "a national disgrace." She is
the self-proclaimed "Queen of Tabloid America" who also guest edited
the *New Yorker.*

These identities have mutated into a series of alternately admired and
reviled public images. First, she was Roseanne Barr: the daughter of a
working-class Jewish-American family, raised with startling incongruity in Mormon Salt Lake City. Then she was Roseanne Pentland, the
agoraphobic wife of motel night watchman, Bill: a mother-of-three, living in a trailer while working as a part-time waitress and an occasional
prostitute. Then she became Roseanne Conner, the central character in

a highly rated, critically acclaimed, prime-time television show that radically transformed situation comedy in the United States. For a while, she was Roseanne Arnold: the megalomaniacal, self-deluded wife of marginally talented, coke-fiend husband, Tom. Now, she is simply "Roseanne": too rich, too famous, and too iconic to need a last name. With significant irony, her identity now matches the title of her show even while critics decry how much Roseanne-the-woman has destroyed Roseanne-the-TV-comedy. As one *New York Times* article noted: "Roseanne the celebrity hovers over Roseanne Conner. . . . A character she no longer inhabits in any convincing way. . . . She has strayed so far from what made the show succeed in the first place, she might as well pick up her cash and celebrity and move on."[2] The many dimensions of Roseanne's personae have made her a one-woman Rabelaisian carnival. As a stand-up comic, she invaded a prohibitively male space, appropriated its language, and proclaimed herself a "Domestic Goddess." This transgression was matched by an appearance, an attitude, and a way of speaking that unequivocally defied socially prescribed definitions of how women should behave in public. She swore profusely, she spat, picked her nose, and belched often. Her voice was shrill and raucous. Her attitude was aggressive and angry. She did not even have the decency to be thin, or at least to be ashamed of her socially unacceptable appearance. Moreover, as she flaunted her disregard for feminine niceties, Roseanne used the power she gained from "acting like a man" to articulate the everyday frustration and barely repressed anger of working-class women in the United States. She describes this moment of self-realization in *My Life as a Woman:* "What excited me, finally, was the thought of a woman, any woman, standing up and saying NO. . . . A huge and cosmic "NO" and the first time I went on stage, I felt *myself* say it, and I felt chilled and free and redeemed."[3]

In the following pages, I will examine how Roseanne overcame the economic, psychological, and social repressions that prevent working-class women from expressing themselves in American culture. At the same time, I will show how her fearless projection of her self-identity was countered by the gender and class hierarchies that control the economics of television production, promote the perspectives of ivy-league educated writers, and define the expectations of middle-class American culture.

Fearlessness

Lots of people come up to me and they go, "Roseanne, you're not very feminine." You know what I say to them? Suck my dick.[4]

From Aristotle to Freud, research into gender and comedy has situated women as the objects rather than the perpetrators of jokes. Studies have usually concluded that while women are certainly capable of Jane Austen-style irony, they can never be comedians in a "broad, physical, or butch" stand-up tradition that is controlled by naturalized phallocentric power.[5] In opposition, Frances Gray offers some psychological advice to women who are potential comics. She recommends: "gentle laughter at the phallus . . . [that will] make a new relationship to comic language possible."[6] Significantly, Roseanne's description of her childhood initiation into comedy reflects this suggestion: "I viewed my first male sexual organ. . . . No penis envy; I thought his guts fell out of his vagina. . . . I thought Daddies were the walking wounded and that is why they had to sit around and be pampered and served—because they were handicapped."[7]

This realization provided the impetus for Roseanne's entry into stand-up comedy. Using material written from her experiences as a wife and mother, she performed her act—and was regularly booed offstage—in male-dominated comedy clubs around the Midwest. Despite finding more supportive environments at all-women revue clubs like "The Black Orchid" in Denver, and at feminist gatherings in the Woman-to-Woman bookstore where she worked, Roseanne was not content to perform her act on the margins of a male-centered mainstream. Instead, she wanted to express herself from within the masculinized language of the stand-up tradition. She modeled herself on such comedians as Richard Pryor, who used humor to project an African-American male perspective to audiences that were often aggressively racist. Roseanne was inspired by Pryor's subversion: "I knew that he was inside the stereotype and fighting against it, that he was going to blow it up from the inside. . . . I thought . . . I'm going to do the same thing being a woman."[8]

From this beginning, Roseanne's stand-up routine became an act of feminist subterfuge. She appropriated material from "consummate male comedians," such as Lenny Bruce, and began to reexpress it from her own perspective.[9] Specifically, Bruce would joke that Jackie Kennedy climbed out of the limousine carrying her assassinated husband to "save her own ass." Roseanne reinterpreted the line: "I'm a woman and I know that is not true, she was sitting there next to her husband, saw his brain blown out into the back of the car, and she was only going out there to clean up the mess."[10] With this retelling, Roseanne illustrated the reactions of a woman confined to an everyday housewife mentality despite her Chanel suit. The joke was the centerpiece of an act that, while acknowledging the restrictive effects of traditional female roles, emphasized women's strength in relation to men. The Jackie Kennedy joke was unique, however, in that Roseanne transposed her comic persona onto an upper-class woman. This conflation highlights an antagonism between femininity and working-class identity that was fundamental to Roseanne's comedy.

Roseanne's initiation into public performance began when she took a job as a cocktail waitress at Bennigans, a restaurant-bar in Denver. Bennigans was Roseanne's first stage, a place where she could actively undermine her role as a female service worker. She was supposed to be ingratiating, polite, submissive, and flirtatious with customers in order to receive the tips that she depended on to support her family. Instead, she responded to the come-ons of male customers with "the meanest comebacks imaginable."[11] At the same time, she refused to submit to the demands of the people she was waiting on. She overcharged on a regular basis, took food from customers' plates, and "forgot" to give change. Ironically, because her aggressive actions were so blatant, customers found them amusing. They assumed, since Roseanne was a working-class woman and therefore not entitled to express herself forcefully in public, that her defiant behavior must have been an act staged for their consumption. In keeping with the reactions of her "audience," Roseanne considered Bennigans to be the first place that she "*really* felt like a star."[12] By transforming her self-identity into a comic performance, Roseanne's existence was validated in a culture where working-class female experiences were otherwise silenced. Roseanne acknowledges this paradox, without irony, in *My Life as a Woman*, noting that Bennigans was the only place where she felt entitled "to tell the truth about my life—because I couldn't tell the truth off the stage."[13]

As a stand-up comedian, Roseanne learned to speak through the male-centered discourses of humor and public performance, and found ways to articulate a self-consciously female perspective. She describes this process as a negotiation within a narrative that was "sad, angry, misogynistic, defiant, misogynistic, titillating, almost obscene and misogynistic."[14] Furthermore, because she was also working-class, she mediated her performance to fit cultural expectations that defined her subjectivity from a middle-class as well as male point of view. Reflecting this double bind, Roseanne was advised to lose forty pounds, to wear clothes that disguised her large body, and to act "more like a lady." She was also pressured to conform to a stereotypical image of working-class identity. After a successful performance at the prestigious "Comedy Store" in Los Angeles, for example, owner Mitzi Shore suggested that Roseanne wear "overalls because yours is kind of a farm-act anyway."[15]

By the time she appeared on the *Tonight Show* in 1985, the distinction between performance and self-expression had been irrevocably obscured. Critical responses such as John Lahr's in the *New Yorker* emphasized the five years Roseanne had spent perfecting the "ungrammatical syntax" and "affectless" mannerisms of her "trailer trash" character.[16] Reflecting this reaction, Roseanne's act included elements of self-parody and ironic references to the "Willie Nelson, jumper cables, cinder blocks, beans and weenies" lifestyle that signifies white working-class culture in the United States.[17] Nevertheless, Lahr's patronizing description of Roseanne's appearance—"a bulky five feet four, in flats and black slacks, with a gardenia corsage pinned to her black-and-orange jacket. She chewed gum and smiled"[18]—also articulates the middle-class perspective that prevented Roseanne from expressing herself when she was not performing. The exclusive effects of this socially inscribed attitude are given resonance in an incident from *My Life as a Woman*. Roseanne recalled leaving a Lily Tomlin show at a New York theater because she was dressed inappropriately. Wearing a black silk dress and rhinestones while everyone else was wearing jeans, Roseanne asked her sister Geraldine a rhetorical question: "Why must we always be . . . doing or dressing or saying the wrong stuff in an effort to rise above our class?"[19] The pathos of this incident highlights a process of articulation and repression that culminated in the *Tonight Show* performance. Television success provided Roseanne with an arena for fearless self-expression. At the same time, the cost of mainstream acceptance was the circumscription and restriction of her self-identity. This dichotomy was fundamental to the success of the *Roseanne* show.

Fear

In a famous episode of *I Love Lucy*, Lucy and Ethel swap roles with their husbands for one week. While Ricky and Fred contend with household chores, the women find employment on a chocolate factory production line. In an acclaimed scene, Lucy struggles to keep up with a silent and inexpressive woman worker. Lucy's incompetence is emphasized by the woman's mechanic—almost robotic—dexterity. Eventually, Lucy becomes overwhelmed by the assembly line and begins throwing chocolates around, spilling them on the ground, and stuffing them in her mouth. As all manner of visual comedy ensues, the scene ends when Lucy hits the woman worker over the head. The woman who performed the role of the worker in this episode was not an actor, but a real chocolate factory production line employee. Evidently, she did not find the episode amusing, and objected to how hard Lucy hit her in the final take.[20] Despite her personal annoyance, however, the woman's silent subjection to the routine of the production line draws attention to Lucy's animation, to her independence, and to her ability to express herself in ways the woman worker cannot comprehend. Representations of working-class women in situation comedy extended from this apparently innocuous scene until the *Roseanne* show first aired in 1988.

Roseanne Conner—the central character of the *Roseanne* show— worked on a production line in a plastic factory with her sister, Jackie, and her friend Crystal. Undermining the juxtaposition in *I Love Lucy*, however, these factory workers hardly ever submit to the dehumanizing routine of their jobs. Despite miserable work conditions, low pay, oppressive time and motion studies, and a series of ignorant and arrogant managers, Roseanne Conner consistently finds ways not to work. Her humor and her self-defiance confuse and disrupt the factory routine. Moreover, her refusal to participate in the production process refutes the implication of the *I Love Lucy* scene: that this work holds any social, economic, or psychological value for the person performing it. In direct contrast to *I Love Lucy*, Roseanne Conner's nonconformity challenges the viewer to admit the creative potential and self-expressive power of working-class women. As a result, the *Roseanne* show constructed a representative space within American popular culture that had previously been ignored.

From this radical position, Roseanne Conner disrupted the traditional narratives of situation comedy by drawing attention to the discrepancy between cultural representation and lived experience. In doing this, Roseanne Conner occasionally referred to sitcom images of housewifely perfection that she could not live up to. Faced with a pile of dirty dishes or an untidy living room, for example, she nodded her head or wiggled her nose, hoping for the kind of instant fix that only a genie or a witch could provide. This self-conscious referral to the distance between "real life" and "television" was fundamental to the success of the *Roseanne* show. In particular, John Lahr notes that its radicalism depended on "a message [that] flies in the face of the vision of consumer contentment conjured up by the show's advertisers."[21] Similarly, Kathleen Rowe contends that the *Roseanne* show also reveals the "realities of working-class family life in the 80s and 90s," in opposition to "the ideals of the New Left and Women's Movements of the 60s and 70s."[22] These interpretations suggest that both mainstream and progressive politics have failed to include the perspectives or express the concerns of working-class women. In this respect, the *Roseanne* show represents what is unrepresentable in American culture. Nevertheless, these optimistic analyses seem to forget that the *Roseanne* show is not "reality" but situation comedy, and therefore that its depiction of working-class female identity is predetermined by the economic, social, and ideological contexts that are fundamental to the production of American popular culture. Consequently, while Roseanne Conner is unprecedented as a television character, she must also ultimately conform to a stereotypical, one-dimensional image of working-class female identity. These culturally inscribed prejudices are highlighted by the narrow ways that the *Roseanne* show has been analyzed by critics who claim to be politically sympathetic to the class and gender issues raised in the story lines.

Even the admirers of the *Roseanne* show have focused intently on the radical potential of Roseanne Conner's body. According to this perspective, her unashamed obesity marks out the physical terrain of working-class female identity in comparison with popular representations of svelte middle-class women. Consequently, Roseanne Conner's size becomes a powerful statement in a culture where nutrition plans and health club memberships are emblematic of the disposability of one's time and money. The critical attention paid to Roseanne Conner's weight is enhanced by a parallel interest in her loudness. John Lahr notes that Roseanne Conner's "voice precedes her, and, like her body, it takes up space."[23] This volume is taken to be another positive proclamation of working-class female identity in a middle-class culture used to more reasonable tones. Compounding this point, Kathleen Rowe suggests that the unfettered yelling in a typical episode of the *Roseanne* show emphasizes the silent absence of working-class women's voices in American culture. Her conclusion that "voices that are not meant to be heard are perceived as loud once they do speak,"[24] is expanded by Roseanne's response: "I just talk louder, and I'm heard."[25]

While superficially supportive, critical concentration on Roseanne Conner's weight and shrillness also compounds the ways in which working-class female identity and self-expression are repressed and marginalized in American culture. From this perspective, a working-class woman can be portrayed on television as sarcastic, defiant, and occasionally insightful, as long as she is also fat and loudmouthed. In the same way, the Conner family can be situated outside the economies of the commercials that frame each episode, as long as they are also seen to aspire to the ideals and values represented in these advertisements. In this way, the radical potential that Roseanne Conner displays as a working-class woman is undercut within a context shaped by economic conservatism. As a result, her capacity for expressing working-class female identity as complex and multidimensional is restricted by an image that ultimately conforms to the stereotypical expectations of a middle-class point of view.

John Lahr suggests that Roseanne Conner's "body . . . and her unladylike talk make her America's bourgeois nightmare come to life."[26] On the contrary, I would suggest that these signifiers of working-class female identity are the very things that make the *Roseanne* show comfortable viewing from a middle-class perspective. Roseanne Conner is not scary because her capacity for self-expression is contained within the reactionary narratives of situation comedy. Tellingly, Roseanne's public image apart from Roseanne Conner is suppressed in the same way. Consequently, although Eric Gilliland, head writer at the *Roseanne* show, is palpably scared of Roseanne—whom he describes as "daunting"—he takes refuge by preferring Roseanne Conner who is "more lovable and wise."[27] Producers Marcy Carsey and Tom Werner are similarly motivated as they hide in their offices while the *Roseanne* show is taped. Their condescending explanation is revealing: "We thought that Roseanne was acting out against authority. . . . So we thought, like the good parents we sometimes are, that when someone is acting out like that, you stay away for a while."[28] Carsey-Werner assert their power as cultural producers by allowing Roseanne to test the boundaries of Roseanne Conner's character, but they expect her eventually to conform to the image they control. Their fear of Roseanne is dissipated by their knowledge that her social impact and her powers of self-expression are limited by a one-dimensional representation of working-class female identity.

In contexts beyond situation comedy, the reflexive fear that is directed toward Roseanne's public persona is even more revealing of the cultural biases that actively marginalize complex representations of working-class women. Specifically, when Roseanne was invited to guest edit a special "women's issue" of the *New Yorker*, a number of writers resigned in disgust. Typical reactions confirmed the impression that Roseanne was a crass, unsophisticated television star who could not possibly understand the import of intellectual writing. More telling, however, was an article that was intended as a sympathetic portrait. In a lengthy piece, John Lahr successfully repudiates the knee-jerk reactions of his colleagues, and suggests that there is more to Roseanne than the white trash character presented in supermarket tabloids. The article sets out the complex paradoxes of her childhood and discusses the impact of her stand-up comedy and its relation to the *Roseanne* show. Nevertheless, even as Lahr acknowledges Roseanne's talents, he simultaneously confines her to a cultural space that is outside the intellectual sophistication, emotional depth, rational understanding, and creative capacities of *New Yorker* readers. From this perspective, "Dealing with Roseanne" simply means middle-class audiences should learn to appreciate what is funny abut Roseanne Conner. It does not mean that Roseanne herself is a complex, multidimensional individual, or that her experiences as a working-class woman have any significance beyond the context that Lahr carefully sets out for her: "Only a walking distance from her soundstage. . . . Is the America [she] speaks for: McDonalds, Winchell's dough-nuts, Blockbuster video, and Du-Par's Restaurant ("Breakfast Served All Day"), where waitresses stand on sore feet and make wisecracks."[29]

Roseanne's route to personal wealth and public notoriety has been "a process of unbecoming."[30] In order for her point of view to be heard, she has had to deconstruct and mediate her identity to fit an image that is ultimately repressive and self-fulfilling. In this respect, the final season of the *Roseanne* show was perfectly apt. The Conner family won the Illinois State lottery, allowing Roseanne Conner to achieve a life of wealth and riches that matched Roseanne's. In an apparent capitulation to the cultural mechanisms that prevented Roseanne from expressing her self-identity beyond the narratives of her television show, Roseanne Conner's fate was portrayed as predetermined in a way that confirmed her disempowerment as an individual working-class woman. In the final episode, however, an audaciously tacky, but nonetheless revealing twist was enacted. In voice-over, Roseanne Conner explained how the lottery win was a fantasy she created as a way of coping with her husband's death at the end of the penultimate season. She also explains how the nine seasons of the *Roseanne* show were a figment of her powerful imagination. This subversive assertion is emphasized by an authoritative narrative technique through which Roseanne's voice combines with Roseanne Conner's to express a creative identity that she explicitly and defiantly describes as female and working-class.

The conclusion of the *Roseanne* show was predictably ridiculed as a "pretentious finale" to a "misbegotten season" that deserved to be "clobbered in the ratings" by an especially touching episode of *Mad about You*.[31] This failed attempt to exert Roseanne Conner's individuality as a working-class woman highlights a defining irony that recalls a past image of Roseanne practicing her stand-up routine in her trailer park home. Her husband had made a mike stand from a wooden box and a broom handle. As she rehearsed the routine that was to become her fearsome stand-up act, Roseanne's husband recalled her "messianic sense of calling." In words that prophetically allude to an economic, social, and cultural process that will systematically deconstruct her self-expressive power, Roseanne remembered her determination was "like somebody saying they're gonna win the lottery."[32]

Notes

1. Roseanne Barr, *Roseanne: My Life as a Woman* (New York: Harper and Row, 1989), 37.

2. Caryn James, " 'Roseanne' Ends Class Act: Blue-Collar Issues Fed 9-Year Show," *New York Times* News Service, 20 May 1997.

3. Barr, *My Life as a Woman,* 152.

4. Rocco Urbisci, *The Roseanne Barr Show,* 60 min., HBO Home Video Comedy Club (1987), videocassette.

5. Frances Gray, *Women and Laughter* (Charlottesville: University of Virginia Press, 1994), 21.

6. Ibid., 36.

7. Barr, *My Life as a Woman,* 6.

8. John Lahr, "Dealing with Roseanne," *New Yorker,* 17 July 1995, 45.

9. Barr, *My Life as a Woman,* 176.

10. Ibid., 177.

11. Lahr, "Dealing with Roseanne," 46.

12. Barr, *My Life as a Woman,* 166.

13. Lahr, "Dealing with Roseanne," 46.

14. Barr, *My Life as a Woman,* 147.

15. Ibid., 183.

16. Lahr, "Dealing with Roseanne," 42.

17. *Roseanne Barr Show* (1987), videocassette.

18. Lahr, "Dealing with Roseanne," 42.

19. Barr, *My Life as a Woman,* 71.

20. Gray, *Women and Laughter,* 52.

21. Lahr, "Dealing with Roseanne," 51.

22. Kathleen Rowe, "Roseanne: Unruly Woman as Domestic Goddess," *Screen* 31, no 4 (winter 1990): 411.

23. Lahr, "Dealing with Roseanne," 54.

24. Rowe, "Unruly Woman as Domestic Goddess," 413.

25. Lahr, "Dealing with Roseanne," 45.

26. Ibid., 42.

27. Ibid., 54.

28. Ibid., 48.

29. Ibid., 48.

30. Sian Mile, "Roseanne Barr: Canned Laughter—Continuing the Subject," in Regina Barreca, ed., *New Perspectives on Women and Comedy* (Philadelphia, Pa.: Gordon and Breach, 1992), 85.

31. Greg Braxton, "Is the Bloom off 'Roseanne'?" *Los Angeles Times,* 19 November 1996.

32. Lahr, "Dealing with Roseanne," 50.

Hog Wars and Pig Politics

Richard P. Horwitz

Our hog farm consisted of 30 sows, so anything over 100
sows, I thought was big. Then I hear these people talking
about thousands of sows. It just blew my mind. Two
nights later we had a meeting and organized opposition,
and we've been going ever since.—Martha Stevens,
co-founder of Partners in Progress[1]

It's kind of an axiom: "What's good for the pigs is good
for the people."—Terry Coffey, head of research and
development for Murphy Farms Inc.[2]

$Oink, $Oink
—Title of an article in *Forbes* on the rapid growth of
Smithfield Foods[3]

For most of the past two decades I have worked two jobs—one full-time
as a professor of American studies and the other part-time as a hired
hand on a hog/grain/cattle farm of more than 2,000 acres near my
home in southeast Iowa. The original attraction in this mix of figurative
and literal manure was the chance to stay in touch with neighbors and
to get some exercise outdoors. But, as it turns out, the commute also
afforded me an opportunity to understand how pigs might provide much
more than midlife salve or a target for silly signifiers like Arnold Ziffel
or Miss Piggy.

During the last couple of decades of the twentieth century, pigs—
the genuine article—actually grabbed some headlines, even outside the
American Swine Belt. In the spring of 1995, for example, they set
the tone for a visit to Iowa by the president of the United States. Iowa
may be the capital of things swinely, but it is normally a flyover state for
leaders of the Free World. Something powerful must have been afoot.

The obvious even if unstated purpose of the president's visit was far
from porcine. Bill Clinton was shooting for enough profile points and
then slam dunks in local caucuses to wow potential contributors to
his 1996 reelection campaign. Iowans are accustomed to hosting such
warmup games every four years. But the excuse for this particular

spectacle was agricultural. He was to lend luster to the opening ceremony of yet another Iowa State University conference on rural life. American policy makers often use such functions to pose as principled, and academics as real-worldly. This one, with its furrowed backdrop, would be especially propitious for the populist pose. He could wax quotably about rugged individuals, the heartland, and other pastoral pieties. Orators have done so since the days of Thomas Jefferson and continued well after most Americans—among them, most Iowans—moved to town and took jobs behind a counter or a desk. But there was reason to worry that this president's photo opportunity might get testy, and the cause was resolutely porcine.

The president would be met, everyone knew, by protesters rallying to protect "family hog farmers" from "vertical integrators," the large, high-tech, multinational operations that took over poultry in the 1970s and that in the 1980s and 1990s set their sights on pigs. With statutes that are perennially reconsidered, the state of Iowa, like other states on the Plains, has long been hospitable to family farms (which diversify by raising animals as well as crops) and relatively inhospitable to factory farms (which diversify by trading grain futures, patents, and packing plants). Citizens were squared off, for and against change to accommodate "the big guys" of pork production. Hence, otherwise calming clichés about yeomen or imagery drawn from *Little House* could turn incendiary. Iowa senator Tom Harkin did his best to chill the crowd, introducing the president with a joke: "No one should be allowed to be president, if they don't understand hogs." Most everyone laughed, though likely for varied reasons.[4]

The tension that Harkin diffused was about the fate of actual animals and their caretakers, but even then they were cast as instruments of symbolic aerial warfare. Rather than evaluating the qualities of particular changes in pork production, people tended to line up on one side or the other of a single, exaggerated divide. From my vantage point, their arguments, which began in the late 1980s and persisted through the '90s, shed about as much light on farming as the World Wrestling Federation sheds on wrestling. Both mainly provided an occasion for a chorus of cheers or jeers as stereotypes were body slammed.

Even when combatants met face-to-face, as they often did (not just in court) to work on their differences, depressingly predictable exchanges would ensue. In 1994, for example, with great fanfare the governor and some state representatives organized a public hearing in Creston, Iowa, where passions were running dangerously high. I was pleased that elected officials were trying to lead Creston back from the brink of blood feud to common interests, if not common sense. But proponents and opponents of corporate hog farming (a.k.a. "progressive producers"/"thieves in the night") seemed only to agree that they could not agree. They lined up on two sides of the room and spent the balance of the session trading invective.[5]

In substance, the divide in most of these disputes resembled that between the "cultural right" and "left" that I already found tiresome in my job at the university. I had hoped to find on the farm some respite from the "culture wars," as presidential aspirant Pat Buchanan dubbed them, of late-twentieth-century America. But allied forces tussled around the hog lot as furiously as they did around the ivory tower. The ammunition was standard-bore.[6]

On one side, you could hear the measured tones of manly "realism." People recall an inspiring past when—distinctly, supposedly—the best Americans (in this case, hog farmers) had the maturity to meet harsh challenges for the benefit of us all. The old days were great, though more in spirit than substance. (Who would want to go back to sod huts and bouts with yellow fever?) A reinvigorated, don't-look-back enterprising spirit will continue to yield bigger and better things, as it always has, and help inspire confidence to face changes that, like it or not, the real world demands. Make way for the big guys.

On the other side, the tone is more "populist" or "progressive." Underdogs or their self-appointed protectors see a less salutary "reality." The past requires pruning for style as well as substance. The first branches to lop are those whose fruits include pollution, arrogance, and injustice for most people and incontestable betterment only for a narrow elite. Hope might best come in restraining consumption and in better distinguishing the short-term interests of robber barons from the long-term interests of the public, the planet, and generations to come. Just say, "Whoa!"[7]

These are familiar and, for many of us in academics, even tedious battle lines. Back-pew arguments and letters to the editor of Swine Belt newspapers resemble the dialogue you might expect, say, between Jesse Helms and bell hooks or the Heritage Foundation and the Brookings Institute.[8] The realist line is most visible in feature stories or editorials facing farrowing-house flooring and dewormer ads in hog trade periodicals. The progressive line is more likely found amid ads for New Age music or radical wear in the Soho or college-town press. For example, after a good deal of success exposing cruelty in veal-calf operations, the Humane Farming Association launched a "campaign against factory farming" from its office suite in San Francisco. The more mainstream press, of course, opted for "balance" of the on-the-one-hand/but-on-the-other variety, as if wisdom lay in fifty-fifty doses of resignation and reform, the journalistic equivalent of Solomonic justice.[9]

But even the mainstream press gave voice to Chicken Little. When, for example, *Time* magazine covered the hog wars in its "Business" section, the story began:

> Colorado farmers Galen Travis and Jim Dober have seen the future, and it stinks. . . . From Colorado to the Carolinas, enterprising growers like [Ronald] Houser and agribusiness giants such as Cargill and Continental Grain are building such livestock factories to mass-produce hogs for packers like Hormel Foods and John Morrell. . . . The vast livestock factories are a long way from the here-a-pig, there-a-pig operations of traditional farms.

Note the forced choice between the Eden of yore and hell 'round the bend. Moreover, the invoked "tradition" only makes sense if your ag experience has been pretty much limited to summer camp choruses of "Old MacDonald Had a Farm." There have been precious few here-and-there-a-pig operations in the United States (next to none capable of supporting a family) for at least a quarter of a century. The choice seems to loom so large in part because the past has been so heavily airbrushed. And the integrators who lead "the march of commerce" are dressed in jackboots:

> Megafarms . . . turn out pigs as if they were piggy banks from football field-length buildings, where the animals are confined to small pens, fed, medicated and monitored with an exacting precision that fattens them to 265 lbs. in six months. . . . [These] porkopolises [are] multiplying like rabbits.

Of course, *Time* does offer some information here that is worth crediting. Modern hog buildings are, in fact, large, often even larger than football fields. Cargill and Continental Grain (though neither Hormel nor Morrell) have been among the key players, as they have been in just about every scrap of food grown, shipped, or processed since World War II. Yes, pigs reach their market weight in six months, but they have been doing so (give or take a couple of weeks) for decades. And animals are confined, fed, and medicated with increasing precision. But are we to gather that their care should be *less* exacting? Is the choice simply between the singular purity of what has been and the stink of what is coming? To hear *Time* tell it, at issue for citizens is nothing less than "a mechanized assault on their way of life."[10]

Such a background of hyperbole may help explain popular acceptance of hallucinatory scenes like the one that opened the film *Babe*. With *film noir* lighting and camera angles, viewers get the impression that Babe, the piglet, was rescued from a state-of-the-art operation that could pass for Treblinka under the *Schutzstaffel*. Sows, we are told, are routinely yanked from their suckling young (who are instead nursed by robots), marched onto pen-side semis, and hauled to slaughter. Only through homespun miracles can Babe live out his/her days with a family that, we are to believe, can make it on home canning and pasturing a couple of dozen sheep (who, incidentally, never go to market).

"Big deal," you might counter. A business story in *Time* or a Hollywood movie (for children, no less) can only be expected to bloat its plot, given a distractible audience. But plots are also distended in otherwise staid periodicals. Look, for example, at the way the topic was covered in a 1996 issue of *U.S. News and World Report*, not in its "Business" section, but in "Culture and Ideas" under the title, "Hog Heaven—and Hell." The story begins with a stock journalistic hook. An innocent (just like you, reader) vaguely recognizes a foul omen. In this case, that innocent is retired farmer Sidney Whaley, who for months forebears "the nauseating odor and clouds of flies from 1200 pigs" on a big guy's farm upwind, Onslow County, North Carolina. Whaley patiently rocks behind closed doors and windows, waiting for a response to letters that he has sent, politely requesting relief from government regulators. He is a model citizen. And then the omen proves prophetic. On 21 June 1995,

> After heavy rains, some twenty-five million gallons of feces and urine flushed from the buildings where the pigs were confined, burst out of the farm's eight-acre waste lagoon. The reddish-brown tide, more than twice the volume of oil spilled by the Exxon Valdez, poured knee deep for two hours across the highway between Whaley's red-brick bungalow and the First Church of God.[11]

Even in the sugar-free, low-sodium prose that is *U.S. News* cuisine, Whaley becomes Job, and his suffering a signal from the Lord.

Actually, churches were receiving prophecy from the hog house well before Onslow County's Armageddon. Back in November 1994, for example, an ecumenical throng gathered at St. Augustine's Church in Des Moines to witness testimony under the title: "Community, Church and Large-Scale Hog Production." The list of speakers was a *Who's Who* of rural activism. Their names dotted front-page stories through the 1980s and 1990s. They were progressives—Methodist, Baptist, Catholic, and academic-agnostic.

Although I could not attend (I had to teach that day), I did buy four hours on videotape and got on their mailing list. And I could not avoid laughing with the participants about the unlikely title of the conference and session subtitles such as "The Theology of Hog Confinement." But these were also people who had to be admired. They were soft-spoken and compassionate, obviously sincere, self-sacrificing, and committed to social justice. Many of them had been drawn into "the battle" by personal experience, growing up in a loving farm family that suffered greatly in prior farm crises. Key institutional participants included the National Catholic Rural Life Conference, which began with the great farm depression in 1923, and Prairie Fire Rural Action, which formed in the foreclosure epidemic of 1985, a period of transformation for many of those in attendance.

Moreover, I greatly admired the savvy coalitions that they were able to build. Several conferees were influential in the self-designated "Citizens' Task Force on Livestock Concentration." Their report, including detailed legislative and regulatory recommendations, was endorsed by an amazingly large and diverse set of interests, ranging from the Diocese of Sioux City to the Iowa AFL and the Sierra Club. It was a model of good sense in countering the governor's version, which was more in-house and accommodative, less a grassroots, leadership affair.

We may not agree that the Lord has chosen to speak through hogs or that your average Midwestern farmer fits among the suffering meek of the world, akin to Mozambique refugees. I, for one, have a hard time restraining my cynicism when clerics put modern farmers at the head of a lineage stretching straight from Jehovah through Isaiah, Jesus, and Thomas Jefferson. They neglect to mention, for example, that the humble farm "community" to which Jefferson belonged was itself a model of vertical integration. And its meek were chattel slaves.

But, quibbling aside, it is hard to resist a clincher moral: "Hey, how many executives of ag multinationals (versus family farmers) live next door to the huge hog barns and manure lagoons they are building? And if they will not, why do they feel entitled to stick them next to someone else?" It is, populists justly insist, a violation of the Golden Rule.

In general, I share their suspicion of high technology, monopoly capital, and rapid change, especially when the profits are so much more visible in suburban office parks than in the countryside or the city. I share their affection for neighborliness, greenery, and agricultural diversity, which I, too, have lived with for most of my life. But my experience with "empowered local communities" has been less inspiring. After all, if locals really had their way, most of the people who plant cotton and rice in the United States would still be slaves, and my immigrant ancestors would likely still be living (or, even more likely, slaughtered) "back where they belong." Rural populists, in particular, have consistently included some of the most vicious bigots in American history. Every time commodity prices take a dip, the grassroots are ablaze with conspiratorial fantasies about Russian or Mexican intrigue and Jewish bankers. Thank goodness, cosmopolites have been willing and able to check some of the ugliest of agrarian impulses.[12] That which is traditional, family, local, and small cannot be so simply set against that which is new, corporate, distant, and large, like catechismic poles, Good and Evil.

This recognition has fueled my determination to parse and evaluate more pointedly the charges and countercharges that arise whenever people get to talking about hogs these days. The commonplace practicalities of "pig production" and pork consumption attract conflicted environmental, social, technical, and spiritual alliances. The issues around which they ally can be very complex, each with its own cadre of specialists who have much to say, surely more than I could adequately cover here. But they deserve sustained, critical—even presidential—attention. The idea is to connect abstractions that pass for "culture" more precisely to circumstances on the ground, and vice versa.[13]

Notes

1. Patty Cantrell, "Is the Family Farm an Endangered Species?" *Ms.*, March/April 1997, 33. *Ms.* readers learn pig politics through the achievements of Martha Stevens, a family farmer and activist from Missouri. Cantrell associates Stevens's passion with "one of her spiritual 'mentors,' Susan B. Anthony, whose image hangs on a shiny medallion around her neck." Prompted by giant new hog operations, courtesy of Continental Grain, thirty miles from her farm in Hatfield, Stevens and a retired schoolteacher, Velda Smith, joined with outraged neighbors to found Partners in Progress, which through the Missouri Rural Crisis Center is affiliated with the National Campaign for Family Farms and the Environment. Cantrell credits Smith and Stevens for having "taken up unpaid positions in the hog wars" (34).

2. Jim Barnett, "Raising a Stink," *Raleigh News and Observer,* 18 July 1993, 10A.

3. The article centers on the success of Smithfield's CEO, Joseph Luter III, who had at that time acquired stock worth $47 million; see Rita Koselka, "$Oink, $Oink," *Forbes*, 3 February 1992, 54–56.

4. Photo caption, *Daily Iowan*, 25 April 1995, 1. Harkin's quip is a standard one in the hog trade, prominently featured among the trivia that NPPC puts in its publicity and credits to former president Harry Truman. In fact, I suspect that Harkin got the quotation from the NPPC, if only because it was otherwise so hard to find. I was unable to find it in any primary

or secondary sources in the university library. Staff whom I asked at the Truman Presidential Library were similarly stumped, and Harkin's staff never responded to my request for sources.

I refer here to the *Little House on the Prairie* books and TV series because they are among the strongest and most popular evocations of "family farming"—self-reliant, intimate, independent. Their image is doubly misleading, not only because they fictionalize the memoirs of Laura Ingalls Wilder, but also because her daughter, Rose Wilder Lane, so revised the memoirs to harmonize with her profound disaffection for New Deal programs. Linda Kerber, "Women and Individualism in American History," *The Massachusetts Review* 30 (winter 1989): 604–5; Stephanie Coontz, *The Way We Never Were: American Families and the Nostalgia Trap* (New York: Basic Books, 1992), 168–76.

5. "Task Force Dragged into Fierce Creston Debate about Hog Lots," *Iowa City Press-Citizen*, 10 September 1994, 5B.

6. See, for example, Cantrell, "Is the Family Farm an Endangered Species?" 33–37.

7. The words "populist" and "progressive," of course, have unique and quite specific referents in American history, especially when capitalized (as in, the Populist or People's Party, which in 1896 endorsed the presidential candidacy of William Jennings Bryan and the Progressive Party, associated with the presidential aspirations of Theodore Roosevelt and then Robert La Follette, 1912–24). I here use them much more loosely and, hence, pretty interchangeably. I generally prefer "populist" to connote a rural, blue-collar, backward-looking, or demagogic quality and "progressive" for a more urbane, bourgeois and hip, forward-looking, or utopian one. But I use both to signal opposition to corporate domination, presumably in defense of humbler folk. Jeff Zimmerman, an epidemiologist at the College of Veterinary Medicine at Iowa State University, provided an example of this usage, as we got to talking about vertical integration: "I have a lot of conflict with it myself because, in the larger sense, I'm a populist. I believe that what works best for society is if everybody owns a piece of the rock. If one guy owns the rock and if everybody else is just working there . . . I don't think it makes for a good society. So, I understand all about efficiency and all the wonderful words you hear, but I think we have a healthier society with a lot of small, independent operators. And whether that's farming or whether it's business, I think it's best," Jeff Zimmerman, interview by author, Ames, Iowa, 3 June 1993.

8. Michael G. Kammen, *Mystic Chords of Memory: The Transformation of Tradition in American Culture* (New York: Knopf, 1991). For a tiny sampler from generals in the 1990s culture wars, see: Roger Kimball, *Tenured Radicals: How Politics Has Corrupted Our Higher Education* (New York: Harper and Row, 1990); bell hooks and Cornel West, *Breaking Bread: Insurgent Black Intellectual Life* (Boston, Mass.: South End Press, 1991); E. D. Hirsch, Jr., *Cultural Literacy: What Every American Needs to Know* (Bos-

ton, Mass.: Houghton Mifflin, 1987); and Henry Louis Gates, Jr., "The Weaning of America," *New Yorker*, 19 April 1993, 113–17.

9. For a nice example of "realism" in the hog trade magazines see the special issue of *National Hog Farmer* (15 May 1994), which was heavily dedicated to the boom outside the Swine Belt and heroic adaptations in the Midwest. For a counterexample in the populist mode, see the press releases from the Humane Farming Association or Lenor Yarger, "Iowa's Hog Hell," *Icon*, 25 January 1996, 4–5, which is based almost entirely on the testimony of Sharon and Ken Petrone, who had long been involved in. organizing to stop vertical integrators in Iowa. See also the "Boss Hog" exposé that first appeared in the [Raleigh, North Carolina] *News and Observer* (19–26 February 1995) and was then posted on the World Wide Web, (http://www.nando.net/sproject/hogs/hoghome.htm) and widely cited elsewhere. Ronald Smothers, "Slopping the Hogs, the Assembly-Line Way," *New York Times*, 30 January 1995, 8A. Journalists touting balance used titles like "Huge Hog Farms Mean Big Dollars, and Foul Odors." For example, the "Business and Farm Section" of the *Waterloo* [Iowa] *Courier* organized a whole series of articles by staff writers under the banner, "Hogging the Market: Are Giant Pork-Producing Farms the Way of the Future for Iowa or Just a Big, Smelly Mess?" *Waterloo Courier*, 17 April 1994, B1, B4. See also Jay P. Wagner, "A Big Year for Agriculture: Stories That Made Headlines on the Farm Pages," *Des Moines Sunday Register*, 1 January 1995) 1J.

10. John Greenwald, "Hogging the Table," *Time*, 18 March 1996, 76. Note also that the name "Porkopolis" was originally coined to refer to the city of Cincinnati because of its packers, not farms. The author apparently collected his most alarming tales from a "Hog Summit" which featured such environmentalists as Nancy Thompson (staff attorney for the Center for Rural Affairs in Walthill, Nebraska), Carla Smalts (Oklahoma "farm wife" who is a leader of legal and grassroots actions against hog expansion), and the Alliance Conserving Tomorrow.

11. Michael Satchell, "Hog Heaven—and Hell," *U.S. News and World Report*, 22 January 1996, 55.

12. "Churches and Hogs," *Des Moines Sunday Register*, 27 November 1994, 3J. I purchased the videotapes, also titled "Community, Church and Large-Scale Hog Production: Theology and Resolution of Hog Production Conflicts in Rural Communities," Church Land Project, Des Moines, Iowa. According to CLP, 130 people registered. *Church Farmland News* 4, no. 3 (April 1995): 2. Among the main speakers were Rev. Jerry Avise-Rouse (Mt. Ayr Larger United Methodist Church, Mt. Ayr, Iowa), Rev. Gil Dawes and Barb Grabner (Prairie Fire Rural Action), Bernard Evans (St. John's University), William Heffernan (Department of Rural Sociology, University of Missouri), Carmen Lampe (First Baptist Church, Mt. Ayr, Iowa), Barb Mathias (Iowa Council for International Understanding), Barbara Ross (Diocese of Jefferson City, Mo.), Mark Schultz (Land Steward-

ship Project, St. Paul, Minn.), Denise Turner (Christian Church, Trenton, Mo.). Citizens' Task Force on Livestock Concentration, *A Citizens Report: Recommendations for the 1995 Iowa Legislature on Concentrated Livestock Production,* 12 October 1994. "Profit Is Only Motive for Some Forms of Ag," *The Bishop's Bulletin,* January 1995, 7.

In viewing the videotape, I was put off by glib contrasts of "family farms" and "corporations," as if their members had different access to God. CEOs were accused of breaking covenants, in the manner of Jerusalem elites starving Palestinians in the eighth century B.C. (Isaiah 5:7–10). It is one thing to say you disagree with people; it is another to presume that there are only two sides, and yours is God's. Furthermore, despite all the talk of leading the downtrodden, by my count, there was only one name on the list of conference registrants that was not Anglo-Saxon, and it was mine. Such quasi-Aryan solidarity plus their awfully easy equation of morality with Christianity made me glad I was absent. "When I say 'we,' I mean the Church. . . . All of us are Christian," a convener announced. For this occasion, ecumenicism meant Catholics and Protestants allying to root out moneyed interests, a solidarity that cannot be very reassuring for a Jew. I do not mean to say that these members of the clergy or their allies were bigots or that they were utterly insensitive to the possibility of abuse. Prairie Fire is to be particularly complimented for its efforts to stop the "Jewish banker" rumors during the 1980s' ag crisis. But my background as a Jew and knowledge of the history of rural populism does leave me wary. I tend to see rural folk both as both more sensible than your average academic and more likely to hang you from the nearest tree. See "Profit Is Only Motive," 7.

Recall that Tom Watson, Huey Long, and other champions of the little guy also pampered racists. On bigotry and its role in U.S. populism in general, see John Higham, *Strangers in the Land: Patterns of American Nativism, 1860–1925* (New Brunswick, N.J.: Rutgers University Press, 1988); V. O. Key, *Southern Politics in State and Nation,* 2nd ed. (Knoxville: University of Tennessee Press, 1984); Catherine McNicol Stock, *Rural Radicals: Righteous Rage in the American Grain* (Ithaca, N.Y.: Cornell University Press, 1996); Walter T. K. Nugent, *The Tolerant Populists: Kansas Populism and Nativism* (Chicago, Ill.: University of Chicago Press, 1963); Jeffrey Ostler, "The Rhetoric of Conspiracy and the Formation of Kansas Populism," *Agriculture History* 69 (winter 1995): 1–27; Jeffrey Ostler, "Why the Populists Party Was Strong in Kansas and Nebraska but Weak in Iowa," *Western History Quarterly* 23 (November 1992): 451–74; and C. Vann Woodward, *Tom Watson: Agrarian Rebel* (London: Oxford University Press, 1938). Historians and political scientists have long debated the relative importance of nativism among rural progressives before the Great Depression. Woodward and Nugent, for example, nicely parse the extremes. Whether fundamental in the grass roots or superficial in the posture of a few leaders, white supremacy, xenophobia, anti-Catholicism, and anti-

Semitism were undeniably evident in otherwise progressive movements through the late nineteenth and early twentieth centuries in the United States. Armed compounds in the Utah or Texas outback—uniformly celebrating the "little guy" and his adamantly Northern European and Protestant lineage—show those connections remain strong today. Chip Berlet and Matthew N. Lyons, *Too Close for Comfort: Right-Wing Populism, Scapegoating, and Fascist Potentials in U.S. Political Traditions* (Boston, Mass.: South End, 1996).

Xenophobia was clearly a resource in the hysteria surrounding Indiana Packers Company, which built a 300,000-square-foot plant in Delphi, Indiana. Among the key complaints was that it was "foreign owned," a joint venture of Ferruzzi of Italy and Mitsubishi of Japan, even though at the time the NPPC was working furiously to remove EC and Japanese barriers to U.S. ventures. See "Communicating the Views of America's Pork Producers," in National Pork Producers Council, *1993–94 Issues Handbook* (Des Moines, Iowa: National Pork Producers Council, 1994), 35.

13. Richard P. Horwitz, *Hog Ties: Pigs, Manure, and Mortality in American Culture* (New York: St. Martin's Press, 1998).

PART VII

FUTUREPHOBIA

Freemasonry and the Illuminati as Archetypes of Fear in America

Brian A. Marcus

The "Plot"

There is a secret society that is the largest and most successful fraternal organization in existence. It is composed of men bound to it by "bonds of brotherhood" and oaths of allegiance. The fraternity's charitable drives and institutions are some of the world's largest and best known, and its membership includes persons from all religions and almost every country on the globe. However, this fraternity's organization has been carefully and methodically infiltrated, with its supposedly neutral meeting places subverted, and then converted, to perpetuate evil across the world.

The secret cabal that has hijacked this larger organization plots amid the fraternity, unbeknownst to most members as it begins to weave a web of deceit and lies. The fraternity is divided into two divergent groups: the first are those in the "inner circle," or the "higher ranks," who are part of this secret plotting. The rest of the members are those who were drawn in by the promise of camaraderie and the fraternity's much heralded charitable works (in the United States, presidents and congressmen, Supreme Court justices and clergy, have all joined this "benevolent society"). However, the members who are not initiates into the "mysteries" only serve to give a veneer of legitimacy and to defer suspicions from the secretive goals of the "insiders."

The cabal of "illuminated" men in the higher ranks not only rule the lodges and structures of their "cover" secret society, but also have been infiltrating the power structures of governments, subverting religions and religious beliefs, and gaining control over the banks and money systems worldwide. The eventual goal of these secretive "men in the shadows," is to break down commonly held ideas of nationhood, nationalism, religion, and morality. As part of the "evolution" these men hope to guide, the beliefs of society at large will be shaped by controlled media, and moved away from "tradition" into a transition towards ungodliness and decadence.

The final aspect of this nefarious plot is the ushering in of an era of universalism, relativism, and "brotherhood," which purports to be peaceful and "a new evolutionary step" in human relations and humankind. A one-world government that will represent and make decisions for all people will be proposed as part of the plan. According to the men behind this plan, the resulting new world order will be the first steps in a millennium of peace and prosperity for the world. However, the reality of this plot is to extend the dominion of Satan across the world and overthrow Christianity, capitalism, and the American way. All of these things will pave the way for the rise of the Antichrist and the end of the world as we know it.

The "Players"

The belief that this plan of world domination and subversion exists and is being implemented by ranking members of Freemasonry has reverberated in political and religious circles for literally hundreds of years. Even a brief outline of the history of Freemasonry in the United States that examines some of the attacks made against it will show the longevity of the fears and paranoia this group has inspired. This overview of Freemasonry and the Bavarian Illuminati will also show that the attacks against these groups have often come from religious sources and utilize religious justifications. The longevity of these fears owes much to the recurrence and reexamination of this topic by various religious persons and groups, as well as the expression of their beliefs, as signified in the religious terminology, that some of the largest and fastest-expanding denominations in the United States utilize.[1]

Protestant warnings of the "dangers" of fraternal groups, combined with the emphasis by various sects and denominations on apocalypticism and prophecy belief, have led a number of Christian groups to focus on interpreting the "signs of the times" in the context of modern events and the actions of various "secret" groups. Freemasons and the Illuminati are two groups that are central to the messages of these apocalyptic visionaries in their decipherment of the events that will unfold at the "End Times." Because of the usefulness of Freemasons and the Illuminati to various "paranoid" groups that seek to explain the context of the secular, religious, social, and political situation as an aspect of prophecy, these two organizations have become archetypes for the twin fears of "modernism" and "liberalism," as well as the purported progenitors and abettors of "godless" communism. These fears have enjoyed great popularity and have been constantly revived throughout American history.

The religious tendencies and beliefs of many of the people in the United States, when combined with a tradition of xenophobia, have led to recurring paranoia about groups believed to be "secretive" or "subversive." These fears have had a significant influence on American society since prior to the founding of the country, and have consumed numerous people and groups as they have attempted (and continue to attempt) discovery and understanding of the "mysteries" behind these "dangerous" organizations. Blaming "others" (foreign or internal "subversives") for introducing changes and ideas believed to be detrimental to the physical, emotional, and spiritual well-being of individuals and the country as a whole has been a constant theme in American history.[2] Certain groups have weighed heavily upon the American psyche, serving as a sort of "grand unified theory" within American history upon which all things considered "un-American" can be (and have been) attached. Freemasonry and its supposed "secret masters," the Illuminati, are two organizations that have been constantly and consistently identified as dangerous, destructive, and downright un-American.

Freemasonry

During the past two centuries there have been numerous charges laid out against Freemasonry. The Freemasons and Illuminati have been linked to virtually every modern conspiracy theory that claims a secretive group is attempting world domination. Communism, secular humanism, international banking, the Federal Reserve, Zionism, Satanism, increased government controls and oversight, lawlessness, godlessness, poor television programming, witchcraft, gun control, public education, ecumenicism, universalism, trilateralization, "liberalization," Jacobinism, and anti-"Real Americanism" are just some of the "plots" that have been linked to these two groups.[3] Virtually every movement, belief, or trend that has been identified as an "evil conspiracy" in the last two-and-a-half centuries has been linked to, and infused with, the fears and suspicions that surround Freemasonry and the Illuminati.

The recent attacks against these groups have been founded upon the belief that they have not only been working at overthrowing the world, but may be close to succeeding.[4]

Attacks by religious groups have often centered upon charges of irreligious actions and beliefs, the supposed fostering and encouraging of "immoral" behavior within the lodge, and questions surrounding the writings and rituals that constitute Freemasonry.[5] Men seeking entry into Freemasonry must profess belief in God to become members, however, no restrictions are placed upon how that term is interpreted by the individual. Because of the fraternity's denial of Christ as the sole means to salvation, and the fact that the Mason's tools (a square and compass) are placed on top of the Bible in the lodge (seen as symbolically "above" the teachings within the text), some conservative interpretations have taken this gesture to mean the fraternity sees itself as a substitute for, even a usurpation of, the "true" religion. The most frequent critics have emerged from denominations and sects that identify themselves as evangelical Christians.[6] Numerous works have attacked Freemasonry from a "Christian" viewpoint, often citing its secrecy and the oaths sworn by initiates to keep that secrecy as central aspects of the "un-Christian" nature of the group.[7]

The fraternity does conduct its meetings in secret, with a guard (the tyler) posted outside the doors to keep out the uninitiated (the cowans). Within the fraternity, initiates do not receive the complete teachings of Masonry until they pass through stages, or degrees. As initiates ascend in the ranks, more answers to the "mysteries" and the teachings of Freemasonry are laid out before them.

The brotherhood of builders who assembled King Solomon's Temple are cited as the original founders of the stonemason guilds and, by extension, the Freemasons themselves. The lodge room is said to be patterned after the Temple of Solomon, and numerous references to the story of the Temple's building are included in the rituals of Masonry.

The stories and rituals apparently use biblical references to give the impression that the foundations of the fraternity are in Scripture. The Bible is not only the source of stories, but also of metaphors and ideas that are translated into modern examples as guides for Masons to follow. The "Great Lights" of Masonry are the Bible, the square, and the compass. The Bible is to guide faith, the square to "square" actions with beliefs, and the compass to draw the boundaries within which the passions must be kept. Because Masonry is concerned with the acceptance of God as an idea, to be seen as the "Grand Architect of the Universe" who presides benevolently over Creation, rather than a particularized version of God, the Bible can be paired with the Koran or other sacred writings of other faiths if the lodge includes members of other religions.

Freemasonry includes three degrees that all full members rise through, each with attendant rituals that impart lessons of morality to the initiate. The degrees occur in a specific order and each is intended to pass on a lesson to the initiate, who takes obligations upon himself to uphold the ideas of morality taught and never to reveal the secrets of the rituals. The rituals seek to test the trust, virtue, and morality of the initiate and to impart the lesson that a Freemason can expect to be helped by brothers who are bound by the same oaths and guided by the same ideals. The rituals are followed by a period when the prospective candidate memorizes the lessons and must show proficiency in them before passing on to the next degree.

The writings, rituals, and books utilized by Masons in their progress are generally available today, so that if nonmembers wish to examine these aspects of Masonry, they can do so.[8] After the member has passed through the three basic degrees in the basic, or "Blue," lodges more advanced degrees and teachings are offered.

Generally, the attacks upon the "hidden" teachings or "secrets" of Masonry are directed at those who are in the degrees beyond the basic (Blue) lodges.[9] The three degrees that are completed by all "Master Masons" are all that is necessary to becoming a full member in a lodge. However, to the attackers of the fraternity, most members of Freemasonry are considered to be dupes, unaware of the evil plots their leaders and high-ranking members are initiating. Only those Masons who have attained the higher degrees and have been deemed trustworthy are supposedly integrated into the plan of attacking the "American" way of life. The plan presupposes that these groups will assist Satan in bringing about a new world order. This "new order of the ages" will give rise to a One World Government that will be the vehicle for the rise of the Antichrist.[10]

These fears are derived from long-standing beliefs in various religious groups that Satan works within the world, and will use certain groups to help instigate the End Times. Shielded by members who do not know of all the secrets and plans of the high-ranking members, Freemasons in the upper echelons can rebuff most investigations and aspersions cast upon them. The lesser ranking members, who only have a part of the picture, defend the group because they do not know of the secret plans that have supposedly been organized and begun by those in the highest ranks. Thus, because members are blind to, or unaware of, the secret plans, outside groups are often the ones who believe they must point out the dangers of the group. And the critics of the fraternity have been sending out warnings and explaining the dangers of the fraternity since its inception.

One charge that Freemasons do not have a definitive defense against are aspersions cast upon the origins of the fraternity. Unlike many other similar fraternal organizations, Freemasons have shrouded their beginnings in mystery, which has even provoked dispute among some Masons.[11]

A number of Masonic scholars and historians purport a lineage that goes back to the builders of Solomon's Temple and extends through various "mystery schools" in Eastern and European history. Some examiners see a development from the guild structures of the Middle Ages into an inclusion of "nonoperative" or "speculative" masons in the working guilds of stonecutters and masons. These guilds had carried the "secrets" of building, architecture, and mathematics (which were necessary for construction and planning of the great cathedrals and buildings across Europe). Those who were interested in these areas, though not employed as masons, were then inducted into the guild as "nonoperative" masons. These men eventually branched off and formed groups of "Free Masons." The speculations and various interpretations have assisted in attacks against the fraternity, as there is no one "genuine" or accepted history for the group.

What is known about the development of Freemasonry is that references were made to "free masons" meeting in England as early as the 1600s.[12] By 1717 the first "Grand Lodge" was convened to organize and systematize the various lodges and rituals that existed in England. In 1723 the bylaws were codified and rituals were established.[13] The lodge system traveled from England to the colonies, where it enjoyed great success. In the American colonies the fraternity was diffused through friendships, migrating members, and traveling lodges within the military.[14] The fraternity enjoyed notable success in the eighteenth century, and key figures in early American history, such as George Washington, Benjamin Franklin, Paul Revere, and the marquis de Lafayette, were members of the fraternity.

However, charges were soon leveled against the fraternity, including that its members attempted to establish an aristocratic system via the formation of the Society of the Order of Cincinnati (with General Washington at its head) shortly after the Revolutionary War.[15] Links were also suspected between the Jacobins and Freemasonry, which tied into the fears that led to the enactment of the Alien and Sedition Acts and beliefs that secretive groups were plotting to overthrow the government, as had supposedly been done in France.[16] In the same vein, the excesses of the French Revolution, especially attacks made against aristocrats and the clergy, were blamed on the influences and plotting of secret organizations such as the Freemasons, the Illuminati, and the Jacobins.

The Illuminati were singled out by American observers as being particularly dangerous, and they have been inextricably and intimately connected with Freemasonry. The Illuminati were charged with subversion and attempting to "overthrow religion and government" both abroad and in the newly formed United States. These charges have continued into the modern era.

The Illuminati

The Illuminati are believed to be the "secret cabal" within Freemasonry that has supposedly been attempting (literally) to take over the world. Founded in Bavaria by Adam Weishaupt (a former professor from the Jesuit University at Ingolstadt) on 1 May 1776, the Illuminati have become the archetypal "subversive" secret society.[17] They began as a utopian, protocommunistic, secretive society of "illuminated" individuals who apparently believed that the systems of religion and government of their day were corrupt. The group was supposed to form "cells" that would exist within a larger organization, multiply and spread, and then seek to guide the organization in accordance with their secret plans. The proposed goals of the Illuminati included the overthrow of monarchies and established churches, as well as the abolition of private property, inheritances, and nationalism.[18]

The Illuminati may have had lofty goals and ideas, but the group had no real way to bring them to fruition. Thus the structure of Freemasonry, along with the belief that Masons would be receptive to their ideas, led the Illuminati to try to "infiltrate" European lodges to further their goals. The plotting of the Illuminati was exposed when copies of their writings were uncovered, though no one has ever determined how successful their plans were. The Bavarian government deemed the group dangerous and officially forced its members to disband in 1790. However, even after the group was "officially" quashed, it supposedly carried on in other guises while continuing to infiltrate organizations and "infect" them.[19]

John Robison was a Mason and a professor in Scotland who was invited by Weishaupt to join the Illuminati. After learning about the group, Robison wrote an exposé that has since become a central source for subsequent attacks against this enlightened band.[20] Another author, the abbé Augusten de Barruel, also exposed the Illuminati in his writings. He wrote a history of the French Revolution that specifically blamed the Illuminati and French Freemasons for the French Revolution, especially the excesses and violence against the aristocrats and priests.[21] Barruel explained in his detailed history of Jacobinism that "there was a 'triple conspiracy' of anti-Christians, Freemasons, and Illuminati to destroy religion and order."[22] Both Robison's and Barruel's books were well received in Europe and America, and apparently were widely read.[23]

The Attacks Begin

The interest stirred up by Robison's and Barruel's books in the United States led to organized attacks against the Illuminati, who had supposedly disbanded years before. The Reverend Jeddidiah Morse of Charlestown, Massachusetts, was one notable preacher who attacked the Illuminati in various speeches. Morse was a Congregationalist preacher who had been given a copy of Robison's book. After reading it, he became quite preoccupied with the idea of the dangers the group supposedly posed and preached a number of sermons about the Illuminati in 1798 and 1799. On 25 April 1799 he gave a sermon marking the National Day of Fasting, in which he stated,

> I have now in my possession complete and indubitable proofs that such societies do exist, and have for many years existed, in the United States. I have, my brethren, an official, authenticated list of the names, ages, places of nativity, professions, etc. of the officers and members of a Society of Illuminati . . . enemies whose professed design is to subvert and overturn our holy religion and our free and excellent government. And the pernicious fruits of their insidious and secret efforts must be visible to every eye. . . . Among these fruits may be reckoned our unhappy and threatening political divisions; the unceasing abuse of our wise and faithful rulers; the virulent opposition to some of the laws of our country and the measures of the Supreme Executive; the Pennsylvania Insurrection; the insidious circulation of baneful and corrupting books . . . and lastly [their intent] to destroy, not only the influence and support, but the official existence of the Clergy.[24]

Freemasonry was soon irrevocably tied to the fears of the Illuminati. The fraternity was popularized as an accomplice in, and abettor of, the evil plans of the Illuminati, which had supposedly infiltrated the lodges and upper hierarchy of the fraternity. The Reverend Nathaniel Emmons wrote in 1799 that "Jeffersonianism, Jacobinism, and Illuminati" were the "cornerstones on which Satan builds his fabric of infidelity."[25] The increasing attacks against Freemasonry and the Illuminati led to organized assaults on the fraternity in social, religious, and eventually political circles.

Antimasonry

The fear and paranoia over Freemasonry and the dangers it supposedly presented erupted in western New York State in the 1820s. Anti-Masonic literature and sermonizing had led to a climate of mistrust among many Americans toward the fraternity.[26] Captain William Morgan, a former Mason who believed he had been slighted by the fraternity, decided to write an exposé of the rituals and initiations of Freemasonry.[27] Books that detailed these aspects of the "secret" society had already appeared in Europe and the United States, but Morgan was threatened by members of the fraternity because he was violating the oaths he had made as a Mason.

The oaths sworn by Masonic initiates are meant to bind the candidate from talking about the rituals and keeping the particulars of the lessons to himself. These oaths include "penalties" that, the candidate swears, can be inflicted upon him if he exposes the "secrets" of Freemasonry. The Entered Apprentice's (the first degree taken) penalty included in the oath that the Mason swears was "no less penalty than having my throat cut across, my tongue torn out by its roots, and my body buried in the rough sands of the sea," which he then confirms by swearing upon the Bible. The Fellow Craft (or second-degree) oath includes the penalties of "having my breast torn open, my heart plucked out and my vitals thrown over my left shoulder to be devoured by the vultures of the air." Second-degree Masons also swear to assist brethren of this degree who make themselves known by the accepted signs. The Master Mason (or third degree) swears to assist fellow Master Masons who make themselves known by the accepted signs, to assist orphans and widows of deceased Masons, to be careful in the making of new Masons (to ensure that none is unfit), and not to cheat or defraud other Masons. The penalty for not keeping the oath is "no less than that of having my body severed in two, my bowels taken from thence and burned to ashes."[28]

As it turns out, Captain Morgan disappeared after a number of incidents of violence against both him and his printer that were apparently meant to frighten him enough so as to not publish the details of Masonic ritual. Morgan was almost certainly kidnapped, and most likely killed, by members of local Free-Masonic lodges.

This incident, known as the "Morgan affair," and the subsequent investigations into Freemasonry, eventually led to a vast outcry against Freemasonry. The first organized anti-Masonic mass movement swept the Northeast during the 1820s–30s. Numerous detractors dredged up the accusations of Illuminati influences in Freemasonry, and often centered attacks upon the "un-Christian" and "irreligious" aspects of the fraternity.[29] The outcry eventually developed into a political party that enjoyed some notable successes, and launched the careers of several key figures in the Antebellum political scene (such as Millard Fillmore, Thurlow Weed, Thaddeus Stevens, and William H. Seward).[30] The party died off quickly but laid a base for subsequent attacks on the fraternity as well as provided a huge volume of literature for later investigations and accusers.

Fears of immigrants and the issue of slavery grew strong enough to drown out most cries against Freemasonry in the mid-1800s; however, the issue of an anti-Masonic party was revisited in the 1870s (but it too died off quickly).[31] The fraternity began to enjoy an upturn in membership as the Victorian era saw a rise in social and fraternal organizations, and began to move into mainstream respectability and acceptance by "mainline" denominations.[32] Whatever attacks were still to be made against Freemasonry generally moved from the political, to the social, and especially to the religious fields during the late nineteenth century.

Linking "Secret Societies"
to Politics and Modern Fears

After the writing of *The Communist Manifesto*, the communist "specter" began to rise in Europe and the United States in the late nineteenth century. Ties were soon made between Freemasonry and communism by detractors.[33] *The Protocols of the Learned Elders of Zion* went another step, linking Freemasonry, the Illuminati, Zionism, international banking concerns, and communism into an integrated plan whereby Jewish-controlled Illuminati would guide Freemasonic lodges, the monetary systems, and eventually the governments in order to overthrow social systems (for example, in Russia, where the *Protocols* were apparently produced) and institute the new world order. Masonry is specifically mentioned in *The Protocols of the Learned Elders of Zion* as a means by which Jews can gain control over the world secretly, shielded by their "goyim" dupes.[34] Thus, the linking of Freemasonry and the Illuminati with Zionism, "international banking," and communism turned the fears of the Illuminati and Freemasons into an all-inclusive "grand unified" evil force. This link, so un-American in design and composition, has become one central aspect of the fears that modern conservative interpreters have seized upon.

Included in the base beliefs of many Americans is the idea that this country was founded as a "Christian" nation and that the United States has been increasingly pulling away from these (somewhat nebulously defined) roots. For some, this pattern has not been seen as a coincidence or social shift—rather it has been part of a plan led by the Illuminati.[35] The longevity of the attacks against Freemasonry and the Illuminati are directly related to the fact that these forces are "identified" and "known" evils, with a long-standing belief that they are (and have been) attacking the "American way of life" since the beginnings of the country, with their most successful instrument as that of communism itself.

Modern Attacks

New outbreaks of anti-Masonry are generally relegated to religiously based outcries against secret organizations and have been tied to the beliefs about millennialism, which are increasingly prevalent in American Christianity. The Prophecy Conferences of the late nineteenth and early twentieth centuries, the rise of Darbyite Dispensationalism, the Fundamentalist movement, the printing of the Scofield *Reference Bible*, and the steadily increasing numbers of Christians identified as "Evangelicals," who follow the tenets of these movements/references, have resulted in an increase in religious attacks against Freemasonry in the last fifty years.[36]

The premillennial shift in Evangelicalism allowed for a worldview that was dominated by the belief in the immanence of the return of Christ, which would be preceded by the rise of the Antichrist. The belief that the Illuminati were the founders and supporters of communism worked quite well in keeping fears of the group alive in the post–World War II era. The fears of the Illuminati as part of an eschatological necessity have also been integrated into various fears that are being popularized in the late 1990s by militia/patriot groups across the United States. The Illuminati are seen as being at the controls of various worldwide organizations, which are seen as precursors to a one-world government that will restrict "traditional" American freedoms. Thus the Illuminati have been integrated into fears about world governing bodies, international banking, communism, ecumenicism, gun control, and even fears of government in general.[37]

Freemasonry and Illuminati are accused of being antithetical to Christianity, and cries have arisen that these groups are not only harbingers of the Antichrist's rule, but that with the inception of their plans the groundwork for the End Times has been laid. These accusations began in the late eighteenth century and have reappeared throughout the following two centuries, but have become increasingly more strident, sophisticated, detailed, and convoluted in the modern era. The Illuminati have been named as the central guiding force behind the very structure of the modern world in areas as diverse as banking, government, schooling and technology, and accusers see them as the force that will lead humanity toward evil in the next millennium, not only through Masonic lodges but also by way of all the groups they have covertly infiltrated and turned.

Organizations and groups believed to have secret goals and plans of world governance and control are often cited as being "puppets" of the Illuminati. The banking system, especially international banking, is often read to be under the control of the Illuminati. Indeed, Revelation prophesied Zionism and the establishment of the state of Israel; thus this policy and event have been linked to the plans of the Illuminati to bring the Antichrist to power—it is seen as a necessary component of the eschatological ends of the Illuminati or, for anti–Semitic detractors, as proof of the Illuminati-led Jewish cabal. In the same vein, universalism and the concept of a one-world government are supposedly embodied in the United Nations. Accordingly, this organization has played a pivotal role in the belief there will be an establishment of a one-world government, which will have a unified monetary system, an identification number (Mark of the Beast), and a one-world church, which will actually be the "synagogue of Satan."

Because U.N. treaties signed by the United States can supersede the Constitution, some believe that an issuance of orders from this world-governing body can result in the whole of the United States being placed under U.N. control. Thus the sightings of "black helicopters" and foreign troops and equipment in the United States; thus the fears of modern militias and patriot movements planning world domination. So often, we find, at the roots of this paranoia lie Freemasonry and the Illuminati, who are "behind it all."[38]

Because of their notoriety, longevity, and popularity, these two groups have become the archetypes of fear within American society. They have been yoked in the minds and beliefs of many individuals and groups that fear the doom of America and "Americanism." Some of these reactionary groups have in fact had a significant impact in American politics, religion, and history. Ultimately, it can be shown that virtually every fear of conspiracy or world domination can be (and has been) traced to fears and paranoia concerning the Free-Masonic institution and the Illuminati. These two groups have been accused of subversion and dangerous activity since the United States was founded. And it is certain that they will continue to be the scapegoats of choice for future conspiracy believers and accusers.[39]

Notes

1. Roger Finke and Rodney Starke, in *The Churching of America, 1776–1990: Winners and Losers in Our Religious Economy* (New Brunswick, N.J.: Rutgers University Press, 1992), note denominations that expanded most rapidly in American history have been those commonly identified as "evangelical." See also Paul Boyer, *When Time Shall Be No More* (Cambridge, Mass.: The Belknap Press of Harvard University Press, 1992). Boyer examines premillennialism (a central part of many evangelical churches' beliefs), biblical literalism, and the impact of "prophecy belief" in American culture. This book is essential reading for an understanding of the depths of premillennial beliefs in the United States, their pervasiveness in American culture, and how much these beliefs have affected politics, religion, foreign and domestic policy, and outlooks on the world, the future, and what America's "proper" role is believed to be.

2. Seymour Lipsett and Earl Raab write in *The Politics of Unreason: Right-Wing Extremism in America, 1790–1977* (Chicago, Ill.: University of Chicago Press, 1978) that conservatives in the early nineteenth century "responded with the basic model of monistic logic which was also to be repeated often in similar circumstances throughout American history: the cause of the distress was a group of evil and conspiratorial—therefore politically illegitimate—men; the remedy was to repress such men by any means, as a matter of high morality" (34–35). David Brion Davis explains in *The Fear of Conspiracy: Images of Un-American Subversion from the Revolution to the Present* (Ithaca, N.Y.: Cornell University Press, 1971) that "because American identity has usually been defined as a state of mind rather than as a familial heritage, Americans have been susceptible to the fear that their neighbors' minds were being seduced by the devil, that their free institutions were being infiltrated by enemies in disguise, and that a hidden society, opposed to every principle of democracy and Christianity, was growing within the very tissues of the existing social order" (1). The statements by these authors seem to be valid appraisals of past actions, as well as present-day situations. Many of the same forces and dynamics are present (and perhaps are even stronger) in the closing years of the twentieth century. The same groups that these authors identified as being feared in the early American period are still often the scapegoats in the modern era.

3. Boyer, *When Time Shall Be No More*, 232–35. Boyer notes a number of religious sources that cite these (and others) as "plots" which show these

groups are paving the way for the rise of the Antichrist. One essential source that links these "plots" to the Freemasons and Illuminati is Arno C. Gaebelein's influential magazine *Our Hope*. George Marsden, in his book *Reforming Fundamentalism* (Grand Rapids, Mich.: Wm. B. Eerdmans Publishing Co., 1987), notes that "the most influential antimodernist doctrine, eventually spreading through most of intradenominational fundamentalism, was dispensationalism[,] a version of premillennialism . . . " (5). Marsden later notes that *Our Hope* was one of the oldest of the dispensationalist journals and that its founder, Arno C. Gaebelein, was "one of the leaders of the old prophecy conference movement out of which had grown much of organized fundamentalism. . . . [R]eading the signs of the times was the main business of *Our Hope*. The widely informed Gaebelein fit each historical event into the drama of the life-and-death conflict between God and Satan. In perhaps the best-known of his many books, *The Conflict of the Ages*, he outlined the satanic conspiracy of lawlessness through the ages, transmitted to America first through the French Revolution and the demonically inspired Illuminati" (71); see Arno C. Gaebelein, *The Conflict of the Ages* (New York: Our Hope, 1933). For a recent book that links Freemasons and the Illuminati to numerous "plots" that are believed to be designed to destroy the United States and Christianity, see Jeffrey A. Baker, *Cheque Mate! The Game of Princes: The New World Order, Dark Conspiracy or Benevolent Master Plan? How It Affects You and the Sovereignty of America* (Springdale, Pa.: Whitaker House, 1993). Baker has been interviewed by such prominent conservative Christians as Randall Terry, Beverly LaHaye, and James Dobson—and he has cited *The Protocols of the Learned Elders of Zion* as one of his central sources of his beliefs and understandings of the "plans" of these groups.

4. Currently on the World Wide Web are thousands of sites that discuss the immanent and present "dangers" of Freemasonry and the Illuminati. Many are linked to well established and respected Christian Websites. One Christian website that includes Illuminati references is "Prophecy Central" (<http://www.bible-prophecy.com:80/index.html> as of 11/15/97). Numerous other sites link to this website, and it has received awards from CLEANWEB, Top 100 Christian Link Page, Golden Crown Award, Christian Web Site of the Day, and a Golden Banner Award for Responsible Content. On the "Prophecy Central" site, the main page includes the "Prophecy Puzzle" graphic. The Prophecy Puzzle includes a section on the new world order that does have a caveat against dogmatic teaching on "controversial issues." The section on the new world order, however, is largely drawn from an extremely conservative source, Gary Kah's book *En Route to Global Occupation* (which is often utilized by militia/patriot groups to justify their fears of the United Nations, the Federal government, etc.). See also the "Dogpile" (<www.dogpile.com>.) multiengine search, as well as, for example, <http://www.prolognet.qc.ca/clyde/illumin.html> (as of 11/15/97).

5. The charges have even included murdering of "apostate" members and originating and disseminating plots to overthrow governments and religious institutions. The Catholic Church condemned Freemasonry with the issuance of a papal bull in 1738, entitled *In eminenti apostolas specula,* which held that denial of Christ's divinity was at the core of Freemasonry. Other early movements against the fraternity often began in churches, especially in the nonestablished Protestant churches (notably Baptist churches) during the latter part of the eighteenth century; see Brian Marcus, *Religion and Antebellum Politics: A Comparison of the Religious Genesis of the Antimasonic and American (Know-Nothing) Parties* (Ann Arbor, Mich.: UMI, 1996).

6. Numerous churches in the nineteenth and twentieth centuries have issued attacks against Freemasonry, including the Church of Jesus Christ-Latter Day Saints, the Southern Baptist Convention, Assemblies of God, Jehovah's Witnesses, Seventh-Day Adventists, various Pentecostal churches, and numerous unaffiliated evangelical churches. For details on religious anti-Masonry there are numerous articles in Freemasonic sources (see especially *The Transactions of the American Lodge of Research*); see also Marcus, *Religion and Antebellum Politics,* 339–41.

7. Literally hundreds of examples exist of Christians writing to attack Masonry, many from the era of the Antimasonic party in the nineteenth century. Acacia Press, Inc., has a significant library of reprint materials currently available; see its website: <http://www.crocker.com/~acacia/antim.html>. Examples of modern books include E. M. Storms, *Should a Christian Be a Mason?* (Fletcher, N.C.: New Puritan Library, 1984); and Pat Robertson, *The New World Order* (Dallas, Tex.: Word Publishing, 1991).

8. Even in Masonry's earliest days there were books that detailed the rituals. Samuel Prichard's *Masonry Dissected* (1730) explained the three basic degrees and detailed their oaths, signs, and rituals; and *Jachin and Boaz* was a similar book that first appeared in 1762, followed by thirty-four editions up to 1800. See William P. Vaughn, *The Antimasonic Party in the United States, 1826-1843* (Lexington: University Press of Kentucky, 1983), 12. Guides such as *Duncan's Masonic Ritual and Monitor* (New York: David Mackay and Company, Inc., 1868) are available today through even major chain bookstores.

9. Differences are even made between the types of higher degrees—with "French" or "Oriental" lodges, Scottish Rite, and Shriners singled out as the most "dangerous" types. Alfred Pike, a Grand Master in the nineteenth century, wrote *Morals and Dogma of the Ancient and Accepted Scottish Rite of Freemasonry* (Richmond, Va.: L. H. Jenkins, Inc. 1871), which outlines the degrees in the Scottish Rite. This work continues to be one of the most frequently attacked Masonic books.

10. This belief is generally centered upon readings from the Bible—especially

the Book of Daniel, Revelation, and sections of the Gospels in the New Testament. Religious groups have attacked the secret ceremonies and meetings of Freemasonry, mainly because this is seen as conflicting with Christ's admonition in John 18:20 ("I spoke openly to the world . . . in secret I have said nothing").

11. See Deed Lafayette Vest, *Pursuit of a Thread* (San Antonio, Tex.: The Watercress Press from Everett & Associates, 1983); see also William T. Still, *New World Order: The Secret Plan of Secret Societies* (Lafayette, La.: Huntington House Publishers, 1990), for a non-Masonic, proconspiracy theory of the fraternity.

12. A diary of Elias Ashmole notes that he and an acquaintance were "made Free Masons" on 16 October 1646, according to John Hamil, *The Craft* (Oxford: Oxford University Press, 1986), 30.

13. In 1723 James Anderson of London systematized and codified the bylaws of the fraternity and published them so that lodges could be brought into conformity; see *Anderson's Constitutions*, reprinted in Peter Ross, *A Standard History of Freemasonry in the State of New York* (New York: Lewis Publishing Company, 1901), 155–65.

14. Traveling lodges were composed of Masons in the military, and the vestments and trappings of the lodge were carried with units as they traveled. The Grand Lodge of Ireland issued the first Traveling Warrant to the 1st Regiment (Foot) in the British army in 1732. The Colonial army included 10 lodges, the largest being the American Union Lodge. By the War of 1812, the British army had over 350 lodges in regiments across the world. See Frederick Adams, *Proceedings of the American Lodge of Research* 2, no. 2: 199.

15. Samuel Adams was one critic who believed the group was a means to establishing a military nobility. The core of those establishing the order were virtually all Masons. See Albert Hart, ed., *American History as Told by Contemporaries* (New York: Davis & Co., 1938), 2:626.

16. The Alien and Sedition Acts were designed to protect the country from supporters of Jacobinism and were specifically concerned with secret or conspiratorial activities. The provisions of the acts included giving the president of the United States the authority to deport aliens who were suspected of "treasonable" acts or "secret machinations" against the government. See Ira M. Leonard and Robert D. Parmet, *American Nativism, 1830–1860* (New York: Van Nostrand Reinhold Co., 1971), 21–23.

17. Thus, two months before the Declaration of Independence, the antithesis of "Americanism" and democracy (according to conservative interpretations) was begun. See Jonathan Vankin, *Conspiracies, Cover-Ups & Crimes* (Lilburn, Ga.: IllumiNet Press, 1996), which discusses the various conspiracy theories in U.S. history, including the Illuminati, who were "behind the French Revolution, the Bolshevik Revolution, the American Revo-

lution, the pope, the Kennedy Assassination, Charles Manson, the Rockefeller dynasty, the New Age Movement, UFO visitations, and the Universal Price Code. The odd inscription '57 Varieties' on Heinz Ketchup has even been called an Illuminati code phrase" (267).

18. Weishaupt believed that Christ spoke in parables that could only be understood by those with special knowledge and that the "secret [of Christ] is to give back to men their original liberty and equality"; quoted in Nesta H. Webster, *Secret Societies and Subversive Movements* (London: Boswell Publishing Co., 1936). See also Still, *New World Order.*

19. See Still, *New World Order,* for one example of a writer who believes this to be true.

20. John Robison, *Proofs of a Conspiracy against All the Religions and Governments of Europe, Carried On in the Secret Meetings of Freemasons, Illuminati and Reading Societies* (New York: Geo. Forman, 1798).

21. Abbé Augusten de Barruel, *Memoirs Illustrating the History of Jacobinism,* 4 vols. (London: T. Burton, 1798).

22. Lipsett and Raab, *The Politics of Unreason,* 35. The abbé Barruel stated in his 1798 book that "in the true Masonic code no other god will be found save mani [*sic*]. He is the god of the cabalist masons, of the ancient Rosicrucians, of the Martinist Masons" (2:xiii).

23. Even George Washington mentioned that he received a copy of Robison's book and thought that the Illuminati had probably spread to the United States—but that they were not very influential in U.S. lodges. Washington wrote to the minister who had sent him the a copy of the book on 25 September 1798: "I have heard much of the nefarious and dangerous plan, and doctrines of the Illuminati, but never saw the Book [Robison's] until you were pleased to send it to me." He later wrote again to the Reverend G. W. Snyder, claiming that "It was not my intention to doubt that, the Doctrines of the Illuminati and principles of Jacobinism had not spread to the United States. On the contrary, no one is more truly satisfied of this fact than I am" (quoted in Still, *New World Order,* 60–61).

24. The Reverend Dr. Jeddidiah Morse, *A Sermon, Exhibiting the Present Dangers and Consequent Duties of the Citizens of the United States. Delivered at Charlestown, April 25, 1799. The Day of National Fast* (Charlestown, Mass.: n.p., 1799), 15–17.

25. Clifford S. Griffin, *Their Brothers' Keepers: Moral Stewardship in the United States, 1800–1865* (New Brunswick, N.J.: Rutgers University Press, 1960), 12–14.

26. See Lee Benson, *The Concept of Jacksonian Democracy: New York as a Test Case* (Princeton, N.J.: Princeton University Press, 1961), for an excellent assessment of the political disruption; William Henry Brackney, "Religious Antimasonry: The Genesis of a Political Party" (Ph.D. diss., Temple University, 1976); Whitney R. Cross, *The Burned-Over District: The Social*

and Intellectual History of Enthusiastic Religion in Western New York, 1800–1850 (New York: Harper & Row, 1950), a classic work on the influence and importance of religion in western New York; Paul Goodman, *Towards a Christian Republic: Anti-Masonry and the Great Transition in New England, 1826–1836* (New York: Oxford University Press, 1988), on the anti-Masonic movement and anti-Masonic political party; Paul E. Johnson, *A Shopkeeper's Millennium: Society and Revivals in Rochester, N.Y., 1815–1837* (New York: Hill & Wang, 1978), an excellent source on revivalism and local anti-Masonry in western New York; and William Preston Vaughn, *The Antimasonic Party in the United States, 1826–1843* (Lexington: University Press of Kentucky, 1983).

27. Cross, *The Burned-Over District*, 113. Cross states that Morgan was made a Mason in Rochester in 1823, but there seem to be no extant records indicating at which lodge Morgan took his first three degrees. See also Vaughn, *The Antimasonic Party in the United States*, 3. Vaughn states that "exhaustive research into the existing records of lodges in the various areas where Morgan lived has failed to unearth any evidence of his having taken any of the three basic, or 'Blue Lodge,' Masonic degrees." See also Brackney, "Religious Antimasonry," which states that Morgan was a "prominent Royal Arch Mason in Batavia Lodge No. 433, where he served as Lecturer to the initiates" (1); however, Brackney cites no specific source for this assertion.

28. Numerous books and tracts have divulged the contents and symbolism of these initiatory rites (see note 11 above). See *Duncan's Masonic Ritual and Monitor* (New York: David Mackay and Company, Inc., 1868), 34–35, 65–66, 94–96, which details the rituals and oaths of the Blue Lodges.

29. Henry Dana Ward edited the *Antimasonic Review and Magazine* and concluded the first number of volume 1 thus: "we have found Free Masonry, by its own showing, carefully collated from its approved writers, and books of constitutions, to be the synagogue of Satan" (34).

30. Early attacks on the fraternity are classic examples of the rise of nativism among Americans, and the defining of an "American" psyche. Ira M. Leonard and Robert D. Parment state that nativism is "defined by historians and sociologists as a deep-seated American antipathy towards internal 'foreign' groups of various kinds—cultural, national, religious, racial—which has erupted periodically into intensive efforts to safeguard America from such perceived 'threats.' " See Leonard and Parmet, *American Nativism*, 6. On the politics of Masonry, see Marcus, *Religion and Antebellum Politics*, 113–55.

31. See Vaughn, *Antimasonic Party*, 190–91; and Lipsett and Raab, *The Politics of Unreason*, 77.

32. See Mark C. Carnes, *Secret Ritual and Manhood in Victorian America* (New Haven, Conn.: Yale University Press, 1989); Mary Ann Clawson, *Con-*

structing Brotherhood: Class, Gender, and Fraternalism (Princeton, N.J.: Princeton University Press, 1989).

33. Some contemporary observers and many modern writers claim that the Il- luminati simply went underground and continued its plans of domination. See Gary Allen, *None Dare Call It Conspiracy* (Rossmoor, Calif.: Concord Press, 1971), a publication of the John Birch Society, which links the Illu- minati to the Baron Rothschild (80); Robertson, *New World Order,* 67–74; George Armstrong, *Rothschild Money Trust* (Palmdale, Calif.: Omni Publi- cations, 1940), which links the Rothschilds (and other powerful Jewish banking families) to communism, Freemasonry, and the Illuminati; and William Guy Carr, *Pawns in the Game* (Palmdale, Calif.: Omni/Christian Book Club, 1958), which details the Illuminati/communist links.

34. See Victor Marsden's translation of *The Protocols of the Learned Elders of Zion* (n.p., 1934), Marsden summarizes each protocol before reprinting it. Marsden ends with a letter that was reprinted from the 1905 version: "the Antichrist—is about to mount the throne of the universal empire. . . . [O]nly the light of Christ and of his Holy Church Universal can fathom the abyss of Satan and disclose the extent of its wickedness. . . . Secular quarrels and schisms would all be forgotten in the imminent need of pre- paring for the coming of the Antichrist" (227–28).

35. Examples abound, but for two popular Christian sources, see Marlin Mad- doux, *America Betrayed* (Lafayette, La.: Huntington House, 1984), and the extremely popular book by David Barton, *The Myth of Separation* (Aledo, Tex.: Wallbuilder Press, 1992). Both see the United States as "pulling away" from "traditional" roots and into godlessness and degeneracy, which they see as part of a planned, calculated, and evil course that has been plotted by "anti-Christian" groups.

36. See Boyer, *When Time Shall Be No More,* 86–100.

37. For examples, see William Cooper, *Behold a Pale Horse* (Sedona, Ariz.: Light Technology Publishing, 1991), which reprints the protocols and spe- cifically instructs readers to notice references to Masons and read "Jews" as "Illuminati" (267); Robert K. Spear's book *Surviving Global Slavery: Living under the New World Order* (Leavenworth, Kans.: Universal Force Dynamics, 1992) for its religious and political discourse on the new world order and its attacks on the plans of "internationalist" groups; and Spear, *Creating Covenant Communities* (Leavenworth, Kans.: Universal Force Dynamics, 1993), in which he advocates forming closed communities to stave off the forces that will be led by the Antichrist against Americans.

38. Some works that include these charges are Jim Keith, *Black Helicopters over America: Strikeforce for the New World Order* (Lilburn, Ga.: IllumiNet, 1994); Robertson, *New World Order;* Des Griffin, *Fourth Reich of the Rich* (Clackmas, Oreg.: Emissary Publications, 1976); Eustace Mullins, *The World Order: Our Secret Rulers* (Staunton, Va.: Ezra Pound Institute of

Civilization, 1992); Mullins, *The Curse of Canaan: A Demonology of History* (Staunton, Va.: Revelation Books, 1987); and Mullins, *The Rape of Justice: America's Tribunals Exposed* (Staunton, Va.: The National Commission for Judicial Reform, 1989).

39. For secondary sources on the militia/patriot movement, see Philip Lamy, *Millennium Rage: Survivalists, White Supremacists, and the Doomsday Prophecy* (New York: Plenum Press, 1996); James Coates, *Armed and Dangerous: The Rise of the Survivalist Right* (1987; reprint, New York: Hill & Wang, 1995); Morris Dees, *Gathering Storm: America's Militia Threat* (New York: Harper Collins, 1996); Kenneth S. Stern, *A Force upon the Plain: The American Militia Movement and the Politics of Hate* (New York: Simon & Schuster, 1996); Michael Barkun, *Religion and the Racist Right: The Origins of the Christian Identity Movement* (Chapel Hill: University of North Carolina Press, 1997); Richard Abanes, *American Militias: Rebellion, Racism & Religion* (Downers Grove, Ill.: InterVarsity Press, 1996); and James Aho, *The Politics of Righteousness* (1990; reprint, Seattle: University of Washington Press, 1995).

Alien Invasion
Ufology and the Millennial Myth

Philip Lamy and Devon Kinne

The mass suicide of the UFO group Heaven's Gate in March 1997 was a tragic example of the ways contemporary millennial groups interpret and enact the currently evolving millennial myth in American culture—this time, as interpreted by a new religious movement within the subculture of ufology. Members of Heaven's Gate believed that by taking their own lives, they would be releasing their alien spirits from their human receptacles in order to link up with a UFO mothership trailing the comet Hale-Bopp. The group maintained that suicide would enable them to achieve a higher evolutionary or cosmic level—just in time to escape the alien destruction of planet Earth.

In basic ways the beliefs of Heaven's Gate mirror classic apocalyptic stories or "millennial myths" that underlie our culture, periodically breaking out under the pressures caused by rapid social and cultural change, including the end of an age or era. The "ufo-theology" of Heaven's Gate was postmodern in the way it fused classic apocalyptic beliefs, such as the imminent destruction of the planet and the return of the "messiah," with modern or "secular" beliefs in extraterrestrial life and intergalactic space travel. Heaven's Gate, like other new religious movements in the ufology subculture, had evolved a fragmented and secularized version of the millennial myth in adaptation to the current age—coinciding, not surprisingly, with the approach of the next millennium.

The millennial myth is derived from ancient Hebrew and Christian apocalyptic literature concerning the ultimate destiny of the world and the cosmic cataclysm in which God destroys the ruling powers of evil

411

and raises the righteous to life in a messianic kingdom. The millennial myth has accompanied the rise and fall of societies and has provoked the development of countless utopian and revolutionary movements throughout the history of Western civilization. With the approach of the new millennium a wide array of new apocalyptic social movements and subcultures have erupted in American society, and indeed the world. From survivalists to Christian fundamentalists, to messianic sects and New Age consciousness, expressions of the millennial myth are in full bloom.[1]

In its modern forms, the myth evolves or "fractures" to fit the current age; its principal components—for example, Tribulation, Armageddon, Messiah—become expressed through current events and social problems. One contemporary expression of the millennial myth is ufology, defined here as a subculture of individuals, groups, and organizations centered around the phenomenon of UFOs, extraterrestrial life, and interplanetary or interdimensional travel and contact. The subculture is extensive and complex; it includes numerous research, recreational, and religious organizations, as well as literature, products, seminars, conventions, and Internet websites.

For this study we examined the Internet websites of eleven religious organizations or movements in the ufology subculture to document the ways the millennial myth becomes altered in form, redefined, and reproduced among the new religious movements in ufology.[2] The power of religious myths such as the millennial myth lie in their persistence and adaptability to changing times. This essay demonstrates how ufology can be interpreted as a millennial subculture which expresses a postmodern form of the classical millennial myth.

Today millennial expressions are found not only in new messianic sects like the Branch Davidians and Japan's Aum Shinrikyo, but also in groups like those in ufology that appear, at least on the surface, not to be religious in orientation. Generally viewed as a nonreligious belief system, secular millennialism has been identified by scholars in a wide variety of political and revolutionary movements in history.[3] Historian Eric Hobsbawm (1959) drew the basic distinctions between religious and secular millennialism in a formative work on millenarian movements entitled *Primitive Rebels*. Religious millenarian movements, like those that have developed in the 2,000-year history of Christianity, have three main features. First, there is a total rejection of the present evil world and a belief in its imminent demise. Second, religious millennialists believe in the supernatural return or "second coming" of a messiah, who, after destroying all evil, will build a new utopian world. Third, the classic religious millennialist is vague about the actual timing and sequence of events leading to the new world, since most of this unfolding will be caused by supernatural intervention.

Hobsbawm contrasts the religiously inspired millenarian movements with the more secular forms, which tend to lack supernatural elements, especially the belief that the Apocalypse will be engineered by God and that the Millennium will be ushered in by the Second Coming of Christ. In the purely secular movements, there are no supernatural beings or divine intervention. Instead, secular millennialists build an organization of ideology, politics, and an alternative plan for society. Like religious millennialists, they also view the collapse of civilization as imminent, and hope to hasten its demise so as to institute a new utopian period. However, for secular millennialists, evil is represented not by supernatural forces but by human ones, generally those who rule or persecute them.[4]

Hobsbawm also suggests that between the "pure" or classical millenarian movement and the more secular kind, all manner of intermediate groups and beliefs systems are possible. Through cultural change and adaptation, the sacred and the secular become redefined and rearranged, and thus the distinctions between them become blurred. This process appears to be the case in American culture today, where elements from the classical apocalyptic tradition merge with modern and secular forms producing a strange array of "postmodern" millennial phenomena.[5] Michael Barkun has used the term "improvisational millennialism" more recently to define millenarian movements, like ufology, that draw meaning from a variety of cultural realms or historical eras.[6] Many of the new religious movements in ufology represent just such intermediate and improvisional forms—where the Antichrist is replaced by sinister "Grey" aliens, and the second coming brings extraterrestrials in spaceships rather than the messiah leading his heavenly crusaders.

The Millennial Myth

The Christian Apocalypse or Revelation of John is the most famous example of the millennial myth. Revelation (Apocalypse in Greek) is the final book in the Bible, presumed to have been written around 95 C.E., during the reign of the Roman emperor Domitian, by the Christian disciple John, who was imprisoned on the island of Patmos. Like John, Christians were being oppressed and imprisoned for their beliefs, especially their refusal to worship the emperor. In his visions John saw Rome as the Antichrist and he wrote to inspire and fortify the young church's resistance to the Romans. While written in a style and with a worldview best understood by John's original audience, "the seven churches of Asia" (Rev. 1.4), Revelation is perhaps the most quoted, most distorted, and most influential book in the Bible.[7]

Through the mythological prism provided by Revelation, the Roman persecutions of Christians reflect the start of a cosmic war between the forces of good and evil. In his visions John saw a parade of catastrophic "tribulations" leading to the end times and climaxing in the rise of the evil false prophet, the Antichrist. Just when all hope is lost, John witnesses the second coming of Christ and his angelic host, who battle and eventually defeat the Antichrist, casting him and his followers into the fiery pit for one thousand years. The Messiah redeems the chosen, creating "a new heaven and a new earth" in the Millennium.

The ambiguities of the book of Revelation have generated countless interpretations, infusing the story with the endurance and power of myth. As derived from Revelation, key structural elements of the millennial myth can be discerned in the following themes: *Tribulation, Babylon, Armageddon, Messiah,* and *Millennium.* The Tribulations that are to accompany the end times will include famine, disease, earthquakes, and war, unleashed on the world by God and other supernatural forces. Babylon, alternately expressed as the whore and the ancient city, also reflects the corrupted people and civilization of the present, both fallen away from God. Armageddon expresses the militaristic and moral imagery of great battles and final war between the forces of Christ and the demonic beasts, dragons and Antichrist—different personifications of Satan. Messiah refers to the belief that a savior or "messianic" figure (Jesus Christ) will come, issuing damnation to the wicked and salvation to the chosen. The Millennium is the final component of the myth— one thousand years of heaven on earth in a new spiritual and physical utopia.

The millennial myth is an ancient and powerful story for explaining the currents of history and everyday life. The myth acts as a powerful metaphor, providing the "big picture" of human history. For both religious and secular millennialists, and "improvisational" groups like ufology, the millennial myth gives meaning and direction, locating believers in a great cosmological plan being played out in their lifetime.

Ufology as an Apocalyptic Subculture

The subculture of ufology has experienced a renaissance in recent years, evidenced by its presence in American popular culture and among new research organizations devoted to understanding the physical dimensions of the phenomenon and new religious movements devoted to understanding its spiritual dimensions.[8] From television programs such as

The X-Files to the summer blockbusters of 1996 and 1997, *Independence Day* and *Men in Black,* respectively, Hollywood's accounts of an invasion of malevolent aliens intent on the destruction of our world have become common popular-culture fare.

In the same week that *Men in Black* was released, more than 200,000 of the faithful and curious descended on Roswell, New Mexico, for the fiftieth anniversary of the alleged flying saucer crashes in July 1947—the unofficial start of the modern UFO era. Roswell has become both a mecca for UFO believers and a popular tourist destination for those interested in UFOs, extraterrestrials, and cosmic conspiracies. A thriving heritage industry has grown up around Roswell, complete with tours of saucer crash sites, UFO museums, gift shops, conferences, and annual celebrations. "Encounter '97: The 50th Anniversary of the Roswell Incident" drew thousands of participants, including John Mack, Bud Hopkins, Stanton Friedman, Linda Moulton Howe, Whitley Strieber, and Eric Von Danieken—the gurus of American ufology.

In addition to the industry of ufology, a quasi-religious contingent has also formed within the subculture.[9] Especially common are the apocalyptic beliefs that many UFO groups seem to hold: that the current era is coming to a dramatic or catastrophic end, and that "messianic" figures from the heavens will destroy evil and redeem the chosen, thereafter instituting a new and better world. Cast through the lens of ufology, and in adaptation to the current age, the final destruction is caused by environmental damage: the messiah is an intergalactic space traveler, and the millennial new world is the attainment of cosmic consciousness.

Aetherius Society	(1954)
Unarius	(1954)
Urantia	(1955)
New World Comforter	(1973)
International Raelian Movement	(1973)
Summum	(1975)
Heaven's Gate	(1975)
Ground Crew Project	(mid-1980s)
Greater Community Way	(1992)
Outpost Kauai	(?)
Armageddon Time Ark Base	(?)

Figure 1. New Religious Ufology Movements on the Internet

By examining the Internet websites of eleven UFO groups (figure 1 above), we will demonstrate the ways in which the five primary themes of the millennial *myth* (*Tribulation*, *Babylon*, *Armageddon*, *Messiah*, and *Millennium*) have been adapted to the emergence of the ufology subculture.

Tribulation

The "Four Horsemen of the Apocalypse" (Rev. 6:1–8) is the classic image of the tribulations that are to accompany the end times. Bearers of conquest, slaughter, famine, and death, the Four Horsemen often ride through the ufological cyberspace that the Internet provides. Signs of the tribulations that signal the end times are today reflected in environmental damage, rapid industrial, technological, and economic change, and globalization. For ufologists, the signs of the times are also reflected in the presumed global increase in the number of alien visitations and UFO sightings. Outpost Kauai, a new religious movement based in Hawaii, points to the cosmological tribulations that will accompany the end times in an article called "What Will You Do as the Curtain Is Raised?"

> We are entering a "heavy" time, a faster-paced concentration of awareness coincidental with your growth . . . the Quickening. Look around at your world. Like salt it flavors your popular culture. People have become more irrational. Your weather grows bizarre. The Earth shakes. UFO's buzz your cities. Mountains blow their tops. Creatures stalk the night. Comets cruise the night sky. The "end" is actually a "beginning. It "was promised there would be signs." There will be.[10]

Many ufologists suggest that humanity bears most of the blame for the current atmosphere of global social and environmental decay. For example, members of the Aetherius Society, founded in 1954 by Sir George King in England, believe that the human race has again reached a crossroad. A document on the website for the Aetherius Society entitled "Why and How Are the Space Masters Helping Us Now" reads: "One road leads to disaster, self-inflicted by his own science and materialism. In these days there is again a danger of his technology, in the hands of the few, causing mass destruction to the many."[11] One does not have to be on the millennial fringe of ufology to appreciate the damage humans have caused to the global environment and ecosystem. Through extraterrestrial communication the Aetherians have come to believe that the aliens will save us from the ultimate destruction of the planet and extinction of humankind.

The International Raelian Movement is a UFO religion and community that was founded in Quebec in 1973 by the French race car driver and journalist Claude Vorilhon, called "Rael" after his meeting and trip to Rael, the home planet of the beings who created humans.[12] To the Raelians the tribulations that wrack the planet are the result of human action. The Raelians contend that war, violence, illness, depression, drug abuse, famine, destruction of the earth's resources, and religious and racial intolerances are precursors to the destruction of humanity and signal the end of the current world system and the human condition itself. According to the Raelians technological advances have brought about the end of the age, fulfilling, in a secular fashion, that which was prophesied in the Bible:

> We are in the age of the Apocalypse, the age when once again we can hope to meet our creators, the Elohim. This age of Apocalypse has been anticipated by religion. For example, in the Bible, it describes how in the age of Apocalypse the blind will be able to see (advanced microsurgery and electronic prosthesis), humanity's voice will be carried beyond the oceans (satellite communication), and humanity will equal itself to "God" (we have already created human genes entirely synthetically).[13]

The threat to the earth's environment and the salvation brought by the aliens are common themes in the alien abduction literature. "Transformation" through environmental pollution, global unrest, and alien manipulation are the hallmarks of this "heavy time," according to Whitley Strieber, author of three books on his own alien abduction.[14]

Babylon

Babylon is the second apocalyptic feature that has its postmodern expression among the new religious movements of the ufology subculture. In Revelation Babylon is expressive of the corrupted civilizations of humanity and signifies the seat of the devil's realm on earth. The destruction of Babylon is the metaphor for the final destruction of the world, which ushers in the Millennium (Rev. 14.8, 16.19, 18.2, 18.21). While Rome had been identified as Babylon by early Christians, millenarian movements throughout history have likened Babylon to the nation and culture of their oppressors.

In the ufology subculture, Babylon assumes various guises, including the current industrial and technological system, the global capitalist order, established religions, the New World Order, and even the planet itself. This pattern is certainly evident in the Weslaco, Texas-based Armageddon Time Ark Base's theology, whose use of millennial mythology is explicit. For example, the article "State of Time Station Earth" describes how the "humatons" have "discarded their ancient perfect factual knowledge, they have substituted and confined themselves in a 'juzgado' of ultimate Babylonian mysteries [and] religious philosophy, based upon the restricted limitations of belief and faith."[15]

Many groups within ufology see in the turn of the millennium the emergence of a new world. Most agree with the New World Comforters' interpretation of Babylon as the "old world order," where humanity has been "stuck in the same old groove, limited by the same old thoughts and emotions."[16] The New World Comforters feel the need to destroy this "old world" to build a new one. "The creation world of Absolute and unlimited mind, will give everyone freedom, security, and abundance, to start with."[17] According to Heaven's Gate leader Marshall "Do" Applewhite, the destruction of the present Babylonian world will occur when the earth is "spaded under." In an article entitled "Last Chance to Evacuate Earth," Applewhite writes:

> [T]his is the End of the Age. At the End of Age, the planet is wiped clean—refurbished, rejuvenated. The mess that the humans have made of it during this civilization will be cleaned up.[18]

Elite political and economic institutions and the "government" are also held responsible by ufologists for the moral bankruptcy of the modern Babylonian civilization. Since the dawning of the modern age of UFOs, the government has been viewed with mistrust by ufologists of both the religious and the secular camps. All manner of conspiracy theories concerning government cover-ups and plots to take over the world, often by conspiring with aliens, can be found on the web pages of ufology. Bearing a remarkable similarity to the conspiracy theories of right-wing militias, ufologists accuse the government of robbing individuals of their rights and selling their freedom to the evil powers of the New World Order. Thus members of the Armageddon Time Ark Base, for example, see in the emergence of national and international political and economic organizations the specter of "Big Brother":

> The jailers who force the humatons to sweat and exist in this stone age "juzgado" are the false prophets of the many of the End Time, who are preventing you from knowing by restricting you to belief and faith, and the Big Brother Police State to insure that you remain in the Dark Stone Age of The Wheel, with its friction, pollution, disease and death as a reward for being a good bondslave.[19]

Armageddon

The place where the kings of the earth are to be collected by the Dragon, the Beast, and the Antichrist to challenge God at the end of human history is called Armageddon (Rev. 16.16). The physical site of Armageddon is less significant than its metaphoric sense as the "spiritual battlefield" between the armies of the Antichrist and those of the Messiah. Generally speaking, Armageddon refers to the conflict itself, both the military and ideological battles that mark the end times.

The UFO group Heaven's Gate provides one of the best examples of the belief that a final Battle of Armageddon will accompany the end times. Members of Heaven's Gate believed that alien visitation was the manifestation of the traditional battle between good and evil. The benevolent aliens, such as the cosmological messiahs Marshall Applewhite and Jesus Christ, had come to warn and prepare the "chosen" for salvation through transformation. The evil aliens, according to Heaven's Gate eschatology, are the "Luciferians"—the forces of the Antichrist attempting to keep humans slaves to this world.

Furthermore, according to Heaven's Gate, "Luciferians" are forming a conspiracy with government authorities to create "a perfect servant to society (THEIR society—of THEIR world)—to the 'acceptable establishment,' to humanity, and to false religious concepts."[20] By "blinding" us with the mundane activities associated with the quest for the American Dream, members of Heaven's Gate believed that the Luciferians were able to conceal their broader motives of conquering and destroying the world.

However, for most millennial ufologists, Armageddon is less about the ultimate battle between good and evil and more about arresting and reversing the decay of the planet. While mass destruction threatens the planet, it can be averted through the intervention of our alien brethren. Like many in the eclectic New Age movement, of which ufology is a part, many new religious movements in ufology see the collapse of the world as a partial, rather than a total, collapse. The evils that now afflict the planet will be altered with help from our benevolent alien saviors.

Ufology groups encountered on the Internet conceive of the passing from the old Babylonian world to the utopian new world of the millennium as a peaceful transition. For example, the website for the New World Comforters, founded in 1973 by Allan Noonan in San Francisco, speaks of this peaceful transition from the old world to the new as a choice to "nonviolently recreate this world as a Space Age Paradise."[21] Elsewhere, Noonan further describes this peaceful transition as "a nonviolent, spiritual revolution . . . accomplished by people uniting to actually create that which takes the place of the existing system."[22] Except for Heaven's Gate, some Christian fundamentalists, and Hollywood movies, most ufologists are less likely to imagine a bloody battle between the forces of good and evil and more likely to see aliens as benevolent beings who are here to help us through this difficult but evolutionary transformation.

Messiah

The coming of a messiah is another apocalyptic feature that has its postmodern expression on web pages of the ufology subculture. Messianism is the belief that a savior or legendary hero will return to conquer the wicked and redeem his faithful followers. Among the Christian fundamentalist churches, the expectation of Christ's Second Coming is still very much a part of church doctrine. However, for many in the subculture of ufology, salvation will be brought by extraterrestrial messiahs.

Most of the new religious movements in ufology argue that the alien visitors are benevolent saviors, sent to help us overcome the restrictions of our "humanness" and assist us in the transition from the old world to a new one. It is evident for followers of the Aetherius Society, for example, that "we are indeed being visited by strange aliens. . . . very advanced extraterrestrials, who consider it their duty to help us and protect us."[23] Members of the Aetherius Society believe that these extraterrestrials "have been helping us for many centuries. They consider us to be their younger, less evolved brothers."[24]

Another UFO group which shares this interpretation of the aliens' intentions is the Ground Crew Project, founded by Sheldon Nidle in Concord, California in the mid-1980s. According to Nidle, in the article "An Urgent Message to Humanity," we are being assisted by "our space brothers and sisters, benevolent and loving Ascended Masters." Their mission is to help with humanity's transition to a higher dimension by providing "counselors, supplies, teachers, and new technology."[25]

The theme of the alien messiah is also evident on the Summum home page. Summum was founded in 1975 by Claude Rex Nowell and is based in Salt Lake City, Utah. Nowell was chosen by the Summa—"extraterrestrial saviors"—to convey their message of hope and salvation to the rest of humanity. This message is reported in the article "The Millennium of Reconciliation has Begun":

I have been with the Summa Individuals many, many times. . . . These advanced Beings work with those ready to take up the labor of universal progression and divine evolution, and within the bounds of natural LAW provide assistance to those willing to take the responsibility of this destiny. Each time the Summa Individuals support and assist in the evolution of Humankind, acting as a catalyst for progression, and always bound by the constraint of the LAW.[26]

The notion of the benevolent, messiah-like alien is central to the millennial cosmology of the Unarians, who believe that aliens possess the advanced technology and wisdom that humanity needs in order to overcome the imminent destruction of our world. Unarius was founded in 1954 by Dr. Ernest L. and Ruth Norman in California. The Unarians' interpretation of the messianic alien visitors is common to many groups within the subculture of ufology. In the article "Who are the Pleiadeans?" the extraterrestrials are described as "Space Brothers who are working for the benefit of humankind . . . and will help to rekindle the flame of spirit through the introduction of advanced electronic devices to correct disease of the mind and the body." These benevolent extraterrestrials will also "provide us with information that will raise the consciousness of humankind."[27]

Another variation on the theme of Messiah is found within the doctrine of Heaven's Gate. Marshall "Do" Applewhite believed that he was the receptacle for the "member of the Kingdom of Heaven," an extraterrestrial entity that inhabited his body, as well as the body of Jesus Christ for some two thousand years. Much like the traditional Christian messiah, Applewhite claimed that the only way to gain salvation in the Kingdom of Heaven was through him:

I am in the same position to today's society as was the One that was in Jesus then. Looking to us, and desiring to be a part of my Father's Kingdom, I can offer to those with deposits, that chance to connect with the Level Above Human, and begin that transition. Your separation from the world and reliance upon the Kingdom of Heaven through its Representatives can open to you the opportunity to become a new creature, one of the Next Evolutionary Level, rightfully belonging to the Kingdom of Heaven.[28]

Like Heaven's Gate, the Urantians apply an extraterrestrial interpretation to their messianic expectations. Founded in 1955, the Urantian Foundation publishes their theology in the Urantia Book. On the Urantia Foundation Home Page a complete "New Age" cosmology is outlined, from our creation by the spiritual forces of the Universe to our certain demise and eventual salvation by an extraterrestrial Christ:

The great hope of Urantia lies in the possibility of a new revelation of Jesus with a new and enlarged presentation of his saving message which would spiritually unite in loving service the numerous families of his present day professed followers. The time is ripe to witness the figurative resurrection of the human Jesus from his burial tomb amidst the theological traditions and the religious dogmas of nineteen centuries.[29]

Millennium

The Millennium is the final apocalyptic element of Revelation that takes a postmodern form in the UFO subculture. In Revelation, the millennium is associated with the one-thousand-year period ushered in by the Messiah upon His return. According to Revelation 20.2–7 the dragon (that is, the Devil) is to be confined in the abyss, while the martyrs, having been raised from the dead, are to reign with Christ.

Most new religious movements within the ufology subculture are optimistic about the possibilities of a new world to be created from the passing of the corrupted Babylonian one. The prevailing conception of the utopia to follow the transformation of the world is one where the current government, economy, and social structure will be rendered obsolete. Members of the Ground Crew Project believe that by ushering in the new world, the old world order will pass away and "the present surface governments and the IRS will cease to exist."[30]

With the coming of the millennium, many groups within ufology believe that human consciousness will be freed from its worldly restrictions to attain a complete acceptance of the unity of all things throughout the universe. The Unarians emphasize the potential for freeing the human mind from our present obsolescence with teaching that allows for the realization of this unity:

Such a joined consciousness extending the principle of love in action would mean the end of all war, poverty, and disease. Technology will then be an arm to the development of the higher consciousness. All institutions that form the culture of society will reflect a new spiritual force in the realization that we are all brothers and sisters of the infinite under the guidance of advanced spiritual beings.[31]

The New World Comforters also see the new world that is emerging as one where everyone will have free use of the planet. According to the article "The New World," this utopian world will be one in which "no one loses anything and everyone gains everything of their greatest dreams."[32] Freeing the human consciousness is a primary theme of the International Raelian Movement. In an article called "Awakening Seminar" the author holds that humanity will "awaken the world by awakening ourselves."[33]

This process will occur "when machines have taken over the menial chores such as food, clothes, consumer goods and luxury production, then there will be no need for money and everything can be free."[34] Only when this freedom is realized, the author writes, "can creativity be really appreciated since people will not invent for commercial purposes, but for pleasure, for utility, and for giving to friends."[35] The Raelians believe that once free from the bonds of materialism, humanity will "create a truly free society based on love, science and harmony adapted to the modern day."[36]

Although an atmosphere of optimism prevails among the new religious movements of ufology, there are groups that take a more cautious approach to the coming Millennium. One example is found within the doctrine of the Greater Community Way, founded by Marshall Via Summers in 1992. Located in Colorado, the Greater Community Way does not completely embrace the new world that is emerging. They see the coming millennium as a time when the societies of planet Earth will be taken in by the "Greater Community" of the extraterrestrials who have been visiting our world. Summers describes this Greater Community in detail:

> The Greater Community will not be a Greater Community that will welcome you. It will not have your best interests at heart necessarily. The Greater Community that you will encounter will be a Greater Community of divergent interests. Those who come to your world will be resource explorers, emissaries of their governments or military forces scouting the possibility of forming an allegiance with your race and with your world. They will not be Divine emissaries, but they will not be evil either. They will simply be fulfilling their own mandates and objectives.[37]

Unlike other millennial ufologists, the Greater Community Way does not embrace the emerging world with optimism. Their theology is wary of the many possible scenarios that could occur with our emergence into the Greater Community of extraterrestrial life.

While a majority of new religious movements within the subculture of ufology are optimistic about the possibilities of the emerging new world, the Heaven's Gate and Armageddon Time Ark Base groups take a more pessimistic view of the future. Both groups believe that the present world has been damaged beyond repair. The only option is to destroy the planet totally and begin again on another planet or in another dimension. Heaven's Gate theology referred to the ultimate destruction of the planet Earth as a "spading under," while Armageddon Time Ark Base sees it as a "chiropractic adjustment of the Earth's spine."[38] The only way to survive this destruction is to evacuate, as the Heaven's Gate group believed they were doing in their mass suicide. The Armageddon Time Ark Base group also predicts the inevitability of planetary collapse, and they will escape the destruction in their "Time Arks" (spaceships), presumably at some time prior to "S-Day, when God begins Armageddon."[39] However, the optimism expressed by a majority of the millennial ufologists exemplifies the hope and excitement that accompany their anticipation of the coming Millennium and the fulfillment of the millennial myth. For many, the current transformations within our society signal the end of an era and the opportunity to participate in the creation of a new world that is free from the problems which plague the present one.

Conclusion

From the tragedy at Waco to the Heaven's Gate suicide, elements of the millennial myth inform the ideology and practices of many new and revitalized social movements and cultural trends in modern society. Ufology provides another contemporary site where the millennial myth has "fractured"—its symbols and meanings reproduced and redefined through the beliefs and experiences of a rapidly growing ufology subculture.

Like all myths, the millennial myth reflects a dual structure. The "downside" of the myth focuses on the evil unleashed in the world during the Apocalypse, as well as tribulations, Armageddon, mass destruction, and death. The "upside," or utopian view of the Millennium concentrates on redemption, salvation, and a future paradise on earth beginning with the Millennium. The subculture of ufology, as seen in the websites of new religious UFO movements, expresses both of these (seemingly contradictory) views of the millennial myth. While both dimensions are crucial to a full understanding of the myth, postmodern and secularized expressions of the myth often emphasize one side over the other.[40] Followers of Heaven's Gate believed that some aliens were "intruders" who harbored sinister intentions towards humans and planet Earth. Similarly, well-known abduction researcher Bud Hopkins promotes the belief that humans are being used in genetic experiments, perhaps as breeding sources.[41] Hopkins furthers suggests that extraterrestrials may be planning an invasion and takeover of the earth in some way.

The belief that the aliens are evil and are bent on destroying or enslaving planet Earth and its human inhabitants is the predominant portrayal in our popular culture as well, where little has changed since H. G. Well's science fiction classic *War of the Worlds*, in which humans and aliens battle it out over the future of the human race and planet Earth. Reproduced live on radio by Orson Wells on 30 October 1938, *War of the Worlds* caused a minor panic among many of those who tuned in on the night of its broadcast. The perception of aliens as evil and destructive remains prevalent today. Recent movies such as *Independence Day* (1996), *Men in Black* (1997), and *Starship Troopers* (1997) serve to reinforce the dominant conception of aliens as sinister entities on a mission to control or destroy our world.

However, as this study of new religious UFO movements on the Internet reveals, a less destructive and more optimistic view of the Millennium prevails. Millennial ufologists such as the Aetherians, Ground Crew Project, New World Comforters, Raelians, and Unarians see the aliens as saviors who have come to help humankind by bringing new technology, messages of peace and love, a plan to save the planet. Perhaps some of these aliens were ancient astronauts to the earth—interpreted by our ancestors as the angelic hosts of biblical legend. These ufologists believe aliens are our creators who have returned to prevent humankind from destroying Earth and to help us achieve a new level of "cosmic consciousness" by having us join the ranks of the intergalactic brotherhood. Many ufologists, perhaps most, are optimistic, clinging to the positive side of the myth, which speaks of redemption, rebirth, and building a millennial new world. However, like the classical millennialist, they wait for the extraterrestrials to do it for us. They do not have a plan of action and do not aspire to solve the social problems of the world themselves, such as environmental damage or rapid social change, since the aliens will save us from ourselves.

As the millennial myth continues to evolve and fracture in the popular culture and among new religious movements, it shows us how certain groups interpret current events through the lens of cultural myth. History has shown that millenarian movements tend to arise during periods of intense social change, often occurring at the end of age or an era. Modern expressions of millennialism mirror the major social changes the world is currently undergoing. The fact that it is occurring with the turn of the millennium might be coincidence, but it helps to fulfill the apocalyptic prophecy: that as the old world declines, a new world is emerging.

Both the destructive potential of current world social problems and new breakthroughs in science, technology, and economics are primary factors infusing the millennial movements in American society today. Famine, war, terrorism, pollution, and AIDS have become the common fare of television news, film drama, and popular literature, reflecting the tribulations of the postmodern age. Simultaneously, what was once science fiction has become science fact, as genetic cloning, the exploration of our solar system, and the search for extraterrestrial life accelerates at a dizzying pace.

The real issues behind these trends (that is, rapid change, environmental degradation, globalization, technological evolution) give credibility to the beliefs of some apocalyptic ufologists regarding global destruction and transformation. However, such changes are neither natural nor supernatural; they are man-made phenomena that are no longer bound by locality or culture, but are often global in their reach and consequences. In this sense visions of the Apocalypse are all too real at the end of the twentieth century, so that, surely, one does not have to be on the millennialist fringe to find them compelling.

Notes

1. The literature on contemporary expressions of millennialism is extensive. The following are a few of the more recent crop of books that take a broad approach to modern millennial and apocalyptic beliefs and movements: Stephen O'Leary, *Arguing the Apocalypse: A Theory of Millennial Rhetoric* (New York: Oxford University Press, 1994); Philip Lamy, *Millennium Rage: Survivalists, White Supremacists and the Doomsday Prophecy* (New York: Plenum, 1996); Thomas Robbins and Susan J. Palmer, eds., *Millennium, Messiahs, and Mayhem: Contemporary Apocalyptic Movements* (New York: Routledge, 1997); Daniel Wojick, *The End of the World as We Know It: Faith, Fatalism, and Apocalypse in America* (New York: New York University Press, 1997). See also the website for the Center for Millennial Studies at Boston University: <www.mille.org>.

2. Most of the Internet references used in our research were initially obtained in April 1997. During the process of editing and revising, it became evident that many Internet references had disappeared from their original locations—a not uncommon phenomenon on the Internet. While some documents and home pages were relocated, others were unable to be located again. We have indicated in our notes those Internet documents and home pages that have been removed from the Internet as of October 1997. Internet sources are referenced by paragraph number.

3. See Norman Cohn, *The Pursuit of the Millennium* (Fairlawn, N.J.: Essen-

tial Books, 1957); Eric J. Hobsbawm, *Primitive Rebels: Studies in Archaic Forms of Social Movements in the Nineteenth and Twentieth Centuries* (New York: Norton, 1959); Edward Hyams, *The Millennium Postponed: Socialism from Sir Thomas More to Mao Tse-tung* (New York: Taplinger, 1974); Philip Lamy, "Millennialism in the Mass Media: The Case of *Soldier of Fortune Magazine*," *Journal for the Scientific Study of Religion* 31, no. 4 (December 1992): 408–24; Arthur L. Greil and Thomas Robbins, "Between the Sacred and the Secular: Research and Theory on Quasi-Religion," *Religion and the Social Order* 4 (1994): 1–23.

4. Hobsbawm, *Primitive Rebels.*

5. Greil and Robbins, "Between the Sacred and the Secular"; Philip Lamy, *Millennium Rage,* 181–84.

6. Michael Barkun, "Politics and Apocalypticism," in John J. Collins, Bernard McGinn, and Stephen J. Stein, eds., *The Encyclopedia of Apocalypticism* (Idyllwild, Calif.: Continuum Press, 1998), forthcoming.

7. *Holy Bible: Revised Standard Edition* (New York: Harper and Brothers, 1952).

8. Secular UFO groups are characterized by their dedication to the scientific study of the UFO phenomenon. Three of the more prominent UFO groups are the Mutual UFO Network (MUFON), the J. Allen Hynek Center for UFO Studies (CUFOS), and the Fund for UFO Research (FUFOR). These three groups comprise the UFO Coalition, a collaborative effort to streamline the investigative and research efforts of the UFO subculture. Other secular UFO groups include the British UFO Research Association (BUFORA), Citizens against UFO Secrecy (CAUS), and the Society for Scientific Exploration (SSE).

9. The religious and spiritual dimensions of ufology have been noted by scholars. See especially Keith Thompson, *Angels and Aliens: UFOs in the Mythic Imagination* (New York: Ballantine Books, 1991); James Lewis, ed., *The Gods Have Landed: New Religions from Other Worlds* (Albany: State University of New York Press, 1995); and Wojick, *The End of the World as We Know It.*

10. C. Jody and Gemini, "What Will You Do as the Curtain Is Raised?" on *Outpost Kauai Home Page,* <http://hoohana.aloha.net/outpost>, paragraph 12, visited April 1997.

11. Brian Keneipp, "Why and How Are the Space Masters Helping Us Now?" on *The Aetherius Society Online,* <http://www.aetherius.org/intro.htm>, paragraph 2, visited June 1997.

12. Susan Jean Palmer, "Women in the Raelian Movement: New Religious Experiments in Gender and Authority," in Lewis, ed., *The Gods Have Landed,* 106.

13. Yahni Saranghey, "The Raelian Lifestyle, Threat or Solution?" on *International Raelian Movement Home Page,* <http://www.rael.org/English/e-digest/raelmsgZZ.html>, 1997, paragraph 10, visited April 1997.

14. Whitley Strieber, *Communion* (New York: Avon Books, 1987); Strieber, *Transformation: The Breakthrough* (New York: William Morrow, 1988); Strieber, *Breakthrough: The Next Step* (New York: Harper, 1995). See also Raymond Fowler, *The Andreasson Affair* (New York: Bantam, 1979); John Mack, *Abduction: Human Encounters with Aliens* (New York: Ballantine Books, 1994); Bud Hopkins, *Missing Time* (New York: Ballantine Books, 1981); and Hopkins, *Intruders: The Incredible Visitations at Copley Woods* (New York: Ballantine Books, 1987).

15. O. T. Nodrog, "State of Time Station Earth," on *Kooks Museum Home Page*, by D. Kossy, <http://www.teleport.com/~dkossy/nodrog.html>, 1997, paragraph 10, visited April 1997.

16. Allen Michael, "The Everlasting Gospel: The New World, Part 1," on *ETI Messenger-New World Comforters Home Page*, <http://www.galactic.org/EG.html>, 1997, paragraph 10, visited June 1997.

17. Ibid.

18. Marshall Applewhite, "Last Chance to Evacuate Earth Before It's Recycled," on *Heaven's Gate Home Page*, <http://www.heavensgatetoo.com/misc/vt092996.htm>, 1996, paragraphs 15, 46, visited April 1997.

19. Nodrog, "State of Time Station Earth," paragraph 10.

20. Applewhite, "Do's Intro: Purpose-Belief," on *Heaven's Gate Home Page*, <http://www.heavensgatetoo.com/Intro>, 1996, paragraph 7, visited April 1997.

21. Michael, "Spirit God's World Master Plan: Introduction," on *ETI Messenger—New World Comforters Home Page*, <http://www.galactic.org/WMP.html>, 1997, paragraph 2, visited October, 1997.

22. Michael, "The Everlasting Gospel," paragraph 3.

23. Brian Keneipp, "Abductions—Some Surprising Answers," on *The Aetherius Society Online*, <http://www.aetherius.org//abduct.htm>, 1997, paragraph 7, visited June 1997.

24. Ibid.

25. Sheldon Nidle, "An Urgent Message to Humanity," on *The Ground Crew Project Home Page*, <http://www.portal.ca/~ground/crew/messhum.htm>, 1997, paragraphs 5, 11, visited April 1997.

26. Claude R. Nowell, "Summum—The Millennium of Reconciliation Has Begun," <http://www.summum.org/summum.htm>, 1997, paragraph 1, visited April 1997.

27. Charles Spiegel, "Who Are the Pleiadeans?" on *Unarius Academy of Science Home Page*, <http://www.unarius.org/et.html>, 1997, paragraph 2, visited June 1997.

28. Applewhite, "Do's Intro," paragraphs 3, 4.

29. Urantia Foundation, <urantia@urantia.org>; "The Urantia Book Description," on *Urantia Foundation Home Page*, <http://www.urantia.org/bookdesc.htm>, 1997, paragraph 5, visited July 1997.

30. Nidle, "Common Questions and Answers," on *Ground Crew*, paragraphs 6, 12.
31. Spiegel. "Who Are the Pleiadeans?" paragraph 8.
32. Michael, "The Everlasting Gospel," paragraph 13.
33. Saranghey, "Awakening Seminars," on *International Raelian Movement*, paragraph 1.
34. Saranghey, "A World without Money," on *International Raelian Movement*, paragraph 1.
35. Ibid.
36. Saranghey, "How to Achieve the Embassy," on *International Raelian Movement*, paragraph 3,.
37. Marshall Summers, "Preparing for the Future," on *Greater Community Way of Knowledge Home Page*, <http://www.greatercommunity.org/booklet.htm>, 1997, paragraph 6, visited October 1997.
38. Nodrog, "A.T.A. Base Operations," on *Alien Religions Home Page*, by D. Hambone, <http://www.io.com/~hambone/guide/rel/ar.html>, 1997, paragraph 1, visited April 1997.
39. Ibid.
40. Lamy, *Millennium Rage*.
41. Hopkins, *Missing Time* and *Intruders*.

Fear of Revelation
Postmillennialism in American Popular Film

James Hewitson

American culture has been especially concerned with things revelatory. Apocalyptism and millennialism have manifested themselves in a series of eruptions throughout American history: from the Millerite movement in the 1830s, to the Dispensationalism formulated by John Darby and popularized by writers such as Cyrus Scofield in the late nineteenth century, to the recent events concerning Heaven's Gate. In the last twenty-five years in particular, Christian prophetic literature has experienced a huge surge of growth. Hal Linsey's *The Late Great Planet Earth* proved to be a commercial breakthrough for the genre, selling 28 million copies since its publication in 1970. Subsequently there has been a general boom in prophetic writings, both in terms of the number of titles published and copies sold. John F. Walvoord's *Armageddon, Oil, and the Middle East Crises* (1974) and Paul Billheimer's *Desired for the Throne* (1975), for example, both have sales figures over 500,000 units, and David Wilkerson's *Set the Trumpet to Thy Mouth* (1985) has passed the million-copy mark.[1]

This tradition has also given rise to a number of popular films that make use of Christian eschatology. Locating apocalyptic plot lines in films constructed according to conventional narrative poetics and for a general audience, however, affects the significance that events are afforded. In particular, there is a reluctance to deal directly with the radical nature of Christ's kingdom as it is understood in fundamentalist or dispensationalist Christian exegeses; such films consistently attempt to refashion or remake the narrative so that its implications are rendered acceptable to mainstream audiences. This process is in itself revelatory:

430

it reflects an unwillingness on the part of contemporary culture to accept the closure implied by revelation and a corresponding insistence on believing in the integrity, autonomy and open-endedness of human history. As I will argue, therefore, in tracing the treatment of the story through a series of such attempts, a process of assimilation becomes apparent, in which the narrative is co-opted by a sensibility radically different from that of fundamentalist Christianity and used to validate an essentially humanistic teleology. That narrative is fashioned into an allegory of humanity's liberation from the constraints of prophecy and supernaturalism, and the millennium it heralds is made an epoch of unlimited human potential.

Millennial belief has taken many forms in history. In the Christian tradition the millennium refers to a long period of unprecedented peace and piety closely associated with the Second Coming of Christ. It is common to distinguish among premillennialist, postmillennialist, and amillennialist understandings of this period and how it will be brought about. Amillennialists believe that biblical references to the millennium should be understood figuratively, as referring to Christ's reign in the hearts of his believers. Postmillennialists hold the position that Christ will return only after humanity has itself achieved a millennium of Christian civilization. Premillennialists, for whom prophecy is most important and who are themselves responsible for the greatest part of the literature on the subject, believe that the Christian millennium will not arrive until Christ returns, defeats the powers opposing Him, and establishes His kingdom on earth. The distinction between post- and premillennialism is significant because each position implies radically different notions regarding the end of history and the potential for human progress. Postmillennialists are compelled to assume a generally optimistic perspective regarding humanity's potential for moral growth: their belief entails that humanity will continue to develop until it becomes capable of receiving Christ as its king. Premillennialists, by contrast, necessarily see world affairs as deteriorating until complete domination by the forces of evil obtains; only Christ's return at the head of an avenging army will be sufficient to effect the world's reform.

Premillennialism further divides into a number of subcategories, and even among exegetes of the same school there is much difference regarding particular details of the last days. However, the larger pattern of events is generally agreed upon. Human efforts to improve society will fail, and the world will decline until the Antichrist gains control of it. Although the timing of the Rapture has been a particularly contentious issue, most premillennialists believe that it will take place just before the Antichrist's ascent: all those who are of Christ's church will be caught up in the air and removed from the world. The Antichrist will then rule on earth for seven years. This period is known as the Tribulation, and during it all those who oppose his rule will be persecuted. At the end of this period Christ shall return to earth and destroy the forces of the Antichrist in the battle of Armageddon. Having bound the power of Satan, Christ will establish his millennial kingdom on earth, which will last for a thousand years. At the end of this period Satan will again revolt, be subdued, and there will then be the resurrection of the dead and the last judgment. God will then create a new heaven and earth for his people.

Although Christian fundamentalist novels about the apocalypse and Christ's second coming have been written since the mid-1930s, *The Omen* (1976) is one of earliest and best-known large-scale treatments of this theme in secular popular film.[2] *The Omen* is about the rise of the Antichrist: it follows his career from his birth from a jackal, through his secret adoption by Jeremy Thorn, a wealthy industrialist and American ambassador to Great Britain, to the death of his adoptive parents and his second adoption by the president of the United States. The film ends with the Antichrist still a child but now poised for future world domination. Throughout the course of the story the Satanists are represented as being extremely well-organized and effective. They easily defeat all attempts to thwart their designs; those opposing them are scattered, weak, and riddled with doubts. Jeremy Thorn comes to know of the true identity of his child only late in the film and resists the implications of that knowledge up until the penultimate scene. His only assistance derives from Father Brennan, a priest who has defected from the coven responsible for the murder of Thorn's natural child, and Keith Jennings, a photographer who accidentally stumbles upon the truth. Both, however, are killed effortlessly through supernatural means. Indeed, the method through which their dispatch is foreshadowed—emulsions visible on photographs taken with high-speed film that indicate the nature of their deaths—heightens the sense of hopelessness and futility that permeates all attempts to halt the Antichrist's rise.

A sense of helplessness before the forces of evil runs throughout the film. Upon first meeting Thorn, Father Brennan demands that he accept Christ and receive communion so as to obtain the strength necessary to combat the Antichrist, but Thorn does not do so and God's influence is never at any point in evidence.[3] Bugenhagen, the exorcist and archaeologist who possesses the knowledge of how to destroy the Antichrist, remains entrenched in a kind of Christian fortress beneath Jerusalem; while he provides Thorn with the utensils necessary for killing the child, he is unwilling himself to venture forth or offer more substantial assistance.[4] Father Brennan too, before his death, papers his apartment walls with pages from the Bible, attempting to hold off the doom he knows will overtake him. The notion of the Rapture has been dropped from the story line altogether and the film's protagonists work constantly to avert Armageddon. There is neither hope for a Christian victory over the Antichrist nor desire for the millennium that such an event would inaugurate. The film's protagonists instead attempt to defeat the powers of evil so as to return to a human history. As such, although *The Omen* uses Christian premillennial eschatology as its setting, this story in fact has no real engagement with the themes deriving from that context. It is a narrative of human termination. On the occasion of their second meeting, Father Brennan repeats a verse to Thorn:

> When the Jews return to Zion.
> And a comet fills the sky.
> And the Holy Roman Empire rises.
> Then you and I must die.[5]

The signs mentioned are indeed those of contemporary premillennialism, but here they prophesy only doom for humanity. The supernaturalism at work is that of conventional horror narratives.

The reluctance to acknowledge millennial Christian aspects of the apocalypse is brought out in greater relief in the film *The Final Conflict* (1981).[6] *The Final Conflict* builds upon the narrative established in *The Omen* and continued in *Damien Omen II* (1978). In this segment of the story the Antichrist has assumed a position of influence in the world. Christ does not come to oppose him as Lord of Hosts in the manner assumed in Christian premillennialist writings, however, but is instead incarnated and born a second time. The story of Herod and the murder of the children are superimposed upon the film, as the Antichrist attempts to destroy the infant Christ by killing all the male babies born on a certain date. A group of monks who have learned the Antichrist's identity are at the same time attempting to kill him so as to ensure the safety of Christ. The film transforms the story utterly, abandoning its earlier premillennialist structure. Christ's second birth is made essentially to reiterate his first birth. The Antichrist in the film is attempting to displace an already existing Christian millennium, and his eventual destruction, at the hands not of Christ but of the mother of one of his disciples, represents a continuation of the world that has existed since Christ's first incarnation. Hence the new structure becomes amillennialist: Christ's kingdom resides in the hearts of his believers, and the premillennialist elements necessary to tell a coherent story dealing with the rise of the Antichrist have, by its ending, all disappeared.

The treatment of Christian eschatology in *The Omen* series and the changes that are made to the story over its three installments reflect an inability to accept its implicit premillennialism. The notion of an end to human history cannot be represented as constituting any kind of good and so must be circumvented. The fear of otherness implied by the ideas of God and the millennium is the subject of John Carpenter's *Prince of Darkness* (1987).[7] While departing significantly from the story line sketched in Revelation, this film nonetheless has a real involvement with popular culture's restructuring of the Christian apocalypse, explicitly delineating the ideological core evident only intermittently and by implication in the structure of the *Omen* series.

Prince of Darkness concerns a glass receptacle within which Satan is imprisoned in the form of a green liquid. This receptacle has been guarded since early Christian times by a secret sect called the Brotherhood of Sleep. As the liquid begins to evince unusual activity, this sect seeks outside assistance, first from the church and then from the scientific community. There is an ancient book describing the receptacle's history, which is translated by a member of the scientific team. This book tells that the receptacle was buried in the Middle East eons ago by the father of Satan, who is described as "a god who walked the earth before man but was somehow expelled to the dark side." The translator continues to read:

> Christ comes to warn us. He was of extra-terrestrial ancestry, but a human-like race. . . . Finally they determine Christ is crazy, but he's also gaining power, converting a lot of people to his beliefs, so they kill him. But his disciples keep the secret and hide it from civilization until man could develop a science sophisticated enough to prove what Christ was saying.[8]

Christ is of an advanced and seemingly sympathetic race, but there is in this film no beneficent divine order. The supernaturalism present is inherently evil and anxious for humanity's destruction, and humanity can only look to itself and its technological and scientific advancement for salvation. When speaking to a priest, the theoretical physicist leading the research team speculates:

> Suppose what your faith has said is essentially correct. Suppose there is a universe of mind controlling everything, a God willing the behavior of every subatomic particle. Now, every particle has an anti-particle, its mirror image, its negative side. Maybe this universal mind resides in the mirror image instead of in our universe

as we wished to believe. Maybe he's anti-God, bringing darkness instead of light.[9]

The notion of the otherness of God has a long history in Christianity. In the *Institutes*, for example, Calvin argues that God is naturally alien to humanity and, indeed, to all of creation. He writes, "to neither angels nor man was God ever Father, except in regard to his only-begotten Son; and men, especially, hateful to God because of their iniquity, become God's sons by free adoption because Christ is the Son of God by nature."[10] Hence, it is only by sharing in Christ's spirit that humanity can be reconciled to God. In *Prince of Darkness*, however, it is precisely the otherness of the supernatural entity—acknowledged in Christian thought through the concepts of personal redemption and the millennium—that is the primary source of evil, and the Second Coming is the work of humanity's dispossession. The force contained in the canister has telekinetic powers, and transforms characters into its thrall by spraying a slimy liquid into their faces. Although the film does not elaborate explicit correlations, there are parallels between this spraying and Christian baptism, as well as between its power to cause mutation and the manner in which the Christian regenerate receives Christ's spirit and becomes the New Man. In this film's ideology, such a change is tantamount to the negating of humanity itself, and so must be resisted. As such, the film in fact formulates a humanistic attack on the whole notion of religious transfiguration. In reflecting on the history of the Church, the priest muses:

> Apparently a decision was made to characterize pure evil as a force even within the darkness within the hearts of men. It was more convenient and that way man remained at the center of things. A stupid lie. We were salesmen, that's all; we sold our product to those who didn't have it. The New Life, reward ourselves, punish our enemies so we could live without truth, substance. Malevolence, that was truth, asleep until now.[11]

The eternal world of "things which are not seen" in Paul (2 Cor. 4:18) becomes here a realm of horror. One of the team assembled to combat this force later states, "I think it's time to stand up for what we are," and from the perspective of humanism such a position entails combating the personal transformation and sense of ending implicit to religious revelation. The New Life is the termination of human life, humanity's forced passage into a world in which it cannot be as it is.

In *Prince of Darkness*, Christ becomes a scientist, providing humanity with theorems and equations that will allow it to defeat the supernaturalism threatening its development. The remaking of Christ's role in this film is consistent with that of other films that have also attempted to restructure the story of the last days. It formulates a reading of Christ's Second Coming that will validate humanity as it presently exists, and so liberate it from the burden of supernatural augury. *The Seventh Sign* (1988) is one such film.[12] In this rendition the world is threatened with termination not because of an apocalyptic struggle between good and evil but because all of the souls that God has created have been spent. In the film's mythology there is a hall in Heaven containing all the souls that are to be born, but the number of souls is finite. Seven signs denote the end of the world, and the last sign is the birth of a soulless child. Christ is again on earth, but only to witness its destruction; although he has attempted to intervene, God refuses to refill the hall with new souls. At the film's climax, Abbie, the protagonist who is pregnant with the soulless child, offers her own life for the life of her baby, and her sacrifice is sufficient to give life to her child and persuade God to refill the hall. The film concludes with Christ leaving the hospital room in which she has just died and telling a boy who has witnessed the event, "Remember it all; write it down. Tell it, so people will use the chance she has given them."[13]

Abbie in effect becomes a female Christ, who, through the birth of her child, provides the hope that the traditional Christ is no longer able to sustain. The only life the film concerns is earthly life, and the figure of the expectant mother becomes the savior, promising humanity the immortality of procreation. Abbie, merely through her belief in the future of humanity, works its reconciliation with God. Her reconciliation, moreover, is achieved for humanity as it is and so does not require its spiritual sanctification or adoption through faith. Prophecy and revelation accordingly become things of the past. *The Seventh Sign* articulates a new covenant between God and humanity, in which the parties agree to leave each other alone. In a sense Abbie's story is the gospel foretold in the representations of the apocalypse in the other films: it is a narrative of humanity's sufficiency to save itself and to continue in its present condition, despite any plans God may have to the contrary.

In each of the popular representations invoking Christian eschatology that I have mentioned, the notion of a millennium consistently collides with a humanism that, in militating against an end to time, insists that history remain perennially open. The inability to accept the notion of a final and completing revelation is reflected in another film, *The Rapture* (1991), which represents the apocalypse as it is understood in Christian premillennialism.[14] This film concludes, however, with its protagonist, Sharon, standing outside of heaven, just beyond the river that washes away all sin, unable to accept heaven and so refusing to proceed any further, preferring to remain in the darkness. As such, *The Rapture* demarcates the limits of humanity's capacity for self-abnegation. Because Sharon cannot dismiss the pain she experienced on earth, she cannot partake of the new life offered by God: divine revelation is no longer capable of speaking to her.

The Rapture complements the rejection of traditional Christian salvation portrayed in *The Seventh Sign* by illustrating the inability of the religious apocalypse to provide fulfillment. Abbie in *The Seventh Sign* sacrifices herself to ensure the perpetuation of the human world, and Sharon in *The Rapture* chooses to remain alone in the twilight of that world rather than accept God's Kingdom. As such, the apocalypse is transformed into what could be termed humanistic postmillennialism. Humanity is presented as having a future that is distinctly its own, but the nature of that future is forever deferred. These films all bear witness to the belief in human potential. *The Rapture* and *The Seventh Sign* are from this perspective the converse of *Prince of Darkness:* liberation from God's prophecy and God's kingdom is as much a good as is the defeat of Satan. In all three films the supernatural element is either rejected or expelled from human history.

Just as popular films cannot represent the end of human time, they cannot ever completely conclude an apocalyptic narrative. *Omen IV: The Awakening* was released in 1991.[15] It chronologically follows *The Final Conflict,* and, although it attempts to link its narrative with the story established in the earlier films, it is essentially a retelling of the first *Omen* film. This retelling, however, reflects the diminishing role afforded supernaturalism in mainstream representations of the apocalypse. In this installment the focal point of evil is a young girl, Delilah, who is the daughter of Damien, the first Antichrist, and is born with the future Antichrist existing in embryo within her womb. As such, this film takes place at a remove from ultimate evil. While Delilah is responsible for some deaths, her malignancy is manifested in such activities as blackening all of the crystals belonging to her nurse and inflaming a New Age fair; her true descent is revealed not by telltale 666 birthmark, but by her possessing a "muddy" aura. In a like manner the film devotes a great deal of attention to the necessary preconditions for the Antichrist's reign. A priest reflects:

We are ushering in the Antichrist to a world of overpopulation, pollution, crime. . . . That part of us that is the worst of us gives him his power[:] . . . leaders who plunder the treasuries of their poor countries, trashing their own people, driving them into

famine, hopelessness, disease. Men who pave over forests that provide the very air we breathe. These are the true apostates; these are
the ones who are laying out the red carpet for the Antichrist.[16]

By stressing the role of humanity in the world's decline the film effectively removes the apocalypse from the realm of the supernatural and
relocates it in the context of human history and agency. Although the
Antichrist still exists as a character, he is primarily the representative of
the destructive elements existing within humanity. As such, the narrative represented in Revelation is made an allegorical representation of
humanity's struggle between its altruistic and selfish tendencies. Humanity is assigned the role of the arbiter of its own fate, and whatever
millennium awaits it is represented as being of its own making.

Omen IV concludes with Delilah, her adoptive father, and the reborn
Damien leaving America for Italy, with the narrative inaugurated in the
first *Omen* film poised to begin again. As such, the film transforms the
story of the Christian apocalypse into a process of continual testing, in
which humanity is perpetually maintaining itself against forces threatening its existence. As with *The Seventh Sign* and *Prince of Darkness*, the
supernatural becomes a realm of dread and potential annihilation. Although *Omen IV* ends ominously, the struggle confronting the world in
fact is not different from before, and the Antichrist is not dissimilar to
other lesser oppressors of the past. Similarly, salvation is to be sought
not in divine deliverance but from humanity's own ability to curb its
destructive impulses and to believe in its own future. In this respect,
Omen IV again accords with the ideology articulated in *The Seventh
Sign* and *Prince of Darkness*. In *The Seventh Sign*, Abbie saves the world
by virtue of her willingness to die for her child, and in *Prince of Darkness* the team of scientists prevails because one member sacrifices herself
to expel the demonic entity. These characters act in this manner because
of their faith in humanity. This faith does not manifest itself in any
particular vision of a future state but merely indicates that these characters are able to imagine some future worthy of sacrifice, as their actions testify to the fact that humanity is capable of sustaining such
belief. As such, it is humanity's faith in itself that provides it with the
strength to prevail against the forces threatening its destruction and
that will likewise allow it to continue to progress.

The apocalyptic narrative that emerges out of secular popular film is
in this way an unveiling of humanity's faith in itself and its future, as
well as its belief in the sufficiency of that faith to preserve it through
adversity. The narrative becomes an articulation of a secular and
humanistic postmillennialism, but one formulated within the context of

a premillennial setting. From this perspective supernatural revelation can only be understood as a coercion and limitation that must be resisted if humanity is to take possession of its future. As the genre evolves through readaptations the possibility of a beneficent divine revelation becomes increasingly alien, eventually receding from film plots altogether. The apocalyptic produced instead becomes a chronicle of termination averted through humanity's belief in its own future.

Notes

1. Paul Boyar, *When Time Shall Be No More: Prophecy Belief in Modern American Culture* (Cambridge, Mass.: Belknap Press of Harvard University Press, 1992), 5–6.

2. Richard Donner, *The Omen* (Twentieth-Century Fox Films, 1976. Both Ira Levin' s novel *Rosemary's Baby* (New York: Random House, 1967) as well as the film based upon it and released one year later represent events relating to the birth of the Antichrist and predate David Selzner's novel *The Omen* (New York: Signet, 1976). They do not, however, deal with the Antichrist's rise to world power or include any of the prophecies emphasized in premillennialist apocalyptics.

3. In the eschatology articulated in the novel *The Omen*, the birth of the Antichrist possibly implies that Christ has also returned as a child. Despite this possibility, however, there is no indication of any beneficent supernatural forces working to counter the influence of the powers of evil.

4. In the novel *The Omen* the sense of the decline of Christian influence in the world receives greater emphasis. Bugenhagen is there identified as descending from a family that has on two previous occasions successfully hindered the coming of the Antichrist and is characterized as a group of "religious zealots, the watchdogs of Christ" (101). Bugenhagen describes himself as " 'the last . . . and the least' " of his family (178).

5. Donner, *The Omen.*

6. Graham Baker, *The Final Conflict* (Twentieth-Century Fox Film, 1981).

7. John Carpenter, *Prince of Darkness* (Alive Films, 1987).

8. Carpenter, *Prince of Darkness.*

9. Carpenter, *Prince of Darkness.*

10. John Calvin, *Institutes of the Christian Religion*, ed. John T. McNeill, trans. Ford Lewis Battles, 2 vols. (Philadelphia, Pa.: The Westminster Press, 1960), 1:488.

11. Carpenter, *Prince of Darkness.*

12. Carl Schultz, *The Seventh Sign* (Tri-Star Pictures and ML Delphi Premier Productions, 1988).

13. Schultz, *The Seventh Sign*.

14. Michael Tolkin, *The Rapture* (New Line Cinema, 1991).

15. Jorge Montesi and Dominique Othenin-Girard, *Omen IV: The Awakening* (Harvey Bernhard Productions, Mace Neufeld Productions and FNM Films, 1991).

16. Montesi and Othenin-Girard, *Omen IV.*

Contributors

Anne M. Baker is a visiting assistant professor of English at Reed College. Her research focuses on nineteenth-century American literature and culture. Her current project is an examination of representations of geographical space in the American Renaissance.

Lee Bernstein is on the faculty of the American Studies Program at the University of Colorado. He is working on a book entitled *The Greatest Menace: Organized Crime in U.S. Culture and Politics, 1946–1963*. His research interests include the history of crime reporting and the history and literature of immigration to the United States.

Kristina Bross is an assistant professor of English at California Polytechnic Institute. She is currently examining the role of John Eliot's biblical translations in shaping the religious expression of his Indian converts.

Anna Creadick is a doctoral candidate in English/American studies at the University of Massachusetts. She uses cultural-studies approaches in her work on postwar cultural history. Her dissertation is an interdisciplinary exploration of "normality" as a keyword of the immediate postwar decades.

María DeGuzmán is a preceptor in the Expository Writing Program at Harvard University. Much of her work focuses on modes of identity construction among Latina/o writers and on the representation of

Hispanicity (including peninsular "Spanishness") in Anglo–American culture.

Elizabeth A. DeWolfe is an assistant professor of anthropology and American studies at the University of New England. Her research interests include religious apostasy, women's history, and print culture—topics which intersect in her current study of the nineteenth-century anti-Shaker author and activist Mary Marshall Dyer.

Jacqueline Ellis is the author of *Silent Witnesses: Representations of Working Class Women in the United States.* She is working on a book about Roseanne and working-class women in popular culture and has taught literature, history, and women's studies in England and the United States.

Amanda Frisken is a graduate student in history at SUNY at Stony Brook. Her work focuses on the cultural politics of post–Civil War American, and specifically on sex radical Victoria Woodhull's controversial role in the decline of Reconstruction.

Matthew Pratt Guterl is a Ph.D. candidate in history at Rutgers University, where he is writing his dissertation, "Investing in Color: A Cultural History of Racial Classification in Modern America." He is particularly interested in the history of race in South Africa, Europe, and the United States.

James Hewitson is a graduate student in English at the University of Toronto. His interests include apocalyptism and millennialism in early and nineteenth-century American literature.

Richard P. Horwitz is a professor of American Studies at the University of Iowa, where he is graduate director of the program. His publications include *The Strip, Exporting America, and Hog Ties: Pigs, Manure, and Mortality in American Culture.* He is currently developing a critical anthology, *The Roots of American Studies.*

Devon Kinne is a graduate of the sociology and philosophy program at Castleton State College in Castleton, Vermont, where he developed interests in culture, religion, and the Internet. He currently works for the Federal Social Security Administration.

Peter Knight is a British Academy Postdoctoral Research Fellow in the School of American Studies at the University of Nottingham, United

Kingdom. He is currently completing a study of contemporary conspiracy culture for Routledge.

Philip Lamy is an associate professor of anthropology at Castleton State College in Vermont. He is the author of *Millenium Rage: Survivalists, White Supremacists, and the Doomsday Prophecy*. His commentaries have appeared in the *Boston Globe* and the *London Times* and on National Public Radio and the BBC.

Jason Loviglio is a Ph.D. candidate in American Studies at the University of Minnesota. His dissertation is a study of network radio's invention of an "intimate public" in the 1930s and 1940s. He teaches American Studies at the University of Massachusetts, Boston.

Brian Marcus is a graduate student in history at Drew University.

Elaine Frantz Parsons is a graduate student in history at Johns Hopkins University. Her research focuses on the intellectual history of non-intellectuals. She is working on her dissertation, "Imagining the Saloon: The Meaning of Drink in the Late Nineteenth Century."

Eve Allegra Raimon is an assistant professor of arts and humanities at the University of Southern Maine. She has published on the teaching of race in an interdisciplinary context and is working on a book on interraciality, nationalism, and the tragic mulatto in nineteenth-century American antislavery fiction.

John Regan is a doctoral candidate in English at the University of Rhode Island in Kingston and a part-time instructor in the writing program at Stonehill College. His dissertation explores representations of gender and class in antebellum anti-Catholic literature.

Corey Robin is a Ph.D. candidate in political science at Yale University. He is currently finishing his dissertation, "Fear: Biography of an Idea," which analyzes how fear has been understood in modern thought and culture.

Nancy Lusignan Schultz is a professor of English at Salem State College in Massachusetts. She is the editor of *A Veil of Fear: Nineteenth-Century Convent Tales by Rebecca Reed and Maria Monk* and is working on a study on the burning of the Ursuline convent in Charlestown, Massachusetts, tentatively titled *Fire and Rose: The Tale of a Convent Burning*.

Mark C. Smith is an associate professor of American studies and history at the University of Texas, Austin. He specializes in the history of American social science and is writing a book on the changing conceptions of the addict in twentieth-century American culture.

Michael Smith is a Ph.D. candidate in history at Indiana University. He is working on his dissertation, which examines the evolving cultural constructions of childhood and nature in the development of outdoor education in the United States in the twentieth century.

Adam Sweeting is an assistant professor of humanities at Boston University. He has written articles on the relationship between literature and the built environment and is the author of *Reading Houses and Building Books: Andrew Jackson Downing and the Architecture of Popular Antebellum Literature.*

Jeffrey W. Taylor is a Ph.D. candidate in religion at Baylor University. His research focuses on the Primitive Baptist movement as a critical outsiders' view of major nineteenth-century religious developments.

J. L. Walsh is currently an unaffiliated scholar. His work encompasses colonial/revolutionary era studies, including the revision of Loyalist identity and a project on the Rev. Andrew Eliot of Boston. He is also preparing a book on the reconstruction of American identity through film.

Rosanne L. Welker is an academic instructor in the Division of Technology, Culture, and Communication in the School of Engineering and Applied Science at the University of Virginia. Her current work examines the American cultural and legal responses to contraceptive technology.

James A. Young is the chair of Administration and Communications at Central Pennsylvania Business School. He has had extensive experience both as a labor leader and as a manager. His scholarly interest has concentrated on labor-management-government relations and their mutual societal roots and effects.

Mari Yoshihara is an assistant professor of American studies at the University of Hawaii at Manoa. She is working on a manuscript on American women and Orientalism from the 1870s to World War II, which examines material culture, literature, and anthropology as sites of Orientalist discourse in the United States.

Index

Index

Index